Research Anthology on Implementing Sentiment Analysis Across Multiple Disciplines

Information Resources Management Association
USA

Volume IV

Published in the United States of America by
    IGI Global
    Engineering Science Reference (an imprint of IGI Global)
    701 E. Chocolate Avenue
    Hershey PA, USA 17033
    Tel: 717-533-8845
    Fax: 717-533-8661
    E-mail: cust@igi-global.com
    Web site: http://www.igi-global.com

Library of Congress Cataloging-in-Publication Data

Names: Information Resources Management Association, editor.
Title: Research anthology on implementing sentiment analysis across
  multiple disciplines / Information Resources Management Association,
  editor.
Description: Hershey PA : Engineering Science Reference, [2022] | Includes
  bibliographical references and index. | Summary: "This reference book of
  contributed chapters discusses the tools, methodologies, applications,
  and implementation of sentiment analysis across various disciplines and
  industries such as the pharmaceutical industry, government, and the
  tourism industry and presents emerging technologies and developments
  within the field of sentiment analysis and opinion mining"-- Provided by
  publisher.
Identifiers: LCCN 2022016823 (print) | LCCN 2022016824 (ebook) | ISBN
  9781668463031 (h/c) | ISBN 9781668463048 (ebook)
Subjects: LCSH: Sentiment analysis.
Classification: LCC QA76.9.S57 R47 2022 (print) | LCC QA76.9.S57 (ebook)
  | DDC 005.1/4--dc23/eng/20220622
LC record available at https://lccn.loc.gov/2022016823
LC ebook record available at https://lccn.loc.gov/2022016824

British Cataloguing in Publication Data
A Cataloguing in Publication record for this book is available from the British Library.

The views expressed in this book are those of the authors, but not necessarily of the publisher.

For electronic access to this publication, please contact: eresources@igi-global.com.

List of Contributors

Aakash, Aakash / *University of Delhi, India*.. 1805
Abdelkader, Mostefai / *Dr. Tahar Moulay University of Saida, Algeria* 367
Acampa, Suania / *University of Naples Federico II, Italy*.................................... 761
Adl, Ammar / *Faculty of Computers and Information, Beni-Suef University, Egypt* 1733
Agarwal, Basant / *Indian Institute of Information Technology, Kota, India* 157
Agarwal, Parul / *Jamia Hamdard, India*.. 1401
Aggarwal, Anu G. / *University of Delhi, India*... 1805
Aggarwal, Sanchita / *University of Delhi, India* 1805
Agrawal, Rashmi / *Manav Rachna International Institute of Research and Studies, Faridabad,
    India*.. 137, 748, 1569
Alamsyah, Kamal / *Universitas Pasundan, Bandung, Indonesia*................................ 1189
Alhalabi, Wadee S. / *Department of Computer Science, King Abdulaziz University, Jeddah,
    Saudi Arabia* 1000
Alharbi, Jamilah Rabeh / *Department of Computer Science, King Abdulaziz University, Jeddah,
    Saudi Arabia* 1000
Alhazmi, Essa Ali / *Jazan University, Saudi Arabia* 1761
Allenki, Ramya / *UnitedHealth Group, India* 864
Alm, Antonie / *University of Otago, New Zealand*... 933
Alowibdi, Jalal S. / *University of Jeddah, Saudi Arabia* 1761
Alshdadi, Abdulrahman A. / *University of Jeddah, Saudi Arabia*............................. 1761
Amala Jayanthi M. / *Kumaraguru College of Technology, India* 1717
Ananthanarayanan, Balamurali / *Tamilnadu Agriculture Department, India* 619
Annaluri, Sreenivasa Rao / *Vallurupalli Nageswara Rao Vignana Jyothi Institute of Engineering
    and Technology, India* 1680
Anu Kiruthika M. / *Anna University, Chennai, India* 398
Arcila-Calderón, Carlos / *University of Salamanca, Salamanca, Spain* 673
Arumugam, Chamundeswari / *SSN College of Engineering, Chennai, India*..................... 484
Asem, Aziza Saad / *Mansoura University, Mansoura, Egypt* 1076
Attili, Venkata Ramana / *Sreenidhi Institute of Science and Technology, India*............ 1680
Bairavel S. / *KCG College of Technology, Chennai, India* 329
Bajaj, Anu / *Department of Computer Science and Engineering, Guru Jambheshwar University
    of Science and Technology, Hisar, India* 256
Bakariya, Brijesh / *I. K. Gujral Punjab Techncial University, India* 1441
Bala, Manju / *Indraprastha College of Women, New Delhi, India*............................ 1219
Balamurali, Anumeera / *St.Joseph's College of Engineering, India*........................ 619

Bansal, Neetika / *College of Engineering & Management, India* 1470

Barigou, Fatiha / *Department of Computer Science, Faculty of Exact and Applied Sciences, Laboratoire d'Informatique d'Oran (LIO), Université Oran1 Ahmed Ben Bella, Oran, Algeria* 1480

Barroso, Haroldo / *Federal University of Sul and Sudeste of Pará, Brazil* 1611

Baskar, S / *Department of Electronics and Communication Engineering, Karpagam Academy of Higher Education, Coimbatore, India* 1064

Batra, Mridula / *Manav Rachna International Institute of Research and Studies, India* 1553

Baulch, Bob / *International Food Policy Research Institute, Malawi* 1923

Behdenna, Salima / *Department of Computer Science, Faculty of Exact and Applied Sciences, Laboratoire d'Informatique d'Oran (LIO), Université Oran1 Ahmed Ben Bella, Oran, Algeria* 1480

Belalem, Ghalem / *Department of Computer Science, Faculty of Exact and Applied Sciences, Laboratoire d'Informatique d'Oran (LIO), Université Oran1 Ahmed Ben Bella, Oran, Algeria* 1480

Bennabi, Sakina Rim / *Ecole Superieure en Informatique, Sidi Bel Abbes, Algeria* 1262

Benslimane, Sidi Mohamed / *LabRI-SBA Laboratory, Ecole Superieure en Informatique, Sidi Bel-Abbes, Algeria* 1262

Bhatnagar, Vishal / *Department of Computer Science and Engineering, Ambedkar Institute of Advanced Communication Technologies and Research, New Delhi, India* 314, 463

Bouarara, Hadj Ahmed / *GeCoDe Laboratory, Algeria* 581

Breda, Zelia / *GOVCOPP, University of Aveiro, Portugal* 1831

Buragohain, Dipima / *Jilin University, China* 1783

Bustos-López, Maritza / *Tecnológico Nacional de México, Mexico & Instituto Tecnológico de Orizaba, Mexico* 637

Canbolat, Zehra Nur / *Istanbul Medipol University, Turkey* 1360

Capolupo, Nicola / *University of Salerno, Italy* 1528

Castro-Pérez, Karina / *Tecnológico Nacional de México, Mexico & IT Orizaba, Mexico* 637

Chang, Victor / *Teesside University, Middlesbrough, UK* 1633

Chaudhari, Vandana V. / *Smt. G. G. Khadse College, India* 63

Chavan, Pallavi Vijay / *Ramrao Adik Institute of Technolgy, India* 1590

Chen, Honglin / *School of Tourism, Sichuan University, China* 1494

Chiplunkar, Niranjan N. / *NMAM Institute of Technology, Nitte, India* 1338

Chuang, Cheng-Tung / *Takming University of Science and Technology, Taipei, Taiwan* 852

Costa, Ana Paula Cabral Seixas / *Universidade Federal de Pernambuco, Brazil* 268

Costa, Rui / *GOVCOPP, University of Aveiro, Portugal* 1831

Curran, Kevin / *Ulster University, Derry, UK* 1650

Dagar, Vibhu / *Vellore Institute of Technology, Vellore, India* 1600

Daud, Ali / *University of Jeddah, Saudi Arabia* 1761

De Falco, Ciro Clemente / *University of Naples Federico II, Italy* 761

Dessouky, Mohamed M. / *University of Jeddah, Saudi Arabia* 1761

Dhawale, Chitra A. / *P. R. Pote College of Engineering and Management, India* 63

Dinis, Gorete / *GOVCOPP, Polytechnic Institute of Portalegre, Portugal* 1831

Djoudi, Mahieddine / *TechNE Laboratory, University of Poitiers, France* 1237

Drall, Gurdeep Singh / *The NorthCap University, Gurgaon, India* 1905

Eldin, Fatma Gamal / *Faculty of Computers and Information Technology, Future University in Egypt, Egypt* 77

Elfergany, Abdelsadeq Khamis / *Faculty of Computers and Information, Beni-Suef University, Egypt* 1733

Elmurngi, Elshrif Ibrahim / *École de Technologie Supérieure, Montreal, Canada* 964

Fainshtein, Elizaveta / *National Research University Higher School of Economics, Russia* 1101

Fernandes, Roshan / *NMAM Institute of Technology, Nitte, India* 1338

Fteimi, Nora / *University of Passau, Germany* 1699

Furey, Eoghan / *Letterkenny Institute of Technology, Donegal, Ireland* 1650

Gadekallu, ThippaReddy / *VIT University, India* 1455

Gali, Suresh Reddy / *Vallurupalli Nageswara Rao Vignana Jyothi Institute of Engineering and Technology, India* 1680

Gallagher, Conor / *Letterkenny Institute of Technology, Donegal, Ireland* 1650

García, Vicente / *Universidad Autónoma de Ciudad Juárez, Mexico* 1280

Garg, Kanwal / *Kurukshetra University, Kurukshetra, India* 892

Garg, Shikhar / *Delhi Technological University, Delhi, India* 1203

Gerrikagoitia, Jon Kepa / *BRTA Basque Research and Technology Alliance, Spain* 1153

Gherbi, Abdelouahed / *École de Technologie Supérieure, Montreal, Canada* 964

Ghosh, Soumadip / *Academy of Technology, Kolkata, India* 17, 174

Gladston, Angelin / *Anna University, Chennai, India* 398

Goel, Lipika / *Ajay Kumar Garg Engineering College Ghaziabad, India* 1871

Goyal, Mahima / *Ambedkar Institute of Advanced Communication Technologies and Research, New Delhi, India* 314

Goyal, Vishal / *Punjabi University, India* 1470

Grover, Arpita / *Kurukshetra University, India* 892

Guerreiro, João / *Instituto Universitario de Lisboa, Portugal* 433

Gupta, Charu / *Department of Computer Science and Engineering, Bhagwan Parshuram Institute of Technology, Delhi, India* 446

Gupta, Divya / *Galgotias University, India* 1032

Gupta, Neha / *Manav Rachna International Institute of Research and Studies, Faridabad, India* 137, 726, 1569

Gupta, Sachin Kumar / *School of Electronics and Communication Engineering, Shri Mata Vaishno Devi University, Jammu, India* 184

Gupta, Sonam / *Ajay Kumar Garg Engineering College Ghaziabad, India* 1871

Hai-Jew, Shalin / *Kansas State University, USA* 342

Hakak, Nida / *Maharshi Dayanand University, Haryana, India* 382

Hamou, Reda Mohamed / *GeCoDe Labs, University of Saida Dr Moulay Tahar, Algeria* 538

Hassan, Hesham Ahmed / *Faculty of Computers and Artificial Intelligence, Cairo University, Egypt* 77

Hazra, Arnab / *Academy of Technology, Kolkata, India* 174

Heuer de Carvalho, Victor Diogho / *Universidade Federal de Alagoas, Brazil* 268

Ho, Tu Bao / *John von Neumann Institute, Vietnam National University, Ho Chi Minh City, Vietnam & Japan Advanced Institute of Science and Technology, Ishikawa, Japan* 519

Hornung, Olivia / *University of Hagen, Germany* 1699

Hu, Ya-Han / *Department of Information Management, National Central University, Taoyuan, Taiwan & Center for Innovative Research on Aging Society (CIRAS), Chiayi, National Chung Cheng University, Taiwan & MOST AI Biomedical Research Center at National Cheng Kung University, Tainan, Taiwan* 800

Huang, Xia / *School of Tourism, Sichuan University, China* 1494

Hussain, Mohammad Anayat / *Ambedkar Institute of Advanced Communication Technologies and Research, New Delhi, India* 314

Idrees, Amira M. / *Faculty of Computers and Information Technology, Future University in Egypt, Egypt* 77

Ilhan, Ibrahim / *Faculty of Tourism, Nevşehir Hacı Bektas Veli University, Turkey* 1506

Ip, Andrew W. H. / *Department of Mechanical Engineering, University of Saskatchewan, Canada* 1422

Jain, Amita / *Department of Computer Science and Engineering, Ambedkar Institute of Advanced Communication Technology and Research, New Delhi, India* 446

Jain, Amith K. / *SDMIT, Ujire, India* 949

Jain, Prithviraj / *SDMIT, Ujire, India* 949

Jaiswal, Arunima / *Indira Gandhi Delhi Technical University for Women, Delhi, India* 1203

Jiménez, Rafael / *Universidad Autónoma de Ciudad Juárez, Mexico* 1280

Johal, Sukhnandan Kaur / *Thapar Institute of Engineering and Technology, India* 918

John, Blooma / *University of Canberra, Australia* 1923

Joshi, Nisheeth / *Department of Computer Science, Banasthali Vidyapith, Vanasthali, India* 446

Jyoti, Vishaw / *Manav Rachna International Institute of Research and Studies, India* 1553

K. R., Kumar / *Adhiyamaan College of Engineering, India* 1750

K., Govardhan / *Vellore Institute of Technology, Vellore, India* 1600

Kalal, Vishakha / *Central University of Rajasthan, India* 1441

Kalra, Vaishali / *Manav Rachna International Institute of Research and Studies, India* 748

Kalyan, Pavan / *SSN College of Engineering, Chennai, India* 484

Kansal, Nancy / *Ajay Kumar Garg Engineering College Ghaziabad, India* 1871

Karas, Vincent / *University of Augsburg, Germany* 27

Karnam, Sudheer / *VIT University, India* 1298

Karthikeyan, Dakshinamoorthy / *SSN College of Engineering, Chennai, India* 484

Kaur, Ramandeep / *Guru Kashi University, Talwandi Sabo, India* 1846

Kautish, Sandeep / *Guru Kashi University, Talwandi Sabo, India* 1846

Kechadi, Mohand Tahar / *Insight Centre for Data Analytics, University College Dublin, Dublin, Ireland* 1384

Khandekar, Sarang / *NIT Raipur, Raipur, India* 836

Khurana, Surinder Singh / *Central University of Punjab, India* 555

Kılıç, Erdal / *Ondokuz Mayıs University, Turkey* 690

Kirmani, Mahira / *Maharshi Dayanand University, Haryana, India* 382

Klouche, Badia / *LabRI-SBA Laboratory, Ecole Superieure en Informatique, Sidi Bel Abbes, Algeria* 1262

Kolhe, Satish R. / *School of Computer Sciences, Kavayitri Bahinabai Chaudhari North Maharashtra University, Jalgaon, India* 496

Krishnamurthy M. / *KCG College of Technology, Chennai, India* 329

Krishnaveni R. / *Hindustan University, Chennai, India* 329

Kumar, Abhishek / *School of Computer Science and IT, Jain University, Bangalore, India* 184

Kumar, Akshi / *Delhi Technological University, India* 1032, 1203

Kumar, Pardeep / *Kurukshetra University, Kurukshetra, India* 892

Kumar, Siddhant / *Delhi Technological University, Delhi, India* 1203

Kumari, Suman / *Swami Keshvanand Institute of Technology, Management, and Gramothan, Jaipur, India* 157

Kuo, Yen-Ming / *Department of Information Management, National Chung Cheng University, Chiayi, Taiwan*.. 800

Kuruva, Lakshmanna / *VIT University, India*... 1455

Law, Kris M. Y. / *School of Engineering, Deakin University, Australia*....................................... 1422

Li, Yuming / *University of Liverpool, Liverpool, UK*.. 1633

Li, Zhiyong / *School of Tourism, Sichuan University, China*.. 1494

Lin, Hao-Chaing Koong / *National University of Tainan, Tainan, Taiwan*............................... 852

López Chau, Asdrúbal / *Universidad Autónoma del Estado de México, Mexico*.......................... 116

López, Abraham / *Universidad Autónoma de Ciudad Juárez, Mexico*...................................... 1280

Loureiro, Sandra Maria Correia / *Instituto Universitário de Lisboa, Portugal*........................ 433

Lu, Ruei-Shan / *Takming University of Science and Technology, Taipei, Taiwan* 852

Ma, Yu-Chun / *National University of Tainan, Tainan, Taiwan*.. 852

Martins, Amandine Angie / *University of Aveiro, Portugal* 1831

Maylawati, Dian Sa'adillah / *UIN Sunan Gunung Djati Bandung, Bandung, Indonesia & Universiti Teknikal Malaysia Melaka, Melaka, Malaysia*... 1189

Mehta, Rupa G. / *Sardar Vallabhbhai National Institute of Technology, Surat, India*.................. 412

Mendoza Carreón, Alejandra / *Universidad Autónoma de Ciudad Juárez, Mexico* 1280

Mi, Chuanmin / *College of Economics and Management, Nanjing University of Aeronautics and Astronautics, China*.. 1887

Mittal, Mamta / *G.B. Pant Government Engineering College, New Delhi, India* 157

Mohana, Rajni / *Jaypee University of Information Technology, India* 918

Mohbey, Krishna Kumar / *Central University of Rajasthan, India*...................................... 1441

Mohsen, Amr Mansour / *Faculty of Computers and Information Technology, Future University in Egypt, Egypt* 77

Muliawaty, Lia / *Universitas Pasundan, Bandung, Indonesia* 1189

Nagesh H. R. / *A.J. Institute of Engineering and Technology, Mangalore, India*.......................... 949

Nantajeewarawat, Ekawit / *Sirindhorn International Institute of Technology, Thammasat University, Pathumthani, Thailand*... 519

Nazeer, Ishrat / *School of Computer Science and Engineering, Lovely Professional University, Jalandhar, India* 184

Ng, C. Y. / *Lee Shau Kee School of Business and Administration, The Open University of Hong Kong, Hong Kong*.. 1422

Ni, Pin / *University of Liverpool, Liverpool, UK* 1633

Nkomo, Larian M. / *University of Otago, New Zealand*... 933

Nosshi, Anthony / *Mansoura University, Mansoura, Egypt*.. 1076

Özen, Ibrahim Akın / *Faculty of Tourism, Nevşehir Hacı Bektas Veli University, Turkey*............ 1506

P., Visu / *Velammal Enginerring College, India* 1750

Pagi, Veerappa B. / *Basaveshwar Engineering College, Bagalkot, India*.................................. 780

Palit, Sandip / *Academy of Technology, Kolkata, India* 17

Panwar, Arvind / *Research Scholar, Guru Gobind Singh Indraprastha University, India* 463

Parikh, Satyen M. / *Ganpat University, India*... 214

Patel, Shreyas Kishorkumar / *Sardar Vallabhbhai National Institute of Technology, Surat, India*.. 412

Phan, Tuoi Thi / *Faculty of Computer Science and Engineering, Ho Chi Minh City University of Technology - VNU-HCM, Hồ Chí Minh, Vietnam*.. 290

Pinarbasi, Fatih / *Istanbul Medipol University, Turkey* 1360

Piscopo, Gabriella / *University of Salerno, Italy*..1528

Plangprasopchok, Anon / *National Electronics and Computer Technology Center, Pathumthani,*
    Thailand...519

Ponce, Alan / *Universidad Autónoma de Ciudad Juárez, Mexico* 1280

Prasad, Guru / *SDMIT, Ujire, India*...949

Priya, Kani / *Hindustan University, Chennai, India*..329

R., Anto Arockia Rosaline / *Department of Information Technology, Rajalakshmi Engineering*
    College, Chennai, India..816

R., Jothikumar / *Shadan College of Engineering and Technology, India* 1750

R., Kumar / *National Institute of Technology, Nagaland, India*...1750

R., Parvathi / *School of Computer Science and Engineering, VIT University, Chennai, India* 816

R., Vijay Anand / *Velloe Institute of Technology, India* 1750

Rahab, Hichem / *ICISI Laboratory, University of Khenchela, Algeria* 1237

Rahmoun, Abdellatif / *Higher School of Computer Science May 8, 1945, ESI Sidi Bel Abbes,*
    Algeria...538

Raj, Abhishek / *Academy of Technology, Kolkata, India* 174

Ramasamy, Subburaj / *SRM Institute of Science and Technology, India*......................................233

Rani, Simpel / *Yadavindra College of Engineering, India* 1470

Rao, Bapuji / *Indira Gandhi Institute of Technology, Sarang, India*...1172

Rashid, Mamoon / *School of Computer Science and Engineering, Lovely Professional*
    University, Jalandhar, India..184

Ribeiro, Dilcielly Almeida / *Universidade Federal do Sul e Sudeste do Pará, Brazil* 1611

Rodrigues, Anisha P. / *NMAM Institute of Technology, Nitte, India* 1338

Rodríguez-Mazahua, Lisbeth / *Tecnológico Nacional de México, Mexico & Instituto*
    Tecnológico de Orizaba, Mexico..637

Ruan, Xiaoyan / *College of Economics and Management, Nanjing University of Aeronautics and*
    Astronautics, Nanjing, China 1887

S., Susi / *Shadan Women's College of Engineering and Technology, India*...................................1750

Sachan, Manoj Kumar / *Computer Science and Engineering, Sant Longowal Institute of*
    Engineering and Technology, India...596

Şahin, Durmuş Özkan / *Ondokuz Mayıs University, Turkey* 690

Sahu, Tirath Prasad / *NIT Raipur, Raipur, India* 836

Salamah, Ummu / *Universitas Pasundan, Bandung, Indonesia*...1189

Salas-Zárate, María del Pilar / *Tecnológico Nacional de México, Mexico & ITS Teziutlán,*
    Mexico 637

Salhi, Dhai Eddine / *LIMOSE Laboratory, University of Mhamed Bougara, Boumerdes,*
    Algeria 1384

Salunkhe, Aditya Suresh / *Ramrao Adik Institute of Technolgy, India* 1590

Sánchez-Cervantes, José Luis / *CONACYT, Mexico & Instituto Tecnológico de Orizaba, Mexico* 637

Sánchez-Holgado, Patricia / *University of Salamanca, Salamanca, Spain*....................................673

Sandoval-Almazán, Rodrigo / *Universidad Autónoma del Estado de México, Mexico* 116

Sanglerdsinlapachai, Nuttapong / *Sirindhorn International Institute of Technology, Thammasat*
    University, Pathumthani, Thailand & Japan Advanced Institute of Science and Technology,
    Ishikawa, Japan...519

Sangwan, Om Prakash / *Department of Computer Science and Technology, Guru Jambheshwar*
    University of Science and Technology, Hisar, India..256

Santos, José / *Federal University of Sul and Sudeste of Pará, Brazil* 1611

Sariki, Tulasi Prasad / *VIT University, India* 1298

Sarkar, Deeptanu / *VIT University, India* 1455

Schuller, Björn W. / *University of Augsburg, Germany* 27

Senousy, Mohammed Badr / *Sadat Academy for Management Sciences, Cairo, Egypt* 1076

Serna, Ainhoa / *University of the Basque Country, Spain* 1153

Serova, Elena / *National Research University Higher School of Economics, Russia* 1101

Seshadri, Karthick / *National Institute of Technology, Tadepalligudem, India* 1314

Seth, Ashish / *INHA University, Tashkent, India* 1

Seth, Kirti / *INHA University, Tashkent, India* 1

Seth, Rakhi / *National Institute of Technology, Raipur, India* 864

Shah, Bisma / *Jamia Hamdard, India* 1119

Shah, Mitali K. / *Ganpat University, India* 214

Shakeel, P Mohamed / *Faculty of Information and Communication Technology, Universiti Teknikal Malaysia Melaka, Malaysia* 1064

Shanthi I., Elizabeth / *Avinashilingam Institution for Home Science and Higher Education for Women, Avinashilingam University, India* 1717

Sharaff, Aakanksha / *National Institute of Technology, Raipur, India* 864

Sharma, Kapil / *Delhi Technological University, New Delhi, India* 1219

Sharma, Tamanna / *Department of Computer Science and Technology, Guru Jambheshwar University of Science and Technology, Hisar, India* 256

Siddiqui, Farheen / *Jamia Hamdard, India* 1119, 1401

Sidhu, Simran / *Central University of Punjab, India* 555

Silva, Priscilla Souza / *Federal University of South and Southeast of Pará, Brazil* 1611

Singh, Shailendra Kumar / *Computer Science and Engineering, Sant Longowal Institute of Engineering and Technology, India* 596

Singh, Vijendra / *The NorthCap University, Gurgaon, India* 1905

Sivamani, Babu Aravind / *SSN College of Engineering, Chennai, India* 484

Smolnik, Stefan / *University of Hagen, Germany* 1699

Somula, Ramasubbareddy / *Vallurupalli Nageswara Rao Vignana Jyothi Institute of Engineering and Technology, India* 1680

Sonawane, Sudarshan S. / *Department of Computer Engineering, Shri Gulabrao Deokar College of Engineering, Jalgaon, India* 496

Soni, Akshat / *VIT University, India* 1455

Srivastava, Ankit / *The NorthCap University, Gurgaon, India* 1905

Sulthana, Razia / *SRM Institute of Science and Technology, India* 233

Tari, Abelkamel / *LIMED Laboratory, University Abderrahmane Mira, Bejaia, Algeria* 1384

Tran, Thien Khai / *Faculty of Computer Science and Engineering, Ho Chi Minh City University of Technology - VNU-HCM, Hồ Chí Minh, Vietnam & Faculty of Information Technology, Ho Chi Minh City University of Foreign Languages and Information Technology, Hồ Chí Minh, Vietnam* 290

Trezza, Domenico / *University of Naples Federico II, Italy* 761

Tripathi, Ashish Kumar / *Delhi Technological University, New Delhi, India* 1219

Tsai, Chih-Fong / *Department of Information Management, National Central University, Taiwan* 800

Tsao, Hsiu-Yuan / *National Chung Hsing University, Taiwan* 852

Uma, V. / *Pondicherry University, India* 198, 1541

Valarmathi B. / *VIT University, India* 1298

Valle-Cruz, David / *Universidad Autónoma del Estado de México, Mexico* 116

Verma, Amber / *Vellore Institute of Technology, Vellore, India* 1600

Verma, Shobhit / *Delhi Technological University, Delhi, India* 1203

Verma, Siddharth / *Manav Rachna International Institute of Research and Studies, India* 726

Vora, Shivani Vasantbhai / *CGPIT, Uka Tarsadia University, Bardoli, India* 412

Vyas, Vishal / *Pondicherry University, India* 198, 1541

Wadawadagi, Ramesh S. / *Basaveshwar Engineering College, Bagalkot, India* 780

Weitzel, Leila / *Fluminense Federal University, Brazil* 1611

Wickramasinghe, Nilmini / *Swinburne University of Technology, Australia & Epworth HealthCare, Australia* 1923

Xiao, Lin / *College of Economics and Management, Nanjing University of Aeronautics and Astronautics, Nanjing, China* 1887

Yadavilli, Vrps Sastry / *National Institute of Technology, Tadepalligudem, India* 1314

You, Zi-Hung / *Department of Nephrology, Chiayi Branch, Taichung Veterans General Hospital, Chiayi, Taiwan* 800

Zerrouki, Kadda / *Higher School of Computer Science May 8, 1945, ESI Sidi Bel Abbes, Algeria* 538, 902

Zitouni, Abdelhafid / *LIRE Laboratory, University of Constantine 2, Algeria* 1237

Table of Contents

Preface..xxviii

Volume I

Section 1
Fundamental Concepts and Theories

Chapter 1
Fundamentals of Opinion Mining... 1
    Ashish Seth, INHA University, Tashkent, India
    Kirti Seth, INHA University, Tashkent, India

Chapter 2
Real Time Sentiment Analysis.. 17
    Sandip Palit, Academy of Technology, Kolkata, India
    Soumadip Ghosh, Academy of Technology, Kolkata, India

Chapter 3
Deep Learning for Sentiment Analysis: An Overview and Perspectives... 27
    Vincent Karas, University of Augsburg, Germany
    Björn W. Schuller, University of Augsburg, Germany

Chapter 4
Sentiment Analysis Techniques, Tools, Applications, and Challenge... 63
    Chitra A. Dhawale, P. R. Pote College of Engineering and Management, India
    Vandana V. Chaudhari, Smt. G. G. Khadse College, India

Chapter 5
Tasks, Approaches, and Avenues of Opinion Mining, Sentiment Analysis, and Emotion Analysis:
Opinion Mining and Extents.. 77
    *Amira M. Idrees, Faculty of Computers and Information Technology, Future University in
        Egypt, Egypt*
    *Fatma Gamal Eldin, Faculty of Computers and Information Technology, Future University in
        Egypt, Egypt*
    *Amr Mansour Mohsen, Faculty of Computers and Information Technology, Future University
        in Egypt, Egypt*
    Hesham Ahmed Hassan, Faculty of Computers and Artificial Intelligence, Cairo University, Egypt

Chapter 6
Sentiment Analysis in Crisis Situations for Better Connected Government: Case of Mexico
Earthquake in 2017 116
    Asdrúbal López Chau, Universidad Autónoma del Estado de México, Mexico
    David Valle-Cruz, Universidad Autónoma del Estado de México, Mexico
    Rodrigo Sandoval-Almazán, Universidad Autónoma del Estado de México, Mexico

Section 2
Development and Design Methodologies

Chapter 7
Integrating Semantic Acquaintance for Sentiment Analysis 137
    Neha Gupta, Manav Rachna International Institute of Research and Studies, Faridabad, India
    Rashmi Agrawal, Manav Rachna International Institute of Research and Studies, Faridabad, India

Chapter 8
A Deep Neural Network Model for Cross-Domain Sentiment Analysis 157
    Suman Kumari, Swami Keshvanand Institute of Technology, Management, and Gramothan, Jaipur, India
    Basant Agarwal, Indian Institute of Information Technology, Kota, India
    Mamta Mittal, G.B. Pant Government Engineering College, New Delhi, India

Chapter 9
A Comparative Study of Different Classification Techniques for Sentiment Analysis 174
    Soumadip Ghosh, Academy of Technology, Kolkata, India
    Arnab Hazra, Academy of Technology, Kolkata, India
    Abhishek Raj, Academy of Technology, Kolkata, India

Chapter 10
Use of Novel Ensemble Machine Learning Approach for Social Media Sentiment Analysis 184
    Ishrat Nazeer, School of Computer Science and Engineering, Lovely Professional University, Jalandhar, India
    Mamoon Rashid, School of Computer Science and Engineering, Lovely Professional University, Jalandhar, India
    Sachin Kumar Gupta, School of Electronics and Communication Engineering, Shri Mata Vaishno Devi University, Jammu, India
    Abhishek Kumar, School of Computer Science and IT, Jain University, Bangalore, India

Chapter 11
Approaches to Sentiment Analysis on Product Reviews 198
    Vishal Vyas, Pondicherry University, India
    V. Uma, Pondicherry University, India

Chapter 12

Classification Approach for Sentiment Analysis Using Machine Learning 214

    Satyen M. Parikh, Ganpat University, India

    Mitali K. Shah, Ganpat University, India

Chapter 13

Applications of Ontology-Based Opinion Mining...233

    Razia Sulthana, SRM Institute of Science and Technology, India

    Subburaj Ramasamy, SRM Institute of Science and Technology, India

Chapter 14

Deep Learning Approaches for Textual Sentiment Analysis 256

    Tamanna Sharma, Department of Computer Science and Technology, Guru Jambheshwar
        University of Science and Technology, Hisar, India

    Anu Bajaj, Department of Computer Science and Engineering, Guru Jambheshwar
        University of Science and Technology, Hisar, India

    Om Prakash Sangwan, Department of Computer Science and Technology, Guru
        Jambheshwar University of Science and Technology, Hisar, India

Chapter 15

Public Security Sentiment Analysis on Social Web: A Conceptual Framework for the Analytical
Process and a Research Agenda...268

    Victor Diogho Heuer de Carvalho, Universidade Federal de Alagoas, Brazil

    Ana Paula Cabral Seixas Costa, Universidade Federal de Pernambuco, Brazil

Chapter 16

Towards a Sentiment Analysis Model Based on Semantic Relation Analysis..................................290

    Thien Khai Tran, Faculty of Computer Science and Engineering, Ho Chi Minh City
        University of Technology - VNU-HCM, Hồ Chí Minh, Vietnam & Faculty of Information
        Technology, Ho Chi Minh City University of Foreign Languages and Information
        Technology, Hồ Chí Minh, Vietnam

    Tuoi Thi Phan, Faculty of Computer Science and Engineering, Ho Chi Minh City University
        of Technology - VNU-HCM, Hồ Chí Minh, Vietnam

Chapter 17

A Novel Aspect Based Framework for Tourism Sector with Improvised Aspect and Opinion
Mining Algorithm..314

    Vishal Bhatnagar, Department of Computer Science and Engineering, Ambedkar Institute of
        Advanced Communication Technologies and Research, New Delhi, India

    Mahima Goyal, Ambedkar Institute of Advanced Communication Technologies and
        Research, New Delhi, India

    Mohammad Anayat Hussain, Ambedkar Institute of Advanced Communication Technologies
        and Research, New Delhi, India

Chapter 18
Analyzing Social Emotions in Social Network Using Graph Based Co-Ranking Algorithm 329
  Kani Priya, Hindustan University, Chennai, India
  Krishnaveni R., Hindustan University, Chennai, India
  Krishnamurthy M., KCG College of Technology, Chennai, India
  Bairavel S., KCG College of Technology, Chennai, India

Chapter 19
Using Computational Text Analysis to Explore Open-Ended Survey Question Responses 342
  Shalin Hai-Jew, Kansas State University, USA

Chapter 20
A Probabilistic Deep Learning Approach for Twitter Sentiment Analysis 367
  Mostefai Abdelkader, Dr. Tahar Moulay University of Saida, Algeria

Chapter 21
Opinion Mining of Twitter Events using Supervised Learning 382
  Nida Hakak, Maharshi Dayanand University, Haryana, India
  Mahira Kirmani, Maharshi Dayanand University, Haryana, India

Chapter 22
Implementation of Recurrent Network for Emotion Recognition of Twitter Data 398
  Anu Kiruthika M., Anna University, Chennai, India
  Angelin Gladston, Anna University, Chennai, India

Chapter 23
Impact of Balancing Techniques for Imbalanced Class Distribution on Twitter Data for Emotion
Analysis: A Case Study 412
  Shivani Vasantbhai Vora, CGPIT, Uka Tarsadia University, Bardoli, India
  Rupa G. Mehta, Sardar Vallabhbhai National Institute of Technology, Surat, India
  Shreyas Kishorkumar Patel, Sardar Vallabhbhai National Institute of Technology, Surat, India

Chapter 24
Unraveling E-WOM Patterns Using Text Mining and Sentiment Analysis 433
  João Guerreiro, Instituto Universitario de Lisboa, Portugal
  Sandra Maria Correia Loureiro, Instituto Universitário de Lisboa, Portugal

Chapter 25
DE-ForABSA: A Novel Approach to Forecast Automobiles Sales Using Aspect Based Sentiment
Analysis and Differential Evolution 446
  Charu Gupta, Department of Computer Science and Engineering, Bhagwan Parshuram
    Institute of Technology, Delhi, India
  Amita Jain, Department of Computer Science and Engineering, Ambedkar Institute of
    Advanced Communication Technology and Research, New Delhi, India
  Nisheeth Joshi, Department of Computer Science, Banasthali Vidyapith, Vanasthali, India

Volume II

Chapter 26

Sentiment Analysis of Game Review Using Machine Learning in a Hadoop Ecosystem 463
>   *Arvind Panwar, Research Scholar, Guru Gobind Singh Indraprastha University, India*
>   *Vishal Bhatnagar, Ambedkar Institute of Advanced Communication Technologies and*
>   *Research, Delhi, India*

Chapter 27

Time Series for Forecasting Stock Market Prices Based on Sentiment Analysis of Social Media 484
>   *Babu Aravind Sivamani, SSN College of Engineering, Chennai, India*
>   *Dakshinamoorthy Karthikeyan, SSN College of Engineering, Chennai, India*
>   *Chamundeswari Arumugam, SSN College of Engineering, Chennai, India*
>   *Pavan Kalyan, SSN College of Engineering, Chennai, India*

Chapter 28

Feature Optimization in Sentiment Analysis by Term Co-occurrence Fitness Evolution (TCFE) 496
>   *Sudarshan S. Sonawane, Department of Computer Engineering, Shri Gulabrao Deokar*
>   *College of Engineering, Jalgaon, India*
>   *Satish R. Kolhe, School of Computer Sciences, Kavayitri Bahinabai Chaudhari North*
>   *Maharashtra University, Jalgaon, India*

Chapter 29

Rule-Based Polarity Aggregation Using Rhetorical Structures for Aspect-Based Sentiment
Analysis 519
>   *Nuttapong Sanglerdsinlapachai, Sirindhorn International Institute of Technology,*
>   *Thammasat University, Pathumthani, Thailand & Japan Advanced Institute of Science*
>   *and Technology, Ishikawa, Japan*
>   *Anon Plangprasopchok, National Electronics and Computer Technology Center,*
>   *Pathumthani, Thailand*
>   *Tu Bao Ho, John von Neumann Institute, Vietnam National University, Ho Chi Minh City,*
>   *Vietnam & Japan Advanced Institute of Science and Technology, Ishikawa, Japan*
>   *Ekawit Nantajeewarawat, Sirindhorn International Institute of Technology, Thammasat*
>   *University, Pathumthani, Thailand*

Chapter 30

Sentiment Analysis of Tweets Using Naïve Bayes, KNN, and Decision Tree 538
>   *Kadda Zerrouki, Higher School of Computer Science May 8, 1945, ESI Sidi Bel Abbes, Algeria*
>   *Reda Mohamed Hamou, GeCoDe Labs, University of Saida Dr Moulay Tahar, Algeria*
>   *Abdellatif Rahmoun, Higher School of Computer Science May 8, 1945, ESI Sidi Bel Abbes,*
>   *Algeria*

Chapter 31

Method to Rank Academic Institutes by the Sentiment Analysis of Their Online Reviews 555
>   *Simran Sidhu, Central University of Punjab, India*
>   *Surinder Singh Khurana, Central University of Punjab, India*

Chapter 32
Sentiment Analysis Using Machine Learning Algorithms and Text Mining to Detect Symptoms of
Mental Difficulties Over Social Media 581
    Hadj Ahmed Bouarara, GeCoDe Laboratory, Algeria

Chapter 33
Classification of Code-Mixed Bilingual Phonetic Text Using Sentiment Analysis 596
    Shailendra Kumar Singh, Computer Science and Engineering, Sant Longowal Institute of
        Engineering and Technology, India
    Manoj Kumar Sachan, Computer Science and Engineering, Sant Longowal Institute of
        Engineering and Technology, India

Chapter 34
Develop a Neural Model to Score Bigram of Words Using Bag-of-Words Model for Sentiment
Analysis 619
    Anumeera Balamurali, St.Joseph's College of Engineering, India
    Balamurali Ananthanarayanan, Tamilnadu Agriculture Department, India

Chapter 35
An Opinion Mining Approach for Drug Reviews in Spanish 637
    Karina Castro-Pérez, Tecnológico Nacional de México, Mexico & IT Orizaba, Mexico
    José Luis Sánchez-Cervantes, CONACYT, Mexico & Instituto Tecnológico de Orizaba, Mexico
    María del Pilar Salas-Zárate, Tecnológico Nacional de México, Mexico & ITS Teziutlán, Mexico
    Maritza Bustos-López, Tecnológico Nacional de México, Mexico & Instituto Tecnológico de
        Orizaba, Mexico
    Lisbeth Rodríguez-Mazahua, Tecnológico Nacional de México, Mexico & Instituto
        Tecnológico de Orizaba, Mexico

Chapter 36
Supervised Sentiment Analysis of Science Topics: Developing a Training Set of Tweets in
Spanish 673
    Patricia Sánchez-Holgado, University of Salamanca, Salamanca, Spain
    Carlos Arcila-Calderón, University of Salamanca, Salamanca, Spain

Chapter 37
An Extensive Text Mining Study for the Turkish Language: Author Recognition, Sentiment
Analysis, and Text Classification 690
    Durmuş Özkan Şahin, Ondokuz Mayıs University, Turkey
    Erdal Kılıç, Ondokuz Mayıs University, Turkey

Section 3
Tools and Technologies

Chapter 38
Tools of Opinion Mining 726
    Neha Gupta, Manav Rachna International Institute of Research and Studies, India
    Siddharth Verma, Manav Rachna International Institute of Research and Studies, India

Chapter 39
Challenges of Text Analytics in Opinion Mining 748
 Vaishali Kalra, Manav Rachna International Institute of Research and Studies, India
 Rashmi Agrawal, Manav Rachna International Institute of Research and Studies, India

Chapter 40
Learning Algorithms of Sentiment Analysis: A Comparative Approach to Improve Data
Goodness... 761
 Suania Acampa, University of Naples Federico II, Italy
 Ciro Clemente De Falco, University of Naples Federico II, Italy
 Domenico Trezza, University of Naples Federico II, Italy

Chapter 41
Sentiment Analysis on Social Media: Recent Trends in Machine Learning 780
 Ramesh S. Wadawadagi, Basaveshwar Engineering College, Bagalkot, India
 Veerappa B. Pagi, Basaveshwar Engineering College, Bagalkot, India

Chapter 42
Integrating Feature and Instance Selection Techniques in Opinion Mining 800
 Zi-Hung You, Department of Nephrology, Chiayi Branch, Taichung Veterans General
  Hospital, Chiayi, Taiwan
 Ya-Han Hu, Department of Information Management, National Central University, Taoyuan,
  Taiwan & Center for Innovative Research on Aging Society (CIRAS), Chiayi, National
  Chung Cheng University, Taiwan & MOST AI Biomedical Research Center at National
  Cheng Kung University, Tainan, Taiwan
 Chih-Fong Tsai, Department of Information Management, National Central University, Taiwan
 Yen-Ming Kuo, Department of Information Management, National Chung Cheng University,
  Chiayi, Taiwan

Chapter 43
Deep Learning for Social Media Text Analytics 816
 Anto Arockia Rosaline R., Department of Information Technology, Rajalakshmi Engineering
  College, Chennai, India
 Parvathi R., School of Computer Science and Engineering, VIT University, Chennai, India

Chapter 44
A Machine Learning-Based Lexicon Approach for Sentiment Analysis..................................... 836
 Tirath Prasad Sahu, NIT Raipur, Raipur, India
 Sarang Khandekar, NIT Raipur, Raipur, India

Chapter 45
Sentiment Analysis of Brand Personality Positioning Through Text Mining............................... 852
 Ruei-Shan Lu, Takming University of Science and Technology, Taipei, Taiwan
 Hsiu-Yuan Tsao, National Chung Hsing University, Taiwan
 Hao-Chaing Koong Lin, National University of Tainan, Tainan, Taiwan
 Yu-Chun Ma, National University of Tainan, Tainan, Taiwan
 Cheng-Tung Chuang, Takming University of Science and Technology, Taipei, Taiwan

Chapter 46
Deep Learning Based Sentiment Analysis for Phishing SMS Detection...864
Aakanksha Sharaff, National Institute of Technology, Raipur, India
Ramya Allenki, UnitedHealth Group, India
Rakhi Seth, National Institute of Technology, Raipur, India

Chapter 47
Improvisation of Cleaning Process on Tweets for Opinion Mining...892
Arpita Grover, Kurukshetra University, India
Pardeep Kumar, Kurukshetra University, Kurukshetra, India
Kanwal Garg, Kurukshetra University, Kurukshetra, India

Chapter 48
Machine Learning in Sentiment Analysis Over Twitter: Synthesis and Comparative Study 902
Kadda Zerrouki, Tahar Moulay University of Saida, Algeria

Chapter 49
Effectiveness of Normalization Over Processing of Textual Data Using Hybrid Approach
Sentiment Analysis 918
Sukhnandan Kaur Johal, Thapar Institute of Engineering and Technology, India
Rajni Mohana, Jaypee University of Information Technology, India

Chapter 50
Chatbot Experiences of Informal Language Learners: A Sentiment Analysis 933
Antonie Alm, University of Otago, New Zealand
Larian M. Nkomo, University of Otago, New Zealand

Chapter 51
A Novel Approach to Optimize the Performance of Hadoop Frameworks for Sentiment
Analysis...949
Guru Prasad, SDMIT, Ujire, India
Amith K. Jain, SDMIT, Ujire, India
Prithviraj Jain, SDMIT, Ujire, India
Nagesh H. R., A.J. Institute of Engineering and Technology, Mangalore, India

Volume III

Chapter 52
Building Sentiment Analysis Model and Compute Reputation Scores in E-Commerce
Environment Using Machine Learning Techniques..964
Elshrif Ibrahim Elmurngi, École de Technologie Supérieure, Montreal, Canada
Abdelouahed Gherbi, École de Technologie Supérieure, Montreal, Canada

Chapter 53
Hybrid Approach for Sentiment Analysis of Twitter Posts Using a Dictionary-based Approach
and Fuzzy Logic Methods: Study Case on Cloud Service Providers 1000
    Jamilah Rabeh Alharbi, Department of Computer Science, King Abdulaziz University,
        Jeddah, Saudi Arabia
    Wadee S. Alhalabi, Department of Computer Science, King Abdulaziz University, Jeddah,
        Saudi Arabia

Chapter 54
Sentiment Analysis as a Restricted NLP Problem 1032
    Akshi Kumar, Delhi Technological University, India
    Divya Gupta, Galgotias University, India

Chapter 55
Automatic Human Emotion Classification in Web Document Using Fuzzy Inference System
(FIS): Human Emotion Classification.. 1064
    P Mohamed Shakeel, Faculty of Information and Communication Technology, Universiti
        Teknikal Malaysia Melaka, Malaysia
    S Baskar, Department of Electronics and Communication Engineering, Karpagam Academy
        of Higher Education, Coimbatore, India

Chapter 56
Hybrid Recommender System Using Emotional Fingerprints Model.. 1076
    Anthony Nosshi, Mansoura University, Mansoura, Egypt
    Aziza Saad Asem, Mansoura University, Mansoura, Egypt
    Mohammed Badr Senousy, Sadat Academy for Management Sciences, Cairo, Egypt

Chapter 57
Using Intelligent Text Analysis of Online Reviews to Determine the Main Factors of Restaurant
Value Propositions 1101
    Elizaveta Fainshtein, National Research University Higher School of Economics, Russia
    Elena Serova, National Research University Higher School of Economics, Russia

Chapter 58
A Novel Algorithm for Sentiment Analysis of Online Movie Reviews... 1119
    Bisma Shah, Jamia Hamdard, India
    Farheen Siddiqui, Jamia Hamdard, India

Chapter 59
Discovery of Sustainable Transport Modes Underlying TripAdvisor Reviews With Sentiment
Analysis: Transport Domain Adaptation of Sentiment Labelled Data Set 1153
    Ainhoa Serna, University of the Basque Country, Spain
    Jon Kepa Gerrikagoitia, BRTA Basque Research and Technology Alliance, Spain

Chapter 60

An Approach to Opinion Mining in Community Graph Using Graph Mining Techniques 1172

    Bapuji Rao, Indira Gandhi Institute of Technology, Sarang, India

Chapter 61

The Concept of Big Data in Bureaucratic Service Using Sentiment Analysis 1189

    Lia Muliawaty, Universitas Pasundan, Bandung, Indonesia

    Kamal Alamsyah, Universitas Pasundan, Bandung, Indonesia

    Ummu Salamah, Universitas Pasundan, Bandung, Indonesia

    Dian Sa'adillah Maylawati, UIN Sunan Gunung Djati Bandung, Bandung, Indonesia &
       Universiti Teknikal Malaysia Melaka, Melaka, Malaysia

Chapter 62

Sentiment Analysis Using Cuckoo Search for Optimized Feature Selection on Kaggle Tweets 1203

    Akshi Kumar, Delhi Technological University, Delhi, India

    Arunima Jaiswal, Indira Gandhi Delhi Technical University for Women, Delhi, India

    Shikhar Garg, Delhi Technological University, Delhi, India

    Shobhit Verma, Delhi Technological University, Delhi, India

    Siddhant Kumar, Delhi Technological University, Delhi, India

Chapter 63

Parallel Hybrid BBO Search Method for Twitter Sentiment Analysis of Large Scale Datasets
Using MapReduce 1219

    Ashish Kumar Tripathi, Delhi Technological University, New Delhi, India

    Kapil Sharma, Delhi Technological University, New Delhi, India

    Manju Bala, Indraprastha College of Women, New Delhi, India

Chapter 64

Sentiment Analysis of Arabic Documents: Main Challenges and Recent Advances 1237

    Hichem Rahab, ICISI Laboratory, University of Khenchela, Algeria

    Mahieddine Djoudi, TechNE Laboratory, University of Poitiers, France

    Abdelhafid Zitouni, LIRE Laboratory, University of Constantine 2, Algeria

Chapter 65

Ooredoo Rayek: A Business Decision Support System Based on Multi-Language Sentiment
Analysis of Algerian Operator Telephones 1262

    Badia Klouche, LabRI-SBA Laboratory, Ecole Superieure en Informatique, Sidi Bel Abbes,
       Algeria

    Sidi Mohamed Benslimane, LabRI-SBA Laboratory, Ecole Superieure en Informatique, Sidi
       Bel-Abbes, Algeria

    Sakina Rim Bennabi, Ecole Superieure en Informatique, Sidi Bel Abbes, Algeria

Chapter 66
Opinion Mining for Instructor Evaluations at the Autonomous University of Ciudad Juarez.......... 1280
    Rafael Jiménez, Universidad Autónoma de Ciudad Juárez, Mexico
    Vicente García, Universidad Autónoma de Ciudad Juárez, Mexico
    Abraham López, Universidad Autónoma de Ciudad Juárez, Mexico
    Alejandra Mendoza Carreón, Universidad Autónoma de Ciudad Juárez, Mexico
    Alan Ponce, Universidad Autónoma de Ciudad Juárez, Mexico

Section 4
Utilization and Applications

Chapter 67
A Survey on Implementation Methods and Applications of Sentiment Analysis 1298
    Sudheer Karnam, VIT University, India
    Valarmathi B., VIT University, India
    Tulasi Prasad Sariki, VIT University, India

Chapter 68
A Survey on Aspect Extraction Approaches for Sentiment Analysis 1314
    Vrps Sastry Yadavilli, National Institute of Technology, Tadepalligudem, India
    Karthick Seshadri, National Institute of Technology, Tadepalligudem, India

Chapter 69
Social Big Data Mining: A Survey Focused on Sentiment Analysis 1338
    Anisha P. Rodrigues, NMAM Institute of Technology, Nitte, India
    Niranjan N. Chiplunkar, NMAM Institute of Technology, Nitte, India
    Roshan Fernandes, NMAM Institute of Technology, Nitte, India

Chapter 70
Using Sentiment Analysis for Evaluating e-WOM: A Data Mining Approach for Marketing
Decision Making 1360
    Zehra Nur Canbolat, Istanbul Medipol University, Turkey
    Fatih Pinarbasi, Istanbul Medipol University, Turkey

Chapter 71
Using E-Reputation for Sentiment Analysis: Twitter as a Case Study 1384
    Dhai Eddine Salhi, LIMOSE Laboratory, University of Mhamed Bougara, Boumerdes, Algeria
    Abelkamel Tari, LIMED Laboratory, University Abderrahmane Mira, Bejaia, Algeria
    Mohand Tahar Kechadi, Insight Centre for Data Analytics, University College Dublin,
        Dublin, Ireland

Chapter 72
Ontology-Based Opinion Mining for Online Product Reviews 1401
    Farheen Siddiqui, Jamia Hamdard, India
    Parul Agarwal, Jamia Hamdard, India

Chapter 73
Assessing Public Opinions of Products Through Sentiment Analysis: Product Satisfaction
Assessment by Sentiment Analysis 1422
    C. Y. Ng, Lee Shau Kee School of Business and Administration, The Open University of Hong
        Kong, Hong Kong
    Kris M. Y. Law, School of Engineering, Deakin University, Australia
    Andrew W. H. Ip, Department of Mechanical Engineering, University of Saskatchewan, Canada

Volume IV

Chapter 74
A Study and Comparison of Sentiment Analysis Techniques Using Demonetization: Case
Study 1441
    Krishna Kumar Mohbey, Central University of Rajasthan, India
    Brijesh Bakariya, I. K. Gujral Punjab Techncial University, India
    Vishakha Kalal, Central University of Rajasthan, India

Chapter 75
Application of Sentiment Analysis in Movie reviews 1455
    ThippaReddy Gadekallu, VIT University, India
    Akshat Soni, VIT University, India
    Deeptanu Sarkar, VIT University, India
    Lakshmanna Kuruva, VIT University, India

Chapter 76
Experimenting Language Identification for Sentiment Analysis of English Punjabi Code Mixed
Social Media Text 1470
    Neetika Bansal, College of Engineering & Management, India
    Vishal Goyal, Punjabi University, India
    Simpel Rani, Yadavindra College of Engineering, India

Chapter 77
Towards Semantic Aspect-Based Sentiment Analysis for Arabic Reviews 1480
    Salima Behdenna, Department of Computer Science, Faculty of Exact and Applied Sciences,
        Laboratoire d'Informatique d'Oran (LIO), Université Oran1 Ahmed Ben Bella, Oran, Algeria
    Fatiha Barigou, Department of Computer Science, Faculty of Exact and Applied Sciences,
        Laboratoire d'Informatique d'Oran (LIO), Université Oran1 Ahmed Ben Bella, Oran, Algeria
    Ghalem Belalem, Department of Computer Science, Faculty of Exact and Applied Sciences,
        Laboratoire d'Informatique d'Oran (LIO), Université Oran1 Ahmed Ben Bella, Oran, Algeria

Chapter 78
Airbnb or Hotel? A Comparative Study on the Sentiment of Airbnb Guests in Sydney – Text
Analysis Based on Big Data 1494
    Zhiyong Li, School of Tourism, Sichuan University, China
    Honglin Chen, School of Tourism, Sichuan University, China
    Xia Huang, School of Tourism, Sichuan University, China

Chapter 79
Opinion Mining in Tourism: A Study on "Cappadocia Home Cooking" Restaurant.......................1506
    Ibrahim Akın Özen, Faculty of Tourism, Nevşehir Hacı Bektas Veli University, Turkey
    Ibrahim Ilhan, Faculty of Tourism, Nevşehir Hacı Bektas Veli University, Turkey

Chapter 80
Communicating Natural Calamity: The Sentiment Analysis of Post Rigopiano's Accident............1528
    Nicola Capolupo, University of Salerno, Italy
    Gabriella Piscopo, University of Salerno, Italy

Section 5
Organizational and Social Implications

Chapter 81
Open Issues in Opinion Mining 1541
    Vishal Vyas, Pondicherry University, India
    V. Uma, Pondicherry University, India

Chapter 82
Feature Based Opinion Mining...1553
    Mridula Batra, Manav Rachna International Institute of Research and Studies, India
    Vishaw Jyoti, Manav Rachna International Institute of Research and Studies, India

Chapter 83
Impact of Deep Learning on Semantic Sentiment Analysis 1569
    Neha Gupta, Manav Rachna International Institute of Research and Studies, Faridabad, India
    Rashmi Agrawal, Manav Rachna International Institute of Research and Studies, Faridabad,
        India

Chapter 84
An Overview of Methodologies and Challenges in Sentiment Analysis on Social Networks..........1590
    Aditya Suresh Salunkhe, Ramrao Adik Institute of Technolgy, India
    Pallavi Vijay Chavan, Ramrao Adik Institute of Technolgy, India

Chapter 85
Sentiment Analysis and Sarcasm Detection (Using Emoticons) 1600
    Vibhu Dagar, Vellore Institute of Technology, Vellore, India
    Amber Verma, Vellore Institute of Technology, Vellore, India
    Govardhan K., Vellore Institute of Technology, Vellore, India

Chapter 86
Impact of Sarcasm in Sentiment Analysis Methodology 1611
    Priscilla Souza Silva, Federal University of South and Southeast of Pará, Brazil
    Haroldo Barroso, Federal University of Sul and Sudeste of Pará, Brazil
    Leila Weitzel, Fluminense Federal University, Brazil
    Dilcielly Almeida Ribeiro, Universidade Federal do Sul e Sudeste do Pará, Brazil
    José Santos, Federal University of Sul and Sudeste of Pará, Brazil

Chapter 87
Recommendation and Sentiment Analysis Based on Consumer Review and Rating.................... 1633
    Pin Ni, University of Liverpool, Liverpool, UK
    Yuming Li, University of Liverpool, Liverpool, UK
    Victor Chang, Teesside University, Middlesbrough, UK

Chapter 88
The Application of Sentiment Analysis and Text Analytics to Customer Experience Reviews to
Understand What Customers Are Really Saying 1650
    Conor Gallagher, Letterkenny Institute of Technology, Donegal, Ireland
    Eoghan Furey, Letterkenny Institute of Technology, Donegal, Ireland
    Kevin Curran, Ulster University, Derry, UK

Chapter 89
Behaviour and Emotions of Working Professionals Towards Online Learning Systems: Sentiment
Analysis 1680
    Venkata Ramana Attili, Sreenidhi Institute of Science and Technology, India
    Sreenivasa Rao Annaluri, Vallurupalli Nageswara Rao Vignana Jyothi Institute of
        Engineering and Technology, India
    Suresh Reddy Gali, Vallurupalli Nageswara Rao Vignana Jyothi Institute of Engineering and
        Technology, India
    Ramasubbareddy Somula, Vallurupalli Nageswara Rao Vignana Jyothi Institute of
        Engineering and Technology, India

Chapter 90
When Emotions Rule Knowledge: A Text-Mining Study of Emotions in Knowledge Management
Research 1699
    Nora Fteimi, University of Passau, Germany
    Olivia Hornung, University of Hagen, Germany
    Stefan Smolnik, University of Hagen, Germany

Chapter 91
Role of Educational Data Mining in Student Learning Processes With Sentiment Analysis: A
Survey 1717
    Amala Jayanthi M., Kumaraguru College of Technology, India
    Elizabeth Shanthi I., Avinashilingam Institution for Home Science and Higher Education for
        Women, Avinashilingam University, India

Chapter 92
Tracking How a Change in a Telecom Service Affects Its Customers Using Sentiment Analysis
and Personality Insight... 1733
    Ammar Adl, Faculty of Computers and Information, Beni-Suef University, Egypt
    Abdelsadeq Khamis Elfergany, Faculty of Computers and Information, Beni-Suef University,
        Egypt

Chapter 93
Sentiment Analysis of Tweets on the COVID-19 Pandemic Using Machine Learning
Techniques 1750
    Jothikumar R., Shadan College of Engineering and Technology, India
    Vijay Anand R., Velloe Institute of Technology, India
    Visu P., Velammal Enginerring College, India
    Kumar R., National Institute of Technology, Nagaland, India
    Susi S., Shadan Women's College of Engineering and Technology, India
    Kumar K. R., Adhiyamaan College of Engineering, India

Chapter 94
Coronavirus Pandemic (COVID-19): Emotional Toll Analysis on Twitter 1761
    Jalal S. Alowibdi, University of Jeddah, Saudi Arabia
    Abdulrahman A. Alshdadi, University of Jeddah, Saudi Arabia
    Ali Daud, University of Jeddah, Saudi Arabia
    Mohamed M. Dessouky, University of Jeddah, Saudi Arabia
    Essa Ali Alhazmi, Jazan University, Saudi Arabia

Chapter 95
General Awareness and Responses to COVID-19 Crisis: A Sentiment Analysis of Twitter
Updates 1783
    Dipima Buragohain, Jilin University, China

Chapter 96
Analyzing the Impact of e-WOM Text on Overall Hotel Performances: A Text Analytics
Approach 1805
    Aakash Aakash, University of Delhi, India
    Anu G. Aggarwal, University of Delhi, India
    Sanchita Aggarwal, University of Delhi, India

Chapter 97
eWOW of Guests Regarding Their Hotel Experience: Sentiment Analysis of TripAdvisor
Reviews 1831
    Zelia Breda, GOVCOPP, University of Aveiro, Portugal
    Rui Costa, GOVCOPP, University of Aveiro, Portugal
    Gorete Dinis, GOVCOPP, Polytechnic Institute of Portalegre, Portugal
    Amandine Angie Martins, University of Aveiro, Portugal

Section 6
Critical Issues and Challenges

Chapter 98
Multimodal Sentiment Analysis: A Survey and Comparison 1846
    Ramandeep Kaur, Guru Kashi University, Talwandi Sabo, India
    Sandeep Kautish, Guru Kashi University, Talwandi Sabo, India

Chapter 99
A Literature Review on Cross Domain Sentiment Analysis Using Machine learning 1871
    Nancy Kansal, Ajay Kumar Garg Engineering College Ghaziabad, India
    Lipika Goel, Ajay Kumar Garg Engineering College Ghaziabad, India
    Sonam Gupta, Ajay Kumar Garg Engineering College Ghaziabad, India

Chapter 100
Microblog Sentiment Analysis Using User Similarity and Interaction-Based Social Relations 1887
    Chuanmin Mi, College of Economics and Management, Nanjing University of Aeronautics
        and Astronautics, China
    Xiaoyan Ruan, College of Economics and Management, Nanjing University of Aeronautics
        and Astronautics, Nanjing, China
    Lin Xiao, College of Economics and Management, Nanjing University of Aeronautics and
        Astronautics, Nanjing, China

Chapter 101
Sentiment Analysis of Twitter Data: A Hybrid Approach 1905
    Ankit Srivastava, The NorthCap University, Gurgaon, India
    Vijendra Singh, The NorthCap University, Gurgaon, India
    Gurdeep Singh Drall, The NorthCap University, Gurgaon, India

Chapter 102
A Sentiment Analysis of the 2014-15 Ebola Outbreak in the Media and Social Media................... 1923
    Blooma John, University of Canberra, Australia
    Bob Baulch, International Food Policy Research Institute, Malawi
    Nilmini Wickramasinghe, Swinburne University of Technology, Australia & Epworth
        HealthCare, Australia

Index... xxxi

Preface

Sentiment analysis is a field that is gaining traction as more organizations and fields discover the myriad benefits and opportunities it offers. Regardless of industry, it is always useful to know what consumers think, whether that be about a product, a service, or a company in general. With sentiment analysis technology, it has never been easier to understand what audiences want and need. Organizations must embrace this technology and integrate it into their business strategies and tactics in order to successfully reach and communicate with their audience.

Staying informed of the most up-to-date research trends and findings is of the utmost importance. That is why IGI Global is pleased to offer this four-volume reference collection of reprinted IGI Global book chapters and journal articles that have been handpicked by senior editorial staff. This collection will shed light on critical issues related to the trends, techniques, and uses of various applications by providing both broad and detailed perspectives on cutting-edge theories and developments. This collection is designed to act as a single reference source on conceptual, methodological, technical, and managerial issues, as well as to provide insight into emerging trends and future opportunities within the field.

The *Research Anthology on Implementing Sentiment Analysis Across Multiple Disciplines* is organized into six distinct sections that provide comprehensive coverage of important topics. The sections are:

1. Fundamental Concepts and Theories;
2. Development and Design Methodologies;
3. Tools and Technologies;
4. Utilization and Applications;
5. Organizational and Social Implications; and
6. Critical Issues and Challenges.

The following paragraphs provide a summary of what to expect from this invaluable reference tool.

Section 1, "Fundamental Concepts and Theories," serves as a foundation for this extensive reference tool by addressing crucial theories essential to understanding the concepts and uses of sentiment analysis in multidisciplinary settings. Opening this reference book is the chapter "Fundamentals of Opinion Mining" by Profs. Ashish Seth and Kirti Seth from INHA University, India, which focuses on explaining the fundamentals of opinion mining along with sentiment analysis and covers the brief evolution in mining techniques in the last decade. This first section ends with the chapter "Sentiment Analysis in Crisis Situations for Better Connected Government: Case of Mexico Earthquake in 2017" by Profs. Rodrigo Sandoval-Almazán, Asdrúbal López Chau, and David Valle-Cruz from the Universidad Autónoma del Estado de México, Mexico, which adapts the methodology of sentiment analysis of social media posts to an expanded version for crisis situations.

Section 2, "Development and Design Methodologies," presents in-depth coverage of the design and development of sentiment analysis for its use in different applications. This section starts with "Integrating Semantic Acquaintance for Sentiment Analysis" by Profs. Rashmi Agrawal and Neha Gupta from Manav Rachna International Institute of Research and Studies, India, which focuses on semantic guidance-based sentiment analysis approaches and provides a semantically enhanced technique for annotation of sentiment polarity. This section closes with "An Extensive Text Mining Study for the Turkish Language: Author Recognition, Sentiment Analysis, and Text Classification" by Profs. Durmuş Özkan Şahin and Erdal Kılıç from Ondokuz Mayıs University, Turkey, which provides theoretical and experimental information about text mining and discusses three different text mining problems such as news classification, sentiment analysis, and author recognition.

Section 3, "Tools and Technologies," explores the various tools and technologies used for the implementation of sentiment analysis for various uses. This section begins with "Tools of Opinion Mining" by Profs. Neha Gupta and Siddharth Verma from Manav Rachna International Institute of Research and Studies, India, which examines how opinion mining is moving to the sentimental reviews of Twitter data, comments used on Facebook, videos, or Facebook statuses. This section closes with the chapter "Opinion Mining for Instructor Evaluations at the Autonomous University of Ciudad Juarez" by Profs. Abraham López, Alejandra Mendoza Carreón, Rafael Jiménez, Vicente García, and Alan Ponce from the Universidad Autónoma de Ciudad Juárez, Mexico, which considers how opinion mining can be useful for labeling student comments as positive and negative and, for this purpose, creates a database using real opinions obtained from five professors over the last four years, covering a total of 20 subjects.

Section 4, "Utilization and Applications," describes how sentiment analysis is used and applied in diverse industries for various applications. The opening chapter in this section, "A Survey on Implementation Methods and Applications of Sentiment Analysis," by Profs. Sudheer Karnam, Valarmathi B., and Tulasi Prasad Sariki from VIT University, India, compares different methods of solving sentiment analysis problems, algorithms, merits and demerits, and applications and also investigates different research problems in sentiment analysis. The closing chapter in this section, "Communicating Natural Calamity: The Sentiment Analysis of Post Rigopiano's Accident," by Profs. Nicola Capolupo and Gabriella Piscopo from the University of Salerno, Italy, aims at understanding the dynamics that led to the exchange and value co-creation/co-production in the interaction between P.A. and citizens during natural calamities and proposes a horizontal communication model in which both actors cooperate to respond to a crisis.

Section 5, "Organizational and Social Implications," includes chapters discussing the impact of sentiment analysis on society and shows the ways in which it can be used in different industries and how this impacts business. The chapter "Open Issues in Opinion Mining" by Profs. V. Uma and Vishal Vyas from Pondicherry University, India, explains the various research issues and challenges present in each stage of opinion mining. The closing chapter, "eWOW of Guests Regarding Their Hotel Experience: Sentiment Analysis of TripAdvisor Reviews," by Profs. Zelia Breda and Rui Costa from GOVCOPP, University of Aveiro, Portugal; Prof. Gorete Dinis from GOVCOPP, Polytechnic Institute of Portalegre, Portugal; and Prof. Amandine Angie Martins of the University of Aveiro, Portugal, focuses on sentiment analysis of comments made on TripAdvisor regarding one resort located in the Algarve region in Portugal.

Section 6, "Critical Issues and Challenges," presents coverage of academic and research perspectives on the challenges of using sentiment analysis in varied industries. Opening this final section is the chapter "Multimodal Sentiment Analysis: A Survey and Comparison" by Profs. Ramandeep Kaur and Sandeep Kautish from Guru Kashi University, India, which provides a full image of the multimodal sentiment analysis opportunities and difficulties and considers the recent trends of research in the field. The closing chapter, "A Sentiment Analysis of the 2014-15 Ebola Outbreak in the Media and Social Media," by Prof. Nilmini Wickramasinghe from Swinburne University of Technology, Australia & Epworth Health-Care, Australia; Prof. Blooma John of the University of Canberra, Australia; and Dr. Bob Baulch from the International Food Policy Research Institute, Malawi, analyzes news articles on the Ebola outbreak from two leading news outlets, together with comments on the articles from a well-known social media platform, from March 2014 to July 2015.

Although the primary organization of the contents in this multi-volume work is based on its six sections, offering a progression of coverage of the important concepts, methodologies, technologies, applications, social issues, and emerging trends, the reader can also identify specific contents by utilizing the extensive indexing system listed at the end of each volume. As a comprehensive collection of research on the latest findings related to sentiment analysis, the *Research Anthology on Implementing Sentiment Analysis Across Multiple Disciplines* provides social media analysts, computer scientists, IT professionals, AI scientists, business leaders and managers, marketers, advertising agencies, public administrators, government officials, university administrators, libraries, instructors, researchers, academicians, and students with a complete understanding of the applications and impacts of sentiment analysis across fields and disciplines. Given the vast number of issues concerning usage, failure, success, strategies, and applications of sentiment analysis, the *Research Anthology on Implementing Sentiment Analysis Across Multiple Disciplines* encompasses the most pertinent research on the applications, impacts, uses, and development of sentiment analysis.

Chapter 74
A Study and Comparison of Sentiment Analysis Techniques Using Demonetization:
Case Study

Krishna Kumar Mohbey
 https://orcid.org/0000-0002-7566-0703
Central University of Rajasthan, India

Brijesh Bakariya
I. K. Gujral Punjab Techncial University, India

Vishakha Kalal
Central University of Rajasthan, India

ABSTRACT

Sentiment analysis is an analytical approach that is used for text analysis. The aim of sentiment analysis is to determine the opinion and subjectivity of any opinion, review, or tweet. The aim of this chapter is to study and compare some of the techniques used to classify opinions using sentiment analysis. In this chapter, different techniques of sentiment analysis have been discussed with the case study of demonetization in India during 2016. Based on the sentiment analysis, people's opinion can be classified on different polarities such as positive, negative, or neutral. These techniques will be classified on different categories based on size of data, document type, and availability. In addition, this chapter also discusses various applications of sentiment analysis techniques in different domains.

DOI: 10.4018/978-1-6684-6303-1.ch074

INTRODUCTION

The aim of sentiment analysis (SA) is to discover the emotional orientation of user opinion or review of the particular topic, product or object. Sentiment analysis is different from traditional text mining in that we focus on a particular topic for mining whereas sentimental analysis is much complex. Sentimental analysis can be considered as a classification process in which opinion or reviews are classified as positive, negative or neutral (Lei et al., 2016). Sentimental analysis has played an important role in various applications of text mining for consumer opinion detection, customer relationship management, brand and product poisoning and reviewed analysis. Based on the sentimental analysis multiple companies can know the status of their product and take different decision to enhance their business.

There are a lot of research has been done in the field of sentimental analysis (Medhat et al., 2014) which is mostly classify reviews based on their polarity. In general, a review can be categorized by different topics, for example, mobile phone reviews most likely discuss topic of a feature such as a price, brand, memory, camera, etc. in sentimental analysis task, users are not only interested in the opinion of review but also interested in the topics discovery. Therefore, it is known that the sentiment polarities are also dependent on various topics. The complete process of sentiment classification is shown in Figure 1.

The classification of sentiments can be performed on three levels such as document, sentence and aspect level. Document-level SA classifies an opinion as positive or negative. Sentence-level SA expresses each sentence as positive or negative opinion. When classifying opinion as document or sentence level, there is no significant difference because sentences are the short documents (Liu, 2012). While aspect level SA classifies entities or objects concerning specific aspect. For example, a different user may have different aspects towards mobile phone such as voice quality, battery life, camera quality, etc. To classify sentiments, it is needed to have a review or opinion information. There are different sources from where the user can collect data for sentiment analysis. Microblogs and social networks are excellent resources for information in these days because they provide an efficient environment to share opinions.

The contribution of this chapter is significant in different dimensions. It provides different applications of SA and fields where it can play an important role. This chapter also describes various SA techniques for opinion classification which is used to make decisions and policy making. Different SA fields such as emotion detection and transfer learning also discussed in this chapter. Finally, this chapter provides various case studies of sentiment analysis. The proposed chapter includes the concept of sentiment analysis, different techniques for sentiment analysis and case studies for opinion mining. It discusses various applications of sentiment analysis and classification in different areas.

This chapter is organized as follows: section 2 includes various applications of sentimental analysis. Section 3 discusses various sentiment classification approaches. In section 4, several feature extraction methods are included that is required for sentiment analysis. Section 5 presents different fields where sentiment analysis used. Sentiment analysis case studies are added in section 6. Lastly, discussion and conclusions are presented in section 7 and 8, respectively.

MOTIVATION

Sentiment analysis or opinion mining is the computational study of people's opinion, thought, attitudes and emotions toward an object. The object can represent individuals, events, topics, tweet or review.

Figure 1. Sentiment analysis process

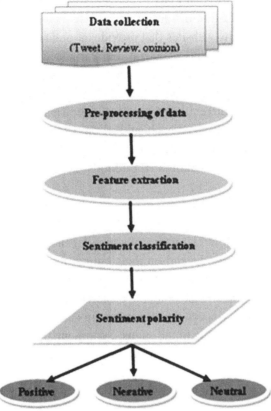

Sentiment analysis identifies the attitude of people expressed in a text then analyses it. The expression of people may belong to acceptance, rejection or neutral regarding any event.

There are different techniques for sentiment analysis and used for different purposes. Sentiment analysis determines the polarity of a tweet, review or user opinion. Based on the user's opinion, polarity can be classified as positive, negative or neutral. According to the identified polarity of opinion, various decisions can be taken by business people or government agencies. There are different methods to classify sentiments in different domains.

Social media is one of the main sources of opinions or review. If we have large amount of review data or tweet in unstructured form. How can we classify it based on sentence polarity or which method is appropriate for it? This is the main point of motivation. Regarding this question there are different techniques and tools are presently available, but the challenge is to apply the appropriate method for available data.

Applications of Sentiment Analysis

Sentiment analysis can be defined as the task of finding the opinions of users about specific objects, reviews or entities. Leaders and decision-makers can make decisions based on opinions of people. For example, if a person wants to purchase any product online he or she will typically start by searching for reviews and opinions written by other people for that product. Similarly, based on people review or opinion one can select a hotel in particular place. There are lots of hottest applications of the sentiment analysis. The most common application of sentiment analysis is in the area of reviews of a products, object, and services. There are many websites that provide automated summaries of reviews about particular products based on different aspects. Amazon, Flipkart, Twitter, and Facebook are a main point of many sentiment analysis applications. The most common application is monitoring the reputation of a specific brand or product before going to buy.

Another important application of sentiment analysis is the financial markets. There are numerous news items, articles, blogs, and tweets about each public company. A sentiment analysis system can use these various sources to find articles that discuss the companies and aggregate the sentiment about them as a single score that can be used by an automated trading system.

Sentiment Analysis in Business

A brand cannot be defined by the product it manufactures or the services it provides. The name and reputation that build a brand majorly depend on their online marketing, social campaigning, content marketing, user feedback and customer support services. Sentiment analysis in business helps in quantifying the perception of the present and the potential customers regarding all these factors. Keeping the negative sentiments of knowledge, you can develop more appealing branding techniques and marketing strategies to switch from torpid to terrific brand status. Sentiment analysis in business can majorly help you to make a quick transition and right decision (Singh et al., 2017).

Electronic Commerce

Sentiment analysis is mostly used in e-commerce activities. Most of the websites allow their customers to submit their experience about shopping and product qualities. The customer can give their suggestions as well opinion in rating bases. Another customer can easily find suggestion and recommendation towards a particular product or service. There are lots of websites which provides a review of different product or services such as travel, hotel, book, etc. Sentiment analysis helps such sites by converting dissatisfied customers into promoters by analyzing this vast volume of opinions (Vohra & Teraiya, 2013).

Customer Satisfaction

Sentimental analysis has the great advantage in customer satisfaction towards any object, product or service. In the business, based on the reviews generated through sentiment analysis, companies can always adjust to the present market situation and satisfy their customers in a better way. Overall, companies can make immediate decisions with automated insights.

Identifying Critics and Promoters

Sentiment analysis can be used for customer service, by spotting dissatisfaction or problems with products. It is also used to find people who are happy with a particular products or services and their experiences can be used to promote your products.

Government Policies

Sentiment analysis can help the government in assessing their strength and weaknesses by analyzing public opinions towards government policies. It may provide facilities to collect public opinion for particular governance of policy. Based on the public opinion, the government can analyze whether the proposed policy is useful or not. Even government can improve their policies for their people (Vohra & Teraiya, 2013).

Preprocessing in Sentiment analysis

Preprocessing analyzes the opinion for syntactical point of view. The main goal of this phase is to remove the noise from the collected opinions. The most common preprocessing techniques are stopped word removal, stemming and POS tagging. Stopword concept was introduced by Luhn (1958). Stop words are the common words and have the higher frequencies in opinion. These words include: a, an, the, that, of, for, to, etc. there are different methods available for stopword removal (Aggarwal & Zhai, 2012). Stop word removal phase enhance the performance of feature extraction methods (Hu & Liu 2004). The stemming process returns the word to its root form. For example, computer, computing, and computation are converted to its root form compute (Aggarwal & Zhai, 2012). Parts of Speech (POS) aim to find adjective because they are an essential indicator of opinion.

Feature Selection in Sentiment Analysis

In sentiment classification, the feature selection is the process of selecting a specific subset of the terms of the training set and using only them in the sentiment classification algorithm. The feature selection process takes place before the training of the sentiment classifier. There are different methods of feature selection towards sentiment analysis. The main advantages of using feature selection algorithms are the facts that it reduces the dimension of opinion data, it makes the training faster, and it can improve accuracy by removing noisy features. As a consequence feature selection can help us to avoid overfitting. Feature selection methods can be divided into statistical methods and lexicon based methods. Statistical methods are automatic and frequently used, while lexicon based methods need human annotation (Whitelaw et al., 2005). The documents are treated as a group of words or strings in the feature selection methods. Feature extraction method creates a smaller set of a feature from the original set of features. Pointwise mutual information (Cover & Thomas, 2012), chi-square (Aggarwal & Zhai, 2012) and latent semantic indexing (Deerwester et al., 1990) is the most frequently used statistical methods of feature extraction. There are other methods such as information gain and Gini index (Aggarwal & Zhai, 2012) which is used in feature extraction.

Sentiment Classification Techniques

Based on the task and available opinion different classification techniques can be applied for sentiment analysis. Sentiment analysis can be employed using both supervised and unsupervised methods of classification. Supervised methods have shown better performance than the unsupervised methods. However, the unsupervised methods are also important because supervised methods required bulky labeled training data that very expensive whereas acquisition of unlabeled data is easy. Sentiment classification methods can be divided into machine learning methods, lexicon based methods, and rule-based methods. Machine learning method uses different machine learning algorithms such as naïve Bayes classification, Bayesian network and so on. The lexicon based methods are based on known and precompiled sentiment terms. A set of rules are modeled in rule-based classification. Fig 2 shows the various sentiment classification methods and algorithm.

MACHINE LEARNING METHODS

Machine learning method uses various machine learning algorithms for sentiment classification. These classifications are same as text classification. These methods use a set of training records where each record indicated as a class. Based on these training records a prediction model can be prepared. This model is used to predict an unknown instance of the class. These methods can be further divided into supervised and unsupervised learning.

Supervised Learning

The supervised learning methods use label training documents to classify sentiments. There are many kinds of supervised classifiers are available for sentiment analysis. Some of the supervised classifiers are discussed below.

Naïve Bayes Classifier

It is a well-known and popular supervised classification approach. It predicts the probability for a tweet to belong to a particular class. This model ignores the possibility of the word in the document while performing classification. This classifier is based on Bayes theorem to predict the probability of a particular tweet (Medhat et al., 2014). When test data is given to this model, it generates positive, negative or neutral sentiment. The Bayes theorem can be defined as:

$$P\left(\frac{C}{x}\right) = \frac{P\left(\frac{x}{C}\right).P(C)}{P(x)} \tag{1}$$

Where

C: specified class
x: tweet wants to classify
$P(C)$ and $P(x)$: prior probabilities

$$P\left(\frac{C}{x}\right): \text{Posterior probability}$$

Given the Naïve assumption which states that a data point $X=\{x_1, x_2, x_3, \ldots, x_i\}$, the probability of each of its feature (independent) occurring in a given class, the equation can be rewritten as:

$$P\left(\frac{C}{x}\right) = P(C).P\frac{x_i}{C} \tag{2}$$

Figure 2. Sentiment classification methods

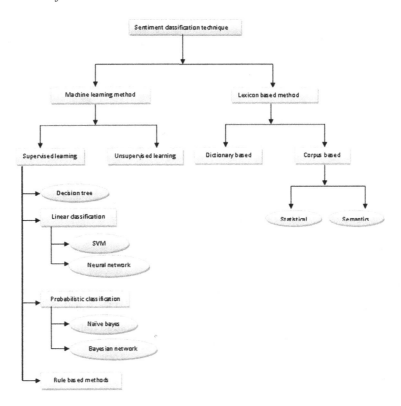

Bayesian Network

The Bayesian network was proposed by Hernandez et al. (2012) for real-world problems. In this model, they have used different target variables to the characterized attitude of the author. This classifier assumes that the features are independent. While other models assume that all the features are dependent. A directed acyclic graph is used in the Bayesian network, in which nodes represent random variable and edges, represents to conditional dependencies.

SVM Classifier

It is a linear classifier used to determine linear separator in the search space. It separates different classes in the best way (Cortes & Vapnik, 1995; Vapnik, 2013). Fig 3 shows an example of SVM classifier. In this figure, there are two classes, and there are three hyperplanes. Hyperplane in dark line provides the best separation among two classes. In this separation the normal distance of any data point is the largest. Therefore it shows the maximum margin of separation.

Figure 3. SVM classification methods

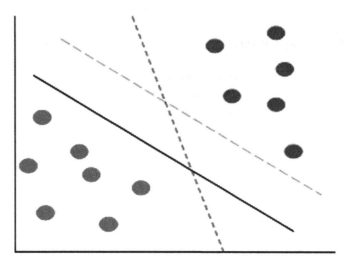

Rule-Based Classifier

This classifier modeled with the set of rules. In these rules, the left-hand side represents a condition on the feature set while the right-hand side represents the class labels. The condition uses presence term not the absence terms because absence terms are not informative in sparse data. Support and confidence are two important criteria in rule-based classifier which is used to generate rules (Ma et al., 1998).

Unsupervised Learning

Supervised learning methods require a large number of labeled training documents. But in the text classification, it is difficult to create labeled training documents, but it is easier to collect unlabeled documents. To classify these unlabeled documents, unsupervised learning classification is used (Ko & Seo, 2000). Xiamghua and Guo (Xianghua et al., 2013) used unsupervised methods to classify Chinese social reviews. There are other unsupervised methods which are based on semantic orientation (Turney, 2002) or lexicon association which measures the similarity between words and polarity prototypes (Read & Carroll, 2009).

Lexicon Based Method

Sentiment classification is based on opinion words which can be positive or negative. Opinion can also be expressed in the form of idioms and phrases that are known as opinion lexicon. There are different methods for collecting opinion word list such as manual, dictionary-based and corpus-based. Manual opinion word collection method is time-consuming and not used in sentiment analysis.

In the dictionary-based methods, a small set of opinion words are firstly manually collected then newly found words are added to this list. The searching process executes up to the level when no new words are found. To remove errors, manual inspection is also required in this method (Hu & Liu, 2004; Kim & Hovy, 2004).

The corpus-based methods are based on syntactic patterns or patterns that occur together along with the list of opinion words. The list of opinion words is finding using available corpus. Corpus-based methods were represented by Hatzivassiloglou and McKeown (1997).

As compared to the dictionary-based method, corpus-based methods are not effective if they are used alone, because large corpus preparation is a typical task. Corpus-based methods are helpful in domain and context specific word finding. Corpus-based methods can be performed using statistical or semantic based methods.

Fahrni and Klenner (2008) have proposed a method to determine posterior polarities using co-occurrence of words in a corpus. This co-occurrence pattern can be found using statistical approaches. The main observation of these methods is that the similar opinion words frequently appear together in the corpus.

Semantic method directly gives the sentiment value and uses the different principle to compute the similarity between words. If the words are semantically close, this principle gave similar sentiment value (Miller et al., 1990). The semantic methods are used in many applications to build a lexicon model that uses verbs, nouns, and adjectives for sentiment analysis (Maks & Vossen, 2012).

Case Study: Demonetization in India

The cash transaction is preferred in India, and only less than half population uses banking system and cash less transactions. As per the announcement on 8th November 2016 by Indian Prime Minister Narendra Modi, the 1000 and 500 rupee notes would cease to be legal tender. With the announcement of this news, many people appreciate this decision while other criticized. The expression of the public can be easily communicated through social media. One of the social media (Twitter) had played an important role in expressing people opinion on demonetization. The expression of people may belong to acceptance, rejection or neutral regarding this event.

In this chapter, sentiment analysis has been performed on public opinion towards demonetization. Sentiment analysis determines the polarity of a tweet, review or user opinion. Based on the user's opinion, polarity can be classified as positive, negative or neutral. According to the identified polarity of an opinion, various decisions can be taken by business people or government agencies. There are different methods to classify sentiments in different domains. Existing methods discover sentiments on document level or sentence levels. Sometimes these techniques do not satisfy user's expectation as per their needs. Therefore, it is required to refine opinion before determining polarity. These opinions can be refining using different attributes or features. Features are important for sentiment analysis because according to these features different user provides their opinion. Table 1 shows some examples of opinion with feature and corresponding polarity.

To perform sentiment analysis on demonetization, twitter data has been collected. This dataset contains 14,940 tweets of different persons. In this dataset, there are 14,940 rows (one row for each tweet) and 15 columns. Figure 4 shows the snapshot of user tweets.

Table 1. Examples of user's opinion on demonetization with feature and polarity

#	Tweet	Feature	Polarity
1.	A badly planned move	badly	negative
2.	Demonetization has long-term benefit	benefit	positive
3.	Demonetization is failure	failure	negative
4.	Things are very fast getting back to normal	normal	positive
5.	Interest rates on loans may go down & higher funding assistance may be possible for young startups	loans, funding	neutral

Figure 4. Snapshot of tweets on demonetization

X	text	favorited	favori	replyT	created	truncated	replyToSID	id	replyToUl	statusSource	screenNa	retweetC	isRetweet	retweeted
1	RT @rssurjewala: Critical question: Was PayTM	FALSE	0	NA	11/23/2016 18:40	FALSE	NA	8.01E+17	NA	<a href="http:/	HASHTAG	331	TRUE	FALSE
2	RT @Hemant_80: Did you vote on #Demonetiza	FALSE	0	NA	11/23/2016 18:40	FALSE	NA	8.01E+17	NA	<a href="http:/	PRAMODK	66	TRUE	FALSE
3	RT @roshankar: Former FinSec, RBI Dy	FALSE	0	NA	11/23/2016 18:40	FALSE	NA	8.01E+17	NA	<a href="http:/	rahulja13C	12	TRUE	FALSE
4	RT @ANI_news: Gurugram (Haryana): Post offic	FALSE	0	NA	11/23/2016 18:39	FALSE	NA	8.01E+17	NA	<a href="http:/	deeptiyvd	338	TRUE	FALSE
5	RT @satishacharya: Reddy Wedding! @mail_to	FALSE	0	NA	11/23/2016 18:39	FALSE	NA	8.01E+17	NA	<a href="http:/	CPIMBadl	120	TRUE	FALSE
6	@DerekScissors1: India's #demonetization: #Bl	FALSE	0	Derek	11/23/2016 18:39	FALSE	NA	8.01E+17	2.59E+09	<a href="http:/	ambazaar	0	FALSE	FALSE
7	RT @gauravcsawant: Rs 40 lakh looted from a b	FALSE	0	NA	11/23/2016 18:38	FALSE	NA	8.01E+17	NA	<a href="http:/	bhodia1	637	TRUE	FALSE
8	RT @Joydeep_911: Calling all Nationalists to	FALSE	0	NA	11/23/2016 18:38	FALSE	NA	8.01E+17	NA	<a href="http:/	KARUNAS	112	TRUE	FALSE
9	RT @sumitbhati2002: Many opposition leaders	FALSE	0	NA	11/23/2016 18:38	FALSE	NA	8.01E+17	NA	<a href="http:/	sumitbha	1	TRUE	FALSE
10	National reform now destroyed even the esser	FALSE	0	NA	11/23/2016 18:38	TRUE	NA	8.01E+17	NA	<a href="https	HelpIndia	0	FALSE	FALSE
11	Many opposition leaders are with	FALSE	1	NA	11/23/2016 18:37	FALSE	NA	8.01E+17	NA	<a href="http:/	sumitbha	1	FALSE	FALSE
12	RT @Joydas: Question in Narendra Modi App w	FALSE	0	NA	11/23/2016 18:37	FALSE	NA	8.01E+17	NA	<a href="http:/	MonishGa	120	TRUE	FALSE
13	@Jaggesh2 Bharat band on 28??<ed><U+00A0>	FALSE	0	Jagges	11/23/2016 18:37	FALSE	8.01E+17	8.01E+17	1.23E+09	<a href="http:/	yuvaraj_k	0	FALSE	FALSE
14	RT @Atheist_Krishna: The effect of	FALSE	0	NA	11/23/2016 18:37	FALSE	NA	8.01E+17	NA	<a href="http:/	PMKejri	45	TRUE	FALSE
15	RT @sona2905: When I explained #Demonetiza	FALSE	0	NA	11/23/2016 18:36	FALSE	NA	8.01E+17	NA	<a href="http:/	hkgupta16	50	TRUE	FALSE
16	RT @Dipankar_cpiml: The Modi app on #DeMor	FALSE	0	NA	11/23/2016 18:35	FALSE	NA	8.01E+17	NA	<a href="http:/	aazaadpar	45	TRUE	FALSE
17	RT @roshankar: Former FinSec, RBI Dy	FALSE	0	NA	11/23/2016 18:35	FALSE	NA	8.01E+17	NA	<a href="http:/	darkdestii	12	TRUE	FALSE
18	RT @Atheist_Krishna: BEFORE and AFTER	FALSE	0	NA	11/23/2016 18:34	FALSE	NA	8.01E+17	NA	<a href="http:/	snooveme	95	TRUE	FALSE
19	RT @pGurus1: #Demonetization The co-operati	FALSE	0	NA	11/23/2016 18:34	FALSE	NA	8.01E+17	NA	<a href="http:/	Vishwaam	76	TRUE	FALSE
20	RT @roshankar: Former FinSec, RBI Dy	FALSE	0	NA	11/23/2016 18:34	FALSE	NA	8.01E+17	NA	<a href="http:/	PoliticalCc	12	TRUE	FALSE
21	RT @Hemant_80: Did you vote on #Demonetiza	FALSE	0	NA	11/23/2016 18:34	FALSE	NA	8.01E+17	NA	<a href="http:/	MdShuaib	66	TRUE	FALSE
22	RT @roshankar: Former FinSec, RBI Dy	FALSE	0	NA	11/23/2016 18:33	FALSE	NA	8.01E+17	NA	<a href="http:/	BharatPar	12	TRUE	FALSE
23	RT @Atheist_Krishna: BEFORE and AFTER	FALSE	0	NA	11/23/2016 18:33	FALSE	NA	8.01E+17	NA	<a href="http:/	ihavnthan	95	TRUE	FALSE
24	RT @MahikaInfra: @narendramodi	FALSE	0	NA	11/23/2016 18:33	FALSE	NA	8.01E+17	NA	<a href="http:/	GajjarBhai	53	TRUE	FALSE
25	RT @Hemant_80: Did you vote on #Demonetiza	FALSE	0	NA	11/23/2016 18:33	FALSE	NA	8.01E+17	NA	<a href="http:/	Rss_chadc	66	TRUE	FALSE
26	RT @roshankar: Former FinSec, RBI Dy	FALSE	0	NA	11/23/2016 18:33	FALSE	NA	8.01E+17	NA	<a href="http:/	mukeshra	12	TRUE	FALSE
27	RT @kapil_kausik: #Doltiwal I mean #JaiChandk	FALSE	0	NA	11/23/2016 18:32	FALSE	NA	8.01E+17	NA	<a href="http:/	mrx565	20	TRUE	FALSE
28	RT @roshankar: Former FinSec, RBI Dy	FALSE	0	NA	11/23/2016 18:32	FALSE	NA	8.01E+17	NA	<a href="http:/	iMirzaG	12	TRUE	FALSE
29	RT @kapil_kausik: #Doltiwal I mean #JaiChandk	FALSE	0	NA	11/23/2016 18:32	FALSE	NA	8.01E+17	NA	<a href="http:/	PontiFukE	20	TRUE	FALSE

Methodology

The process of sentiment analysis has shown in figure 1. Before applying sentiment analysis, data pre-processing is required because it contains a lot of noise in collected tweets. Preprocessing step contains stop word removal, special character removal, stemming and negation handling, etc. After completion of this step data is ready for analysis, now sentiment classification can be performed.

Experimental Results

The experiments of this study have been performed on demonetization tweets dataset. This dataset contains 14,940 opinions of different persons. The classifier is implemented in R language. This experiment of demonetization sentiment analysis has performed on the Pentium Dual-core 3.3 GHz processor with 8GB RAM.

Sentiment Analysis Approach

In this approach, sentiment score is calculated for each tweet based on positive and negative word counts. According to calculated sentiment, score tweet can be classified as positive, negative or neutral. Also, a dictionary of positive and negative words also used. There are different methods to calculate sentiment score; here it is calculated using following formula.

Score =sum (positive words) - sum (negative words)
If score==0 then "neutral tweet"
If score>0 then "positive tweet"
If score<0 then "negative tweet"

The analysis result on demonetization data has shown in figure 4.

Figure 5. Analysis result on demonetization tweet data

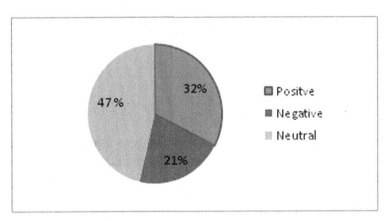

Figure 5 shows that 47% opinion is neutral for demonetization while 32% opinion is considered positive step and 21% people take this initiative as a negative step.

OTHER FIELDS OF SENTIMENT ANALYSIS

Some of the topics discussed below come under sentimental analysis:

Emotion Detection

To find an opinion about the entity, sentiment analysis can be considered sometime as natural language processing task. Since it is unclear about the opinion, sentiment and emotion differences. Therefore, opinion is defined as a transitional concept that reflects an attitude toward an entity. Sentiment means feeling or emotion and emotion shows attitude (Tsytsarau & Palpanas, 2012). Plutchik (1980) told about the first eight basic emotions which are: joy, sadness, anger, fear, trust, disgust, surprise and anticipation. Emotion detection can be considered as a sentiment analysis task. Sentiment analysis is mainly concerned with specifying positive or negative opinion while emotion detection is related to detecting different emotions from the text. Using machine learning or lexicon based methods emotion detection can be implemented as sentiment analysis task. Lexicon based method is frequently used for it. Lu (Lu et al., 2010) gave emotion detection on a sentence level. This method was related to the probability distribution of common mutual actions between subject and the object of an event. By using machine learning or lexicon based methods, Balahur et al. (2012) proposed a method based on commonsense knowledge stored in the emotion corpus knowledge base since emotions are related to real life situation.

Transfer Learning

In sentiment analysis with the use of transfer learning, sentiment classification can be transferred from one domain to another (Wilson et al., 2005) or to build a bridge between two domains (Wu & Tan, 2011). The entropy-based algorithm was proposed by Tan and Wang (2011) to find out high-frequency domain based specific feature. For classifying cross-domain sentiment Wu and Tan (2011) gave two stage frameworks. The first stage is to obtain most confidently labeled document in the target domain by making a bridge between the source and target domain. In the second stage, intrinsic structures are prepared for target domain data.

CONCLUSION

This chapter presented a comparative study of sentiment analysis using demonetization case study. To solve sentiment classification problems, naïve Bayes classifier and support vector machines are mostly used machine learning algorithms. Different people, opinion, and reviews can be easily collected from different social networking sites, blogs, and forums. These social media sites played an important role in expressing people's opinion towards any product, service, and object. Today, micro blogging such as twitter, facebook is the most significant source of sentiment opinions. In addition, based on the sentiment analysis, it is concluded that most of the people have a neutral opinion towards demonetization initiative in India 2016.

REFERENCES

Aggarwal, C. C., & Zhai, C. (Eds.). (2012). *Mining text data*. Springer Science & Business Media. doi:10.1007/978-1-4614-3223-4

Balahur, A., Hermida, J. M., & Montoyo, A. (2012). Detecting implicit expressions of emotion in the text: A comparative analysis. *Decision Support Systems*, *53*(4), 742–753. doi:10.1016/j.dss.2012.05.024

Cortes, C., & Vapnik, V. (1995). Support-vector networks. *Machine Learning*, *20*(3), 273–297. doi:10.1007/BF00994018

Cover, T. M., & Thomas, J. A. (2012). *Elements of information theory*. John Wiley & Sons.

Deerwester, S., Dumais, S. T., Furnas, G. W., Landauer, T. K., & Harshman, R. (1990). Indexing by latent semantic analysis. *Journal of the American Society for Information Science, 41*(6), 391–407. doi:10.1002/(SICI)1097-4571(199009)41:6<391::AID-ASI1>3.0.CO;2-9

Fahrni, A., & Klenner, M. (2008, April). Old wine or warm beer: Target-specific sentiment analysis of adjectives. *Proc. of the Symposium on Affective Language in Human and Machine,* 60-63.

Hatzivassiloglou, V., & McKeown, K. R. (1997, July). Predicting the semantic orientation of adjectives. In *Proceedings of the eighth conference on European chapter of the Association for Computational Linguistics* (pp. 174-181). Association for Computational Linguistics. 10.3115/979617.979640

Hu, M., & Liu, B. (2004, August). Mining and summarizing customer reviews. In *Proceedings of the tenth ACM SIGKDD international conference on Knowledge discovery and data mining* (pp. 168-177). ACM.

Hu, M., & Liu, B. (2004, July). Mining opinion features in customer reviews. AAAI, 4(4), 755-760.

Kim, S. M., & Hovy, E. (2004, August). Determining the sentiment of opinions. In *Proceedings of the 20th international conference on Computational Linguistics* (p. 1367). Association for Computational Linguistics.

Ko, Y., & Seo, J. (2000, July). Automatic text categorization by unsupervised learning. In *Proceedings of the 18th conference on Computational linguistics* (vol. 1, pp. 453-459). Association for Computational Linguistics. 10.3115/990820.990886

Lei, X., Qian, X., & Zhao, G. (2016). Rating prediction based on social sentiment from textual reviews. *IEEE Transactions on Multimedia, 18*(9), 1910–1921. doi:10.1109/TMM.2016.2575738

Liu, B. (2012). Sentiment analysis and opinion mining. *Synthesis Lectures on Human Language Technologies, 5*(1), 1-167.

Lu, C. Y., Lin, S. H., Liu, J. C., Cruz-Lara, S., & Hong, J. S. (2010). Automatic event-level textual emotion sensing using mutual action histogram between entities. *Expert Systems with Applications, 37*(2), 1643–1653. doi:10.1016/j.eswa.2009.06.099

Luhn, H. P. (1958). The automatic creation of literature abstracts. *IBM Journal of Research and Development, 2*(2), 159–165. doi:10.1147/rd.22.0159

Ma, B. L. W. H. Y., & Liu, B. (1998, August). Integrating classification and association rule mining. *Proceedings of the fourth international conference on knowledge discovery and data mining.*

Maks, I., & Vossen, P. (2012). A lexicon model for deep sentiment analysis and opinion mining applications. *Decision Support Systems, 53*(4), 680–688. doi:10.1016/j.dss.2012.05.025

Medhat, W., Hassan, A., & Korashy, H. (2014). Sentiment analysis algorithms and applications: A survey. *Ain Shams. Engineering Journal (New York), 5*(4), 1093–1113.

Miller, G. A., Beckwith, R., Fellbaum, C., Gross, D., & Miller, K. J. (1990). Introduction to WordNet: An on-line lexical database. *International Journal of Lexicography, 3*(4), 235–244. doi:10.1093/ijl/3.4.235

Ortigosa-Hernández, J., Rodríguez, J. D., Alzate, L., Lucania, M., Inza, I., & Lozano, J. A. (2012). Approaching Sentiment Analysis by using semi-supervised learning of multi-dimensional classifiers. *Neurocomputing*, *92*, 98–115. doi:10.1016/j.neucom.2012.01.030

Plutchik, R. (1980). A general psychoevolutionary theory of emotion. *Theories of Emotion, 1*(3-31), 4.

Read, J., & Carroll, J. (2009, November). Weakly supervised techniques for domain-independent sentiment classification. In *Proceedings of the 1st international CIKM workshop on Topic-sentiment analysis for mass opinion* (pp. 45-52). ACM. 10.1145/1651461.1651470

Singh, V., Saxena, P., Singh, S., & Rajendran, S. (2017). Opinion Mining and Analysis of Movie Reviews. *Indian Journal of Science and Technology*, *10*(19), 1–6. doi:10.17485/ijst/2017/v10i19/112756

Tan, S., & Wang, Y. (2011). Weighted SCL model for adaptation of sentiment classification. *Expert Systems with Applications*, *38*(8), 10524–10531. doi:10.1016/j.eswa.2011.02.106

Tsytsarau, M., & Palpanas, T. (2012). Survey on mining subjective data on the web. *Data Mining and Knowledge Discovery*, *24*(3), 478–514. doi:10.100710618-011-0238-6

Turney, P. (n.d.). Semantic Orientation Applied to Unsupervised Classification of Reviews. *Proceedings of ACL-02, 40th Annual Meeting of the Association for Computational Linguistics*, 417-424.

Vapnik, V. (2013). *The nature of statistical learning theory*. Springer Science & Business Media.

Vohra, M. S., & Teraiya, J. (2013). Applications and challenges for sentiment analysis: A survey. *International Journal of Engineering*, *2*(2), 1–5.

Whitelaw, C., Garg, N., & Argamon, S. (2005, October). Using appraisal groups for sentiment analysis. In *Proceedings of the 14th ACM international conference on Information and knowledge management* (pp. 625-631). ACM.

Wilson, T., Wiebe, J., & Hoffmann, P. (2005, October). Recognizing contextual polarity in phrase-level sentiment analysis. In *Proceedings of the conference on human language technology and empirical methods in natural language processing* (pp. 347-354). Association for Computational Linguistics. 10.3115/1220575.1220619

Wu, Q., & Tan, S. (2011). A two-stage framework for cross-domain sentiment classification. *Expert Systems with Applications*, *38*(11), 14269–14275.

Xianghua, F., Guo, L., Yanyan, G., & Zhiqiang, W. (2013). Multi-aspect sentiment analysis for Chinese online social reviews based on topic modeling and HowNet lexicon. *Knowledge-Based Systems*, *37*, 186–195. doi:10.1016/j.knosys.2012.08.003

This research was previously published in Sentiment Analysis and Knowledge Discovery in Contemporary Business; pages 1-14, copyright year 2019 by Business Science Reference (an imprint of IGI Global).

Chapter 75
Application of Sentiment Analysis in Movie reviews

ThippaReddy Gadekallu
https://orcid.org/0000-0003-0097-801X
VIT University, India

Akshat Soni
VIT University, India

Deeptanu Sarkar
VIT University, India

Lakshmanna Kuruva
VIT University, India

ABSTRACT

Sentiment analysis is a sub-domain of opinion mining where the analysis is focused on the extraction of emotions and opinions of the people towards a particular topic from a structured, semi-structured, or unstructured textual data. In this chapter, the authors try to focus the task of sentiment analysis on IMDB movie review database. This chapter presents the experimental work on a new kind of domain-specific feature-based heuristic for aspect-level sentiment analysis of movie reviews. The authors have devised an aspect-oriented scheme that analyzes the textual reviews of a movie and assign it a sentiment label on each aspect. Finally, the authors conclude that incorporating syntactical information in the models is vital to the sentiment analysis process. The authors also conclude that the proposed approach to sentiment classification supplements the existing rating movie rating systems used across the web and will serve as base to future researches in this domain.

DOI: 10.4018/978-1-6684-6303-1.ch075

INTRODUCTION

Necessity is the mother of invention.

We are drowning in data, but starving for knowledge!

The present era of Internet has become a huge Cyber Database which hosts gigantic amount of data which is created and consumed by the users. The data mining has been growing at an exponential rate giving rise to a new industry filled with it, in which users express their opinions across channels such as Face-book, Twitter etc. Opinions which are being expressed in the form of reviews provide an opportunity for new explorations to find collective likes and dislikes of cyber community. One such domain of reviews is the domain of movie reviews which affects everyone from audience, film critics to the production company. The movie reviews being posted on the websites are not formal reviews but are rather very informal and are unstructured form of grammar. Opinions expressed in movie reviews give a very true reflection of the emotion that is being conveyed. The presence of such a great use of sentiment words to express the review inspired us to devise an approach to classify the polarity of the movie using these sentiment words.

Sentiment Analysis is the process of determining whether a piece of writing is positive, negative or neutral. It's also known as opinion mining, deriving the opinion or attitude of a speaker. A common use case for this technology is to discover how people feel about a particular topic.

Sentiment Analysis is a technology that will be very important in the next few years. With opinion mining, we can distinguish poor content from high quality content. With the technologies available we can know if a movie has more good opinions than bad opinions and find the reasons why those opinions are positive or negative. Much of the early research in this field was centred around product reviews, such as reviews on different products on Amazon.com, defining sentiments as positive, negative, or neutral. Most sentiment analysis studies are now focused on social media sources such as IMDB, Twitter and Face-book, requiring the approaches be tailored to serve the rising demand of opinions in the form of text. Furthermore, performing the phrase-level analysis of movie reviews proves to be a challenging task.

Social media sentiment analysis can be an excellent source of information and can provide insights that can:

- Determine marketing strategy
- Improve campaign success
- Improve product messaging
- Improve customer service
- Test business KPIs
- Generate leads

In a nutshell, if done properly, social media sentiment analysis can improve your bottom line. However, if you are making decisions using incorrect sentiment analysis data, the results can be catastrophic. Most social media analysis vendors will admit (if you push them hard enough) that their sentiment analysis algorithm will be, at best, 50-60% accurate.

Types of Sentiment Analysis

Manual Processing

Human interpretation of sentiment is definitely the most mature and accurate judge of sentiment. However, it still isn't 100% accurate. Very few vendors still use this process without the additional use of a tool. This is due to the prolific growth of social media. According to Seth Grimes, social is the fastest growing source of enterprise analytical data.

Therefore, if you are going to use social media to determine sentiment, it is becoming less practical to use human processing and more likely you will need to automate the process.

Keyword Processing

Keyword processing algorithms assign a degree of positivity or negativity to an individual word, then it gives and overall percentage score to the post. For example, positive words, great, like, love or negative words: terrible, dislike

The advantages of this method are that it is very fast, predictable and cheap to implement and run.

However, there are numerous disadvantages including dealing with double negatives or positives, or different meanings of words, for example: the use of a word such as 'sick' (to mean either "ill" or to mean "awesome"). Not to mention, different researchers may assign difference percentages of positive or negative to word. More often the issue is that it does not deal with multiple word/context issues or non-adjective words.

Natural Language Processing

(NLP also called: text analytics, data mining, computational linguistics)

NLP refers to computer systems that process human language in terms of its meaning. NLP understands that several words make a phrase, several phrases make a sentence and, ultimately, sentences convey ideas. NLP works by analysing language for its meaning. NLP systems are used for in a number of areas such as converting speech to text, language translation and grammar checks

It can be likened to programming an algorithm to interpret the English language (or any language for the matter) with the rules that you were taught in English class.

Although NLP may seem to be far superior to keyword processing, it still has its limitations. Sarcasm a well known Australian trait, is very difficult to detect using NLP as is hyperbole (exaggerated statements) and social media acronyms (e.g. OMG, BFF, BTW etc) or social jargon such as:

- **Youturn:** To follow another person on social media with the intention of unfollowing them once they have you followed back, esp. on Twitter
- **Wallflower:** A person who regularly consumes the social media of others but never posts
- **Face Crawling**: Begging for Facebook likes, online or offline
- **Hash-Browning:** The excessive use of hashtags within a single post
- **Metapals:** Social media connections that have never personally met

People express opinions in complex ways for example: the difference between "I'm fine!!!" and "I'm fine.". Also, changing topic mid post can be confusing.

The Future of Sentiment Analysis?

- We can assume that the future of sentiment analysis will plug the existing gaps in being able to interpret meaning.
- Increased accuracy when compared to human processing
- The ability to interpret human emotions: according to research by Glasgow University. there are six basic emotions of happiness, sadness, fear, anger, surprise and disgust.
- Improvements in machine learning accuracy
- Predictive analytics – once we have extracted sentiment and believe it to be accurate we can then predict future trends and behaviour.

Below are some interesting ideas from Phil Wolff via Quora:

- **Longitudinal Analysis:** Where are the cycles and patterns in sentiment? How does Phil's attitude change during the day, year?
- **Root Cause Analysis:** What activities or people affect Phil and how? If we can see what Phil reads, where he goes, who he talks to, how much he moves, music he hears, what he eats, can we identify likely triggers for sentiment and affect changes?
- **Realtime Scoring:** At scale, limited only by latency.
- **Scoring Reflect New Models of Cognition:** Neuroscience and cogsci will inform what and how we measure, analys e and report. How likely is it that new social gestures will amplify patterns discovered through brain imaging?
- **Analysis of Non-Textual Inputs:** Facial microexpressions captured in Skype chats, body language in YouTube videos, gestures in Google Glass, typing speed/interval/error patterns in Bing search, stress analysis in voice calls, clickstreams in Chrome, check-ins in FourSquare, physiology from Quantified Self loggers – all will complement text analysis.
- **Micropublic Reporting:** How are the people attending this meeting in two hours feeling now? This is aggregating sentiment for smaller, defined groups.
- **Predictive Sentiment Analysis:** How will they feel when the meeting starts in two hours? What are likely causes of drift?
- **Sentiment Streaming:** Sentiment as realtime presence. Phil's mobile emits a stream of Phil's happiness, engagement, focus when he's awake.

In this work, the authors applied Classification and Prediction algorithm to determine the overall polarity of the movie review. The authors analyze and study the features that affect the sentiment score of the movie review text. Also, the authors use the state of the art classification algorithms for the evaluation of performance and accuracy of the approach used. Also, the authors not only study the approach but try to have a deeper understanding of the problem domain.

Sentiment Analysis Uses

Sentiment analysis is extremely useful in social media monitoring as it allows us to gain an overview of the wider public opinion behind certain topics. Social media monitoring tools like Brandwatch Analytics make that process quicker and easier than ever before, thanks to real-time monitoring capabilities.

The applications of sentiment analysis are broad and powerful. The ability to extract insights from social data is a practice that is being widely adopted by organisations across the world.

Shifts in sentiment on social media have been shown to correlate with shifts in the stock market.

The Obama administration used sentiment analysis to gauge public opinion to policy announcements and campaign messages ahead of 2012 presidential election.

The ability to quickly understand consumer attitudes and react accordingly is something that Expedia Canada took advantage of when they noticed that there was a steady increase in negative feedback to the music used in one of their television adverts.

Sentiment analysis conducted by the brand revealed that the music played on the commercial had become incredibly irritating after multiple airings, and consumers were flocking to social media to vent their frustrations.

A couple of weeks after the advert first aired, over half of online conversation about the campaign was negative.

Rather than chalking up the advert as a failure, Expedia was able to address the negative sentiment in a playful and self-knowing way by airing a new version of the advert which featured the offending violin being smashed.

Contextual Understanding and Tone

But that is not to say that sentiment analysis is a perfect science at all.

The human language is complex. Teaching a machine to analyse the various grammatical nuances, cultural variations, slang and misspellings that occur in online mentions is a difficult process. Teaching a machine to understand how context can affect tone is even more difficult.

Humans are fairly intuitive when it comes to interpreting the tone of a piece of writing.

Consider the following sentence: "My flight's been delayed. Brilliant!"

Most humans would be able to quickly interpret that the person was being sarcastic. We know that for most people having a delayed flight is not a good experience (unless there's a free bar as recompense involved). By applying this contextual understanding to the sentence, we can easily identify the sentiment as negative.

Without contextual understanding, a machine looking at the sentence above might see the word "brilliant" and categorise it as positive.

LITERATURE SURVEY

Sentiment analysis is basically concerned with analysis of emotions and opinions from text (Neethu et al., 2013). We can refer sentiment analysis as opinion mining. Sentiment analysis finds and justifies the sentiment of the person with respect to a given source of content. In this work the authors propose a highly accurate model of sentiment analysis of tweets with respect to latest reviews of upcoming Bollywood or Hollywood movies. With the help of classification and prediction algorithm we are correctly classifying these tweets as positive, negative and neutral to give sentiment of each tweet.

Social Networks such as Facebook, Twitter, Linked In etc… are rich in opinion data and thus Sentiment Analysis has gained a great attention due to the abundance of this ever growing opinion data (Mejova et al., 2009). In this work the target set is movie reviews. The authors are going to apply some pre-processing techniques and compare the accuracy using Classification algorithm. This work illustrates a comparative study of sentiment analysis of movie reviews using Naïve Bayes Classifier.

We can refer sentiment analysis as opinion mining. Sentiment analysis finds and justifies the sentiment of the person with respect to a given source of content (Sentiment analysis of this largely generated data is very useful to express the opinion of the mass. We know that the maximum length of each tweet in Twitter is 140 characters. So it is very important to identify correct sentiment of each word. In this work the authors are proposing a highly accurate model of sentiment analysis of tweets with respect to latest reviews of upcoming Bollywood or Hollywood movies.

In this work authors aim to use Sentiment Analysis on a set of movie reviews given by reviewers and try to understand what their overall reaction to the movie was, i.e. if they liked the movie or they hated it (Turney, 2004). The authors aim to utilize the relationships of the words in the review to predict the overall polarity of the review. The dataset that authors are using in this work contains 50,000 training examples collected from IMDb where each review is labelled with the rating of the movie on scale of 1-10. As sentiments are usually bipolar like good/bad or happy/sad or like/dislike, the authors categorized these ratings as either 1 (like) or 0 (dislike) based on the ratings. If the rating was above 5, the authors deduced that the person liked the movie otherwise he did not.

Various measures, including Information gain, simple chi-square, feature relation network, log-likelihood ratio, and minimum frequency thresholds, have previously been used as feature selection methods in sentiment analysis and classification (Troussas et al., 2013).

The following four step process is followed to analyze the sentiment of each movie review:

- Pre-processing and breaking the review into parts of speech
- Identifying subjective and objective sentences
- Classifying subjective sentences into those expressing positive and negative sentiments
- Aggregating the overall sentiment.

The user of this software can type in a query that is any entity and the system mines the web for public opinion about that entity and generates a sentiment score (Pong-inwong et al., 2014). A positive score represents a positive public sentiment about that entity and negative score represents a negative sentiment or opinion. It is fair to say that people are generally very interested in what other people think about global entities. Also, public opinion about entities help people form their own opinions. It also helps people make their decisions. Like a company looking for a new brand ambassador would want to select a personality with the highest positive sentiment among people.

Sentiment analysis is a well-known task in the realm of natural language processing. Given a set of texts, the objective is to determine the polarity of that text (Akaichi et al., 2013). It provides a comprehensive survey of various methods, benchmarks, and resources of sentiment analysis and opinion mining. The sentiments can consist of different classes. In this study, the authors consider two cases: 1) A movie review is positive (+) or negative (-). This is similar to, where they also employ a novel similarity measure. 2) A movie review is very negative (- -), somewhat negative (-), neutral (o), somewhat positive (+), or very positive (+)

Sentiment analysis is language processing task that uses a computational approach to identify opinionated content and categorize it as positive or negative (Bollen et al., 2011). The unstructured textual data on the Web often carries expression of opinions of users. Sentiment analysis tries to identify the expressions of opinion and mood of writers. A simple sentiment analysis algorithm attempts to classify a document as 'positive' or 'negative', based on the opinion expressed in it. This work presents the experimental work on a new kind of domain specific feature-based heuristic for aspect-level sentiment analysis of movie reviews.

In Sentiment mining or opinion mining, we basically try to analyse the results or predict outcomes that are based on customer feedback or opinion (Rahn et al., 2000). Especially applications involving stock prediction, movie and product review analysis. The study involves automated text mining which in turn includes understanding the meaning of the sentence. Movie review analysis is one of the most popular fields to analyse public sentiment. One more application is also in the field of politics where politicians can come to know about the sentiment of the people regarding certain policies and rallies. It helps while decision making and prediction procedures.

The authors attempted to classify movie reviews by using various measures of similarity between each pair of reviews (Harish, 2009). The measure uses the number of occurrences of various part-of-speech tags in the reviews. The authors then incorporated a suitable graph algorithm to obtain the classification. The key objective is to design an algorithm that can learn 'certain' information from the already classified data set (learning set) and then classify a review as positive or negative.

This work addresses the problem of sentiment analysis in twitter; that is classifying tweets according to the sentiment expressed in them: positive, negative or neutral (Pang, 2009). Twitter is an online micro-blogging and social-networking platform which allows users to write short status updates of maximum length 140 characters. It is a rapidly expanding service with over 200 million registered users - out of which 100 million are active users and half of them log on twitter on a daily basis - generating nearly 250 million tweets per day. Due to this large amount of usage the authors hope to achieve a reflection of public sentiment by analysing the sentiments expressed in the tweets. Analysing the public sentiment is important for many applications such as firms trying to find out the response of their products in the market, predicting political elections and predicting socioeconomic phenomena like stock exchange. The aim of this work is to develop a functional classifier for accurate and automatic sentiment classification of an unknown tweet stream.

Millions of users share opinions on diverse aspects of life and politics every day using micro blogging over the internet (Pang et al., 2004). Micro blogging websites are rich sources of data for belief mining and sentiment analysis. In this dissertation work, the authors focus on using Twitter for sentiment analysis for extracting opinions about events, products, and people and use it for understanding the current trends or state of the art. The authors proposed naïve bayes classifier algorithm in that case. It classifies the tweets in positive and negative classes respectively. Experimental results demonstrate the superiority of hybrid naïve bayes on multi-sized datasets consisting of variety of keywords over existing approaches yielding >90 percent accuracy in general and 98.59 percent accuracy in the best case.

Over the past decade humans have experienced exponential growth in the use of online resources, in particular social media and micro blogging websites such as Twitter (Agarwal et al., 2005). Many companies and organisations have identified these resources as a rich mine of marketing knowledge. This work focuses implementing machine learning algorithms to extract an audience's sentiment relating to a popular television program. A major focus of this study was on comparing different machine learning algorithms for the task of sentiment classification. The major findings were that out of different machine learning algorithm classification provide the highest accuracy for this domain.

A novel FFBAT algorithm is proposed by Thippa Reddy, G., & Khare, N, (2016) to improve the classification of heart disease dataset. The same authors have proposed another novel method OFBAT based Classification (Tumasjan et al., 2010) to classify heart disease datasets.

Example Application of Sentiment Analysis

It is common to classify sentences into two principal classes with regard to subjectivity: objective sentences that contain factual information and subjective sentences that contain explicit opinions, beliefs, and views about specific entities.

As an example, here is a review about a hotel in Manhattan.

The king suite was spacious, clean, and well appointed. The reception staff, bellmen, and housekeeping were very helpful. Requests for extras from the maid were always provided. The heating and air conditioning functioned well; this was good as the weather was variable. The sofa bed was the best I've ever experienced. The king size bed was very comfortable. The building and rooms are very well soundproofed. The neighborhood is the best for shopping, restaurants, and access to subway. Only "complaint" has to do with high-speed Internet access. It's only available on floors 8–12.

Overall the review is very positive about the hotel. It refers to many different aspects of the hotel including: heating, air conditioning, staff courtesy, bed, neighborhood, and Internet access. Sentiment analysis systems must be able to provide a sentiment score for the whole review as well as analyze the sentiment of each individual aspect of the hotel.

METHODOLOGY

The aim of this work is to study and compare some of the methods used to evaluate the reputation of items using sentiment analysis. The challenge of the increasing amount of data available on the Internet is explained and the role of sentiment analysis in mining this information. Recent solutions are classified into different categories based on techniques, document approach, and rating methods.

Tools Used

- Python
- Beautiful soup
- Algorithms- classification and association rule mining.
- NLP (Natural language processing)
- NLTK(python library)
- Twitter API

Process

Part 1

Millions of tweets are made every day out of which some are related to movies. So the tweets will used for analysis.

The authors will be collecting the tweets for related movie and will try to analyze the tweets as positive, neutral or negative tweet.

Using classification algorithm the authors will find the percentage of each type of tweets.

By seeing the percentage of tweet one can rate the movie.

Also sentimental analysis will be performed.

Part 2

The authors will collect review for movie from different movie review sites.

For collection of movie review from internet web scrapping using python library scrappy will be used. Then data is collected in database.

Then NLP will be applied on these reviews and algorithms to separate the positive and negative comments about the movie.

Then sentimental analysis of movie will be done i.e. how the movie is doing with passing days or which type of people are liking movie etc.

Pre-Processing Using NLP

- Stop words removal- text which does not have any meaning. Ex: a, an etc.
- Stemming- removal of words which gives same meaning ex: ride, riding.
- Chunking- grouping of words into meaningful sentences.
- Chinking- Removal of some irrelevant text.
- Identifying verbs, adjectives, nouns etc.

Part 3

- Create the account on twitter using twitter API.
- This will provide consumer key, access token, access token key to uniquely identify the twitter account.
- Follow some of the movie review pages like IMDB, rotten tomatoes, movies official pages etc.
- Now each time run the code for some movie code will gather all the tweets related to this movie and then will do the sentiment analysis on these tweets by separating positive, negative and neutral tweets.

The results generated by twitter sentiment analysis can be compared and scrapped data from different movie review sites. By comparing we can get the accurate movie rating.

SCREEN SHOTS

Below shown screenshots (Figure 1, Figure 2, Figure 3, Figure 4, Figure 5) is of the code used to connect twitter with the python code. For this the authors have used NLTK (natural language tool kit) library of python.

Figure 1.

Figure 2.

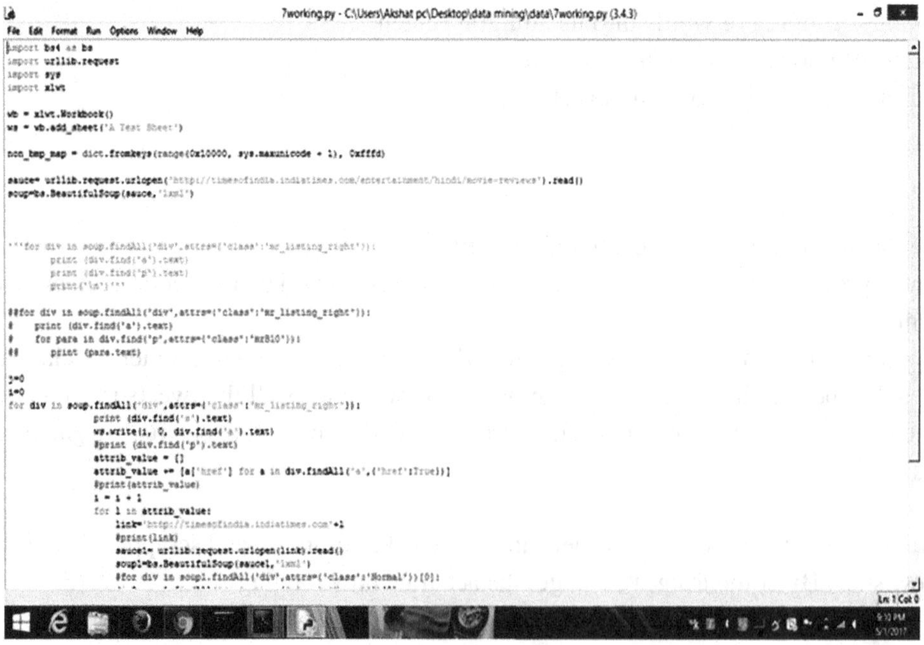

Figure 3.

Figure 4.

Figure 5.

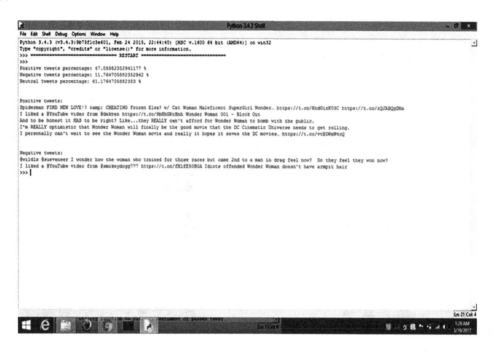

Above screenshots shows the sentiment analysis for migureovie name-"Baahubali-2". Results are:

- Positive sentiment percentage- **48**
- Neutral sentiment analysis percentage-40
- Negative sentiment analysis percentage -11

Just below this is top 5 positive and negative tweets. We can also get top 10 tweets or more according to our need but limiting to 5 or 10 is better as for more number of tweets processing will take more time.

Above screenshots shows the sentiment analysis for movie name-"wonder woman". Results are:

- Positive sentiment percentage- **47**
- Neutral sentiment analysis percentage-41
- Negative sentiment analysis percentage -11

Just below this is top 5 positive and negative tweets.
Similarly we can continue this process for all the movies.

ADVANTAGES OF SENTIMENT ANALYSIS

1. We can also compare the success between different movies using sentiment analysis. Success rate is directly proportional to the interest shown by audience and critics. Advantage of using tweets

for sentiment analysis is we can get the combined result i.e. we can get the tweets from critics and common audience and by doing sentiment analysis of this tweets we can get the common ratings.

2. We can get day by day success of movies. Daily there will be tweets from different viewers and results can be generated using these tweets. We can calculate the gain or drop in interest of people for movie. As the movie becomes old the number of tweets related to movie will be reduced by which we can calculate the rate at which movie is losing or gaining interest.

3. Sentiment can be applied in many fields. Sentiment analysis using twitter can be used for getting people opinion on different issues like elections, electronic gadgets, any current affair etc.

CONCLUSION

The authors conclude that the machine learning technique is very easier and efficient. These techniques are easily applied to twitter sentiment analysis. Twitter sentiment analysis is difficult because it is very tough to identify emotional words form tweets and also due to the presence of the repeated characters, slang words, white spaces, misspellings etc. To handle these problems the feature vector is created. Before creating features vector pre-processing is done on each tweet. Then features are extracted in two phases: First phase is the extraction of the twitter specific word. Then they are removed from the text. Now extracted feature vector is transformed into normal text. After that, features are extracted from tweet which is normal text without any hash tags or slang words. And these extracted features are then added to form feature vector. There are different machine learning classifiers to classify the tweets. From the results, the authors have shown that Naïve Bayesian machine performs well and also provide higher accuracy. The results show that 65% accuracy is achieved from Naïve Bayesian classifier. So we can increase the accuracy of classification as we increase the training data. By this work we can say that feature vector performs better for tweets related to Movie reviews. For sentimental analysis the authors mainly use lexicon based approach which includes statistical and semantic analysis.

REFERENCES

Agarwal, A., & Bhattacharya, P. (2005). Sentiment Analysis: A new approach for effective use of linguistic knowledge and exploiting similarities in a set of documents to be classified. In *Proceedings of the 4th International Conference on Language Resources and Evaluation (LREC 2004)* (vol. 4, pp. 1115-1118). European Language Resources Association.

Akaichi. (2013). Social Networks Facebook Statuses Updates Mining for Sentiment Classification. *Proceedings of SocialCom/PASSAT/BigData/EconCom/BioMedCom.*

Alec, G. (2009). *Twitter Sentiment Classification using Distant Supervision. Project Technical Report.* Stanford University.

Biffet & Frank. (2010). Lecture Notes in Computer Science: Vol. 6332. *Sentiment Knowledge Discovery in Twitter Streaming Data.* Discovery Science. doi:10.1007/978-3-642-16184-1_1

Boiy, E., Hens, P., Deschacht, K., & Moens, M. (2007). Automatic sentiment analysis in on-line text. *11th International Conference on Electronic Publishing*, 349360.

Bollen, J., Mao, H., & Pepe, A. (2011). Modeling public mood and emotion: Twitter sentiment and socio-economic phenomena. *International Conference on Web and Social Media.*

Harish, R. (2009). "Lexical analysis-a brief study." Stamatatos, Efstathios. "A survey of modern authorship attribution methods. *Journal of the American Society for Information Science and Technology, 60*(3), 538–556. doi:10.1002/asi.21001

Kouloumpis, E., Wilson, T., & Moore, J. (2012). Twitter Sentiment Analysis: The Good the Bad and the OMG! *Proceedings of AAAI Conference on Weblogs and Social Media (ICWSM).*

Mejova. (2009). *Sentiment analysis: An overview*. Ymejova Publications.

Neethu, M. S., & Rajasree, R. (2013). Sentiment analysis in Twitter using Machine Learning Techniques. *4th International Conference on Computing, Communication and Networking Technologies.*

Pak, A., & Paroubek, P. (2010). Twitter as a Corpus for Sentiment Analysis and Opinion Mining. *Proceedings of international conference on Language Resources and Evaluation (LREC).*

Pang, B., & Lee, L. (2004). A sentimental education: Sentiment analysis using subjectivity summarization based on minimum cuts. *Proceedings of the ACL*, 271–278. 10.3115/1218955.1218990

Pang, B., Lee, L., & Vaithyanathan, S. (2002). Thumbs up? Sentiment Classification using Machine Learning Techniques. *Proceedings of the Conference on Empirical Methods in Natural Language Processing (EMNLP).*

Pang. (2002). Thumbs up? Sentiment classification using machine learning techniques. *EMNLP*, 79-86.

Pong-Inwong & Songpan. (2014). TeachingSentiLexicon for Automated Sentiment Polarity Definition in Teaching Evaluation. *Proceedings of Semantics, Knowledge and Grids (SKG), 2014 10th International Conference.*

Rahn, W. M. (2000). Affect as information: The role of public mood in political reasoning. *Elements of reason: Cognition, choice, and the bounds of rationality*, 130-50.

Reddy, G. T., & Khare, N. (2017). An efficient system for heart disease prediction using hybrid OFBAT with rule-based fuzzy logic model. *Journal of Circuits, Systems, and Computers, 26*(4), 1750061. doi:10.1142/S021812661750061X

Tan, C., Lee, L., Tang, J., Jiang, L., Zhou, M., & Li, P. (2011). User Level Sentiment Analysis Incorporating Social Networks. *Proceedings of ACM Special Interest Group on Knowledge Discovery and Data Mining (SIGKDD)*. 10.1145/2020408.2020614

Thippa Reddy, G., & Khare, N. (2016). FFBAT-optimized rule based fuzzy logic classifier for diabetes. International Journal of Engineering Research in Africa, 24, 137-152.

Troussas, C., Virvou, M., Espinosa, K. J., Llaguno, K., & Caro, J. (2013). Sentiment Analysis of Facebook statuses using Naïve Bayes classifier for language learning. *Proceedings ofInformation, Intelligence, Systems and Applications (IISA), 2013 Fourth International Conference.*

Tumasjan, A., Sprenger, T. O., Sandner, P. G., & Welpe, I. M. (2010). Predicting Elections with Twitter: What 140 Characters Reveal about Political Sentiment. *Proceedings of AAAI Conference on Weblogs and Social Media (ICWSM).*

Turney, P. (2002). Thumbs Up or Thumbs Down? Semantic orientation applied to unsupervised classification of reviews. *40th annual meeting on association for computational linguistics, 417424.*

This research was previously published in Sentiment Analysis and Knowledge Discovery in Contemporary Business; pages 77-90, copyright year 2019 by Business Science Reference (an imprint of IGI Global).

Chapter 76
Experimenting Language Identification for Sentiment Analysis of English Punjabi Code Mixed Social Media Text

Neetika Bansal
College of Engineering & Management, India

Vishal Goyal
Punjabi University, India

Simpel Rani
Yadavindra College of Engineering, India

ABSTRACT

People do not always use Unicode, rather, they mix multiple languages. The processing of codemixed data becomes challenging due to the linguistic complexities. The noisy text increases the complexities of language identification. The dataset used in this article contains Facebook and Twitter messages collected through Facebook graph API and twitter API. The annotated English Punjabi code mixed dataset has been trained using a pipeline Dictionary Vectorizer, N-gram approach with some features. Furthermore, classifiers used are Logistic Regression, Decision Tree Classifier and Gaussian Naïve Bayes are used to perform language identification at word level. The results show that Logistic Regression performs best with an accuracy of 86.63 with an F-1 measure of 0.88. The success of machine learning approaches depends on the quality of labeled corpora.

DOI: 10.4018/978-1-6684-6303-1.ch076

INTRODUCTION

According to statistical data reports, there are 525.3 million internet users currently in India. The use of social networking media has gained popularity since decades. Facebook is emerging as the most popular social networking site in the country. Other Social media networks include WhatsApp, Google+, and Skype. India ranks third with the most Instagram users with 69 million users. As per July 2019 statistical data, Instagram is one of the most popular social networks worldwide, especially where youngsters share selfies or other photographic content such as travel pictures, and moreover they try to keep up with favorite athletes and celebrities. Facebook and YouTube accounted for the largest penetration, both at 30 percent each as of the third quarter of 2017. T-Series is reported as the most subscribed YouTube channel till April 2019, with 92.38 million subscribers.

The number of people using social media as a part of their daily life is noticeably high and they use these platforms merely to share their experiences, preferences and opinions regarding the products or services of some brands. With analytics of data the buyers as well as sellers can enhance future decisions and actions. Electronic Word of Mouth (EWOM) has become important source of information for consumers and website owners. The analysis of data gives insight into consumer choice, brands and products. Sentiment analysis here emerges as a field for the digital world and helps website owners to design marketing strategies to increase the revenues.

Customer reviews available online have become valuable for customers and firms. The product reviews by users act as a valuable source of information for buyers in making product choices. On the contrary, reviews posted online act as feedback for firms as it requires huge advertising and huge investments. These firms attain publicity at large that too with no additional cost.

The post-visit brand image and the pre-visit image of a destination through EWOM has become important source for destination planning. Interested consumers use websites when planning their trips to a destination. Thus, businesses owners can utilize make the best use of such data. Furthermore, online reviews left by guests have business value in terms of understanding customer perceptions of hotel products and services attributes. Hoteliers can use this information to set priority rules for making improvements and use the generated electronic word of mouth effect from online customer reviews to enhance their performance. Online customer reviews have strong information. Online customer ratings and their likes and dislikes can be considered as indication of customer satisfaction.

Sentiment Analysis is used for analyzing trends, evaluation of public opinions, identifying ideological bias, targeting advertisements, analyzing reviews of a product and services, opinions and reactions to ideas. English being the dominant language around the world, therefore the work in the field of Sentiment Analysis is predominantly in English. There is absence of large volume of datasets, linguistic and lexical resources for Indian languages; posing challenges ahead. With the use of advanced Artificial Intelligence Techniques and advancements in deep learning algorithms, there has been considerable improvement in the field of sentiment analysis of textual data. Sentiment analysis has achieved higher accuracies with deep learning algorithms and the language identification work performed by authors can be used as base for Sentiment analysis.

LITERATURE REVIEW

Language identification is an essential prerequisite for automatic text processing. It is a preprocessing task for computational tasks for code switching and is considered as almost a solved problem for monolingual text in which n-gram approaches, character encoding detection or stop word lists can reach up to 100% accuracy. Researchers use simple dictionary method or machine learning techniques such as Naive Bayes, Support Vector Machines (SVM), and Conditional Random Forests (CRF), Convolutional Neural Networks (CNN) etc. Language systems fail due to style of writing and brevity of texts. Language detection is a difficult and unsolved problem due to Anglicism, code mixing, code switching, lexical borrowings (all terms being used interchangeably).

Beesley (1988) developed a prototype for language identifier of online text based on cryptanalysis. (Cavnar & Trenkle, 1994) used character n-gram frequency lists to determine the language of a new piece of text in the underlying algorithm of TextCat, an automatic LID system developed by vanNoord. The results were reported are 99.8% accuracy for language models of more than 300 n-grams.

Dunning (1994) followed similar approach except the tokenization of the text to build the n-grams. The language models were generated with assumption that the data are sequences of Bytes. For 50 KB on training data this approach identified correctly 92% for test documents of length 20 Bytes and 99.9% for longer texts with 500 Bytes.

Baldwin and Lui (2010) tested language identification on Wikipedia pages. It has been deduced that the performance improves with growing document length. Accuracy for longer documents reported is 90%, whereas for shorter documents it was found to be only 60–70%.

Pavan et al. (2010) proposed a Romanized text language identification system (RoLI) which uses an n-gram based approach and also exploits sound-based similarity of words. RoLI has been claimed with an accuracy of 98.3%, despite the spelling variations as well as sound variations in Indian languages.

Lui and Baldwin (2012) developed langid.py, an off-the-shelf language identification tool with an embedded model which covers 97 languages. The model has been trained for 5 long document datasets, and 2 belong to the microblog domain. langid.py maintains consistently high accuracy across all domains,

(Carter et al., 2013) also used Maximum Entropy Model and a character n-gram distance metric. They collected tweets in five different European languages (Dutch, English, French, German, and Spanish) and performed language identification at post-level only. The accuracy is reported 92.4%.

(King and Abney 2013) used weakly supervised methods as a sequence labeling problem with monolingual text samples for training data. They have also used CRF model trained with generalized expectation, a Hidden Markov Model (HMM) trained with expectation maximization (EM) and a logistic regression model trained with generalized expectation criteria. The best performer has been Naive Bayes Classifier with 93% accuracy. (Lignos and Marcus 2013) analyzed millions of Spanish-English twitter messages in a simple way with crowd sourcing for annotation. They have used the ratio of the word probability and achieved 96.9% and 92.3% accuracy at the word-level and monolingual data respectively.

(Nguyen and Dogruoz 2013) analyzed Turkish-Dutch posts from an online chat forum. They have compared dictionary-based methods with language models, adding logistic regression and linear-chain CRF. This system has been found to be the best with word-level accuracy of 97.6%, with a substantially lower accuracy on post-level at 89.5%.

(Barman et al. 2014) used English-Bengali & English-Hindi chat mixed Corpora of Indian student community between the 20-30 years age group. Approaches used are simple dictionary based, word-level classification using supervised machine learning with SVM without contextual information and word-level classification, using supervised machine learning with SVM and sequence labeling using CRFs, both with contextual information. CRF model performed best with accuracy of 95.76%. (Gamback and Das 2014) used Code Mixing Index to measure the level of mixing between languages [36]. They have developed a system to separate multiple languages using n-gram pruning with SVM for word level language identification with 98% accuracy for English-Hindi and 60% accuracy for English-Bengali using 10 fold cross validation on training set.

(Chittaranjan et al.2014) described a CRF based system for word-level language identification using lexical, contextual, character n-gram, and special character features like capitalization etc. For four language pairs, namely, English-Mandarin (En-Cn), English-Nepali (En-Ne), English- Spanish (En-Es), and Standard Arabic-Arabic (Ar-Ar) Dialects; the performance was found to be best against the test sets provided by the shared task on code-mixing (Solorio et al., 2014). For first three language pairs the accuracy was near 95% and for Ar- Ar dataset only up to 85% accuracy has been reported.

(Voss et al.2014) have worked to separate Romanized Moroccan Arabic (Darija), English and French tweets used a Maximum Entropy classifier and achieved accuracy of 92.8%, 89.2% and 84.6% for English, French, and Darija respectively.

(Sharma et al. 2016) have annotated data with three types of tags: 'hi', 'en' and 'rest'. The feature set comprised of BNC: normalized frequency of the words in British National Corpus (BNC), LEX-NORM: binary feature indicating presence of the word in the lexical normalization dataset released by Han et al. (2011). HINDI DICT: binary feature indicating presence of the word in a dictionary of 30,823 transliterated Hindi words as released by Gupta (2012). NGRAM: word n-grams. AFFIXES: prefixes and suffixes of the word. All features were combined using a context window of n-words, compared a linear SVM and CRF. CRF reported with greater accuracy of 93.98%.

(Jamatia et al., 2018) performed deep learning-based language identification in English-Hindi, English -Bengali, English-Hindi-Bengali code-mixed data. Accuracies reported are 88.27%, 86.97% and 88.27% with LSTM for English-Bengali, LSTM for English-Hindi as and Bi-directional LSTM for English-Hindi-Bengali dataset respectively.

CHALLENGES

Language Identification (LID) is considered as one of the well-studied tasks among computational code-switching approaches. Two main challenges faced in Language Identification are language annotation and mixing of languages inside a word. Language annotation becomes difficult when the mixed languages are closely related either linguistically or share common platform. Examples: college, canteen etc. are used in both the languages (English and Punjabi). Furthermore it becomes difficult to decide the language tag of a particular token when a word exists in both languages. Example: *"Sat_shri akal*, my dear friends". Here, sat (means greeting in Punjabi or verb form of sit or Saturday in short). *Second* challenge is mixing of two languages inside a single word. Normally, people use words in native language with plural as suffix or vice versa. Some of the examples are kumbals, samosas, computeran. This word level code mixing poses challenges ahead. Example: "Seminar *te main confusa gaya si*" (main means I in Punjabi and main means important in English).

DATA COLLECTION

The data has been collected from Twitter and Facebook by using twitter API (Application programming Interface) and Facebook graph API respectively. In addition, some data has been collected from whatsapp messages and web links where Romanized Punjabi text is available. The dataset consists of around 40000 tokens which contains 1825 URLs and 1329 hashtags that have been removed during preprocessing. The preprocessing of text also includes removal of symbols, unwanted spaces and Unicode characters and punctuation marks. The single characters existing in the dataset are also preserved. Examples: k means ok, c means see and many more.

Annotation is the main preprocessing task for language identification. Experiments have been done to test the data by manually annotating the dataset with seven categories of tags. The different tags assigned are: en (English), pb (Punjabi), univ (Universal), mixed (mixing of two languages inside a word), ne (Named Entity), acro (Acronyms), rest (none of earlier mentioned tags).

Example: Dr/acro Ambedkar/ne ne/pb apni/pb book /en "/univ Problem/en of/en Rupee/en "/univ vich/pb kiha/pb s/pbi ki/pb bhrishtachar/pb nu/pb khatam/pb karan/pb layi/pb 10/univ salan/pb vich/pb note/pb badal/pb dene/pb chahide/pb han/pb"

Translation: Dr. Ambedkar wrote in his book "Problem of Rupee" that in order o remove corruption the currency should be changed every 10 years.

The tokens which are part of English Dictionary are tagged as 'en' and Punjabi Romanized text are tagged as 'pb'. All the words containing numbers, universal expressions like haha, yo have been tagged as 'univ'. The acronyms used commonly like lol, rofl have been tagged as 'acro'. The word level code mixing inside single words like Samosas (a Punjabi word with English plural marker -s) are tagged as 'mixed'. All the names of places, persons or any other entities have been tagged as 'ne'. Additional label 'rest' is used to accommodate words that did not strictly belong to any of earlier mentioned tags. The details of frequencies of tags are shown in Table 1. Ambiguous words have been tagged according to the context in the current utterance. It is depicted in the example as: "Seminar/en *te/pb main/ambigous confuse/mixed gaya/pb si/pb*" (main means I in Punjabi and main means important in English). Here, 'main' will be tagged as Punjabi as per meaning of the sentence.

Table 1. Statistics of the dataset

Tags	No. of words
En	19004
Pb	15992
Univ	2803
Acro	297
Undef	285
Mixed	12

PROPOSED METHODOLOGY

The proposed language identification system uses a pipeline approach which is a combination of vectorizer and a classifier. The Dictionary Vectorizer has been used to find the existence of word in the corresponding dictionary. In addition, the classifier is used to classify every token into different label on the basis of the features as a training data. The Pyenhant Dictionary has been used to find the existence of a word in the English Dictionary. Experiments have been done using three Classifiers namely Logistic Regression, Decision Tree Classifier and Gaussian Naive Bayes. 80% of the dataset is trained and rest 20% is used for testing.

The system acts as a baseline for language identification of code mixed English Punjabi text. The feature set used for training set includes GDLC approach used by (Barman, 2014). Using contextual clues, the first and foremost features includes N-gram approach (G). N-gram approach has been commonly used by researchers for language identification. 1 to 5-character slices of a long token are used. The Dictionary approach (D) is used as a feature for storing the presence of a word in the dictionary. Length(L) feature is used to train decision trees and corresponding nodes are used to create Boolean features. In the last capitalization (C) uses three Boolean features to train the concerned dataset: whether any letter in the word is capitalized, whether all letters in word are capitalized, whether first letter is capitalized.

All the features have been used with different combination and the results are depicted in the Table 2.

Table 2. System performance using different features

Feature Used	Accuracy (%)
G	85.55
GL	85.55
GC	85.61
GD	86.32
GLC	85.58
GDL	86.33
GDC	86.52
GDLC	86.63

RESULTS

The English Punjabi code mixed dataset of 40000 tokens have been trained and tested using the described pipeline. Out of all three classifiers namely Logistic Regression, Decision Tree Classifier and Gaussian Naive Bayes Classifiers, the Logistic Regression performs best with an accuracy of 86.63% and F-score of 0.88 with 8000 tokens as the test data. Table 3 depicts the results of pipeline with classifier used and the performance.

Figure 1, 2, 3 depict the confusion matrix for Logistic Regression Classifier, Decision Tree classifier and Gaussian Naive Bayes Classier respectively. The confusion matrix shows predicted tags on x-axes and true tags on y-axes. It is clearly seen that Logistic Regression and Decision Tree classifiers perform really better than Gaussian Naive Bayes Classier. But the Gaussian NB performs better for named entities tags.

Table 3. System performance on test data

Model	Precision	Recall	F-Score	Accuracy (%)
Logistic Regression	0.91	0.87	0.88	**86.63**
Decision Tree Classifier	0.89	0.86	0.87	85.9
Gaussian Naive Bayes	0.62	0.66	0.62	65.88

Figure 1. Logistic regression

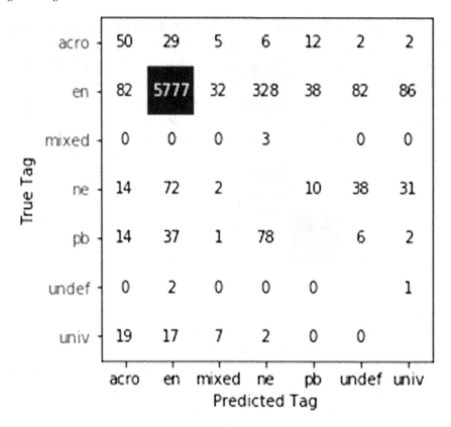

CONCLUSION

This article presents an initial baseline approach for language identification with English Punjabi code mixed social media text. From the experimental results it is concluded that character N-gram feature predominates all other features; still incorporating the N-gram feature blended with other features provides higher accuracy levels. This work represents a preliminary study and in near future it will be experimented using supervised CRF and TF_IDF vectorizer. This work can be used as strong input for sentiment analysis of code mixed Social Media Text. The ambiguous words have been assigned tags using the contextual information and tag 'wlcm' has been handled separately. Besides using such a robust dataset, the accuracy achieved is acceptable.

Figure 2. Decision tree classifier

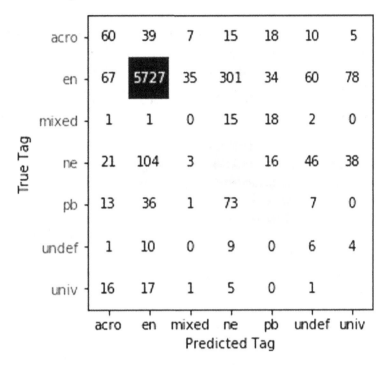

Figure 3. Gaussian NB classifier

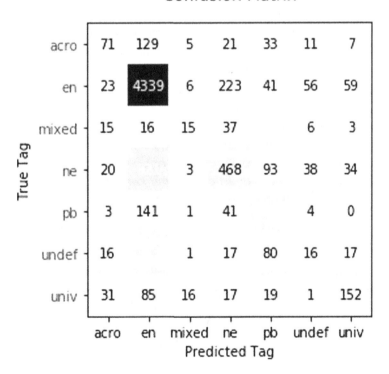

REFERENCES

Barman, U., Das, A., Wagner, J., & Foster, J. (2014, October). Code mixing: A challenge for language identification in the language of social media. In *Proceedings of the first workshop on computational approaches to code switching* (pp. 13-23). Academic Press. 10.3115/v1/W14-3902

Beesley, K. R. (1988, October). Language identifier: A computer program for automatic natural-language identification of on-line text. In *Proceedings of the 29th annual conference of the American Translators Association* (p. 54). Academic Press.

Carter, S., Weerkamp, W., & Tsagkias, M. (2013). Microblog language identification: Overcoming the limitations of short, unedited and idiomatic text. *Language Resources and Evaluation, 47*(1), 195–215. doi:10.100710579-012-9195-y

Cavnar, W. B., & Trenkle, J. M. (1994, April). N-gram-based text categorization. In *Proceedings of SDAIR-94, 3rd annual symposium on document analysis and information retrieval*. Academic Press.

Dunning, T. (1994). *Statistical identification of language*. Las Cruces, NM: Computing Research Laboratory, New Mexico State University.

Gella, S., Sharma, J., & Bali, K. (2013). Query word labeling and back transliteration for Indian languages: Shared task system description. *FIRE Working Notes, 3*.

Gokul Chittaranjan. Y. V., Bali, K., & Choudhury, M. (2014). A framework to label code-mixed sentences in social media. In *Proceedings of the First Workshop on Computational Approaches to Code-Switching*. ACL. Retrieved from https://www.statista.com/

Han, B., & Baldwin, T. (2011, June). Lexical normalisation of short text messages: Makn sens a# twitter. In *Proceedings of the 49th Annual Meeting of the Association for Computational Linguistics: Human Language Technologies* (Vol. 1, pp. 368-378). Association for Computational Linguistics.

Jamatia, A., Das, A., & Gambäck, B. (2019). Deep Learning-Based Language Identification in English-Hindi-Bengali Code-Mixed Social Media Corpora. *Journal of Intelligent Systems, 28*(3), 399–408. doi:10.1515/jisys-2017-0440

King, B., & Abney, S. (2013, June). Labeling the languages of words in mixed-language documents using weakly supervised methods. In *Proceedings of the 2013 Conference of the North American Chapter of the Association for Computational Linguistics: Human Language Technologies* (pp. 1110-1119). Academic Press.

Lignos, C., & Marcus, M. (2013, January). Toward web-scale analysis of codeswitching. In *Proceedings of annual meeting of the Linguistic Society of America*. Academic Press.

Lui, M., & Baldwin, T. (2012, July). langid. py: An off-the-shelf language identification tool. In *Proceedings of the ACL 2012 system demonstrations* (pp. 25-30). Association for Computational Linguistics.

Nguyen, D., & Doğruöz, A. S. (2013, October). Word level language identification in online multilingual communication. In *Proceedings of the 2013 conference on empirical methods in natural language processing* (pp. 857-862). Academic Press.

Prager, J. M. (1999). Linguini: Language identification for multilingual documents. *Journal of Management Information Systems*, *16*(3), 71–101. doi:10.1080/07421222.1999.11518257

Sequiera, R. D., Rao, S. S., & Shambavi, B. R. (2014). Word-Level language identification and back transliteration of romanized text: a shared task report by BMSCE.

Sharma, A., Gupta, S., Motlani, R., Bansal, P., Srivastava, M., Mamidi, R., & Sharma, D. M. (2016). Shallow Parsing Pipeline for Hindi-English Code-Mixed Social Media Text. 10.18653/v1/N16-1159

Tromp, E., & Pechenizkiy, M. (2011, May). Graph-based n-gram language identification on short texts. In *Proceedings of 20th Machine Learning conference of Belgium and The Netherlands* (pp. 27-34). Academic Press.

Voss, C. R., Tratz, S., Laoudi, J., & Briesch, D. M. (2014, May). *Finding Romanized Arabic Dialect in Code-Mixed Tweets*. In LREC (pp. 2249–2253). .

Yamaguchi, H., & Tanaka-Ishii, K. (2012, July). Text segmentation by language using minimum description length. In *Proceedings of the 50th Annual Meeting of the Association for Computational Linguistics* (Vol. 1, pp. 969-978). Association for Computational Linguistics.

This research was previously published in the International Journal of E-Adoption (IJEA), 12(1); pages 52-62, copyright year 2020 by IGI Publishing (an imprint of IGI Global).

Chapter 77
Towards Semantic Aspect–Based Sentiment Analysis for Arabic Reviews

Salima Behdenna

https://orcid.org/0000-0001-9872-2877

Department of Computer Science, Faculty of Exact and Applied Sciences, Laboratoire d'Informatique d'Oran (LIO), Université Oran1 Ahmed Ben Bella, Oran, Algeria

Fatiha Barigou

https://orcid.org/0000-0001-5444-4000

Department of Computer Science, Faculty of Exact and Applied Sciences, Laboratoire d'Informatique d'Oran (LIO), Université Oran1 Ahmed Ben Bella, Oran, Algeria

Ghalem Belalem

https://orcid.org/0000-0002-9694-7586

Department of Computer Science, Faculty of Exact and Applied Sciences, Laboratoire d'Informatique d'Oran (LIO), Université Oran1 Ahmed Ben Bella, Oran, Algeria

ABSTRACT

Sentiment analysis is a text mining discipline that aims to identify and extract subjective information. This growing field results in the emergence of three levels of granularity (document, sentence, and aspect). However, both the document and sentence levels do not find what exactly the opinion holder likes and dislikes. Furthermore, most research in this field deals with English texts, and very limited researches are undertaken on Arabic language. In this paper, the authors propose a semantic aspect-based sentiment analysis approach for Arabic reviews. This approach utilizes the semantic of description logics and linguistic rules in the identification of opinion targets and their polarity.

DOI: 10.4018/978-1-6684-6303-1.ch077

INTRODUCTION

As a result of the rapidly increasing number of opinionated posts on different social media such as (blogs, Face book, discussion groups,…), analysis people's opinion has gained considerable attention recently.

"Sentiment analysis, or opinion mining, is the field of study that analyzes people's opinions, sentiments, evaluations, appraisals, attitudes, and emotions towards entities and their attributes" (Liu, 2012). The growing field resulted in the emergence of three levels of granularity: (i) document level, (ii) sentence level and (iii) aspect level:

1. **Document Sentiment Classification:** The goal of document level sentiment analysis is to classify the sentiment expressed in the whole opinion document as positive or negative (Liu, 2012). This level provides an overall opinion of the document on a single entity (Behdenna, Barigou, & Belalem, 2016);
2. **Sentence Subjectivity and Sentiment Classification:** The goal of this level is to classify the sentiment expressed in each sentence as positive, negative or neutral (Liu, 2012);
3. **Aspect-Based Sentiment Analysis:** Both document level and sentence level do not find what exactly people liked and did not like. Aspect level yields very fine-grained sentiment information. The goal of this level of analysis is to discover and summarize people's opinions expressed on entities and/or their aspects. The difficulty of Aspect-based Sentiment Analysis (ABSA) tasks is due to the following reasons: (i) the opinion can be expressed on entity explicitly or implicitly (Qiu, 2015). (ii) Many sentences without opinion words can also imply opinions (Liu, 2012). (iii) The difficulty in locating the opinion target; where Opinion targets is entity and their aspects about which opinions have been expressed (Qiu, Liu, Bu, & Chen, 2011).

The most commonly used approaches for sentiment analysis are: Machine Learning (ML) and Lexicon-based approaches. Machine Learning approaches require labeling a corpus in advance, and several supervised-based techniques are used (Zhang, Wang, Wu, & Huang, 2007). Lexicon-based approaches exploit a sentiment lexicon which is either built from existing dictionaries, or generated from the corpus (Oard, Elsayed, Wang, Wu, Zhang, Abels,, … & Soergel, 2006). Sentiment analysis approaches is summarized in Figure 1 inspired from (Ibrahim, & Salim, 2013).

On the other hand, most researches' effort in Sentiment analysis deals with English texts and very limited researches are undertaken on Arabic language. Arabic is the official language of 22 Arab countries (Korayem, Aljadda, & Crandall, 2016), spoken by around 422 million people[1], it is the fastest-growing language on the web (Korayem, Aljadda, & Crandall, 2016). Therefore, the need for a designing system for Arabic language is increasing.

The current paper focuses on aspect based sentiment analysis (ABSA) for the Arabic language. More specifically, this work considers two ABSA tasks: Extraction of the opinion target (implicit or explicit) and detecting their polarity. To this end, the authors propose to employ linguistic rules combined with ontology (they employ T-Box and A-Box to describe the ontology).

The main contributions of this work are:

- First, an ontology development, the authors employ Description Logic (DLs) to describe the ontology. To the best of their knowledge, this is the first Arabic research work to address aspect based sentiment analysis using description logic (DLs);

- Second, identify the opinion target employing description logic combined with linguistic rules (inspired from (Ding, & Liu, 2007));
- Third, determining polarity of ambiguous words by refinement and enriching of A-Box.

The rest of this paper is organized as following. In the section 2 the authors introduce some important preliminaries required for the next sections .The section 3 presents Related Work. The section 4, details the proposed approach. Finally the section 5 discusses conclusions and future contributions.

Figure 1. Sentiment analysis approaches

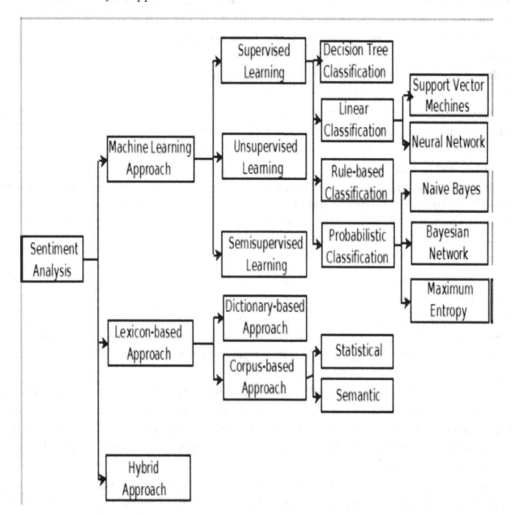

PRELIMINARIES

Definition 1(Entity): An entity e is a product, service, topic, issue, person, organization, or event. It is described with a pair, *e*: (T, W), where T is a hierarchy of parts, sub-parts, and so on, and W is a set of attributes of *e*. Each part or sub-part also has its own set of attributes (Liu, 2012).

Example 1: Laptop has a set of attributes, e.g., speed processor, price, size, and weight, and a set of parts, e.g., motherboards, screen, and battery.

Definition 2(Explicit Aspect Expression): If an aspect explicitly mentioned in the sentence, is called explicit aspect expression (aspect is a part or attribute of an entity) (Liu, 2012).

Example 2: In "*the battery life of this laptop is too short*", *battery life* is explicit aspect expression as it is explicitly mentioned in the sentence.

Definition 3 (Implicit Aspect Expression): Aspect expressions that are not nouns or noun phrases are called implicit aspect expressions (Liu, 2012).

Example 3: In "*This laptop is expensive*", *price* is implicit aspect expression.

Definition 4 (Polarity-Ambiguous Word): The same words have varying polarities in different contexts (Xia, Cambria, Hussain, & Zhao, 2015).

Example 4: Sentence 1, "*high price*" (Martın-Wanton, Balahur-Dobrescu, Montoyo-Guijarro, & Pons-Porrata, 2010), *high* has a negative polarity. Sentence 2, "*high performance*" (Martın-Wanton, Balahur-Dobrescu, Montoyo-Guijarro, & Pons-Porrata, 2010), *high* has a positive polarity.

Definition 5 (Opinion Lexicon or Sentiment Lexicon): An opinion lexicon or sentiment lexicon is a dictionary providing opinion words with their polarity values to indicate the positive or negative sentiments (Agarwal, Mittal, Bansal, & Garg, 2015).

Example 5: There are several sentiment lexicons, such as SentiWordNet (Baccianella, Esuli, & Sebastiani, 2010), Senti Strength[2], and MPQA (Multi-Perspective Question Answering)[3].

Definition 6 (Description Logic (DLs)): Knowledge representation system based on Description Logic (DLs) consists of two components – T-Box and A-Box[4]. The T-Box describes terminology, i.e., the ontology in the form of concepts and roles definitions, while the A-Box contains assertions about individuals using the terms from the ontology. Concepts describe sets of individuals; roles describe relations between individuals.

RELATED WORKS

With the increase in the volume of Arabic opinionated posts on different social media, Arabic sentiment analysis is viewed as an important research field. Most researches in Arabic sentiment analysis to conduct both the document level and the sentence level. But few studies exist for aspect-based sentiment analysis.

In (Tamchyna, & Veselovská, 2016), the authors propose a new system for aspect based sentiment analysis for Arabic Language. The focus of this work is aspect category detection. For each sentence, the goal is to identify all aspect categories which are mentioned. Each category is composed of an entity and its attribute. They propose to utilize neural networks and they apply their system on several languages (Arabic, Dutch, English, French, Russian, Spanish and Turkish). Experiments showed that their system was the best for Russian and Turkish but did not achieve interesting results on other languages.

In (Al-Sarhan, Al-So'ud, Al-Smadi, Al-Ayyoub, & Jararweh, 2016), the authors aim at fostering the domain of Arabic affective news' analysis by providing: (a) a benchmark of annotated Arabic dataset of news for affective news analysis. The dataset consists of 2,265 news posts. The dataset has been prepared and annotated to provide important information for all tasks related to the Aspect-Based Sentiment Analysis (ABSA) based on SemEval-2014 Task 4 guidelines (Pontiki, Galanis, Pavlopoulos, Papageorgiou,

Androutsopoulos, & Manandhar, 2014). The four tasks under consideration are: aspect terms extraction (T1), aspect term polarity identification (T2), aspect category selection (T3) and aspect category polarity identification (T4). (b) A baseline approach for four ABSA tasks, with a common evaluation framework to compare future research results with the baseline ones. (c) A lexicon-based approach for aspect term extraction (with 12% improvement in the F1 measure) and aspect term polarity estimation (with 1% improvement in accuracy).

As a result of limitation in availability of appropriate datasets, Human Annotated Arabic Dataset (HAAD) presented in (Al-Smadi, Qawasmeh, Talafha, & Quwaider, 2015) is the first aspect-based sentiment analysis dataset publicly available for Arabic language. The dataset (HAAD) consists of 1513 books review sentences selected from the LABR dataset (Aly, & Atiya, 2013). The dataset has annotated based on SemEval-2014 Task 4 guidelines (Pontiki, Galanis, Pavlopoulos, Papageorgiou, Androutsopoulos, & Manandhar, 2014). And it has been prepared to support a set of research tasks such as aspect extraction and polarity detection, aspect category identification and category polarity detection.

Another work focuses on the aspect-based sentiment analysis for the Arabic language is proposed in (Al Smadi, Obaidat, Al-Ayyoub, Mohawesh, & Jararweh, 2016), the authors develop several lexicon-based approaches for two Aspect-Based Sentiment Analysis (ABSA) tasks: aspect category determination and aspect category polarity determination and makes use of the publicly available human annotated Arabic dataset (HAAD) (Al-Smadi, Qawasmeh, Talafha, & Quwaider, 2015). Experiments showed an enhancement of 46% in the task aspect category polarity determination. This result was achieved by the lexicon-based approach, where this approach was built gradually following three phases. A similar approach was developed for Task T3; however, the improvements are not as impressive as Task T4 (an enhancement of 9%).

In (Alkadri, & ElKorany, 2016), the authors propose a feature-based opinion mining framework for Arabic reviews. This framework uses the semantic of ontology and lexicons in the identification of opinion features and their polarity. This approach is composed of five components: Ontology and lexicon Development, Semantic Feature Identification, Polarity Identification, Feature Polarity Identification and Opinion Mining. Experiments showed that this approach achieved a good level of performance. The accuracy improved to be much better than the result achieved by baseline approach.

An aspect-based sentiment analysis (ABSA) approach to evaluate Arabic news posts affect on readers was proposed in (Al-Smadi, Al-Ayyoub, Al-Sarhan, & Jararweh, 2016), the authors focus on the tasks related to aspect terms. They investigated machine learning approach to address these tasks. The features considered include Part of Speech (POS) tagging, Named Entity Recognition (NER), and N-Grams. The considered classifiers are: Conditional Random Fields (CRF), Decision Tree (J48), Naive Bayes (NB) and K-Nearest Neighbor (IBk). The results show that J48 performs the best for the task of aspect terms extraction whereas CRF and NB are slightly better in the task aspect terms polarity identification.

The work presented in (Ibrahim, & Salim, 2016) focuses on evaluating Arabic tweets for restaurant services. The authors constructed a prototype for sentiment analysis of Arabic tweets with corresponding Arabic Opinion Lexicon (AOL) and Arabic Tweet Sentiment Analyzer (ATSA). The prototype has been designed and tested using customer's opinions obtained from tweeter; it accepts tweets as input, generates polarity, and determines the tweet target as outputs. Additionally, the prototype can ascertain the type of tweet as subjective, objective, positive, or negative and give a summarization of tweet polarity.

PROPOSED APPROACH

The goal of Aspect based Sentiment analysis (ABSA) is to:

- Identify the opinion target, where an Opinion target is entity, their aspects or a part of entity about which opinions have been expressed (Qiu, Liu, Bu, & Chen, 2011);
- Identify the sentiment polarity for each mentioned aspect[5].

But the difficulty of ABSA tasks is due to both the high semantic variability of the opinions expressed, the diversity of the aspect and the polarity of opinion words used to depict them (Balahur, & Montoyo, 2009). For this reason, the authors propose:

- To use the domain ontology to identify entities, main aspects of domain and to resolve the high semantic variability of the opinions expressed;
- To address the problems of:
  - Opinion target extraction (implicit or explicit);
  - Determining polarity of the sentiment ambiguous words.

The main goals of the proposed approach in this paper are to improve aspect-based sentiment analysis for a specific domain by employing Description Logic (DLs) combined with linguistic rules inspired from (Ding, & Liu, 2007) for extraction of opinion target, and determine the sentiment polarity for each mentioned aspect.

In the proposed approach, the authors chose to use Description Logic (DLs) to describe the ontology. The motivation of this choice is double-handed: on the one hand, the entities of the domain and their attributes are described by concepts, roles using the concept and role constructors provided by the particular DL (Baader, Horrocks, & Sattler, 2005). On the other hand, DLs are based on a formal, logic-based semantics (Shu, Rana, Avis, & Dingfang, 2007).

The architecture proposed by authors is shown in Figure 2.

This architecture consists of the following two phases:

Phase 1: Ontology Development: In aspect-based sentiment analysis, the aim of using ontology is to identify entities, aspects and opinions (Nguyen, &Quan, 2014). In the proposed approach, the authors employ Description Logic (DLs) to describe the ontology; i.e. they use the concept of T-Box and A-Box, and regard their domain ontologies as Books Ontologies. Figure 3 shows a simplified version of the taxonomy. The T-Box (assertions on concepts) introduces the terminology, i.e. consists of a set of concept axioms and role axioms (Figure 4). The A-Box (assertions on individuals) consists of a set of concept assertions and role assertions. Figure 5 gives an example of A-Box of this book's ontology.

Phase 2: Aspect Based Sentiment Analysis: This second phase is composed of six main components: sentence splitting, tokenization, morpho-syntactic analysis, Subjective analysis, Opinion target extraction and Polarity identification. However, before describing in detail these components; they must first present the linguistic resources such as: linguistic rules, Corpus and opinion lexicon, which are required in their approach.

Figure 2. Architecture proposed by authors

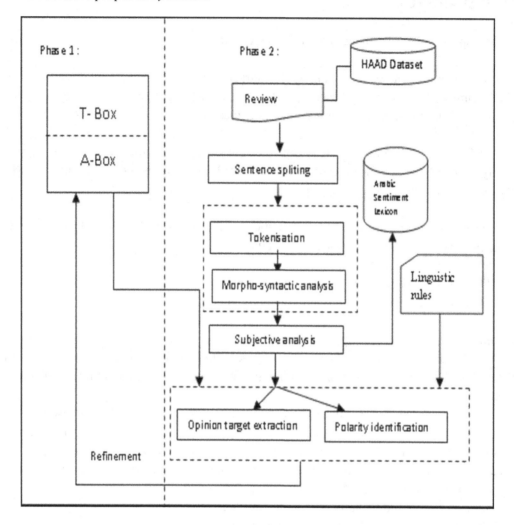

Linguistic Resources

Researches in the field of sentiment analysis rely on Opinion lexicons and annotated corpus. Unfortunately, there are very few available resources for Arabic sentiment analysis. In the proposed approach, the authors use ArSenL (Badaro, Baly, Hajj, Habash, & El-Hajj, 2014), the first publicly available lexicon constructed for the Arabic language and HAAD Dataset (Al-Smadi, Qawasmeh, Talafha, & Quwaider, 2015). Moreover, the authors propose to use linguistic rules inspired from (Ding, & Liu, 2007) combined with A-Box to disambiguate the polarity of the polarity-ambiguous word. These linguistic rules can be used to infer opinions:

- Intra-sentence conjunction rule: For example: "إنه كتاب رائع و مهم جدا" "It's a great book and very important";
- Pseudo intra-sentence conjunction rule: one can use an implicit conjunction, for example: "إنه كتاب رائع, مهم جدا" "It's a great book, very important";

- Inter-Sentence Conjunction Rule;
- Synonym and Antonym Rule: If a word is considered positive (or negative) in a context for an aspect, its synonyms are also considered positive (or negative), and its antonyms are considered negative (or positive) (Ding, & Liu, 2007).

Figure 3. Book domain ontology

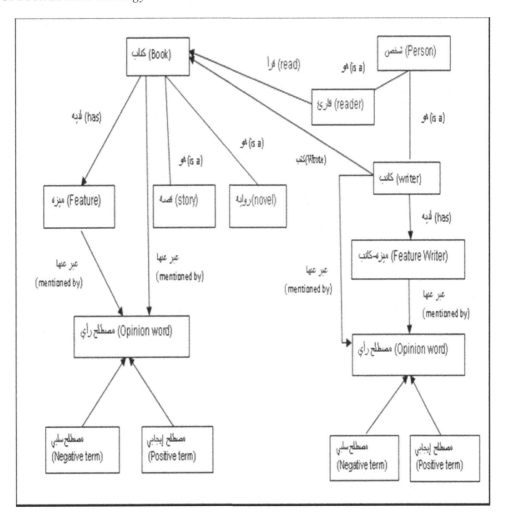

Sentence Splitting

First, the authors need to split the text of the review to separate sentences and keep the conjoined sentences and neighboring sentences to apply the linguistic rules and infer opinions.

Figure 4. TBox

كتاب ≡ T (Book≡ T)

شخص ⊓ كتاب. كتب ∃ ≡ كاتب (Writer ≡ ∃ wrote.Book ⊓ Person)

شخص ⊓ كتاب. قرأ ∀ ≡ قارئ (Reader ≡ ∀ read.Book ⊓ Person)

مصطلح سلبي ⊔ مصطلح إيجابي ≡ مصطلح رأي (Opinion word ≡ Positive term ⊔ Negative term)

مصطلح سلبي ⊓ مصطلح إيجابي ≡ ⊥ (Positive term ⊓ Negative term ≡ ⊥)

ميزة. لديها ∃ ≡ كتاب (Book ≡ ∃ has. Feature)

مصطلح رأي عبر عنها ∃ ≡ كتاب (Book ≡ ∃ mentioned by. Opinion word)

مصطلح رأي عبر عنها ∃ ≡ ميزة (Feature ≡ ∃ mentioned by.Opinion word)

ميزة-كتاب. لديه ∃ ≡ كاتب (Writer ≡ ∃has. Feature Writer)

مصطلح رأي عبر عنها ∃ ≡ كاتب (Writer ≡ ∃ mentioned by.Opinion word)

مصطلح رأي عبر عنها ∃ ≡ ميزة-كاتب (Feature Writer≡ ∃ mentioned by.Opinion word)

قصة ⊆ كتاب (Story⊆ Book)

رواية ⊆ كتاب (Novel ⊆ Book)

Figure 5. ABox

(جميل جداً) مصطلح إيجابي ;) "Positive term(very nice)"

(ممتع) مصطلح إيجابي ;) "Positive term(enjoyable)"

(جميل جداً،الكتاب) عبر عنها ;) "Mentioned by(book, very nice)"

(ممتع،أجواء) عبر عنها ;) "Mentioned by(Ambiance, enjoyable)"

(ضعيفة) مصطلح سلبي ;) "Negative term(weak)"

(ضعيفة،رواية) عبر عنها ;) "Mentioned by(novel, weak)"

(متدفقة) مصطلح إيجابي ;) "Positive term(gushing)"

Preprocessing

In order to identify opinion target and extract opinions from reviews, several NLP techniques must be utilized, including Tokenizer, to tokenize every sentence into words. After removing the special characters, the words are tagged using Stanford Arabic part of speech tagger.

Subjective Analysis

In order to identify if the sentence has expressed or not an opinion, opinion lexicon must be used. In the proposed approach, the authors use the Arabic sentiment lexicon (ArSenL) to determine whether a sentence is subjective or objective.

Opinion Target Extraction

An opinion target can be mentioned explicitly, it can be extracted by simple projection of the lexical component of the ontology. Example: "عئار باتك" "It's a great book". As well as an opinion target can be mentioned implicitly in several instances:

Instance 1: The difficulty in locating the opinion target because of the presence of several candidates' entities around the opinion word.

Instance 2: There is no explicit mention of the entity.

Instance 3: The difficulty in locating the opinion target because of several forms of the unique entity.

In these instances, the authors use the ontology semantic relationships between concepts.

Polarity Identification

For polarity identification, the authors use the Arabic sentiment lexicon (ArSenL) to determine the polarity of the extracted opinion words in reviews. To deal with the problem of the polarity-ambiguous word, they propose to use linguistic rules inspired from (Ding, & Liu, 2007) combined with A-Box.

Refinement

In literature, most works focus on enriching the opinion lexicon but the semantic orientations of many words are context dependent as they have outlined in section2 example 4. For this reason, the authors propose to enrich description logics with aspect-opinion pair for each disambiguated polarity-ambiguous word, Figures 6 and 7 show examples of several reviews noticed in several cases and situations. From review 1, they can extract the opinion targets by simple projection of the lexical component of the ontology, and use the Arabic sentiment lexicon to determine their polarity.

From review 2, they can extract the opinion target and their polarity by using the ontology semantic relationships between concepts, linguistic rules inspired from (Ding, & Liu, 2007) and the A-Box.

Figure 6. Example 1

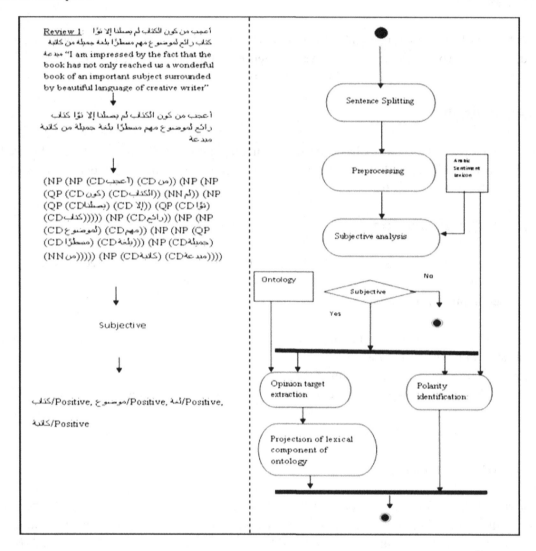

CONCLUSION

In a review, Opinions can be expressed explicitly or implicitly. Whereas in other cases, it is difficult to locate the opinion target. Aspect based Sentiment analysis (ABSA) intends to: Identify the opinion target, and identify the sentiment expressed towards each aspect. Most researches effort in this field deal with English texts and very limited researches exist on the Arabic language. In this paper, the authors propose a semantic aspect based sentiment analysis approach for Arabic reviews. This approach utilizes the semantic of Description logics and linguistic rules in the identification of opinion aspects and their polarity.

The authors intend to implement the proposed approach and they plan to apply this approach in book domain using HAAD Dataset.

Figure 7. Example 2

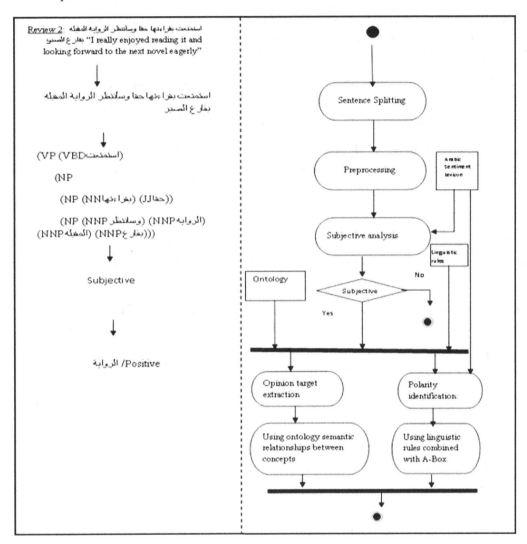

REFERENCES

Agarwal, B., Mittal, N., Bansal, P., & Garg, S. (2015). Sentiment analysis using common-sense and context information. *Computational Intelligence and Neuroscience, 2015*, 30. doi:10.1155/2015/715730 PMID:25866505

Al-Sarhan, H., Al-So'ud, M., Al-Smadi, M., Al-Ayyoub, M., & Jararweh, Y. (2016). Framework for affective news analysis of arabic news: 2014 gaza attacks case study. In *Information and Communication Systems (ICICS), 2016 7th International Conference on* (pp. 327-332). IEEE.

Al-Smadi, M., Al-Ayyoub, M., Al-Sarhan, H., & Jararweh, Y. (2016). An Aspect-Based Sentiment Analysis Approach to Evaluating Arabic News Affect on Readers. *JUCS, 22*, 630-649.

Al Smadi, M., Obaidat, I., Al-Ayyoub, M., Mohawesh, R., & Jararweh, Y. (2016). Using Enhanced Lexicon-Based Approaches for the Determination of Aspect Categories and Their Polarities in Arabic Reviews. *International Journal of Information Technology and Web Engineering, 11*(3), 15–31. doi:10.4018/IJITWE.2016070102

Al-Smadi, M., Qawasmeh, O., Talafha, B., & Quwaider, M. (2015). Human annotated arabic dataset of book reviews for aspect based sentiment analysis. In *Future Internet of Things and Cloud (FiCloud), 2015 3rd International Conference on* (pp. 726-730). IEEE. 10.1109/FiCloud.2015.62

Alkadri, A. M., & ElKorany, A. M. (2016). Semantic Feature Based Arabic Opinion Mining Using Ontology. *International Journal of Advanced Computer Science and Applications, 7*(5), 577–583.

Aly, M. A., & Atiya, A. F. (2013). LABR: A Large Scale Arabic Book Reviews Dataset. In ACL (pp. 494-498). Academic Press.

Baader, F., Horrocks, I., & Sattler, U. (2005). Description logics as ontology languages for the semantic web. In *Mechanizing Mathematical Reasoning* (pp. 228–248). Springer. doi:10.1007/978-3-540-32254-2_14

Baccianella, S., Esuli, A., & Sebastiani, F. (2010). SentiWordNet 3.0: An Enhanced Lexical Resource for Sentiment Analysis and Opinion Mining. In LREC (Vol. 10, pp. 2200-2204). Academic Press.

Badaro, G., Baly, R., Hajj, H., Habash, N., & El-Hajj, W. (2014). A large scale Arabic sentiment lexicon for Arabic opinion mining. *ANLP, 2014*(165), 165–173. doi:10.3115/v1/W14-3623

Balahur, A., & Montoyo, A. (2009). Semantic approaches to fine and coarse-grained feature-based opinion mining. In *International Conference on Application of Natural Language to Information Systems* (pp. 142-153). Springer.

Behdenna, S., Barigou, F., & Belalem, G. (2016) Sentiment Analysis at Document Level. In Smart Trends in Information Technology and Computer Communications. SmartCom 2016 (vol. 628). Springer. doi:10.1007/978-981-10-3433-6_20

Ding, X., & Liu, B. (2007). The utility of linguistic rules in opinion mining. In *Proceedings of the 30th annual international ACM SIGIR conference on Research and development in information retrieval* (pp. 811-812). ACM. 10.1145/1277741.1277921

Ibrahim, M. A., & Salim, N. (2013). Opinion analysis for twitter and arabic tweets: A systematic literature review. *Journal of Theoretical & Applied Information Technology, 56*(3).

Ibrahim, M. A., & Salim, N. (2016). Aspect Oriented Sentiment Analysis Model of Arabic Tweets. *International Journal of Computer Science Trends and Technology, 4*(4), 342-353.

Korayem Korayem, M., Aljadda, K., & Crandall, D. (2016). Sentiment/subjectivity analysis survey for languages other than English. *Social Network Analysis and Mining, 6*(1), 75. doi:10.100713278-016-0381-6

Liu, B. (2012). Sentiment analysis and opinion mining. *Synthesis Lectures on Human Language Technologies, 5*(1), 1-167.

Martın-Wanton, T., Balahur-Dobrescu, A., Montoyo-Guijarro, A., & Pons-Porrata, A. (2010). Word sense disambiguation in opinion mining: Pros and cons. *Natural Language Processing and Its Applications, 119*, 358.

Nguyen, T. T., & Quan, T. T. (2014). A sentiment analysis model using ontology-enriched conceptual graph and operational rules. In *Proceedings of International Conference on Advances in Computing, Electronics and Electrical Technology - CEET 2014, Malaysia* (pp. 34 – 38). Academic Press.

Oard, D., Elsayed, T., Wang, J., Wu, Y., Zhang, P., Abels, E., & Soergel, D. (2006). *TREC-2006 at Maryland: Blog, enterprise, legal and QA tracks.* Maryland Univ College Park Inst for Advanced Computer Studies. doi:10.21236/ADA463747

Pontiki, M., Galanis, D., Pavlopoulos, J., Papageorgiou, H., Androutsopoulos, I., & Manandhar, S. (2014). Semeval-2014 task 4: Aspect based sentiment analysis. *Proceedings of SemEval*, 27-35.

Qiu, G., Liu, B., Bu, J., & Chen, C. (2011). Opinion word expansion and target extraction through double propagation. *Computational Linguistics, 37*(1), 9–27. doi:10.1162/coli_a_00034

Qiu, L. (2015). An opinion analysis model for implicit aspect expressions based on semantic ontology. *International Journal of Grid and Distributed Computing, 8*(5), 165–172. doi:10.14257/ijgdc.2015.8.5.16

Shu, G., Rana, O. F., Avis, N. J., & Dingfang, C. (2007). Ontology-based semantic matchmaking approach. *Advances in Engineering Software, 38*(1), 59–67. doi:10.1016/j.advengsoft.2006.05.004

Tamchyna, A., & Veselovská, K. (2016). UFAL at SemEval-2016 Task 5: Recurrent Neural Networks for Sentence Classification. *Proceedings of SemEval*, 367-371.

Xia, Y., Cambria, E., Hussain, A., & Zhao, H. (2015). Word polarity disambiguation using bayesian model and opinion-level features. *Cognitive Computation, 7*(3), 369–380. doi:10.100712559-014-9298-4

Zhang, Q., Wang, B., Wu, L., & Huang, X. (2007). FDU at TREC 2007: Opinion Retrieval of Blog Track. In TREC (pp. 500-274). Academic Press.

ENDNOTES

[1]   UNESCO World Arabic Language Day, 2012. UNESCO http://www.unesco.org/new/en/unesco/events/prizes-and-celebrations/celebrations/international-days/world-arabic-language-day/

[2]   http://sentistrength.wlv.ac.uk/

[3]   http://mpqa.cs.pitt.edu/lexicon/subj_lexicon/

[4]   https://www.obitko.com/tutorials/ontologies-semantic-web/description-logics.html

[5]   http://alt.qcri.org/semeval2014/task4/

This research was previously published in the International Journal of Information Systems in the Service Sector (IJISSS), 12(4); pages 1-13, copyright year 2020 by IGI Publishing (an imprint of IGI Global).

Chapter 78
Airbnb or Hotel?
A Comparative Study on the Sentiment of Airbnb Guests in Sydney – Text Analysis Based on Big Data

Zhiyong Li
School of Tourism, Sichuan University, China

Honglin Chen
School of Tourism, Sichuan University, China

Xia Huang
School of Tourism, Sichuan University, China

ABSTRACT

Advances in information technology have hugely influenced the tourism industry. Many tourists can generate and share their travel tips through social media, and people consult online reviews before making travel arrangements because they could access these sources of information easily. Either positive or negative reviews could increase consumer awareness of Airbnb. Using the approach of text mining and sentiment analysis, examining whether guests' emotions are positive or negative, this study investigates the attributes that influence Airbnb consumers' experiences compared with their previous hotel experiences by analysing big data of guests' online reviews. Findings reveal that the factors of guests' positive sentiment are the atmosphere, flexibility, special amenities, and humanized service; the factors of guests' negative sentiment are not value for money, have to clean the room before leaving, sharing amenities and space with strangers, disturbed by hosts' noisy recreational activities, and troubled by hosts' requesting good reviews.

DOI: 10.4018/978-1-6684-6303-1.ch078

INTRODUCTION

The sharing economy, also called the collaborative consumption, based on peer-to-peer activity to share goods and services through Internet, moved by growing shared values of the public and increasing technological advancement of Internet platforms, including services like Couchsurfing, Uber as well as Airbnb (Hamari et al., 2016). Airbnb, founded in 2008, is one of the largest peer-to-peer (P2P) accommodation platforms in the sharing economy, has enjoyed significant worldwide growth in more than 81,000 cities and 191 countries. It allows ordinary people to rent residences such as an entire apartment or a private room to tourists, exists to create a world where anyone can belong anywhere and provides healthy travel that is local, authentic, diverse, inclusive and sustainable (Airbnb, 2019). Given its popularity in the tourism industry, researchers have begun undertaking studies on the Airbnb phenomenon, mainly focusing on the issues about Airbnb's impacts on the traditional hospitality sector, attributes comparison between Airbnb and hotels and Airbnb guests' motivations for using the service (Birinci, Berezina, & Cobanoglu, 2018; Guttentag, 2015; Guttentag & Smith, 2017; Neeser, 2015; Tussyadiah, 2015; Yannopoulou, 2013), however, it seldom involves the comparative study of tourists' emotional characteristics between Airbnb and hotels based on the sentiment analysis.

With the rapid development of information technologies, online social media and we-media, a massive new source of data called user-generated content (UGC) have come into being and been shared (Kaplan & Haenlein, 2010). Most of the UGC data at present are the travel photos, travel vlogs and tourist reviews of scenic spots, accommodations, caterings and the overall destinations, through which tourists could know about the tourism information more veritably and objectively. Several recent studies explore the issue of online reviews, or electronic word-of-mouth, focusing mainly on matters such as motivations of, and social dynamics between, users and contributors of review sites (Hennig-Thurau, Gwinner, Walsh, & Gremler, 2004). Yet, previous studies primarily rely on surveys, personal interviews, and other communication-based methods, but not made full use of this UGC (Xiang, Schwartz, Gerdes, & Uysal, 2015). The present sentiment analysis based on travelers' online reviews has mainly restricted the processing of unstructured text especially Airbnb guests' comments needs to be further studied and developed.

As a result, based on the theory of sentiment analysis, this study uses online reviews of world tourists to Australia and selects LIWC dictionary and text analysis instrument to compare the sentiment characteristics of Airbnb users and their previous hotel experience, to investigate the influencing factors of their positive and negative reviews. This study is an attempt to explore the sentiment of tourists based on the tourism big data. For tourists, it is helpful for them to obtain useful information from the huge amount of information before making reservations. For the managers and hosts of the Airbnb platform, it would be useful to perceive tourists' sentiment demands so that they can promote the quality of the accommodation products and services provided during their stay.

REVIEW OF LITERATURE

Comparisons Between Airbnb and Hotel

Various studies have attempted to investigate Airbnb's impacts on traditional hotel accommodation industry. And some researchers have compared Airbnb's attributes with hotels (Belarmino, Whalen, Koh,

& Bowen, 2017; Guttentag & Smith, 2017; Zhang, Cui, Cheng, Zhang & Li, 2019). For example, given the small sample capacity, Belarmino et al. (2017) made a preliminary comparison between Airbnb and hotel to see how significant the connection of tourist and hosts is. By using guest reviews, Zhang et al. (2019) found some nuanced attributes between Airbnb and hotels: Airbnb's distinctive attributes compared with hotels include pets, atmosphere, flexibility, value for money and so on. The similar attributes are cleanliness, location, services as well as amenities. These research not only certifies prominent attributes of Airbnb that have been found in preceding studies (e.g. Cheng & Jin, 2019) but also supplement researches with the content that to what extent Airbnb is considered as a good alternative for hotels.

Specifically, a few researchers have made a comparison of users' experiences between Airbnb and Hotel, on the one hand, some studies considered the "social communications" and "authentic experience" as the central point of the Airbnb costumers' experience (Festila & Müller, 2017; Yannopoulou, 2013). For instance, Yannopoulou (2013) studied two brands of Airbnb and Couchsurfing, finally found four themes, including the environment of privacy, humanism, the interaction between guests and hosts which is meaningful as well as authenticity. On the other hand, "cheaper price" (Guttentag & Smith, 2017), "convenient location" (Tussyadiah & Zach, 2016), "home amenities" (Guttentag, 2015) and "cleanliness" (Bridges and Vásquez2016) are of critical importance. However, there is very little literature on the emotional characteristics of Airbnb and hotel's customers from the perspective of sentiment analysis. Besides, there is also a lack of in-depth research on the influencing factors of sentiment comparing Airbnb's guests with traditional hotels.

Big Data and Online Reviews

Tourism has been recognized as the most popular sector in online engagement, traditional approaches are insufficient to academic research because of the volume, velocity, and variety of big data (McAbee et al., 2017), so that the use of big data is rapidly emerging in the tourism research (Fuchs, Höpken, & Lexhagen, 2014). There is a growing literature on social media analysis that combines web crawling, computational linguistics and machine learning to collect and analyze the big data for business purposes such as tracking trending topics as well as identifying opinions about products (Fan & Gordon, 2014). Online consumer review comments, vary significantly in terms of their linguistic characteristics as well as semantic features (Xiang, Du, Ma & Fan, 2017), widely considered big data source that naturally reflects consumer evaluation of products and experiences, often reflecting consumer's sentiments such as happiness, anxiety, sadness and some others (O'Leary, 2011), have been acknowledged and used by researchers to understand a range of research problems in hospitality and tourism (e.g., Abbie-Gayle & Barbara, 2017; Brochado et al., 2017; He et al., 2013; Kozinets, 2010; Schuckert, Liu, & Law, 2015b; Tussyadiah & Zach, 2017; Xiang et al., 2015). Belarmino et al. (2017) compared relevant online reviews to investigate guests' motivations behind staying in P2P accommodations rather than hotels; XXX., however, the tourism and hospitality field has few relevant articles based on big data from a sentiment perspective using online reviews (Fuchs et al., 2014; Xiang et al., 2015).

Sentiment Analysis

The sentiment is an emotional psychological reaction produced in the human perception process, which is situational and unstable, changing with the external environment. After many times of emotional changing, people will form a more rational and organized attitude. From this level, we can understand that tourism commentary expressed by written language is the expression of sentiment.

There are two main orientations in the current sentiment theory, including the categorical approach and dimensional approach. Categorical orientation is enlightened by Darwin's evolutionism, which holds that emotions can be divided into basic emotions (happiness, sadness, anger, disgust, fear and surprise) and complex emotions. Dimensional orientation holds that emotions are not composed of basic emotions and complex emotions, but depend on the influence of three vector dimensions: valence, arousal and power (Ekman and Friesen,1971; Russell, 1980).

Sentiment analysis is a type of text mining that measures people's sentiments on whether they are positive, negative or neutral toward a particular topic through extracting and analyzing people's subjective information but not objective information (Ma, Cheng, & Hsiao, 2018; Zhou, Yang, Bao, & Huang, 2016), for that objective reviews usually do not contain those words that can be classified as positive or negative in a sentiment dictionary. When Compared with traditional questionnaires, using sentiment analysis to evaluate customer satisfaction has become a more objective approach in the marketing and consumer behavior field (Das & Chen, 2007; Mady, 2011). Therefore, it is emerging as an automated process of examining semantic relationships and meaning in reviews.

At present, mature analysis techniques include semantic localization and machine learning. Semantic localization method is to classify words by measuring the distance between positive and negative words, while machine learning method is to mine ideas and analyze emotions through prior supervisory training tests, which includes Naive Bayesian, Support Vector Machine and so on (Pang and Lee, 2008). Sentiment analysis can be explored at the word, sentence, paragraph and document levels. Relatively less research has focused on sentence-level analysis since it is more difficult to exemplify from words compared with paragraphs and documents (Schmunk et al., 2014). Data collection, cleaning, mining and evaluating of the data results are the major steps in most of the sentiment analysis in tourism (Hippner & Rentzmann, 2006; Schmunk et al., 2014). There are three considerations in these steps: 1) the data collection source should be distinguished, researchers have typically studied two types of online content for analysis including professional tourism platforms such as TripAdvisor and social media like micro-blog and Facebook, these online text are usually limited, for instance, micro-blog in China allows no more than 140 characters in length; 2) in data cleaning, some meaningless words, repetitive words and non-text content should be filtered out initially; 3) in the data mining process, three sentiment analysis methods can be selected, that is machine learning (supervised and unsupervised machine learning), dictionary-based (rely on the use of comprehensive sentiment lexicons and sets of fine-tuned rules created either by humans or by machine) and hybrid approaches.

Although the study of judging consumer satisfaction through the evaluation of tourists' emotions is becoming a new hot spot in recent years, there is still a lack of sentiment analysis based on big data to compare the hotel and Airbnb users, so that here we choose dictionary-based sentiment analysis method on account that it can more flexibly interpret Airbnb users' comments on the Internet, and more suitable for the analysis of tourism phenomena.

RESEARCH METHODS AND DATA

Research Area and Data Collecting

This paper focused on the tourism city of Sydney in Australia for two reasons. One is that Sydney is the largest city in Australia with spectacular natural scenic spots and rich cultural tourism resources located on the east coast. The other is that the Sydney has seen an explosive increase in the number of Airbnb listings (about 23,615) by December 2016, which is ranked the fourth most popular destination for Airbnb in the world (Stuart, 2017), therefore, it has important research value to mine the potential influencing factors behind.

This study used the data available on Inside Airbnb website in Sydney. With the help of a web crawler tool, the researchers collected 181263 online reviews in total. To directly investigate the dissimilarity between Airbnb guests' and the hotel's in preferences and sentiment characteristics, only reviews with the keyword 'hotel' in English were selected, which commendably reflect Airbnb guests' direct comparison with their previous hotel experiences because these relevant reviews were derived from the same respondents. Therefore, 2938 online reviews of 331997 words posted between 24 July 2010 and 4 December 2016 were retained for analysis.

Processing Methods

The first necessary step was to use the TextBlob to process textual data and calculate the emotional scores of the guests' review. TextBlob is a Python library which provides a simple API for diving into common natural language processing (NLP) tasks (Loria, 2018). It has various features such as noun phrase extraction, classification (naive Bayes, decision tree), spelling correction, tokenization and sentiment analysis. TextBlob can break reviews can into words or sentences and the sentiment property returns a named tuple of the form Sentiment(polarity, subjectivity). The polarity score is a float within the range [-1.0, 1.0], if the score of one review was positive, it would be categorized as a positive review and vice versa. The subjectivity ranges between 0.0 and 1.0 where 0.0 is very objective and 1.0 is very subjective. In the tourism field, "positive" and "negative" may respectively mean "satisfied" and "unsatisfied", but further research to link sentiment with satisfaction still under explored.

Second, to analyze tourists' preference and understand what features customers are mainly concerned about, the researchers utilize the ROST CM6 instrument to carry out high-frequency word analysis. ROST Content Mining is a tool of content analysis, developed by professor Shenyang of an information management institute in Wuhan university in China. This system can not only assist various disciplines in scientific research, but also carry out text and content analysis from a large number of data. At present, it can be used to analyze papers, micro-blogs, blogs, forums, web pages, e-mails, chat records and other content files composed of text. The software has many powerful functions such as word classification, word frequency, word type and word frequency, emotional analysis from simple to complex, citation and citation analysis. The frequency of words is called word frequency, moreover, before using this tool to analyze the frequency of words, we should deal with the data of online reviews in advance, that is delete the pictures, emoticons, wrongly written character, unknown adverbs, singular and plural numbers in the comments for modification and replacement at first, and then filter out meaningless prepositions and articles.

Third, to further analyze tourists' preference and impact factors of the positive and negative review, each of the classified reviews, filtering the neutral reviews, went through the LIWC (Linguistic Inquiry and Word Count) program. The way that the LIWC program works is reading a given text and counting the percentage of words that reflect different emotions, thinking styles, social concerns, and even parts of speech. And LIWC2015 is the most recent evolution in which the heart is default LIWC2015 Dictionary, composed of almost 6,400 words, word stems, and select emoticons (Pennebaker, Booth, Boyd, & Francis, 2015). For each text file, approximately 90 output variables are written as one line of data to an output file. This data record includes the file name and word count, 4 summary language variables (analytical thinking, clout, authenticity, and emotional tone), 3 general descriptor categories (words per sentence, percent of target words captured by the dictionary, and percent of words in the text that are longer than six letters), 21 standard linguistic dimensions (e.g., prepositions, conjunctions, negations, etc.), 41 word categories tapping psychological constructs (e.g., affective processes, social processes, drives, etc.), 6 personal concern categories (e.g., work, home, money, etc.), 5 informal language markers (assents, fillers, swear words, netspeak and nonfluencies), and 12 punctuation categories (colons, question marks, etc.). This study applied LIWC2015 in two steps: (1) selecting the categories the researchers want to analyze and (2) color-coding the words in the dictionary from selected categories.

RESULTS AND DISCUSSIONS

After the process of the above methods, this study extracts 2872 positive, 10 neutral and 56 negative online reviews respectively, of which positive sentiments are the main ones, accounting for 97.75% of the total number of online comments.

Next, we extract the top 150 high-frequency words of the Airbnb guests' online comments, as shown in Table 1. As we can see, the top ten words are "hotel", "stay", "great", "place", "apartment", "Sydney", "location", "room", "host" and "walking", their words frequency are all more than 1000, of which the highest is "hotel" of 3160 in total, hence we could conclude that guests care about "location", "amenities" and "host". First, guests not only emphasize place's convenience such as near the station (ranking No.25 of 778 words frequency), airport (ranking No.33 of 684 words frequency), restaurant (ranking No.54 of 464 words frequency) and shops (ranking No.64 of 373 words frequency) and CBD (ranking No.102 of 220 words frequency), but also prefer Airbnb's superiority that they can easily have a fantastic landscape of beautiful beach (ranking No.42 of 568 words frequency) and cultural harbor (ranking No.97 of 231 words frequency). Second, "hotel", "apartment", "room" are bout Airbnb listings' quality and type because they're the basic element, on the other hand, they put emphasize on houses' specific amenities, for instance, "bed" ranks No.17 of 922 words frequency, "kitchen" ranks No.54 of 464 words frequency, "bathroom" ranks No.57 of 435 words frequency. Third, the high ranking of "stay", "great" and "host" indicate that Airbnb guest regard the great experience of connecting to hosts during their stay as exactly important, the atmosphere is of vital importance because the word "home", "feel", "comfortable", "nice", "lovely", "helpful", "friendly", "wonderful" and "happy" well reflected the feelings or emotions that tourists have when staying in Airbnb listings and communicating with hosts, this fully illustrates the important value of sentiment analysis based on LIWC sentiment lexicon of the third step of processing method.

Table 1. Top 150 high frequency vocabulary of tourists' online reviews

No.	words	words frequency	No.	words	words frequency	No.	words	words frequency
1	hotel	3160	51	beautiful	486	101	work	221
2	stay	2828	52	back	485	102	CBD	220
3	great	2162	53	love	471	103	extremely	219
4	place	2063	54	restaurant	464	104	central	216
5	apartment	2002	55	need	463	105	nearby	211
6	Sydney	1654	56	kitchen	441	106	park	210
7	location	1586	57	bathroom	435	107	new	205
8	room	1469	58	accommodation	431	108	balcony	203
9	host	1258	59	enjoy	422	109	price	195
10	walking	1148	60	highly	404	110	flat	194
11	clean	1062	61	wonderful	402	111	modern	193
12	house	1047	62	use	399	112	warm	192
13	home	1030	63	fantastic	395	113	food	187
14	feel	962	64	shops	373	114	living	186
15	recommend	941	65	after	372	115	parking	181
16	everything	929	66	check	370	116	WIFI	173
17	bed	922	67	private	366	117	kind	171
18	really	873	68	trip	362	118	amenity	170
19	well	866	69	short	359	119	fresh	168
20	me	866	70	booking	349	120	water	167
21	staying	859	71	most	343	121	quality	162
22	comfortable	831	72	best	342	122	communication	161
23	nice	805	73	provide	338	123	unit	157
24	time	804	74	looking	335	124	fridge	155
25	station	778	75	street	332	125	early	153
26	perfect	723	76	star	304	126	far	152
27	thanks	719	77	people	302	127	equipment	151
28	they	717	78	friends	300	128	large	150
29	good	720	79	family	297	129	public	149
30	lovely	700	80	bus	294	130	couple	147
31	experience	699	81	excellent	285	131	TV	146
32	her	686	82	breakfast	277	132	road	146
33	airport	684	83	studio	272	133	guest	146
34	when	680	84	weekend	269	134	tidy	144
35	easy	665	85	arrival	266	135	room	141
36	better	640	86	happy	264	136	information	135
37	helpful	637	87	small	262	137	appreciate	133

continues on following page

Table 1. Continued

No.	words	words frequency	No.	words	words frequency	No.	words	words frequency
38	city	620	88	super	257	138	old	131
39	close	611	89	convenient	255	139	awesome	129
40	space	579	90	neighborhood	252	140	describe	128
41	quiet	577	91	local	252	141	facility	128
42	beach	568	92	visit	251	142	extra	127
43	Airbnb	565	93	value	244	143	service	123
44	area	563	94	enough	244	144	floor	122
45	minutes	561	95	distance	242	145	safe	120
46	your	522	96	towel	233	146	darling	118
47	coffee	509	97	harbor	231	147	free	117
48	first	505	98	shower	224	148	noise	115
49	view	493	99	question	224	149	bar	114
50	friendly	489	100	access	223	150	business	113

Theoretically, the ways people use words and expressions can provide abundant information about their faiths, dreads, thinking styles, social connections, and their own characteristics (Dunphy, Stone & Smith, 1965; Gottschalk & Glaser, 1969; Weintraub, 1989). According to all of the categories of LIWC2015 dictionary,first of all, the category of "affective processes" includes positive emotion words (such as nice, love, and sweet) and negative emotion (anxiety, sadness and anger) words (such as annoyed, worried and hurt), and through this dictionary's filter, in the column of positive emotion, the biggest number is 35.29, which means that the proportion of positive emotion words in the total online reviews is 35.29%, for example, review No.42 states that "fantastic location and great value when compared to nearby Manly hotels, I would definitely come back again", in this sentence, "fantastic", "great value" and "definitely" are colored red by LIWC sentiment lexicon, that is, these words belong to affective processes words. In review No.40 "very welcoming host, spacious and clean bedroom, comfy bed, good wifi...", and the red color words are "welcoming" and "good". Review No.97 said: "Stuart was the perfect host, really helpful, couldn't have been better. Best visit to bondi ever. Will never use a hotel again." This review's affective processes words are "perfect", "helpful", "better" and "best". And in review No.446 "Thiago's place is in a great location and very modern and nice. The bed is amazingly comfortable - easily as good as any 5-star hotel I've been in. Communication was quick and easy, and Thiago was very helpful and friendly. I would gladly stay here again", the sentiment words are "great", "nice", amazingly", "comfortable", "easy", "helpful" and "friendly". Also, No.951 said: "The room is clean, nice and cozy. 15minutes walk from Central station. Hazel and Gareth are very nice, they even gave me AC on my second day. I ordered food from restaurant downstairs and got 30% discount (works like in-room dining at the hotel). Amenities like towel, bedsheet, tissue, wifi, TV and xbox available in the room. Overall, I am very satisfied with my experience staying here." The colored word in this review is "satisfied", consequently, we can infer that why the guest is pleased is that the quality of house is good, the attitude and service of host is great, the location is very convenient to eating and the amenities are well-considered. In summary, factors affecting the positive emotions of tourists include the atmosphere (e.g. home feeling, authentic feeling and friendly feeling), flexibility (e.g. earlier check-in and late check-out), special amenities (e.g. kitchen) and humanized service (e.g. allowing to bring pets in, offering coffee and local food, providing travel tips and advice, lending bicycle or car, etc.). These factors are unique compared to their previous hotel experience.

Moreover, in the column of negative emotion, the highest proportion of negative emotion words is 12.5%, including 3.57% of "anxiety", 3.23% of "anger" and 12.5% of "sadness". For instance, the No.355 described that "just felt not comfortable to stay in there. Have to wipe the floor by ourselves, it is ridiculous! Did you hear that before when you stay in hotel, the staff ask you wipe the wet floor after shower? Same in here, right?" We can see that the factor of guest's negative emotion is cleaning the place before check-out. In addition, the No.105 review of "the apartment was smaller than expected and there was no air-condition, We found the apartment quite expensive compared to a hotel with breakfast included" and the No.89 review of "this is a budget hotel, not an apartment, the room and furnishings were old and worn. Dirty carpet and very poor wifi" both reflected that the lower-than-expected housing quality will bring to dissatisfaction. Review of No.383 wrote:" accommodation trap, not suitable for any serious guest. Poor check-in process, very noise hosts. Had to leave 12:00 Pm and stay are hotel accommodation, bed was incredibly uncomfortable. This is serious, the positive comments below must be not genuine. Do not stay!" This remark strongly expresses the guest's complaints and distrust, demonstrating that the poor service of host seriously affects customer sentiment. On the whole, factors affecting the negative emotions of tourists include that not value for money, have to clean the room before leaving, sharing amenities and space with strangers, disturbed by hosts' noisy recreational activities such as party, troubled by hosts requesting good reviews and so on.

CONCLUSION AND RECOMMENDATIONS

Either positive or negative reviews could increase consumer awareness of Airbnb. Using the approach of text mining and sentiment analysis, examining whether guests' emotion is positive or negative, this study identified the attributes that influence Airbnb consumers' experiences compared with their previous hotel experiences by analysing big data of guests' online reviews, findings reveal that the factors of guests' positive sentiment are the atmosphere, flexibility, special amenities and humanized service; the factors of guests' negative sentiment are not value for money, have to clean the room before leaving, sharing amenities and space with strangers, disturbed by hosts' noisy recreational activities and troubled by hosts requesting good reviews.

The study's theoretical contribution lies in demonstrating how big data can be used and visually interpreted in tourism and hospitality studies, it not only makes a useful supplement to the sharing platform Airbnb in the tourism accommodation industry, but also provides guests' direct experience comparisons between Airbnb and hotel through sentiment analysis, reveals the main factors affecting the positive and negative emotions of Airbnb guests, laying the foundation for further theoretical discussions.

The major contribution of this study is practical. It is of great value to use massive UGC such as tourist reviews for that it not only helps tourists make better reservations but also provides important managerial guidance for Airbnb developers, operators and hosts to grasp guests' sentiment preference and strengthen their competitive advantages in tourism marketing and management field.

Notwithstanding this study's contributions, this study is not without limitations. First, the online reviews were restricted to the people who are Internet surfers and capable of using Airbnb app to make tour bookings. Carrying out some in-depth interviews offline could be more comprehensive. Second, this study was limited to a collection of data from only one city, i.e., Sydney. Therefore, different data sets of Airbnb collected in other cities in Australia would help to generalize the findings. Third, researchers could make comparisons to Xiaozhu in China as well as the cultural varieties leading to the differences in reservation preference in the future. Also, a specific lexicon in the tourism and hospitality industry needs to be conducted.

REFERENCES

Abbie-Gayle, J., & Barbara, N. (2017). Airbnb – An exploration of value co-creation experiences in Jamaica. *International Journal of Contemporary Hospitality Management, 29*(9), 2361–2376. doi:10.1108/IJCHM-08-2016-0482

Airbnb. (2018). *About us*. Retrieved from: https://press.airbnb.com/about-us/

Belarmino, A., Whalen, E., Koh, Y., & Bowen, J. T. (2019). Comparing guests' key attributes of peer-to-peer accommodations and hotels: Mixed-methods approach. *Current Issues in Tourism, 22*(1), 1–7. doi:10.1080/13683500.2017.1293623

Birinci, H., Berezina, K., & Cobanoglu, C. (2018). Comparing customer perceptions of hotel and peer-to-peer accommodation advantages and disadvantages. *International Journal of Contemporary Hospitality Management, 30*(2), 1190–1210. doi:10.1108/IJCHM-09-2016-0506

Bridges, J., & Vásquez, C. (2018). If nearly all Airbnb reviews are positive, does that make them meaningless? *Current Issues in Tourism, 21*(18), 2057–2075. doi:10.1080/13683500.2016.1267113

Brochado, A., Troilo, M., & Aditya, S. (2017). Airbnb customer experience: Evidence of convergence across three countries. *Annals of Tourism Research, 63*, 210–212. doi:10.1016/j.annals.2017.01.001

Das, S. R., & Chen, M. Y. (2007). Yahoo! For amazon: Sentiment extraction from small talk on the web. *Management Science, 53*(9), 1375–1388. doi:10.1287/mnsc.1070.0704

Dunphy, D. C., Stone, P. J., & Smith, M. S. (1965). The general inquirer: Further developments in a computer system for content analysis of verbal data in the social sciences. *Behavioral Science, 10*(4), 468. PMID:5838381

Ekman, P., & Friesen, W. V. (1971). Constants across cultures in the face and emotion. *Journal of Personality and Social Psychology, 17*(2), 124–129. doi:10.1037/h0030377 PMID:5542557

Fan, W., & Gordon, M. D. (2014). The power of social media analytics. *Communications of the ACM, 57*(6), 74–81. doi:10.1145/2602574

Fuchs, M., Höpken, W., & Lexhagen, M. (2014). Big data analytics for knowledge generation in tourism destinations–A case from Sweden. *Journal of Destination Marketing & Management, 3*(4), 198–209. doi:10.1016/j.jdmm.2014.08.002

Gottschalk, L. A., & Gleser, G. C. (1969). *The measurement of psychological states through the content analysis of verbal behavior*. University of California Press.

Guttentag, D. (2015). Airbnb: Disruptive innovation and the rise of an informal tourism accommodation sector. *Current Issues in Tourism*, *18*(12), 1192–1217. doi:10.1080/13683500.2013.827159

Guttentag, D. A., & Smith, S. L. (2017). Assessing Airbnb as a disruptive innovation relative to hotels: Substitution and comparative performance expectations. *International Journal of Hospitality Management*, *64*, 1–10. doi:10.1016/j.ijhm.2017.02.003

Hamari, J., Sjöklint, M., & Ukkonen, A. (2016). The sharing economy: Why people participate in collaborative consumption. *Journal of the Association for Information Science and Technology*, *67*(9), 2047–2059. doi:10.1002/asi.23552

He, W., Zha, S., & Li, L. (2013). Social media competitive analysis and text mining: A case study in the pizza industry. *International Journal of Information Management*, *33*(3), 464–472. doi:10.1016/j.ijinfomgt.2013.01.001

Hennig-Thurau, T., Gwinner, K. P., Walsh, G., & Gremler, D. D. (2004). Electronic word-of-mouth via consumer-opinion platforms: What motivates consumers to articulate themselves on the internet? *Journal of Interactive Marketing*, *18*(1), 38–52. doi:10.1002/dir.10073

Hippner, H., & Rentzmann, R. (2006). Text mining. *Informatik-Spektrum*, *29*(4), 287–290. doi:10.100700287-006-0091-y

Kaplan, A. M., & Haenlein, M. (2010). Users of the world, unite! The challenges and opportunities of Social Media. *Business Horizons*, *53*(1), 59–68. doi:10.1016/j.bushor.2009.09.003

Kozinets, R. V. (2010). *Netnography: Doing ethnographic research online*. London: Sage.

Loria, S. (2018). Textblob Documentation. Technical report.

Ma, E., Cheng, M., & Hsiao, A. (2018). Sentiment analysis – a review and agenda for future research in hospitality contexts. *International Journal of Contemporary Hospitality Management*, *30*(11), 3287–3308. doi:10.1108/IJCHM-10-2017-0704

Mady, T. T. (2011). Sentiment toward marketing: Should we care about consumer alienation and readiness to use technology? *Journal of Consumer Behaviour*, *10*(4), 192–204. doi:10.1002/cb.329

McAbee, S. T., Landis, R. S., & Burke, M. I. (2017). Inductive reasoning: The promise of big data. *Human Resource Management Review*, *27*(2), 277–290. doi:10.1016/j.hrmr.2016.08.005

Neeser, D., Peitz, M., & Stuhler, J. (2015). *Does Airbnb hurt hotel business: Evidence from the Nordic countries*. Universidad Carlos III de Madrid.

O'Leary, D. E. (2011). The use of social media in the supply chain: Survey and extensions. *Intelligent Systems in Accounting, Finance & Management*, *18*(2-3), 121–144. doi:10.1002/isaf.327

Pang, B., & Lee, L. (2008). Opinion mining and sentiment analysis. *Foundations and Trends? Information Retrieval*, *2*(1–2), 1–135. doi:10.1561/1500000011

Pennebaker, J. W., Boyd, R. L., Jordan, K., & Blackburn, K. (2015). *The development and psychometric properties of LIWC2015*. Austin, TX: University of Texas at Austin.

Russell, J. A. (1980). A circumplex model of affect. *Journal of Personality and Social Psychology, 39*(6), 1161-1178.

Schmunk, S., Höpken, W., Fuchs, M., & Lexhagen, M. (2014). Sentiment analysis: Extracting decision-relevant knowledge from UGC. In Information and Communication Technologies in Tourism 2014. Springer.

Schuckert, M., Liu, X., & Law, R. (2015). Hospitality and tourism online reviews: Recent trends and future directions. *Journal of Travel & Tourism Marketing, 32*(5), 608–621. doi:10.1080/10548408.20 14.933154

Stuart, R. (2017). *Sydney Is Airbnb's Australian Boomtown, but Not Everyone Is Celebrating the Website's Success.* Retrieved from https://www.abc.net.au/news/2017-01-31/airbnb-booming-in-sydney-but-it-could-be-pushing-up-rents/8223900

Tussyadiah, I. P., & Zach, F. (2017). Identifying salient attributes of peer-to-peer accommodation experience. *Journal of Travel & Tourism Marketing, 34*(5), 636–652. doi:10.1080/10548408.2016.1209153

Weintraub, W. (1989). *Verbal behavior in everyday life.* Springer.

Xiang, Z., Schwartz, Z., Gerdes, J. H. Jr, & Uysal, M. (2015). What can big data and text analytics tell us about hotel guest experience and satisfaction? *International Journal of Hospitality Management, 44*, 120–130. doi:10.1016/j.ijhm.2014.10.013

Yannopoulou, N. (2013). User-generated brands and social media: Couchsurfing and Airbnb. *Contemporary Management Research, 9*(1), 85–90. doi:10.7903/cmr.11116

Zhang, G., Cui, R., Cheng, M., Zhang, Q., & Li, Z. (2019). A comparison of key attributes between peer-to-peer accommodations and hotels using online reviews. *Current Issues in Tourism*, 1–8.

Zhou, J., Yang, Y., Bao, X., & Huang, B. (2016). Combining user-based and global lexicon features for sentiment analysis in twitter. *International Joint Conference on Neural Networks.*

This research was previously published in the International Journal of Tourism and Hospitality Management in the Digital Age (IJTHMDA), 4(2); pages 1-10, copyright year 2020 by IGI Publishing (an imprint of IGI Global).

Chapter 79
Opinion Mining in Tourism:
A Study on "Cappadocia Home Cooking" Restaurant

Ibrahim Akın Özen
https://orcid.org/0000-0003-1172-5448
Faculty of Tourism, Nevşehir Hacı Bektas Veli University, Turkey

Ibrahim Ilhan
https://orcid.org/0000-0002-6614-9356
Faculty of Tourism, Nevşehir Hacı Bektas Veli University, Turkey

ABSTRACT

In the tourism sector, online tourist reviews analysis is one of the methods to evaluate the products and services offered by businesses and understand the needs of tourists. These reviews take place in social networks and e-commerce sites in parallel with the developments in information and communication technologies. Tourists generate these reviews during or after their use of the products or services. In the literature, these reviews are referred to as UGC (User Generated Content) or eWOM (electronic word-of-mouth). The scientific evaluation of the textual contents in tourist reviews is done by text mining, which is a sub-area of data mining. This chapter discusses the methods and techniques of opinion mining or sentiment analysis. In addition, aspect-based sentiment analysis and techniques to be used in the application are discussed. A case study was carried out using aspect-based sentiment analysis method. In the application "Cappadocia home cooking" restaurant used tourist reviews.

INTRODUCTION

In tourism sector, online tourist reviews analysis is one of the methods of evaluating the products and services offered by businesses and of understanding the needs of tourists. These reviews take place in social networks and e-commerce sites in parallel with the developments in information and communication technologies. Tourists generate these reviews during or after their use of the products or services. In the literature, these reviews are referred to as UGC (User Generated Content) or eWOM (electronic

DOI: 10.4018/978-1-6684-6303-1.ch079

word-of-mouth). For businesses, these reviews are of understanding the emotions of tourists and at the same time being able to solve future problems (He, Zha, & Li, 2013). In addition, these reviews are becoming more and more important for other tourists to develop their travel plans (Lei & Law, 2015). The most important reason for this situation is that tourists are more confident in the tourist's reviews that have been experienced before, rather than the information obtained from the other information sources available on the internet. Tourists consider such reviews impartial and honest (Nowacki, 2019). Before tourists decide to buy, they give importance to the ideas of other tourists (Misner & Devine, 1999). The scientific evaluation of the textual contents in tourist reviews is done by text mining, which is a sub-area of data mining. Text mining is defined as the process of extracting the implicit knowledge from textual data (Feldman & Sanger, 2006). The text classification, clustering, and association are the typical tasks of text mining (T. Jo, 2019).

Reviews on the web are collected under two categories. These categories are information that expresses facts or opinions. Facts express objective sentences that contain no emotions. Opinions are about people's natural and general subjective definitions of events and assets (Agarwal & Mittal, 2016).

Many studies in the literature have been conducted using NLP (natural language processing) method of text mining of the texts reflecting the facts. Text analyzes that express opinions are very limited. Opinion mining (OM) or sentiment analysis (SA) is a field of study that analyzes people's opinions and thoughts about assets (products, services, etc.) through texts. In other words, sentiment analysis performs the classification of an opinion as positive, neutral or negative (Mostafa, 2013). In previous studies, opinion mining is also referred to as sentiment analysis (Can & Alatas, 2017; Liu, 2012; Medhat, Hassan, & Korashy, 2014).

This study consists of two main parts. The first section discusses the methods and techniques of opinion mining or sentiment analysis. In addition, aspect-based sentiment analysis (ABSA) and techniques to be used in the application are discussed. In the second part, a case study was carried out using aspect-based sentiment analysis method. In the application "Cappadocia home cooking" restaurant tourist reviews are used.

BACKGROUND

In this part, opinion mining or sentiment analysis, sentiment analysis techniques, opinion mining in tourism, challenges of opinion mining in tourism are defined and explained.

Opinion Mining or Sentiment Analysis

The concepts Opinion Mining (OM), Sentiment Analysis (SA) and Subjectivity Analysis are broadly used as synonyms. According to some researchers, these concepts are explained as follows:

An opinion might possibly be merely thought as a positive or negative sentiment, view, attitude, emotion, or assessment about an entity (product, person, event, business or subject) or an aspect of this entity from a consumer or group of users (Serrano-Guerrero, et al., 2015)..

Opinions are ordinarily subjective expressions that exposit fill's sentiments, appraisals or feelings toward entities, events and their properties. A little amount of opinionated texts was available before the recent World Wide Web expansion. (Wiebe & Riloff, 2011).

Opinion mining is used to identify subjective information from text (Kaur & Chopra, 2016).

Opinion mining or sentiment analysis is a study that analyzes people's ideas and thoughts about assets such as products and services in the text. (Agarwal & Mittal, 2016).

Sentiment analysis instead known as opinion mining is definite as a technique of identifying the positive/negative course of a text (Nasim & Haider, 2017).

As can be seen from the above definitions, SA or OM is often used interchangeably. However, OM makes polarity detection, whereas SA focuses on emotion recognition. Because the identification of sentiment is often exploited for detecting polarity, the two fields are usually combined under the same umbrella or even used as synonyms.(Cambria, et al., 2013).

The online textual information is of two sorts: Facts and opinions claim. Facts are goal sentences regarding the entities and don't display any sentiments. Opinions are subjective in character and generally describe the people's sentiments towards events and entities. The majority of the existing research with all the available on-line text continues to be emphasized about the truthful data in a variety of natural language processing (NLP) jobs, e.g., information retrieval, text classification (Forman, 2003) and so forth. Research on digesting the opinionated sentences continues to be very limited because of a large numbers of challenges mixed up in field (Cambria, et al., 2013).

OM or SA research is categorized as document level (Wilson, Wiebe, & Hoffmann, 2005), sentence level (Meena & Prabhakar, 2007) and aspect / feature-level sentiment analyzes (Y. Jo & Oh, 2011).

Document-Level Sentiment Analysis: Document-level sentiment analysis classifies an assessment document as containing positive or negative polarity. It views a record as an individual unit (Agarwal & Mittal, 2016). This level is linked to the job called document-level sentiment classification. Nevertheless, if a document presents several sentences coping with different aspects or entities, then your sentence level is more desirable (Serrano-Guerrero, et al., 2015).

Sentence-Level Sentiment Analysis: Sentence-level sentiment analysis is closely related to document-level sentiment analysis. Because the document has a structure consisting of sentences (Wilson, et al., 2005). Sentiment analysis at the sentence level expresses the opinion or sentiment expressed in the sentence. Both the document-level and the sentence-level sentiment analysis do not detect what exactly people liked and did not like (Agarwal & Mittal, 2016).

Aspect-Based Sentiment Analysis (ABSA): In opinion mining, it is often not enough to determine the opinion or polarity of the opinion that is mentioned in a text alone. It is also necessary to find out on which entities the opinion is expressed. Aspect-based sentiment analysis is the process of finding out for which entities the opinions in a document or sentence are specified (Liu, 2012). Aspect based sentiment analysis is also called feature-level opinion mining (Hu & Liu, 2004; Thet, Na, & Khoo, 2010). A text example applied aspect-based sentiment analysis can be given as follows;

For instance, "although the service isn't that good, I still like the food"; with this example, "service" and "food" are two entities regarding which thoughts and opinions are indicated. Aspect-based sentiment analysis model, first of all, recognizes these entities, and furthermore, opinions regarding these entities will be identified. (Hu & Liu, 2004; Liu, 2012).

Sentiment Analysis Techniques

There are two main approaches in current scientific studies in the field of sentiment analysis. These are machine learning and lexicon sentiment analysis approaches.

Machine Learning Approaches

In machine learning methods, algorithms and linguistic features are used to make text classification. The machine learning approach is examined in two categories as supervised and unsupervised learning methods.

The supervised learning method aims to model the function that includes these data and results, using data that has already been observed and whose results are known (labeled). Unsupervised learning includes methods based on the discovery of patterns hidden from unlabeled data, unlike supervised learning (Agarwal & Mittal, 2016). Regarding supervised methods, Maximum Entropy (ME), Support Vector Machines (SVM), Naive Bayes (NB) are a few of the most typical approaches used (Chenlo & Losada, 2014; Rushdi Saleh, et al., 2011). While semi-supervised and unsupervised methods are suggested when it's impossible with a preliminary group of tagged documents/opinions to categorize the others of things (Xianghua, et al., 2013). Besides, hybrid methods, combining supervised and unsupervised techniques, or semi-supervised techniques even, can be utilized to categorize sentiments.

Lexicon-Based Approaches

Two subclassifications can be found here: Dictionary-based and Corpus-based approaches.

Dictionary-Based Approach: The dictionary-based approach depends on uncovering opinion seed words, and then searches the dictionary of their synonyms and antonyms. The dictionary-based approach focuses on compiling word lists based on synonyms and antonyms for every word. This process begins by obtaining a small set of words with known positive or negative emotion and an algorithm is utilized to increase this list using on-line dictionaries (Buzova, Sanz-Blas, & Cervera-Taulet, 2018). For this purpose, many dictionaries that give positive, negative or neutral opinions to words or phrases on the internet have been developed. In this study, some of the known online dictionary databases are presented in the Table 1. In this study, we will look at most known dictionary databases.

Corpus-Based Approaches: Corpus-based approaches mainly depend on the method to see the polarity of the words (Agarwal & Mittal, 2016). These dictionaries are produced from a mates of seed thoughts and opinions cost that grows throughout the operation of incidental status by implementation of the employment of either listing or semantic techniques (Serrano-Guerrero, et al., 2015). Making use of the corpus-based strategy alone isn't as effectual as the dictionary- based approach since it is hard to get ready an enormous ensemble to cover almost all English terms, but this method includes a main advantage that will help to discover domain and context particular opinion phrases and their orientations utilizing a domain name corpus (Medhat, et al., 2014).

Opinion Mining in Tourism

In the literature, the first attempt on opinion mining (sentiment analysis) is document-level by Turney (2001). The first study on aspect/feature-based sentiment analysis was conducted by Hu and Liu (2004).

In recent years, important studies have been carried out on the opinion mining in the domain of tourism (Dolnicar & Otter, 2003).

Ttripadvisor.com reviews of 2510 hotel customers in Sarasota, Florida were evaluated through the text mining method. Online reviews of satisfied and dissatisfied customers were compared. According to the findings of the research, it revealed some common categories used in both positive and negative

Table 1. Online dictionary databases

Name	Number of words and phrases	Analysis Group	Opinion words	Sentiment Score	Web
Liu and Hu lexicon	Around 6800	Words and phrases	Positive, negative and subjectivity	-1 and +1	https://www.cs.uic.edu/~liub/FBS/sentiment-analysis.html#lexicon
SentiWord Net v3	117000 synonymous	Nouns, verbs, adjectives and adverbs	Positive, negative and objectivity	-1 and +1	https://sentiwordnet.isti.cnr.it/
Natural Language Processing (SentiWords)	Around 155,000 English	Words and phrases	Positive, negative	-5 and +5	http://www2.imm.dtu.dk/pubdb/views/publication_details.php?id=6010
WordStat	9164 negative -4847 positive English	Word patterns	Positive, negative	Rule Based	https://provalisresearch.com/products/content-analysis-software/wordstat-dictionary/sentiment-dictionaries/
SenticNet	50000	Natural language concepts	Pozitif-negatif	-1 and +1	https://sentic.net/
The Whissell Dictionary of Affect in Language	348000	Spoken English	Word	Standard deviation	https://www.god-helmet.com/wp/whissel-dictionary-of-affect/index.htm

Source: (Davydova, 2017)

reviews, including workplace (eg hotels, restaurants and clubs), rooms, furniture, members and sports. The desire to recommend a hotel to others refers to the intangible aspects of hotel stays, such as staff members, more often than dissatisfied customers. On the other hand, dissatisfied customers often mention tangible aspects such as hotels accommodation and financing (Berezina, et al., 2016).

Xiang, et al., (2017) compared online reviews on three major online review platforms (TripAdvisor, Expedia and Yelp) in terms of information quality for all hotels in Manhattan, New York. They used Latent Dirichlet Allocation (LDA), one of the text analysis methods. They discovered five main topics: Basic Service, Value, Landmarks / Attractions, Food- Experience and Core Item.

Marrese-Taylor, Velásquez, & Bravo-Marquez (2014), argue that the aspect-based opinion mining approach applied in the literature will not be applied in the field of tourism. The basis of the claim is that the products in the field of tourism do not consist entirely of physical products. Researchers have analyzed TripAdvisor reviews for the Los Lagos region of Chile with their new model. The new model confirmed that it was particularly effective in determining the emotional aspect of interpretations.

Xiang, et al., (2015) were looking for semantic relationships between words to deconstruct hotel consumer experiences by combining aspect extraction approaches and also statistical analysis, factor and regression analysis.

Tsytsarau & Palpanas (2012) have examined methods related to sentiment analysis and opinion mining in their studies in recent years and they proposed machine-learning, dictionary-based, semantic and statistical approaches. Schuckert, Liu, & Law (2015) suggested using supervised machine learning algorithms (Naive Bayes, Support Vector Machine, and N-gram) in their online review analysis.

Schmunk, et al., (2013) compared dictionary-based and machine learning methods in opinion mining. They found that SVM method in machine learning methods provides very important results in determining sentiment polarity and sentiment classification.

In the literature, the studies using aspect-based sentiment analysis technique in restaurant reviews are presented in Table 2.

In this case study, aspect-based sentiment analysis will be applied to restaurant reviews.

Table 2. Restaurant reviews and ABSA related studies

References	Method	Data source
(Brody & Elhadad, 2010)	Aspect Detection and Sentiment Analysis.	Online restaurant reviews from Citysearch New York
(Zhang, et al., 2011)	Sentiment Analysis	Restaurant reviews
(Afzaal & Usman, 2016)	Aspect-Based Opinion Classification	Twitter (tourist place)
(Afzaal, Usman, & Fong, 2019)	Aspect-Based Sentiment Classification	TripAdvisor restaurants reviews
(Lei & Law, 2015)	Content Analysis and Taxonomy	TripAdvisor Reviews on Restaurants in Macau
(Nasim & Haider, 2017)	Aspect-Based Sentiment Analysis	Yelp restaurant review
(Amalia, Putri, & Alamsyah, 2017)	Opinion Mining	TripAdvisor (hotel-restaurant)
(Weismayer, Pezenka, & Gan, 2018)	Aspect-Based Sentiment Detection	TripAdvisor (hotel-restaurant)
(Xiang, et al., 2015)	Text Analytics	Expedia (hotel-restaurant)
(Alkalbani, et al., 2017)	Opinion Mining	Cloud service
(Saeidi, et al., 2016)	Aspect Based Sentiment Analysis	SentiHood
(Blair-Goldensohn, et al., 2008)	Aspect-Based Summarization	Local service and restaurant

Challenges of Opinion Mining in Tourism

Opinion mining conducted in the field of tourism is provided from different data sources. These data are collected from three primary data sources. **(1) UGC data**: The first and most important data source consists of the reviews of tourists about products and services. Such reviews are called user-generated context (UGC) such as online review data and online image data. **(2) Device and sensor data:** Data collected from devices and sensors used in tourist areas such as GPS, mobile data and Bluetooth data, Rfid data, Wifi data. **(3) Operational data:** Operational data provided during tourism activities such as web search data, on-line booking data, webpage visiting data (Li, et al., 2018).

The data obtained from these data sources are used in different tourism studies. UGC data is generally used in tourist sentiment analysis, tourist behavior analysis, tourism marketing and tourism recommendation research. Device data has gained a significant advantage in investigating the spatial-temporal behavior of tourists. Operational data is rarely used in tourism research since it is under state and private sector protection (Li, et al., 2018).

Although it provides significant advantages with the data set used in tourism research, it has some disadvantages. These disadvantages are related to data quality, privacy and data cost. Table 3 presents the advantages and disadvantages of the data sets used in tourism research.

Table 3. Several types of data sets used in tourism research

Dataset Source	Dataset type	Topics focused on tourism research	Advantages	Disadvantages
UGC data	Tourists online textual data	Opinion mining for tourists	Low cost; Multiple information inclusion	Data quality problem
	Online picture data	Sentiment analysis Tourist behavior analysis Tourist recommendations		
Device and Sensor data	Devices GPS data	Data possibility in tourism Tourist spatial-temporal behavior Tourist tracking systems Tourism reference Effect estimation of weather on tourism	Global High precision Crowded indoor availability	High cost Privacy concerns Small-range coverage
	Mobile roaming data			
	Bluetooth data			
	RFID data			
	WIFI data			
	Weather data			
Operational data	Operations WEB search data	Tourism demand prediction Search engine optimization	Low cost; Reflecting community attention	Data privacy problem
	Transaction data	Tourist behavior analysis; Tourism promotion	Operations in tourism marketplaces	

Source: Adapted from (Li, et al., 2018)

Data quality: Although there is sufficient data set in tourism research, quality is seen as a problem. The factors affecting data quality in tourism research are explained below.

1. **Fake Reviews:** Tourists can create fake reviews in online textual data. This reduces the reliability of the data set (Filieri, 2016; Kapucugil & Özdağoğlu, 2015).
2. **Irony Reviews:** Tourist reviews can include sarcastic remarks and irony. A very challenging job in extracting opinion is irony detection (Medhat, et al., 2014; Mostafa, 2013; Serrano-Guerrero, et al., 2015).
3. **Multiple Domains or Languages:** Extracting opinions from textual data from multiple languages and domains may require special algorithms and techniques (Boiy & Moens, 2009; Rushdi Saleh, et al., 2011; Serrano-Guerrero, et al., 2015).
4. **Information Loss:** Reduction methods applied in high volume data sets may cause loss of information (Marjani, et al., 2017).
5. **High Performance Requirements:** Dynamically generated data on devices require high performance. In addition, methods supported by advanced analysis provide interactive graphics on laptops, desktops, or mobile devices such as smartphones and tablets (Marjani, et al., 2017).

Data Privacy: Due to confidentiality, there are barriers to access to data sets created during the operations of tourism stakeholders (tourists, online travel agencies, hotels, government sectors) (Li, et al., 2018).

Data Cost: Data collection devices (e.g., GPS loggers and Bluetooth sensors) in tourism research constitute high cost (Li, et al., 2018).

MAIN FOCUS OF THE CHAPTER

In this part methodology, software and components used in research, data collection and generation, research model are defined and explained.

Methodology

Aspect-based sentiment level and unsupervised machine learning technique were used in the study. When non-structural data are used in sentiment analysis, unsupervised learning technique yields successful results (Brody & Elhadad, 2010). There are many restaurants serve local dishes accompanied by training in Cappadocia Tourism Region. The subject of this research is one of them, the Cappadocia Home Cooking Restaurant serving regional cuisine for tourists in region. The reviews of tourists on TripAdvisor about products and services offered will be evaluated. The main purpose of the study is to analyze tourists' reviews of "Cappadocia Home Cooking Restaurant" on "Tripadvisor.com" using aspect-based sentiment analysis method and the sample is limited to a single restaurant.

Software and Components Used in Research

RapidMiner: In 2001, YALE (Yet Another Learning Environment) is the first software that was announced. It can be used in a very wide area with its hundreds of add-on options as well as keeping up with the current developments. It has the capacity to perform 99% of the processes such as machine learning, data mining and text mining. Rapid Miner is written in Java and it can work with other languages / environments such as Python, Weka or R. In addition to the paid and commercial version, there is also a community version that is promised to be free forever and is distributed under the AGPL license. It is also possible to obtain an academic license for use for academic purposes (Hofmann & Klinkenberg, 2013).

Aylien API: It is an API application that can perform semantic analysis of texts obtained from social media and blogs. It can be preferred in field dependent text analysis. It is an API specialized in aspect-based sentiment analysis such as cars, hotels, airlines and restaurants. In this research, Aspect-based sentiment analysis component presented by Aylien was used. The component is compatible with RapidMiner software. The component is built into Rapidminer software. The component called Analyze Aspect-based sentiment evaluates tourist comments at sentence level. The component identifies a positive, negative, and neutral view for each entity in the sentence.

This api is offered by Aylien company and 1000 comments are made daily free of charge. Since 174 datasets were used for this research, the analysis was made free of charge (Alkalbani, et al., 2017).

Data Collection and Generation

The data set used in the analysis was obtained from the TripAdvisor website by web scraping (web harvesting or web data extraction). Web scraping technique can be defined as the process of collecting data from web sites with the help of computer programs or APIs (Thelwall, 2001).

As a result, the data set consisting of tourist reviews containing 174 lines was recorded in the excel file. RapidMiner text analysis program has the ability to import excel files.

Research Model

A model was created for the processing of the data set that was transferred to RapidMiner software. The model to be applied and its contents are given in Figure 1.

Figure 1. Model for analysis of tourists' reviews

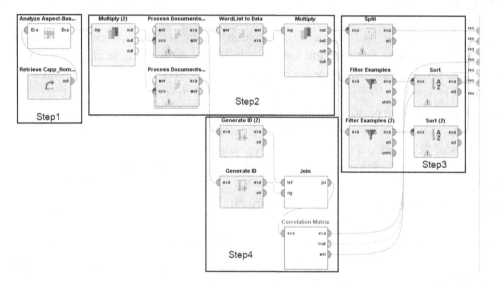

The analysis model created in the RapidMiner software in Figure 1 consists of 5 steps. These steps are as follows:

Step 1: Aspect-based sentiment analysis.
Step 2: Prepping the results. Realize the top aspects mentioned and their sentiment (positive, negative or neutral).
Step 3: Splitting and filtering results.
Step 4: Correlation analysis on the words and aspects.
Step 5: Visualization of findings.

Step 1: Aspect-based sentiment analysis: In this step, the excel file obtained during data collection and generation was transferred to RapidMiner software. There are 174 lines of reviews for each tourist in the transferred excel file. Aspect based sentiment analysis (ABSA) was applied to the data set via Aylien component. ABSA is the most important component of this model. By using this component, the sentiment polarity (positive, negative, neutral) of tourist reviews was determined.

Table 4. Example of the result obtained from ABSA

Review	Rating	Aspects
My mom and I last minute decided we wanted to do a cooking class in Cappadocia. ...	5	food: positive, desserts: positive, value: negative, drinks: positive
A spectacular restaurant find in an out of the way little sleepy village....	5	food: positive, value: positive, drinks: positive
Tolga and his wife Tuba and his mother welcomed us into their home where we were able to experience a fun lesson in simple Turkish home cooking....	5	food: positive, menu: positive, staff: positive
We had wonderful time during the cooking class. Owners were amazing, took great care of us and made us feel at home!...	5	food: positive, menu: positive, staff: positive
We had such a good night with Tolga and his family, learning to cook new dishes and making new friends..	5	food: positive, location: positive, value: positive
The food is very homey, and quite different from the food you would get in the restaurants. Every dish was delicious and we were fairly happy with the food! The portion is huge and definitely more than enough.	4	food: positive, value: negative, staff: positive

The output obtained as a result of ABSA applied to tourist reviews is given in table 4. According to Table 4, the assets included in the reviews were identified and evaluated as positive, negative or neutral according to the tourist perspective.

Step 2: Prepping the results: Data set tokenization was performed using the Process Documents from Data component. This component is used to create word vectors by means of text processing operators. Before running tokenization, the data was duplicated using the Multiplication Operator to perform two parallel types of analysis using the same data (Figure 2).

In Figure 2, the document processing stage took place in 2 stages. These were; (a) Process documents from data and (b) Process documents from data.

a) **Process Documents From Data:** In the new column obtained as a result of Aspect-based sentiment analysis in Table 3, if the "aspect: polarity" pair has a feature, then 1 weight will be assigned. "Binary Term Occurrences" parameter is used in the "process documents from data (a)" component (Figure 3).

b) **Process Documents From Data:** Under the process documents from data (2) component, the text processing process consists of 5 steps. "Term Occurrences" parameter is used in the "process documents from data (b)" component (Figure 4).

The functions of the subcomponents of Figure 4 are described below.

- Step 1: Tokenize: This component breaks down the review text into words and phrases. The component's parameters are specified as non-letters, character specification, and regular expression. Non-letter mode was used in this study.
- Step 2: Transform Cases: In this component, all words are converted to small characters in order to ensure the integrity of meaning in the review text. For instance, if the review text contains terms like "wonderful" or "Wonderful" or "WONDERFUL", then each one of these words are changed into the same case and so are all treated the same.

Figure 2. Multiply operator

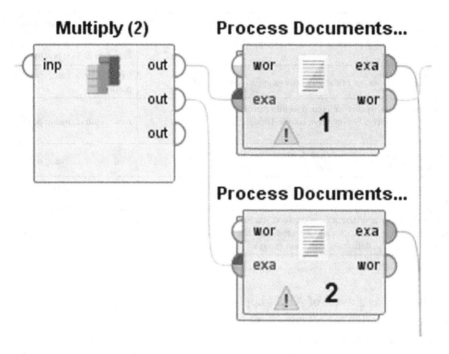

Figure 3. Process documents from data (1)

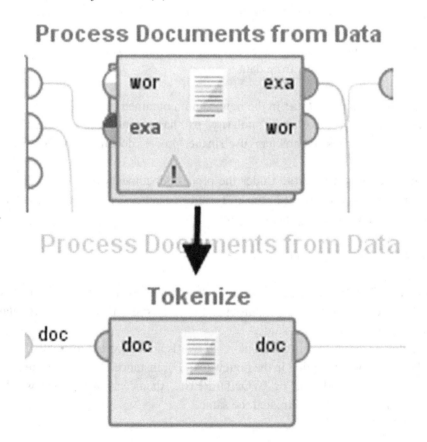

- Step 3: Filter tokens (by context): Meaningless signs in the text are removed.
- Step 4: Filter Tokens (by length): This component specifies the minimum and maximum number of meaningless characters in the review text.
- In this research, words less than three and larger than twenty-five characters were removed.
- Step 5: Filter stop words (English): The words in the reviews but not adding meaning to the sentence were removed. Such as "a," "this," "and," and other similar terms.

Figure 4. Process documents from data (2)

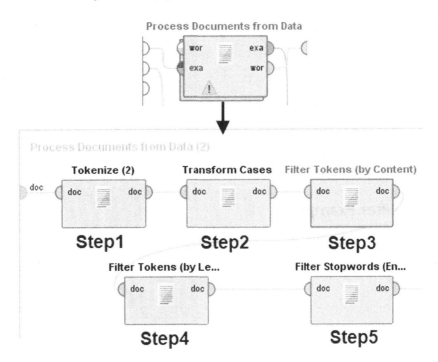

Step 3: Splitting, filtering and sort results: Figure 5 shows the components related to the splitting, filtering and sort of the results obtained.

ABSA analysis applied to the review texts was separated with split component (Table 4). The ":" sign is selected in the split component parameter. In Table 5, word_1 (aspect) and word_2 (polarity) are separated into columns.

Negative and positive polarity properties were classified using the filter component. As a result, it is ranked according to the number of repetitions. Table 6 below shows the positive aspect and Table 7 shows the negative aspect.

In Table 6, the most repetitive and positive outlooks among all the reviews of tourists are presented in 12 categories.

According to the results of the analysis, the dimensions that have caused the tourists' positive point of view have emerged (Table 6). From the positive point of view of the tourists, the fact that the "food" dimension is considerably high shows that it creates value suitable for the real purpose of the enterprise. Tourists seem to be pleased with the local dishes on offer. In the second place, it was seen that the dimension which caused the positive point of view of the tourists was the "staff". The high "staff" dimension indicates that the employees in the enterprise perform their duties well. Tourists were pleased with the staff. The third perceived positive dimension is the "value". It is understood that according to the value dimension, the expectations of tourists are met according to the cost they endure. The fourth and fifth positive dimensions show the satisfaction of tourists from the "desserts" and "drinks" offered. A positive menu dimension indicates that the content of the menu is appropriate. Other positive dimensions are "reservation", "location" "ambience", "busyness", "cleanness", and "quietness". Although these dimensions are low, they lead to a significant positive perspective for the enterprise.

Figure 5. Splitting, filtering and sorting

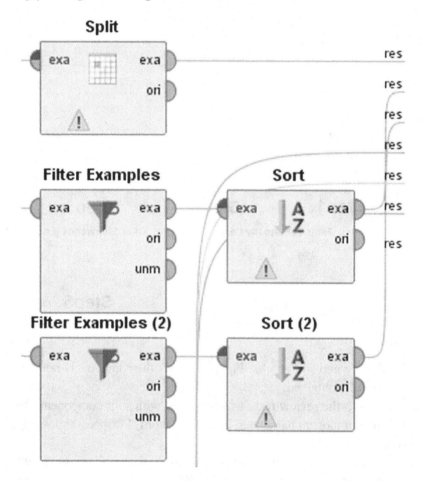

In Table 7, the most repetitive and negative outlooks among all the reviews of tourists are presented in 10 categories.

According to the results of the analysis, the dimensions that caused the negative point of view of the tourists for the business have emerged (Table 7). It is seen that tourists have a very low level of negative view of the business. While the "food" dimension of the establishment leads to a low negative point of view, it is seen that the tourists do not have a negative point of view regarding the menu dimension. Although the "value" dimension leads to the negative perspective in the first place, it is not significant when compared to the "value" dimension in the positive perspective.

Table 5. Example set (splitting, filtering)

In Documents	Total	Word1	Word2
12	12	ambience	positive
10	10	busyness	positive
5	5	cleanliness	positive
25	25	desserts	positive
24	24	drinks	positive
163	163	food	positive
15	15	location	positive
23	23	menu	positive
2	2	quietness	positive
20	20	reservations	positive
38	38	staff	positive
29	29	value	positive
1	1	desserts	positive
2	2	drinks	positive
2	2	food	positive
1	1	menu	positive
1	1	reservations	positive
1	1	value	positive

Table 6. Sorted dataset (positive aspect)

Row No.	Word	In Documents	Total
1	food: positive	163	163
2	staff: positive	38	38
3	value: positive	29	29
4	desserts: positive	25	25
5	drinks: positive	24	24
6	menu: positive	23	23
7	reservations: positive	20	20
8	location: positive	15	15
9	ambience: positive	12	12
10	busyness: positive	10	10
11	cleanliness: positive	5	5
12	quietness: positive	2	2

Step 4: Correlation Analysis: Correlation analysis results. The correlation coefficients between the offered product, service categories and related words are shown in the Table 8. The values with high correlation coefficient are considered in the Table 8.

Table 7. Sorted dataset (negative aspect)

Row No.	Word	In Documents	Total
1	Value: negative	8	8
2	Busyness: negative	5	5
3	Location: negative	5	5
4	Food: negative	4	4
5	Reservations: negative	3	3
6	Staff: negative	1	1
7	Ambience: negative	1	1
8	Cleanliness: negative	1	1
9	Drinks: negative	1	1
10	Facilities: negative	1	1

Table 8. Negative and positive aspect of the words related to the correlation table

	Desserts Positive (r)	Drinks pos.	Menu pos.	Staff pos.	Ambience: pos.	Reservation pos.	Facilities Neg.	Cleanliness: neg.
dessert	0,862							
tea		0,824						
local cuisine			0,793					
stuffed			0,517					
soup			0,406					
friendly				0,777				
atmosphere					0,772			
book						0,648		
things							0,484	
actually								0,482

Correlation coefficients (r) in Table 8 will be evaluated. Evaluation of correlation coefficients determines the weak ($0 < r <= 0.3$), moderate ($0.3 < r <= 0.7$) and strong ($0.7 < r <= +1$) positive relationships between the variables (Gürbüz & Şahin, 2014).

According to the results obtained from the correlation analysis, the main categories (positive and negative) obtained from tourist comments and the words associated with these categories are shown in the correlation table.

- **Positive Aspect-Based Sentiment:** The reason for the positive aspect of tourists towards desserts seems to be a strong correlation with the word "dessert" (r = 0.862). In Table 6, where positive dimensions are presented, "desserts" have a positive effect in the fourth place. But it is seen that the word "dessert", which affects the size of the desserts, has the highest correlation in the correlation table. In the positive dimension of sweets, the most repeated word was "dessert". This is thought to be due to the fact that tourists do not know the local dessert names offered in the menu. Therefore, the correlation coefficient was found to be high. It is understood that the positive aspect of tourists towards drinks is significantly correlated with the word "tea" (r = 0.824). The reason why the word "tea" constitutes a significant positive perspective in terms of drinks is that the region's teas are offered to tourists. Especially teas made from dried fruits are offered to tourists in the region. The positive aspect of the menu appears to be significantly correlated with the word's "local cuisine", "stuffed", "soup" (r = 0.793, r=0,517, r= 0,406). It is seen that the tourists' point of view of the menu is due to the local cuisine. It seems that soup and stuffing are the most popular local cuisine dishes. It is understood that the soup and stuffing that are unique to the region have gained the appreciation of tourists. The positive aspect towards the staff appears to be significantly correlated with the word "friendly" (r = 0.777). Another point of view that tourists consider the business as positive is that the business is "pro-friend". Business staffs have been successful in communicating with tourists. In this way, tourists see themselves as part of that business. The positive aspect for reservation appears to be significantly correlation with the word "book" (r = 0.648). Tourists consider the booking facilities sufficient.
- **Negative Aspect-Based Sentiment:** The negative aspect of the facilities seems to be moderate correlation with the word "things" (r = 0.484). The negative aspect for "cleanliness" appears to be moderately correlated with the word "actually" (r = 0.482). As a result of the analysis, although the tourists have a positive view of the business in many ways, they think that the business is generally not clean and the facilities are insufficient.

Step 5: Visualization of Findings: In Rapidminer software, visualization of the findings can be done using graphics or advanced graphics in the results tab.

SOLUTIONS AND RECOMMENDATIONS

In this research, tourist reviews of "Cappadocia home cooking" a local food and beverage business in Cappadocia, were analyzed. Tourist reviews were collected automatically from the TripAdvisor website. Text mining method and ABSA technique were used in the analysis. As a result of the analysis, positive aspects consisting of 15 categories were also determined. In addition, the negative aspect consists of 10 categories. The main factors that cause positive opinions in tourists have been local "foods", "drinks" and "friendly" behaviors. Moreover, the reason for negative opinions were seen as "value". Correlation levels between categories and words were also determined. The most correlated words that cause positive opinion among tourists were determined as "dessert" and "tea". According to the results of the analysis, businesses will provide the opportunity to evaluate themselves according to the tourism perspective. Thus, companies will be able to develop a strategy that considers their positive and negative aspects.

Tourism is an information-intensive sector (Doolin, Burgess, & Cooper, 2002). The tourism sector should consider online tourist reviews to improve their products and services. Extracting meaningful relationships from these reviews provides an important source of information for all stakeholders. Tourist reviews from other online platforms can be analyzed by considering other stakeholders in the tourism sector.

Online tourist reviews and opportunities for stakeholders can be listed as follows;

Opportunities for destinations;

- Opportunity to understand and interpret the destination
- Opportunity to understand and interpret tourist needs

Opportunities for tourism businesses;

- Opportunity to evaluate products and services offered to tourists: Discovering negative aspects, discovering positive aspects, opportunity to manage customer relationships.
- Opportunity to understand and evaluate competitors: Providing product and service advantage, product and service development or improvement, providing a price advantage (price determination).

Opportunities for tourists;

- Opportunity to make travel plans.

FUTURE RESEARCH DIRECTIONS

Aspect-based sentiment analysis is a method that can express opinion for each entity or phenomenon that exists in the document. Previous studies have mostly taken into account the opinion of sentence or document. This generalization makes it difficult to discover information in unstructured texts.

In text mining, opinion extraction is divided into two areas: Domain dependent and domain independent. Domain dependent opinion extraction can be performed by creating a dictionary about the area to be analyzed. In this direction, it is aimed to develop the research. In the future, a special dictionary will be used for local restaurants. Developing the domain dependent dictionary for local restaurants is presented to the attention of researchers.

CONCLUSION

In this study, the methods of determining opinions from online tourist reviews were examined. Determination of opinions from textual content is done using sentiment analysis (alternatively known as opinion mining) techniques. Sentiment analysis is applied at document-level, sentence-level and aspect-based sentiment levels.

Aspect-based sentiment level is thought to be a more effective technique than other levels (Medhat, et al., 2014; Nasim & Haider, 2017). The most important reason for this is that the text analysis using ABSA technique has the ability to determine opinions for each entity/event in the document. Therefore, aspect-based sentiment level was used in the case study.

REFERENCES

Afzaal, M., & Usman, M. (2016). A novel framework for aspect-based opinion classification for tourist places. *The 10th International Conference on Digital Information Management, ICDIM 2015*, (Icdim), 1–9. 10.1109/ICDIM.2015.7381850

Afzaal, M., Usman, M., & Fong, A. (2019). Predictive aspect-based sentiment classification of online tourist reviews. *Journal of Information Science*, *45*(3), 341–363. doi:10.1177/0165551518789872

Agarwal, B., & Mittal, N. (2016). *Prominent feature extraction for sentiment analysis* (N. Mittal, Ed.)., doi:10.1007/978-3-319-25343-5

Alkalbani, A. M., Gadhvi, L., Patel, B., Hussain, F. K., Ghamry, A. M., & Hussain, O. K. (2017). Analysing cloud services reviews using opining mining. *Proceedings - International Conference on Advanced Information Networking and Applications, AINA*, 1124–1129. 10.1109/AINA.2017.173

Amalia, N., Putri, S., & Alamsyah, A. (2017). *Opinion Mining of Tripadvisor Review Towards Five-Star Hotels in Bandung City.*, *4*(1), 4.

Berezina, K., Bilgihan, A., Cobanoglu, C., & Okumus, F. (2016). Understanding Satisfied and Dissatisfied Hotel Customers: Text Mining of Online Hotel Reviews. *Journal of Hospitality Marketing & Management*, *25*(1), 1–24. doi:10.1080/19368623.2015.983631

Blair-Goldensohn, S., Neylon, T., Hannan, K., Reis, G. A., McDonald, R., & Reynar, J. (2008). Building a sentiment summarizer for local service reviews. *Workshop on NLP in the Information Explosion Era.*

Boiy, E., & Moens, M. F. (2009). A machine learning approach to sentiment analysis in multilingual web texts. *Information Retrieval*, *12*(5), 526–558. doi:10.100710791-008-9070-z

Brody, S., & Elhadad, N. (2010). An Unsupervised Aspect-Sentiment Model for Online Reviews. *HLT '10 Human Language Technologies: The 2010 Annual Conference of the North American Chapter of the Association for Computational Linguistics.*

Buzova, D., Sanz-Blas, S., & Cervera-Taulet, A. (2018). Does culture affect sentiments expressed in cruise tours' eWOM? *Service Industries Journal*, 1–20. doi:10.1080/02642069.2018.1476497

Cambria, E., Schuller, B., Xia, Y., & Havasi, C. (2013). New avenues in opinion mining and sentiment analysis. *IEEE Intelligent Systems*, *28*(2), 15–21. doi:10.1109/MIS.2013.30

Can, U., & Alatas, B. (2017). Duygu Analizi ve Fikir Madenciliği Algoritmalarının İncelenmesi. *Int. J. Pure Appl. Sci*, *3*(1), 75–111.

Chenlo, J. M., & Losada, D. E. (2014). An empirical study of sentence features for subjectivity and polarity classification. *Information Sciences*, *280*, 275–288. doi:10.1016/j.ins.2014.05.009

Davydova, O. (2017). Sentiment Analysis Tools Overview, Part 1. Positive and Negative Words Databases. Retrieved June 15, 2019, from https://medium.com/@datamonsters/sentiment-analysis-tools-overview-part-1-positive-and-negative-words-databases-ae35431a470c

Dolnicar, S., & Otter, T. (2003). Which Hotel attributes Matter? A review of previous and a framework for future research. *Proceedings of the 9th Annual Conference of the Asia Pacific Tourism Association (APTA)*. Academic Press.

Doolin, B., Burgess, L., & Cooper, J. (2002). Evaluating the use of the Web for tourism marketing: A case study from New Zealand. *Tourism Management, 23*(5), 557–561. doi:10.1016/S0261-5177(02)00014-6

Feldman, R., & Sanger, J. (2006). The Text Mining Handbook. In The Text Mining Handbook. doi:10.1017/CBO9780511546914

Filieri, R. (2016). What makes an online consumer review trustworthy? *Annals of Tourism Research, 58*, 46–64. doi:10.1016/j.annals.2015.12.019

Forman, G. (2003). An Extensive Empirical Study of Feature Selection Metrics for Text Classification George. *Journal of Machine Learning Research*. doi:10.1162/153244303322753670

Gürbüz, S., & Şahin, F. (2014). Sosyal bilimlerde araştırma yöntemleri. In Seçkin Yayıncılık. Ankara, Turkey.

He, W., Zha, S., & Li, L. (2013). Social media competitive analysis and text mining: A case study in the pizza industry. *International Journal of Information Management, 33*(3), 464–472. doi:10.1016/j.ijinfomgt.2013.01.001

Hofmann, M., & Klinkenberg, R. (2013). RapidMiner: Data mining use cases and business analytics applications. Boca Raton, FL: CRC Press.

Hu, M., & Liu, B. (2004). Mining and summarizing customer reviews. *Proceedings of the 2004 ACM SIGKDD International Conference on Knowledge Discovery and Data Mining - KDD '04*, 168. 10.1145/1014052.1014073

Jo, T. (2019). *Text Mining*. Cham, Switzerland: Springer; doi:10.1007/978-3-319-91815-0

Jo, Y., & Oh, A. H. (2011). Aspect and sentiment unification model for online review analysis. *Proceedings of the Fourth ACM International Conference on Web Search and Data Mining - WSDM '11*, 815. 10.1145/1935826.1935932

Kapucugil, A., & Özdağoğlu, G. (2015). Text Mining as a Supporting Process for VoC Clarification. *Alphanumeric Journal, 3*(1). doi:10.17093/aj.2015.3.1.5000105108

Kaur, A., & Chopra, D. (2016). Comparison of text mining tools. *2016 5th International Conference on Reliability, Infocom Technologies, and Optimization, ICRITO 2016: Trends and Future Directions*, 186–192. 10.1109/ICRITO.2016.7784950

Lei, S., & Law, R. (2015). Content analysis of TripAdvisor reviews on restaurants: A case study of Macau. *Journal of Tourism, 16*(1), 17–28. Retrieved from http://search.ebscohost.com/login.aspx?direct=true&db=hjh&AN=111435361&site=ehost-live

Li, J., Xu, L., Tang, L., Wang, S., & Li, L. (2018). Big data in tourism research: A literature review. *Tourism Management, 68*, 301–323. doi:10.1016/j.tourman.2018.03.009

Liu, B. (2012). Sentiment Analysis and Opinion Mining. *Synthesis Lectures on Human Language Technologies*, *5*(1), 1–167. doi:10.2200/S00416ED1V01Y201204HLT016

Marjani, M., Nasaruddin, F., Gani, A., Karim, A., Hashem, I. A. T., Siddiqa, A., & Yaqoob, I. (2017). Big IoT Data Analytics: Architecture, Opportunities, and Open Research Challenges. *IEEE Access: Practical Innovations, Open Solutions*, *5*, 5247–5261. doi:10.1109/ACCESS.2017.2689040

Marrese-Taylor, E., Velásquez, J. D., & Bravo-Marquez, F. (2014). A novel deterministic approach for aspect-based opinion mining in tourism products reviews. *Expert Systems with Applications*, *41*(17), 7764–7775. doi:10.1016/j.eswa.2014.05.045

Medhat, W., Hassan, A., & Korashy, H. (2014). Sentiment analysis algorithms and applications: A survey. *Ain Shams Engineering Journal*, *5*(4), 1093–1113. doi:10.1016/j.asej.2014.04.011

Meena, A., & Prabhakar, T. V. (2007). Sentence Level Sentiment Analysis in the Presence of Conjuncts Using Linguistic Analysis. In Advances in Information Retrieval (pp. 573–580). doi:10.1007/978-3-540-71496-5_53

Misner, I., & Devine, V. (1999). *The world's best-known marketing secret: building your business with word-of-mouth marketing*. Retrieved from https://scholar.google.com.tr/scholar?hl=tr&as_sdt=0%2C5&q=The+world's+best+known+marketing+secret%3A+Building+your+business+with+word-of-mouth+marketing.&btnG=

Mostafa, M. M. (2013). More than words: Social networks' text mining for consumer brand sentiments. *Expert Systems with Applications*, *40*(10), 4241–4251. doi:10.1016/j.eswa.2013.01.019

Nasim, Z., & Haider, S. (2017). ABSA Toolkit: An Open Source Tool for Aspect Based Sentiment Analysis. *International Journal of Artificial Intelligence Tools*, *26*(06). doi:10.1142/S0218213017500233

Nowacki, M. (2019). World Cities' Image in TripAdvisor Users' Reviews. *Ereview of Tourism Research*, *16*(2–3). Retrieved from https://journals.tdl.org/ertr/index.php/ertr/article/view/327

Rushdi Saleh, M., Martín-Valdivia, M. T., Montejo-Ráez, A., & Ureña-López, L. A. (2011). Experiments with SVM to classify opinions in different domains. *Expert Systems with Applications*, *38*(12), 14799–14804. doi:10.1016/j.eswa.2011.05.070

Saeidi, M., Bouchard, G., Liakata, M., & Riedel, S. (2016). *SentiHood: Targeted Aspect Based Sentiment Analysis Dataset for Urban Neighbourhoods*. 1546–1556. Retrieved from http://arxiv.org/abs/1610.03771

Schmunk, S., Höpken, W., Fuchs, M., & Lexhagen, M. (2013). Sentiment Analysis: Extracting Decision-Relevant Knowledge from UGC. In Information and Communication Technologies in Tourism 2014 (pp. 253–265). doi:10.1007/978-3-319-03973-2_19

Schuckert, M., Liu, X., & Law, R. (2015). Hospitality and Tourism Online Reviews: Recent Trends and Future Directions. *Journal of Travel & Tourism Marketing*, *32*(5), 608–621. doi:10.1080/10548408.2014.933154

Serrano-Guerrero, J., Olivas, J. A., Romero, F. P., & Herrera-Viedma, E. (2015). Sentiment analysis: A review and comparative analysis of web services. *Information Sciences*, *311*, 18–38. doi:10.1016/j.ins.2015.03.040

Thelwall, M. (2001). A web crawler design for data mining. *Journal of Information Science*, *27*(5), 319–325. doi:10.1177/016555150102700503

Thet, T. T., Na, J. C., & Khoo, C. S. G. (2010). Aspect-based sentiment analysis of movie reviews on discussion boards. *Journal of Information Science*. doi:10.1177/0165551510388123

Tsytsarau, M., & Palpanas, T. (2012). Survey on mining subjective data on the web. *Data Mining and Knowledge Discovery*, *24*(3), 478–514. doi:10.100710618-011-0238-6

Weismayer, C., Pezenka, I., & Gan, C. H.-K. (2018). Aspect-Based Sentiment Detection: Comparing Human Versus Automated Classifications of TripAdvisor Reviews. In Information and Communication Technologies in Tourism 2018 (pp. 365–380). doi:10.1007/978-3-319-72923-7_28

Wiebe, J., & Riloff, E. (2011). *Finding mutual benefit between subjectivity analysis and information extraction*. IEEE Transactions on Affective Computing; doi:10.1109/T-AFFC.2011.19

Wilson, T., Wiebe, J., & Hoffmann, P. (2005). Recognizing contextual polarity in phrase-level sentiment analysis. *Proceedings of the Conference on Human Language Technology and Empirical Methods in Natural Language Processing - HLT '05*, 347–354. 10.3115/1220575.1220619

Xiang, Z., Du, Q., Ma, Y., & Fan, W. (2017). A comparative analysis of major online review platforms: Implications for social media analytics in hospitality and tourism. *Tourism Management*, *58*, 51–65. doi:10.1016/j.tourman.2016.10.001

Xiang, Z., Schwartz, Z., Gerdes, J. H. Jr, & Uysal, M. (2015). What can big data and text analytics tell us about hotel guest experience and satisfaction? *International Journal of Hospitality Management*, *44*, 120–130. doi:10.1016/j.ijhm.2014.10.013

Xianghua, F., Guo, L., Yanyan, G., & Zhiqiang, W. (2013). Multi-aspect sentiment analysis for Chinese online social reviews based on topic modeling and HowNet lexicon. *Knowledge-Based Systems*, *37*, 186–195. doi:10.1016/j.knosys.2012.08.003

Zhang, Z., Ye, Q., Zhang, Z., & Li, Y. (2011). Sentiment classification of Internet restaurant reviews written in Cantonese. *Expert Systems with Applications*. doi:10.1016/j.eswa.2010.12.147

ADDITIONAL READING

Alaei, A. R., Becken, S., & Stantic, B. (2019). Sentiment analysis in tourism: Capitalizing on big data. *Journal of Travel Research*, *58*(2), 175–191. doi:10.1177/0047287517747753

Cambria, E., Das, D., Bandyopadhyay, S., & Feraco, A. (Eds.). (2017). *A practical guide to sentiment analysis*. Cham, Switzerland: Springer International Publishing. doi:10.1007/978-3-319-55394-8

Dwivedi, R. K., Aggarwal, M., Keshari, S. K., & Kumar, A. (2019). Sentiment Analysis and Feature Extraction Using Rule-Based Model (RBM). In *International Conference on Innovative Computing and Communications* (pp. 57-63). Springer, Singapore. 10.1007/978-981-13-2354-6_7

Liu, B. (2012). Sentiment analysis and opinion mining. *Synthesis lectures on human language technologies, 5*(1), 1-167.

Salloum, S. A., AlHamad, A. Q., Al-Emran, M., & Shaalan, K. (2018). A survey of Arabic text mining. In *Intelligent Natural Language Processing: Trends and Applications* (pp. 417–431). Cham: Springer. doi:10.1007/978-3-319-67056-0_20

Shirsat, V. S., Jagdale, R. S., & Deshmukh, S. N. (2019). Sentence Level Sentiment Identification and Calculation from News Articles Using Machine Learning Techniques. In *Computing, Communication and Signal Processing* (pp. 371–376). Singapore: Springer. doi:10.1007/978-981-13-1513-8_39

Vyas, V., & Uma, V. (2019). Approaches to sentiment analysis on product reviews. In *Sentiment Analysis and Knowledge Discovery in Contemporary Business* (pp. 15–30). IGI Global. doi:10.4018/978-1-5225-4999-4.ch002

KEY TERMS AND DEFINITIONS

Aspect-Based Sentiment Analysis: is the level of determining opinions in the text analyzed. At this level of analysis, the sentiment polarity is determined separately for each entity or event in the document. Used for detailed document analysis.

Machine Learning: Machine Learning is the general name of computer algorithms (Decision Trees, Naïve Bayes, Logistic Regression, Random Forest) that model a given problem according to the data obtained from the problem environment. Since it is an intensively studied subject, many approaches and algorithms have been proposed.

NLP (Natural Language Processing): The natural language processing tools can be used to facilitate the SA process. It gives better natural language understanding and thus can help produce more accurate results of SA.

Sentiment Polarity: It is the expression that determines the sentimental aspect of an opinion. In textual data, the result of sentiment analysis can be determined for each entity in the sentence, document or sentence. The sentiment polarity can be determined as positive, negative and neutral.

Supervised Learning: Machine learning is one of the methods. The data is taken from systems that operate on the principle of response to the effect and organized in the input-output order.

SVM (Support Vector Machine): It is one of the most effective and simple machine learning methods used in classification. For classification, it is possible to separate the two groups by drawing a boundary between the two groups in one plane. Where this boundary is drawn should be the farthest from the members of both groups. SVM determines how to draw this limit.

Unsupervised Learning: Machine learning is one of the methods. It aims to explore groups within the data that are either non-class or not.

This research was previously published in the Handbook of Research on Smart Technology Applications in the Tourism Industry; pages 43-64, copyright year 2020 by Business Science Reference (an imprint of IGI Global).

Chapter 80
Communicating Natural Calamity:
The Sentiment Analysis of Post Rigopiano's Accident

Nicola Capolupo
University of Salerno, Italy

Gabriella Piscopo
University of Salerno, Italy

ABSTRACT

This chapter aims at understanding the dynamics that led to the exchange and value co-creation/co-production in the interaction between P.A. and citizens during natural calamities. In addition, it proposes a horizontal communication model in which both actors cooperate to respond to crisis, a semantic and semiotic space on the net able to satisfy their information needs. When natural disasters occur, citizens' primary need is to reach as much information as possible about the status of loved ones possibly involved in the accident, road traffic, how to give an effective contribution to the cause without hindering, etc. On the other hand, P.A. and rescuers need to know as much information as possible about the reports, on the site of the disaster so as to intervene promptly to help the population in danger. Therefore, P.A. and citizens are called upon to cooperate to guarantee crisis containment, crisis management, and also future crisis prevention.

INTRODUCTION

When natural disasters occur, citizens primary need is to gather as much information as possible (relatives involved in the accident, road traffic, how to give an effective contribution to the cause without hindering et al). On the other hand, Public Administration and rescuers need to know as much information as possible about the reports, on the site of the disaster to intervene promptly to help the population in danger.

DOI: 10.4018/978-1-6684-6303-1.ch080

In this scenario, all the actors involved in this dynamic interaction tends to create a system in which value is seen as a systemic process generated/produced as a consequence of that dynamical relation. Accordingly, appeared particularly relevant to the author to make a distinction between the concept of generating and co-producing value. By addressing the most relevant literature in this field, they found both interesting correlation and even consistent differences. As a matter of fact, the review pointed out that authors such Whitaker (1980), Levine and Fisher (1984) associate the term 'co-production' to citizens active participation in improving public services. On the contrary, *'co-creation'* – according to Gebauer H. (2010) is due to the involvement of customers, and in this case the producer is asked to *'create value'*. Therefore, co-production is an active process of citizens' involvement in improving - together with public administration - public services to promote a better experience of their daily life. Value co-creation, instead, is a natural propensity to interact to achieve needs, as Vargo and Lusch (2008) suggest: the customer is 'always a co-creator of value'.

Co-creation is a spontaneous process which benefits the players involved in the dynamic interaction that occur when P.A. and citizens went to communicate. Public administration needs are to manage logistically and communicatively the phenomenon to avoid daily life challenges (live time traffic information, hospital structures available etc.), to better coordinate volunteers and provide as much as possible effective services for citizens, to favor a long-lasting trust. Citizens, on the other hand, when facing a catastrophe, must be aware of the risks they are going through, specific information on facilities, unavailable services, and so long. They both have to cooperate to achieve their survival by exchanging information with each other, so to improve all the processes available in those situations.

It follows that the active players are called to cooperate to establish a horizontal communication model in which they can talk to each other to satisfy their information needs.

Social media, nowadays, allow the community to be active part of the current crisis communication response. As a matter of fact, the social network Twitter was mostly used to quickly share information and updates during the 2007 and 2008 California wildfires, 2008 Mumbai massacre, 2009 crash of US Airways Flight 1549, 2010 Haiti earthquake and so long (Veil S.R. et al., 2011).

The effort that this work wants to produce and the contribution that it aims to give to literature and to the academic community is, therefore, to connect the theoretical framework of value co-creation (once its distance from the concept of co-production of value has been marked) to the constant dialogue between public administration and citizens during natural crisis, analyzing it through the use of Sentiment Analysis on Twitter. Authors will use Twitter because tool to set the communication model. As a matter of fact, thanks to its immediacy and syntax, it represents the most suitable tool to build and strengthen the link between citizens and relief efforts.

The chosen case study – that of post-Rigopiano's accident – it is important to verify authors assumption:

- To what extent sentiment analysis allows both practitioners and scholars to understand citizens/ P.A. interaction?

The effort that this work wants to produce and the contribution that it aims to give to literature is, therefore, to connect the theoretical framework of value co-creation to the constant dialogue between public administration and citizens during natural crisis.

THEORETICAL BACKGROUND

Value Co-Creation and Co-Production

As previously mentioned, the introduction on value co-creation and co-production showed a particular interest of academy on the themes of value co-creation, which has been tackled and implemented over time. For instance, Osborn (2010, 2011, 2013) has been the first author who postulates a distinction of four different types of value '*which are co-created in public service delivery by the dynamic interaction of service users and/or service professionals with public service delivery systems*' (Osborn et al., 2016). They can be classified in four pivotal points:

- The co-creation of value by the meeting of an individual social need (or of groups of individuals) through co-production in a way that adds to society – such as enabling individuals with disabilities to enhance their lives (Type I).
- The co-creation of value by the meeting of community needs through co-production in a way that adds to society – such as through a community regeneration scheme (Type II).
- The co-creation of value by the individual well-being created through type I or type II activities, such as the well-being created for individuals as a result of helping them resolve the impact of a disability upon their life (Type III).
- The co-creation of social capital in an individual and/or community through co-production that co-creates capacity to resolve problems in the future – such as developing the skills and/or confidence of individuals with disabilities or local communities, as a consequence of Type I or Type II activities, and that enable them to address and resolve other issues in the future (Type IV).

To explain this classification, authors investigated the systemic literature on value co-creation and co-production, stressing those theoretical issues in other scientific works (Capolupo N., Piscópo G., Annarumma C., *forthcoming*) which represent a starting investigation point: according to several scholar, the first one has been processed as a natural, spontaneous moment (Chandler and Lusch, 2015) in which the service user generate value through its personal desire of achieving that good/service, thinking at how can be positively affect its own experience and upon their life (type 1 and/or 3). Contrariwise, value co-production represents a different matter: it is identified as '*the conscious will of individual and/or social communities to improve specific service issues*' (Bovaird and Loeffler, 2012) and generate a value that somehow adds to the entire society, as point 2 and 4 suggests. Moreover, co-created value occurs when customer contributions, network support, and macro environmental conditions are synergized: '*Customers must be active participants in service coproduction in order to optimize value co-creation*' stated Black and Gallan (2015). The literature, instead, provide a definition of co-produced that can be expanded far beyond the simple idea of service provision. Although considered by several scholars similar to value co-creation process, it requests the active participation of citizens in identifying a common issue which affect a community daily life, organizing as a social group of people – as Osborn point out (2010) - which act as one but to achieve a universally usable value, delivering and better performing public services.

The distinction between co-production and co-creation leads consequently to face other several key concepts, such as that of globalization and active citizenship, understood as citizens' ability to organize themselves in several social groups, with the aim to mobilize resources and to act in the public sphere in order to protect rights and take care of common goods. 'Active citizenship usually does not start from government interventions but operates somewhat independently from public authorities. It is also referred to as self-organisation, self-governance, Do-It-Yourself democracy, or bottom-up governance' (Buijs et al., 2016). Nevertheless, this process must not be seen as a degeneration of democracy into ochlocracy, or a '*coup d'etat*' to the Public Administration and the State. Self-organization means instead, as Vicari suggests (1998), '*the ability to act without resorting to hierarchy or coordination mechanisms. The elements that lead to self-organization can be individuals or formal or informal groups. What matters is that they collaborate and compete with each other.*' Moreover, the agents and the interconnections between them are fundamental (Olson and Eoyang, 2001). It is not a matter of leaving absolute freedom, but of stimulating a context in which self-organization can arise. Therefore, authority and power are no longer centred or hierarchically structured, instead are delegated to every single person. Control, in the broadest sense of the systemic governance, is distributed between the parties and not concentrated in one or a few. This suggests that it is crucial adopting a widespread responsibility and interdependence of feedback mechanisms, logics no longer predominantly top-down but bottom-up (De Toni, 2011).

Social-Mediated Crisis Communication (SMCC) Theory

The literature review conducted by the authors in another aimed also at pointing out which were the most relevant theoretical strands that connect crisis communication and value co-production during crisis. This effort was by all means oriented to contextualize the practical communication model proposed by the authors in the following chapters.

Hence, the review found that social-Mediated crisis communication (SMCC) theory represents the most suitable theoretical approach in which contextualize both the emergency communication model and the value co-production field of study. It is not a coincidence that, according to the Pew Research Centre's Internet & American Life study (2006), when affording crises, audiences' social media use increases,, '*and audiences perceive social media to be more credible than traditional mass media*' (Procopio & Procopio, 2007). The literature arguments also that this model is divided into two different parts which explain how the source and form of crisis information affect organizations' response options and recommended social-mediated crisis response strategies. paper (Capolupo N., Piscopo G., 2018).

When crisis information source occurs, this model depicts the interaction between a given organization experiencing a given crisis and three types of publics who produce and consume crisis information via social media, traditional media, and offline word-of-mouth communication (Liu et al., 2011).

Austin (2012) proposes a classification of three different actors which possess different values/scopes. The first ones are '*influential social media creators*', who generate crisis information for others to consume; the second ones are '*social media followers*', players that consume the influential social media creators' crisis information; lastly, '*social media inactive*', who '*may consume influential social media creators 'crisis information indirectly through word-of-mouth communication with social media followers and/or traditional media who follow influential social media creators and/or social media followers*'. (Austin et al., 2012). Thence, is necessary contextualizing them in the active relation between the citizen and P.A. on the net and, in particular, on social media, by classifying them for their polarity:

- Influential social media creators: active polarity LEADER
- Social media followers: mid-active polarity FOLLOWER
- Social media inactive: passive polarity UNFOLLOWERS

By addressing this kind of approach and- in particular – adopting social media as the ideal field in which analyse those relations and polarity, it follows an exponential increase of indicators like efficiency, convenience, accountability, transparency, citizens involvement and improved trust and democracy. (Chang & Kanan, 2008; Cromer, 2010; Dorris, 2008; Kuzma, 2010).

As a matter of fact, the use of social media – like the vast majority of literature (Graham M.W. et all, 2014) – allows governments to communicate more efficiently with publics nowadays than with more traditional media and are often capable of saving resources including time and money (Kingsley, 2010; Kuzma, 2010). In addition, this mediated communication stream generates a value-in-use from which both Public Administration and citizens may benefit over time, because on the one hand, P.A. is able to manage the crisis through the mediation of active users (classified according to the above-mentioned roles and polarities), and citizens may be able to reach all the information they need to survive the crisis.

MAIN FOCUS OF THE CHAPTER

Methodological Issues

Sentiment analysis, also called opinion mining, is the field of study which examines opinions, feelings, values, attitudes, and emotions of people to entities such as products, services, organizations, individuals, issues, events and their attributes (Bing Liu, 2012). *'The two-way relationship which occurs between producer and consumer, accomplices in a mutual exchange of co- creation of the product, born from the needs of developing new businesses and social organizations, the need for which is to draw the views of consumers or the public about their products and services, and those of individual consumers who also want to know the opinions of an existing product before buying it'*. (Capolupo N., Basile G., Scozzese G., 2017)

Several authors (Wiebe J., Wilson T., et al., 2004) propose a methodology of automatic learning of sentiment analysis which applies the techniques of categorization of parts of a given text to analyze the subjective portions of the document. It is mainly composed of two moments:

1. Label the phrases in the document both subjective and objective, discarding the latter;
2. Apply a classifier machine learning standards for the part extracted.

The chosen case vignette is the Rigopiano avalanche, occurred on the afternoon of 18th January, 2017: a major avalanche occurred on Gran Sasso d'Italia massif, one of the mountains above Rigopiano, hitting a 4-star hotel in Pescara, in Abruzzo region. 'The avalanche struck the luxury resort Hotel Rigopiano, killing twenty-nine people and injuring eleven others'.

Nevertheless, applying sentiment analysis to the present case study it will be fundamental not to focus our attention on how events occurred and the communication stream is managed, but to explain how the proposed communication model during natural disaster works.

Therefore, the research has been conducted and contextualized on Twitter from the 3rd to the 11th of April 2018, for two main reasons: firstly, to demonstrate how – even more than one year far from the timeline of the catastrophe – the attention of public opinion and users/citizens to the argument seems to remain pivotal on the net; secondly, to analyse the episode occurred after Easter which has mobilized public outrage regarding the landslide areas.

Although not need it at this stage, authors used a free data extractor software called Tweet Reach, which allowed to collect Tweets with the hashtag #Rigopiano. The analysis found 100 Tweets in this 8-days period, that authors then classified for their polarity in neutral (35%, press, news and general information), negative (60%, sense of outrage and shame for the Easter Monday celebrations on the sites of the disaster) and positive (5% memory and celebration of the heroes who have helped during the avalanche).

The following Tweets, translated in English by the authors, are clear example of negative, neutral and positive polarity of users' feedback.

Matteo Grittani @mdimagritt 3ʳᵈ Apr I'll say it once again. The problem isn't Italy itself, which is a wonderful country. The real problem is 'Italians' as such, a people of saints, poets and sailors. The problem is this generation of Italians, which is for a large part damaged goods. #Rigopiano

The user Matteo Grittani defines as 'damaged goods' this Italian people generation because of the celebration of Easter Monday close to Rigopiano's hotel. Both the repetition of the word 'problem', the use of stereotypes ('people of saints, poets and sailors') and the expression 'damaged goods' clearly suggest a negative polarity of the Tweet, which have been retweeted 92 times, commented 24 times and liked 216 times.

What's Trending? @breakingnewsit 3rd April Few minutes ago #BREENT, #Rigopiano, #20Mediaset, #AllianzStadium and #Invalsi Twitter trend topic

Concerning neutral polarity, feedbacks were majorly on news and updates. What's Trending? account reminded that the hashtag #Rigopiano became trend topic in Italian Twitter rating.

carlasicuro @CarlaSicuro1 RT @4Paguz2: 9 km on skis and then get to the hotel and start digging, these are the true heroes. I honor you. #Rigopiano

The user Carla Sicuro on the 11ᵗʰ of April decided to retweet a message of another user on January 2017, precisely when rescuers arrived at Hotel Rigopiano. Words like heroes and the expression 'I honor you' express the positive polarity of the Tweet, even shared over time by other users.

Furthermore, the report pointed out several interesting aspects which should be taken into account to positively evaluate the accuracy of the chosen methodology:

1. From 3ʳᵈ to 11ᵗʰ of April 162,305 of Twitter's accounts have been reached by using the hashtag #Rigopiano, achieving 194,254 impressions:
2. The top 3 #Rigopiano Tweet contributors achieved 21,5k impressions, 30 retweets and 30 mentions. Moreover, the most retweeted Tweets seems to have negative (expressing rage and shame) polarity.

Figure 1. Tweet reach estimated reach and exposure

Figure 2. Tweet reach top contributors and most retweeted tweets

More Practical Issues

Given these points, authors agreed on the fact that Twitter in a first stance may be used as the pivotal tool to set the Emergency communication model. As a matter of fact, thanks to its immediacy and syntax, it represents the most suitable tool to build and strengthen the interaction between citizens and relief efforts.

Therefore, the communication model between P.A./rescuers and citizens should be structured in different agents and moments:

1. P.A./rescuers, who receive the information sorted by the filter and coordinate the support or respond to requests for information from citizens.
2. Citizens, which help to report in a verified way (with the help of photos and videos) the requests for assistance and information during the natural catastrophe or the consequent disservices.
3. The 'filter', a team of communicators and IT analysts which have the task of identifying the hashtags on the network that uniquely mark the help request; check that the reports are true and send them to the rescue units.

This circular model could be represented as follow:

Figure 3. Twitter-based emergency model according to authors view

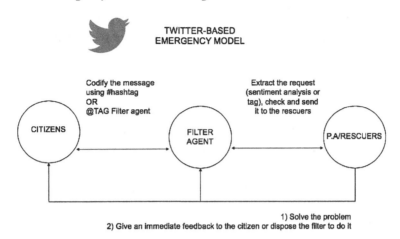

The first moment concern the report of the natural disaster and related problems to it through the use of unique hashtag (for example, #Rigopianohelp) or tagging the filter account @RescueTeam. Citizens must be able, when asked, to prove the reporting. They could ask for information about viability, their family conditions etc.:

Mario Rossi, @MarioRossi 3rd Apr, #Rigopianohelp and/or @RescueTeam Send help to the Hotel Rigopiano, address Contrada Rigopiano 65010 farindola (Pescara). Avalanche in progress. I enclose videos/photos

Mario Rossi, @MarioRossi 3rd Apr #Rigopianohelp and/or @RescueTeam which road may I take to reach Pescara driving from...

By checking citizens report, discarding the whole information which does not produce added value for relief efforts, the filter communication team will be in charge of contacts by tag and hashtag rescuers and P.A. to convey – both online and offline if not applicable - only those verified information that can be useful for reporting and solving the problem:

Rescue Team, @RescueTeam 3rd Apr #Rigopianohelp @Protezione Civile VERIFIED HELP REQUEST, Hotel Rigopiano, address Contrada Rigopiano 65010 farindola (Pescara). Avalanche in progress.

Rescue Team, @RescueTeam 3rd Apr #Rigopianohelp @Autostradeperlitalia Are there any alternative routes to reach Pescara from...?

Rescue Team, @RescueTeam 3rd Apr #Rigopianohelp Thanks for your report @MarioRossi, we are contacting Civil Protection Unit to send help immediately at the coordinates you sent us / You can reach Pescara by taking the Highway...

P.A./rescuers will provide relief on the basis of the indications received from the filter and citizens, will be in contact with the filter in order to receive as many indications as possible and – once rescue operations has been settled – answer to those citizen's question through the filter mediation.

FUTURE RESEARCH

In the last decade crisis management studies have largely stressed the importance of co-producing value implementing processes and technologies available to both citizens and rescuers to support them during crisis and catastrophes. Social media, in this sense, played a pivotal role to crisis management, allowing citizens to be active protagonists in crisis mediation, and to public administration to use this activism and participatory being to improve its services and better coordinate the emergence. In this connection, literature use to confirm that value co – production occurs if organizations and their stakeholders, P.A. and citizens cooperate with each other in order to develop systems, products or services, 'reinforcing the idea that consumer experience is central to enterprise value creation and innovation' (Prahalad and Ramaswamy's, 2004). Therefore, it can be stated that the main stakeholder and the most interested external partner of an organization is its consumer - citizen, in the specific case (Izvercianua M., Șerana S.A., Branea A., 2014). Thus, it happened that citizens and P.A. / rescue units, thanks to the proposed communication model, establish a horizontal profitable dialogue between each other, creating a sub-system autonomous, self-reliant and dependent, interactive vertically and characterized by rules of behaviour, that is called 'holon' (Mella P., 2007). According to Koestler (1968), the holon is self-organization characterized by its ability to interact and coordinate with other superordinate and subordinate holons (integrative tendency) – which derives from its being both included and inclusive, and by its ability for self-preservation. The effort that this work aims to bring forward consists in contextualizing the new methodologies of rescue and management of natural disasters, starting from a qualitative methodology – i.e. sentiment analysis - to build around its I.T. logic a communication model that, through the contribution of multiple actors, aims to co-produce value which can be universally used over time. As mentioned above, from this interaction emerges a sub-system of civil society in which people share at the same level the same aims, and collaborate with each other to reach them.

CONCLUSION

The sentiment analysis methodology shown – both in the case vignette and applied to the twitter-based communication model – that there could be a strong bond between presented is nothing but a simple targeted re-use of a social network with specific characteristics that are extremely suitable for the prompt reporting of large-scale problems. It represents an interesting interactive platform between active citizenship and P.A., within which there are no hierarchies and both its actors play their part in order to achieve the same result and co-produce value. Nevertheless, requires timeliness and skills concerning the filter communicators; active citizens Twitter knowledge and accuracy in reporting the catastrophes; collaboration and cooperation with P.A. and rescue units specifically in charge of this activity. In order to overcome these issues, authors will structure the Rescue team as a non-governmental organization that works on multiple levels autonomously but working synergistically with the relevant stakeholders: on the one hand, training internal staff and making it ready for sorting and filtering help requests, conveying them to rescuers; on the other hand, organizing free training courses through local communities and territories aimed at both citizens (thus teaching them how to report the problem) as well as rescuers and PA (creation of territorial reporting networks, help agreements, knowledge of IT tools).

REFERENCES

Austin, L., Fisher, B. L., & Jin, Y. (2012). How Audiences Seek Out Crisis Information: Exploring the Social-Mediated Cisis Communication Model. *Journal of Applied Communication Research, 40*(2), 188–207. doi:10.1080/00909882.2012.654498

Bing, L. (2012). *Sentiment Analysis and Opinion Mining. In Synthesis Lectures on Human Language Technologies*. Morgan and Claypool Publishers.

Black, H. G., & Gallan, A. S. (2015). Transformative service networks: Cocreated value as well-being. *Service Industries Journal, 35*(15-16), 826–845. doi:10.1080/02642069.2015.1090978

Bovaird, T., Stoker, G., Jones, T., Loeffler, E., & Pinilla Roncancio, M. (2016). Activating collective co-production of public services: Influencing citizens to participate in complex governance mechanisms in the UK. *International Review of Administrative Sciences, 82*(1), 47–68. doi:10.1177/0020852314566009

Buijs, A. E., Mattijssen, T., Vander Jagt, P., Ambrose-Oji, N., Andersson, B., Elands, E., ... Møller, M. (2016). Active citizenship for urban green infrastructure: Fostering the diversity and dynamics of citizen contributions through mosaic governance. *Current Opinion in Environmental Sustainability, 22*, 1–6. doi:10.1016/j.cosust.2017.01.002

Capolupo, N., Basile, G., & Scozzese, G. (2017). Sentiment Analysis as a Tool to Understand the Cultural Relationship between Consumer and Brand. In *Handbook of Research on Intelligent Techniques and Modelling Applications in Marketing Analytics*. Hershey, PA: IGI Global. doi:10.4018/978-1-5225-0997-4.ch011

Capolupo, N., & Piscopo, G. (2018), Value Co-Production in the Interaction between P.A. and Active Citizenship. Social Media as Tool to Communicate Natural Calamity. *Proceedings IFKAD 2018 13th International Forum on Knowledge Asset Dynamics*, 742-754.

Capolupo, N., Piscopo, G., & Annarumma, C. (in press). Value co-creation and co-production in the interaction between citizens and Public Administration. A Systematic Literature Review. *Kybernetes*.

De Toni, F. (2011). Teoria della complessità e implicazioni manageriali: Verso l'auto-organizzazione. *Sinergie, 81*(10), 77–96.

Gebauer, H., Johnson, M., & Enquist, B. (2010). Value co-creation as a determinant of success in public transport services. *Managing Service Quality, 20*(6), 511–530. doi:10.1108/09604521011092866

Izvercianua, M., Șerana, S. A., & Branea, A. (2014). Prosumer-oriented Value Co-creation Strategies for Tomorrow's Urban Management. *Procedia: Social and Behavioral Sciences, 24*, 149–156. doi:10.1016/j.sbspro.2014.02.471

Koestler, A. (1968). *The ghost in the machine*. Oxford, UK: Macmillan.

Levine, C. H., & Fisher, G. (1984). Citizenship and service delivery: The promise of coproduction/ response/discussion. *Public Administration Review*, *44*, 178–189. doi:10.2307/975559

Mella, P. (2007). *The Holonic Revolution Holons, Holarchies and Holonic Networks. The Ghost in the Production Machine*. Pavia University Press.

Olson, E. E., & Eoyang, G. H. (2001). *Facilitating Organization Change. Lessons from Complexity Science*. San Francisco, CA: Jossey-Bass/Pfeiffer.

Osborne, S. P. (2010). Delivering public services: Time for a new theory? *Public Management Review*, *12*(1), 1–10. doi:10.1080/14719030903495232

Osborne, S. P., & Brown, L. (2011). Innovation, Public Policy and Public Service Delivery in the UK: The word that would-be king? *Public Administration*, *89*(4), 1335–1350. doi:10.1111/j.1467-9299.2011.01932.x

Osborne, S. P., Radnor, Z., & Nasi, G. (2013). A New Theory for Public Service Management? Toward a (Public) Service-Dominant Approach. *American Review of Public Administration*, *43*(2), 135–158. doi:10.1177/0275074012466935

Osborne, S. P., Radnor, Z., & Strokosch, K. (2016). Co-Production and the Co-Creation of Value in Public Services: A suitable case for treatment? *Public Management Review*, *18*(5), 639–653. doi:10.1080/14719037.2015.1111927

Pew Internet & American Life Project. (2006), *Blogger callback survey*. Retrieved from http://www.pewinternet.org

Procopio, C. H., & Procopio, S. T. (2007). Do you know what it means to miss New Orleans? Internet communication, geographic community, and social capital in crisis. *Journal of Applied Communication Research*, *35*(1), 67–87. doi:10.1080/00909880601065722

Vargo, S. L., & Lusch, R. F. (2008). Service-dominant logic: Continuing the evolution. *Journal of the Academy of Marketing Science*, *36*(1), 1–10. doi:10.100711747-007-0069-6

Veil, S. R., Buhener, T., & Palenchar, J. (2011). A Work-In-Process Literature Review: Incorporating Social Media in Risk and Crisis Communication. *Journal of Contingencies and Crisis Management*, *19*(2), 110–122. doi:10.1111/j.1468-5973.2011.00639.x

Vicari, S. (1998). *La creatività dell'impresa.Tra caso e necessità*. Milan, Italy: Etas.

Whitaker, G. P. (1980). Coproduction: Citizen participation in service delivery. *Public Administration Review*, *40*(3), 240–246. doi:10.2307/975377

Wiebe, J., Wilson, T., Bruce, R., Bell, M., & Martin, M. (2004). Learning Subjective Language. *Computational Linguistics*, *30*(3), 277–308. doi:10.1162/0891201041850885

ADDITIONAL READING

Alves, H. (2013). Co-creation and innovation in public services. *Service Industries Journal*, *33*(7-8), 671–682. doi:10.1080/02642069.2013.740468

Chatfield, A. T., Jochen Scholl, H. J., & Brajawidagda, U. (2013). Tsunami early warnings via Twitter ingovernment: Net-savvy citizens' co-production of time-critical public information services. *Government Information Quarterly*, *30*(4), 377–386. doi:10.1016/j.giq.2013.05.021

Coombs, T. W., & Holladay, S. J. (1996). Communication and Attributions in a Crisis: An Experimental Study in Crisis Communication. *Journal of Public Relations Research*, *8*(4), 279–295. doi:10.12071532754xjprr0804_04

Janowski, T. (2015). Digital government evolution: From transformation to contextualization. *Government Information Quarterly*, *32*(3), 221–236. doi:10.1016/j.giq.2015.07.001

Spence, P. R., Lachlan, K. A., & Rainear, A. M. (2016). Social media and crisis research: Data collectionand directions. *Computers in Human Behavior*, *54*, 667–672. doi:10.1016/j.chb.2015.08.045

Szkuta, K., Pizzicannella, R., & Osimo, D. (2014). Collaborative approaches to public sector innovation: A scoping study. *Telecommunications Policy*, *38*(5–6), 558–567. doi:10.1016/j.telpol.2014.04.002

Takahashi, B., Tandoc, E. C. Jr, & Carmichael, C. (2015). Communicating on Twitter during a disaster: An analysis of tweets during Typhoon Haiyan in the Philippines. *Computers in Human Behavior*, *50*, 392–398. doi:10.1016/j.chb.2015.04.020

Zhao, D., Wang, F., Wei, J., & Liang, L. (2013). Public reaction to information release for crisis discourse by organization: Integration of online comments. *International Journal of Information Management*, *33*(3), 485–495. doi:10.1016/j.ijinfomgt.2013.01.003

KEY TERMS AND DEFINITIONS

Crisis Communication: The effort of communicating with the public and stockholders when an unexpected event occurs that could have a negative impact on the organization reputation.

Disaster Management: The attempt to understand the driving mechanisms of natural disasters.

Holon: An autonomous self-reliant unit.

Leader: A person who holds a dominant or superior position within its field, capable of exercising a high degree of control or influence over others.

Sentiment: An idea or feeling that someone expresses in words.

Twitter: A social networking website, which allows users to publish short messages that are visible to other users.

Value: The worth of all the benefits and rights arising from ownership.

This research was previously published in Exploring the Power of Electronic Word-of-Mouth in the Services Industry; pages 352-363, copyright year 2020 by Business Science Reference (an imprint of IGI Global).

Section 5
Organizational and Social Implications

Chapter 81
Open Issues in Opinion Mining

Vishal Vyas
Pondicherry University, India

V. Uma
iD https://orcid.org/0000-0002-7257-7920
Pondicherry University, India

ABSTRACT

Opinions are found everywhere. In web forums like social networking websites, e-commerce sites, etc., rich user-generated content is available in large volume. Web 2.0 has made rich information easily accessible. Manual insight extraction of information from these platforms is a cumbersome task. Deriving insight from such available information is known as opinion mining (OM). Opinion mining is not a single-stage process. Text mining and natural language processing (NLP) is used to obtain information from such data. In NLP, content from the text corpus is pre-processed, opinion word is extracted, and analysis of those words is done to get the opinion. The volume of web content is increasing every day. There is a demand for more ingenious techniques, which remains a challenge in opinion mining. The efficiency of opinion mining systems has not reached the satisfactory level because of the issues in various stages of opinion mining. This chapter will explain the various research issues and challenges present in each stage of opinion mining.

INTRODUCTION

Opinion mining (OM)/Sentiment Analysis (SA) is related to deriving insight through analysis of user's thoughts (reviews, posts, blogs etc.) about entities such as products, movies, people etc. Evaluation of reviews posted by users on e-commerce and social networking is of much use as it contains highly rated information. Calculation of average inclination of opinion towards any entity not only helps business organizations to gain profits but also helps an individual in getting the right opinion about something unfamiliar.

DOI: 10.4018/978-1-6684-6303-1.ch081

Natural Language Processing (NLP) deals with actual text element processing. The text element is transformed into machine format by NLP. Artificial Intelligence (AI) techniques are applied on information provided by NLP to determine whether text sentence is positive or negative. Text mining can also be used in extracting the opinion. The difference is that, in text mining, data mining techniques are used to identify the opinion.

In both the techniques, content from the text corpus is pre-processed and opinion word extraction is performed before the opinion is derived. The raw text contains unwanted words which have no contribution to the opinion and such words are removed in preprocessing. The clean data is the output of the preprocessing stage. Various issues such as noise removal, missing values etc. are to be dealt in preprocessing stage. Many methods are available for pre-processing of text in opinion mining. The time complexity involved in pre-processing is high as compared to proceeding stages. High usage of abbreviations is normal when it comes to publishing more information using fewer characters. For instance in Twitter, only 280 characters are allowed in single post. Though various acronym dictionaries such as netlingo, urban dictionary are available, to deal with emerging slangs is a difficult task. Real-time updation of such dictionaries is the need of the hour.

Considering the next stage in opinion mining, the objective to create a predictive model for opinion mining can be fulfilled effectively by proper feature selection. Better feature selection not only produces accurate results but it also reduces the time complexity. In-depth knowledge of the problem domain is a prerequisite for feature selection. Filter, wrapper and embedded methods are used for feature selection in text mining. Presently, selection of a feature is a big issue, as the orientation of opinion changes with respect to the domain. Opinion mining is not limited to textual data but extending it to data in different formats such as real-time video, audio etc. is a real challenge.

Analysis being the next stage in OM, with what sentiment the author of the text is giving the opinion is identified through classification of the text. The chapter discusses the following challenges involved in classification of text for opinion mining. Researchers mainly use online reviews on movies and products for opinion mining. It is hard to identify whether the content is authentic or fake. Singh (2018) discussed a model to classify whether the review is authentic or fake. For better opinion mining, the elimination of spam content is necessary. The chapter discusses issues in the application of opinion mining for spam detection. Sentiment detection of the writer is important to get the accurate opinion from content. It ultimately tells the reputation of the writer. Identification of duplicates, sentiment detection of writer/ reviewer from outliners by knowing the reputation of the content generator is still a challenging task in opinion mining. In online reviews, most of the times we come across mixed opinions. Consider the sentence, *"The car looks good but its interiors are not up to the mark"*. With aspect-based opinion mining, it is possible to get an opinion on particulars rather than getting an aggregate opinion in case of mixed reviews. There is still an effort required to raise the accuracy score while dealing with mixed reviews.

NLP and text mining play a vital role in OM. The ultimate goal is to the fill the gap how the humans communicate (natural language) and what the computer understands (machine language). User generated online content from social networking websites is easy to access and preferable for opinion mining but there exists social media imposed challenges such as cross-lingual opinion mining, sarcasm, negation handling and relevance. A huge amount of study has been carried out in English language. Hence, a lot of resources such as dictionaries and methods are available in English language for opinion mining. Opinion mining for Non- English languages is still a less explored area. The mapping of available resources in English language to other languages which is cross-lingual analysis is still a challenge in opinion mining. Opinion mining helps political organizations to get a better understanding of their competitors. Political debates, posts and discussions contain sarcastic sentences. An advanced NLP approach to deal with sarcasm detection is still not available. The chapter will briefly cover the issues viz. cross-lingual OM, sarcasm detection, relevance and negation handling which are some of the challenges imposed by social media.

Various research issues and challenges restrict efficiency of opinion mining system, because of which there isn't any satisfactory opinion mining system. The essence of opinion mining is to help people in decision making. The unstructured text, different writing styles, usage of sarcasm etc., in social media, e-commerce assigns a high percentage of difficulty in deriving opinion. E-commerce is not just selling and buying online. Utilizing opinion mining in e-commerce helps in recommending products to customers which will increase the efficiency of organizations and help in competing with other giants in the market. Thus, the necessity of opinion mining is increasing gradually. Hence, this chapter discusses the various issues and research challenges involved in opinion mining.

VARIOUS APPROACHES TO OPINION MINING (OM) /SENTIMENT ANALYSIS (SA)

Sentiment analysis is used to identify the feeling expressed by an individual whereas; opinion mining is used to identify the user's view. The approaches used are mostly common.

There are specific approaches to OM/SA that are important in designing a system that gives an accurate result while deriving opinion. These approaches are Document-level sentiment analysis, Sentence level sentiment analysis, Aspect-Based sentiment analysis and Comparative-Based sentiment analysis.

1. In Document level Sentiment Analysis, whole document is considered as single information unit and classified as positive, negative or neutral sentiment polarity. Supervised learning and unsupervised learning are the main approaches used in solving document level Sentiment Analysis.
2. Sentence level Sentiment Analysis considers each sentence as one information unit. Before real analysis of polarity, each sentence is determined to be Subjective or Objective. Only subjective sentences are further analysed. The sentiment polarity of the whole document is known after examining each sentence.
3. In Aspect-Based Sentiment Analysis, classification of sentiment concerns particular Sentiment Aspect/Entity. Firstly, aspects and their entities are identified. For instance, in the opinion about a car "Mileage of the car is very low but it is equipped with high-end safety features", "Mileage" and "Safety features" are two aspects of entity "Car."
4. In comparative-based Sentiment Analysis, rather than having a direct opinion about a product, text has comparative opinions such as "Most of the features in Audi car are better than BMW." Firstly, comparative sentences are identified in the text and then preferred entities are extracted. Focus on words like "more", "less", "most", "better", "superior" etc. help in identifying comparative sentences.

ISSUES INVOLVED IN PREPROCESSING

Anomalies in the assembled data from different online sources are the biggest issue in achieving accurate opinion. Product reviews and social networks which are a valuable source of data are usually preferred to acquire content for opinion mining. Online text is generally created by humans and it is heterogeneous in nature for e.g. different styles to write the date, name, etc. It is naïve to use unstructured data as it degrades the performance of any technique which is used for opinion mining.

Preprocessing is the first step in the process of opinion mining which aims at refining online content. Preprocessing involves some distinct steps which are (a) Data cleaning. (b) Data Integration. (c) Data Transformation.

Issues in Data Cleaning

Raw data are incomplete and contain noise which steers to irregularities in the dataset for opinion mining. Extraction of useful information (opinion) from online content is only possible when the acquired data is clean. Data cleaning provides consistent data for opinion mining.

Dealing With Missing Data

Ignoring a record with missing values is not a right option as it may affect the accuracy of the model for opinion mining. Manually entering missing values is the most accurate approach but it is time-consuming. The other option one can think of is, inserting predicted values in place of missing data but it may inject bias in the data. The said method is beneficial for validating results procured by snubbing records with missing values. Missing data account for inaccurate opinion mining system. Data extracted for opinion mining is human input. Different mindset or limit of words such as 280 words in Twitter are some of the reasons which leave a possibility of small, incorrect words etc. that give nil or wrong opinion. It is necessary to deal with missing values to get an accurate opinion mining system.

Dealing With Noisy Data

The content extracted for opinion mining is generally a manual entry by people of different mindset. Lexical accuracy in online content (Reviews, Blogs, and Posts etc.) remains an issue when it comes to getting an automated opinion. Challenges arise while data is extracted from social media websites as it is erroneous, unstructured and of dynamic nature. Online data contains abbreviations which an author of the text furnishes it according to its requirement of his/her mindset. Using slangs and transliterating etc. usually incorporate inconvenience to the opinion mining system. Such kind of content increases the difficulty level to mine the opinion and it is still a challenging task for researchers to deal with noisy data.

Various approaches namely binning methods, clustering and machine learning are being used for data smoothing. JHam et al. (2006) have described these approaches of data preprocessing. There is still a need for better data smoothing technique to get accurate insight from the data during opinion mining.

Issues in Data Integration

Data cleaning and data integration are important steps to get a reliable data set. Data is extracted from different sources and combining heterogeneous data sources is still an open issue. A data warehouse is used where extract, transform and load (ETL) process is repeated continuously to synchronize the data. Sometimes, the problem occurs when there is no access to full data and query is triggered. The different data formats to address similar items in various data sources are a big issue. For example, in a sentence which discusses a mobile phone "my phone" and "her phone" may occur. To deal with such kind of issues, NLP techniques such as parsing, word sense disambiguation and co-reference are being used. These are classic problems in NLP but there is still no accurate solution present to deal with the issue of data integration.

Issues in Data Transformation

The raw data extracted for analysis is not suitable for analysis. It is to be transformed into a format that is best suitable to derive opinion. The difference between the source (raw) data and the final (required) data tells the complexity of data transformation. The steps which are being applied to transform the data are (a) Data discovery (b) Data mapping (c) Code generation (d) Code execution and (e) Data review. Each step is equally important based on the complexity of the transformation required. The other possible option to get the data in user format is by applying normalization, aggregation and generalization. With the increase in the data, there is a need for advanced techniques to deal with data transformation, which is still a research challenge in the field of opinion mining.

ISSUES INVOLVED IN FEATURE EXTRACTION

While dealing with reviews of products, the text contains information about different characteristics of the reviewing entity. For example, *"Considering the mileage, Maruti's car is above all but it lacks in safety features"*. In above example "Mileage" and "Safety" are the two different characteristics/feature of an entity "Maruti car". Till now, noun-based approach is used to get the features from product reviews. Frequently used nouns are extracted and are identified as features of the entity. Liu (2011) discussed an approach that can identify nouns that imply the opinion. Identification of verb is a complex task but it can also be the characteristic/feature. Identification of contributing feature always remains a challenging task.

ISSUES INVOLVED IN CLASSIFICATION

Online content is rich and contains hidden information. It is necessary to derive opinion from such content. Classification is a form of data analysis that is used to extract models to describe data classes. Classification is a machine learning approach used to predict group membership (positive/negative incase of OM/SA) for data instances.

Different Writing Style

Mining opinion from online content which includes web forums, posts and reviews etc. is a challenging task. The content we get online is usually a manual entry from people of a different mindset. Expression of opinion differs from person to person. The difference in the text comes when people use abbreviations, negative/positive words as per their ease. Sometimes the word is identified as an abbreviation which is in original a half-written word. Anna Stavrianou and Jean-Hugues Chauchat. (2008) have discussed the opinion mining issues in the online forum and Christopher (2008) addressed the issue of mining consumer opinion from the online web using linguistic and NLP techniques. However, it is found that these techniques are not suitable for user-generated text in online forums. Class association rules are suggested for getting insight from the online text and through and their result showed that content mining approach is better than NLP approach. Research focus is required to address this issue.

Requirement of World Knowledge

World knowledge requires being integrated into the opinion mining system. Consider the following example:

He is living with a Frankenstein without any awareness.

The sentence derives negative opinion but one has to have the knowledge of "Frankenstein". There is a need for a lexicon of words with their usage. The lexicon can incorporate the Knowledge required to derive opinion from the sentences where it becomes difficult to get the insight.

Synonym Grouping

The issue which occurs while dealing with product reviews to get an opinion is the usage of dissimilar words that are used to refer to same features of different products. Synonyms are to be identified and grouped together. The issue of synonym grouping requires serious attention as it is not well addressed in the past. Zhai et al. (2010, 2011) addressed the issue of synonym grouping using semi-Supervised and constrained LDA (Latent Dirichlet Allocation) respectively. Pham et al. (2011) discussed the issue and gave a solution to group Vietnamese synonym feature words in product reviews.

Spam Detection

False positive opinions to mislead users are normal these days. Bogus opinions are given to online users either to promote some product or to damage the reputation of any entity. Spams are mainly intended to confuse people between true positive and false negative opinions. Detecting these spams is a tedious but an important task. Jindal and Liu (2007, 2008) discussed review spam detection and opinion spam detection. Indurkhya et al. (2010) broadly classified spams into Email spam and Web spams. An email spam refers to unsought commercial emails which are intended to sell, promote or advertise something. Web spam refers to the use of illicit means to increase the search rank position of web pages. By exploiting the weakness of current search ranking algorithms some businesses are helping other by improving their page ranking. Such businesses are known as "search engine optimization" (SEO). Detecting fake reviews is a research challenge in opinion mining. Singh et al. (2018) discussed a model to detect fake or spam reviews.

Table 1. Theoretical and technical challenges in opinion mining/ sentiment analysis

Reference	Theoretical/Technical	Opinion Mining /Sentiment Analysis Challenge	Technique Used
Bas et al. (2011)	Theoretical	Negation	Parts of speech (POS)
Yulan et al. (2011)	Theoretical	Domain dependence	Naïve Bayes and Support vector machine
Maral (2011)	Theoretical	Negation	Bag of words (BOWs) term frequencies
Svetlana et al. (2014)	Theoretical	Domain dependence	SemEval-2013
Alexandra et al. (2013)	Theoretical	Domain dependence	WordNet- lexicon based
Lucie et al. (2015)	Technical	Bi-polar words	n-grams
Emitza and Walid (2014)	Technical	Feature and keyword extraction	POS tagging with fine-grained app
Qingxi and Ming (2014)	Theoretical	Spam and fake reviews	Combine lexicon and use shallow dependency parser
Mohammad et al. (2014)	Theoretical & Technical	Domain dependence and NLP overheads	Lexicon-based method depends on POS tagging
Doaa et al. (2015)	Theoretical & Technical	Lexicon, feature extraction, negation and world knowledge	Enhanced BOW model
Jiang and Min (2011)	Theoretical	Domain dependence	n-grams
Walter and Mihalea (2011)	Theoretical & Technical	Extracting features and domain dependence	Character n-grams instead of terms
Myle et al. (2011)	Theoretical	Spam and fake reviews	POS tagging similarities and n-gram algorithm
Ning Luo et al(2018)	Theoretical	Fake reviews	Multi-aspect Feature based Neural Network Model
Shehnepoor et al. (2017)	Theoretical	Spam detection	NetSpam Framework

CHALLENGES IMPOSED BY SOCIAL MEDIA

In addition to the research challenges discussed earlier, Social media imposes various issues on opinion mining. The text element (reviews, blogs etc.) can be analysed using NLP and text mining. It is still not possible to have a generalized opinion mining system for any kind of text. The text extracted from social media is a human input and therefore, it has a lot of ambiguity. Some of the issues which are imposed by social media are discussed here.

Cross-Lingual Opinion Mining

Much of the literature on opinion mining is focused on English text. Hence, most of the resources developed are in English language. Existing resources are utilized for opinion mining of content source language. Exploiting the present resources for other languages is domain adaptation. Deshmukh and Tripathi (2018) discussed entropy based classifier for cross domain opinion mining. Lo et al. (2017) discussed challenges in multilingual sentiment analysis and provided a framework to deal with scarce resource languages.

Relevance

Identification of relevant pages is not always correct. Comment threads in social media usually diverge into un-associated topics. In the forum of a topic, there remains a possibility of comments on other topics too. On Twitter, people talk about diverse fields. It is difficult to have a single lexical model of "interesting tweets" as it differs from person to person. Mynard et al. (2012) discussed the challenges in having opinion mining tool for social media.

Dealing With Sarcasm and Irony

In the presence of sarcasm and irony, opinion mining gives erroneous results. The senses of positive and negative words do not remain the same as in normal sentences. Firstly, sarcastic and ironical sentences are needed to be identified. Identification of a sentence with sarcasm is a challenging task in opinion mining. Gonzalez-Ibanez (2011) addressed sarcasm in microblog website, Twitter. Filatova (2012) conceived a corpus to handle irony and sarcasm using crowdsourcing, Reyes(2013) addressed irony in Twitter using a multidimensional approach and Bharti et al. (2016) streamed tweets in real time and detected sarcastic sentiments. Following example shows how a sentence can have a positive/negative opinion without bearing an opinion word.

How can anyone travel on this bus?

The above sentence is not carrying any negative word but it is a sentence of negative opinion. It shows opinion mining is not only achieved by syntax detection but identification of semantics is the need of the hour.

Negation Handling

Negation changes the truth value of the premise. Words such as "not" and "never" are used to express negation which changes the opinion in its scope. In opinion mining, negation handling is a challenging task. Farooq (2017) discussed negation handling at the sentence level. The approach which is usually applied to handle negation is reversing the polarity of the words that
appear after negative word. In the example, *"I do not like the camera which I received as a gift"*, *"Like"* has appeared after a negative word "not". Using the classic approach it would *become "Like not"* but this approach does not work. In case of *"I do not like the camera which I received as a gift, but it has got nice features"*. Here it is required to consider the scope of the negative word which extend till

the conjunction the word but. The issue does not stop here. In the example sentence, *"Not only did I like the car but I loved its features"* there is no need to change the polarity of the word appearing after the negative word. There is a need for a generalized algorithm, as manually it is very difficult to consider all the different cases.

MATHEMATICAL APPROACHES USED IN ADDRESSING THE ISSUES

In E-commerce, it is usually seen that for the same product or its feature, customer express their feeling with different word or phrases. Opinion from such unstructured online reviews is usually derived by clustering product features and applying supervised and unsupervised methods. Jiajia et al. (2016) proposed a constrained orthogonal non-negative matrix factorization (CONMT) model to categorize features. Here, three assumptions are exploited to build feature-opinion namely relation matrix, cannot-link constrain matrix and must-link matrix. These three matrices are incorporated into CONMT model. The model outperformed several baseline methods. Irrespective of applying machine learning algorithm to assess sentiment in micro-blogging messages, Chan et al. (2013) provides an efficient tool utilizing the rough set theory by Pawlak (1982) for deriving new perspectives of sentiment analysis from micro-blogging messages. More specifically, they introduced the use of rough set theory to formulate sentimental approximation spaces based on keywords for assessing sentiment of micro-blogging messages. Various other researches are being carried out worldwide in addressing the issues.

CONCLUSION

With the advancements in Web 2.0, web content is increasing every day. There is a demand for more ingenious techniques and it is a challenge in opinion mining. With the advancement in internet related applications, opinion mining has become an interesting research area in NLP community. Opinion mining is beneficial for a business organization, as they analyse social media and get insight from ongoing activities. Merely, with their online presence, they can get overall performance utilizing the opinions mined. Popular individuals can benefit by knowing the audience attitude and this is possible through opinion mining. This chapter discusses the open issues in opinion mining. The data extracted from the web is unstructured and data cleaning is required at this preprocessing step. The chapter discussed the issues involved in data cleanings such as dealing with missing data and noise.

The cleaned data is not a final input for opinion mining system hence the issues data integration and data transformation are briefly explained in the chapter. Various issues involved in opinion mining such as different writing style, world knowledge, synonym grouping and spam detection are elaborated in the chapter. The data for opinion mining is usually extracted from social media hence there is also an explanation about the challenges imposed by the source of data extraction. This chapter has given an overall idea about the challenges that exist in opinion mining. The development of a novel approach to achieve a satisfactory opinion mining system is still an open challenge.

REFERENCES

Al-Kabi, M. N., Gigieh, A. H., Alsmadi, I. M., Wahsheh, H. A., & Haidar, M. M. (2014). Opinion mining and analysis for Arabic language. *International Journal of Advanced Computer Science and Applications*, *5*(5), 181–195.

Alexandra, B., Ralf, S., Mijail, K., Vanni, Z., Erik, V. D. G., Matina, H., ... Jenya, B. (2013). Sentiment analysis in the news. *Proceedings of the Seventh International Conference on Language Resources and Evaluation (LREC'10)*.

Bharti, S. K., Vachha, B., Pradhan, R. K., Babu, K. S., & Jena, S. K. (2016). Sarcastic sentiment detection in tweets streamed in real time: A big data approach. *Digital Communications and Networks*, *2*(3), 108–121. doi:10.1016/j.dcan.2016.06.002

Chan, C. C., & Liszka, K. J. (2013). Application of rough set theory to sentiment analysis of microblog data. In *Rough Sets and Intelligent Systems-Professor Zdzisław Pawlak in Memoriam* (pp. 185–202). Berlin: Springer. doi:10.1007/978-3-642-30341-8_10

Dadvar, M., Hauff, C., & de Jong, F. M. (2011, February). Scope of negation detection in sentiment analysis. In *Proceedings of the Dutch-Belgian Information Retrieval Workshop, DIR 2011*. University of Amsterdam.

Deshmukh, J. S., & Tripathy, A. K. (2018). Entropy based classifier for cross-domain opinion mining. *Applied Computing and Informatics*, *14*(1), 55–64. doi:10.1016/j.aci.2017.03.001

El-Din, D. M., Mokhtar, H. M., & Ismael, O. (2015). Online paper review analysis. *International Journal of Advanced Computer Science and Applications*, *6*(9).

Farooq, U., Mansoor, H., Nongaillard, A., Ouzrout, Y., & Qadir, M. A. (2017). Negation Handling in Sentiment Analysis at Sentence Level. *JCP*, *12*(5), 470–478. PMID:28097676

Filatova, E. (2012, May). Irony and Sarcasm: Corpus Generation and Analysis Using Crowdsourcing. In LREC (pp. 392-398). Academic Press.

Flekova, L., Preoţiuc-Pietro, D., & Ruppert, E. (2015). Analysing domain suitability of a sentiment lexicon by identifying distributionally bipolar words. In *Proceedings of the 6th Workshop on Computational Approaches to Subjectivity, Sentiment and Social Media Analysis* (pp. 77-84). Academic Press. 10.18653/v1/W15-2911

González-Ibánez, R., Muresan, S., & Wacholder, N. (2011, June). Identifying sarcasm in Twitter: a closer look. In *Proceedings of the 49th Annual Meeting of the Association for Computational Linguistics: Human Language Technologies: Short Papers-Volume 2* (pp. 581-586). Association for Computational Linguistics.

Guzman, E., & Maalej, W. (2014, August). How do users like this feature? a fine grained sentiment analysis of app reviews. In *Requirements Engineering Conference (RE), 2014 IEEE 22nd International* (pp. 153-162). IEEE. 10.1109/RE.2014.6912257

Han, J., Kamber, M., & Pei, J. (2006). *Data preprocessing. Data mining: concepts and techniques* (pp. 47–97). San Francisco: Morgan Kaufmann.

He, Y., Chenghua, L., & Harith, A. (2011). Automatically extracting polarity-bearing topics for cross-domain sentiment classification. *Proceedings of the Annual Meeting of the Association for Computational Linguistics.*

Heerschop, B., van Iterson, P., Hogenboom, A., Frasincar, F., & Kaymak, U. (2011). Accounting for negation in sentiment analysis. In *11th Dutch-Belgian Information Retrieval Workshop (DIR 2011)* (pp. 38-39). Academic Press.

Indurkhya, N., & Damerau, F. J. (Eds.). (2010). *Handbook of natural language processing* (Vol. 2). CRC Press.

Jiajia, W., Yezheng, L., Yuanchun, J., Chunhua, S., Jianshan, S., & Yanan, D. (2016, June). Clustering Product Features of Online Reviews Based on Nonnegative Matrix Tri-factorizations. In *Data Science in Cyberspace (DSC), IEEE International Conference on* (pp. 199-208). IEEE. 10.1109/DSC.2016.32

Jindal, N., & Liu, B. (2007, May). Review spam detection. In *Proceedings of the 16th international conference on World Wide Web* (pp. 1189-1190). ACM. 10.1145/1242572.1242759

Jindal, N., & Liu, B. (2008, February). Opinion spam and analysis. In *Proceedings of the 2008 International Conference on Web Search and Data Mining* (pp. 219-230). ACM.

Kasper, W., & Vela, M. (2011, October). Sentiment analysis for hotel reviews. In Computational linguistics-applications conference (Vol. 231527, pp. 45-52). Academic Press.

Kiritchenko, S., Zhu, X., & Mohammad, S. M. (2014). Sentiment analysis of short informal texts. *Journal of Artificial Intelligence Research*, *50*, 723–762.

Lau, R. Y., Li, C., & Liao, S. S. (2014). Social analytics: Learning fuzzy product ontologies for aspect-oriented sentiment analysis. *Decision Support Systems*, *65*, 80–94. doi:10.1016/j.dss.2014.05.005

Liu, B. (2012). Sentiment analysis and opinion mining. *Synthesis Lectures on Human Language Technologies, 5*(1), 1-167.

Lo, S. L., Cambria, E., Chiong, R., & Cornforth, D. (2017). Multilingual sentiment analysis: From formal to informal and scarce resource languages. *Artificial Intelligence Review*, *48*(4), 499–527. doi:10.100710462-016-9508-4

Luo, N., Deng, H., Zhao, L., Liu, Y., Wang, X., & Tan, Z. (2017, July). Multi-aspect Feature based Neural Network Model in Detecting Fake Reviews. In *2017 4th International Conference on Information Science and Control Engineering (ICISCE)* (pp. 475-479). IEEE. 10.1109/ICISCE.2017.106

Maynard, D., Bontcheva, K., & Rout, D. (2012). Challenges in developing opinion mining tools for social media. *Proceedings of the@ NLP can u tag# usergeneratedcontent*, 15-22.

Ott, M., Choi, Y., Cardie, C., & Hancock, J. T. (2011, June). Finding deceptive opinion spam by any stretch of the imagination. In *Proceedings of the 49th Annual Meeting of the Association for Computational Linguistics: Human Language Technologies-Volume 1* (pp. 309-319). Association for Computational Linguistics.

Pawlak, Z. (1982). Rough sets. *International Journal of Computer & Information Sciences, 11*(5), 341-356.

Penalver-Martinez, I., Garcia-Sanchez, F., Valencia-Garcia, R., Rodriguez-Garcia, M. A., Moreno, V., Fraga, A., & Sanchez-Cervantes, J. L. (2014). Feature-based opinion mining through ontologies. *Expert Systems with Applications, 41*(13), 5995-6008.

Peng, Q., & Zhong, M. (2014). Detecting Spam Review through Sentiment Analysis. *JSW, 9*(8), 2065–2072. doi:10.4304/jsw.9.8.2065-2072

Pham, H. T., Vu, T. T., Tran, M. V., & Ha, Q. T. (2011, December). A solution for grouping Vietnamese synonym feature words in product reviews. In *Services Computing Conference (APSCC), 2011 IEEE Asia-Pacific* (pp. 503-508). IEEE. 10.1109/APSCC.2011.48

Reyes, A., Rosso, P., & Veale, T. (2013). A multidimensional approach for detecting irony in Twitter. *Language Resources and Evaluation, 47*(1), 239–268. doi:10.100710579-012-9196-x

Shehnepoor, S., Salehi, M., Farahbakhsh, R., & Crespi, N. (2017). NetSpam: A network-based spam detection framework for reviews in online social media. *IEEE Transactions on Information Forensics and Security, 12*(7), 1585–1595. doi:10.1109/TIFS.2017.2675361

Singh, M., Kumar, L., & Sinha, S. (2018). Model for Detecting Fake or Spam Reviews. In *ICT Based Innovations* (pp. 213–217). Singapore: Springer. doi:10.1007/978-981-10-6602-3_21

Stavrianou & Chauchat.(2008). *Opinion Mining Issues and Agreement Identification in Forum Texts.* Academic Press.

Yang, C. C., & Wong, Y. C. (2008, May). Mining Consumer Opinions from the Web. In WEBSITE (2) (pp. 187-192). Academic Press.

Yang, J., & Hou, M. (2010). Using Topic Sentiment Sentences to Recognize Sentiment Polarity in Chinese Reviews. *CIPS-SIGHAN Joint Conference on Chinese Language Processing.*

Zhai, Z., Liu, B., Xu, H., & Jia, P. (2010, August). Grouping product features using semi-supervised learning with soft-constraints. In *Proceedings of the 23rd International Conference on Computational Linguistics* (pp. 1272-1280). Association for Computational Linguistics.

Zhang, L., & Liu, B. (2011, June). Identifying noun product features that imply opinions. In *Proceedings of the 49th Annual Meeting of the Association for Computational Linguistics: Human Language Technologies: short papers-Volume 2* (pp. 575-580). Association for Computational Linguistics.

This research was previously published in Extracting Knowledge From Opinion Mining; pages 283-297, copyright year 2019 by Engineering Science Reference (an imprint of IGI Global).

Chapter 82
Feature Based Opinion Mining

Mridula Batra

Manav Rachna International Institute of Research and Studies, India

Vishaw Jyoti

Manav Rachna International Institute of Research and Studies, India

ABSTRACT

Opinion mining is the estimated learning of user's beliefs, evaluation and sentiments about units, actions and its features. This method has several features matched with data mining techniques, language processing methods and feature oriented data abstraction. This seems to be extremely difficult to mine opinions from analysis those exist in common human used language. Views are very essentials when one desires to construct a judgment. Data abstraction is an important characteristic for decision making applicable to individuals and organization of different nature. While selecting and purchasing a particular product, it is always beneficial for an individual to collect other views for correct decision making. One association wants to conduct surveys and gather opinions to develop their product excellence. Internet as a source of information, having a number of websites available with the customer reviews as a number of products, it is easy to extract the features from these opinions, sentiments and view, is a task comes under feature-based opinion mining.

INTRODUCTION

Web is playing an important role in advertising information regarding products. Web sites are also used by the consumers to express their views related to a product. Customer can say what they think (positive/negative) about the product. It is a good medium to collect consumer feedback, reviews and comments. These costumer responses in the form of reviews and comments are very useful as information that can be further utilized as a base for future analysis of product sales and revenue. The common example is hotel booking, an online customer can check the reviews for setting his sentiments regarding the preference of the hotel likely to be booked.

DOI: 10.4018/978-1-6684-6303-1.ch082

Therefore customer is utilizing large number of information available on the net (in form of reviews and comments) to improve their decision making process for example in their hotel booking. This is also called as Sentiment analysis. The various web application works on client opinion. Generally, it is seen that a web application approach to the customer is according to its area of interest. This is mined on the basis of customer reviews blogs and search on the internet.This help to analyze customer's inclination on a particular product choice.

Opinion mining process has three basic components

1. **Customer or Opinion Holder:** The customer is the person who has his own view related to a particular object and has the power to communicate those views and opinions.
2. **Product:** An object like goods and services about which views can be formed.
3. **Opinion:** These are views or thoughts or sentiments on an object given by the customer.

For marketing view point, selling the product on the internet with the help of the websites are largely influenced by the sentiments of the customer expressed in the form of reviews. Generally sentiments are related to less cost of the product and good opinion given the other customers on the same products because it is human behavior that people always try to know other people's thoughts and opinions before drawing any conclusion. It is often seen that most of the businesses try to collect and analyze customer reviews regarding their goods and services and try to enhance or modify them as per the customer need e.g. In restaurants individual's reviews in relation to food quality taste and services are collected to enhance the performance . Consumer opinions about the object can be either positive or negative which is referred as the sentiment orientation or the polarity of the sentiment. The internet is utilized for large amount of review collection and to develop the review database. These reviews act as a foundation for decision making.

Feature based opinion mining is the process of extracting the relevant information regarding the product and the services e.g., website of Trivago does the feature based opinion mining; they collect the reviews of various hotel booking and then extract the relevant hotel list that meets the customer satisfaction. There are two basic methods of opinion mining

1. **Direct Opinion:** This method has no comparison value. The subjective opinions on the products are given by the customers and these opinions are evaluated to check the worth of the product.
2. **Comparison Opinion:** This method is largely used in advertising industry. Here the objective opinions are taken related to the product and compared for relative analysis and then these opinions are used for the further promotion of the product.

The expensive utilization of opinion mining is in online sales of products, goods and services. This single platform can provide customers with a large variety of products having reasonable prices and interesting offers and discounts. But with the passage of time competition with the websites are increased due to almost having same kind of product and services. Now the opinion of individual customers is valuable for promotion and sales. As no professional staff assistance is provided for appropriate selection, this sentimental analysis plays a vital role. Every online sale has a platform for customer reviews and rating that will help future customers for buying. The challenge is that the most of the reviews are opaque and it is hard to be believed by the customer. So, the best methods to evaluate these reviews are feature based opinion mining or sentiment analysis.

The process can be initiated as follows:

1. Find the feature of the product depends upon its nature for e.g. for clothes the feature will be type of fabric, style, length etc. The feature should be written correctively in word phrases. It should be not expressed in sentence form.
2. Collect the reviews of the customer on the product. Reviews expressed can be subjective or objective
3. For feature extra.ction, from the customer reviews extract the feature word for negative and positive opinion.
4. Next step is to find the polarity of the feature. The feature can be positively inclined related to opinion or it can be negatively inclined.
5. The formation of feature opinion pairing will be done.
6. Then feature based clustering is used for handling the customer's sentiments for sales of the product.

Hence feature based opinion mining method would be used to mine the customer's knowledge by evaluating their reviews on products and then focusing on making opinion profiles for each products, that can be used for product evaluation and comparison with similar products . This leads to ultimate increase in the brand value of the product.

Extract of the information from the opinions is the key issue because from the subjective opinions key feature of the product is extracted. Product feature extraction is an important task of review mining and summarization. Generally, these kinds of tasks are carried out with the help of text feature extraction.

Applications of Feature Based Opinion Mining

1. **Customer Reviews:** Sentiment analyses analyze the user's opinion data, this analysis is based on one of the three levels: (a) Document Level, (b) Sentence Level, and (c) Attribute Level:
    a. **Document Level:** At this level, customer's review can be positive or negative. The problem of this level is that the complete review is based on a single topic. At this level single review is not considered on multiple topics. This level focuses on opinion sentence polarity identification. This method forecasts the direction of an opinion sentence. For example: "This is not good phone" This sentence holds opinion word 'good' which communicates positive opinion. But sentence communicates negative opinion since there is negation word 'not'. So when opinion word polarity identification is found, it is essential to locate polarity of opinion sentence. For opinion sentence polarity identification a list of negation words such as 'no', 'not' etc. can be set and negation policy can be created.
    b. **Sentence Level:** At this level, customer's review can be positive, negative or neutral. In neutral review no opinion and unrelated words are considered. The categorization of chore at this level can be subjective or objective. Objective sentences describe accurate information while subjective sentences describe slanted opinions. This level focuses on opinion word polarity identification method. In this method significant direction of each opinion word is identified, which means it has to be identified whether opinion word is describing positive, negative of neutral opinion.
    c. **Attribute Level:** The above two levels do not represent the exact linking of the people. It describes the fact that user can express his or her opinion on a particular feature. This level focuses on product feature extraction method of customer review. In feature extraction method,

product features are taken out from every sentence. These are basically nouns that are why every noun is taken out from sentence. In review, features can be referred unambiguously or absolutely by the reviewer. Features which are referred in a sentence directly are called as explicit features and features which are referred indirectly are called implicit features. For example, "Battery Life of a phone is less" In this sentence reviewer has pointed out battery life directly so it is explicit feature. It is easy to extract such features. Now consider following sentence, "This phone needs to charge many times in a day" In sentence reviewer is talking about battery of phone but it is not mentioned directly in the sentence. So here battery is implicit feature. It is difficult to understand and extract such features from sentence (Mishra & Jha, 2012). Product feature extraction method has two approaches: Supervised and Unsupervised. The Supervised product feature extraction approach needs a set of preannotated review sentences as training examples (Mishra & Jha, 2012). A supervised learning approach is useful to create an extraction model, which is able to identify product features from new consumer reviews. The supervised approach is practically useful in organizing training examples but this approach is time consuming. The Unsupervised approach repeatedly pulls outs product featured from consumer reviewers without concerning training examples.

2. **Shopping:** Feature based opinion mining is also applied in online shopping. With the fast growth of e-commerce platform, online shopping on the products has improved. Many online shopping websites gives permission to users to react or give their opinion on products. A customer can see the analysis of the product and judge against its features. If the review is mined and result is available in pictorial representation so there will be an ease for the customer to compare its features. Towards the huge variety of products and suitable shopping practice with smart offers, these podiums have become admired for customers and manufacturers but it is very difficult for the customers to acquire the help from the specialized sales personnel to purchase the product. One approach is used to overcome this problem is that merchant provides meta data for products which are sold online. Merchants have prepared a forum which assists the customers to find out the reviews of the product and expresses their opinions about the product, but there are hundred reviews are available for a particular product, so it is difficult to find out to read every customer's review and take the decision on purchasing the product and if customer reads only some reviews and take the decision on those reviews then it will be biased.

3. **Entertainment:** This opinion mining technique is also applied in entertainment. A database named Internet Movie Database which provides the review about movies or television show. This is an online database; this site facilitates registered users to offer new objects and edits to existing opening. However, most of the data is checked, especially if it is submitted by new users, there may be errors in the system. Users with a confirmed track record of submitting realistic data are given immediate sanction for slight add-ons. Users can also give rating to any film on a scale of 1 to 10, and the totals are changed into a weighted mean-rating that is displayed next to each title.

4. **Government:** Government can also take the opinions or reviews of public on their public policies. Public policies are mined online and the online feedback of the general public can be taken against the existing of new policies. Discussions about the bang of public opinion on public policy are planned about what should be there and what is there. Each and everyone have the same point of view that in a democracy public policy should be sturdily exaggerated by public opinion.

5. **Research and Development:** Customers also give their reviews on the features of product which is beneficial for the manufacturer and research and development department, so that R & D department can improve the features of their product.

6. **Education:** Now a day's tutorials or study materials are available on line, known as e-learning. This is very popular amongst students and they use it very frequently. Students also give their opinions or reviews about that study material which is very helpful to improve that service.

7. **Business and Organization:** In the current scenario, businesses spend a large amount of funds to find out consumer's sentiments and reviews. They hire consultants and take the surveys of a particular group of people to find out the opinion of their product so that they can improve their products. This is known as product and service benchmarking and market intelligence. Opinion mining tools permit businesses to take customer's reactions on large scale.

8. **Individuals:** An individual opinion's matters a lot in every field whether it is purchasing a product or using a service of any company and it is also considered on political issues.

9. **Ads Placement:** An advertisement of a product is placed in user-generated content to take the review or opinion of the feature of the product. An advertisement is also placed online when one customer admires or appreciates the product and if a competitor criticizes the product then also advertisement is formed, with fast expansion of user-generated content on the internet symbolized by blogs; Wikipedia's etc. opinion mining tools examine the web data.

Model/Architecture of Feature Based Opinion Mining

Our motivation is to build a model for feature based opinion mining. In this model customer's reviews will be gathered and the features from these reviews will be extracted and refined in another level of the model these features will be classified and ranked for their polarity. Figure 1 represents the proposed model.

The various parts of this model are:

1. **View Collection:** Various opinions from customers are both subjective and objective in nature. Subjective opinions and views are generated from feedbacks, opinions and emotional statements. Objective views are fact based. They provide the concise information regarding object. A systematic method will be used to classify subjective and objective opinions. The opinion first required to be divided into tokens and these tokens can be analyzed for classification. Data base is prepared from these views.

2. **View Refinement:** Opinion can be wanted or unwanted, so opinions are refined for the next level. During data refining process unwanted and non-satisfactory statements or phrases will be eliminated. The preprocessing of the opinions will help to recover the accurate and the relevant opinions.

3. **Feature and Opinion Extraction:** During this phase each opinion is analyzed for finding a feature in the view. Generally, Noun and Noun phrases of opinions are used to find the valuable feature. Each feature has valuable information given by the customer for the product.

4. **Feature Classification:** After the feature extraction process a list of features are prepared. these features are further classified as characteristic set and word set for rating these features. These features list are further passed from a parser to categories them into positive feature and negative feature.

5. **Score Allocation:** For each negative and positive feature quantitative value is assigned to calculate the orientation or the inclination of the opinion. A priority score is assigned to each positive feature to polarize an opinion for future decision making.

6. **Summary of Feature Set:** At the final stage of this model a list of finalized opinion words with their score and polarity will be generated.

7. **Performance Evaluation:** The performance of these opinions will then have evaluated. These reviews are required to be interpreted for their negative and positive polarity with the help of certain parameters. These parameters are accuracy and precision. Accuracy is the degree to which opinion will be helpful in decision making. Precision is the correctness of the opinion. Sometimes an opinion can be defined with negative polarity where it can be used for positive polarity. The change in the polarity can affect decision making. The rating mechanism will help to quantize feature polarity. The correctness of opinion is required for feature based opinion mining.

Figure 1. Architecture of feature based opinion mining

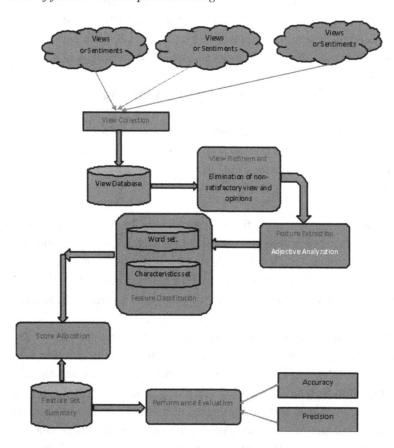

Mining Classifications of Feature Based Opinion Mining

Feature based Opinion mining trails the outlook, thoughts or review of the community about a specific matter, goods or service. The all kind of information available in the whole world of internet can be divided into two categories of reviews and numerical figures that can represent factual data.

The numerical and statistical data are used to represent real world entities and their characteristics where, reviews are textual data and this terminology is used to represent people's or consumer's reviews, sentiments for the different characteristics of real world objects. According to the latest scenario, it is assumed through the engines that the statistical data are accurate and can be combined with key features or key adjectives whereas while searching data with the help of search engines opinions are not a good choice because depending on opinions with key features make the searchers complicated, so their ranking approaches are not correct or opinion reclamation. Currently the web has drastically altered its mode on public comments and their reviews on goods and services. Consumers use websites and other mechanisms of internet like blogs and forums to give their views and sentiments about goods and services provided by the producer. This opinion database generated by user holds useful information that helps in decision making. Such website remarks are not partial but these are prolonged on worldwide level. Now a day, if the consumer needs the opinion of a specific product then his/ her circle is not limited as he/she can receive the view of that product on the internet throughout assorted assessment or remarks. Feature based opinion mining has many reasons for someone else to react angrily or emotionally. The number one issue required to cater is, in some cases reviews are treated in favor while in another case it is treated as negative. The second issue is that people do not affirm the opinions in a similar mode for all time. The assessment of opinion can be made in two ways:

1. **Direct Opinion:** It provides positive or negative view about the product directly. For example, "The speed of 2G is slow", articulates a direct opinion.
2. **Comparison:** It compares the product with some other alike product. For example, "The speed of 4 G is better than 2 G and 3 G", this describes a comparison.

Feature based opinion mining can be classified on various mining techniques:

1. **Text review and Fact Review Analyzing:** A customer can give both subjective and objective reviews. Prejudiced stuffs characterize customer's view, feelings, reactions etc. and objective contents reveals realistic information. So, the aim of subjectivity/objectivity categorization is to limit needless objective transcript from further processing. For that reason, every assessed text statement is symbolized into noun and noun phrases, after dividing text statements a process is applied to extract the adjective words from these statements and sentences in order to classify between subjective opinions and objective opinions. To set up the effectiveness of the known features for subjectivity purpose, a variety of important classifiers are defined such as Naive Bayes etc.
2. **Feature and Opinion Learning Techniques:** This component is developing of a variety of perspectives for information module (includes feature, modifier, and view) pulling out from subjective analysis sentences pulled out in the preceding pace. For one perspective, the feature mining procedures are instigated through the help of a numerical parser and progressed by a predefined rules mechanism to recognize applicant information modules in supplementary investigation. Additionally, a variety of opinions information are missing because of non availability of noun and

noun phrases pairs at sentence level. So, for one more perspective, a review mechanism has offered in order to recognize words that are already referred in previous text which are applicable precursor which subsists in earlier sentences to requisite feature-opinion pairs. Both the perspectives are standard and are implemented on analysis phrases which affects to other goods and services field and there is no earlier information is not required to recognize the product features and customer's opinions articulated over them.

3. **Sentimental Analyzing:** In accumulation to the mining of feature-opinion pairs from assessment credentials, one further vital chore linked with the growth of a relevant feature extracting system in order to categorize emotion that may be in support, against or having no emotions in the reviews. Opinion based databases acts as source of information. A sentimental parser is prepared having predefined rules that is capable of classifying positive and negative reviews from the sentence phrases by the customers. This classification is useful to establish the emotions of prejudiced words maintained after viability investigation.

4. **Feasibility Analyzing:** Throughout information module pulling out phase, various nouns, verbs and adjectives are taken out which are not pertinent product features, modifiers, and opinions. Also, anaphora antecedent binding caused noisy feature-opinion pairs extractions that are not relevant for feature-opinion binding task. In line with Agrawal and Batra (2013), feasibility analysis technique is applied to eliminate noisy feature-opinion pairs based on reliability scores generated through a customized version HITS algorithm, which molds feature-opinion pairs and evaluate article as a bipartite graph which considers feature opinion pairs as core and appraisal credentials as establishment. A superior score value of a pair reproduces a stretched veracity of the two modules in a pair. This score decides the amount of consistency of an opinion uttered over a product feature.

The responsibility of estimation withdrawal is in the direction of discovering the view of an entity that may be in favor or no favor and the characteristics it portrays, characteristics are appreciated etc. The mechanism of an opinion is:

- **Opinion Holder:** Opinion holder is a person who provides a precise view on an entity.
- **Object:** Object is article, by an opinion is articulated by consumer
- **Opinion:** This is a vision, emotion, or assessment of an entity done by consumer.

Pictorial Representation of Mining Techniques

The mining at different levels have different features to be evaluated and summary is generated for future references and help in decision making. All these mining techniques can be combined to form a process to refine the feature set and further enhance the decision-making process.

Responsibilities of Opinion Mining at Manuscript Stage

This estimation withdrawal categorizes on whole estimation obtainable via creators in complete manuscript since in favor, no favor or having no views regarding definite entity. Statement in use at manuscript stage be to facilitate every manuscript states about solitary entity and holds the estimation of a single estimation owner. Some author states vocation support on remoteness assess of characteristics originated in entire manuscript which recognized the division that is outstanding or poor. The author gives the description of algorithm having three stages i.e. First stage describes that characteristics are taken out by the side of an expression that presents suitable information. Another stage describes that, the literal meaning direction be confined via calculating remoteness as of expressions of recognized division. The last stage, the pseudo code calculates the regular literal course of every expression which organizes an appraisal since suggested or not.

Figure 2. Pictorial representations of mining techniques

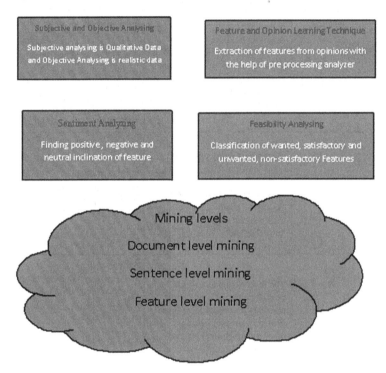

Responsibilities of Opinion Mining at Ruling Stage

This stage of estimation withdrawal is having two responsibilities. The very first responsibility investigates about the existing task whether it is subjective or objective. The second task discovers view of dogmatic verdict may be in favor, no favor or having no review. Supposition can be considered at ruling stage be so as to verdict holds merely single view e.g., "The speed of 2G is slow."

Responsibilities of Opinion Mining at Characteristic Stage

The task of opinion mining at feature level is to extract the features of the observation object and thereafter conclude the opinion of the object, it can be positive or negative and then cluster the feature synonyms and creates the outline description. To recognize the direction of opinion the lexicon based approach is used. This loom utilizes opinion words and phrase in a sentence to decide the view. The working of lexicon based approach is explained in following steps

- Identification of opinion words
- Role of Negation words
- But –clauses (Mishra & Jha, 2012)

Table 1. Responsibilities of opinion mining at various stages

Categorization of Opinion mining at various stages	Hypothesis of Opinion mining at various stages	Responsibilities at various stages
Opinion Mining at Ruling Stage	A verdict holds just single view placed via one estimation owner; that may not be accurate in some situations. The ruling edge is clear in the certain manuscript.	Responsibility 1: recognize the particular verdict as prejudiced or intolerant module: objective and Intolerant. Responsibility 2: View categorization of the specified verdict. module: optimistic Unconstructive and unbiased.
Opinion Mining at Manuscript stage	Every manuscript has a focal point on a solitary entity and holds view placed by a solitary view owner. This is not appropriate for discussion position because there may be several views of numerous substances of these basis.	Responsibility 1: view categorization of evaluation module: optimistic Unconstructive and unbiased.
Opinion Mining at Characteristic stage	The facts have a focal point on characteristics of a sole entity placed by a solitary view owner. This is not appropriate for discussion position because there may be several views of numerous substances of these basis.	Responsibility 1: Recognize and pull out entity characteristics which have been remarked via a view owner. Responsibility 2: module: optimistic Unconstructive and unbiased. Responsibility 3: Cluster characteristic synonyms. create a feature- based opinion synopsis of several evaluations.

(Mishra & Jha, 2012)

Algorithm of Feature Based Opinion Mining

The Algorithm for feature based opinion mining is divided in to two phases:

- **Phase 1**: This phase will identify the important reviews. The algorithm is called as High Noun and Noun Phrase Count Algorithm (HNNPC). In this phase the algorithm will check the noun and noun phrase associated with it. If any noun has a noun phrase then its adjective is collected and the count of feature will be increased by one. High count features will be passed in to phase two for priority assignment. The steps of algorithm are:
  - **Step 1:** Start
  - **Step 2:** Read Review

- ○ **Step 3:** Set Score _count to zero.
- ○ **Step 4:** For complete sentence of review do
  - ▪ Scan Noun and Noun Phrase.
  - ▪ If Noun and Noun Phrase pair is found
  - ▪ Then increase Score _count by 1.
- ○ **Step 5:** For Each objective review do
  - ▪ Scan a factual value associated with objective.
  - ▪ If numeric value is found then increase Score _count by 1.
- ○ **Step 6:** Save the Score _count and pass it to phase two.
- **Phase 2:** This phase is used to allocate the priority of the feature. This algorithm is called as Priority Allocation algorithm. The score _count value from the phase one is received and then further priority is assigned. For each feature word assign a priority between values of -5 to +5. A negative priority indicates Negative view, zero priority indicates neural opinion and a positive priority indicates positive view that can be further used as valuable source for decision making. The steps of this algorithm are:
  - ○ **Step 1:** Receive score _count from phase 1.
  - ○ **Step 2:** Receive the feature list.
  - ○ **Step 3:** If score _count is less than thresh hold values than allocate a negative priority to the feature word and go to step 6.
  - ○ **Step 4:** If score _count is zero then feature is neutral and no priority will be assigned to the feature word and go to step 6.
  - ○ **Step 5:** If score _count is more than thresh hold values than allocate a positive priority to the feature word and go to step 6.
  - ○ **Step 6:** Repeat step 3 to 5 until feature list is empty.
  - ○ **Step 7:** Receive refined feature list for decision making.
  - ○ **Step 8:** Stop.

This algorithm is future evaluated on a number of parameters for feature evaluation. These parameters are precision and accuracy. The main difference between feature extraction algorithm and simple word count algorithm is that a weight is assigned to each feature word to as priority for further analysis and evaluation.

Applications of Opinion Mining in Web Text Mining

Estimation withdrawal engages content withdrawal and verbal communication and content categorization. Content withdrawal conquers the existing insufficiency. Unluckily, natural language processing come across a variety of complexity because of complicated personality of individual speech. in addition, the region of estimation withdrawal includes trouble of content categorization, that is entirely dissimilar to the standard content withdrawal. Standard content categorization recognizes subject, while in estimation withdrawal, reaction categorization is made that has the focal point of reviewing author's emotions in the direction of the subject matter. Sentiments are not adequately examined with keyword based techniques. Text mining procedures shapeless information, it takes out significant numeric indices from the text, and constructs the information enclosed in the text available to a variety of data mining algorithms. Information can be taken out from the recapitulated terms of the credentials, so the terms can be investigated and also the resemblance between terms and credentials can be determined. On the whole, text mining translates text into statistics that can be incorporated in other study like predictive data mining projects, clustering etc. Text mining is also recognized as text data mining, which submits the procedure of developing superiority information from text. Superiority information is consequent during the statistical pattern learning. Text mining involves the procedure of organizing the input text like parsing and other successive insertion into a database. It derives patterns within the structured data, calculates them and lastly creates the output. It takes explanation of text classification, text clustering, sentiment analysis, document summarization, and entity relation modeling. Text mining is a procedure that utilizes a set of algorithms for adapting unstructured text into structured data objects and the quantitative methods used to analyze these data objects.

Applications of Text Mining

There are a variety of applications of Text mining like default dispensation of messages and emails. For example, it is probable to "clean" out automatically "junk email" on the basis affirms conditions; those messages are repeatedly removed. These default schemes for organizing electronic messages can too be helpful in applications when messages are required to be running automatically to the most suitable section.

Analyzing warranty or insurance claims, diagnostic interviews. In some business domains, the major information is composed in textual form. For example, guarantee asserts or preliminary medical (patient) discussions can be sum up in concise narratives needs to be fixed responses. Ever more, such comments are composed electronically; therefore, such kinds of narratives are voluntarily accessible for input into text mining algorithms.

Analyzing open-ended survey responses. Survey feedback form holds two categories of questions: open -ended and closed-ended. Closed-ended questions describe a distinct set of reactions from which to choose. Such kinds of reactions are simply measured and evaluated but open -ended questions permits the respondent to answer a question in his own words. These kinds of unstructured responses frequently offer comfortable and appreciated information than closed-ended questions.

Web Mining

Now a day, huge amount of data is accessible on web so, WWW is known as usual region for data mining. This study is having the turning point of study from numerous research societies like database, information retrieval, and Artificial Intelligence.

As web acquaintance is sprinkled and because of absence of any standardized format, web mining is a not an easy job to engage any issues.

This is the procedure of pertaining data mining methodologies for finding out prototypes from the Web. Web mining is alienated into three diverse types, these are Web usage mining, Web content mining and Web structure mining.

1. **Web Usage Mining:** This is the procedure of determining the user's perspective that he needs to observe on the Internet. Several customers are fascinated in textual data but some are interested to explore multimedia data. This is completed by making use of user logs.
2. **Web Structure Mining:** This is the procedure of taking out information from web pages by giving focus on the formation. Web structure mining is alienated into two types:

a. **Extracting Patterns From Hyperlinks in the Web:** A hyper link is a structural module which attaches the web page to a diverse place.

b. **Mining the Document Structure:** In this type the tree-like structure of page formation to portray HTML or XML tag custom is evaluated.

3. **Web Content Mining:** This procedure aspires to pull out practical information from contents of the web page. It engages scrutinizing of every content on a web page to discover its significance with the investigated inquiry.

Terminologies

- **Text Mining vs. Data Mining:** In Text Mining, prototypes are taken out from natural language text but in Data Mining prototypes are taken out from databases.
- **Text Mining vs. Web Mining:** In Text Mining, the participation is amorphous text, but in Web Mining web foundations are prearranged. (Rashmi Agrawal and Mridula Batra, 2013)

Figure 3. Web Mining Categories (Seerat, 2012)

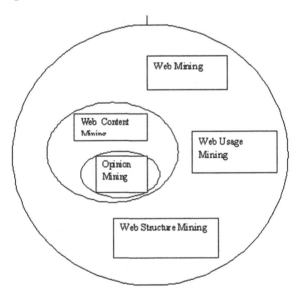

The major applications of Opinion mining and sentiment analysis in web text mining are the following:

1. **Purchasing Product or Service:** When a customer is buying a product, then taking accurate choice is not hard chore. Through this method, users can effortless class other's views and have knowledge about any product or service and too he/she can simply evaluate the rival brands because every data is available on the web and customers give their feedback on the web about the product. So, there is no need for the users to depend on outside advisor. The Opinion mining and pulls out public opinion form the internet and examines it and then offers to them in planned and comprehensible mode.

2. **Quality Improvement in Product or Service:** By this technique of feature-based opinion mining, the producer can gather the opponent's estimation and constructive view about their manufacturing goods and so they can enhance the quality of their product. They can create use online product evaluation from websites such as Amazon and CNet, etc.

3. **Marketing Research:** The outcome of sentiment analysis methods can be employed in marketing research. By this method, the current inclination of customers regarding some product can be studied. Likewise, the current approach of common public towards some new government policy can also be simply studied. So, the entire consequences can be added to combine intellectual study.

4. **Recommendation Systems:** By giving or filling the feedback forms of the product on line the user's view can be found positive or negative about the product, this scheme can easily find out which one ought to be suggested and which one ought not to be suggested.

5. **Detection of "Flame":** The observations of newsgroups, blogs and social media are simply probable by opinion mining. Opinion mining can notice egotistical terms over intense words or abhorrence speech used in emails or tweets on different internet resources by default.

6. **Opinion Spam Detection:** As internet is accessible to everyone, so anybody can place everything on internet, this amplified the opportunity of spam content on the web. People can write down spam content to deceive the public. Opinion mining can categorize the internet content into' spam' content and 'not spam' content.

7. **Policy Making:** During Opinion Mining, strategy creator may take people's point of view regarding some policy and they can use this information in generating new public forthcoming policy.

8. **Decision Making:** User's views and skills are very helpful ingredients in decision making procedure. Opinion mining provides examined people's judgment which can be successfully adopted for decision making. (Rahmath, 2014)

CONCLUSION

Opinion mining is a valuable task now a day. Due to increase in market competition among the producers of goods and services, mining of customer interest can improve in sales and generation of profits. Feature based opinion mining is an efficient tool for extracting customer interest. To extract this information, it is required to mine the customer's reviews on products. From theses reviews the adjective words are mined to find the inclination of the customer towards the product. The websites and internet has played a great role in review generation. In current market maximum product sale is on line and it increases the capture of global market for each individual manufacturer easily. The process starts from collecting the objective and subjective reviews of the customer given for the similar nature of the products. These reviews are classified in to separate list of characteristic set and word set, where characteristic set belongs to objective features and word set is belongs to subjective features. From this word set the adjective words are identified. A score is assigned to each feature. Then theses reviews are pre-processed for feature extraction. These features can have negative polarity or positive polarity. Positive polarity features are valuable to increase product sale and to improve the market competition among the producers. Feature extraction opinion mining can be used in some number applications ranges from product production to marketing and sales. This technique is also an area of research for researchers to further improve the web mining contents.

REFERENCES

Agrawal, R., & Batra, M. (2013). A detailed study on text mining techniques. *International Journal of Soft Computing and Engineering, 2*(6), 118–121.

Mishra, N., & Jha, C. K. (2012). Classification of opinion mining techniques. *International Journal of Computers and Applications, 56*(13).

Rahmath, H. (2014). Opinion mining and sentiment analysis-challenges and applications. *International Journal of Application or Innovation in Engineering & Management, 3*(5).

ADDITIONAL READING

Ding, X., & Liu, B. (2008). A holistic lexicon-based approach to opinion mining. In *Proceedings of the International Conference on Web Search and Web Data Mining, WSDM'08* (pp. 231–240). 10.1145/1341531.1341561

Guo, H., & Zhu, H. (2009). Address standardization with latent semantic association. In *Proceedings of the 15th ACM SIGKDD International Conference on Knowledge Discovery and Data Mining* (pp. 1155–1164). ACM.

Hu, M., & Liu, B. (2004). Mining opinion features in customer reviews. In *Proceedings of the 19th National Conference on Artificial Intelligence AAAI'04* (pp. 755–760).

Kim, S.-M., & Hovy, E. (2004). Determining the sentiment of opinions. In *Proceedings of the 20th International Conference on Computational Linguistics COLING'04.* 10.3115/1220355.1220555

Liu, B., & Cheng, J. (2005), Opinion observer: Analyzing and comparing opinions on the web. In *Proceedings of the 14th International Conference on World Wide Web, WWW'05* (pp. 342–351). 10.1145/1060745.1060797

Meena, A., & Prabhakar, T. V. (2007). Sentence level sentiment analysis in the presence of conjuncts using linguistic analysis. In *Proceedings of the 29th European Conference on IR Research, ECIR'07.* 10.1007/978-3-540-71496-5_53

Miao, Q., & Li, Q. (2008), An integration strategy for mining product features and opinions. In *Proceeding of the 17th ACM Conference on Information and Knowledge Management, CIKM'08* (pp. 1369-1370). 10.1145/1458082.1458284

Mishra, N., & Jha, C. K. (2012). An insight into task of opinion mining. In *Second International Joint Conference on Advances in Signal Processing and Information Technology – SPIT.*

Nasukawa, T., & Yi, J. (2003), Sentiment analysis: Capturing favorability using natural language processing. In *Proceedings of the 2nd International Conference on Knowledge Capture K-CAP'03* (pp. 70-77).

Seerat, B., & Azam, F. (2012). Opinion Mining: Issues and Challenges (A survey). *International Journal of Computers and Applications, 49*(9).

Tian, P., Liu, Y., Liu, M., & Zhu, S. (2009, October). Research of product ranking technology based on opinion mining. In *Second International Conference on Intelligent Computation Technology and Automation ICICTA'09* (Vol. 4, pp. 239-243). IEEE.

Zhai, Z., & Liu, B. (2010). Grouping product features using semi-supervised learning with soft-constraints. In *Proceedings of the 23rd International Conference on Computational Linguistics, COLING'10* (pp. 1272–1280).

Zhang, W., & Yu, C. (2007), Opinion retrieval from blogs. In *Proceedings of the 16th ACM Conference on Conference on Information and Knowledge Management, CIKM'07* (pp. 831–840). 10.1145/1321440.1321555

Chapter 83
Impact of Deep Learning on Semantic Sentiment Analysis

Neha Gupta

https://orcid.org/0000-0003-0905-5457

Manav Rachna International Institute of Research and Studies, Faridabad, India

Rashmi Agrawal

https://orcid.org/0000-0003-2095-5069

Manav Rachna International Institute of Research and Studies, Faridabad, India

ABSTRACT

Online social media (forums, blogs, and social networks) are increasing explosively, and utilization of these new sources of information has become important. Semantics plays a significant role in accurate analysis of an emotion speech context. Adding to this area, the already advanced semantic technologies have proven to increase the precision of the tests. Deep learning has emerged as a prominent machine learning technique that learns multiple layers or data characteristics and delivers state-of-the-art output. Throughout recent years, deep learning has been widely used in the study of sentiments, along with the growth of deep learning in many other fields of use. This chapter will offer a description of deep learning and its application in the analysis of sentiments. This chapter will focus on the semantic orientation-based approaches for sentiment analysis. In this work, a semantically enhanced methodology for the annotation of sentiment polarity in Twitter/ Facebook data will be presented.

1. INTRODUCTION

1.1 Introduction to Deep Learning

G.E Hinton in 2006 proposed the concept of deep learning & was also the founder of the Deep Neural Network machine learning (Day & Lee, 2016). The human brain is influenced by the neural network and contains many neurons which make up an impressive network. Deep learning (DL) simulate the structure of the human brain hierarchically, processes data from the lower to the upper level and gradu-

DOI: 10.4018/978-1-6684-6303-1.ch083

ally produces more and more semantic concepts. In developing the technology of big data and artificial intelligence, deep learning has been increasingly explored as a machine learning paradigm. Deep learning networks can provide both supervised and unsupervised training (Vateekul & Koomsubha, 2016). The architecture of deep learning demonstrates maximum potential when dealing with different functions and involves large numbers of labeled samples to collect data across deep architectures. Deep learning networks and techniques are widely implemented in various fields such as visual recognition, pedestrian tracking, off-road robot navigation, category artifacts, acoustic signaling & in the prediction of time series (Arnold et.al, 2011). In natural language processing the dynamic multi-tasking, including syntactic and semantic labeling, can be highly performed using deep architectures.

1.2 Introduction to Sentiment Analysis

Opinions or ideals have become an essential component in making judgement or alternatives for people or businesses. The rapid boom of Web 2.0 over the last decade has improved online organizations and enabled humans to put up their reviews or evaluation on a variety of topics in public domains. This user-generated content (UGC) is an essential statistics supply to help clients make shopping decision, however also provided treasured insights for shops or manufacturers to enhance their marketing strategies and products (Pang & Lee, 2008) . Sentiment evaluation deals with the computational treatment of critiques expressed in written texts (Kalra & Agrawal, 2017) .In the era of Information explosion, there may be a huge quantity of opinionated statistics generated each day. These generated statistics leads to unstructured records and the analysis of these records to extract useful information is a hard to achieve task. The need to address these unstructured opinionated statistics naturally causes the upward push of sentiment analysis. The addition of already mature semantic technologies to this subject has increased the consequences accuracy. Evaluation of semantic of sentiments is precisely essential method in the internet now days. Discovering the exact sense and understanding in which a specific sentence was written on the net is very important as there might not be any physical interaction to discover the significance of the sentence. There are a number of techniques to classify the specified sentiment as bad or terrible. This categorization helps us honestly discover the context of a sentence remotely (Gupta & Verma, 2019). The crucial troubles in sentiment evaluation is to express the sentiments in texts and to check whether or not the expressions indicate superb (favorable) or negative (unfavorable) opinions toward the challenge and to evaluate the correctness of the sentences that are classified.

1.3 Sentiment Analysis and Deep Learning

Deep learning plays a major role in both unsupervised and supervised learning, and many researchers use deep learning to perform sentiment analysis. Deep learning model is comprised of numerous efficient and common models, which are used to effectively solve the various problems (Ouyang, 2015). The most prominent example of deep learning is used by Socher where he has used Recursive Neural Network (RNN) to analyze the sentiments in film reviews (Socher et.al, 2011). Following the efforts of (Mikolov, 2013), many researchers have carried out a sentiment classification using neural networks, for instance, Kalchbrenner (Kalchbrenner et.al, 2014) anticipated a complex DyCNN(Dynamic Convolution Neural network) that uses an activity of pooling, i.e., dynamic k-max pooling on linear sequences. Similarly, Kim (Kim, 2014) uses CNN to learn sentence vectors of sentiments.

The motivation of writing this chapter is to understand the concepts related to deep learning, sentiment analysis and the importance of semantic in sentiment analysis. The present chapter starts with introduction to deep learning, basic of ontologies and their relation to sentiment analysis. The chapter further discusses semantic ontologies with concept forms and their relationships along with steps to develop a baseline model for simple analysis of sentiment using NLP. At the end of the chapter case study related to the sentiment analysis using R programming on the protests for CAA and NRC in India during December 2019 has been presented. The corpus of the case study has been built by collecting related articles from the Times of India and other leading newspapers of the India. Real time data has been extracted from twitter by applying the most frequent words as hash tags. Finally sentiment analysis techniques have been applied on twitter data to know the opinions of the people of country on the issue of NRC and CAA protest.

2. ONTOLOGY AND THE SEMANTIC WEB

Today the Internet has become a critical human need. People depend heavily on the Internet for their day-to-day tasks. World Wide Web (WWW) has rapidly become a massive database with some information on all of the interesting things. Most of the web content is primarily designed for human read, computers can only decode layout web pages (Kaur & Agrawal, 2017). Machines generally lack the automated processing of data collected from any website without any knowledge of their semantics.

This has become a concern because users spend a great deal of time comparing multiple websites. Semantic Web provides a solution to this problem. Semantic web is defined as a collection of technologies that enable computers to understand the meaning of metadata based information, i.e., information about the information content. Web Semantic can be applied to integrate information from heterogeneous sources and improve the search process for improved and consistent information (Jalota & Agrawal, 2019). The Semantic technologies allow the ontology to refer to a metadata.

Ontology is a description of a domain knowledge that includes various terminologies of a given domain along with the relationship between existing terms.

Ontology is designed to act as metadata. Ontologies can help to create conceptual search and navigation of semantics for integration of semantically in-order feature. The language structures used to constructs ontologies include: XML, XML Schema, RDF, OWL, and RDF Scheme.

OWL has benefits over other structure languages in that OWL has more facilities to express meaning and semantic than XML and RDF / s. Ontologies built using RDF, OWL etc. are linked in a structured way to express semantic content explicitly and organize semantic boundaries for extracting concrete information (Kalra & Agrawal, 2019).

A semantic ontology can exists as an informal conceptual framework with concept forms and their relationships named and described, if at all, in natural language, Or it may be constructed as a formal semantic domain account, with concept types and systematically defined relationships in a logical language.

However, within the Web environment ontology is not merely a conceptual construct but a concrete, syntactic structure that models a domain's semantics – the conceptual framework – in a machine-understandable language (Gupta & Verma, 2019).

For the purpose of comprehensive and transportable machine understanding, the semantic web relies heavily on the structured ontologies that structure underlying data. Consequently, the performance of the semantic Web is highly dependent on the proliferation of ontology that requires quick and easy ontology engineering and the avoidance of a bottleneck of information gain (Pang & Lee, 2008). Conceptual structures which define the underlying ontology are German to the concept of machine processable data on the semantic Web. By identifying mutual and specific theories of the domain, ontology lets both people and machines interact precisely in order to facilitate semantic exchange. Ontology language editors aid in the development of semantic Web. Thus, the cheap and rapid creation of a domain-specific ontology is crucial to the semantic Web's success.

2.1 Limitations of Semantic Ontologies

Ontology helps in delivering solutions for database identification, end-to-end application authentication, authorization, data integrity, confidentiality, coordination and exchange of isolated pieces of information issues (Agrawal & Gupta, 2019). Some of the drawbacks of semantic ontologies are

1. Natural language parsers can function on only single statement at a particular time.
2. It is quite impossible to define the ontology limits of the abstract model of a given domain.
3. Automatic ontology creations, automatic ontology emergence to create new ontologies, and the identification of possible existing relationships between classes to automatically draw the taxonomy hierarchy are needed.
4. Ontology validators are limited and unable to verify all kinds of ontologies, e.g. validation of ontologies on the basis of complex inheritance relations.
5. Domain-specific ontologies are highly dependent on the application domain, and it is not possible to determine the general purpose ontologies from them because of this dependency.
6. The reengineering of semantic enrichment processes for web development consists of relational metadata, which must be built at high speed and low cost based on the abundance of ontologies, which is not currently possible (Agrawal & Gupta, 2019).

Because of these limitations in ontology, it is not currently possible for Semantic Web to achieve the actual objectives of completely structured information over the web in a computer process-able format and making advanced knowledge modeling framework.

3. NLP AND SENTIMENT ANALYSIS

Sentiment analysis (Pang and Lillian 2008) is a kind of text classification that is used to handle subjective statements. Natural language processing (NLP) is used to gather and study opinion or sentiment words. Determining subjective attitudes in big social data maybe a hotspot in the field of data mining and NLP (Hai et al. 2014). Makers are additionally intrigued to realize which highlights of their items are increasingly well known out in the open, so as to settle on profitable business choices. There is an immense archive of conclusion content accessible at different online sources as sites, gatherings, internet based life, audit sites and so forth. They are developing, with increasingly obstinate content poured in constantly. In the past, manual strategies are used to investigate millions of sentiments & reviews and aggregated them toward a quick and efficient decision making (Liu, 2006). Sentiment analysis strategies carry out the project via automated procedures with minimum or no consumer support. The datasets that are available online may also comprise of objective statements, which no longer make effective contributions in sentiment analysis. These Type of statements are usually segregated at pre-processing stage. Binary Classification can be used to recommend the outcome of sentiment analysis. It may be considered as a multi-class classification problem on a given scale of likeness. Because text is considered as a complex community of words which might be uniquely related to every sentiment therefore graph based definitely evaluation techniques are used for NLP tasks. Opinion mining involves NLP, to retrieve semantics from phrases and words of opinion. NLP will, however, have open problems that may be too challenging to be handled quickly and correctly up to date. Because sentiment analysis frequently uses NLP really well in large scale, it reflects this complicated behavior (Agrawal & Gupta, 2019). NLP's definitions for categorizing textual source material now don't fit with opinion mining, because they are different in nature. Documents with vastly disproportionate identical frequency of words do not always have the same polarity of sentiment. This is because, a fact can be either morally right or wrong in categorizing textual content, and is commonly accepted by all. Because of its subjective existence, a number of opinions may be incorrect about the same thing. Another distinction is that opinion mining is responsive to individual words, in which an unmarried word like NOT can change the meaning of the entire sentence. The transparent challenging conditions are prepositional phrases without the use of NOT words, derogatory and hypothetical sentences, etc. The latter section includes an in-depth overview of NLP problems surrounding the assessment of sentiments. The online resources consists of subjective content material having basic, composite, or complex sentences. Plain sentences have approximately one product's unmarried view, whereas complex sentences have multiple opinions on it (Agrawal & Gupta, 2019). Long sentences have an implied mean and are difficult to test. Standard assessments pertain only to an unmarried person, even though comparative articles have an object or a variety of its aspects examined as opposed to some other object. Comparative viewpoints may be either empirical or contextual. An example of a subjective comparison sentence is "Game X's visual effects are much better than game Y's," while an example of objective comparison expression is

"Game X has twice as many control options as that of Game Y". Opinion mining anticipates an assortment of sentence types, since individuals follow different composing styles so as to communicate in a superior manner.

Normally, conclusion examination for content information can be figured on a few levels, remembering for an individual sentence level, section level, or the whole archive in general. Frequently, notion is registered on the archive overall or a few collections are done subsequent to processing the supposition for singular sentences. There are two major approaches to sentiment analysis (Gupta & Verma, 2019).

- Supervised machine learning or deep learning approaches
- Unsupervised lexicon-based approaches

Usually we need pre-labeled facts for the first strategy, although we do not also have the luxury of a well-labeled training dataset in the second technique. We would therefore want to use unsupervised approaches to predict sentiment through the use of knowledge bases, ontologies, databases, and lexicons with distinctive details, primarily curated and prepared for analysis of sentiment. A lexicon is an encyclopedia, a wordbook or an e-book. Lexicons, in our case, are special dictionaries or vocabularies created to interpret sentiments (Gupta & Agrawal, 2020). Some of these lexicons provide a list of wonderful and terrible polar terms with a few grades aligned with them along with the use of different techniques such as the position of terms, phrases, meaning, sections of expression, phrases, and so on, .

Rankings are given to the text documents from which we need to determine the sentiments. After these scores have been aggregated we get the very last sentiment.

TextBlob, along with sentiment analysis, is an excellent open-supply repository for efficient working of NLP tasks. It is additionally a sentiment lexicon (in the form of an XML file) that enables to offer rankings of polarity as well as subjectivity. The polarity rating is a float inside the [-1.0, 1.0] range. The subjectivity is a float in the range [0.0, 1.0] where zero.0 could be very objective and 1.0 may be very subjective.

Following the trends of artificial intelligence, the number of programs built for the processing of natural languages is growing every day with aid of the day. NLP-developed applications would allow for a faster and more effective implementation of infrastructures to remove human strength in many jobs (Niazi & Hussain, 2009). The following are common examples of NLP applications

- Text Classification (Spam Detector etc)
- Sentiment Analysis & Predictions
- Author Recognition systems
- Machine Translation
- Chatbots

3.1 Steps to Develop a Baseline Model for Simple Analysis of Sentiment Using NLP

Following steps needs to be followed to develop a baseline model for analysis of sentiment using NLP. The implementation is in python with standard libraries and tools:

1. Identifcation of Dataset
2. Name of the data set: Sentiment Labelled Sentences Data Set
3. Source of data set: UCI Machine Learning Library
4. Basic Information about the data set: 4.This information kit was generated through a user analysis of 3 websites (Amazon, Yelp, Imdb). Such remarks include impressions of restaurants, movies and goods. Two separate emoticons appear in each record in the data set (PORIA & GELBUKH 2013). These are 1: good, 0: bad.
5. Creation of a model of sentiment analysis with the above-mentioned data.
6. Create a Python based Machine Learning model with the sklearn and nltk library.
7. Code writing by library imports. For instance:

```
import pandas as pnd
import numpy as nmp
import pickle
import sys
import os
import io
```

8. Now upload and view the data set. For Example:

```
input_file = "../data/amazon_cells_labelled.txt"
amazon = pnd.read_csv(input_file,delimiter='\t',header=None)
amazon.columns = ['Sentence','Class']
```

9. Statistical analysis of the data on the basis of following parameters.
    a.   Total Count of Each Category
    b.   Distribution of All Categories
10. For a very balanced dataset that is having almost equal number of positive and negative classes then pre processing the text by removing special characters, lower string, punctuations, email address, IP address, stop words etc
11. Data pre-cleaning makes the data inside the model ready for use..
12. Build the model by splitting the dataset to test (10%) and training(90%).
13. Test the model with test data and examine the accuracy, precision, recall and f1 results.
14. To test the accuracy of the calculations, create the confusion matrix. Link to plot a confusion matrix can be seen at

```
#source: https://www.kaggle.com/grfiv4/plot-a-confusion-matrix
```

4. SEMANTIC SEARCH ENGINE

Current keyword-based search engines such as Google can identify internet pages by matching correct tokens or words with tokens or words in internet content inside the consumer's query (Ye & Zang, 2009). There are many disadvantages to this method.

1. Tokens or tokens-like words inside the User Search shall not be taken into account when looking for net sites.
2. The key-word based search engine gives equal importance to all key phrases whereas consumers challenge them as they think of one category of keywords as important.
3. To get the correct applicable end result, customers might also also want to enter numerous synonyms on his very own to get the desired records which would possibly result into the omission of many treasured net pages.
4. Another trouble is of information overloading. The traditional keyword based absolute search engines like google make it very tedious for user to locate the useful facts from a massive list of search results.

To remedy the above mentioned problems that the customers face, Ontology based semantic steps were developed.

Ontology is primarily based on Semantic Search Engine that which recognizes the meaning of the consumer query and gives the results in a comparative sense.

It is not principally easy to return built-in keyword pages but also the pages which can be used to provide the means available by using the Ontological synonym dataset, created using WordNet, to enter keywords from the user. First the Ontology Synonym Collection uses WordNet and then invokes the provider. In addition, if the similarity is 100%, extra keywords are taken into account to provide the user with the appropriate and accurate results. Approximately the meta facts like URL is provided by the meta-processor.

Following are the components of a basic semantic search engine:

1. Development of Ontology: Ontology with. OWL or. DAML extensions are developed in plain text format.
2. Crawler for Ontology: Ontology crawler discovers new ontological content on the web and add it to the library of ontology.
3. Ontology notepad: It is used for the purpose of annotating and publishing web pages to ontologies.
4. Web Crawler: Crawls across the web to find Web pages annotated with ontologies and create knowledge base on Ontology instances.
5. Semantic Searching: understands the context and logical reasoning of the content on the website and offers objective results.
6. Query Builder: Query builder is used to construct the user search queries.
7. Query Pre-processor: It pre-process the queries and send the queries to the inference engine.
8. Inference Engine: Reasoning of the search queries using ontology database and the knowledge base is done by the inference Engine.

5. SEMANTIC RESOURCES FOR SENTIMENT ANALYSIS

Sentiment and Semantic analysis is an important resource in our network today. It is necessary to find a suitable context and meaning for a selected sentence on the internet because the real meaning of the sentence can not be discovered by physical contact (Tsai & Hsu, 2013). There are large variety of methods and techniques used to identify and classify the argument as good or bad in quality. Such classification virtually helps in defining the context of the sentence (Liu, 2006). The essential questions of sentimental analysis is to identify the expressions of feelings in texts and to check whether the expressions indicate wonderful (favorable) or negative (unfavorable) opinions closer to the subject and how successfully and efficaciously sentences are classified. In the detailed interpretation of the meaning of the expression, Semantics plays a critical role. The role of semantics is studied from two perspectives:

1. The manner in which semantics is represented in sentimental tools like lexica, corpora and ontology.
2. The manner in which automatic systems conduct sentiment evaluations of social media data.

For example, context-dependence and a finer detection of feelings that lead to the assignment of feeling values to elements or to the layout and use of an extensive range of effective labels or to the use of current techniques for finer-grained semantical processing. In the case of semantics, lexical elements should be paired with logical and cognitive problems and other aspects that are concerned about emotions.

Many works in sentiment evaluation try to utilize shallow processing techniques. The not unusual element in a lot of these works is that they merely attempt to pick out sentiment-bearing expressions. No effort has been made to discover which expression simply contributes to the overall sentiment of the text.

Semantic evaluation is critical to recognize the exact meaning conveyed inside the textual content. Some words generally tend to mislead the which means of a given piece of text. For Example:

I like awful boys.

Here the phrase 'like' expresses fine sentiments while the word awful represent negative sentiments. WSD (Word Sense Disambiguation) is a technique that could been used to get the right sense of the word. Syntactic or structural homes of textual content are used in many NLP applications like gadget translation, speech recognition, named entity recognition, etc.

In general, techniques that are using semantic analysis are high-priced than syntax-based techniques because of the shallow processing involved within the latter. Therefore it is incredibly essential for us to ascertain the precise significance of the expression or else it may result in unfortunate knowledge (in many cases altogether different) on the matter. The key issues in the sentiment assessment are the manner in which sentiments are interpreted in texts and how words indicate a positive or negative (unfavorable) view of the subject. In the present situation, feelings of good or bad polarities for particular topics are extracted from a report instead of the whole document being marked as good or bad in order to include a massive quantity of statistics from one individual paper.Most of their applications aim to classify an entire report into a file subject, which is either specifically or implied. For example, the film form evaluates into wonderful or terrible, implies that all the expressions of sentiment in the evaluation directly represent sentiments towards that film and expressions that contradict it. On the contrary, by studying the relationships between expressions of sentiment and subjects, we can investigate in detail what is and is not required (Niazi & Hussain, 2009). These approaches, therefore, provide a wide variety of incentives for different applications to reach beneficial and unfavorable views on particular topics. It provides strong functions for aggressive research, reputation assessment and the identification of undesirable rumours. For example, huge sums are spent on the evaluation and examination of customer satisfaction. However, the efficacy of such surveys is usually greatly limited (Pang and Lee 2008), considering the amount of money and attempts spent on them, both due to sample length limitations and due to the problems associated with making successful questionnaires. There is thus natural preference for detecting and evaluating inclination, instead of making specific surveys, inside online archives, including blogs, chat rooms and news articles. Human views of these electronic files are easy to understand. Therefore there may have been also significant issues for some organisations, as these documents may have an impact on the general public and terrible rumors in online documents. Let us take an example to interpret the realistic application of sentiment investigation: "Product A is good however expensive." This declaration incorporates a aggregation of statements: "Product A is good" "Product A is expensive" We suppose it's smooth to agree that there is one assertion, Product A is good, it gives a good strong impression, and another statement, product A, is expensive and it has a negative thought. Therefore, we seek to extract any assertion of support additionally to research the benefit of the full context and present it to abandon users who use the findings in line with their program requirements. Sentiment Analysis research therefore involves:

- Sentiment expressions recognition.
- Polarity and expressive power.
- Their relation to the subject.

They are interrelated elements. For example, "XXX beats YY" refers to a positive meaning for XXX and a negative sense for YYY. The word "beats" refers to XXX.

6. SEMANTIC ORIENTATION AND AGGREGATION

6.1 Semantic Orientation

The semantic response to a function f shows whether the view is positive, negative or neutral. Here the view represent the opinion of the user. Wide variety of literature has been studied for semantic approach to sentiment analysis that classify the semantic orientation into two kinds of approches, i.e.

1. corpus based
2. dictionary or lexicon or knowledge based.

Figure 1. Sentiment Classification Techniques

Corpus-based approach suggests data-driven approaches that not only have access to the sentiment labels, but can also be used for the advantage in an ML algorithm. This may simply be a rule-based technique or even a combination of NLP parsing. Corpus also has some specific domain, which will tell the Machine learning algorithm about the variety of the sentiment label for a word depending on its context / domain. Full semantic orientation requires large data sets to satisfy the polarity of the phrases and hence the feeling of the text.

The key drawback with the method is that it is based on the polarity of words contained within the training corpus, and the polarity of word is determined according to the terms in the corpus. Because of the simplification of this approach, this method was well studied in the literature. This method first eliminates sentiment expressions from the unstructured text and then measures the polarity of the words. Most of the sentiment-bearing terms are multi-phrase features in contrast to bag-of-words, e.g., "good movie," "satisfactory cinematography," "satisfactory actors," etc. In literature, the efficiency of a semantic orientation based technology was restricted because of by an insufficient availability of multi-word features.

Dictionary based approach suggests the judging of sentiment based on presence of signaling sentiment words (and perhaps some shorter context, like negations in the front of them) + some kind of counting mechanism to reach at sentiment prediction. In literature, dictionary based method is usually called the most effective (and subsequently of much less accuracy) one. Word based sentiment analysis is a statistical method for evaluating the feeling of a document. In the most successful case, feelings are binary: high or low, but they can be extended to more than one dimension, like anxiety, depression, rage, happiness, etc. This approach is largely based on the predefined list of sentences (or dictionary).

Dictionary-based approach works by identifying the words (for which an opinion has been given), from reviewed textual content then reveals their synonyms and antonyms from dictionary. WordNet or SentiWordNet or any another word network can be used as a dictionary. Corpus based approach helps locate the words of opinion in a particular context orientation, begin with the list of the words of opinion and then locate another word of opinion in a broad corpus. The most useful dictionary to use is Senti-WordNet 3.0. It is publicly accessible lexical tools consisting of "synsets," each with a positive and a negative numerical score of 0 to 1. This score is allocated from the WordNet automatically. This uses a semi-supervised learning process and an iterative algorithm for random walks. The above mentioned method works as follows:

First of all, the system needs to collect the simple and easy to understand sentiment words that have well defined positive or negative orientations. This collection is further extended by the algorithm by searching for its synonyms and antonyms in the WordNet or another online dictionary. The words searched by the algorithm are further added into the seed list to enlarge the collection. Included in the seed list are the following terms. The algorithm continues with the iterations. The cycle stops when new words can no longer be identified. A manual inspection is conducted to clean the list after the cycle had been completed.

6.2 Semantic Aggregation

Every review related to a product (shall we take an example of a camera) is mapped with its precise polarities in the product ontology. Product attributes that are at the higher level of the tree overpower the attributes that are at the lower level. When a reviewer talks about certain features of the product that are more advantageous or terrible within the ontology, he is weighting that feature more in comparison to other statistics of all child nodes (ex- light, resolution, coloration and compression). This is because the function of the parent class abstracts data and the characteristics of its child class. The value of the function is captured in the ontological tree by increasing the height of the characteristic node. In case of neutral polarity of the parent function, the polarity of the characteristic node is attributed to the polarities of its younger nodes. Thus data in a particular node is generated by his own data and by the weighted information of all its younger nodes.

In order to assess the record content of the base ode and the polarity of the analysis, the accurate propagation is carried out from the bottom to the top.

Let us create an ontology tree TR(V1,E1) where $V1_i \in V1$ which is used for setting up a product attribute.

```
attribute.
```

The attribute set of a product V1i consists of the V1i tuple

$V1_i = \{f1_i, p1_i, h1_i\}$

Where $f1_i$ is represented as the feature of the product
$P1_i$ represents the polarity score of the product recieved after the review in relation to $f1_i$ and $h1_i$
$H1_i$ represents the height attribute of the product
$E1_{ij} \in E1$ is s a relationship attribute

$F1_i \in V1_i,$

$F1_i \in V1_j$

$V1_i, V1_j \in V1$.

Let $V1_{ij}$ be the jth child of $V1_i$

The positive sentiment weight (PSW) and negative sentiment weight (NSW) of a vertex $V1_i$ can be calculated using the formula:

$PSW(V1_i) = h1_i * p1_i$

$NSW(V1_i) = h1_i * p1_i$

The product review polarity is estimated using expected sentiment-weight (ESW) of the ontology tree defined as,

$ESW\ (root) = PSW\ (root) + NSW\ (root)$

7. SEMANTIC APPROACH TO LEXICON ADAPTATION

The sentiment of a term isn't always static, as located in general-cause sentiment lexicons, however rather relies upon at the context wherein the term is used, i.e., it relies upon on its contextual semantics (Liu, 2006). Therefore, the lexicon adaptation technique functions in two predominant step

First, given a corpus and a sentiment lexicon, the approach builds a contextual semantic representation for each particular term in the corpus and ultimately uses it to derive the time period's contextual sentiment orientation and strength. The SentiCircle representation version is used to this end. Following the distributional inference, the words co-occurring in specific ways appear to have a common meaning, with certain words within the same corpus, SentiCircle derives the word's contextual semantics from its co-occurrence-styles. Such patterns are then interpreted as a Geometric Circle & are used to measure the word's conceptual meaning, using simple trigonometric identities. For each single duration m within the corpus in particular, we are constructing a two Dimensional geometric circle, in which the center of the circle is the time span m and each factor is described as a background c_i (i.e., a time period that happens with m inside the identical context).

Secondly, rules are applied, mostly in line with the correspondent contextual sentiments, in order to change the previous feelings of the words within the lexicon.

The adaptation process uses a series of antecedent-consistent regulations which determine how their previous feelings in Thelwall-Lexicon are to be up to date in accordance with their SentiMedians' positions (i.e. their contextual feelings). For a term m, it checks, particularly,

1. the prior SOS value of the SentiCircle quadrant in Thelwall-Sexicon and
2. the SentiMedian of m.

The method then chooses the most suitable rule to update the previous feeling and/or opinion of the word.

8. CASE STUDY: SENTIMENT ANALYSIS ON CAA AND NRC PROTESTS IN INDIA - 2019

To perform the sentiment analysis on the protests held for CAA and NRC in India during December 2019, we created one corpus by collecting related articles from the Times of India and other leading newspapers of the India. The corpus was created for the articles of December 2019 and January 2020 during the peak of the protest.

The aim of this case study is to show the technique of sentiment analysis using R programming. The first objective of this study is to plot a word cloud and identify the most frequent words from the corpus along with the sentiments of these words. These words are used as hash tags to extract the data from the twitter. We extracted real time data from twitter by applying the most frequent words as hash tags. Then we applied sentiment analysis on twitter data to know the opinions of the people of country on the issue of NRC and CAA protest.

a) Installing Packages and Library

First step for implementing sentiment analysis on R is to install the relevant packages and their corresponding libraries. Some of the important packages which are used in sentiment analysis are-tm, SnowballC, SentimentAnalysis and wordcloud. We read the corpus as text file and loaded the data as corpus.

```
docs <- Corpus(VectorSource(text))
First few lines of corpus is shown below-
<<SimpleCorpus>>
Metadata:  corpus specific: 1, document level (indexed): 0
Content:  documents: 192
[1] 20-12-2019 25,000 Citizens Protest CAA At August Kranti
[2] Call for "azaadi" or freedom dominated the student-driven protest of over
25,000 Mumbaikars, including 7,000 women, against the Citizenship Amendment
Act (CAA) and the proposed National Register of Citizens (NRC) at the historic
August Kranti Maidan at Grant Road on Thursday. The protest was supported by
political parties and activists.
[3] While organisers said more than one lakh protesters had turned up, police
pegged the number at over 25,000.
[4] Students from Tata Institute of Social Sciences (TISS), IIT-Bombay and
Mumbai University mobilised their peers and other citizens from across the
city. "The first call was given on my Twitter handle on December 11 and though
I have only a few thousand followers, the tweet was seen by over one lakh in-
dividuals," said Fahad Ahmad, PhD student of TISS who was one of the main or-
ganisers. "I am on 24 WhatsApp groups coordinating with students from across
the city."
```

The sample text is an evidence for the extracted article from Times of India dated 20-12-2019. Before applying the text analysis, the text needs to be transformed. Hence text transformation is an important step while analyzing the text. Here we applied the tm_map() function for text transformation to replace the special characters like- "/", "@" and "|" with space in the text. Subsequent to changeover of special characters with space, text cleaning is done with the same tm_map() function where the content_transformer(tolower) is used to convert all capital letters into lowercase letters and removeNumbers is used to remove the digits from the text.

To remove the common stop words, an inbuilt English stopwords dictionary is used by R which can be accessed as –

```
stopwords("english")
```

The common stopwords are-

```
'but' 'if' 'or' 'because' 'as''we\'re' 'they\'re'  'until' 'while' 'of' 'at'
'by' 'for' 'with' 'about' 'against' 'between' 'into' 'i' 'me' 'my' 'myself'
'we' 'our' 'ours' 'ourselves' 'you' 'your' 'yours' 'yourself' 'yourselves' 'he'
'him' 'his' 'through' 'during' 'before' 'after' 'above' 'below' 'to' 'from'
'up' 'down' 'in' 'out' 'on' 'off' 'over' 'more' 'most' 'other' 'some' 'such'
'no' 'nor' 'not' 'only' 'own' 'same' 'so' 'than' 'too' 'very' 'under' 'him-
self' 'she''her' 'hers' 'herself' 'it' 'its' 'itself' 'they' 'them' 'their'
'theirs' 'themselves' 'what' 'which' 'who' 'whom' 'this''that' 'these' 'those'
'am''is' 'are''was' 'were' 'be' 'been' 'being' 'have' 'has' 'you\'ll' 'he\'ll'
'she\'ll' 'we\'ll' 'they\'ll' 'isn\'t' 'aren\'t''wasn\'t' 'weren\'t' 'hasn\'t'
'haven\'t' 'hadn\'t' 'had' 'having' 'do''does' 'did' 'doing' 'would' 'should'
'could' 'ought' 'i\'m' 'you\'re' 'he\'s''she\'s' 'it\'s' 'i\'ve' 'you\'ve'
'we\'ve' 'they\'ve' 'i\'d' 'you\'d' 'he\'d' 'she\'d' 'we\'d' 'they\'d' 'i\'ll'
'again' 'further' 'then' 'once' 'here' 'there' 'when' 'where' 'why' 'how'
'all' 'any' 'both' 'each' 'few'
'doesn\'t' 'don\'t' 'didn\'t' 'won\'t' 'wouldn\'t' 'shan\'t' 'shouldn\'t'
'can\'t' 'cannot' 'couldn\'t' 'mustn\'t'
'let\'s' 'that\'s' 'who\'s' 'what\'s' 'here\'s' 'there\'s' 'when\'s' 'where\'s'
'why\'s' 'how\'s' 'a' 'an' 'the' 'and'
```

To add more stopwords we need to specify our stopwords as a character vector. In this case we find "said" and "also" as the stopwords and we removed them by applying the following function-

```
docs <- tm_map(docs, removeWords, c("said", "also"))
```

Subsequently punctuation and white spaces are also eliminated. First few lines of the transformed corpus are shown below-

```
<<SimpleCorpus>>
Metadata:  corpus specific: 1, document level (indexed): 0
```

```
Content:  documents: 192
  [1]  citizens protest caa august kranti


  [2] call "azaadi" freedom dominated studentdriv-
en protest mumbaikars including women citizenship amendment act
caa proposed national register citizens nrc historic august kranti
maidan grant road thursday protest supported political parties activists


  [3]  organisers one lakh protesters turned police pegged number


  [4] students tata institute social sciences tiss iitbombay mum-
bai university mobilised peers citizens across city " first call giv-
en twitter handle december though thousand followers tweet seen
one lakh individuals" fahad ahmad phd student tiss one main or-
ganisers " whatsapp groups coordinating students across city"


  [5] apart three institutions organis-
ers got support students st xavier's college internation-
al institute population sciences iips wilson college among others



  [6] appeals attend rally made protests places " can see people mumbra mira
road govandi bhendi bazaar outraged know allow inequality constitution stop "
activist teesta setalvad
```

To build a term document matrix we applied the following function-

```
D_t_m <- TermDocumentMatrix(docs)
mat <- as.matrix(d_t_m)
var<- sort(rowSums(mat),decreasing=TRUE)
doc <- data.frame(word = names(var),freq=var)
head(doc, 10)
```

This has resulted the output as frequency of each word in descending order. We have shown only first 10 lines of the output by via head().

Using this word frequency table we plotted the frequency table of words as shown in figure and generated the word cloud as shown in Figures 2 and 3.

To carry out sentiment analysis of these frequent words we used the SentimentAnalysis package and its library where we used the above generated document term matrix. First few lines of sentiments generated are-

Every document has a word count, a negativity score, a positivity score, and the overall sentiment score.

Table 1. Word frequency table

Word	Freq	
caa	caa	32
citizenship	citizenship	29
nrc	nrc	28
police	police	27
india	india	26
modi	modi	24
people	people	23
delhi	delhi	23
law	law	20
minister	minister	19

Figure 2. Word Frequency Plot

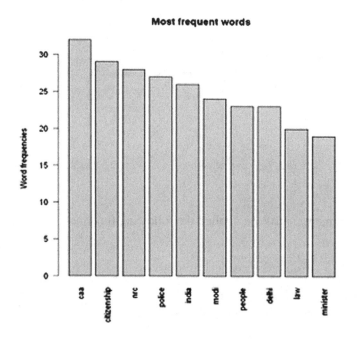

The distribution of overall sentiment can be seen as-

```
        summary(sent$SentimentGI)
Min.  1st Qu.   Median     Mean 3rd Qu.     Max.     NA's
-0.33333  0.00000  0.00000  0.01538  0.05518  0.33333        34
```

After adding the column of words with the sentiment score-

Figure 3. Word cloud

Table 2. Sentiment Analysis of Frequent Words

WordCount	SentimentGI	NegativityGI	PositivityGI
5	-0.20000000	0.20000000	0.00000000
30	0.00000000	0.06666667	0.06666667
8	0.00000000	0.00000000	0.00000000
42	0.04761905	0.00000000	0.04761905
18	0.05555556	0.00000000	0.05555556
24	0.12500000	0.00000000	0.12500000

Table 3. Sentiment score of the words

d[1:6, 1]	WordCount	SentimentGI	NegativityGI	PositivityGI
protest	5	-0.20000000	0.20000000	0.00000000
caa	30	0.06666667	0.10000000	0.16666667
citizenship	8	-0.25000000	0.25000000	0.00000000
india	44	0.06818182	0.00000000	0.06818182
nrc	18	0.11111111	0.00000000	0.11111111
police	26	0.07692308	0.11538462	0.19230769

b) Performing Sentiment Analysis on Twitter Data Based on Hashtags

In 21st century, there has been an exponential rush forward in the online commotion of people across the world. One of the online social platforms is Twitter when people freely express their sentiments. There are several challenges in performing sentiment analysis on the data extracted from the twitter as inhabitants have a dissimilar way of writing and while posting on Twitter, people are least bothered about the correct spelling of words or they may use a lot of slangs which are not proper English words but are used in casual conversations. Hence it has been an interesting research area among researchers from one decade.

By motivating from the above, we have generated the most frequent words from the corpus collected in the above section from various articles in news papers during December 2019 and January 2020 on NRC and CAA and these words have been used as hashtags to extract the relevant data from twitter. Using the twitter API in R we performed data extraction by passing most frequent word as hashtag and extracted top 250 tweets. These tweets were stored as a data frame. First few lines of text of this dataframe can be seen as-

```
head(tweets.df$text)
```

1. 'RT @ShayarImran: Participated in KSU protest march and public meeting against #CAA #NRC at Calicutt, Kerala \n@RamyaHaridasMP \n@srinivasiyc…'
2. '@hfao5 @AnjanPatel7 @SyedAhmedAliER @KTRTRS @trspartyonline @TelanganaCMO @ asadowaisi Hyderabadi\'s must protest KCR… https://t.co/T53DB7do14'
3. 'RT @GradjanskiO: Novi protest ce obeleziti puteve Vesicevih rusevina.\n\nUrbicid! Mrznja prema gradjanima!\n\n15.02.2020\n\u23f0 18h\nPlato\n\nDo pobede…'
4. 'RT @SwamiGeetika: #DelhiAssemblyElections2020 \n\nYouth gathered in large numbers to protest after TMC barred distributing Hanuman Chalisa an…'
5. 'RT @anyaparampil: Workers w Venezuelan airline Conviasa tell @ErikaOSanoja their protest of Guaidó\'s arrival in Venezuela is part of "defen…'
6. 'RT @JamesRu55311: We've known for a long time that BBC is already lost, and that they were complicit in their own downfall. Watching them s…'

Figure 4. Total Positive And Negative Words In The Twitter Text

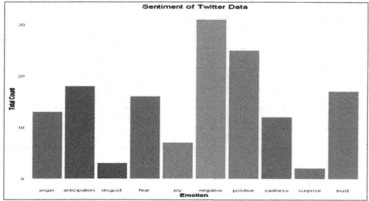

This data frame is first converted into a vector and then preprocessing is applied before sentiment analysis. The function get_nrc_sentiment() is used to identify the positive and negative words. We then computed the total positive and negative words in the twitter text and the a plot is drawn as shown in figure below. This plot shows the sentiments attached with the corresponding text.

As we can discover here, in the given case more number of negative words are found hence it represents the negative sentiments of the people. Thus we can easily identify and analyse the sentiments of the people based on the key words.

CONCLUSION

The chapter discusses the concepts related to deep learning, sentiment analysis and the importance of semantic in sentiment analysis. The present chapter has illustrated the basic of ontologies and their relation to sentiment analysis. The chapter has further discussed semantic ontologies with concept forms and their relationships along with steps to develop a baseline model for simple analysis of sentiment using NLP. At the end of the chapter case study related to the sentiment analysis using R programming on the protests for CAA and NRC in India during December 2019 has been presented. The corpus of the case study has been built by collecting related articles from the Times of India and other leading newspapers of the India. Real time data has been extracted from twitter by applying the most frequent words as hash tags. Finally sentiment analysis techniques have been applied on twitter data to know the opinions of the people of country on the issue of NRC and CAA protest. This work can be extended further by applying various sentiment analysis techniques to improve the accuracy of the predicted words. More work is also required to preprocess the data in order to improve the accuracy.

REFERENCES

Agrawal, R., & Gupta, N. (Eds.). (2018). *Extracting Knowledge from Opinion Mining*. IGI Global.

Arnold, L., Rebecchi, S., Chevallier, S., & Paugam-Moisy, H. (2011) An Introduction to Deep Learning. *ESANN 2011 Proceedings, European Symposium on Artificial Neural Networks, Computational Intelligence and Machine Learning*, 477-488.

Day, M., & Lee, C. (2016). *Deep Learning for Financial Sentiment Analysis on Finance News Providers*. Academic Press.

Gupta, N., & Agrawal, R. (2020). Application and Techniques of Opinion Mining. In *Hybrid Computational Intelligence*. Elsevier. doi:10.1016/B978-0-12-818699-2.00001-9

Gupta, N., & Agrawal, R. (2017). Challenges and Security Issues of Distributed Databases. In *NoSQL* (pp. 265–284). Chapman and Hall/CRC.

Gupta, N., & Verma, S. (2019). Tools of Opinion Mining. In *Extracting Knowledge From Opinion Mining* (pp. 179–203). IGI Global. doi:10.4018/978-1-5225-6117-0.ch009

Hai, Z., Chang, K., Kim, J. J., & Yang, C. C. (2013). Identifying features in opinion mining via intrinsic and extrinsic domain relevance. *IEEE Transactions on Knowledge and Data Engineering, 26*(3), 623–634. doi:10.1109/TKDE.2013.26 doi:10.1109/TKDE.2013.26

Jalota, C., & Agrawal, R. (2019). Ontology-Based Opinion Mining. In Extracting Knowledge From Opinion Mining (pp. 84-103). IGI Global. doi:10.4018/978-1-5225-6117-0.ch005 doi:10.4018/978-1-5225-6117-0.ch005

Kalchbrenner, N., Grefenstette, E., & Blunsom, P. (2014). *A convolutional neural network for modelling sentences.* arXiv preprint arXiv:1404.2188. doi:10.3115/v1/P14-1062

Kalra, V., & Aggarwal, R. (2017). Importance of Text Data Preprocessing & Implementation in Rapid-Miner. In *Proceedings of the First International Conference on Information Technology and Knowledge Management–New Dehli, India* (Vol. 14, pp. 71-75). 10.15439/2017KM46

Kalra, V., & Agrawal, R. (2019). Challenges of Text Analytics in Opinion Mining. In *Extracting Knowledge From Opinion Mining* (pp. 268–282). IGI Global. doi:10.4018/978-1-5225-6117-0.ch012

Kaur, S., & Agrawal, R. (2018). A Detailed Analysis of Core NLP for Information Extraction. *International Journal of Machine Learning and Networked Collaborative Engineering, 1*(01), 33–47. doi:10.30991/IJMLNCE.2017v01i01.005

Kim, Y. (2014). *Convolutional neural networks for sentence classification.* arXiv preprint arXiv:1408.5882. doi:10.3115/v1/D14-1181

Liu, B. (2006). Mining comparative sentences and relations. In AAAI (Vol. 22). Academic Press.

Medhat, W., Hassan, A., & Korashy, H. (2014). Sentiment analysis algorithms and applications: A survey. *Ain Shams Engineering Journal, 5*(4), 1093–1113. doi:10.1016/j.asej.2014.04.011

Mikolov, T., Chen, K., Corrado, G., & Dean, J. (2013). *Efficient estimation of word representations in vector space.* arXiv preprint arXiv:1301.3781.

Niazi, M., & Hussain, A. (2009). Agent-based tools for modeling and simulation of self-organization in peer-to-peer, ad hoc, and other complex networks. *IEEE Communications Magazine, 47*(3), 166–173. doi:10.1109/MCOM.2009.4804403

Ouyang, X., Zhou, P., Li, C. H., & Liu, L. (2015). *Sentiment analysis using convolutional neural network. In 2015 IEEE international conference on computer and information technology; ubiquitous computing and communications; dependable, autonomic and secure computing; pervasive intelligence and computing.* IEEE.

Pang, B., & Lee, L. (2008). Opinion mining and sentiment analysis. *Foundations and Trends in Information Retrieval, 2*(1–2), 1–135. doi:10.1561/1500000011

Poria, S., Gelbukh, A., Hussain, A., Howard, N., Das, D., & Bandyopadhyay, S. (2013). Enhanced SenticNet with affective labels for concept-based opinion mining. *IEEE Intelligent Systems, 28*(2), 31–38. doi:10.1109/MIS.2013.4

Socher, R., Lin, C. C., Manning, C., & Ng, A. Y. (2011). Parsing natural scenes and natural language with recursive neural networks. In *Proceedings of the 28th international conference on machine learning (ICML-11)* (pp. 129-136). Academic Press.

Tsai, A. C. R., Wu, C. E., Tsai, R. T. H., & Hsu, J. Y. J. (2013). Building a concept-level sentiment dictionary based on commonsense knowledge. *IEEE Intelligent Systems*, *28*(2), 22–30. doi:10.1109/MIS.2013.25

Vateekul, P., & Koomsubha, T. (2016). A Study of Sentiment Analysis Using Deep Learning Techniques on Thai Twitter Data. *13th International Joint Conference on Computer Science and Software Engineering (JCSSE)*, 1-6. 10.1109/JCSSE.2016.7748849

Ye, Q., Zhang, Z., & Law, R. (2009). Sentiment classification of online reviews to travel destinations by supervised machine learning approaches. *Expert Systems with Applications*, *36*(3), 6527–6535. doi:10.1016/j.eswa.2008.07.035

This research was previously published in Examining the Impact of Deep Learning and IoT on Multi-Industry Applications; pages 97-117, copyright year 2021 by Engineering Science Reference (an imprint of IGI Global).

Chapter 84

An Overview of Methodologies and Challenges in Sentiment Analysis on Social Networks

Aditya Suresh Salunkhe
Ramrao Adik Institute of Technolgy, India

Pallavi Vijay Chavan
Ramrao Adik Institute of Technolgy, India

ABSTRACT

The expeditious increase in the adoption of social media over the last decade, determining and analyzing the attitude and opinion of masses related to a particular entity, has gained quite an importance. With the landing of the Web 2.0, many internet products like blogs, community chatrooms, forums, microblog are serving as a platform for people to express themselves. Such opinion is found in the form of messages, user-comments, news articles, personal blogs, tweets, surveys, status updates, etc. With sentiment analysis, it is possible to eliminate the need to manually going through each and every user comment by focusing on the contextual polarity of the text. Analyzing the sentiments could serve a number of applications like advertisements, recommendations, quality analysis, monetization provided on the web services, real-time analysis of data, analyzing notions related to candidates during election campaign, etc.

INTRODUCTION

The Cambridge dictionary defines sentiments as, "an opinion, thought, or an idea based on a feeling about a particular situation, or an approach of thinking about something" (Cambridge University Press, 2008).

Types of Sentiments

There are primarily two ways one can classify the sentiments being expressed in text.

DOI: 10.4018/978-1-6684-6303-1.ch084

1. **Opinions:** This is something that the subject believes/decides. For instance, liked/disliked/expensive/low quality/affordable etc.
2. **Emotions:** This is something that the subject perceives or feels. For instance, happy/sad/satisfied/relaxed etc.

In this chapter we shall focus only on the opinions rather than emotions. Merriam-Webster dictionary has defined an opinion as ''a judgment, a view or appraisal formed in the mind about a particular entity'', or ''a belief that is stronger than an impression but less strong than positive knowledge''

Thus there are 2 types of opinions:

- Judgement opinion: desirable/undesirable/disgusting/good/bad.
- Belief opinion: Possibly/likely/mostly/probably/true/false

Their internal structure can be defined with the help of a quadruple at minimum (Hovy, 2015).

- Topic = topic which is being considered.
- Holder = individual, group, institution holding or making the opinion.
- Claim = statement which is in regard with the topic.
- Valence (judgment opinions): – Positive/Negative/Neutral.
- Valence (belief opinions): – Believed/Disbelieved/Unsure/Neutral.

Figure 1. General classification of sentiments

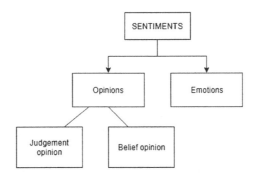

- **Definition:** Opinion is a decision made by the holder i.e. person, group or an organization as a whole about a topic. One can add additional factors such as strength, facets, and conditions to the quadruple to extend the structure.
- Strength of opinion: It is difficult to establish strength across different holders.
- Facet of topic: It is used for narrowing down the topic and differentiate between its sub-facets. For example, not the "overall delivery time" but the time required for "product dispatch" for a particular goods delivery company.
- Argument/Reasoning: This opens up the argument structure. "I find the service quality poor because, (reason)"

Sentiment Analysis through Emoticons:

Apart from above two, emoticons are also been used nowadays while expressing opinions And highly reflect the attitude of the subject, for example has stated emoji having effect on results of elections, stocks etc. (Ljubesic and Fiser, 2016). Pairing writer's sentiment to the use of the emoticons can provide a better understanding of user sentiments. Another major advantage is the limited sets of emoji compared to infinite possibility of words. We can take advantage of this and introduce a template database with annotations for every possible emoji. Further rules to correlate the sentiment based on a set/combination of emoji could be used.

Table 1. Categorical classification of emoticons

Emoji	Description	Category
😃	A simple round face with open eyes and broad smile. Conveys humour, pleasure and good vibes.	Smileys and People
☕	A cup of a hot beverage usually represents tea or coffee. Used to express sentiments related to food, restaurants, warmness, hunger, appetite. etc.	Food and Beverages
⚽	A round, black and white ball used in the game of football usually used to express sports related sentiments.	Sports & Activities.
✈	Airplane transcending upwards. Used to represent travel, overseas vacation or phone/device on airplane mode.	Travel & Places.
🚩	Contains a range of internationally recognised flags of countries & organisations. Usually used while conveying national/international news/events, political opinions etc.	Flags and Countries

BACKGROUND

Defining the opinion is one of the major challenge in sentiment analysis. Many linguists of different times have tried to define subjectivity. One of the prominent definition among existing definitions is been given by Randolph Quirk. Quirk has defined private state as "something that is not accessible to verification or objective" (Quirk, Greenbaum, and Syartyik, 1985). Emotions, personal opinions, attitude, speculations and many more form these private states. A pioneer in Natural Language Processing (NLP), Weibe has used this definition of Quirk where private state is narrative. According to her, private state is a tuple defined as: (p, attitude, object, and experiencer) (Pang and Lee, 2008). For practical purposes, a simpler version of this definition where only the polarity and goal state are in focus is used. In general terms, sentiments are positive or negative individual opinions with several unique properties that set them apart from the general text.

SENTIMENT ANALYSIS METHODS

Sentimental Analysis can be carried out majorly in 3 different ways: Supervised, Semi supervised, unsupervised techniques. Naïve Bayesian, SVM and decision trees are the most predominantly used supervised approaches.

Use of Semi-Supervised Polarity Dictionary

- **Polarity (Definition):** Cambridge dictionary has defined polarity as: "the quality of having two poles/extreme opposite values" (Cambridge University Press, 2008).

To determine the sentimental polarity of any news or online blog response, we first create a polarity dictionary, consisting of terms and their respective polarities. This polarity dictionary uses a semi-supervised dictionary approach in which first a dictionary of considerably small size is constructed using a few seed words. The polarity to the seed words are assigned manually. After which, we add new words to the polarity dictionary using co-occurrence frequency with words in a polarity dictionary.

Polarity Dictionary Construction

Bootstrap method is used for construction of polarity dictionary of semi-supervised nature. A bootstrap method focuses on both small unlabelled data and large unlabelled data, the small labelled data is basically the initial dictionary with few seed words entered manually. Here we assume that all sentences in an article are of the same polarity. This assumption is strict because some sentences may include adversative conjunction & negation. Since the expressions change a context in an article, our assumption is not correct. Under the assumption candidates which are added in the polarity dictionary are selected according to co-occurrence frequency with words in the polarity dictionary. We begin by making a small initial polarity dictionary which has some words present in that polarities determined manually. Hence, human efforts are required to make the initial dictionary. The dictionary consists of both positive and negative words. We call a dictionary for positive words a 'positive polarity dictionary' and a dictionary for negative words a 'negative polarity dictionary'. After that, we measure how many times a new word which is not added in the dictionary occurs with words in positive or negative polarity dictionary in the same sentence. If a word occurs with positive words and negative words in the same sentence, we count co-occurrence frequency for both polarities. Many words occur with words in a positive polarity dictionary and in a negative polarity dictionary though we exclude sentences including negation and adversative conjunction. Thereby to measure a bias of co-occurrence we use a rate of co-occurrence with a positive or a negative polarity dictionary. And based upon the rate of co-occurrence we estimate a polarities of a word not added in the polarity dictionary. Finally we determine the polarity of word that became candidates after previous operation and add them to the polarity dictionary. In this approach we determine two thresholds, T1 and T2. Where T1 and T2 represent positive and negative thresholds. When R1 of a word is over T1, the word is added in the positive polarity dictionary, When R2 of a word is greater than T2, and we add the word to the negative polarity dictionary. The thresholds lie in between 0.5-1.0 (Ljubesic and Fiser, 2016). We don't use words whose occurrence frequency is less than 10 since co-occurrence frequency for such words is not reliable. This process is repeated several times to increase the size of the polarity dictionary. The process terminates when it reaches the saturation point i.e. no new words are being added to the dictionary. In case the process isn't stopping, we can introduce a maximum loop condition.

Sentimental Analysis Using Polarity Dictionary

We begin by counting the frequency of the positive words and negative words. Then we compare them quantitatively. If a text has more positive words as compared to negative words, the polarity of the entire article is positive. When there are more negative words compared to positive ones, the polarity of the article is negative. When the frequency of the positive and negative words is same or when there are no positive or negative words at all the article is considered as neutral. Hence, all article are classified as either positive, negative, or neutral. We explain a process to determine a polarity of an article using an example:

"The product is very good, after sales service is supreme but price is unaffordable"

Here the words "good" and "supreme' account for positive polarity whereas "unaffordable" accounts for negative polarity. Since the number of positive polarities are greater than negative polarities, the overall polarity of the sentence is considered as positive. In this step we neglect impact, negation and adversative conjunction and use all sentence to decide polarity of articles. This methodology was experimented for data acquired from Centillion Co. and an accurate polarity of 45% of total news was obtained (Ljubesic and Fiser, 2016).

Sentiment Classification Based on Support Vector Machine (SVM)

In this approach, the sentence is first splitted into 3 parts: the starting part of the comment, the middle part of the comment and the terminating/concluding part of the comment. Then mark the sentences with labels according to their position in the comment. The first sentence is marked as 'f', the middle sentence which forms the centre of the comment is marked as 'm' and the last sentence is marked as 'l'. Then through Jeiba Chinese Software, the words were segmented. To improve the accuracy, noun, verb, adjective, adverb etc. were introduced (Mizumoto, Yanagimoto, and Yoshioka, 2012). Every forum review set ri where $\mathbf{R}= \{\mathbf{r1}, \mathbf{r},..., \mathbf{rm}\}$ of several completed sentences$<si1,si2,...sin>$ (Wang, Zheng, Liu, 2012). In the next step, the review is divided into 3 parts: the first sentence, middle sentence, last sentence. The weight is then calculated based on the part of the sentence at the paragraph following to which polarity is calculated of the review 'i'

$(ri)=\Sigma(sij)wij n j=1$. Suppose two sentiment labels are used *Rpos* and the other is *Rnega*. When $sij \in Rpos, (sij)=1$; else if $sij \in Rnega, P(sij)=-1$. If $(ri)>0, ri$ is the +1. Else, ri is the -1. We can acquire weights as wij through the formula as follows: $wi= ((r \in Rpos \wedge si \in Rpos) \vee (r \in Rneg \wedge si \in Rneg))$. Following to this, we use SVM as classifier to train the model. This method when tested for shares trading on SSE and SZSE. At first, the information crawling software to get comments of every stocks on Easymoney stock forum was used. When compared to the traditional semantic method which gave an accuracy of 53.1%, this method gave an accuracy of 80.7% (Wang, Zheng, Liu, 2012).

Sentence Level Sentiment Analysis

A rule base analysis is essential for performing sentence level sentiment analysis. This method focuses on analysing the various intricacies and levels of granularity (Zhang and Bu, 2017). Negation rules are used here for the purpose of sentiment extraction. Thus the presence of words like no, never, not, negative etc. account for negative polarity of the sentence. Further various combinations of verbs or adjectives such as unstable, inefficient, stop etc. can be put to use to improve accuracy.

Feature Level Sentiment Analysis

This method is used when an overall or aggregate notion about the product/service to improve knowledge about predicting its stock outcomes is to be found. In this intelligent analysis, each feature is assigned some score/weightage. For instance, a positive review is assigned a positive weightage score. A more positive comment/review is assigned a more weighted score. In similar fashion, a negative feature is assigned a negative score. The overall/ aggregate review is judged on the factor of aggregate of the individual scores. Thus if the aggregate score is positive, the entire review is considered positive. If the aggregate score is negative, the entire review is considered negative. Feature analysis is an approach based on the mathematical formula or statistics which acts as a base for the entire prediction of the sentiment feature.

Word Level Sentiment Analysis

One of the most widely used and high performance sentimental analysis technique. Encoding is done effectively between the classes and the words. For instance, (Satisfactory, good, excellent, brilliant) => positive sentiments. A number of databases are used that represent a relationship between adjectives and its respective classes. Extraction of adjectives comes under lexical analysis of the sentiment (Zhang and Bu, 2017). Two classes are formed for the purpose of identifying the positive and negative reviews. The overall efficiency of Word-level Sentiment Analysis approach depends on the wholesomeness of the wordlist/adjective database put to use.

The steps further involved are as follows:

Relevant documents are considered.

- Irrelevant words such as are, we, am, for etc. are eliminated and keywords are extracted.
- From these extracted keywords, adjectives and keywords that reflect opinions are identified.
- Opinion class is determined and weightage is designated to each keyword. The opinion class comprising of higher number of keywords is assigned a higher weightage and vice versa.
- Overall/ aggregate weight depends on each opinion class based on which overall resulting decision is taken.

It is an effective, simple technique and thereby quite extensively used algorithm for document classification.

Challenges in Sentiment Analysis

1. Fast paced change in data sets: Creating a robust classifier that works for the ever changing mentality and opinions reflected through the reviews and comments online is difficult. Thus features used for classification so far may soon become irrelevant in near future. The amount and the type of user data collected every day is changes at an unprecedented rate. Another drawback could be people expressing their views towards the utility or service implicitly with no or less words of sentiments rather than doing it explicitly. This worsens the situation and furthermore makes it challenging. Another problem that may make the problem more difficult is it is difficult to differentiate transient important features from recurring ones. It is important to keep a track of these features as they may disappear and reappear in the future. Another problematic situation arises when there is inconsistency in the datasets. Machine learning often assumes clean, well-distributed data sets for the purpose of experimentation. However the real life datasets aren't that well-distributed (Raghuvanshi and Patil, 2016).

2. Each product is referred using different names sometimes in same document and many a times across various documents. This is a serious issue of entity resolution and is not yet solved. Anaphora handling is another major challenge in sentiment analysis. For instance, the terms "mileage" and "fuel efficiency" have same meanings and refer to same aspects of a car.

3. Texts with spelling mistakes, grammatical errors, improper use of tense, punctuation mistakes, use of slangs etc. account as noisy data. Classification of such a data is still a major challenge in sentiment analysis.

4. Many a times, statements which put forth the factual aspects of the products are made. Currently, the approaches which are employed focuses only on the subjective nature of the statements. There's a need of algorithms that could attach context scores & focus on the objective (factual) part of the statement for efficient classification and better understanding.

5. Challenges related to interpretation: There has been lack of harmony in the online behaviour of the masses and their actual behaviour in practice. For instance, a person/group writing negative comments about the online food delivery service may still continue to use it despite of their opinion on internet perhaps because it's the only service available in their neighbourhood. This thus doesn't affect monetarily and neither hampers the sales.

6. Presence of links: If we take an example of twitter, many a times the tweets redirect the readers to certain websites, profiles, articles etc. through browser links. While the parent tweet may fail to reflect sentiments of the users, it may be contained in the redirected site. These links cannot be identified by the current methods. Those links are crucial and represent the tweet in its complete sense. Without referring two those links, it becomes impossible to detect the sentiments even for a human annotator (Ebrahimi, Yazdayar, and Sheth, 2017).

7. Content related challenges: Recently there has been an advent in the use of hashtags. These hashtags are quite volatile in nature and hence need distant control which is training a dataset on periodically labelled training set (Ebrahimi, Yazdayar, and Sheth, 2017).

People tend to use a quite access of these hashtags on various online platforms such as twitter to express their opinion about a product or entity. Hashtags are also used for emotion detection through machine learning approach (Go, Bhayani, and Huang, 2009). Due to its dynamic nature, the quantity, quality and freshness of the labelled data plays an important role in constructing a robust classifier with reliability.

8. Many a times the presence of bots on social media platform hamper the authenticity of the data obtained for sentiment analysis. A bot is a computer generated algorithm that tries to imitate the human behaviour by generating biased content on social & news distribution related platforms (Wang et. al, 2012). Though measures are been taken to track down and ban bots, this still poses a serious threat to the idea of sentiment analysis.

9. Use of sarcasm can be an issue while mining responses for the analysis. For instance, the classifier may consider both the comments "I love the way the after sales service of car 'X' ignores me" and "I love the in-built music stereo system of car X" as similar when in practical world, they clearly don't comply similar notions (Lee, Eoff, Cayerlee, 2011).

10. Unclear target of emotion could also lead to ambiguity. For instance, for a company 'X' trying to find about the opinions of masses about a newly released feature in their car, comments like "I hate the traffic outside showroom X" or "The music taste of employees working in day-shift of showroom X is poor" might lead to problems while classification.

MISINFORMATION IN SENTIMENTS OVER SOCIAL MEDIA

These days most of the review sites, public discussions, forums etc. are affected more & more due to widespread of misinformation. Misinformation usually aims at hampering the business or goodwill of an individual, group or an organization by misleading them & thereby causes anomalies in the sentiment analysis. To tackle this, several data-driven solutions have been suggested since reviews can strongly affect the decisions of uninformed people visiting the website for advice. Today with the introduction to the Web 2.0, it is possible for every individual to diffuse his/her opinions over internet without requiring any form of trusted security verifications. One of the proposed methodology is analysis of the features connected to the reviewers and reviews & to learn about their distinct characteristics. Literature shows that it has led to it has led to successful identification of malicious or falsely generated content. One method is to compare the features of a singleton review ad check for the occurrence of multiple reviews with similar features which then is used to determine the creditability factor. For instance, if there's single negative review among a set of hundreds of positive reviews, the creditability of that single review is low. However if there are multiple reviews of same nature, the creditability factor increases (Fontanaraya, Pasi, Viviani, 2017).

From a historical point of view creditability is often associated with truth worthiness, reliability, accuracy etc. The features or the characteristics which are considered for the purpose of evaluation are linguistic parameters associated with the text. One of the approach is to analyze the reviews based on the meta-data. For instance analyzing the reviews based upon its rating (1-5 stars) or the period during which the review/comment was made (Fontanaraya, Pasi, Viviani, 2017). The latter is done to ensure that the comments/reviews made far in the past on a particular service/ product aren't considered especially since several updates have been already done to it. The classifiers used for the same are supervised and unsupervised. Unsupervised classifiers are in general less effective but useful in cases where a pre-determined dataset is not required. Supervised classifiers are in general more effective and employ review & reviewer centric features. To evaluate this a supervised model based on Random Forests has been developed. This model can be used efficiently on large public datasets.

FUTURE RESEARCH DIRECTIONS

For future research, we would evaluate the effectiveness of each of the above proposed methodologies against various test scenarios for the purpose of sentence and phrase-level analysis of sentiments. We also aim to employ these methods individually on different types of content such as stock markets, news articles, twitter feed, product reviews and test their effectiveness on an individual level. Further this research could also be directed for analyzing the abstract features of a document such as topic, genre, type of content etc.

Works which have been previously done have mostly focused on the semantic and syntactic features there has been a minimal use of the stylistic features such as vocabulary rich measures, character/word length, frequencies of special characters, lexical features at word level etc. Thus more light could be thrown on these parameters (Abbasi, Chen, and Salem, 2008).

Web-based crawling for sentiment analysis has a potential of research extension since most of the web-pages with undiscovered content contain diverse sentiments. Discovery of such mixed sentiments is important in various domains especially sales, politics, marketing etc. New metrics can be designed to gather, identify & evaluate such diverse emotions (Gural et. al, 2014).

CONCLUSION

This chapter gives a brief insight to the understanding of the term 'sentiment'. Further, the need to analyse the user generated data reflecting their opinions about a utility/service to get insights of their reviews were discussed. Various methodologies that can be employed for the classification of the data mined from the internet along with their efficiencies were discussed. SVM of all the discussed methods turned out to give most accurate results. Lastly we came up with the various challenges related to the classification of the data. Sentiment analysis is a promising field and overcoming these challenges and moving towards a more robust classifier would result in better mining of human sentiments from an industrial standpoint.

REFERENCES

Abbasi, A., Chen, H., & Salem, A. (2008). Sentiment Analysis in Multiple Languages: Feature Selection for Opinion Classification in Web Forums. ACM Transactions on Information Systems, 26(3), 12. doi:10.1145/1361684.1361685

Cambridge University Press. (2008). Cambridge online dictionary. Author.

Ebrahimi, M., Yazdavar, A., & Sheth, A. (2017). Challenges of Sentiment Analysis for dynamic events. IEEE Intelligent Systems, 32(5), 70–75. doi:10.1109/MIS.2017.3711649

Fontanarava, J., Pasi, G., & Viviani, M. (2017). Feature Analysis for Fake Review Detection through Supervised Classification. International Conference on Data Science and Advanced Analytics. 10.1109/DSAA.2017.51

Go, A., Bhayani, R., & Huang, L. (2009). Twitter sentiment classification using distant supervision. CS224N Project Report, 1(12).

Hovy, E. H. (2015). What are Sentiment, Affect, and Emotion? Applying the Methodology of Michael Zock to Sentiment Analysis. Springer International Publishing Switzerland. doi:10.1007/978-3-319-08043-7_2

Joshi, A., Bhattacharya, P., & Mark, J. (2017). Automatic Sarcasm Detection: A Survey. ACM Computing Surveys, 50(5).

Lee, K., Eoff, B. D., & Caverlee, J. (2011). Seven Months with the Devils: A Long-Term Study of Content Polluters on Twitter. ICWSM.

Ljubesic, N., & Fiser, D. (2016). A global analysis of emoji usage. ACL.

*Mizumoto, K., Y*anagimoto, H., & Yoshioka, M. (2012). IEEE/ACIS 11th International Conference on Computer and Information Science. IEEE.

Pang, B., & Lee, L. (2008). Opinion mining and sentiment analysis. Foundation and Trends in Information Retrieval, 2(1-2), 1–135.

Quirk, R., Greenbaum, S. G. L., & Svartvik, J. (1985). A comprehensive grammar of the English language. Longman.

Raghuvanshi, N., & Patil, J. M. (2016). A Brief Review on Sentiment Analysis. International *Conference on Electrical, Electronics, and Optimization Techniques (ICEEOT). IEEE Conferences.*

Vural, A. G., Cambazoglu, B. B., & Karagoz, P. (2014). Sentiment-Focused Web Crawling. ACM Trans-*actions on the Web, 8(4), 22. d*oi:10.1145/2644821

Wang, H. W., Zheng, L. J., & Liu, Z. Y. (2012). Sentiment feature selection from Chinese online reviews. China J*ournal of Information Systems, 11.*

*Wa*ng, W. (2012). Harnessing twitter big data for automatic emotion identification. Priv*acy, Security, Risk and Trust (PASSAT), Int*ernational Conference on Social Computing (SocialCom) IEEE.

Zhang, Y., & Bu, H. (2017). Can extracted features from stock forum amount for the stock return? I*n-ternational Conference on Service Systems and Service Management.*

Chapter 85
Sentiment Analysis and Sarcasm Detection (Using Emoticons)

Vibhu Dagar
Vellore Institute of Technology, Vellore, India

Amber Verma
Vellore Institute of Technology, Vellore, India

Govardhan K.
Vellore Institute of Technology, Vellore, India

ABSTRACT

Sentiment analysis is contextual mining of text which identifies and extracts subjective information in source material and helps a business to understand the social sentiment of their brand, product, or service while monitoring online conversations. However, analysis of social media streams is usually restricted to just basic sentiment analysis and count-based metrics. This is akin to just scratching the surface and missing out on those high value insights that are waiting to be discovered. Twitter is an online person-to-person communication administration where overall clients distribute their suppositions on an assortment of themes, talk about current issues, grumble, and express positive or on the other hand negative notions for items they use in life. Hence, Twitter is a rich source of information for supposition mining and estimation investigation.

INTRODUCTION

Internet based Social Media websites, for example, Twitter enable clients to post short and casual messages, communicate their suppositions on a wide assortment of points and express their feelings. Clients express their assessments on the world of politics, strict convictions, purchaser items what's more, individual issues in a couple of words. Twitter is a rich asset from which you can pick up bits of knowledge by performing assessment examination. Supposition investigation is significant as it has some genuine

DOI: 10.4018/978-1-6684-6303-1.ch085

applications. Corporate associations need to reveal bits of knowledge for better client the board. They need to hold old clients and pull in new ones.

Supposition investigation enables organizations to perform statistical surveying to assess client input, without having to convey polls or overviews. Political decision gatherings need to contemplate the move in popular conclusion about their up-and-comers. Notwithstanding, any standard calculation may neglect to catch genuine estimations covered up in the printed piece of tweets. There is the test of discovery of mockery or incongruity in the writings and it can prompt wrong classification of tweets.

With various settings they can mean various things. Incorrectly spelled words and linguistic mistakes can include to the clamor in the informational collection. Tweets containing a blend of positive and negative words can be wrongly classified as nonpartisan conclusion. Subsequently, recognizable proof of genuine feelings dependent on just literary piece of tweets isn't adequate as it is essential to comprehend the real plan of the creator of the tweet. Estimation examination, otherwise called Opinion mining, can be improved a lot further by utilizing emoticons. Emoticons were included to web based life destinations to speak to facial highlights of a creator and to zest up enthusiastic signs to instant messages. Numerous mind boggling thoughts can be passed on through basic emoticons. While customary notion investigation decides if a book is certain or negative (extremity), an additional layer of emoticons investigation can help in arranging messages into further classifications like love, happiness, shock, outrage, misery, dread, and so on. emoticons can likewise help in better characterization in instance of wry writings.

This examination expects to research the assumptions of tweets utilizing emoticons. By performing emoticons investigation, this examination fills a hole between the territory where most research has been centered distinctly around the literary piece of tweets. These emoticons can also be used to identify sarcasm in some cases. Sarcasm is in the tone of a person but sometimes its the emoticons that bring it out. Tweets with text portraying certain meaning can mean different altogether when seen in contrast with the emoticons. We have tried to capture this aspect of tweets in our research.

ML-Based: Classifies the content as certain, uncertain or impartial utilizing Machine Learning grouping calculations and etymological highlights.

Vocabulary Based: Makes utilization of opinion dictionaries, assessment vocabularies are assortments of clarified and preprocessed assumption terms. Conclusion esteems are alloted to words that portray the positive, negative and impartial demeanor of the speaker. It is additionally named:

Word Reference Based Strategy: It utilizes a little arrangement of seed words and an online word reference. The procedure here is beginning seed set of words with their realized directions are gathered and afterward online word references are looked to locate their plausible equivalents and antonyms. The example is arranged dependent on the presence of such flagging opinion words.

Corpus-Based Technique: Uses corpus information to distinguish notion words. Despite the fact that it isn't as successful as word reference based plan, it is useful in finding the area and setting of explicit opinion words against the corpus information. The calculation will approach not exclusively to estimation names, yet in addition to a unique situation.

Hybrid: It is a blend of both Machine Learning and dictionary based methodologies.

In view of an investigation of online message sheets, Russell S, Norvig P. (2003) proposes that females utilize less emoticons than guys, and use them in progressively shifted settings, with guys generally utilizing them for mockery and prodding. In any case, these discoveries ought to be seen circumspectly, since the impacts are probably going to have been vigorously affected by the themes of the message sheets analyzed. While the male commanded message board was about football, the theme of the female overwhelmed message board was "dietary issue support," a region probably not going to be related with mockery or emoticons use in general.Our point is to uncover how emoticons are utilized in explaining wry versus exacting plan. Mockery (and incongruity all in all) is particularly liable to be misconstrued in composed correspondence, as it includes unraveling an implying that is regularly something contrary to what is said. According to Manning, Surdeanu, Bauer, Finkel, Bethard, and McClosky (2014) rather than rating explicit emoticons or looking over a set, the two examinations talked about here enable members to openly create emoticons. This will empower us to see which emoticons are favored when expressly stamping wry and exacting analysis and snide and strict applause, just as the scope of emoticons utilized by members. We expect members will utilize a wide scope of emoticons, with a smaller subset being used most frequently.

Figure 1.

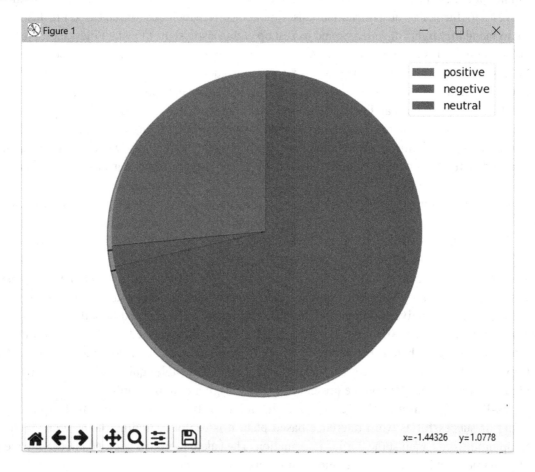

LITERATURE SURVEY

Emojis were initially utilized in Japanese electronic messages and spreading outside in various other areas of Japan. According to Baccianella, Esuli, and Sebastiani (2010) the characters are utilized a lot of like emojis, albeit a more extensive territory is given. The ascent of prominence of emojis is because of its being joined into sets of characters accessible in cell phones. Apple, Android and other portable working frameworks incorporated a few emojis character sets. emojis characters are likewise remembered for the Unicode standard. According to Novak, Smailović, Sluban and Mozetič (2015) the fundamental issue is the way to extricate the rich data that is accessible on Twitter and how might it be utilized to draw significant bits of knowledge. To accomplish this, first we have to manufacture an exact estimation analyzer for tweets, which is the thing that this arrangement expects to accomplish. As a product to information dissect can be utilized SAS Text Miner, SAS Visual Analysis or different devices. The test stays to get modified Tweets and clean information before any content or image mining. SAS Visual Analysis permits direct import of Twitter information, yet to utilize SAS Text Miner and different devices, information must be downloaded and converted.

Various people have proposed Characteristic Language Processing (NLP) systems to address this test and concentrate low-level syntactic highlights from the content of tweets, for example, the nearness of explicit sorts of words and grammatical forms, to build up a classifier to recognize tweets which add to situation mindfulness and tweets which don't. Consequently separating such tweets from those that reflect feeling or on the other hand assumption is a non-inconsequential test, for the most part due to the very little size of tweets and the casual manner by which tweets are composed, with a great deal of emoticons, contractions, etc.

Examinations over tweets identified with four various calamity occasions demonstrate that the proposed highlights distinguish situation mindfulness tweets with fundamentally higher precision than classifiers dependent on standard pack of-words models alone. Sen, Rudra, and Ghosh (2015) proposed a similar examination of Fuzzy C-Means versus K-Means on the Iris data set. They play out a period multifaceted nature correlation between the calculations for modest number of highlights. The outcomes demonstrate that FCM works better than K-implies for modest number of highlights.

Stoyanov, Cardie, and Wiebe (2005) present a similar investigation of K- implies and Soft K-Means(Fuzzy) on the BIRCH and Wine dataset from UCI, which contains 100 and 3 bunches individually.

Vibhu Dagar and Amber Verma, students of Vellore Institute of technology, along with Prof. K Govardhan have worked on this topic to come up with an efficient solution to solve the complicated sentimental analysis problem with the help of emoticons and almost exactly segregate tweets on the basis of exact sentiment score.

PROPOSED WORK

With the help of a python library (tweepy), we gathered the latest 93124 tweets from the twitter stream, sifting the tweets based on the language, the emoticons present and whether they were retweets. Twitter uncovered a stream API to gather such information with channel parameters, for example, language and question. We gathered tweets with around 20 chose emoticons. From these we evacuated all tweets which are retweets or were rehashed. We at that point expelled all tweets with under 5 words to guarantee an exact extremity score. We were left with around 15652 tweets coordinating the above determinations. In these lone 6 emoticons were available, in numbers surpassing an edge of around 2000 tweets.

Along these lines, we chose to diminish the quantity of emoticons to 6 and evacuate all tweets with different emoticons. A sum of 1621 tweets were left, where every emoticon has around 3000 tweets each except for affection, which had around 2400 tweets. Hyperlinks, user names and prevent words were expelled from each tweet, and every one of the characters were changed over to lowercase. Hashtags and emoticons in each tweet were isolated. On the off chance that hashtags were found in camel cased structure, each word will be treated as a different hashtag.

In addition to the above information, we utilized extremity scores from the site which contained a rundown of 8221 positive and negative words. This was to check our tweets for precision. The stop-words in each tweet were distinguished by utilizing the Stanford NLP site, which has around 257 stop-words. We additionally utilize the Snowball stemmer from nltk if there should arise an occurrence of action words, to search for positive or negative words.

Figure 2.

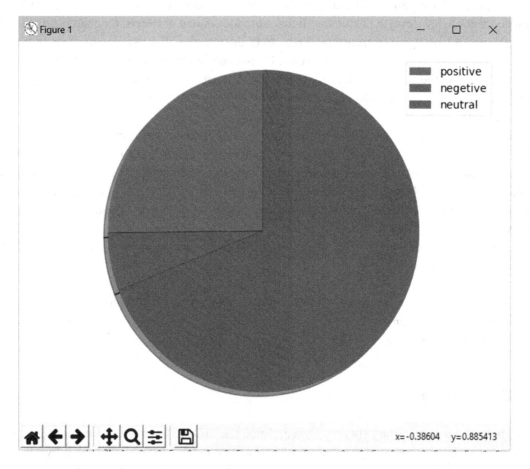

EMOTICON BASED METHOD

Previous studies have shown that maostly the distribution of scores primarily based on the intensity of the emotions being analyzed as an integer polarity. We select 6 of the most commonly used emoticons from a list of 751 emoticons with respect to their frequency and distinction in the emoticons scores. These researched scores are the basis of our approach. The scores are mentioned below:

Table 1. Emoticon based scores

EMOTICON	SYMBOL	SCORE
laughing emoji	😄	0.221
wink emoji	😉	0.445
heart emoji	💜	0.746
crying emoji	😢	-0.093
angry emoji	😠	-0.173
confused emoji	😕	-0.397

SENTIMENT SCORE

Scoring Parameters and Logic

1. Since soft-clustering doesn't need extensive training and works on-the-go, we had to ensure that we cover all features of tweets/text. Apart from the general text pre-processing and considering emoticons and hashtags together, we are focusing on patterns in parts-of-speech(POS), rather than merely judging on the basis of the tag. We check for noun-adjective pairs, and stemmed verbs for helpful understanding of the potential subjectivity of the tweet.

2. Since all noisy parts of data have been removed in pre-processing, we are left with emoticons, hashtags and list of keywords in each twee

3. We had to decide on the amount of data to be shifted for positive or negative words encountered. Rather than using integer polarity to express intensity of words, we use emoticon scores. Since we are using emoticons Sentiment Ranking as our basis, we take average of all the emoticons scores to get 0.124833. We refer to this value as Change In Sentiment. This will be the value used for increasing or decreasing sentiment score

Scoring Components

(1) Emoticons - For each emoticon, assign the sentiment score corresponding to its value in the emoticons ranking site.

(2) Hashtags - If a hashtag is encountered, if its a positive word, increment by 2*averageChangeInSentiment and by - 2*averageChangeInSentiment for a negative word.

(3) POS tags(nltk POS tagger) -

    a) If a noun is encountered - if its preceded by an adjective, then we increment or decrement by 2*averageChangeInSentiment depending on polarity of the word, else we add or subtract the value of averageChangeInSentiment

    (b) If a verb is encountered, stem it and check for positive or negative polarity and assign 2*averageChangeInSentiment. Repeat the same for adjective without the stemming.

METHODOLOGY

Firstly we have segregated all of the tweets from twitter and stored them into a text file. Then we read all these tweets one by one form the text file and removed any mentions or hyperlinks to any websites from the tweets. After lemmatization of these tweets was done. Stop words were removed to make the processing easy. Nltk library is used for lemmatization.

Two methods are used to calculate the score of the tweets. The first one is done using the library TextBlob. This library can classify text into positive, negative or neutral form and display it in the form of scores ranging from -1 to 1, below 0 for negative and above 0 for positive.The second method is the one in which each word is compared to a list of positive and negative words, and then the respective scores are updated for each sentence.

After calculating the scores from both the methods, they are analyzed to accurately predict the final scores. The scores are also analyzed using pie charts. After this the same file containing the tweets are opened in Unicode 16 format so as to make the emoticons readable rather than Unicode 8. Then the emoticons are read one by one for each tweet and converted into text using the emoticons library. Then these specific texts are analyzed to calculate the final score and are combined with the text scores of each tweet with lesser weight.

RESULT ANALYSIS

Final Analysis was made using the final scores obtained from both the methods and analyzing the pie chart along with sentiment percentages.

Figure 3. Pie chart is constructed using positive and negative word search method

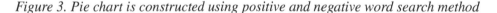
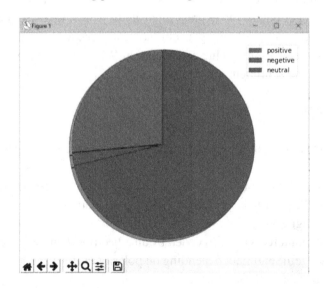

Figure 4. Pie chart is constructed using the TextBlob library.sdd

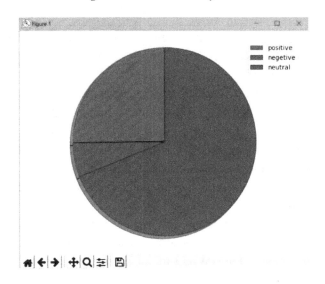

Percentages for both the methods are given below.

```
Percentages Score 1 :
   Positive :  26.400000000000002
   Negetive :  2.1
   Neutral :  71.5
Percentages Score 2 : (TextBlob)
   Positive :  25.2
   Negetive :  5.800000000000001
   Neutral :  69.0
```

Final scores and sarcasm values.

```
[0.0, 0.05, 0.08000000000000002, -0.05, 0.0,
[-0.093, 0.221, -0.093, 0.445, 0.746, 0.001,
[-1.0, 1.0, -1.0, 1.0, 1.0, 1.0, -1.0]
['yes', 'no', 'yes', 'yes', 'yes', 'yes', 'no
>>> |
```

CHALLENGES

Sentiment analysis may not be all that swish in the end. There are many problems associated with Sentiment analysis that could result in the loss of recognition of the technique. It tends to be difficult to comprehend for a machine as well as for a human. The consistent variety in the words utilized in mocking sentences makes it hard to effectively prepare assumption investigation models. Basic points, interests, and chronicled data must be shared between two individuals to make mockery accessible.

- Opinion spam: Sentiment analysis are often employed by competitors to portray negative image of a corporation. Once sentiment analysis gains quality as a metric to measure performance and complete image of a corporation, such mal- practices could become quite common which can result in weakened quality.
- Result measure: The outputs of Sentiment analysis are helpful as a reactive measure. It can't be accustomed to predict the performance of a corporation or alternative metrics. In some cases, Sentiment analysis are often redundant and might be solely a coverage live once the harm has been done.
- Biased results supported the sources: The sources of extracting info are often a serious roadblock in sentiment analysis. Analysis of a state of affairs on incomplete info will result in inclined results. Sources like Twitter, Facebook are often strip- mined to urge complete info.
- Negation Detection: There is no fixed size for the extent of influenced words. For instance, in the sentence "The amazing show was not extremely fascinating," the extension is just the following word after the invalidation word. Be that as it may, for sentences as "I don't consider this film a satire film," the impact of the nullification word "not" is until the finish of the sentence. The first importance of the words changes if a positive or negative word falls inside the extent of nullification—all things considered, inverse extremity will be generated.
- Word ambiguity: Word vagueness is another entanglement you'll confront dealing with a conclusion examination issue. The issue of word vagueness is the inconceivability to characterize extremity ahead of time on the grounds that the extremity for certain words is emphatically reliant on the sentence setting.
- Multiple polarity: Once in a while, a given sentence or report or whatever unit of text we might want to examine, this will show various extremity. In these cases, having just the all out consequence of the investigation can be deceiving, especially like how a normal can once in a while conceal important data pretty much all the numbers that went into it.

But, alternative sources like blogs, posts, forums etc are often tough to retrieve info from that may result in a biased result-set.

CONCLUSION

We are getting high accuracy on maximum occasions when comparing to the TextBlob to our code. That by no means, concludes that we have solved the Sentiment Analysis problem. There are multiple reasons for this result:

(1) Heavy text pre-processing - Out of around a million tweets, we only chose the ones which had the emoticons with clear distinction on the emoticons ranking website

(2) Emoticons - All the tweets included the emoticons, so it is bound to converge to all the clusters. Also, we couldn't impose heavy penalty on positive or negative words or that would change the whole context of sentences.

If we could add subjectivity pre-processing before feeding it to clustering algorithms, it is possible to use these techniques on a much more diverse dataset and get more realistic results. TextBlob algorithms can be very effective if proper structured dataset is fed to them, and in many cases, they can be faster than Machine Learning techniques like Neural Networks etc. without the pains of tuning required.

FUTURE WORK

In future, there can be some changes and modifications done. There can be specific sets of emoticons to judge different type of texts or tweets based on the maximum used emoticons. Also the possibility for adding new emoticons is endless. By collecting more and more data we can correctly predict the scores for each newer emoticon and run it with the adjusted scores of other emoticons to get more efficient results

The work done in this exploration is just identified with order opinion into two of the classes (double grouping) that is a positive class and negative class. Later on advancement, a multiclass of assessment grouping, for example, positive, negative, nonpartisan, etc may be mulled over. In this work, the emphasis is on discovering highlights that show up expressly as things or thing phrases in the surveys. The finding of certain highlights is left to future work. As gathering learning strategies need a great deal of figuring time, parallel processing procedures ought to be investigated to handle this issue. A significant impediment of group learning strategies is the absence of interpret ability of the outcomes and the information learned by outfits is hard for people to get it.

In this way improving the interpretability of gatherings is another significant research course. Future conclusion mining frameworks need more extensive and more profound normal and realistic learning bases. This will prompt a superior comprehension of regular language conclusions and will all the more proficiently overcome any issues between multimodal data and machine processable information. Mixing logical speculations of feeling with the commonsense building objectives of investigating slants in characteristic language content will prompt more bio-enlivened ways to deal with the structure of clever supposition mining frameworks equipped for taking care of semantic information, making analogies, adapting new full of feeling learning, and identifying, seeing, and "feeling" feelings.

REFERENCES

Baccianella, S., Esuli, A., & Sebastiani, F. (2010). *SentiWordNet 3.0: An enhanced lexical resource for sentiment analysis and opinion mining* (Vol. 10). LREC.

Dagar, V., Verma, A., Govardhan, K. (2019). *Sentiment analysis and sarcasm detection (using emoticons)*. Academic Press.

Kolchyna, O., Souza, T. T. P., Treleaven, P. C., & Aste, T. (2015). *Twitter Sentiment Analysis: Lexicon Method, Machine Learning Method and Their Combination.* arXiv preprint arXiv:150700955

Manning, Surdeanu, Bauer, Finkel, Bethard, & McClosky. (2014). The Stanford CoreNLP Natural Language Processing Toolkit. Association for Computational Linguistics (ACL).

Novak, P. K., Smailović, J., Sluban, B., & Mozetič, I. (2015). Sentiment of emoticons. *PLoS One, 10,* 12.

Russell, S., & Norvig, P. (2003). *Artificial Intelligence: A Modern Approach* (2nd ed.). Prentice Hall.

Sen, A., Rudra, K., & Ghosh, S. (2015). Extracting situational awareness from microblogs during disaster events. *2015 7th International Conference on Communication Systems and Networks (COMSNETS).* 10.1109/COMSNETS.2015.7098720

Stoyanov, Cardie, & Wiebe. (2005). *Multi-perspective Question Answering Using the OpQA Corpus.* doi:10.3115/1220575.122069

This research was previously published in Applications of Artificial Intelligence for Smart Technology; pages 164-176, copyright year 2021 by Engineering Science Reference (an imprint of IGI Global).

Chapter 86
Impact of Sarcasm in Sentiment Analysis Methodology

Priscilla Souza Silva

Federal University of South and Southeast of Pará, Brazil

Haroldo Barroso

Federal University of Sul and Sudeste of Pará, Brazil

Leila Weitzel

Fluminense Federal University, Brazil

Dilcielly Almeida Ribeiro

Universidade Federal do Sul e Sudeste do Pará, Brazil

José Santos

Federal University of Sul and Sudeste of Pará, Brazil

ABSTRACT

Sentiment of analysis is a study area applied to numerous environments (financial, political, academic, business, and communication) whose purpose is to search for messages posted on social media, and through these to identify and classify people's opinions about particular item as positive or negative. Rating the sentiment expressed in opinionated messages is such an important task that currently companies invest a lot of money in collecting this type of information and the development of methods and techniques to classify the sentiment that they express, so that they can use the results as useful information in preparing marketing and sales strategies efficiently. However, one of the major problems facing the feelings of analysis is the difficulty of methods to properly analyze messages with sarcastic and/or ironic content, as these linguistic phenomena have the characteristic of transforming the polarity or meaning of a positive or negative statement into its opposite.

DOI: 10.4018/978-1-6684-6303-1.ch086

INTRODUCTION

With the advent of the Web, and increased use of online channels (such as social networks, blogs, social networking sites, online newspapers, forums, recommendations websites and online business tools that allow users to register their opinions on goods and services) in which users exchange information and share their knowledge, criticism, opinions and feelings about a topic of interest, made in the last decade the amount of textual information written in natural language reached gigantic proportions. As Cambria et al. (2013), extract and process properly all this mountain of information has become something extremely interesting to the business world, because through this data companies can get a continuous and faster feedback on the opinion of the public about their products and brand. The academic world in turn is largely responsible for the development of tools and methods to treat such data.

However, despite the relevance of such information, collect and analyze resulting web opinions became an impractical task for the human being in time due to the large amount of textual data published. So to treat and automatically analyze the opinions and sentiments expressed in this type of data has emerged an area called Sentiments Analysis (AS) also called Opinion Mining (LIU, 2010a).

The sentiment analysis according to Benvenuto, Ribeiro and Araújo (2015), is a field of study that uses computer processing to define automated techniques to extract subjective information from texts in natural language, such as opinions and feelings in order to create knowledge structured that can be used by a support system or decision maker. Basically these techniques identify the sentimentthat users have regarding any interest entity (a specific product, a company, a place, a person, among others) based on the Web shared texts, allowing a user to get a report containing what people comment on any item, without having to seek and read all the reviews and news about manually.

Currently companies like Walmart, MCDonalds and IBM, are investing in research groups in sentiment analysis, it realized the value of the opinions expressed in social media and how these views may affect them positively or negatively (CHEN, Zimbra, 2010). Other emerging sectors interested in these data are: a policy to keep its members informed about public opinion regarding their actions; famous accompanying its level of popularity among Internet users; producers interested in knowing about the acceptance of the films produced, among other sectors.

Among the different data sources used by the AS, social networks represent the most conducive environment to identify opinions and feelings about different entities, since they are places where people argue about everything expressing political opinions, religious or even about brands, products and services. In addition to these opinions when properly collected and analyzed, allow not only to understand and explain many complex social phenomena, but also provides them.

However, despite the Web and especially social networks facilitating access and distribution of opinionated information, the task of identifying, classifying, and summarizing data views in text format, it is not trivial and has many challenges, which induce inconsistencies the results generated by sentiment analysis applications. Generally, these challenges are related to the difficulty that computers have to automatically process natural language (human). The automation of processing of human language has its principles in the study area called Natura Language Processing (NLP). This area relates directly with AS, they share the study of unstructured data (LIU; HOGAN; CROWLEY, 2011).

Natural language in turn is somewhat complex mainly when it comes to social networking as there are many nuances in a text message. This complexity is a challenge that are factors of human language, such as words and / or phrases with ambiguous meanings, sarcasm and irony, slang, spelling mistakes, regionalism, dialects, among others.

Given these challenges, it is important to consider that studies on automatic detection and classification of sarcasm and / or irony are still at the beginning. However, a difficulty of analysis is one that has an ability to transform a polarity of a positive or negative statement into its opposite or change its meaning (GONZÁLEZ-IBANEZ, MURESAN, WACHOLDER, 2011). For this, the elements that characterize the language figures, use simple language techniques such as word games, which have a capacity for analyzing applications of analysis of feelings (LUNANDO, PURWARINTI, 2013).

Thus, the recognition and treatment of sarcasm and / or irony are of utmost importance for better performance of methods, algorithms and techniques that make up the systems used for the determination of polarity in messages with opinion, available in great quantity on the Web (KALAMKAR, PHAKAT-KAR, 2013).

Currently, several scientific studies in computing and other areas of knowledge, such as linguistics (Cheang, PELL, 2011), is turning its efforts to the characterization, detection and sarcasm rating and irony in informal dialogues shared on the Web. The authors (BUSCHMEIER; CIMIANO; KLINGER, 2014), for example, presented an analysis of the funds invested in irony detection in a set of data from this product on the reviews on the Amazon.com site. Veale and Hao (2010), pointed out a linguistic approach to separate ironic expressions not ironic figurative expressions, comparing more than one smiles corpus collected on the Web.

In Reyes, Rosso and Veale (2013), the problem of irony detection is addressed only to you share posts on Twitter, where a set of textual features is used to recognize the irony linguistic level. Already in Riloff et al. (2013), the focus is on identifying the sarcastic tweets that express a positive sentimenttoward a negative situation. A model for classifying sarcastic tweets using a set of lexical features is shown in (Barbieri; SAGGION; RONZANO, 2014).

A recent episode that illustrates the importance of studying the sarcasm in social media occurred in 2014, when the agency Secret Service of the United States announced the hiring developers for the construction of a sarcasm detector system in online social networks, the objective was automate real-time analysis of what is published on social networks especially on Twitter (BBC, 2014).

According Benevenuto, Ribeiro and Araújo (2015), the broad applicability of sentiment analysis in various segments has led many companies and researchers from different areas to employ time and money on solutions that perform the extraction of affective factors (thoughts and feelings) in messages shared by the public in social networks, focusing primarily on the identification and orientation of a text classification as positive, negative or neutral.

However, as Maynard and Greenwood (2014) and Gonçalves et al. (2013th), many existing methods in the literature, has been employed in the development of applications without a concrete understanding of its applicability in different contexts, its advantages, limitations and compared efficiency to other methods, and that several of them have never been evaluated in a context involving sarcasm and / or irony. And most importantly, after a thorough analysis of the work in which they are presented methods in such a context, it is clear that there are few efforts to evaluate and quantitatively compare the performance of these methods in a context involving messages with sarcastic content or ironic.

In this context, taking into account the possible impact that the sarcasm presence / irony may have on the performance of sentiment analysis methods, the objective of this study was to evaluate and compare in quantitative terms the performance of different analysis methods feelings sort polarity messages with sarcastic content removed from Twitter, and identify the impact of sarcasm presence on the performance of these methods.

Sentiment Analysis

For Liu (2010a) sentiment analysis a way to automate the analysis of opinions, feelings, evaluations, attitudes, affections, visions, emotions, and subjectivities expressed in the web in text format, for someone about something. Several approaches can be related to AS as Web of opinion extraction mainly from social networks; classification of the extracted opinion as to its polarity (positive, negative or neutral); comparison messages as the opinions they express, etc.

Some scholars such as Liu (2010a) identify the sentiment analysis task as what you might call classification feelings or classification polarity of feelings. However researchers from AS not only restrict the sentiments of classification. Examples of studies linked the area, but they are not facing the sort of feelings or polarity is the research on subjectivity detection (identify if a particular piece of text or posting on Web channels, has opinionated content) as shown at work Pang and Lee (2004), and others such as improving summarization stage, or applying aS the answers and questions systems (SOUZA, 2012).

To perform the classification task usually feelings analysis uses techniques based on areas of Natural Language Processing (NLP) and text mining, for determining whether a given text is expressing a positive, negative or neutral. This is because these areas are pioneers in the treatment of natural language through machines in specific information in text format. PLN is a set of computational techniques for analyzing and representing natural occurrences of text in one or more levels of linguistic analysis. Your goal is to achieve a processing similar to human language, so that computer systems are able to perform different kinds of tasks that involve communication between man and machine or simply by processing useful way of texts and creating value for the user (LIDDY, 2003). In short, it is an area that deals with diverse linguistic elements and grammatical structures, such as morphology, syntax, semantics, among others. Some of his techniques can be used to assist in the pre-processing of textual data step (extremely important step for sentiment analysis task), such as stopwords removal technique, segmentation of words stemming, among others (CARVALHO FILHO, 2014). These techniques are applied in order to improve the structure and organization of data to be analyzed.

The text mining, also known as mining text data is the pattern extraction area, trends or interesting knowledge and non-trivial unstructured data through a set of methods used to browse, organize and find information large textual databases (BERRY, Kogan, 2010). Performs tasks such as sorting, grouping, information extraction, categorization and summarization. When coupled with sentiment analysis it has currently been used for monitoring social media in order to identify what is said about brands on enterprises, mainly (PANG; Lee, 2008). It is in the NLP techniques and text mining that sentiment analysis is based to accomplish their tasks.

Basically, the architecture of a complete system of sentiment analysis is complex, so it is usually divided into large steps. For Angulakshmi and Chezian (2014), these steps include: data recovery, classification and summarization (presentation of results). Figure 1 illustrates the relationship between the steps.

Understanding Sarcasm and Irony

Typically, but not exclusively, sarcasm and irony are figures of speech that occur frequently in content generated by Internet users on blogs, forums, social networks and online microposts like Twitter, Facebook, Myspace and Youtube, especially in English. In this environment, automatically identify when someone is being sarcastic or ironic is a challenge, since human language writing involves complex elements and difficult to understand by machines because as mentioned in the previous section computers do not process accurately messages and words according to the context in which they were written (RILOFF et al., 2013).

Figure 1. Steps of sentiment analysis

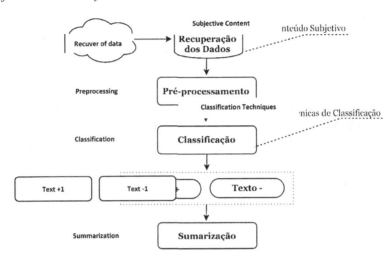

According to the English dictionary NTC's American Inglês (SPEARS, GROUP 1998, our translation), Sarcasm is the "activity of saying or writing the opposite of what you mean, or speak in a way in order to make someone feel stupid or show you that you are angry. " Generally, the sarcasm there is the use of indirect language tools for ridicule or mockery, often considered rude and offensive, being used for destructive purposes and of hypocritically manipulated and false politeness. Sarcasm example can be seen in the tweet "This is my brilliant son, who failed out of college #sarcasm" (the Portuguese translation would be "This is my brilliant son, who could not get out of #sarcasmo college"), in which it is found a sense of thanks to the emergence of a negative setback in a disapproving dialogue.

The irony in turn is "a form of humor that you use words to express the opposite of what the words really mean" (SPEARS, GROUP 1998, our translation). It can be regarded as a discrepancy between what you say and what you feel, or what is expected and what actually occurs (Singh, 2012). This kind of message is usually accompanied by a playful tone and has less offensive weight than sarcasm. For example, "I loved my iPhone 6s! #irony" ("I love my iPhone 6s! #irony"), In this post funny tone the user shows his disapproval towards the mobile device, taking into account problems the model presented during its launch.

In the view of Conz (2010), the sarcasm and irony have a close connection, as both tend to be used to make a statement that has an emotional sense. Often people say that something is ironic when in reality it is sarcastic and vice versa. However, in reality sarcasm is a concept that makes use of irony. In most cases, the subtle difference between the two is that sarcasm is almost cruel scathing order, often hurting the sensitivity of the person who receives it, while the irony is more polite and subtle. Traditionally the distinction between the two is that sarcasm is an irony more explicitly.

Today, especially in social networks, sarcasm and irony are generally used in statements in which people "say the opposite of the truth, or the opposite of their true feelings in order to be funny, to emphasize a point or mock something or someone "(MAYNARD, GREENWOOD, 2014).

To Gonçalves et al. (2015), one of the main difficulties for the identification task or sarcastic or ironic messages Web classification is the lack of agreement among most researchers (sociologists, psychologists, computer scientists, etc.) on how to define or differentiate ironic sarcasm. While several studies suggest that sarcasm and irony are terms associated with the same linguistic phenomenon (Conz, 2010; INGLE et al., 2014; MAYNARD, GREENWOOD, 2014), other researchers and Singh (2012) argue that these phenomena differ.

Therefore, considering that the database used in this study has messages (tweets) of users who do not differentiate irony sarcasm, this research as well as Maynard and Greenwood (2014) and Ingle et al. (2014) defines a sarcastic and / or ironic statement as "one where the opposite meaning of the sentence is intentional," because this is the dominant use of the work and also what tends to influence / impact the polarity of the sentiment expressed in the messages. For example, "I love walking to work in the rain # #irony sarcasm," it would be interpreted as a negative polarity message on her sarcastic and ironic sense. Thus the irony and sarcasm terms were treated in this paper as similar.

In this context that involves sarcasm and / or irony web, in view of Riloff et al., (2013), feelings of analysis can be easily fooled by the presence of words that have a strong polarity, which are used as sarcasm, the it means that the opposite polarity was intentional. For example, the following tweet that includes the words "yay" (oba) and "thrilled" (enthusiastic) are strong words, but actually express a negative feeling: "yay it's a holiday weekend and I'm on call for work! Could not be more thrilled! #sarcasm. " ("Wow! A long holiday and I'm on duty at work! It could not be more excited! #sarcasmo"). In this case, the #sarcasm hashtag reveals the intended sarcasm, but not always the methods used to classify feelings have the benefit of explicit nature sarcasm tags in a message.

Hashtags are usually used as metadata in tweets, is to express a pragmatic information in textual form, as irony, or evaluation (eg the #not hastags, #win, #fail), or to classify them on the topic (eg #google, #android, etc.). Research in the area AS exploit the use of hashtags as feelings of labels, i.e., the methods classify the orientation of the polarity of messages according to keywords within hashtags having.

For automatic identification of these linguistic phenomena, some studies suggest the creation of methods to seek for common grammatical factors in sarcastic / ironic phrases (eg, interjections and adverbs). In Kreuz and Caucci (2007), were created patterns and grammatical formulas for sarcasm identification and irony. Another strategy for identification of sarcasm / irony in messages posted on social networks, is the filtering technique for hashtags that denote sarcasm. For example, Gonzalez-Ibañes et al. (2011), created a textual database only sarcasm satisfaction messages, each message was kneecap with #sarcasm and #sarcastic hashtags.

Correlated Works

In the research of Gupta and Yang (2017), a system was developed that performs an analysis of shared sentiment through SemEval-2017. This system has the main characteristic of the ability to detect sarcasm in order to improve performance when classifying sentiment in text. For this was constructed an affect-cognition-sociolinguistic characteristics of sarcasm and, this model was trained with the SVM algorithm to detect sarcastic expressions in various tweets. As a result, the authors identified in the features derived from the detection of sarcasm have consistently benefited as key evaluation analysis metrics to varying degrees in four A-D subtasks.

In Poria, Cambria, Hazarika and Vij (2016), a structure was proposed that learned sarcasm automatically from a corpus of sarcamo, using a convolutive neural network called CNN, pre-trained to extract characteristics of sentiment, emotion and personality for a detection of sarcasm. Such features, along with network baseline capabilities, are proposed models that outperform the state of the art in reference datasets.

METHODS APPLIED IN THE SEARCH SCOPE

In the literature there are several methods of analysis of feelings, which are differentiated by the classification techniques they use to determine the sense or polarity expressed in a message. Among these techniques there may be mentioned approaches based on lexical dictionaries, machine learning, natural language processing, psychometric scales that hybrid methods (combination of different methods) and advanced linguistic and statistical techniques.

In Pang vision and Lee (2008), current detection methods and / or feelings or polarity Web posted messages classification, can be divided basically into two groups based on techniques lexical dictionaries and machine learning. The methods based on machine learning commonly rely on manually labeled databases to train (teach) algorithms called classifiers. On the other hand, methods using lexical dictionaries and lists of words associated with specific feelings (Benevenuto; RIBEIRO; Araujo, 2015).

Dictionary lexicon of feelings, is a kind of dictionary words or terms that instead of having as content the meaning of each word, has in place a quantitative meaning (ie, can be a number between -1 to 1, where - 1 is the most negative sentimental value and 1 the most positive value) or qualitative value (ie positive / negative, happy / sad, love / hate). approaches assume that lexical individual words have what is called prior polarity, which is an independent semantic context and guidance that can be expressed with a numerical value or polarity of class (TABOADA et al., 2011).

In addition to the lexical dictionaries another technique used for sorting or messages polarity analysis, is the Machine Learning. It consists of a subfield of artificial intelligence (AI) applied to development of algorithms and techniques that allow computers to be able to learn and evolve their performance on certain tasks, through experience gained in the repetition of such tasks (MITCHEL, 2006). Simon (1983) also defines learning machine (AM) as any change and a system to improve its performance in an automatic way at a later repetition of the same task or another task using the same database. According to Becker and Tumitan (2013), the main purpose of machine learning techniques is automatically find general rules (ie, standards) in large databases that allow find information implicitly represented. In general, the techniques and AM algorithms can be divided into two types: supervised learning and unsupervised learning.

The following are the twelve methods of AS that were evaluated in this study, as well as the polarity classification techniques or sense in which they are based.

- **SentiWordNet:** It consists of a lexical base in text file format used for feelings of classification. It was developed by the Bank of English language words WordNetnota (Miller, 1995), which consists of nouns, verbs, adjectives and adverbs cognitive synonyms grouped in sets (synsets), each expressing a different concept. The synsets are interconnected by means of conceptual-semantic and lexical relations. The SentiWordNet is the result of automatic annotation of each synsets of WordNet, which was assigned to each word three numerical values indicating which P (Positive), N (negative) O (neutral) the terms contained in each sysnet are. Currently SentiWordNet is in version 3.0, available at <http://sentiwordnet.isti.cnr.it/>.

- **PANA-t:** A lexicon method is adapted from an expanded version of a scale well known in psychology called the Positive and Negative Affect Schedule (Watson, CLARK; Tellegen, 1985). It aims to detect the users mood fluctuations on Twitter through the posts. It consists of a psychometric scale based on a broad lexicon of words associated with 11 categories of humor: cheerfulness, confidence, serenity, surprise, fear, sadness, guilt, hostility, shyness, fatigue and attention. It is designed to detect any increase or decrease of feelings of levels over a period. The table in Figure 7 summarizes the items that make up the PANAS-t range (GONÇALVES; PAINS; Benevenuto, 2012).

- **Emolex:** The EmoLex Mohammad and Turney (2013th), is a lexicon created from the Amazon Mechanical Turk Servicenota in which people were paid to sort the terms. Each entry is associated with 8 basic feelings in English: joy, sadness, anger, etc. The base was built using EmoLex terms of Macquarie Thesaurusnota and words of General Inquirernota and Wordnet. The words that compose it include some nouns, verbs, adjectives and adverbs most common of the English language. The method also includes not only the presence but also of unigrams various bigramasnota, which are commonly used in texts.

- **NRC Hashtag:** Developed by Mohammad Kiritchenko and Zhu (2012), consists of a dictionary of words with associations for positive and negative feelings, linked to eight emotion categories: happiness, sadness, anger, fear, trust, disgust, anticipation and surprise . The lexicon is distributed in three files: unigrams-pmilexicon.txt (54.129 terms), bigrams-pmilexicon.txt (316.531 terms) and peer-pmilexicon.txt (480.010 terms). To create this lexicon thousands of tweets were automatically labeled based on the occurrence of hashtags linked to positive and negative words. From the auto-labeling found with relatively simple scores, which words occur more frequently in positive or negative tweets.

- **Opinion Lexicon:** Also known as Sentiment Lexicon (HU; LIU, 2004), is a lexical database publicly available, it contains approximately 6,800 words, and in 2006 with positive semantic orientation and 4783 negatively. It was initially built from Wordnet, a word database in English grouped into sets of synonyms (synsets).

- **VADER:** Proposed by (HUTTO; GILBERT, 2014) VADER (Valence Aware Dictionary for Sentiment Reasoning) is a method for sentiment analysis developed for the context of social media. In its construction the authors created a list of words based on dictionaries already well established as LIWC, ANEWnota and GInota. Then they were added numerous lexical present buildings in microblogs such as emoticons, acronyms and slang to express feelings, resulting in 9000 new candidates to be included in the dictionary. Then, it was found through the "knowledge of crowds" (AMT) which of these actually had applicability through score by Turkers ranging from -4 (extremely negative) to 4 (extremely positive). Finally, remaining 7000 lexical constructions in the dictionary that is to include the average between the evaluations obtained from the AMT should be different from 0 (neutral) and standard deviation of the scores below a threshold established by the authors. The word "okay" for example has a score of 0.9, while "great" has the value 3.1 and "horrible" is -2.5 (Benvenuto; RIBEIRO, ARAUJO, 2015).

- **Sentiment140:** Sentiment140-Lexicon or simply Sentiment140 (MOHAMMAD; KIRITCHENKO; ZHU, 2013b), is a lexicon of words associated with positive and negative feelings. The method was created with a database consisting of about 1.6 million tweets labeled as positive or negative. The corpus used to create this method can be found in http://saifmohammad. com/Lexicons/Sentiment140-Lexicon-v0.1.zip

- **SentiStrength:**It is a tool to estimate the polarity of short texts in informal language, for it uses a lexicon labeled by humans and is automatically enhanced by machine learning. Your main language is English, but also has implementations that allow the classification in other languages. It also uses classification techniques based on machine learning that enable its improvement automatically. It also has a dictionary of terms based on an optimized version for social networks LIWC dictionary. This form is characterized as a hybrid method (Thelwall, 2013). Given a message, said tool classifies its polarity within a range of [-5, 5] -5 which represent the most negative scores and 5 the most positive. It is available for download at <http://sentistrength.wlv.ac.uk/>.

- **Combined Method:** Developed by (Goncalves et al, 2013th.) Combined Methos (in Portuguese, Method Combined) is a method which is the combination of 7 methods used in the literature for the task of analyzing feelings, being: PANAS-t, emoticons, SentiStrength, SentiWordNet, SenticNet, SASA and Happiness Index. It analyzes the harmonic mean (F-measure) the precision and recall of each method and distributes different weights for each. To evaluate the performance of the method, the developers tested on SentiStrength database consisting of labeled messages by human, then they calculated the F-measure, and the average coverage on such data.

- **AFINN:** AFINN (Nielsen, 2011), is a lexicon that provides a list of English words associated with an affective valence or score, is list includes words with feelings, internet slang and obscenities. The scores (scores) of the words vary on a scale of -5 indicating a very negative feeling, 5 indicating a very positive feeling. Currently there are two versions: AFINN-111 latest version with 2477 words and phrases, and AFINN-96 with 1468 words and original sentences in 1480 lines.

- **Pattern.en:** It is a package of python programming language to deal with natural language processing. One of its modules is responsible for inferring the sentimentin the text. Designed to be fast it is based on polarities associated with WordNet. This module is called "text" and contains: a quick labeler part-of-speech into English (which identifies nouns, adjectives, verbs, etc. in a sentence), tools for verb conjugation and noun, individualization and pluralization in English, a WordNet interface; a lexicon with 8,500 common English verbs and their conjugated forms, and analyze feelings (Smedt; NIJS; Daelemans, 2014). The Pattern.en packs a lexicon of adjectives (eg, good, bad, amazing, annoying, ...) which often occur in product reviews, annotated with the scores for a sense of polarity (positive negative ↔) and subjectivity (↔ goal subjective).

Support Vector Machine. Support Vector Machine (SVM) consists of a machine learning method for supervised binary classification based on the theoretical foundations of statistical learning developed by Vapnik (1995). A method is implemented by algorithms which visualize the data as input two sets of vectors in an N-dimensional much space (N is the number of vector attributes), and attempt to classify correctly new data (Goncalves, 2010).

The idea behind the SVM is to find optimal separation hyperplane, that is, debt and better differentiates two classes (categories) of data. To do this, first the algorithm must manually receive labeled data for training (if the message classification these data are the vectors of words or terms), and after performing various intelligent training tests with labeled data is the same as points in the feature space, and then build hyperplanes capable of separating the different classes identified in the labeled data, so that new input data which are not part of the test set are sorted correctly (HASTIE; TIBSHIRANI; FRIEDMAN, 2008).

COLLECTION AND HANDLING OF DATA

To validate the proposed approach was counted using a database of short messages (tweets) labeled (classified) manually as positive, negative or neutral, comprised of several subjects. To collect the data necessary to carry out the experiments with the methods, the microblogging service launched was used in 2006, Twitter, one of the reasons for choosing this social network was to be a dissemination tool of information responsible for a lot real-time available opinionated content, in addition to its wide use for academic work with the same line of research of this work. One of its main features is the maximum size prefixed in 140 characters to post tweets. Thus, we have a positive point, posting short messages that emit sentimentabout only one object.

The collection resulted in a total of more than 3,000 tweets. This complete a manual filtration was performed with the purpose to separate and select messages that compose the database being used in experiments. After this initial screening process performed manually, the database is initially collected summed to a total of 1137 tweets.

The data collected initially passed through a treatment (pre-processing) in order to remove the inconsistencies that could disrupt the classification process performed by methods and algorithm. In addition to that second (SANTOS, 2010; Benevenuto; RIBEIRO, ARAUJO, 2015) preprocessing is an integrated and essential step of the AS task. Thus, 1137 tweets resulting from the previous step under-gone a treatment where considered structures were discarded irrelevant to the process of classification of the polarity of data, called tokens. These structures included: irrelevant words stopwords calls, present terms specifically Twitter, punctuation and special characters.

Messages that made each tweet were also classified (labeled or tagged) manually by creating so labels to identify the sentiment expressed by each message as positive, negative or neutral. The labeled data took two tasks: comparison basis for the results generated by the methods (ie a point of comparison between the actual polarity of the messages and trial methods), and as a basis for experiments with SVM algorithm, since this uses data labeled to train the algorithm. Possible labels were:

- **Positive:** Messages that do not express any opinion or feeling;
- **Negative:** Messages that express a negative feeling, but are written with the structure of positive texts;
- **Neutral:** Messages that do not express any opinion or feeling.

Experiments Done

After preparation of the data were performed experiments with the methods provided by iFeel Web tool and Support Vector Machine algorithm. These experiments were performed in two ways: the first messages were submitted to the algorithm and methods in the presence of hashtags (markers) that indicate sarcasm, in the second test were removed from these hashtags messages and the base resubmitted for classification.

The first experiment consisted in sentiment analysis performed by the 11 methods provided by the Web iFeel system, on the set of 1137 tweets collected and properly treated in the previous steps. The methods used were SentiWordNet, PANAS-t, Sentistrength, EmoLex, NRC Hashtag, Opinion Lexicon, Pattern.en, AFINN, VADER, Sentiment140 and Combined Method. We are chosen specifically for these methods use different polarity classification techniques allowing diversity in the results generated. The objective of this experiment was basically to test the performance of the methods mentioned above, to correctly classify the polarity (feeling) messages (tweets) positive, neutral and mostly negative. For the messages labeled as negative (representing the sarcastic nature of messages), they are in fact sentences written with words and key terms that have a positive character, but express a negative sentimentwhen analyzed according to the context in which they were written ie are the messages that suffered from the reverse polarity caused by the presence of sarcasm.

The second experiment in turn, was the classification of the set of tweets with and without the presence of sarcastic nature of hashtags, the algorithm based on learning SVM machines, whose goal was was also to test the performance of classifying the polarity sarcastic nature messages. This experiment was divided into two tasks: classification of tweets with the presence of sarcastic nature of hashtags and without the presence of these.

An important note is the fact that the experiments with the SVM algorithm neutral tweets had to be discarded, since the aforementioned standard for algorithm disregards goals texts (neutral polarity) as the default output generated by it is binary, which means that text is likely to belong to only one of two classes - negative (0) or positive (1). Then, after the disregard of neutral tweets set 1137 tweets, the database resulted in a total of 906 tweets for experiments with the algorithm.

Finally the results of the classifications made by the methods and algorithm, and with the correct labeling of messages in the test base, it was estimated then performance evaluation metrics: recall, precision, F-measure and accuracy. The values were used to compare the performance of the methods and organize the results in the shape of tables and graphs. These metrics are best addressed in the next section.

Metrics for Performance Comparison

A key aspect in the evaluation of methods for analyzing feelings regards used metrics. In this context, four key metrics are commonly used to validate the efficiency of a method, they are: precision, recall, F-measure and accuracy. Specifically in sentiment analysis area these metrics are used in the literature for methods of assessment and detection algorithms or polarity classification of feelings (Sokolova, Lapalme, 2009; Gonçalves et al, 2015;. RIBEIRO, 2015). These metrics were used for performance evaluation of the methods tested in this research.

- **Precision (P):** Measures portion of samples of a class that were classified correctly, ie, evidence the percentage of messages belonging to a class of polarity that were correctly classified by taking into consideration the method of trial and error method for this class. To find the precision of a class X must divide the number of messages classified correctly by the total of classified messages as belonging to class X. As shown by the following equation (Sokolova, Lapalme, 2009).

$$Precision = \frac{\text{TP}}{\left(\text{TP} + \text{FP}\right)}$$

TP is the total of true positive of the class is calculated and FP total false positives class in question.

- **Recall (R):** The recall measure (R) measures the proportion of classified samples as a class in relation to all kind of samples, that is, the percentage of messages of a certain polarity class that were correctly classified by the method from total messages comprising the particular class. Their percentage evidence adjustment capability of the method to the total of messages belonging to certain polarity class. This percentage is calculated according to the following equation (Sokolova, Lapalme, 2009).

$$Recall = \frac{TP}{\left(TP + FN\right)}$$

TP is the total of true positive of the class which is the total FN calculating and false negative of the class in question.

- **F-Measure:** It is the harmonic mean or balance between precision and recall. Feelings commonly used in analysis area to assess the classification ability of a method to determined polarity class. Its result provides one measure of comparison that allows comparison of the classification capacity between different methods. Thus, the better the method evaluated closer to 1 is the metric value, and if the method has a low rating capacity it will have a value of F-measure closer to 0 (Sokolova, Lapalme, 2009).

$$F - measure = \frac{2 \cdot \left(Precision \cdot Recall\right)}{\left(Precision + Recall\right)}$$

Applied to the scope of this work, this metric was used to directly compare the overall performance classification of the different methods and tested algorithm.

- **Accuracy:** The measurement accuracy (A) the accuracy English, denotes the proportion (percentage) Total method hit regardless of the polarity class, that is, the sum of the hits of all the polarity classes divided by the total number classified messages (Sokolova ; Lapalme, 2009). In this research the accuracy was used in comparing the performance of the methods globally on all the problem of sentimentclasses. It is calculated according to the following equation.

$$Accuracy = \frac{TP}{\left(TP + FP + FN\right)}$$

It is noteworthy that the F-measure is a weighted measure of precision and recall and was used to measure the overall ability of the method of classification for a particular class, that is, the most important measure to evaluate the performance of the methods and algorithm studied

COMPARISON RESULTS

This section presents the quantitative results as a percentage of polarity classification performed by the 11 methods and algorithm. These results are: the recall, precision and F-measure, obtained by each method for each class polarity (positive, negative, and neutral) exists in the test data base.

Each following diagram, shows the values of precicion, recall and F-measure er achieved by each of the 11 methods implemented on the Web iFeel tool, according to two tests carried out on the satisfaction test based on the 1137 tweets: the first test was the classification of tweets with the presence of sarcastic nature of hashtags and the second test was the classification without the presence of sarcastic nature of hashtags. For each table there is a chart corresponds, allowing for better visualization and comparison of results. The y-axis (represented by a scale of 0 to 100) equals the percentage achieved by any method each evaluation metric (i.e., the method of classification performance), while the x-axis represents the sentimentanalysis method tested

The following charts bring the results of the classifications made by the methods of the Test Base with and without the presence of sarcasm die hashtags.

Figure 2. Comparison of test results hashtags (tweets positives)

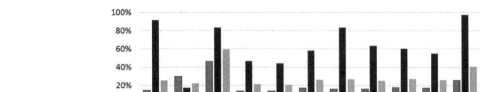

Figure 3. Comparison of test results without hashtags (Neutral tweets)

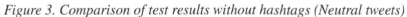
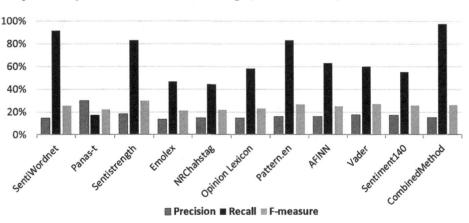

For the classification of tweets with positive polarity, the methods with greater precision, recall and F-measure, respectively:

- Sentistrength, more precisely at a rate 46.30%, in the experiment with the presence of sarcastic nature of hashtags;
- Increased recall was the PANAS-t (17.50%) in both tests;;
- Emolex (20.97%), had a higher F-measure, the test without hashtags.

Figure 4. Comparison of test results with hashtags (negative tweets)

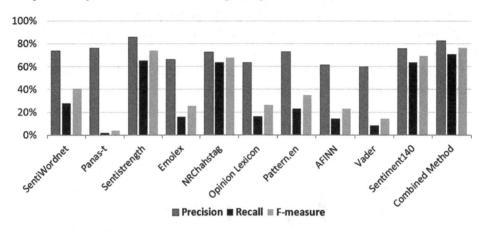

Figure 5. Comparison of the test results without hashtags (negative tweets)

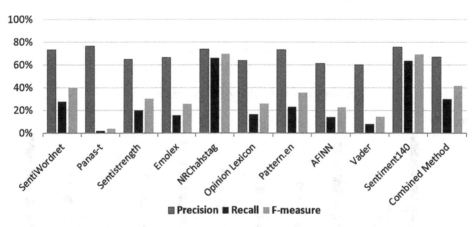

In the ranking of 786 negative tweets that had sarcastic content from the first test (negative tweets with the presence of sarcastic nature of hashtags) and the second test (negative tweets without hashtags), the results were as follows:

- **Precision:** The first test Sentistrength method (85.64%) had the highest accuracy rate. As for the second test the best was the Pattern.en with 76.19%. The method Vader got the worst rate in both tests - 59.81% (with hashtags) and 60.19% (no hashtags);
- **Recall:** For the first test the Combined Method (71.12%) reached better recall, in the second test NRChashtag (66.03%) was the best. The method as poor recall in both tests was PANAS-T at the rate of 2.04%;
- **F-Measure:** With a percentage of 76.47% the Combined Method was the best performing method to classify the class of negative tweets, however for the second test was the best NRChashtag with 69.52%. The worst performance was in the NAPA-T (3.97%) in both tests.

Figure 6. Comparison of the test results with hashtags (neutral tweets)

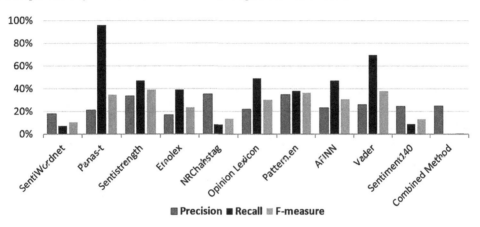

Figure 7. Comparison of the test results without hashtags (neutral tweets)

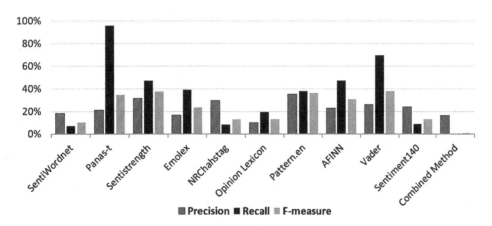

Taking into consideration the total of 231 neutral tweets labeled in accordance with the tables and graphs presented above:

- The method with higher accuracy in the test was hashtags NRChashtag the rate of 35.09%, since the test without hashtags the highest rate was achieved by Pattern.en (35.20%);
- The PANAS-T had the highest recall in both tests (96.10%), and Combined Method worse in both tests (0.43%);
- The highest percentage of F-measure to the test with hashtags was hit by Sentistrength (39.42%), as the test without hashtags Vader fared better with 37.97%. The worst result of F-measure was the Combined Method method (0.85% and 0.84%).

The graph in Figure 8 shows the results of the classifications carried out by the SVM algorithm for the experiments with and without the presence of sarcasm die hashtags.

Figure 8. Results obtained by the SVM algorithm

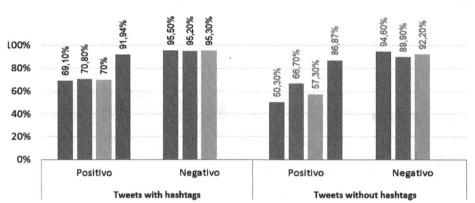

In tests with the Support Vector Machine algorithm (SVM), and with the methods implemented in the Web iFeel tool, the algorithm performed better to sort the tweets in the presence of sarcastic nature of hashtags. As the graph in Figure 8.

Figure 9. Accuracy experiment with sarcastic nature of hashtags

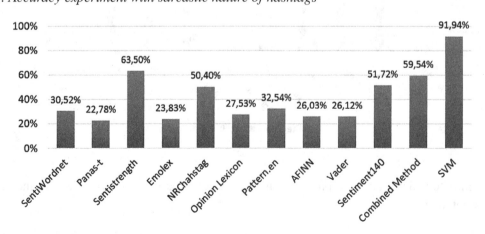

For further enrichment of this work was also carried out to compare the performance of methods in terms of accuracy, which is to hit rate on the three polarity classes, to experiment with hashtags (Figure 8) and without hashtags (Figure 9) .

Figure 10. Accuracy of experiment without sarcastic nature of hashtags

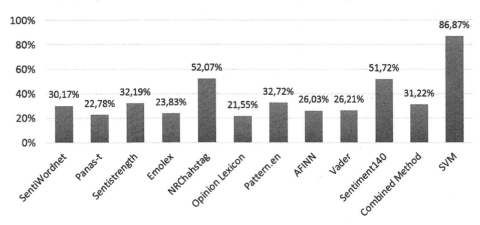

As the chart 9, among the methods implemented in iFeel system to the test with presence of hashtags, the method with the highest percentage of correct answers was the Sentistrength (63,50%). Have the lowest percentage of correct answers was with the PANAS-T method (22.78% performance). As for the test on the tweets hashtags after removal of the NRChashtags method was better with a percentage of 52.07%, while Opinion Lexicon (21.55%) achieved the worst percentage. However when comparing the SVM algorithm with other methods implemented in iFeel, it is observed that the SVM had a higher rating performance, with a lead of 34.08% over the NRChashtags method, the classification without hashtags.

Analyzing the results also realize is that the most accurate rate achieved was when the methods classified the tweets even with the hashtags.

FUTURE RESEARCH DIRECTIONS

As future work, we intend to study the semantic and syntactic structure of tweets with sarcastic content in order to find a pattern that can identify sarcasm and other figures of speech, commonly used in short messages posted on social networks. In addition to performing the evaluation and comparison of performance of a greater number of feelings analysis methods. It is also intended to test this more and equalized database, ie, a base in which the amount of polarity samples for each class are equal.

CONCLUSION

In this work we tried to evaluate 12 different methods of analysis of feelings existing in the literature, and how different performances they present to classify a polarity of messages with sarcastic content, taken from Twitter. The approach adopted was to quantitatively identify the performance of these methods in the context of sarcasm.

Following are two tables. Table 1 with the result of the classification performed by the methods with the presence of sarcasm and, table 2 without the presence of hashtags.

Table 1. Performance of all methods tested with hashtags

Method	F-Measure (Positive)	F-Measure (Negative)	F-Measure (Neutral)
SentWordNet	25,49%	40,55%	10,43%
Panas-t	22,11%	3,97%	34,77%
Sentistrength	59,52%	74,08%	39,42%
Emolex	21,01%	25,49%	23,70%
NRChashtag	20,10%	67,84%	13,89%
Opinion Lexicon	26,22%	26,09%	30,36%
Pattern.en	26,49%	35,17%	36,36%
AFINN	25,17%	22,96%	31,01%
Vader	27,02%	14,33%	37,97%
Sentiment140	25,93%	69,20%	13,25%
Combined Method	40,55%	76,47%	0,85%

Table 2. Performance of all methods tested without hashtags

Method	F-Measure (Positive)	F-Measure (Negative)	F-Measure (Neutral)
SentWordNet	25,26%	39,96%	10,56%
Panas-t	22,11%	3,97%	34,77%
Sentistrength	29,90%	30,52%	37,85%
Emolex	20,97%	25,49%	23,73%
NRChashtag	21,95%	69,52%	13,42%
Opinion Lexicon	23,22%	26,09%	13,49%
Pattern.en	26,46%	35,49%	36,59%
AFINN	25,17%	22,96%	31,01%
Vader	27,07%	14,54%	37,97%
Sentiment140	25,98%	69,20%	13,21%
Combined Method	26,09%	41,58%	0,84%

Through the results obtained for an F-measure metric, it was possible to verify that among 12 methods of analysis of quality feelings, which obtained a higher capacity of classification of the messages (tweets) with sarcastic content, in the presence or not of sarcastic hashtags (SVM) with the confidence values of 95.35% and 92.94% (Figure 8). What characterizes what is best classified as messages even without the help of hashtags, which help you in identifying sarcasm. While that obtained the classification performance for the PANAS-method with a percentage of 3.97% performance (Figures 4 and 5).

Another important point observed from the results found, which strengthened an idea of the impact caused by the sarcasm, was the fact that the methods Sentistrength, combined method and SVM had in their results a considerable reduction of performance, when classifying the tweets with meaning sarcastic (tweets negatives) Without the presence of sarcastic hashtags. As shown in the graphs of Figures 4 and 8, the three methods cited obtained the following performance when classifying negative tweets with the presence of hashtags: 74.08%, 76.47% and 95.35% respectively, but after performing the (Tables 5 and 8), respectively. The results obtained in this study were similar to those of the F-measure. According to these results it is possible to conclude that the Sentistrength suffered a performance decrease of 43.56% in its performance performance, the Combined Method a reduction 34.89% and the SVM a decrease of 3.11%.

These phenomena observed within the scope of this research reveal that some of the tested methods presented inconsistent classification results when compared to the manually classified database (labeled) by humans. Thus, it is possible that different methods of feeling analysis found in the literature may present inconsistent results due to the inversion of polarity caused by the presence of sarcasm in shared messages in social media. This performance drop occurred mainly when the methods classified the messages without the presence of sarcastic hashtags, which are labels with words that aid some methods in identifying the polarity inversion present in the messages. Thus, the complexity of identifying and classifying polarity in sarcastic messages is shown.

Finally, it is emphasized that the identification of these changes in the performance of the methods are of high importance when it comes to organizations that use the results generated by methods of analysis of feelings to guide their decision making.

REFERENCES

Angulakshmi, G., & Chezian, R. (2014). Article. *International Journal of Advanced Research in Computer and Communication Engineering*, *3*(7), 5.

Barbieri, F., Saggion, H., & Ronzano, F. (2014). Modelling sarcasm in twitter, a novel approach. *WASSA, ACL, 2014*, 50.

BBC. (2014). *US Secret Service seeks Twitter sarcasm detector*. Retrieved from http://www.bbc.com/news/technology-27711109

Becker, K., & Tumitan, D. (2013). Introdução à mineração de opiniões: Conceitos, aplicações e desafios. *Lectures of the 28th Brazilian Symposium on Databases*.

Benevenuto, F. Ribeiro, F., & Araújo, M. (2015). Métodos Para Análise de Sentimentos em Mídias Sociais. *Brazilian Symposium on Multimedia and the Web (Webmedia)*.

Berry, M., & Kogan, J. (2010). Text Mining: Applications and Theory. Wiley. doi:10.1002/9780470689646

Buschmeier, K., Cimiano, P., & Klinger, R. (2014). An impact analysis of features in a classification approach to irony detection in product reviews. *Proceedings of the 5th Workshop on Computational Approaches to Subjectivity, Sentiment and Social Media Analysis*, 42–49. 10.3115/v1/W14-2608

Cambria, E. (n.d.). New avenues in Opinion mining and sentiment analysis. *IEEE Intelligent Systems, 28*(2), 15–21.

Carvalho Filho, J. A. (2014). *Mineração de Textos: Análise de Sentimentos Utilizando o Tweets Referentes a Copa do Mundo* (Dissertação de Mestrado). Universidade Nova de Lisboa, Quixadá.

Cheang, H. S., & Pell, M. D. (2011). Recognizing sarcasm without language: A cross-linguistic study of English and Cantonese. *Pragmatics & Cognition, 19*(2), 203–223. doi:10.1075/pc.19.2.02che

Chen, H., & Zimbra, D. (2010). AI and Opinion Mining. *IEEE Intelligent Systems, 25*(3), 74–80.

Conz, J. (2010). IRONIA VERBAL: Teorias e Considerações (Graduação em Letras). Universidade Federal do Rio Grande do Sul, Porto Alegre.

Gonçalves, M. A. (2010). *Abordagens para Avaliação Automática da Qualidade de Conferências científicas: um estudo de caso em ciência da computação* (Dissertação de Mestrado). Universidade Federal de Minas Gerais, Belo Horizonte.

Gonçalves, P. (2013a). Comparing and combining sentiment analysis methods. In *Proceedings of the First ACM Conference on Online Social Networks (COSN '13)*. New York, NY: ACM. 10.1145/2512938.2512951

Gonçalves, P., Dores, W., & Benevenuto, F. (2012). Panas-t: Uma escala psicométrica para medição de sentimentos no twitter. *Proceedings of the Brazilian Workshop on Social Network Analysis and Mining (BraSNAM)*.

Hastie, T., Tibshirani, R., & Friedman, J. (2008). The elements of statistical learning: data mining, inference and prediction (2nd ed.). Springer.

Hu, M., & Liu, B. (2004). Mining opinion features in customer reviews. In *Proceedings of the 19th National Conference on Artifical Intelligence*. AAAI Press.

Hutto, C. J., & Vader. (2014). A parsimonious rule-based model for sentiment analysis of social media text. *Eighth International AAAI Conference on Weblogs and Social Media*.

Ingle, A. (2014). Sentiment analysis: Sarcasm detection of tweets. Nagpur.

Kalamkar, P. N., & Phakatkar, A. G. (2013). Opinion mining in figures of speech in text. *International Journal of Scientific Engineering Research, 4*(10), 1132–1134.

Kreuz, R. J., & Caucci, G. M. (2007). Lexical influences on the perception of sarcasm. In *Proceedings of the Workshop on Computational Approaches to Figurative Language*. Stroudsburg, PA: Association for Computational Linguistics. 10.3115/1611528.1611529

Liu, B. (2010b). Sentiment analysis: Amultifaceted Problem. *IEEE Intelligent Systems, 25*(3), 76–80.

Liu, K., Hogan, W. R., & Crowleya, R. S. (2011). Natural language processing methods and systems for biomedical ontology learning. *Journal of Biomedical Informatics, 44*(1), 163–179. Retrieved from http://migre.me/thZEQ

Lunando, E., & Purwarianti, A. (2013). Indonesian social media sentiment analysis with sarcasm detection. *Advanced Computer Science and Information Systems (ICACSIS), 2013 International Conference,* 195–198. 10.1109/ICACSIS.2013.6761575

Maynard, D., & Greenwood, M. A. (2014). *Who cares about sarcastic tweets? Investigating the impact of sarcasm on sentiment analysis.* LREC.

Miller, G. A. (1995). Wordnet: A lexical database for English. *Commun. ACM, 38*(11), 39–41.

Mitchell, T. (2006). *The discipline of machine learning.* Academic Press.

Mohammad, S. (2012). #emotional tweets. In **SEM 2012: The First Joint Conference on Lexical and Computational Semantics – Volume 1: Proceedings of the main conference and the shared task, and Volume 2: Proceedings of the Sixth International Workshop on Semantic Evaluation (SemEval 2012).* Montréal, Canada: Association for Computational Linguistics.

Mohammad, S. M., Kiritchenko, S., & Zhu, X. (2013b). *Nrc-canada: Building the state-of-the-art in sentiment analysis of tweets.* Academic Press.

Mohammad, S. M., & Turney, P. D. (2013a). Crowdsourcing a word-emotion association lexicon. Academic Press.

Pang, B., & Lee, L. (2004). A sentimental education: Sentiment analysis using subjectivity summarization based on minimum cuts. *Proceedings of the ACL,* 271–278. 10.3115/1218955.1218990

Poria, S. (2016). *A Deeper Look into Sarcastic Tweets Using Deep Convolutional Neural Networks.* Nanyang Technological University.

Raj, K. G., & Yinping, Y. (2017). CrystalNest at SemEval-2017 Task 4: Using sarcasm detection for enhancing sentiment classification and quantification. In *Proceedings of the 11th International Workshop on Semantic Evaluation.* Vancouver, Canada: SemEval '17.

Reyes, A., Rosso, P., & Veale, T. (2013). *A multidimensional approach for detecting irony in twitter. In Language Resources and Evaluation* (pp. 1–30). Springer Netherlands.

Riloff, E. (2013). *Sarcasm as contrast between a positive sentiment and negative situation.* EMNLP.

Santos, F. (2013). *Mineração de Opinião em Textos Opinativos Utilizando Algoritmos de Classificação* (Graduação). Universidade de Brasilia, Brasilia.

Simon, H. A. (1983). Machine learning: An artificial intelligence approach. Springer Berlin Heidelberg.

Smed, T. D., Nijs, L., & Daelemans, W. (2014). Creative Web Service with Pattern. Academic Press.

Sokolova, M., & Lapalme, G. (2009). A systematic analysis of performance measures for classification tasks. *Inf. Process. Manage., 45*(4), 427–437.

Souza, M. V. S. (2012). *Mineração de Opiniões Aplicada a Mídias Sociais* (Dissertação de Mestrado). Universidade Católica do Rio Grande do Sul, Porto Alegre. Retrieved from http://migre.me/thZxK

Spears, R. (1998). *NTC's American English learner's dictionary: The essential vocabulary of American language and culture.* NTC Pub. Group.

Taboada, M. (2011). Lexicon-based methods for sentiment analysis. Computational Linguistics, 37(34), 267–307.

Thelwall, M. (2013). *Heart and Soul: Sentiment Strength Detection in the Social Web With SentiStrength.* Academic Press.

Vapnik, V. N. (1995). *The nature of statistical learning theory.* New York, NY: Springer-Verlag New York, Inc. doi:10.1007/978-1-4757-2440-0

Veale, T., & Hao, Y. (2010). Detecting ironic intent in creative comparisons. *ECAI, 215,* 765–770.

Watson, D., Clark, L. A., & Tellegen, A. (1988). Development and validation of brief measures of positive and negative affect: The panas scales. *Journal of Personality and Social Psychology, 54*(6), 1063–1070. doi:10.1037/0022-3514.54.6.1063 PMID:3397865

Chapter 87
Recommendation and Sentiment Analysis Based on Consumer Review and Rating

Pin Ni
https://orcid.org/0000-0003-4516-1249
University of Liverpool, Liverpool, UK

Yuming Li
https://orcid.org/0000-0003-2219-9033
University of Liverpool, Liverpool, UK

Victor Chang
https://orcid.org/0000-0002-8012-5852
Teesside University, Middlesbrough, UK

ABSTRACT

Accurate analysis and recommendation on products based on online reviews and rating data play an important role in precisely targeting suitable consumer segmentations and therefore can promote merchandise sales. This study uses a recommendation and sentiment classification model for analyzing the data of beer product based on online beer reviews and rating dataset of beer products and uses them to improve the recommendation performance of the recommendation model for different customer needs. Among them, the beer recommendation is based on rating data; 10 classification models are compared in text sentiment analysis, including the conventional machine learning models and deep learning models. Combining the two analyses can increase the credibility of the recommended beer and help increase beer sales. The experiment proves that this method can filter the products with more negative reviews in the recommendation algorithm and improve user acceptance.

DOI: 10.4018/978-1-6684-6303-1.ch087

1. INTRODUCTION

Online review and rating, as the two most important customer reference factors in online shopping platforms, have a greater influence on consumers' willingness to buy. At the same time, e-commerce platforms or online advertising agencies also need to use these data as a basis to make accurate recommendations or advertising for customers with different preferences. However, rating data cannot reflect the specific characteristics of the product. And in many cases, reviews that lack rating data often make it difficult to judge the user's specific tendency of the product (especially in the case of ambiguous, overly simplistic or worthless reviews). Therefore, how to comprehensively use these two types of data to support the construction of a more intelligent recommendation system is a subject worth exploring.

This paper mainly analyses the data based on users' reviews on beer. However, the current researches focus on the intrinsic quality of the beer, and there are few researches on beer review and rating mining. Analyzing online reviews can not only help manufacturers develop products that are more in line with consumer preferences, but also promote sales. Therefore, the study is based on beer rating data and recommends beer products through the Spark-ALS collaborative filtering algorithm and compared 10 classification models including conventional machine learning and deep learning for consumer review analysis. Finally, a recommendation model based on Spark-ALS and LSTM was built to provide more accurate and credible recommendations.

Our main contributions are as follows:

1.   We combine customers' review text data and rating data to support the construction of recommendation model and improve its effectiveness. Experiments have shown that our method achieves effective performance on beer product recommendation task;

2.   Comparing 10 classifiers including mainstream conventional machine learning methods and deep learning methods for sentiment analysis task of recommendation model 3. We conducted a relatively comprehensive literature review of previous research in customer review mining, product rating analysis, and provided some technical and application analysis and suggestions for related business intelligence fields.

The rest of the article is structured as follows: Section 2 reviews the related works and is followed by the methodology in Section 3. The experiment description is presented in Section 4. Next, Sections 5 reports the result of the experiment. 5. Section 6 illustrates the limitations of the study, discusses, and analyzes the value of related tasks from both technical and application perspectives. Finally, the last section is the conclusion.

2. LITERATURE REVIEW

The reputation of the product has become an important factor for consumers to influence purchase intention. To a certain extent, it can be regarded as a filter in the current Internet environment with massive consumption information to help people make better decisions. Online reviews are one of the most important mediums that reflect the reputation of the product. And as an emerging field of Web information mining, online reviews' sentiment analysis involves a wide range of research topics, e.g., identifying the attributes of the products being reviewed, determining the attitudes of customers, and mining online reviews of products.

2.1. Mining for Customers' Review

Customers' review has become an essential reference for consumer consumption in today's product consumption (Duan, Gu, & Whinston, 2008). Therefore, the role of customers' reviews in business has attracted the attention of scholars in many fields. Customers' reviews are the most valued information for companies and manufacturers to understand customers' feedback on their products so that they could use this information to improve the quality of their products (Chong, Ch'ng, Liu, & Li, 2017). Customer reviews also can provide retailers with a better way to understand the specific preferences of each customer. Furthermore, consumers' review reflects the process of their purchase decisions, and by exploring the key factors that led them to purchase, it can help improve product sales (Wei, Chen, Yang, & Yang, 2010).

Park et al. (Park, Lee, & Han, 2007) used a likelihood model to explain how the degree of online product reviews and product participation affect consumer behavior, and the result was that the quality of reviews has a positive influence on consumers' purchase intentions, and low-engagement consumers are affected by the number, not the quality of the reviews. Ifrach et al. (Ifrach, Maglaras, Scarsini, & Zseleva, 2019) proposed that in a certain price range, users usually use Bayesian models to infer product quality inversely based on product ratings, thereby conducting research on product pricing issues. Singh et al. (Singh et al., 2017) established a machine learning model that uses the characteristics of the text to predict the contributions of consumer reviews to potential users. The results of the study encourage buyers to write more effective reviews, thereby assisting other consumers in making purchasing decisions, and also help merchants improve their product websites. Salehan et al. (Salehan & Kim, 2016) conducted big data statistics and sentiment analysis on the evaluation of online users. The experimental results show that reviews with a higher degree of positive emotions will be read by more users, and the reviews with a neutral emotion in the text are also considered more helpful. Proserpio et al. (Proserpio & Zervas, 2017) analyzed user reviews in the hotel industry and concluded that when hotels respond to the customers, the hotel will receive fewer negative reviews. Lee et al. (Lee, Yang, Chen, Wang, & Sun, 2016) proposed an approach of mining perceptual mapping to automatically construct perceptual maps and radar charts from online consumer reviews. This approach can help related merchants to positioning new products' market and formulate corresponding marketing strategies. Additionally, customers' reviews may include not only text reviews but also product ratings and other sales information. Chen et al. (L. Chen, Li, Liu, Zhang, & Woodbridge, 2017) proposed a product recommendation algorithm based on Apache Spark. This machine-learning algorithm can recommend the most suitable product to users according to the customers' ratings. Filieri et al. (Filieri, Hofacker, & Alguezaui, 2018) used a detailed likelihood model to study consumer perceptions and found that long length reviews might not necessarily be helpful, while highly relevant reviews and products ranking scores were considered two important pieces of information.

2.2. About Sentiment Analysis in Online Reviews

According to different types of texts, sentiment analysis can be divided into subjective text analysis and objective text analysis (Witten, 2004), including text sentiment polarity analysis and text sentiment polarity intensity analysis. The polarity of sentiment is divided into positive and negative poles, and some scholars have joined the neutrality pole. Although this classification method is simple, it can meet the needs of most practical applications, such as judging whether consumers are positive or negative reviews of goods and whether they support or oppose some opinions. However, the multi-classification of sentiment is a difficult task in classification.

Cao (Cao, Duan, & Gan, 2011) analyzed the semantic features in the review text and found that the semantics in the review could more effectively influence consumers' decisions. Moreover, the reviews with more extreme language expressions were more influential. Jonathan et al. (Jonathan, Sihotang, & Martin, 2019) study the restaurant reviews in a restaurant scoring application named Zomato and used them for sentiment analysis. This article uses the term frequency-inverse frequency (TF-IDF) to create word feature. The accuracy of the positive, negative, and neutral emotions obtained in the experiments is 92%, 93%, and 96%, respectively. Ruder et al. (Ruder, Ghaffari, & Breslin, 2016) proposed using a hierarchical bidirectional LSTM model to model the content of customer reviews, and then used aspect-based sentiment analysis to process. The experimental results show that this model has obtained results that compete with the most advanced results and surpasses the most advanced technology on multilingual and multi-domain datasets. Zhang et al. (Zhang, Zhou, Duan, & Chen, 2018) proposed a bidirectional GRU-based sentiment analysis model for multi-label sentiment analysis tasks, and experiments proved the effectiveness of the model in computing efficiency. Chen et al. (H. Chen et al., 2018) used the LSTM network to perform fine-grained sentiment analysis on customer reviews on online shopping platforms. The experimental results achieved an accuracy of 90.74% and an F1 score of 65.47%, proving the feasibility and effectiveness of the LSTM network. In addition, the performance of LSTM networks in fine-grained sentiment analysis is significantly better than conventional machine learning methods. Jebbara et al. (Jebbara & Cimiano, 2016) divided the emotion analysis task into two sub-tasks: aspect extraction and specific sentiment extraction. Compared with the conventional single-task sentiment analysis, this method is more flexible and more practical. It has been well verified in the ESWC-2016 semantic sentiment analysis challenge.

3. METHODOLOGY

The user review data in the dataset consists of two parts: the user's rating of the beer and the other part is the user's text review on the beer. The data mining of the data is also divided into two parts: one is to build a recommendation mechanism based on the rating data; the other is sentiment polarity analysis based on the textual review.

3.1. Analysis of Rating Data

The Spark-ALS based collaborative filtering recommendation algorithm is used to recommend beers to users. The ALS recommendation algorithm is a matrix-based decomposition method that considers both User and Item aspects (Xie, Zhou, & Li, 2016). In general, users only buy a minimal number of products in the item and score it. Such a rating matrix containing users and products is quite sparse. Using the matrix decomposition function in the Spark MLlib machine learning library (Meng et al., 2016), find a k-dimensional (low-order) matrix similar to the "user-item" matrix, which is a matrix of $m \times n$ is obtained by multiplying two matrices of $m \times k$ and $k \times n$ ($k << m,n$):

$$A_{m \times n} = U_{m \times k} \times V_{k \times n} \tag{1}$$

These two matrices one for representing the user $m \times k$-dimensional matrix, and a $k \times n$-dimensional matrix that characterizes the item. These two matrices are called factor matrices, which are multiplied to get a rating for each product for each user.

The task of machine learning is to find $U_{m \times k}$ and $V_{k \times n}$. It can be seen that $u_i^T v_j$ is the preference of user i for commodity j, and the Frobenius norm is used to quantify the error generated by reconstructing U and V. Since many places in the matrix are blank, i.e., the user does not score the product, for this case we do not need to calculate the unknown element, only the observed (user, commodity) set R (Winlaw, Hynes, Caterini, & De Sterck, 2015).

U and V are coupled to each other in the objective function, so an alternating square algorithm is used. That is, the initial value $U^{(0)}$ of U is assumed first, so that the problem is transformed into a least-squares problem. $V^{(0)}$ can be calculated according to $U^{(0)}$, and $U^{(1)}$ is calculated according to $V^{(0)}$, this iteration continues until iterates a certain number of times, or converges:

$$\left\| A - UV^T \right\|_F^2 \to min \sum_{(i,j) \in R} \left(a_{ij} - u_i^T v_j \right)^2 \tag{2}$$

3.2. Sentiment Analysis for Review Data

The sentiment polarity analysis of product reviews can meet the basic needs of the platform or user in practical applications (Mostafa, 2018). According to the user's overall rating of the product, the sentiment polarity of the text data set is annotated, and the polarity of the sentiment is mainly divided into three types of positive, negative, and neutral. Pre-processing the already annotated text data set mainly removes duplicate data and fills in null values during the pre-processing process.

After the processed dataset is obtained, each piece of text is segmented, and the characters and stop words are removed. Use the Word2Vec, a word embedding model to vectorize words in the text. Compared with the conventional natural language statistical modeling methods, it solves the problems of the dimensional explosion, word similarity and model performance to some extent (Liu, 2019).

The combination of the deep learning algorithm and text sentiment analysis can provide a better solution for sentiment polarity classification (Da Silva, Hruschka, & Hruschka Jr, 2014). This paper will compare the conventional machine learning classification model and the neural network classification model through experiments to obtain a better solution in the sentiment analysis of text reviews.

3.2.1. Convolutional Neural Network

Convolutional neural network (CNN) is a feed-forward neural network, which has an excellent performance in large-scale image processing and has been widely used in image classification, text classification, and other fields. The CNN is constructed by imitating the biological visual perception mechanism and can perform supervised learning and unsupervised learning. The sharing of convolution kernel parameters in the hidden layers and the sparseness of the connection between layers enable the convolutional neural network to learn grid-like topology features (e.g., pixels and audio) with a small amount of computation.

And it has a stable effect and no additional feature engineering requirements for the data. The overall structure of Convolutional Neural Network mainly includes three layers:

- **Convolutional layer:** This layer consists of filters and activation functions. Generally, the hyper-parameters to be set include the number, size, and step size of filters, and whether the padding is "valid" or "same", and what activation function is selected;
- **Pooling layer:** The parameters of this layer have been set, such as MaxPooling or Average pooling. In addition, it is needed to specify the hyper-parameters, including whether it is Max or average, the window size, and the step size;
- **Fully Connected layer:** This layer is a row of neurons. This layer is called "fully connected" because each unit is connected to each unit in the previous layer.

3.2.2. Recurrent Neural Network

Recurrent Neural Network (RNN) has the characteristics of parameter sharing, memory, and Turing completeness, and it has great advantages in learning the nonlinear characteristics of the sequence. As a significant model of deep learning, it has been widely used in the field of natural language processing (e.g., language modeling, machine translation, speech recognition, etc.) and time series related prediction tasks. The RNN constructed after introducing the convolutional neural network can be used to solve computer vision tasks with sequence input. RNN is a type of neural network used to process time-series data. Time-series data refers to data collected at different points in time; this type of data reflects the changing state of a thing or phenomenon over time or degree. The reason why RNN is called recurrent neural network is that the current output of a sequence is also related to the previous output. The specific manifestation is that the network memorizes the previous information and applies it to the current output calculation, that is, the nodes between the hidden layers are not connected but the layers are fully connected, and the input of the hidden layer includes not only the output of the input layer. It also includes the output of the hidden layer from the previous moment. It mainly consists of an input layer, a hidden layer, and an output layer.

Suppose $t-1$, t represents time series, X is the input sample, S_t is the memory of the sample at time t, W is the input weight, U is the weight of the input sample at the current moment, and V is the output sample weight. The final output value can be obtained by:

$$h_t = Ux_t + WS_{t-1} \tag{3}$$

$$s_t = f(h_t) \tag{4}$$

$$o_t = g(VS_t) \tag{5}$$

Among them, f and g are activation functions. And f can be $tanh$, *relu*, sigmoid and other activation functions, g can be *sotfmax* or other. And W, U, V are always equal, also defined as weight sharing.

3.2.3. Long Short-Term Memory

Long Short-Term Memory (LSTM) networks, a variant RNN network, is designed to solve the problem of long dependence (e.g., Forget the key information of long-distance context. It can also be regarded as "Gradient disappearance problem" of RNN). It is suitable for processing and predicting important events with relatively long intervals and delays in time series (e.g., a special reference in context). The LSTM network can delete or add information to the cell state through a structure called a gate, and the gate can selectively decide which information to pass. LSTM controls the state of cells by three gates, which are called forget gate, input gate, and output gate.

The first step in LSTM is to decide what information needs to be discarded from the cell state. This part of the operation is handled by a sigmoid unit called the forget gate. It uses h_{t-1} and x_t information to output a vector between 0-1. The 0-1 value in this vector indicates which information in the cell state C_{t-1} is retained or discarded.

The next step is to decide what new information to add to the state of the cell. First, use h_{t-1} and x_t to decide which information to update through an operation called an input gate. Then use h_{t-1} and x_t to obtain new candidate cell information $\widetilde{C}_t$ through a tan$h$ layer, and this information may be updated into the cell information.

After updating the cell state, it needs to determine which state characteristics of the output cell according to the inputs h_{t-1} and x_t. Then the input is passed through a sigmoid layer called an output gate to obtain a judgment condition. Then the cell state is passed through the tanh layer to obtain a vector between -1 and 1, which is multiplied with the judgment condition obtained by the output gate to obtain the final output of the LSTM unit.

4. EXPERIMENTS

4.1. Dataset

The dataset from Craft Beer dataset (Kaggle.com)[1], which mainly describes users' reviews on beer from 1999 to 2012. The Beer dataset file (CSV) has 37,500 rows and 19 columns. The user's review data includes textual reviews of beer and ratings of four features (aroma, appearance, taste and palate) and overall for beer. The information about the reviewers, such as age and gender, and other data columns irrelevant to the experiment, were excluded in this work. In the sentiment analysis experiment, the text dataset is classified according to the overall rating in the data, which is divided into three categories: neutral, positive, and negative (Table 1).

4.2. Experiment of Rating Data

1. Pyspark library is used to get a matrix <user, item, rating>;
2. Count the number of unique users and beer and calculate the sparsity of the matrix;
3. Training ALS model (Hidasi & Tikk, 2012) in pyspark.ml.recommendation library;
4. Training and get the score of each beer from each user, sort the score of each beer from the user, and recommend a beer to the user;

5.   By comparing the ALS recommendation model, the SVD recommendation model (Ba, Li, & Bai, 2013) and KNN-based recommendation model (Resnick, Iacovou, Suchak, Bergstrom, & Riedl, 1994), select the optimal recommendation algorithm.

Table 1. Data description

Column Name	Quantity	Type
beer/beerId	37500	int64
beer/brewerId	37500	int64
beer/name	37500	object
beer/style	37500	object
review/appearance	37500	float64
review/aroma	37500	float64
review/overall	37500	float64
review/palate	37500	float64
review/taste	37500	float64
review/text	37490	object
user/profileName	37495	object

4.3. Sentiment Analysis Experiment for Text Review

4.3.1. Contrast Experiments

There are conventional machine learning classification models (Pedregosa et al., 2011), including the Decision Tree model, Random Forest model, Extra Trees model, Naive Bayesian model, and Logistic Regression model and Stochastic Gradient Descent classification model:

1.   Decision Tree is a tree structure in which each internal node represents a judgment on an attribute, each branch represents the output of a judgment result, and each leaf node represents a classification result;
2.   Random Forest refers to a classifier that uses multiple trees to train and predict samples. In which randomness is mainly reflected in two aspects: random sampling (row random) and random selection features (column random), which can prevent the occurrence of overfitting; multiple decision trees can prevent the occurrence of low generalization of the model;
3.   Extra Trees algorithm has more randomness. When selecting the optimal split value for continuous variable features, the effect of all split values will not be calculated to select the split feature. Instead, for each feature, within its feature value range, a split value is randomly generated and then calculated to see which feature is selected for splitting;
4.   Naive Bayes method is a classification method based on Bayes' theorem and independent assumptions of feature conditions. It is simplified based on the Bayesian algorithm, that is, it is assumed that the attributes are independent of each other when given target value;

5. Logistic Regression is a machine learning method for solving binary classification (0 or 1) problems. It is used to estimate the probability of certain events.

Deep Learning models: CNN (Kim, 2014), RNN (Mikolov, Karafiát, Burget, Černocký, & Khudanpur, 2010), LSTM (Sundermeyer, Schlüter, & Ney, 2012) classification model.

The detail of the above 3 Deep Learning models has been introduced in 3.2.1, 3.2.2 and 3.2.3.

4.3.2. Experiment Process

- Text Pre-processing uses the Tokenizer in the NLTK library to segment the text and get the word list for each textual review;
- Use the stop word dictionary in NLTK library to remove stop words, numbers and special symbols also removed from the list;
- Use the Word2vec model to learn the word vector of the data, using the default parameter settings. The pre-processed word sequence is entered into the learning word vector in the model;
- Use the generated word vector to input into each classification model for learning classification, and all models classify the data into three categories.

5. RESULT AND ANALYSIS

In the preliminary analysis of the data, the correlation matrix is shown in Figure 1.

Figure 1. Correlation Matrix

	review/appearance	review/aroma	review/palate	review/taste	review/overall
review/appearance	1	0.538076	0.555833	0.531676	0.498733
review/aroma	0.538076	1	0.608922	0.711809	0.616117
review/palate	0.555833	0.608922	1	0.732092	0.69722
review/taste	0.531676	0.711809	0.732092	1	0.78522
review/overall	0.498733	0.616117	0.69722	0.78522	1

It indicated that the most relevant to the overall rating of beer is the taste rating, followed by the palate rating. The least relevant is the appearance rating of beer.

Through the ALS recommendation model, beer can be recommended for each user. For example, the results of recommending beer for users 11 are as follows (Figure 2).

The beer recommendation system is a comprehensive recommendation based on the overall rating and four features' rating (aroma, appearance, palate and taste) to recommend beers for each user. Compared to the recommendation algorithm recommended only by one kind of rating, Users may likely to accept the beer recommended by the former system. However, due to the imbalance of the user rating data in the database, the accuracy rate of the ALS recommendation algorithm is 62%.

Figure 2. Recommendation results

```
User 11's Recommendations:
+-------+-------+----------+--------------------+
|beer_id|user_id|prediction|         beer/name|
+-------+-------+----------+--------------------+
|     39|     11| 4.2370405|Founders CBS Impe...|
|     14|     11|  4.250751|Barrel Aged B.O.R...|
+-------+-------+----------+--------------------+
```

Compared with other SVD recommendation algorithms and KNN-based recommendation algorithms, the RMSE results are 0.65 and 0.82, respectively. The KNN-based recommendation algorithm is based on finding neighboring users and making recommendations based on items purchased by neighboring users. This method has a higher RMSE value of 0.82. Both the SVD recommendation model and the ALS model use the decomposition matrix to calculate the user's predicted score for the item. While the SVD first fills the entire sparse matrix and then calculates the dimensionality of the matrix by calculating the percentage of the square of the odd value. The RMSE values of the SVD model and the ALS model are similar in this dataset. However, the SVD model is not only computationally complex but also consumes a considerable amount of storage space. Thus, by comparison, the ALS recommendation model is best suited for this beer dataset.

In the experiment of sentiment analysis, the classification metrics (accuracy, recall, F1-Score) obtained by the conventional machine learning classification model shown in Table 2.

Table 2. Conventional model results

	Accuracy	Recall	Precision	F1-Score
Decision Tree	0.666	0.686	0.667	0.674
Random Forest	0.675	0.695	0.675	0.684
Extra Tree	0.676	0.697	0.676	0.679
Naive Bayes	0.614	0.631	0.647	0.634
Logistic Regression	0.677	0.697	0.677	0.679
SGD Classifier	0.677	0.697	0.676	0.679
MLP Classifier	0.676	0.697	0.676	0.680

It can be seen from Table 2 that the accuracy of Logistic Regression, SGD Classifier, MLP Classifier, Extra Tree, Decision Tree and Random Forest model are all around 0.67, and the values of Precision and

Recall are similar (around 0.69 and 0.67, respectively). The difference is the F1-Score value, which is the harmonic average of accuracy and recall. In the above four models, the highest F1-Score value is the Random Forest model, the Recall value is 0.695, and the recall values of the remaining five models is 0.69.

Overall, the best performing conventional machine learning model is the Random Forest model.

In comparative experiments, CNN, RNN and LSTM models were used to classify text sentiments. In order to facilitate experimental comparison, the main parameters of the three deep learning models are the same. the main parameters are shown in Table 3.

Table 3. Parameter list

batch size	32
vocab dim	100
kernel size	3
dropout	0.5
num classes	3
epochs	100

The changes in the accuracy and loss of the LSTM model are shown in Figures 3 and 4.

The LSTM model has approached stationary in about 60 steps, which indicates that the model converges around 60 steps. The accuracy of the model reaches 0.75, which has been greatly improved compared to the conventional machine learning model. The second model of this experiment is the CNN model. As can be seen from Figures 5 and 6, the CNN model converges faster than the LSTM model and has converged in about 20 steps. However, the accuracy of the model is far less than that of the LSTM model, and its accuracy is 0.67. The accuracy is the same as that of the conventional machine learning model, but the complexity of the model is larger than the conventional machine learning model.

The last model in this experiment is the RNN model. The loss of the RNN model did not converge well within the 100 steps (Figure 7). However, it can be seen in Figure 8 that the model has converged after 40 steps, and the accuracy is the same as the CNN model of 0.67.

Figure 3. The Epoch accuracy of LSTM training process

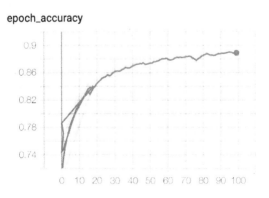

epoch_accuracy

Figure 4. The Epoch loss of LSTM training process

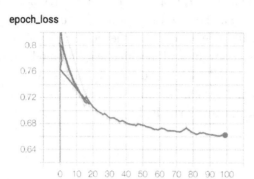

Figure 5. The Epoch loss of CNN training process

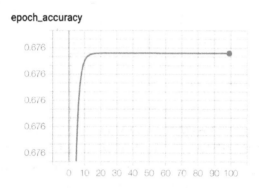

Figure 6. The Epoch loss of CNN training process

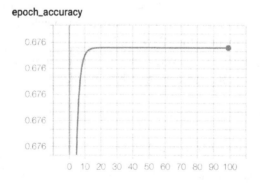

Table 4. Example results

Beer Type	Recommend	Negative	Neutral Positive
Nine Man Ale Golden Ale	14%	36%	50%
Benchwarmer Porter	3%	28%	69%
Strike Out Stout	9%	40%	51%
Amstel Light	51%	35%	14%

Figure 7. The Epoch loss of RNN training process

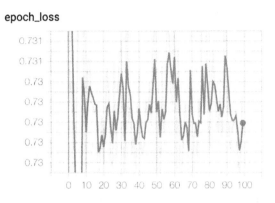

Figure 8. The Epoch accuracy of RNN training process

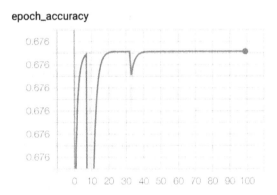

Comparing all the classification models in the experiment, the LSTM model performed best and achieved an accuracy of up to 0.75.

The recommendation system combined with the LSTM sentiment analysis system could increase the credibility of the recommended beer. According to the recommended beer by the recommendation algorithm, the LSTM model conducts a sentiment analysis of the reviews on these recommended beers. Although the recommendation algorithm is based on the user's recommendation for beer ratings, if the recommended beer has a lot of negative sentiments due to some other factors, these beers should also be removed from the recommended beer list. The beer recommended by the results of the integrated LSTM sentiment analysis system and recommendation algorithm can increase the user's acceptance. For example, according to the beer recommendation results of user No.62, after the LSTM sentiment analysis, the negative sentiments of the first three beer were less than 20%, and the positive reviews were higher than 50%. But the negative reviews on the fourth beer were as high as 51%, and the positive reviews were only 14%. Therefore, the beer of the fourth kind should be removed from the recommended beer list. Through the combination of the two analysis methods, the credibility of the recommendation system can be increased, and the probability that the user accepts the recommended product becomes larger. This is beneficial for users who buy beer online and can also help e-commerce to increase beer sales (Table 4).

5. LIMITATIONS AND DISCUSSIONS

Rating data is a measure that can directly quantify the quality of products in customer evaluation. As a typical quantitative data, products can be directly sorted through statistical forms. This is one of the most intuitive and effective data types for recommendation systems, but it also has many shortcomings: 1. Rating data is affected by sales, and there is a statistical preference for products with fewer samples but higher average rating data. This is often unfair for products with a larger rating sample available. 2. Rating data represents the preferences of most customers, but it does not have a high reference value for customers with special preferences. Therefore, the single rating type of data cannot comprehensively reflect the real situation of the product. At the same time, there is a lack of more dimensional information for modeling. Therefore, customer review data, as a more comprehensive content carrier, contains richer details of the product. By combining review data and other product quantitative indicators (e.g. rating data, etc.) and other types of data into the recommendation agent, it can provide more accurate recommendations for customer groups with special preferences.

As a carrier of user questions, suggestions, and attitudes, the review data is extremely valuable for product evaluation, improvement, and optimization. Merchants can use text analysis to analyze user's concerns, main discussion topics, user's sentiment tendencies, and the main subject of reviews, etc. Therefore, this distillation processing of massive unstructured data can also transform complex and abstract semantics into quantifiable semi-structured or structured data. After such refined processing, a large amount of information implied in the textual review data can be effectively used. In particular, the potential multi-dimensional information in the reviews can be used to improve the recommendation effect of the recommendation model through dimensional modeling. In addition, the information extracted from the review text can also be directly presented to the user in a variety of report forms, which can include heat maps for sentiment analysis, radar chart of users' evaluation, word cloud, etc.

In the future study, the text mining task of reviews will be enriched more and more fine-grained (e.g. fine-grained topic analysis, etc.). At the same time, more quantitative data can be introduced into the recommendation model (e.g. other purchase record data of customers with different special preferences, and the duration of online browsing of related products, etc.). These sales-related data are an important reference source for consumers to quickly judge from mass products to meet their own needs. As a typical method of using Collective Intelligence, the recommendation model can use a collaborative filtering mechanism to discover a small number of products that match the preferences of target users from a large number of users. Compared with Collective Intelligence in the traditional sense, this collaborative filtering mechanism retains the characteristics of individuals (i.e. individual preferences) to a certain extent, so it can be used as the core idea of personalized recommendation algorithms. By adding more types of data as model inputs, the recommendation model can make more precise recommendations for their specific needs when serving the customer group with more complex and diverse preferences. This will undoubtedly enable merchants to track the appropriate target customer group better and faster, promote the purchase rate and favorable rate of related products, and provide efficient and high-quality services for customers with different needs.

6. CONCLUSION

By including more dimensions of online sales data, the effect of the online product recommendation system can be improved, and more accurate and high-quality product recommendations can be provided to customers with different preferences. It is a potentially feasible solution by combining customer rating data (quantitative type data) and review data (unstructured data) for recommendation system construction and performance improvement. This paper analyzes the rating and reviews of the beer dataset, and through the analysis of the rating, a beer recommendation system was constructed, which recommended beer according to four features' rating. Sentiment analysis of text reviews can effectively let the brewery or sales platform understand the consumer's feelings about a specific beer. By comparing the ten machine learning classification models, the LSTM model performed best, and the accuracy of data classification reached 0.75, which was about 0.1 higher than the accuracy of other models. By combining the LSTM sentiment analysis model with the recommendation algorithm, the credibility of the recommended beer can be increased, allowing the user to accept the recommended beer, thereby facilitating the purchase and sale of the beer.

ACKNOWLEDGMENT

This work is partly supported by VC Research (VCR 0000044).

REFERENCES

Ba, Q., Li, X., & Bai, Z. (2013). *Clustering collaborative filtering recommendation system based on SVD algorithm.* Paper presented at the 2013 IEEE 4th International Conference on Software Engineering and Service Science.

Cao, Q., Duan, W., & Gan, Q. (2011). Exploring determinants of voting for the "helpfulness" of online user reviews: A text mining approach. *Decision Support Systems, 50*(2), 511–521. doi:10.1016/j. dss.2010.11.009

Chen, H., Li, S., Wu, P., Yi, N., Li, S., & Huang, X. (2018). Fine-grained Sentiment Analysis of Chinese Reviews Using LSTM Network. *Journal of Engineering Science & Technology Review, 11*(1), 174–179. doi:10.25103/jestr.111.21

Chen, L., Li, R., Liu, Y., Zhang, R., & Woodbridge, D. M.-k. (2017). *Machine learning-based product recommendation using apache spark.* Paper presented at the 2017 IEEE SmartWorld, Ubiquitous Intelligence & Computing, Advanced & Trusted Computed, Scalable Computing & Communications, Cloud & Big Data Computing, Internet of People and Smart City Innovation (SmartWorld/SCALCOM/UIC/ATC/CBDCom/IOP/SCI). 10.1109/UIC-ATC.2017.8397470

Chong, A. Y. L., Ch'ng, E., Liu, M. J., & Li, B. (2017). Predicting consumer product demands via Big Data: The roles of online promotional marketing and online reviews. *International Journal of Production Research, 55*(17), 5142–5156. doi:10.1080/00207543.2015.1066519

Da Silva, N. F., Hruschka, E. R., & Hruschka, E. R. Jr. (2014). Tweet sentiment analysis with classifier ensembles. *Decision Support Systems*, *66*, 170–179. doi:10.1016/j.dss.2014.07.003

Duan, W., Gu, B., & Whinston, A. B. (2008). Do online reviews matter?—An empirical investigation of panel data. *Decision Support Systems*, *45*(4), 1007–1016. doi:10.1016/j.dss.2008.04.001

Filieri, R., Hofacker, C. F., & Alguezaui, S. (2018). What makes information in online consumer reviews diagnostic over time? The role of review relevancy, factuality, currency, source credibility and ranking score. *Computers in Human Behavior*, *80*, 122–131. doi:10.1016/j.chb.2017.10.039

Hidasi, B., & Tikk, D. (2012). *Fast ALS-based tensor factorization for context-aware recommendation from implicit feedback.* Paper presented at the Joint European Conference on Machine Learning and Knowledge Discovery in Databases. 10.1007/978-3-642-33486-3_5

Ifrach, B., Maglaras, C., Scarsini, M., & Zseleva, A. (2019). Bayesian social learning from consumer reviews. *Operations Research*, *67*(5), 1209–1221. doi:10.1287/opre.2019.1861

Jebbara, S., & Cimiano, P. (2016). *Aspect-based sentiment analysis using a two-step neural network architecture.* Paper presented at the Semantic Web Evaluation Challenge. 10.1007/978-3-319-46565-4_12

Jonathan, B., Sihotang, J. I., & Martin, S. (2019). *Sentiment Analysis of Customer Reviews in Zomato Bangalore Restaurants Using Random Forest Classifier.* Paper presented at the Abstract Proceedings International Scholars Conference. 10.35974/isc.v7i1.1003

Kim, Y. (2014). *Convolutional neural networks for sentence classification.* arXiv preprint arXiv:1408.5882

Lee, A. J., Yang, F.-C., Chen, C.-H., Wang, C.-S., & Sun, C.-Y. (2016). Mining perceptual maps from consumer reviews. *Decision Support Systems*, *82*, 12–25. doi:10.1016/j.dss.2015.11.002

Liu, H. (2019). Agricultural Q&A System Based on LSTM-CNN and Word2vec. *Revista de la Facultad de Agronomía*, *36*(3).

Meng, X., Bradley, J., Yavuz, B., Sparks, E., Venkataraman, S., Liu, D., ... Owen, S. (2016). Mllib: Machine learning in apache spark. *Journal of Machine Learning Research*, *17*(1), 1235–1241.

Mikolov, T., Karafiát, M., Burget, L., Černocký, J., & Khudanpur, S. (2010). *Recurrent neural network based language model.* Paper presented at the Eleventh annual conference of the international speech communication association.

Mostafa, M. M. (2018). Mining and mapping halal food consumers: A geo-located Twitter opinion polarity analysis. *Journal of Food Products Marketing*, *24*(7), 858–879. doi:10.1080/10454446.2017.1418695

Park, D.-H., Lee, J., & Han, I. (2007). The effect of online consumer reviews on consumer purchasing intention: The moderating role of involvement. *International Journal of Electronic Commerce*, *11*(4), 125–148. doi:10.2753/JEC1086-4415110405

Pedregosa, F., Varoquaux, G., Gramfort, A., Michel, V., Thirion, B., Grisel, O., ... Dubourg, V. (2011). Scikit-learn: Machine learning in Python. *Journal of Machine Learning Research*, *12*(Oct), 2825–2830.

Proserpio, D., & Zervas, G. (2017). Online reputation management: Estimating the impact of management responses on consumer reviews. *Marketing Science*, *36*(5), 645–665. doi:10.1287/mksc.2017.1043

Resnick, P., Iacovou, N., Suchak, M., Bergstrom, P., & Riedl, J. (1994). GroupLens: an open architecture for collaborative filtering of netnews. *Proceedings of the 1994 ACM conference on Computer supported cooperative work.* 10.1145/192844.192905

Ruder, S., Ghaffari, P., & Breslin, J. G. (2016). *A hierarchical model of reviews for aspect-based sentiment analysis.* arXiv preprint arXiv:1609.02745

Salehan, M., & Kim, D. J. (2016). Predicting the performance of online consumer reviews: A sentiment mining approach to big data analytics. *Decision Support Systems, 81,* 30–40. doi:10.1016/j.dss.2015.10.006

Singh, J. P., Irani, S., Rana, N. P., Dwivedi, Y. K., Saumya, S., & Roy, P. K. (2017). Predicting the "helpfulness" of online consumer reviews. *Journal of Business Research, 70,* 346–355. doi:10.1016/j.jbusres.2016.08.008

Sundermeyer, M., Schlüter, R., & Ney, H. (2012). *LSTM neural networks for language modeling.* Paper presented at the Thirteenth annual conference of the international speech communication association.

Wei, C.-P., Chen, Y.-M., Yang, C.-S., & Yang, C. C. (2010). Understanding what concerns consumers: A semantic approach to product feature extraction from consumer reviews. *Information Systems and e-Business Management, 8*(2), 149–167. doi:10.100710257-009-0113-9

Winlaw, M., Hynes, M. B., Caterini, A., & De Sterck, H. (2015). *Algorithmic acceleration of parallel ALS for collaborative filtering: Speeding up distributed big data recommendation in spark.* Paper presented at the 2015 IEEE 21st International Conference on Parallel and Distributed Systems (ICPADS). 10.1109/ICPADS.2015.91

Xie, L., Zhou, W., & Li, Y. (2016). Application of improved recommendation system based on spark platform in big data analysis. *Cybernetics and Information Technologies, 16*(6), 245–255. doi:10.1515/cait-2016-0092

Zhang, L., Zhou, Y., Duan, X., & Chen, R. (2018). *A hierarchical multi-input and output Bi-GRU model for sentiment analysis on customer reviews.* Paper presented at the IOP Conference Series: Materials Science and Engineering. 10.1088/1757-899X/322/6/062007

ENDNOTE

[1]   https://www.kaggle.com/applied-computing/beers

This research was previously published in the International Journal of Business Intelligence Research (IJBIR), 11(2); pages 11-27, copyright year 2020 by IGI Publishing (an imprint of IGI Global).

Chapter 88

The Application of Sentiment Analysis and Text Analytics to Customer Experience Reviews to Understand What Customers Are Really Saying

Conor Gallagher
Letterkenny Institute of Technology, Donegal, Ireland

Eoghan Furey
Letterkenny Institute of Technology, Donegal, Ireland

Kevin Curran
Ulster University, Derry, UK

ABSTRACT

In a world of ever-growing customer data, businesses are required to have a clear line of sight into what their customers think about the business, its products, people and how it treats them. Insight into these critical areas for a business will aid in the development of a robust customer experience strategy and in turn drive loyalty and recommendations to others by their customers. It is key for business to access and mine their customer data to drive a modern customer experience. This article investigates the use of a text mining approach to aid sentiment analysis in the pursuit of understanding what customers are saying about products, services and interactions with a business. This is commonly known as Voice of the Customer (VOC) data and it is key to unlocking customer sentiment. The authors analyse the relationship between unstructured customer sentiment in the form of verbatim feedback and structured data in the form of user review ratings or satisfaction ratings to explore the question of whether customers say what they really think when given the opportunity to provide free text feedback as opposed to how they rate a product on a scale of one to five. Using various Sentiment Analysis approaches, the authors assign a sentiment score to a piece of verbatim feedback and then categorise it as positive, negative, or

DOI: 10.4018/978-1-6684-6303-1.ch088

neutral. Using this normalised sentiment score, they compare it to the corresponding rating score and investigate the potential business insights. The results obtained indicate that a business cannot rely solely on a standalone single metric as a source of truth regarding customer experience. There is a significant difference between the customer ratings score and the sentiment of their corresponding review of the product. The authors propose that it is imperative that a business supplements their customer feedback scores with a robust sentiment analysis strategy.

1. INTRODUCTION

Increasingly, leading modern businesses are looking to gain more insights from customer verbatim data they collect. Unfiltered customer feedback provides a tremendous opportunity to learn more about customer sentiment in relation to products and their end-to-end experience with a company. It also gives the business an opportunity to understand how they can 'close-the-loop' on any poor feedback they may receive and conversely how they can capitalise on positive feedback from customers. One of the drawbacks of online customer verbatim is its quality and quantity of data (Maritz, 2018). How do businesses mine and analyse data to ensure it reveals key insights that can ultimately drive profits in the right direction. Once a business recognises the benefit of analysing its customer feedback data, the question becomes, how? Identifying customer verbatim as unstructured data is the first step and secondly using a 'Big Data' approach such as text mining will allow the business to employ a more sophisticated and advanced modelling technique to uncover patterns in the data, employing sentiment analysis to identify key themes from the feedback. However, businesses will continue to use structured quantitative data gathering techniques such as asking customers to rate customer/client interactions, products and employees on various scales i.e. 1-5 Stars, 0 – 11-point scales and so on. These methods cannot be solely replied upon and it is key for a business to critically analyse its unstructured data whether than be on social media channels, ad-hoc emails to the business, letters and customer surveys.

All businesses need customers to prosper and grow. They are the main source of revenue for most businesses. It can be argued that the success of a business is directly proportional to its ability to acquire customers (Smith, 2016), keep customers happy, identify issues or irritants and consequently drive more selling opportunities. But for a business to achieve this it needs to identify the key indicators that will provide insights to facilitate this. There are many variables that a business needs to identify, the who, what, why, and how. Who are the potential customers in the marketplace? What do they want? Why do they want a product? How as a business can they retain customers and grow their market share. Examples of where a business can utilise their customer data are sales demographics, product and channel product preferences, social media or website sentiment and interactions and transaction behaviours. Customer analytics is becoming one of the key enablers available to companies to facilitate the translation of raw data into useful insights about their customers. This research intends to highlight the importance of customer analytics in the delivery of customer insights back to the business to drive decision making (Fiedler, et al., 2016). 60% of companies said that organisational silos were a major obstacle to improving customer experience (Google, 2016). Companies are finding it difficult to understand what customer data they have and often are underutilising the customer data that they do have (Department of Industry, 2018). The most successful companies have found ways around this and are actively implementing Customer Experience strategies i.e. building Customer Experience teams that are agile and can pivot based on business needs and goals (Hollyoake, 2009). While any company can use data to report financials or drive cost savings, the key differentiation comes from how this data can be used to drive business insights. While businesses are quite good at tracking structed feedback i.e. numerical ratings such as 1 - 5-star ratings they need to improve on understanding what customers are saying about their products and experiences with the company. This poses a serious challenge and difficulty increases as a business grows its customer base (Parasuraman, et al., 1991). With that in mind it seems impossible for a business to contact every potential and current customer individually to understand their sentiment. There are many methods or channels in which customers can interact with a business, for example, social media, email, customer satisfaction surveys, registering satisfaction via IVRs, capturing feedback on calls via Speech Analytics. So, the challenge for the business is how to accurately capture, store, analyse and obtain insights from this data. This becomes more difficult as the customer base grows, and it seems very unlikely that a business will create a touchpoint with every single customer they have.

In today's high-tech marketplace, customers have more options for products and services than ever before (International, 2017). The barriers of choice have come down as technology and the internet has advanced and this leaves the business with a conundrum of how to accurately predict what their customers will do in the future before their competitors. To achieve this, they need to predict customer behaviour. This is where predictive analytics becomes the answer. To get ahead of the curve and ultimately their competitors (LaValle et al., 2011) argue that a business needs to proactively employ advanced data analytics techniques and drive a strategy that will provide insight into what their customers might do in the future. What products are customers buying? What is the likelihood that a customer will churn and move to a competitor? Are customers satisfied with the products, if not why? Are there irritants that customers find when dealing with the business? There are a multitude of questions the business will have, and predictive analytics can go some way in providing insights. Using advanced data analytics techniques, a business can use their customer data to build predictive models. These models have the potential to predict future customer behaviour. It aids businesses to identify customers at risk of leaving, potential issues with products or services. With predictive analytics, businesses can gain a competitive advantage over rivals if used properly. There is a trend towards prescriptive analytics and a move away from descriptive analytics (S. Kaisler, 2013). This allows the business to focus on what could happen, based on predictive modelling methods rather than what has already happened. There is obviously a requirement for descriptive analytics, businesses will always have to report what has happened at a certain point of time hence the need to capture metrics and KPIs but the notion of utilizing this data to predict what will happen shows a forward-thinking mindset (Steger, 2013). The opportunity for exploring predictive customer analytics today is better than ever before. Data sources such as customer satisfaction surveys, social media channels, chatbots, voice calls using speech analytics all provide a rich source of opportunity. And naturally Big Data technology has kept pace with the exponential growth in data and is capable of handling large-scale data processing, storage and integration needed to capitalize on these uncovered insights (EMC, n.d.) To begin to understand what the customers think and feel a business needs to understand the type of data it has and build the technological infrastructure to be able to mine the data to build effective models (McKinsey, 2016). Only at this point can the business develop these models effectively and drive their analytics strategy forward

We examine if it is possible for a business to rely solely on a single point Customer Satisfaction metric through the value of sentiment contained within customer feedback as an indicator of customer satisfaction and/or advocacy with a company or product. Essentially, we investigate if a customer sentiment provides a truer reflection of the customers experience with a service or product.

2. RELATED WORK

Text analytics provides a set of techniques to make trends visible, dynamic, and to reveal relationships between data points that may have been difficult to uncover by a human due to the scale and quantity of the data (Miner, 2012). Numeric ratings remain the most generic form of data collection in customer surveys and unstructured feedback such as customer verbatim continues to increase in importance. Rather than attempting to manually review reams of customer comments, tools like text analytics and speech analytics allow companies to turn this verbatim feedback into valuable insights they can analyse and measure more efficiently than manually reviewing the data (Verint, 2016). The end to end Text mining process has many stages all of which are key to the end goal of deriving insights from the textual data. Figure 1 gives an idea of how this would look as a process flow.

Figure 1. End to End Text Mining Process (Harris, 2018)

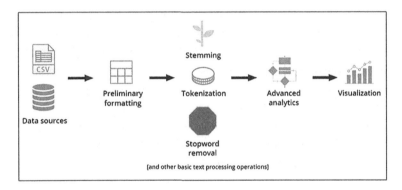

It is key that the data needs to be in a processable format. Multiple data sources can be used, a large amount of textual data may be available via free text format on social media platforms, customer surveys and speech analytics tools would also convert conversations into a raw format. Preliminary formatting is preparing the data by removing dirty or erroneous data. This improves the data and lessen the chance of errors although can be time consuming (Natarajan K., 2010). Other formatting procedures can be applied to the data as required. Textual data contains lots of small yet highly frequently-used words: "at," "the," "or," "for" etc. To analyse the frequency of words in a text block, these types of words will always occur. Stop word removal is the process of filtering out these words to look for longer, more significant words. Python for example comes with built-in stop word dictionaries for different languages (Upadhyay, 2017). "Tokenization looks at the spaces between the words as word boundaries to 'cut' words from the text string at those points." (Ott, 2018). Tokenization is a crucial step in the process of structuring text for further analysis, as otherwise text is treated as an unstructured "string." The idea is to break the string into individual words or tokenize, the sentence or piece of text. This allows for the determination of word frequency in the document and begin identifying relationships between words. The intention for a business for example would be to ensure that frequently-used words are tokenized properly with a view to further analysis. Most of text-mining tools allow users to create customized tokenization rules. The Bag-of-words process, also known as a vector space model, breaks down a document into its constituent words, regardless of grammar and order. This is a crucial step as there is the likelihood of receiving additional textual data which require be broken down in similar fashion to allow for further analysis (Robert P. Schumaker, 2012). Stemming (a.k.a. "lemmatization") is the process by which words are reduced in a document to their basic form. Taking the English language as an example, words have many forms rather than one single form based on their grammatical purpose. For instance, "was," "are," "is," etc., are all forms of the verb "to be." As with Tokenization above, once you perform a process like stemming then the data is prepared for further analytics which can be applied to textual data to recognize patterns (Mejova, 2012). One example of an advanced analytics technique associated with the text mining process is Cluster analysis. In the context of the text mining process, cluster analysis involves classifying words into groups, such that words in each group are more related to one another than they are to words in other groups. (Kochut, et al., 2017) This is done through the application of algorithms such as k-means and x-means clustering. Using K-means clustering the variable 'K' represents the number of clusters you want. You could potentially segment data into four groups, eight groups — then the algorithm understands that and executes based off that 'K' number. For x-means the number of optimal clusters is unknown and here you would specify a max and min number of clusters. The algorithm will then run an analysis and output the optimal number of clusters. Clustering is a powerful way to identify relationships and trends in copious amounts of textual data (Allahyari, 2017). It can also be used as part of the sentiment analysis process. Data Visualization plays a key role in allowing a business or researcher to identify key trends or insights from the data. There are multiple methods to visualise data, one could use the inbuilt features of a programming language e.g. Python has matplotlib for creating charts ad visuals from data. There are a vast range of Data Visualisation software available from a Business intelligence point of view, i.e. Tableau is an industry leader in Data Visualisation (Ajenstat, 2017), Microsoft's offering of PowerBI is an up and coming challenger to Tableau (Molag, 2017). These business intelligence tools can link to multiple data sources i.e. excel, csv, SQL server, json and interestingly they now can link directly to Python or R scripts, so that users can run scripts inside the tool and then create visuals and ultimately dashboards to aid in the insight exploration of the data. This is extremely beneficial in a business scenario where companies can have dedicated Data Visualization analysts who create and maintain these types of dashboards. As part of this research the author plans to utilise and promote the benefits of visualising the data so that the reader can understand how this would play out in a business environment.

Text mining can be utilized to evaluate customer satisfaction from verbatim feedback rather than relying solely on a numerical indicator from a customer satisfaction survey-based (Hosseini, et al., 2010) proposed a data-mining model using monetary (RFM) attributes and K-means clustering to evaluate customer loyalty and customer lifetime value (CLV). The research investigated the degree to which customer loyalty influenced bottom line profits for an organization. The model developed showed a clear improvement in the accuracy of the customer loyalty measurement. This study had limitations as the model relied too heavily on combining data-mining techniques alone and did not consider the impact of textual data such as verbatim comments from customers, which are now generated at many touchpoints in the customer's journey. (Pang & Lee, 2002) employed text mining methods to extract insights from customer data using sentiment analysis to try to improve customer loyalty measurement. Another example of using text analytics to understand the dimensions of product alignment to gain insight into brand positioning was used by (Tirunillai & Tellis, 2014). (Ordenes, et al., 2014) found that text analytics could be used to analyse customer feedback to capture insights of the customer experience. This model captured customer sentiment from the data and tagged it as either complaints, compliments or suggestions/feedback. This allowed them to propose insights to suggest efficiencies for the company and its resources. Their research, however did not combine the qualitative data and quantitative data to assess and predict customer loyalty. Where the research proved useful was in relation to the computation methods applied that could produce findings that can be expressed quantitatively, and this for example aids the desired outcome to conduct statistical modelling, data visualization, and machine learning algorithms to derive further insights.

Businesses have two kinds of customer feedback data that they store, analyse and measure: structured and unstructured data. Structured data is information that is clearly defined and easy to report on. It is the kind of data that is generally found in a survey and can be organized in a spreadsheet: name, location, age, and rating (3 out of 5 stars, for example, or a 10 for "most satisfied" versus a 1 for "least satisfied") (Taylor, 2018). Unstructured data as it exists today in the context of Customer experience data is, basically, text or free form customer verbatim, although it can also include other media such as audio, photos, or videos. Unstructured data can be captured in an email, the "additional comments" section of a survey, voice recordings of customer interactions e.g. Speech Analytics tools, a post on a customer review site e.g. Amazon, in social media, and in a multitude of other places. (Taylor, 2018). Analysing all this data correctly is critical, because it reveals everything from buying trends to product flaws and provides a significant business advantage. (Aswani, 2017) Organizations often struggle to do this analysis, however, because unstructured data is significantly harder to categorize and report on than structured data. It can be hard to parse due to grammatical errors or slang, it frequently contains multiple unrelated ideas, and it can represent various levels of sentiment related to each idea (e.g. "I couldn't complete the registration process online, I didn't understand the website, but the rep was very patient and talked me through the process."). Unstructured data is, by its natural harder to navigate than structured data. Anecdotally it is thought that 95% of customer feedback data is unstructured (Kemper, 2008) and it contains a wealth of information to aid in the understanding of customer sentiment and opinion. Daunting as it may seem to businesses, this type of feedback is predicted to continue to grow, as millions of people increase their use of online (Clarabridge, 2015). Customer satisfaction is one of the most critical issues concerning business organization of all types, which is justified by the customer-oriented philosophy and the principles of continues improvement in modern enterprise (Arokiasamy, 2013) see Figure 2.

Figure 2. Basic American Customer Satisfaction Index model (ACSI, 2018)

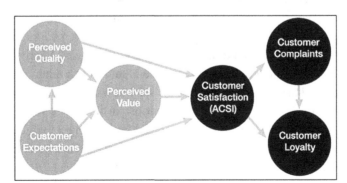

Net Promoter Score (NPS) is a measure of customer loyalty and is often held as the leading customer experience metric. NPS is still a popular customer loyalty measurement despite recent studies arguing that customer loyalty is multidimensional. Therefore, firms require new data-driven methods that combine behavioural and attitudinal data sources. Measured on a 0 -10 scale, it is broken down where a score of 0 – 6 is classified as Detractors, unhappy customers how are very unlikely to recommend the business to friends or family. A score of 7 – 8 is classified as Passives, those customers who are happy enough with the service but not enough to actively encourage others and a score of 9 – 10 is classified as Promoters, those customers who are loyal and would recommend the business or product to friends and family (Qualtrics, 2018).

Sentiment analysis plays a key role in the development of predictive and machine learning models. It has developed into a wider all-encompassing process that involves analysing textual data and applying a 'sentiment score' to that text (Mejova, 2012) One of the most widely used approaches is using machine learning strategies to develop and build an algorithm using a training data set before applying a test or 'real' data set. Machine learning techniques first trains the algorithm with some inputs with known outputs so that later it can work with new unknown data (Devika, et al., 2016). SVM or Support Vector Machines are defined as a supervised machine learning algorithm normally used for regression and classification processes. SVM uses a non-probabilistic classifier in which a large amount of training set is required. It is done by classifying points and identifying a (d-1)-dimensional hyper plane. SVM looks for the hyper plane that best segregates the classes (Devika, et al., 2016). Support Vector Machines make use of the concept of decision planes that define decision boundaries. A decision plane is one that best differentiates between a set of objects having different class membership. Support Vector Machines are considered a powerful classification algorithm. When used in conjunction with other techniques such as random forest and other machine learning tools, they give a very different aspect to ensemble models (Srivasta, 2014). There is an argument that SVM do not perform well with larger data sets due to the high training time required, they do however perform well with clear margin of separations between objects (Brownlee, 2016).

In the context of sentiment analysis or text mining, an n-gram is a neighbouring sequence of n items from a given sequence of text or speech. N Items can be letters, words, pairs of words for example and are typically collected from a sequence of text or speech corpus. Figure 3 shows how a sentence can be broken up into various formats i.e. words, pairs of words, etc. N-gram sentiment analysis considers the sentence as a whole (Ghiassi et al., 2013).

In Machine learning, Naïve Bayes is termed as a family of "probabilistic classifiers" based on the use of Bayes Theorem. Naïve Bayes classifiers are highly scalable and are mainly used when the size of the training set is less. The conditional probability that an event X occurs given the evidence Y is determined by Bayes rule shown in Equation (1). Unlike Naïve Bayes, Maximum Entropy Classifier does not assume that the features are conditionally independent of each other. Uncertainty is maximum for a uniform distribution and the measure of uncertainty is known as entropy. Maximum Entropy Classifier can be used to solve a variety of text mining scenarios particularly sentiment analysis (Vryniotis, 2013). Maximum Entropy Classifier uses a parameterized set of weights which when combined, join the features that are generated from a set of features by an encoding. This encoding then maps each pair of feature set and labels them to a vector (McCallumzy & Nigamy, 1998). ME classifiers are known as the exponential or log-linear classifiers and because they work by extracting sets of features from the input data, combining them in a linear fashion and then using this sum as the exponent (Daume III & Marcu, 2006). (Pang & Lee, 2002) used the approach that each document is represented with an array of 1's and 0's that indicate if a word exists in the text of the document. This plays on the BoW (Bag of Words) theory commonly used in NLP and text mining.

Figure 3. N-Gram example (Maiolo, 2015)

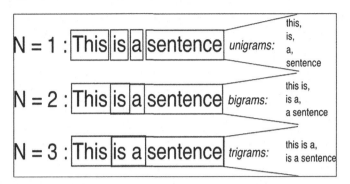

$$P\left(c \mid x\right) = \frac{P\left(x \mid c\right) \; P\left(c\right)}{P\left(x\right)}$$

$$P\left(c \mid x\right) = P\left(x_1 \mid c\right) \times P\left(x_2 \mid c\right) \times \ldots \times P\left(x_n \mid c\right) \times P\left(c\right) \tag{1}$$

The K-Nearest Neighbour (KNN) technique is based on the notion that the classification of an instance will be in some way like those nearby it in the vector space hence the term nearest neighbour. (Srivastav & Singh, 2014) researched weighted k-Nearest Neighbour where they assumed weightage to those objects in the training set and then used these weights for their calculation of sentiment of text in word by word fashion. In a weighted k-NN analysis (Srivastav & Singh, 2014) the sentences of the tweets captured were tokenised and then stop words were removed. The algorithm developed a positive score to each review after the first parse. For the second parsing process a neutral review is input. This score is then modified if required allowing for better positivise determination and creating an output file that consists of the review ID and its associated positive score. Weighted combinations of feature sets can be quite effective in the task of sentiment classification, since the weights of the ensemble represent the relevance of the different feature sets (e.g. n-grams, POS, etc.) to sentiment classification, instead of assigning relevance to each feature individually (Xia et al., 2011). (Balahur & Montoyo, 2008) investigated the notion of assigning products classes to textual data sets and extracting general features from the products and then in turn assigning sentiment to the features.

A Rule based approach (Liu, et al., 2005) to extract opinion from a textual data set by defining various rules tokenized each sentence in every document of the data set and tested for the presence of each token or word. If the presence of the word is confirmed and has a positive sentiment, then a "+1" rating is applied to it. Each piece of text starts with a neutral score of zero and was considered positive. In (Devika, et al., 2016) for example, if the input sentence contains any word which is not present in the database then it will be added to the database. This is a supervised learning approach in which the system is trained to learn if any new input is given. Rule-based approaches tend to use heuristics to determine sentiments and linguistics research to analyse sentiments. They tend to have very poor generalization, but within a narrow domain they tend to perform well (Medhat et al., 2014). In machine learning this is known as overfitting and the aim is to avoid this problem and conversely with rules-based systems it's considered largely unavoidable. (Devika et al., 2016) employed a machine learning data driven approach which used a labelled corpus of texts with their respective sentiments for prediction.

A Lexicon based approach uses dictionaries of words tagged with their semantic polarity and sentiment strength (Yadav & Elchuri, 2013) These scores are then used to calculate the polarity and/or sentiment of the textual data. It is said that this technique allows for high precision but low recall. Lexicon Based techniques work on an inference that the aggregated semantic polarity of a sentence or tokens is the sum of polarities of the individual phrases or words. At the ROMIP 2012 conference the lexicon-based method proposed in (Chetviorkin & Loukachevitch, 2013) was used. The authors employed an emotional research technique for sentiment analysis dictionaries for each of the domains. Using appraised words from the appropriate training set, the domain dictionaries were reloaded with the highest weighted words

3. METHODOLOGY

We built a classification model using predictive variables. The steps were:

1. Apply a linguistic text mining approach (Ordenes et al., 2014) to determine the category of each customers review by mining the review verbatim thus dividing customer reviews into three groups of positive, neutral or negative. This sentiment analysis will facilitate the process of modelling the sentiment score generated against the customer rating score, hence attempting to predict the likelihood that the customer has rated the product 1 thru 5.
2. Apply a Naive Bayes Machine Learning Algorithm to predict the rating of the reviews as this is found to work well with the text data.
3. Prepare the textual data for vectorization by removing the punctuations and then converting into lower case and all stop words removed from the sentences.
4. Convert Review' text data to a token (which has punctuations and stop words removed). Using Scikit-learn's Count-Vectorizer functionality the text is then converted into a matrix of token counts. It effectively is a 2D matrix where each row is a unique word, and each column is a review.
5. Develop the prediction model using a Naïve Bayes algorithm to predict customer satisfaction scores accuracy.
6. Evaluate the model by testing the predicted values against the actual ratings in the data using a confusion matrix and classification report from the Scikit-learn toolkit. The data is run through the model and the efficiency of the model is noted and commented upon.
7. Test the output from the model to confirm that predictions are accurate and line up with the expected results. This involves testing random reviews and noting the predicted outcome from the model and comparing with the actual rating in the data.

3.1. Data Transformation

The data set was sourced from Kaggle[1]. It comprised mobile phone reviews from the Amazon website (n=413,840) with only 62 not having a verbatim comment in the 'Review' column. The key component we looked for was the rating (start rating or 1-5 rating for example) and a corresponding review from the customer. We wanted a wide-ranging variance in the types of reviews left by the customers so that there is some degree of subjectivity as differing views are important to aid the design and development of the sentiment model. Therefore, there is an expectation to see different results from the sentiment analysis of this dataset compared to that of datasets about technology products. The variables were Product Title, Brand, Price, Rating & Review text and number of people who found the review helpful. Python was used as it has a considerable variety of text mining and sentiment analysis packages (Bird, et al., 2009) and packages that allow the visualisation of the data and it has a solid range of predictive analytics packages.

Transforming customer satisfaction data into customer insights requires a formal system by which measures are included as part of a data collection and analytics process. The aim was to investigate the correlation between the sentiment analysis score and that of the customer rating score and predict with a degree of certainty the likelihood of the rating based of the sentiment? Therefore, rather than relying on the survey-based CSAT measurement, we applied big data techniques to the mobile phone customer data to evaluate the link between satisfaction and sentiment. The basis of this analysis is to study the customer feedback from the 'Review' column in the data containing the textual feedback, to understand the sentiment behind their commentary and to identify key themes and words within this data. To do this there are several stages required and this follows the Cross-Industry Process for Data Mining (CRISP-DM) (Chapman, et al., 2000). The CRISP-DM process is the "de facto standard for developing data mining and knowledge discovery projects" (Marbán et al., 2009). This multi-layered research methodology has 5 key components of which this process utilizes some but not all the elements of the framework: (Marbán et al., 2009).

Customers who purchased a phone from Amazon were invited to rate the phone i.e. Customers Satisfaction score or 'Rating' as per the data, provide a review of the product via a free form text box i.e. 'Reviews' and as per the amazon website other users could react to the review and 'up-vote' the feedback given by the customer on the product. The customer experience strategy of capturing data like this has been touched upon previously but it is relevant to understand how it is applicable in a business context. As a business there must be some understating of how customer react to products and in this data set there are two key variables that provide insight into this i.e. Rating and Reviews. We note that this is an amazon data set and not company specific data i.e. Apple do not own this data for example and whilst they could carry out analysis on the data do not have sole ownership of it.

The data set can be considered longitudinal customer data covering attitudinal data elicited from the customer survey, which includes Satisfaction ratings ('Rating') and qualitative customer verbatim comments ('Reviews'), behavioural data (transactional data i.e. price) and product data across multiple products for all major mobile phone companies. The data source did not have any date/time references associated with the records. Therefore, the opportunity to conduct time-series analysis is unavailable, this would be an area where the author deems future work would be recommended. There was a total of 413,840 product review records.

The key predictive variables in the data sets that are considered for analysis were, Rating and Review. It should be noted that there will be descriptive analysis performed on the all the other variables within the data set to look for additional insights from the data. The intention is to allow the business to accurately predict the likelihood that a customer will rate a product the way they have. The process will involve identifying those customers who rated the products 1 thru 5 and then using a predictive modelling technique output the accuracy using a classification report.

3.2. Analysis

Pearson and Spearman correlation plots ascertain where there are correlations both positive and negative in the data and this will then help decision making easier when deciding which variables to look at as part of the descriptive analysis in later sections. Data correlations help to identify related variables and can be used by investigating the relationship between two quantitative, continuous variables. Pearson's correlation coefficient (r) is a measure of the strength of the association between the two variables and the interval level ranges between -1 to +1. We use Spearman's correlation which is the nonparametric version of the Pearson correlation. Spearman's correlation coefficient, (ρ, also signified by rs) measures the strength and direction of association between two ranked variables (Hauke & Kossowski, 2011).

The first part of the analysis was done using the matplotlib library and a comparison was run between the Review and Review length variables to get an understanding if there was any significant correlation between the length of a review given by the customer and the subsequent rating. Histograms were generated representing each review category i.e. 1 -> 5 showing the distribution of review lengths for each rating. A comparison was carried out to analyse how the rating and price affected each other. Using the Seaborn library, a scatter graph with a regression line was created for each rating in relation to the corresponding price. For this analysis the heatmap functionality from the seaborn library was used and this produced a heat map graphic that grouped the numerical variables in the data (Price, Review Votes and Review Length) and assigned a colour and correlation score to each relationship indicating the strength of the correlation. This is useful in the sense that it allows the reader to spot any important positive or negative correlations between the data points that may not have been obvious when eyeballing the raw data. Based on the results one could then decide on how best to continue analysing the data.

A scatter chart from the seaborn library was used in this analysis to look at the distribution of review lengths across each rating. In this scenario the data is plotted using a scatter plot and the reason for this is to identify if there are any outliers in the data across the 5 ratings. To investigate the Ratings distribution of the data a KDE (Kernel Density Estimation) plot was used to visualise the ratings. In statistics, KDE is a non-parametric way to estimate the probability density function of a random variable, in this case the Rating given by customers. KDE attempts to smooth the data where assumptions about the population are made based on a finite data set as shown below in Equation (2).

$$\hat{f}_h\left(x\right) = \frac{1}{n}\sum_{i=1}^{n} K_h\left(x - x_i\right) = \frac{1}{nh}\sum_{i=1}^{n} K\left(\frac{x - x_i}{h}\right) \tag{2}$$

where K is the kernel, a non-negative function that integrates to one and $h > 0$ is a smoothing parameter called the bandwidth In Equation (2), the kernel K with subscript h is called the scaled kernel. Ideally one would look to select the h value as small as is feasible for the data; however, there is always a trade-off between the bias of the estimator and its variance. The bandwidth (h) controls how tightly the estimation is fitted to the data, very much like the bin size in a histogram. The KDE plot is very similar to a histogram, it estimates the probability density of a continuous variable, in this case the probability of a rating from 1 to 5. In this case a univariate or kernel density estimate is plotted. A comparison between Apple and Samsung was plotted in two separate graphs allowing for the analysis of the distribution of ratings between the two brands. A side by side comparison can be valuable in determining any obvious differences between the brands with future analysis in mind. Staying with KDE plots and using Samsung again as an example, a plot was created to visualise the distribution by Price of the Samsung products using the Seaborn library as in the previous two sub sections.

3.3. Sentiment Analysis

Using the TextBlob library, we conducted sentiment analysis on each comment for each dataset using TextBlob and assigned each 'Review' a polarity score of between -1 -> 1. The ranges for Positive, Negative and Neutral were Positive Sentiment Score: >0.1 to 1, Neutral Sentiment Score: between -0.1 and 0.1 and Negative Sentiment Score: -1 to <-0.1. These ranges represent the various categories of sentiment polarity. A data frame named 'df_polarity_desc' was used to output a table with the columns Review, Sentiment and Polarity. This enabled the reader to view the output from the sentiment analysis and to put some context around the actual Sentiment Polarity scores for each individual review. Two separate word clouds were created to visual both 'Positive Words' and 'Negative Words'. Both 'Positive Reviews', 'Neutral Reviews' and 'Negative Reviews' were defined based on the numerical ranges discussed. This allowed the author to categorise the Reviews into the three 'buckets' described.

Using the Word Cloud function, two words clouds were visualised for both Positive and Negative reviews i.e. the most used words in each categorisation. A word cloud with a black background was produced for the Positive Review words and a world cloud with a white background for the negative review words. The Sentiment Polarity score was generated on a -1 to 1 scale based on the corresponding 'Review'. The intention is to test whether the sentiment polarity score is related to the rating provided for the corresponding text comment from the customer. To achieve this the Sentiment score has been normalised from a -1 to 1 scale to a 1 to 5 scale to mimic the ratings scale available to the customer. To normalize the data, Equation (3) was used and applied to the 'Polarity' score and the normalised data was named 'Polarity_Norm'.

$$x_{new} = \frac{x - x_{min}}{x_{max} - x_{min}} \tag{3}$$

The Polarity scores were normalized as per the above to scores between 1 and 5 to allow for direct comparison to the corresponding rating score Once the Polarity score has been normalised, the mean and standard deviation of 'Polarity_Norm' is used to create several charts analysing the probability distribution for each Rating category. The two main rating categories that have been identified throughout the research have been Rating 1 and Rating 5. A plot of the polarity distribution is created to explore the sentiment from the reviews in terms of the actual rating and this provides a key insight into the data.

Word frequencies are gathered from the Reviews textual data set into a document-term matrix thus allowing the extraction of features from the Reviews sub dataset. We can employ a feature extraction technique that allows for transforming arbitrary data, in this case the Review text, into numerical features usable for machine learning. The vectorization process turns the collection of text documents into numerical feature vectors. This technique employs tokenization, counting and normalization of the data and is commonly referred to Bag of Words or "Bag of n-grams" representation. Using 'bow_transformer. vocabulary' a classification technique is carried out on the data. Since the vectorization process provided discrete features i.e. the word counts from the Review data the next step is to employ Multinomial Naïve Bayes with the feature counts (Huang, 2017). This helps us calculate the probability of two ratings categories, Rating 1 and Rating 5, using Bayes theorem. Using Reviews as the second variable in the testing, the probability and accuracy of predicting a Rating of 1 and 5 based on the reviews will be obtained. To do this the data is split into a testing and training set. We take 30% of the data and use that as the testing set. Using a confusion matrix, we summarise the performance of the classification algorithm. The number of correct and incorrect predictions are summarized with count values and broken down by each class. We run the confusion matrix for 1 and 5 Ratings and then all Ratings i.e. 1 thru 5. Due to the nature of the confusion matrix it is expected that the accuracy will drop when the 5 classes are modelled.

4. EVALUATION

The Pearson Correlation showed a slight correlation between Rating and Review Votes (see Figure 4). This would suggest that as the Rating increases the price increases and the number of Review votes given to the product increases also. Which would make sense but since there is not a strong correlation the thought is that this would be not worth exploring with further analysis. Using the Spearman correlation in Figure 5, one can observe very similar correlations with a slight negative correlation between Rating and Review votes which, as with the Pearson test, does not warrant deeper analysis.

Figure 4. Pearson Correlation

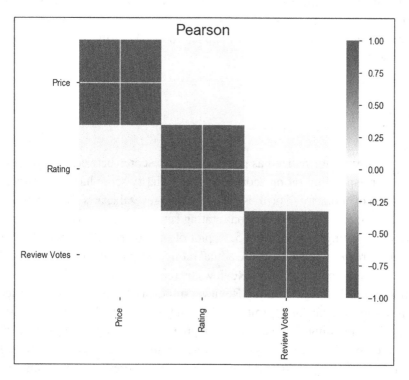

Figure 5. Spearman Correlation

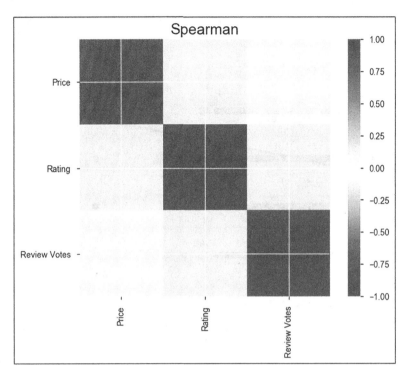

The correlation between variables showed a negative correlation between Price and Polarity which would suggest that the sentiment of the review tends to be more negative as the price goes up. This potentially could indicate that customers are less happy with their more expensive phones and expect better from the product. Polarity and Review votes have a positive correlation with each other, indicating that the more a Review is 'up-voted' the higher the more positive the sentiment seems to be, which would make sense form a logical standpoint (see Figure 6).

Figure 6. Review v Review Length by Ratings

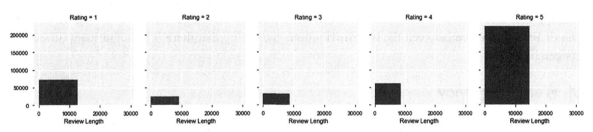

We created histograms to compare review lengths against each rating to help us note the number of reviews and which buckets the review length belong to for each rating. This is reveals that there is an overwhelming number of reviews for Rating 5 and a considerable number of reviews for Rating 1. This will be useful going forward in determining which Ratings should be more closely looked into. Figure 7 is quite interesting as is displays the distribution of price points across each Rating value. As expected, many price points exist below the $1000 rang with a small number of outliers upwards of $2000.

Figure 7. Regression Plot of Price v Rating

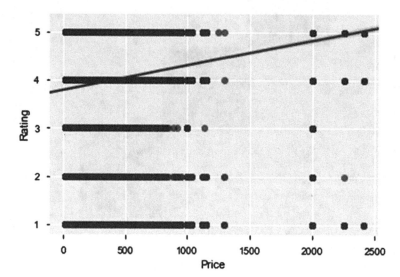

Using a heat map to look at correlations between the variables it is noticeable that there are negative correlations of -0.91 between Price and review length which would indicate that the greater the price the shorter the review and vice versa. This could be attributed to the fact that there are more reviews at the lower price level as noted previously in Figure 8 and therefore this finding it not at all surprising. Like other charts, it was felt that a closer look should be taken at Review length v Rating. (see Figure 9). What is observed here is the distribution of reviews by Length v Rating and it shows that there is a slight tendency for customers to comment more about phones that they are happy with hence the distribution in Figure 10.

To get a sense for the multivariate density of the ratings the chart in Figure 11 shows the high density of % ratings across the reviews. There is a smaller but significant population of 1 Star reviews and this will supplement the previous charts for further investigation. Comparing Figure 11 with Figure 12 there is no distinct difference between the two distributions indicating that there is no significant difference between brands.

4.1. Word Frequency

The word phone is by far the most common. Some other interesting outputs from this are the occurrences of the words Great and Good which would lead to a possible conclusion that there may be an overwhelming number of positive reviews in the data. Figure 13 shows the Top 7-words.

As another visual alternative Figure 14 shows a word cloud of word frequencies. This gives an impactful visual of the occurrences of the top 100 words in the review feedback.

Figure 8. Heat Map

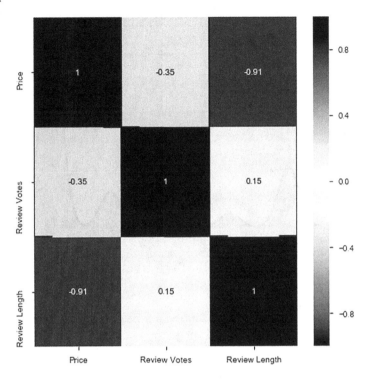

Figure 9. Rating v Review Length Regression plot

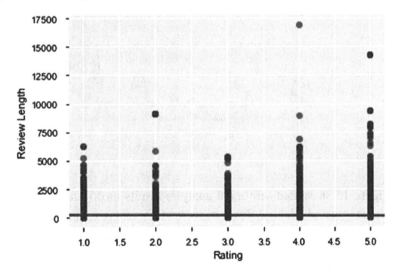

Using the TextBlob library the intention is to give each 'Review' a sentiment score of between -1 -> 1. These define the various categories of sentiment. There is an overwhelming number of positive reviews and this follows from the exploratory analysis above showing the high frequency of 5-star ratings. This does not tell the whole story so further analysis on the sentiment is required.

Figure 10. Kernel Density Estimate

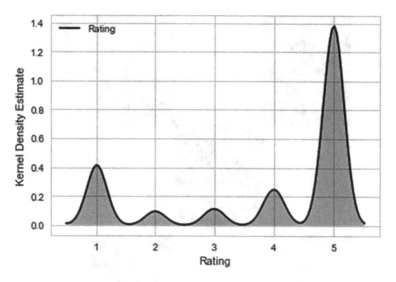

Figure 11. Samsung Kernel Density Estimate

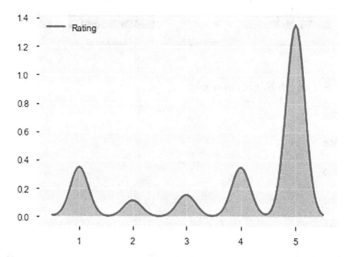

The results in Figure 15 show that sentiment analysis results mostly fall into the Positive Review category based on the range used. Neutral Reviews seems to have a reasonable volume with the narrow range taken into consideration and there are a smaller number of Negative reviews compared to the other categories. This would suggest that most customers were reasonably happy with their purchases. Interestingly, a Rating of 1 had the second highest volume but as per the above there are significantly less Negative reviews which on the face of it suggests that those who gave a Rating of 1 their corresponding sentiment score may be higher and not directly related to the rating, this is for now a question to be explored further. Interestingly the observable trend for Rating scores of 5 and Positive reviews seem fairly aligned so further analysis on this is needed.

Figure 12. Apple Kernel Density Estimate

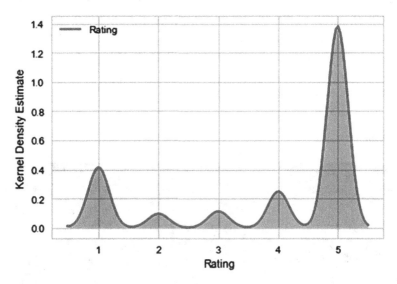

Figure 13. Word Frequency Chart

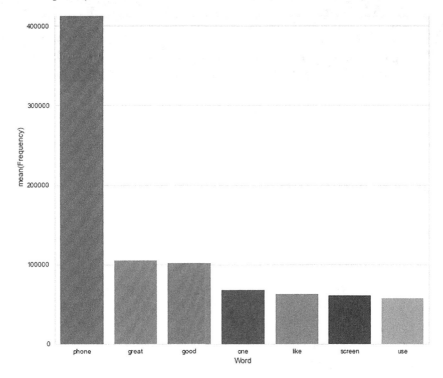

Figure 16 shows a small cohort of reviews with the corresponding Sentiment and Polarity scores. This gives the reader a very quick taste of output from the code showing how each piece of text is given a score. A very brief scan of the results shows that it 'seems' accurate, taking record [2] as a positive review i.e. 'Very Pleased' and conversely looking at record [5] with the word problems mentioned the sentiment is -0.3 which seems to fit. This is obviously not indicative of the total population of reviews but gives some insight into the results. Figure 17 shows the word cloud for Positive Reviews and here is it noticeable that key words such as 'Great', 'Love' and 'Good' are quite prevalent in the data and this is something that would be expected. Reviewing Figure 18, the word cloud for negative reviews it is noticeable that there are many occurrences of the words 'Disappointed', 'Broken' and 'Bad' which would tend to be on the negative side and again something that would be expected to see in the analysis.

Figure 14. Word Cloud

Figure 15. Sentiment Frequency Chart

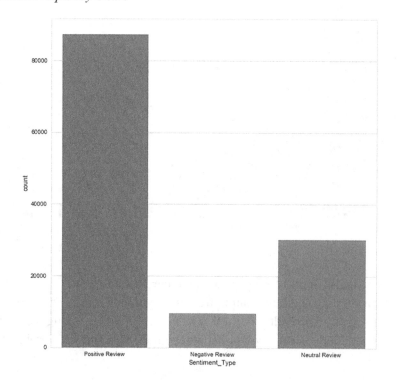

Figure 16. Reviews, Sentiment and Polarity Table

	Review	Polarity
0	I feel so LUCKY to have found this used (phone...	0.180952
1	nice phone, nice up grade from my pantach revu...	0.449259
2	Very pleased	0.650000
3	It works good but it goes slow sometimes but i...	0.452500
4	Great phone to replace my lost phone. The only...	0.214583
5	I already had a phone with problems... I know ...	-0.300000
6	The charging port was loose. I got that solder...	0.019814
7	Phone looks good but wouldn't stay charged, ha...	0.516460
8	I originally was using the Samsung S2 Galaxy f...	0.267692
9	It's battery life is great. It's very responsi...	0.222222
10	My fiance had this phone previously, but cause...	0.358333
11	This is a great product it came after two days...	0.182500
12	These guys are the best! I had a little situat...	0.282500
13	I'm really disappointed about my phone and ser...	-0.083333
14	Ordered this phone as a replacement for the sa...	0.191591
15	Had this phone before and loved it but was not...	0.236111
16	I was able to get the phone I previously owned...	0.416667
17	I brought this phone as a replacement for my d...	0.473611

Figure 17. Positive Review Word Cloud

The multinomial Naive Bayes classifier is suitable for classification with discrete features (e.g., word counts for text classification). The multinomial distribution normally requires integer feature counts. However, in practice, fractional counts such as tf-idf also work. The Multinomial Naïve Bayes model had a 93% accuracy rate when predicting a Rating of 1 and a 96% accuracy rate when predicting a Rating of 5, with an overall model accuracy of 96% The f1-score of 90% and 97%, with an overall core of 96% represent the weighted average of the precision and recall scores indicating that the model is accurate when attempting to predict if a customer will score the review a 1 or 5.

Figure 18. Negative Review Word Cloud

The model was trained on the entire data set including all 5 ratings. Figure 19 shows the precision and recall output from the Multinomial Naïve Bayes modelling and Figure 20 shows the accuracy and averages. It is noticeable that when the model is run with the entire population of the data the accuracy drops quite significantly to an overall score of 74%. This indicates that the data for Ratings 2, 3 & 4 has a significant impact on the models' accuracy. It is noteworthy that Ratings 1 and 5 remain quite high and this is potentially due to the large volumes of Ratings in these categories compared with the other categories.

Figure 19. Confusion Matrix (additional variables)

```
[[ 5026    18    65   140   751]
 [  876   176    34   190   388]
 [  554    17   341   292   918]
 [  249     7    32  1252  3283]
 [  280    13    61   456 21196]]
```

	precision	recall	f1-score	support
1	0.72	0.84	0.77	6000
2	0.76	0.11	0.19	1664
3	0.64	0.16	0.26	2122
4	0.54	0.26	0.35	4823
5	0.80	0.96	0.87	22006
avg / total	0.74	0.76	0.72	36615

Figure 20. Accuracy and Weighted Average Table

Rating	Accuracy	Weighted Average
1	72%	77%
2	76%	19%
3	64%	26%
4	54%	35%
5	80%	87%
Avg/Total	74%	72%

4.2. Normalisation of Polarity

Using the mean and standard deviation of the Polarity_Norm, each rating was matched with its corresponding normalised polarity score. Figure 21 is interesting for many reasons as it can be observed that a customer's rating of 5 will have approximately a 60% probability that the sentiment score will be 4. Secondly there is a noticeable distribution between 3 and 4 which is in and around the neutral sentiment category. This slight shift away from a polarity score of 5 suggests that while most of sentiment may be positive there is a significant cohort of reviews that have a slight negative or neutral tone which would indicate an area for further exploration from a business perspective.

Figure 21. Normalised Polarity Distribution for Rating 5

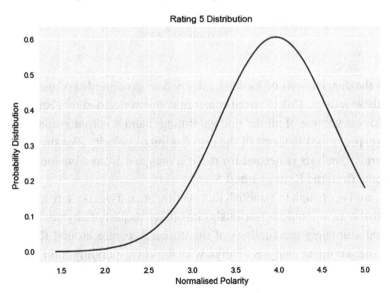

The same method was applied when plotting the graph in Figure 22. Considering that these are the probability distributions for Ratings of 1, one could be forgiven for thinking these were the results for a Rating of 3. It is significant to observe that the polarity or sentiment of 1 Ratings are tending towards slightly negative and natural, this could be down to many reasons. The model itself may be unable to identify negative words, or customers tend to not be overly critical when commenting.

Figure 22. Normalised Polarity Distribution for Rating 1

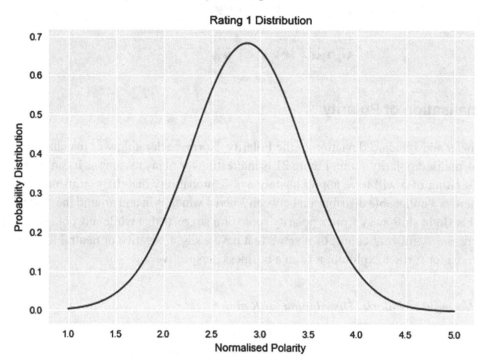

Figure 23 shows the distributions of Ratings 1,3,4 & 5 to give an idea of the how the sentiment has been measured for these ratings. Due to space constraints it was decided that Rating 2 would be left out and it also had the lowest volume of all the ratings. Rating 3 and 4 output graphs seem to be consistent and in line with the expectations in terms of the distribution of polarity. For that reason, the suggestion would be that no further analysis is needed for these scores and from a business perspective the most valuable insights come from the Ratings 1 and 5.

The model was intuitive enough to establish that sentiment analysis is a key indicator of the customer experience and for that reason should be seriously considered as part of any businesses metrics strategy. The key analysis and ultimately the findings of this research centre around the normalisation of the polarity score from the sentiment analysis to align with the corresponding rating given by the customer for that product. It was noticeable that a large distribution of ratings fell into the '1' and '5' buckets. For that reason, it was prudent to examine the associated polarity with these scores more closely than the other rating scores. The analysis, supplemented with the visualisations showed that for a Rating of 5, the sentiment distribution was skewed towards a score of 4 with a slight emphasis on 3 also. This showed that while customers were rating the products 5/5 their actual sentiment regarding the product was not so overwhelmingly positive. Conversely the same can be said of customers giving the products a rating of '1'. The results showed that while customers rated some products poorly the overall sentiment fell into the somewhat negative and neutral bands. What we show is that there can be an over reliance on using the Ratings score as a single point of truth for a business, when big data analytics techniques are employed it is possible to drill down into the real feelings of customers and get a clearer picture of products and services. The predictive analytics model used multinomial Bayesian networks to predict customer ratings using the sentiment review score. The results of the research highlight the short-comings of the ratings score as a single customer experience metric, thereby supporting the notion that a business cannot rely solely on this metric. The result from the prediction phase is a model that is capable of correctly predicting 74 per cent of customers ratings based on their reviews. This is not remarkably high percentage in terms of accuracy and backs up the claim above that the ratings cannot be used as an accurate predictor of sentiment alone. On this basis of the results, this research recommends that businesses are discouraged from using the CSAT or ratings scores as a single point of truth for customer experience. Although these metrics are important, they do not provide an insight into the opinion of customers regarding the experience they have had with a business or a product. The approach employed here demonstrates that a data-driven approach to exploring customer sentiment via text mining helps form a clearer picture for the business and it is important that firms capitalize on this type of data.

Figure 23. Rating 1,3,4 & 5 Polarity Distribution

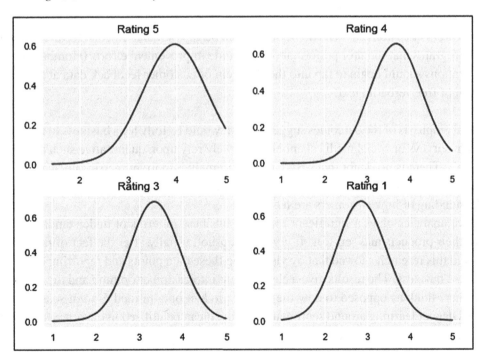

5. CONCLUSION

Quantitative survey questions such as Customer Satisfaction will always remain widely popular with businesses when attempting to take the pulse from their customers on products and customer experience (Hague & Hague, 2018). To overly rely on single customer metrics such as customer experience or net promoter score is a risky strategy and the suggestion is that business should focus upon a more nuanced multidimensional approach to predicting customer behaviour (Zaki et al., 2016).

We explored the notion of focussing and adopting a more scientific approach to measure customer sentiment by mining verbatim feedback and applying a sentiment analysis methodology to determine how customers feel about the products as opposed to the score they gave the product based on the constrictive 1 to 5 rating. We provided a framework to understand how a customer experience process can be developed to provide insights into the Voice of the Customer.

Key recommendations are as follows:

- Establishing and maintaining a positive customer experience for customers is imperative for any company's long-term goals and ultimately their success as a business.
- There needs to be buy-in at a senior management level to embrace a customer-centric metrics strategy which includes development of a robust process to measure customer sentiment.
- Text mining and sentiment analysis play a key role in understanding how customers feel about the products they purchase or the experience they had with a company (Fan, 2014).
- While survey-based metrics gathering will always remain an important process in measuring leading indicators of customers' behaviour, this should be supplemented with a formal customer experience programs that monitor performance and guide improvement efforts (Homburg et al., 2015).
- Organizations should begin to tap into the rich vein of customer feedback data at their disposal in the form of free verbatim text.

The central emphasis of the outcomes suggests that it would be folly for a business to ignore customer feedback from surveys or social media channels and solely rely upon quantitative such as customer satisfaction CSAT. There is no doubt that CSAT is an extremely important metric and should continue to be measured however businesses need to capitalise on customer data points such as sentiment to really get an understanding of how customers are feeling.

Descriptive analytics plays a significant role for a business in terms of understanding what is happening with their products and services. It gives a snapshot, usually after the fact of performance and experience and this research showed that by visualising these data points and reporting out on them can be valuable to a business. The results give a clear insight into customer opinion and the nuances around which customers think as opposed to how they rate a product on a limited 5-point scale. The findings point towards deeper learning around sentiment and how it can be utilised in other areas of the business and with additional data points not present in this research. This strategy could be employed in a business scenario and the results and findings would prove valuable in helping build a customer experience strategy for a business. The key findings are that it is unwise to rely solely on CSAT or NPS scores without examining customer feedback.

REFERENCES

ACSI. (2018). *American Customer Satisfaction Index.* Retrieved from http://www.theacsi.org/about-acsi/the-science-of-customer-satisfaction

Ajenstat, F. (2017). Tableau five years a leader in Gartner's Magic Quadrant for Analytics. *Tableau.* Retrieved from https://www.tableau.com/about/blog/2017/2/tableau-five-years-leader-gartners-magic-quadrant-analytics-66133

Allahyari, M., Pouriyeh, S., Assefi, M., Safaei, S., Trippe, E. D., Gutierrez, J. B., & Kochut, K. (2017). A brief survey of text mining: Classification, clustering and extraction techniques. arXiv:1707.02919

Arokiasamy, A. (2013). The impact of customer satisfaction on customer loyalty. *Journal of Commerce,* *5*(1), 14–21.

Aswani, S. (2017). Analyzing Customer Feedback Data: Manual Analysis vs NLP. *Clarabridge.* Retrieved from https://www.clarabridge.com/blog/analyzing-customer-feedback-data-manual-analysis-vs-nlp/

Baars, H., & Kemper, H. G. (2008). Management support with structured and unstructured data—an integrated business intelligence framework. *Information Systems Management,* *25*(2), 132–148.

Balahur, A. & Montoyo, A. (2008). A feature dependent method for opinion mining and classification.

LaValle, S., Lesser, E., Shockley, R., Hopkins, M. S., & Kruschwitz, N. (2011). Big Data, Analytics and the Path From Insights to Value. *MIT Sloan Management Review,* *52*(2), 21–32.

Bird, S., Klein, E., & Loper, E. (2009). Natural language processing with Python: analyzing text with the natural language toolkit. In *Natural language processing with Python: analyzing text with the natural language toolkit* (pp. 1–34). O'Reilly Media Inc.

Broan, S.E. & Steger, A.J. (2013). Key performance indicators are not just about profit. CFMA. Retrieved from http://www.cfma.org/content.cfm?ItemNumber=1899

Brownlee, J. (2016). *Support Vector Machines for Machine Learning.* Retrieved from https://machine-learningmastery.com/support-vector-machines-for-machine-learning/

Cappelli, A. (2017). *Natural Language Processing with Stanford CoreNLP.* Retrieved from https://cloudacademy.com/blog/natural-language-processing-stanford-corenlp-2/

Chapman, P., Clinton, J., Kerber, R., Khabaza, T., Reinartz, T., Sherer, C., & Wirth, R. (2000). Cross industry standard process for data mining (CRISP-DM) 1.0.

Chen, H., Chiang, R., & Storey, V. (2012). Business intelligence and analytics: From big data to big impact. *Management Information Systems Quarterly,* *1*(1), 1165–1188. doi:10.2307/41703503

Chetviorkin, I. & Loukachevitch, N. (2013). Evaluating sentiment analysis systems in Russian.

Chowdhury, G. (2005). Natural language processing. *Annual Review of Information Science & Technology,* *37*(1), 51–89. doi:10.1002/aris.1440370103

Clarabridge. (2015). Retrieved from www.clarabridge.com

Cran Project. (2018). *CRAN Task View: Natural Language Processing.* Retrieved from https://cran.r-project.org/web/views/NaturalLanguageProcessing.html

Daume, H. III, & Marcu, D. (2006). Domain adaptation for statistical classifiers. *Journal of Artificial Intelligence Research, 26,* 101–126. doi:10.1613/jair.1872

Department of Industry, Australian Government. (2018). Understand your customers. [REMOVED HYPERLINK FIELD]Retrieved from https://www.business.gov.au/info/plan-and-start/start-your-business/what-is-customer-service/understand-your-customers

Devika, M. D. C, S. & Ganesha, A., 2016. Sentiment Analysis:A Comparative Study On Different Approaches. Chennai, Tamil Nadu, India, Department of CSE, Vidya Academy of Science and Technology.

EMC. (n.d.). [REMOVED HYPERLINK FIELD]Big Data storage [white paper]. Retrieved from https://www.emc.com/collateral/white-papers/idg-bigdata-storage-wp.pdf

Schumaker, R. P., Zhang, Y., Huang, C. N., & Chen, H. (2012). Evaluating sentiment in financial news articles. *Decision Support Systems, 53*(3), 458–464. doi:10.1016/j.dss.2012.03.001

Fiedler, L., Großmaß, T., Roth, M., & Vetvik, O. J. (2016). [REMOVED HYPERLINK FIELD]Why customer analytics matter. *McKinsey.* Retrieved from https://www.mckinsey.com/business-functions/marketing-and-sales/our-insights/why-customer-analytics-matter

FoundationP. S. (2018). Get it. *Python.* Retrieved from http://www.python.org/getit/

Ghiassi, M., Skinner, J., & Zimbra, D. (2013). Twitter brand sentiment analysis: A hybrid system using n-gram analysis and dynamic artificial neural network. *Expert Systems with Applications, 40*(16), 6266–6282. doi:10.1016/j.eswa.2013.05.057

Think with Google. (2016). Why cutomer analytics are the key to creating value. Retrieved from https://www.thinkwithgoogle.com/intl/en-gb/marketing-resources/data-measurement/why-customer-analytics-are-the-key-to-creating-value/

Harris, D. (2018). What Is Text Analytics? We Analyze the Jargon. *Software advice.* Retrieved from https://www.softwareadvice.com/resources/what-is-text-analytics/

Hauke, J., & Kossowski, T. (2011). Comparison of values of Pearson's and Spearman's correlation coefficients on the same sets of data. *Quaestiones Geographicae, 30*(2), 87–93. doi:10.2478/v10117-011-0021-1

Hollyoake, M. (2009). The four pillars: Developing a 'bonded' business-to-business customer experience. *Journal of Database Marketing & Customer Strategy Management, 16*(2), 132–158. doi:10.1057/dbm.2009.14

Hosseini, S., Maleki, A., & Gholamian, M. (2010). Cluster analysis using data mining approach to develop CRM methodology to assess the customer loyalty. *Expert Systems with Applications, 37*(7), 5259–5264. doi:10.1016/j.eswa.2009.12.070

Huang, O. (2017). *Applying Multinomial Naive Bayes to NLP Problems: A Practical Explanation.* Medium. Retrieved from https://medium.com/@Synced/applying-multinomial-naive-bayes-to-nlp-problems-a-practical-explanation-4f5271768ebf

Telus International. (2017). Customer First Magazine. Retrieved from https://www.telusinternational.com/media/TI-CustomersFirstMagazine-I04.pdf

Kaisler, S. (2013). Big Data: Issues and Challenges Moving Forward. In *Proceedings of the 46th Hawaii International Conference on System Sciences* (pp. 995-1004). 10.1109/HICSS.2013.645

Kim, E. (2017). *Everything You Wanted to Know about the Kernel Trick.* Retrieved from http://www.eric-kim.net/eric-kim-net/posts/1/kernel_trick.html

Liu, B., Hu, M., & Cheng, J. (2005, May). Opinion observer: analyzing and comparing opinions on the web. In *Proceedings of the 14th international conference on World Wide Web* (pp. 342-351). ACM.

Loria, S. (2018). *TextBlob.* Retrieved from http://textblob.readthedocs.io/en/dev/

Maiolo, A. (2015). Comparing n-gram models. *Recognize Speech.* Retrieved from http://recognize-speech.com/language-model/n-gram-model/comparison

Marbán, Ó., Mariscal, G., & Segovia, J. (2009). A data mining & knowledge discovery process model. In *Data mining and knowledge discovery in real life applications.* IntechOpen.

Maritz. (2018). Maximise verbatims with text analytics [white paper]. Retrieved from https://www.maritzcx.com/blog/wp-content/uploads/2014/11/Maritz-White-Paper-Maximise-verbatims-with-text-analytics.pdf

McCallumzy, A. K., & Nigamy, K. (1998, July). Employing EM and pool-based active learning for text classification. In *Proc. International Conference on Machine Learning (ICML)* (pp. 359-367).

Medhat, W., Hassan, A., & Korashy, H. (2014). Sentiment analysis algorithms and applications: A survey. *Ain Shams Engineering Journal, 5*(4), 1093–1113. doi:10.1016/j.asej.2014.04.011

Mejova, Y. A. (2012). *Sentiment analysis within and across social media.* University of Iowa. doi:10.17077/etd.zze4b252

Miner, G. (2012). *Practical text mining and statistical analysis for non-structured text data applications.* Oxford: Academic Press.

Molag, T. (2017). Power BI vs Tableau. *Encore Business.* Retrieved from https://www.encorebusiness.com/blog/power-bi-vs-tableau/

Natarajan, K., Li, J., & Koronios, A. (2010). Data mining techniques for data cleaning. In *Engineering Asset Lifecycle Management* (pp. 796–804). Springer London.

NTLK.org. (2017). Retrieved from http://www.nltk.org/

Ordenes, F., Theodoulidis, B., Burton, J., Gruber, T., & Zaki, M. (2014). Analyzing customer experience feedback using text mining: A linguistics-based approach. *Journal of Service Research, 17*(3), 278–295. doi:10.1177/1094670514524625

Ott, T. (2018). What is text analytics. *Software Advice*. Retrieved from https://www.softwareadvice.com/resources/what-is-text-analytics/

Pang, B., & Lee, L. (2002). Thumbs up? Sentiment Classification using. *Machine Learning*.

Parasuraman, A., Berry, L. L., & Zeithaml, V. A. (1991). Understanding Customer Expectations of Service. *Sloan Management Review*, *32*(3), 39.

Project, C. (n.d.). *Cran r-project*. Retrieved from https://cran.r-project.org/

Qualtrics. (2018). *What is the Net Promoter Score (NPS)*. Retrieved from https://www.qualtrics.com/experience-management/customer/net-promoter-score/

Rapidminer. (2018). *Rapidminer*. Retrieved from https://rapidminer.com/

ŘehůřekR. (2018). *gensim*. Retrieved from https://radimrehurek.com/gensim/about.html

SAS. (2017). *Natural Language Processing*. Retrieved from https://www.sas.com/en_us/insights/analytics/what-is-natural-language-processing-nlp.html

Smith, E. (2016). Everything you need to know about customer success. *Cobloom*. Retrieved from https://www.cobloom.com/blog/everything-you-need-to-know-about-customer-success

Spacy.io. (n.d.). *Industrial-Strength NLP*. Retrieved from https://spacy.io/

Srivastava, A., & Singh, D. M. (2014). Supervised SA of product reviews using Weighted k-NN Algorithm. In *2014 11th International Conference on Information Technology*.

Srivastava, T. (2014). Support vector machine simplified. Retrieved from https://www.analyticsvidhya.com/blog/2014/10/support-vector-machine-simplified/

Tamilselvi, A. & Parveen Taj, M. (2013). Sentiment Analysis of Micro blogs using Opinion Mining Classification Algorithm. *International Journal of Science and Research*, *2*(10), 2319–7064.

Taylor, C. (2018). [REMOVED HYPERLINK FIELD]Structured vs unstructured data. *Datamation*. Retrieved from https://www.datamation.com/big-data/structured-vs-unstructured-data.html

Tirunillai, S., & Tellis, G. (2014). Mining marketing meaning from online chatter: Strategic brand analysis of big data using latent dirichlet allocation. *JMR, Journal of Marketing Research*, *51*(4), 463–479. doi:10.1509/jmr.12.0106

Upadhyay, P. (2017). Removing stop words NLTK python. *Geeksforgeeks.com*. Retrieved from https://www.geeksforgeeks.org/removing-stop-words-nltk-python/

Verint. (2016). *Verint Text Analytics*. Retrieved from https://www.verint.com/Assets/resources/resource-types/datasheets/text-analytics-datasheet.pdf

Vryniotis, V. (2013). Machine Learning Tutorial: The Max Entropy Text Classifier. *Datumbox*. Retrieved from http://blog.datumbox.com/machine-learning-tutorial-the-max-entropy-text-classifier/

Wichmann, M. (2017). *The Python Wiki*. Retrieved from https://wiki.python.org/moin/

Xia, R., Zong, C., & Li, S. (2011). Ensemble of feature sets and classification algorithms for sentiment classification. *Information Sciences*, *181*(6), 1138–1152. doi:10.1016/j.ins.2010.11.023

Yadav, V., & Elchuri, H. (2013). Serendio: Simple and Practical lexicon based approach to Sentiment Analysis. In *Proceedings of the Second Joint Conference on Lexical and Computational Semantics* (pp. 543-548).

ENDNOTE

[1]   https://www.kaggle.com

This research was previously published in the International Journal of Data Warehousing and Mining (IJDWM), 15(4); pages 21-47, copyright year 2019 by IGI Publishing (an imprint of IGI Global).

Chapter 89
Behaviour and Emotions of Working Professionals Towards Online Learning Systems:
Sentiment Analysis

Venkata Ramana Attili
Sreenidhi Institute of Science and Technology, India

Sreenivasa Rao Annaluri
Vallurupalli Nageswara Rao Vignana Jyothi Institute of Engineering and Technology, India

Suresh Reddy Gali
Vallurupalli Nageswara Rao Vignana Jyothi Institute of Engineering and Technology, India

Ramasubbareddy Somula
Vallurupalli Nageswara Rao Vignana Jyothi Institute of Engineering and Technology, India

ABSTRACT

Student behaviour in the classroom depends on various influential factors (such as family, friends, locality, habits, etc.). Once a student enters into professional life after completing the graduation, it finds it difficult to get back to the learning process due to a variety of issues. In such situations, most of the students go for online courses to improve their skills or to get a promotion at work by upgrading their academic degrees. The tendency of working professionals attending online classes is increasing rapidly due to the vast development in technology in recent times and due to the demand for innovative Secunderabad, e technologies. In this paper, a detailed study on a variety of participants from different work domains was carried out to study the sentiments of working professionals by analysing their behaviour and emotions using Hadoop, big data, and R-Language. Using the RFacebook API, the functioning of the students was analysed in this work by using R programming. Results have shown that the behaviour of 89% working professionals is positive, and emotionally, 75% were satisfied with online courses. However, the tendency of being lazy was also expressed by many for online courses.

DOI: 10.4018/978-1-6684-6303-1.ch089

1. INTRODUCTION

Student learning system (SLS) is changing with time and innovation for a good reason to adopt the best suitable provisions for the students to address the real-time challenges. With the changing systems and applications developed based on computers and mobiles with the support of internet connectivity, it becomes a great challenge for educational institutions. These challenges include the student behaviour in the classroom, overlooking the teaching staff with limited experience and exposure, underestimating the importance of book reading, undermining the traditional teaching methodologies, etc. Such a kind of behavioural changes in the student community demands careful monitoring towards their attitude for learning in the classroom, methods they follow while learning online using web applications on their computers and mobile phones at home, etc. In the recent times, various programs by professors from IIT's, NIT's are available online by centre for the development of advanced computing (C-DAC), national program on technology enhanced learning (NPTEL), etc. providing various certification courses are funded by HRD Ministry, Government of India. Such initiations are made by various governments globally, nationally and regionally to ensure that the youngsters are well trained to suit and fulfil the requirements of the industry to sustain with the daily life challenges in the technological world.

1.1. Recent Work on Sentiment Analysis

In recent times, the purpose of monitoring student performance was obtained by using educational data mining (EDM) by taking the feedbacks and by analyzing student behaviour and sentiments (Altrabsheh et al., 2013). The feedback systems in the educational institutions included response systems, short message services (SMS), and different types of mobile applications, according to Altrabshesh et al. using data mining. Later Altrabshesh et al., experimented with predicting the emotions related to learning by taking feedback via Twitter. The purpose of this experiment is to understand the individual student behaviour using Twitter as compared to the feedback given by students in groups (Altrabsheh et al., 2015). Such an investigation revealed that the emotions of the students are different when they are giving feedback individually and when they are in groups. Apart from Twitter, in an experiment with another popular social network site (SNS), Facebook (FB) was considered by Zamani et al. to determine the sentimental analysis for the emotions of the people (Zamani et al., 2013). In this work, the authors tried to extract both English and Malay words from FB and experimented to find opinion mining and sentimental analysis. Similar work was carried out by Teja et al. movie reviews using machine learning algorithms (Teja et al., 2018). This study helped most of the administrators to keep track of events in their employee's life, which may influence the workplace.

However, these behavioral changes depending on the gender, student level, and their approach to using mobile phones were critically analyzed by Abdulsalami et al. by using four lexical resources (Abdulsalami et al., 2017). The results from this work revealed that the student sentiments are always influenced based on their association with different groups and people in their real lives. In a critical method, Jo et al. built a sentiment analysis model using deep Convolutional Neural Network (CNN) algorithms (Jo et al., 2017), and later experiments are carried out with different psychological measurements (Sharma, 2017). Using the movie review data, the models were trained with the summaries as a part of the concept of transfer learning. The results of this experiment revealed that some of the sentiments were appropriately analysed but could not relate most of the psychological measurements (Bhattacharya et al., 2020; Gadekallu et al., 2020; Reddy et al., 2020).

To understand and address the problems of students related with confusion and boredom the sentimental analysis was carried out by Altrabsheh et al. using different data mining techniques such as Naïve Bayes, Complement Naïve Bayes (CNB), Support Vector Machines (SVM), etc. (Altrabsheh et al., 2014). In this work, the SVM found to be more accurate (94%) followed by CNM with 84%. With a keen interest towards the education system, the potential application of the sentimental analysis has been carried out by Koehler et al. to compare the friendliness two different conferences carried out by educational institutions (Koehler et al., 2015). The authors used Twitter and FB as a platform for collecting a massive set of data. Such an experiment helped to discourse communities, controversies, issues and opinion in the educational institutions. So far, it was seen to understand the student's behaviour and sentiments. However, Kagklis et al. performed similar experiments on the students studying in distance education (Kagklis et al., 2015). To conduct this study, the authors used text mining techniques by processing student information from social network analysis techniques. The authors remarked to have a regular watch on the student sentiments during the entire course time.

In an attempt to understand the sentiments on identities and behaviours based on the social events texts that were published in newspapers were examined by Joseph et al. using Affect Control Theory (ACT) (Joseph et al., 2016). This work helped to perceive the actions of individuals and helped to understand the effect of the language and words used in different conversations. A similar attempt was made on student's texts comments by Aung using lexicon-based sentiment analysis (Aung, 2016). The database was created for sentimental analysis using a lexical source for obtaining the polarity of words.

Later, the performance of medical students was evaluated by Izzo and Maloy using Microsoft Cognitive Services (MCS), which is an SVM trained with preliminary data from twitter (Izzo & Maloy, 2017). The algorithm designed in this work found to be correct with 66% and incorrect with 34%; mean sentiment scores are well correlated with overall grades but do not have any relationship between grads and sentiments of free-form texts.

1.2. Importance Features of Online Learning System

As discussed in the literature, a series of events will take place in every individual life, and they influence a person so that the behaviour may change with time. Sometimes such changes in behaviour may lead to give an advantage or even may become a negative impact on someone's life as well. Notably, the students will be having a variety of experiences during their course time with a lot of new challenges in the form of exams, subjects, laboratories, experiments, research, and finally facing the interviews for a bright career. Sometimes students feel a kind of a shy and (or) shame to speak up in the traditional classrooms and prefer to go for online courses. Some students are very good at listening and understanding the lecturers in the classrooms, but the same may find it difficult while taking online courses. Some of the critical suggestions were summaries by Bishop and Verleger towards flipped classrooms (Bishop & Verleger, 2013). Some of the student comments are summarized here in online education. Some of the drawbacks are also listed, along with the benefits of online education systems (Song et al., 2004).

Benefits:
- Learning can be done at own phase and convenient;
- Very much helpful for working employees;
- Easy to access;
- Pressure free environment for students in a relaxed way;

- ◦ No need of buying the books anymore;
- ◦ Allows you to spend more time for individuals to thinking;
- ◦ Flexible towards selecting the courses and independent schedules;
- ◦ No worries due to any kind of illness or absence.

Drawbacks:

- ◦ Slow instructor feedback;
- ◦ Learning accountability is always a question mark;
- ◦ Opportunity to meet peers is very less;
- ◦ Lack of observation by a teacher is always a concern;
- ◦ Develops poor time management in most of the students;
- ◦ Procrastination will become a part of life;
- ◦ More confusions due to lack of guidance;
- ◦ Lack of communication skills due to no interactions with professors and teachers;
- ◦ Distractions may dominate due to unnecessary browsing or due to unfamiliar technologies.

1.3. Objectives of This Work

In this work, detailed research is being carried out among the working professionals to identify their response towards online learning system using a survey. This survey is just a preliminary stage of opinion collection where the participants will express the data. Similarly, this paper evaluated the text and sentiment analysis of working professionals based on Facebook posts and messages using the R language. The results are analyzed using data mining techniques to understand the students who are working in part-time or distance courses in various universities. The outcomes of this work will help both institutions and people opting for distance education to understand the individual strategies to get maximum benefits.

2. PROPOSED APPROACH

The overall work in this research is based on the response of people on various social websites. The patterns of this work are derived by using the reactions of students responding online in different social networking platforms. In Figure 1, different steps involved analyzing the student behaviour and their emotions for online education systems are presented.

2.1. Data Collection

In this work, data collection was mostly made from Facebook accounts of different participants involved in online training with their choice of courses. To import data from Facebook, an account was created and using RFacebook package and later, the data analysis was done. These days' social networking sites are providing various inbuilt supporting tools for data collection and using them for different study purposes (Sharma, 2017).

2.2. Data Pre-Processing

The data pre-processing is very much essential to collect the specific words used by the participants to express their opinion towards online education. Selective data must be considered in a particular scenario's which are related to their course interests and towards sharing their likes, dislikes, opinions, frustrations, etc. (Jindal & Sharma, 2018). In the process of analyzing the participant behaviour, the Part_of_Speech (POS) tagging plays a vital role. Here POS is going to identify the nature of different words that form a sentence. It will help to determine the keywords used by the participants while expressing their feelings on Facebook.

Datasets are available online from different sources for analyzing the sentiments and behaviour of people using Facebook. LINDAT/CLARIN data & tools from the University of West Bohemia collected a corpus which consists 10,000 Facebook posts with references to sentiments with 2,587 positive, 5,174 neutral, 1,991 negatives and 248 bipolar posts (CUCIS, n.d.; LINDAT/CLARIN, 2018). The datasets containing different types of Facebook comments are used from CUCIS as a reference dataset for the sentimental analysis in this work (CUCIS, n.d.).

2.3. Identifying the Features

There are two types of features a person exhibits, they are structural features (includes posts on the Facebook timeline and usage of different kinds of texts); and behavioural characteristics (includes nine various factors such as qualifications, frequency, duration, friends, gender, age, area, status of the posts, the state of the shares (Soundarya et al., 2017). Later the clustering technique will be applied using K-Means to find the clusters.

2.4. Extracting the Semantic Feature

After identifying all the features from participant texts on Facebook, semantic-based filtering is needed to identify a reasonable featuring set. The latent semantic technique may be well suitable for finding relevant data semantically from Facebook data. This method proved to be accurate while dealing with Twitter data, according to Chodhary et al. (2016).

The Facebook posts are collected by using the Facebook API by using the query string hashtags. For conducting the sentiment analysis two sets of datasets are prepared to i) collect the posts or feedback given by the participants based on a particular topic as defined in the dataset; and ii) to remove unnecessary data such as website links, markup's, hashtags, punctuations, white spaces, symbols, etc. After completing the data cleaning process in the above two steps, the Facebook posts based on a specific topic is tested for sentiments of the users by extracting the topical words (i.e. bigram) in the post by using item response theory (Ravichandran et al., 2015). The usage of specific topics helps to relate the post based on topic sentiments and topic-based sentiment lexicon approach can be developed. Such an approach helps to measure the sentiments by using a few curving lexicons agreement. In this method, a group of dictionary words is used that are associated with different polarity scores as per the training corpus. All these words from the dictionary will be compared with the terms used in the lexicon.

The success rates of a lexicon offering the best results are to estimate the sentiments and are due to a) domain-specific, b) dictionary-based, and c) corpus-based lexicons. It is essential to note that in the case of a dictionary-based lexicon, the external elements are added to the corpus to improve preassembled lexicons. Now by using lexicon-based sentimental analysis frequency of the number of words that are similar to that of the external words added to enhance the lexicons. Lexical tokens are compared with vocabulary by using the training samples using the following equations:

$$p\left(\omega\mid+\right)=\frac{M_{\omega}}{\left|N^{+}\right|} \tag{1}$$

$$p\left(\omega\mid-\right)=\frac{M_{\omega}}{\left|N^{-}\right|} \tag{2}$$

where, N^{+} and N^{-} are a score of positive and negative sentiments.

In this work, the sentence messages "*m*", the log likelihood ratio is calculated by using:

$$S_{m}=\sum_{i=1}^{n}\log\left(\frac{p\left(\omega\mid-\right)}{p\left(\omega\mid+\right)}\right) \tag{3}$$

where ω is the lexical unit of dictionary and n is representing the total number of words that are included in the dictionary.

Figure 1. The flow diagram to conduct the sentimental analysis of student behaviour and emotions

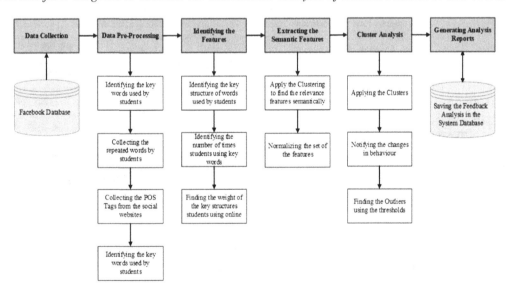

2.5. Cluster Analysis

From the incoming entities, the pattern matching is achieved by using the vector space model, and the space density computation approach was used in this cluster analysis. To identify outliers, K-means clustering technique was used for forming the clusters. Changes in the behaviour of participants will be realised at the time of cluster formations. Based on the changes in the data points, the clusters are analysed.

2.6. Generating Analysis Reports

Now it is the time to analyse the emotions and behaviour of the participants from the analysis reports and the same are saved in the database for further analysis.

3. DATA COLLECTION AND METHODOLOGY

An experiment was carried out with a group (128) of individuals working at different places during the summer vacations in 2018 from different backgrounds of subject interests. The 128 participants registered for the online course was with an average age of 32.17188 and a standard deviation of 7.576496. There were no face-to-face interactions between the participants and trainers at any time.

Figure 2. Shows the response of the participants for different parameters under test

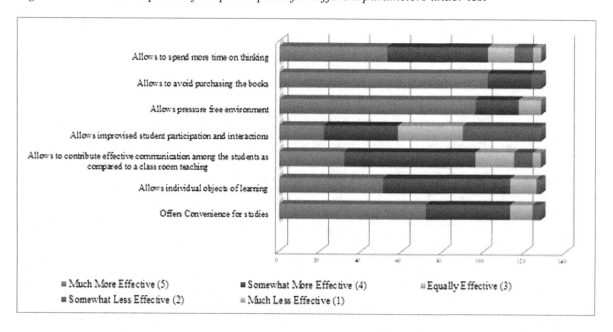

The data considered were collected from these professionals recognised to test sentiment analysis on their behavioural changes and emotions. An assignment was given to the participants, along with material, shared online using Facebook. Facebook was used as a medium to understand their experience with the course, material and their opinions in different formats, such as posts and messages. The training participants were asked to submit the assignment along with a simple questionnaire to understand their response is shown in Figure 2. Most of the participants (88%) expressed positive intent or opinion towards the online learning system. However, they also expressed a shaky response (40%) towards fulfilling the objectives of individual learning as they find it challenging to address the challenges that come in the process of learning online without the support of a teacher physically. Otherwise, most of the participants were happy that they need not purchase books, avoid travelling time, and are very much relaxed due to the free environment. However, some participants expressed their concerns over distractions, laziness, and relaxation in time schedules while taking online training.

3.1. Using RFacebook for Sentiment Analysis

In the process of conducting online training, the participants were made to use Facebook actively for sharing information to interact with friends and teachers for any inputs or suggestions. Initially, a Facebook page was created and invited the participants to access the page and allowed them to access the information related to their course material. For Sentimental analysis, follow the below steps to use R language using Facebook.

Need to install the Rfacebook package by using install.package ("RFacebook") to get the library(Rfacebook).

To get the data from the facebook used the graph API explorer using https://developers.facebook.com/tools/explorer.

Create an app to get started.
Select the developer tools option and in that select Graph API Explorer.
Click on the Get Token button.
Select the permissions for specific information from the Facebook API.
Generate the token and use it in the program using the R language.

The sentiment analysis conducted in this work was based on corpus level, sentence level and on the text used by the participants. However, the opinion words used by the participants were considered with top priority and such words are identified from the feedback and opinions of the participants on Facebook. To get information about the participants to use my_friends <-getFriends(token) in the R program. One can also observe the reactions of people from the recent posts by using fb_page <-getReactions(post=fb_page$id(Altrabsheh et al., 2013), token, api= "v2.8"). Also, the emotions of people using the symbols also can be counted by using the syntax such as post_reaction$likes_count and post_reaction$angry_count, etc. using different types of syntaxes available in the R language. By using all the above the sentiment analysis can be done using the R language. Some of the participants were more active and some were less active. Based on their performance and activeness the relevance of the outcome is defined. See Figure 3, with the interaction between the participants and online tutors.

Very few participants and tutors were involved actively for online posts and communication using messages. During online training, the concern of good communication between the experts and participants was always a concern as discussed by various authors in the literature. Due to a lack of proper communication or guidance, most of the participants will be in their own impression on the subject matters and the impact was seen in their performance after submitting the assignments (Song et al., 2004).

However, few participants were actively involved in discussing the course topic on Facebook towards getting their problems solved for further progress. Both messages and posts were shared by participants who were good in numbers but by very few people. On the other side, some of the tutors were involved in this process to share the events using posts and messages. Few tutors contributed their opinions with a lot of suggestions and solutions using the posts for some of the personal messages as well, so as to ensure a mass communication of information is in the process of online courses/training. Almost 60% of the participants were involved in communicating with messages on Facebook and when it comes to the posts even reduced to 53% only. Hardly, 6-8% of the people participated with the maximum number of posts and messages. The tendency of people using social networking sites seems to be based on their interests/hobbies and other interests.

Figure 3. Shows number of messages and posts shared between participants and tutors during the online training

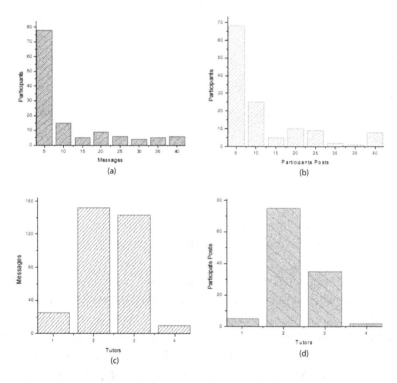

The number of posts or messages posted by the participants was found to be more when the deadlines for submitting the assignment were nearing. Some expressed their emotions of not having adequate interaction with the experts in their flexible timings due to their work hours and individual busy schedules. Most of the participants were working professionals and they expressed an opinion of professors to be available in the evening hours so as to communicate and get interaction when they're using different software applications at home. While working on the assignments some of the participants even expressed that there is a lot of gap between each activity that is related to studies. Reading the concepts and practicing/working on the programming used to takes place with a lot of gaps due to leniency and easy going habit that comes with the flexibility of an online education system. Most of the participants used to forget what they have read after a while, and when it comes to the programming tasks they feel it very difficult to recollect or adjust with the challenges or sometimes gave up the tasks for other easy methods.

3.2. Applications of R-Language as an Analysis Tool

In recent years, R-Language has become very popular to deal with statistics and along with various forms of analyzing tools. Here, the R-Language is used along with Hadoop (RHadoop) tool. RHadoop helps to process larger amounts of data since the R interface is not capable of processing huge data. In this work, the role of Rhadoop is useful at the time of text analysis for the data collected from the RFacebook API. To proceed further with the sentimental analysis using Facebook API, the following flow process may be applied as shown in Figure 4.

3.2.1. Steps Involved in the Flow Process are as Follows

1. Facebook Authentication is needed for using the Facebook API (FAPI), so creating an account with a username and password is essential. Once the registration and login process completed, the handshake process is completed with FAPI and the Facebook server allows accessing the data for the usage of analysis;
2. The content obtained from the Facebook server contains a lot of words in shortcuts, a variety of emotions, pictures, web site contents, etc. Pre-processing helps to filter all the unnecessary content and removes the data or words with hashtags. A total new data set will be available once the process of removing unnecessary data completed. Now from the complete data set each word will be compared to understand the behavior or emotions of a participant;
3. Now the sentiments of participants from each post on the website will be collected and based on the number of positive words or texts used will be deciding the overall emotions or behavior of a participant. All this information will be stored for further process of changes in the curriculum or methodology for future online training programs;
4. The classification of user sentiments is stored to assess the overall response in terms of positive, negative and neutral.

Figure 4. The flow process to proceed further for sentimental analysis of participant's behavior using Facebook API

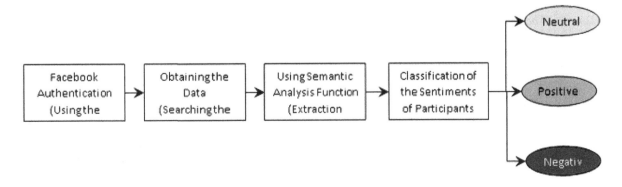

3.3. Using Rhadoop in the Present Scenario

The text content generated on Facebook in the form of posts, messages, and comments will be huge, in the sense, it can be considered as a big data analysis. So in such context Hadoop platform is used to deal with big data and R Language to deal with data analytics. Therefore the integration of R and Hadoop is possible by using a variety of connectors like Rhadoop, Hadoop streaming, and Rhipe.

3.3.1. For Sentiment Analysis to Use R Language Use Following Steps

Step 1: Install and load different packages like RFacebook, ROAuth, Plyr, Stringr, ggplot2, etc. Further, there are some more dependency software's available such as httr, httput, dplyr, etc.

Step 2: Create a Facebook account to connect with Facebook API.

Step 3: For valid user authentication, download the certificate file from the web browser on Facebook API.

Step 4: Fetch the required data from the Facebook server by following the instructions from Facebook.

Step 5: Extract meaningful and useful information by filtering the unnecessary data from the posts and messages.

Step 6: Finally, output scores based on the fetched information will be analyzed to identify the sentiments and emotions of people.

3.3.2. Now to Use R Language and Hadoop the Following Steps are Used

Step 1: Install Rhadoop (i.e. install Hadoop, R, rJava, Rhadoop and set up all environment variables).

Step 2: For setting up the system to operate, load all Rhadoop and R packages to R Console for data analysis.

Step 3: Crawl the posts and messages from participants using search Facebook() and save them into a .csv extension file.

Step 4: Load the file content into the Hadoop distributed file system (HDFS) so as to use the data by using some of the commands available from rhdfs package.

Step 5: From the R language apply sentimental function.

Step 6: By using the command fetch the files to be analysed fro HDFS (Ex: Plot_data<-read.csvfile="C:/ Users/Venkat_Ramana/ Desktop/ Plot_data.csv, header=TRUE, sep=",").

Step 7: Finally calculate the scores and analyze using the R language.

Figure 5. The code used to retrieve information from the Facebook

```
RStudio
File  Edit  Code  View  Plots  Session  Build  Debug  Profile  Tools  Help

Go to file/function          Addins

Venkat Ramana Final Work.R    2 Venkat.R    Venkat.R

Source on Save                                           Run      Source

1  facebook.S4::facebook.current.accounts("Venkat Ramana")
2  facebook.S4::facebook.participants("Ramesh", "umesh jadav", "Baldev singh", "Prem Andrews", "Rajashe
3  facebook.S4::facebook.search("bad", "poor", "good", "excellent")
4
```

Now for sentimental analysis on the behavior of participants the following code formats as shown in Figure 5 was used to connect with Facebook and retrieve the required specific data.

The code shown in Figure 6 was used to remove different types of unnecessary words, graphics, hashtags, etc. from the retrieved content of Facebook as a part of pre-processing. Also, it will help to obtain the vector of different sentences from the posts on Facebook.

Figure 6. Code used to identify different word formats defined in the corpus from Facebook content

```
RStudio
File  Edit  Code  View  Plots  Session  Build  Debug  Profile  Tools  Help

Venkat Ramana Final Work.R    2 Venkat.R    Venkat.R

Source on Save                                          Run    Source

 1  score.sentiment = function(sentences, pos.words,
 2                              neg.words, .progress='none')
 3 - {
 4    require(plyr)
 5    require(stringr)
 6    scores = laply(sentences, function(sentence, pos.words,neg.words)
 7    ## Three line of above code is used for obtaining vector of sentense from facebook data.
 8 -  {
 9      sentence = gsub('[[:punct:]]', '', sentence)
10      sentence = gsub('[[:cntrl:]]', '', sentence)
11      sentence = gsub('\\d+', '', sentence)
12      sentence = tolower(sentence)
13      word.list = str_split(sentence, '\\s+') ##used for splitting sentences into different words
14      words = unlist(word.list)
15      pos.matches = match(words, pos.words)
16      neg.matches = match(words, neg.words)
17      pos.matches = !is.na(pos.matches)
18      neg.matches = !is.na(neg.matches)
19      score = sum(pos.matches) - sum(neg.matches)
20    return(score)
21    },
22    pos.words, neg.words, .progress=.progress )
23    scores.df = data.frame(score=scores, text=sentences)
24    return(scores.df)
25  }
26
```

4. EXPERIMENT RESULTS AND ANALYSIS

In this section, a detailed analysis of the overall participants and their organizations are considered for the analysis. At the same time, the emotions expressed by them towards online training and education system will be analyzed based on different types of responses and keywords using the statistical analysis.

The number of participants involved in online training from different organizations is shown in Figure 7. As a part of the experiment, some of the feedback posts from the participants were collected from the Facebook database and pre-processed (as shown in Figure 11) to use it for text analysis. In this work, 30 keywords were selected for testing the behaviour and emotions of the participants, as listed in Table 1. The overall participant's response can be seen in Figure 8 for different words they used to express their feelings about the online training and their experience.

Figure 7. The histogram shows the number of participants participated in the online training program

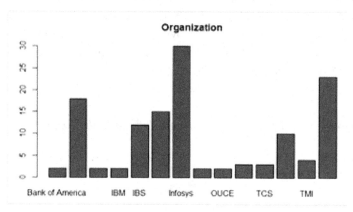

Table 1. Showing the response of participants based on the comments they used the messages with different behavioural aspects are shown below from processed data

Sl. No	Word	Response
1	Impressed	Positive
2	Best	Positive
3	World Class	Positive
4	Helpful	Positive
5	Informative	Positive
6	Well Organized	Positive
7	Good	Positive
8	Clear	Positive
9	Opportunity	Positive
10	Provided	Positive
11	Good Job	Positive
12	Power Failure	Positive
13	Real Life	Positive
14	Meaningful	Positive
15	Clearly	Positive
16	Rushed	Positive
17	Great	Positive
18	More Examples	Positive
19	Easy to Understand	Positive
20	Knowledge	Positive
21	Time Wastage	Negative
22	Information	Positive
23	Covered	Positive
24	Approach	Positive

continues on following page

Table 1. Continued

Sl. No	Word	Response
25	Participants learn the material	Positive
26	Excellent Trainer	Positive
27	Poor	Negative
28	Hard	Negative
29	Conduct	Negative
30	very patient	Positive

4.1. Testing for the Behaviour of Participants

From Table 1, the nature of response for different words is defined and they are based on the overall feedback data retrieved from the Facebook server. The results after executing the data show that 89% of the participants expressed their positive intent for the overall online course and its outcomes shown in Figure 8 and 9.

Figure 8. The response after executing the pre-processed data

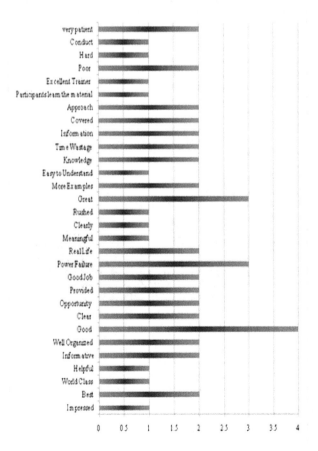

Figure 9. Code used to identify different word formats defined in the corpus from Facebook

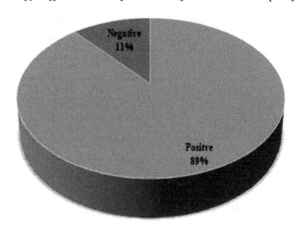

4.2. Testing for Emotions of the Participants

Here, the Facebook data posted in the form of messages and wall posts from all the participants for online training was considered. The emotions of the 128 participants were tested and the results are as shown in Figure 10. 75% expressed their happiness to attend such online courses, 12% expressed their mixed emotions due to various individual reasons. However, 10% of the people did not react in any way on Facebook. However, few participants (3%) started using some slang words to express their unhappiness (Figures 11-12).

Figure 10. The response rate on Facebook for online training from the 128 participants

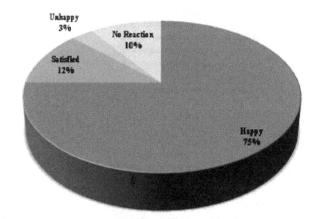

4.3. Discussion

From the above work it is seen that online training is contributing a lot for the employees working in different organizations and at different far-end locations. They are provided with personalized guidance and needful technical skills for the professional advancement in their career. The role of emotional states, priorities and personalities are playing a vital role to understand the sentiments analysis of the students.

Figure 11. The feedback from the posts retrieved from Facebook after pre-processing

DR. SNEHA MURTHY

Seminar: Hadoop and Big Data
Comments: Sneha was hands down the best instructor I've ever worked with! Her knowledge, professionalism and presentation skills are simply world class!
From: Ramesh, TCS

Seminar: R Language and Python
Comments: An extremely helpful and informative course, especially in R Language with graphic plotting. Training materials were well organized and provided good case studies. Instructor was extremely professional and pleasant to learn from.
From: Umesh Jadav, Wipro

Seminar: Hadoop and Big Data
Comments: The training was clear and detailed. I like Sneha's style of teaching as the recurrent training is a thorough review of the Big Data. Every opportunity for the student to ask questions was provided.
From: Baldev Singh, Wipro

Seminar: R Language and Python
Comments: Sneha did an exceptional job presenting the material. She set up by explaining what she was going to teach us, summarized, and proceeded to teach, providing relevant real life examples on Big Data. She found out what we handled and catered examples to us to make the course meaningful. I am a software engineer and have taken many similar courses - this was very well done, which I attribute primarily to the instructor and secondarily to the quality materials.
From: Prem Andrews, Infosys

Seminar: Hadoop and Big Data
Comments: Sneha and team did a very good job simplifying difficult material. Thank you.
From: Rajashekar Kasturi, FDI

Seminar: R Language and Python
Comments: Sneha conducted the class in a very professional manner. Her examples were very relevant and I feel that I gained a lot from the updated materials this year.
From: Aruta Aurora, Bank of America

Seminar: Hadoop and Big Data
Comments: Sneha handled the course with a good pace and orderly. I have been to other courses where the instructor clearly appeared rushed/ anxious, since there is a lot of info to cram in the limited time. Side Note: I was very surprised with the material offered online with more examples. Great!
From: Priya Gill

Seminar: R Language and Python
Comments: Sneha was a great instructor. Thanks Sneha for making the training easy to understand. A lot of information was covered. She made the approach easy to follow.
From: Devender Gattu, SBI

Seminar: R Language and Python
Comments: Sneha Murthy wants to make sure that her students walk away from her course with a good working knowledge of Python and how to use the regulations. She is an excellent trainer and cares that all of her participants learn the material.
From: Rajender Chetkuri, LIC of India

Seminar: Hadoop and Big Data
Comments: This is my third training class - the quality of training I receive continues to be excellent. Although I do not ship hazardous materials very often, your training helps me to know where to find the information I need, when I need it, as well as helping me and my company in compliance. Thanks again for the great job. I'll be back.
From: Karan Tapa, The Republic

Seminar: Hadoop and Big Data
Comments: Sneha is very thorough and professional. She made the code very understandable. I was very impressed with Sneha's teaching methods and presentation of the Hadoop. Sneha is the best!
From: Dhasharath, OUCE

Figure 12. The processed data of participants with (a) Age in scatter plot; (b) Age in histogram; (c) Cluster analysis using a k-mean cluster with K=3; and (d) Response of the people saying a good job

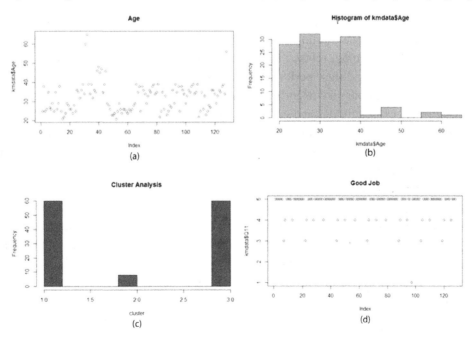

For online learning, the emotional factors of the people working in industry are mostly influenced by the learning process, learning contexts, and flexibility of online training timings. Most of the times, it is also seen that pressure at the work place also impact most of the employees towards online training. Some of them with lack of clarity with the main objectives of the training sessions end up with a poor performance at the end. They express deep concern over the facilities, study materials, timings, etc. as a reason for their poor performance. The behaviour and emotions of such students going through online training working in industry, express most of the time their dissatisfaction due to lack of eye to eye contact with the tutor. In general, the traditional classroom includes a positive communication between the students and teachers by linguistic approach and eye to eye contact as well. Such things help the students to forget or ignore the previous situations while listening to a good lecture added with some of the gestures, body actions and frequent interactions as well. However, in the recent times the participants involved in online training courses are out of their job profile requirements and new challenges in most of the software companies due to the competition among the employees and drastic changing behaviour of customer demands and technology up gradations. Therefore, the sentiments of the working people is always towards obtaining maximum information useful for their next project at work or profession make them to be more active for acquiring quality information from the online training courses.

The tendency of their response is now purely based on the subject knowledge shared by the tutor and from this work on sentimental analysis it is found that maximum participants are joining these types of courses with a positive intent and are satisfied with the present course. The role of R-language in the sentiment analysis played a critical role towards analysing the sentiments of the participants by extracting the information from Facebook. The obtained results in this work using different parameters to study the sentiments analysis revealed that online training is strongly and positively received/accepted by most of the participants.

5. CONCLUSION

In this work, applications of Rhadoop and R-Language were used to analyse the sentiments of working professionals towards online training courses. It is quite evident that most of the participants expressed the attitude of easy going, relaxed nature while training, laziness, etc. are going to influence the overall learning process and their performance too. On the other hand, listening to lectures online help to avoid negative emotions like anger due to any kind of personal interaction between a teacher and student. The changes in attitudes and emotions influence the behavioural aspects of working professionals. These are going to impact the emotions (as per the results 75%) of people in the long run. It is also very important to note that defining the corpus data played a vital role in the calculation of the accuracy of the behavioural changes and emotions as they vary with different groups of people. In this work, 30 parameters were considered to test the sample data retrieved from Facebook posts. The role of R-Language and Rhadoop was crucial to execute larger amounts of data and care must be taken to have sufficient memory for a smooth process of the data. To get information about the participants used my_friends <-getFriends(token) in the R program. The reactions of people from the recent posts are observed by using fb_page <- getReactions(post=fb_page$id(Altrabsheh et al., 2013), token, api= "v2.8"). Also, the emotions of people using the symbols also can be counted by using the syntax such as post_reaction$likes_count and post_reaction$angry_count, etc. using different types of syntaxes available in the R language. Further, this work can be extended towards the sentiments of people based on religious sentiments, habits evolved from the geography and environmental changes.

REFERENCES

Abdulsalami, A. O., Ahmad, B. I., Umar, M. A., Abubakar, A. H., Jauro, F., Kufena, A. M., & Ekoja, E. A. (2017). Sentiment analysis of students' perception on the use of smartphones: A cross sectional study. In *Informatics and Computing (ICIC), 2017 Second International Conference on*, 1-5.

Altrabsheh, N., Cocea, M., & Fallahkhair, S. (2014). Learning sentiment from students' feedback for real-time interventions in classrooms. In *Adaptive and Intelligent Systems* (pp. 40–49). Springer.

Altrabsheh, N., Cocea, M., & Fallahkhair, S. (2015). *Predicting learning-related emotions from students' textual classroom feedback via Twitter.* Academic Press.

Altrabsheh, N., Gaber, M., & Cocea, M. S. A.-E. (2013). Sentiment analysis for education. *International Conference on Intelligent Decision Technologies, 255*, 353-362.

Aung, K. Z. (2016). A Lexicon Based Sentiment Analyzer Framework for Student-Teacher Textual Comments. *International Journal of Scientific and Research Publications, 6*(3), 277–280.

Bhattacharya, S., Kaluri, R., Singh, S., Alazab, M., & Tariq, U. (2020). A Novel PCA-Firefly based XGBoost classification model for Intrusion Detection in Networks using GPU. *Electronics (Basel), 9*(2), 219. doi:10.3390/electronics9020219

Bishop, J. L., & Verleger, M. A. (2013). The flipped classroom: A survey of the research. *ASEE National Conference Proceedings, 30*(9), 1-18.

Chodhary, S. G., Jagdale, R. S., & Deshmukh, S. N. (2016). Semantic analysis of tweets using LSA and SVD. *International Journal of Emerging Trends and Technology in Computer Science, 5*(4), 39–42.

CUCIS. (n.d.). *Social Media Data for Sentimental Analysis.* http://cucis.ece.northwestern.edu/projects/Social/sentiment_data.html

Gadekallu, T. R., Khare, N., Bhattacharya, S., Singh, S., Reddy Maddikunta, P. K., Ra, I. H., & Alazab, M. (2020). Early detection of diabetic retinopathy using PCA-firefly based deep learning model. *Electronics (Basel), 9*(2), 274. doi:10.3390/electronics9020274

Izzo, J. A., & Maloy, K. (2017). 86 Sentiment Analysis Demonstrates Variability in Medical Student Grading. *Annals of Emergency Medicine, 70*(4), S35–S36. doi:10.1016/j.annemergmed.2017.07.111

Jindal, S., & Sharma, K. (2018). Intend to analyze Social Media feeds to detect behavioral trends of individuals to proactively act against Social Threats. *Procedia Computer Science, 132*, 218–225. doi:10.1016/j.procs.2018.05.191

Jo, H., Kim, S. M., & Ryu, J. (2017). *What we really want to find by Sentiment Analysis: The Relationship between Computational Models and Psychological State.* arXiv preprint arXiv:1704.03407

Joseph, K., Wei, W., Benigni, M., & Carley, K. M. (2016). A social-event based approach to sentiment analysis of identities and behaviors in text. *The Journal of Mathematical Sociology, 40*(3), 137–166. doi:10.1080/0022250X.2016.1159206

Kagklis, V., Karatrantou, A., Tantoula, M., Panagiotakopoulos, C. T., & Verykios, V. S. (2015). A learning analytics methodology for detecting sentiment in student fora: A Case Study in Distance Education. *European Journal of Open, Distance and E-learning, 18*(2), 74–94. doi:10.1515/eurodl-2015-0014

Koehler, M., Greenhalgh, S., & Zellner, A. (2015). Potential Applications of Sentiment Analysis in Educational Research and Practice–Is SITE the Friendliest Conference? In *Society for Information Technology & Teacher Education International Conference*. Association for the Advancement of Computing in Education (AACE).

LINDAT/CLARIN. (2018). *Facebook data for sentimental analysis*. https://lindat.mff.cuni.cz/repository/xmlui/handle/11858/00-097C-0000-0022-FE82-7

Ravichandran, M., Kulanthaivel, G., & Chellatamilan, T. (2015). Intelligent topical sentiment analysis for the classification of e-learners and their topics of interest. *The Scientific World Journal*, 1–8. doi:10.1155/2015/617358 PMID:25866841

Reddy, G. T., Reddy, M. P. K., Lakshmanna, K., Kaluri, R., Rajput, D. S., Srivastava, G., & Baker, T. (2020). Analysis of Dimensionality Reduction Techniques on Big Data. *IEEE Access: Practical Innovations, Open Solutions, 8*, 54776–54788. doi:10.1109/ACCESS.2020.2980942

Sharma, S. (2017). Text Analysis and Sentiment Analysis using Facebook in R Language: Case Studies. *International Journal of Computer & Mathematical Sciences, IJCMS, 6*, 200–214.

Song, L., Singleton, E. S., Hill, J. R., & Koh, M. H. (2004). Improving online learning: Student perceptions of useful and challenging characteristics. *The Internet and Higher Education, 7*(1), 59–70. doi:10.1016/j.iheduc.2003.11.003

Soundarya, V., Kanimozhi, U., & Manjula, D. (2017). Recommendation System for Criminal Behavioral Analysis on Social Network using Genetic Weighted K-Means Clustering. *JCP, 12*(3), 212–220. doi:10.17706/jcp.12.3.212-220

Teja, J. S., Sai, G. K., Kumar, M. D., & Manikandan, R. (2018). Sentiment Analysis of Movie Reviews using Machine Learning Algorithms – A Survey. *International Journal of Pure and Applied Mathematics, 118*(20), 3277–3284.

Zamani, N. A. M., Abidin, S. Z., Omar, N., & Abiden, M. Z. Z. (2013). *Sentiment analysis: Determining people's emotions in Facebook*. Universiti Teknologi MARA.

This research was previously published in the International Journal of Gaming and Computer-Mediated Simulations (IJGCMS), 12(2); pages 26-43, copyright year 2020 by IGI Publishing (an imprint of IGI Global).

Chapter 90
When Emotions Rule Knowledge:
A Text–Mining Study of Emotions in Knowledge Management Research

Nora Fteimi
University of Passau, Germany

Olivia Hornung
University of Hagen, Germany

Stefan Smolnik
University of Hagen, Germany

ABSTRACT

Although emotions play an important role in human behavior and knowledge studies, knowledge management (KM) research considers them from specific angles and, to date, has lacked a comprehensive understanding of the emotions dominating KM. To offer a holistic view, this study investigates the presence of emotions in KM publications by applying a sentiment analysis. The authors present a sentiment dictionary tailored to KM, apply it to KM publications to determine where and how emotions occur, and categorize them on an emotion scale. The considerable amount of positive and negative emotions expressed in KM studies prove their relevance to and dominance in KM. There is high term diversity but also a need to consolidate terms and emotion categories in KM. This study's results provide new insights into the relevance of emotions in KM research, while practitioners can use this method to detect emotion-laden language and successfully implement KM initiatives.

DOI: 10.4018/978-1-6684-6303-1.ch090

INTRODUCTION

Emotions are as much a part of human behavior as reason and play an important role in intelligence and knowledge (Martínez-Miranda & Aldea, 2005). Managing knowledge in organizations has proved to be very useful since successful knowledge management (KM) leads to significant improvements in their scientific, economic, and social aspects (Cao et al., 2012). Nonetheless, knowledge is often viewed merely as just another manageable organizational resource (Alavi & Leidner, 2001). Owing to its context-specificity and boundedness to human beings (Nonaka, 1994), however, it cannot be separated from human emotions and, thus, has to be approached differently than other organizational resources (Kuo et al., 2003). Consequently, the role played by emotions, which help to both express and understand knowledge (Davenport & Prusak, 1998), requires attention from within the information systems (IS) domain in general and from KM researchers in particular.

IS researchers have started to pay attention to the presence and role of emotions (Chau et al., 2020; Beaudry & Pinsonneault, 2010; Gregor et al., 2014). Likewise, KM studies on emotion-related topics are critical to acknowledging emotions and the role emotional concepts play in KM (Scherer & Tran, 2003; van den Hooff et al., 2012). Nonetheless, these studies also show how compartmentalized KM research on emotions is. It only focuses on single emotions and limited subtopics from emotion research while neglecting an overall and holistic perspective that would help to develop common ground in this area. For instance, concerning KM processes, the roles of emotional intelligence (Decker et al., 2009; Peng, 2013; Trong Tuan, 2013) and emotional obstacles (Lin et al., 2006; Pemberton et al., 2007) have been investigated. However, an integrated and comprehensive overview of emotions, unbiased by any particular single topic, is still lacking, and it is necessary to consolidate research on single emotions and emotional concepts (Hornung & Smolnik, 2018), and in which nexus they are displayed in KM research – with a taxonomy of emotions in KM research as the ultimate goal. To arrive at a comprehensive taxonomy of emotions in KM and close the aforementioned gap, it is crucial to understand which emotions are prevalent in and dominate KM research. Sentiment analyses, which have often been used to detect words associated with either positive or negative emotions in the context of politics, finance, and (social media) marketing (Matthies, 2016; Yassine & Hajj, 2010), are a useful instrument to gain a broader understanding of emotions. As a special type of text mining, sentiment analyses support the authors' goal of analyzing the underlying sentiment of a text that "can encompass investigating both the opinion and the emotion behind that unit" (Yadollahi et al., 2017, p. 2). Sentiment analyses also enable the exploration of vast amounts of data. They are also effective at revealing which emotions prevail in written KM publications and can, therefore, help to answer the following research questions:

RQ1: Which emotions dominate research on KM?
RQ2: How can these emotions be categorized according to emotion scales?

The sentiment analysis in this study relies on a dictionary-based approach in which KM-specific dictionaries 1) are created based on Hu and Liu (2004) and 2) applied to a comprehensive sample of 6,017 scientific KM publications to detect existing emotions. The analysis results are then 3) categorized and structured using an appropriate emotion scale.

RESEARCH BACKGROUND

Emotion Theories

Emotions are the primary motivational system for human beings (Leeper, 1948; Mowrer, 1960). Thus, an emotional component drives human actions and interactions, which also display emotions in communication through IS (Rice & Love, 1987). Psychology researchers have focused heavily on emotions as a research object, which has led to not one universal but many different definitions and conceptualizations (Chaplin & Krawiec, 1979; English & English, 1958). Definitions range from broad views, such as emotions directing cognitive activities (Clark & Fiske, 1982; Mandler, 1975), to specifically seeing emotion as the complex reaction to a stimulus (Plutchik, 1984). In this study, an emotion is considered a chronologically unfolding sequence: After exposure to a stimulus, a human perceives a state of "feeling" and, consequently, displays externally visible behaviors or emotional outputs (Elfenbein, 2007).

The ambiguity of definitions in various disciplines has also led to emotions often being blended with strongly related but different concepts, such as mood or feeling (Rottenberg, 2005) – two terms that are often used interchangeably in extant research (Beedie et al., 2005). Therefore, the authors of this study initially include what they classify as emotions, feelings, moods, and sentiments to grasp the full extent of emotion-related words in KM research before assigning each of these words an appropriate emotion.

To firmly embed this research in existing emotion theory, the authors apply a comprehensive model to classify emotions. While there are several well-established models in research, some – like Plutchik's wheel of emotion (1980), which includes emotions such as *terror* and *grief*, and Richins's consumption-related emotions (1997), including emotions such as *envy* or *loneliness* – encompass too many other emotions that are not relevant to the KM context. Other models, such as the computer emotion scale by Kay and Loverock (2008), have a strong focus on negative emotions like *anger*, *anxiety*, and *sadness*, with only *happiness* as a positive counterpart, and are inappropriate for exploratory studies because it is essential to clearly distinguish and focus on both positive and negative emotions (Aviezer et al., 2012). Thus, the authors of this study decided to apply the well-established model by Izard (1977), called the differential emotion scale (DES), which involves the following 10 emotions: *interest, joy, surprise, sadness, anger, disgust, contempt, fear, shame*, and *guilt*. The DES includes not only a comprehensive yet manageable number of emotions but also universal emotions, for example, those expressed in a similar manner across different cultures (Izard, 1977).

Emotions and Sentiment Analysis In KM Research

KM is a well-established discipline with many journals and conference tracks dedicated to investigating and advancing academic KM research (Serenko & Bontis, 2017). Between 1993, when the KM discipline emerged, and 2012, there were 12,925 KM-related publications (Qiu & Lv, 2014) – a number that has since continued to rise. Besides this theoretical significance, KM and its success are critical to any organization's advancement (Jennex & Olfman, 2010). To achieve goals, add value, and improve an organization's situation, KM comprises all conscious and organized efforts to develop, preserve, and utilize knowledge (Holsapple & Joshi, 2004).

KM researchers within the IS domain have used a vast array of research methods and approaches (Ioannis & Belias, 2020) to examine KM theories, processes, technologies (Fteimi & Lehner, 2016), and successes (Jennex & Olfman, 2005). To date, KM research on emotions has been insightful but without a holistic view. Previous studies on single emotions have revealed the significance of *trust* (Kauffmann & Carmi, 2017; Song & Teng, 2008; Swift & Hwang, 2013), *pride* (van den Hooff et al., 2012), and *fear* (Khalil & Shea, 2012) in KM or shown how related concepts such as *emotional intelligence* can improve KM (Decker et al., 2009; Geofroy & Evans, 2017; Tuan, 2016). More studies have investigated positive emotions as a contributor to successful KM (Aarrestad et al., 2015; Marshall, 2000; Tenório et al., 2017; Trenck et al., 2015) than negative emotions as a hindrance to successful KM use and outcomes (Lin et al., 2006; Peng, 2013), which is one the main drivers to conduct a comprehensive investigation and classify both positive and negative emotions.

Text-mining analysis in KM has previously not been applied to uncover emotions but rather to uncover different KM topics (Qiu & Lv, 2014). For instance, the mechanics behind text analysis for organizational KM have been analyzed (Ur-Rahman & Harding, 2012), and Fteimi and Basten (2015) developed a KM-specific dictionary using text-mining approaches. While it is popular to analyze social media data and research (Bojja et al., 2020; Yassine & Hajj, 2010), a domain that is connected to KM, applying sentiment dictionaries to KM research is still in its early stages.

RESEARCH PROCESS AND METHODS

In a multistep research process (cf. Figure 1), a sentiment analysis was applied using a dictionary-based approach (also known as a bag-of-words model).

Figure 1. Multistep sentiment analysis

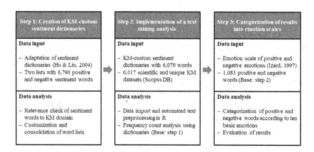

The authors customized sentiment dictionaries (step 1) and used them as input for step 2 to implement a matching algorithm that maps the dictionary's contents against those of the dataset (Li, 2010). Subsequently, in step 3, the authors categorized the results of step 2 into 10 basic emotions according to Izard's emotion scale (Izard, 1977).

CREATION OF KM-CUSTOM SENTIMENT DICTIONARIES

The authors referred to the dictionaries of Hu and Liu (2004) to create customized KM sentiment dictionaries that initially contained two separate lists containing 2,007 positively and 4,783 negatively connoted sentiment words. Following the recommendation that the application of dictionaries always take into account the respective application domain (Krippendorff, 2013; Matthies, 2016), two of the co-authors first performed a manual relevance check of all the words on both dictionary lists for the KM domain. Consequently, 147 positive words and 691 negative words that both coders deemed irrelevant (e.g., colloquial slang words) were removed. The respective intercoder-reliability values of 0.7 for the positive words list and 0.68 for the negative words list indicate strong reliability in the agreement of both coders (Landis & Koch, 1977). Furthermore, the lists were extended by the respective British spelling variants of 127 words (e.g., *dishonour* vs. *dishonor*), since the datasets in the subsequent text-mining analysis include texts using either American or British spelling. The result of this overall customization led to a positively connoted dictionary list of 1,911 words and a negatively connoted dictionary list of 4,168 words. The overall customization process resulted in a reduction rate of 5% for the positive-word list and 13% for the negative-word list.

IMPLEMENTATION OF A TEXT-MINING ANALYSIS

The sentiment dictionaries developed in the previous step served as input for the text-mining analysis. Following the process-oriented understanding of text mining as a holistic approach to knowledge discovery, the analysis was performed over several main phases, starting with data selection and proceeding to its analysis and subsequent interpretation (cf. Figure 2). This results in interfaces to steps 1 and 3 of the overarching research process depicted in Figure 1 as the developed dictionaries and subsequent categorization according to emotions are linked to the text-mining process.

Figure 2. Phases of text-mining process with links to steps 1 and 3

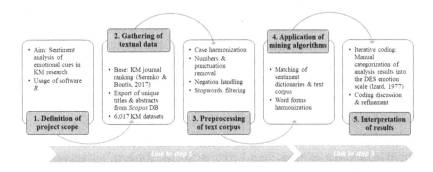

The analysis was conducted using the top 10 KM journals as ranked by Serenko and Bontis (2017). All datasets consisting of available titles and abstracts representing a comprehensive summary of a paper's main findings were obtained from the Scopus database (by December 2018). Editorials, duplicates, and datasets where no abstract was available were excluded. The subsequent analysis included 6,017 unique datasets. Table 1 provides a detailed overview of the journals included and the corresponding number of datasets considered, which vary because of different publication frequencies.

The analysis was performed using *R*, a statistical data analysis software with a variety of packages and functionalities to implement text mining, among others (Venables et al., 2014).

Table 1. Corpus description

Journal Title	Ranking	Period	# items
Journal of Knowledge Management	A+	1997–2018	1,262
Journal of Intellectual Capital	A+	2000–2018	664
The Learning Organization	A	1994–2018	704
Knowledge Management Research & Practice	A	2006–2018	461
Knowledge and Process Management	A	1997–2018	421
VINE: The Journal of Information and Knowledge Management Systems	A	1985–2018	1,040
International Journal of Knowledge Management	A	2005–2018	275
Journal of Information and Knowledge Management	B	2002–2018	543
International Journal of Learning and Intellectual Capital	B	2004–2018	366
International Journal of Knowledge and Learning	B	2005–2018	281
Σ			**6,017**

In any textual analysis, different preprocessing steps are necessary to handle data effectively (Elder et al., 2012). First, to ensure a consistent analysis of similar words (e.g., *Fear* vs. *fear*), cases were harmonized by transforming all the letters to lower case. Second, punctuation marks, special characters (e.g., copyright symbols), and numbers were removed from the corpus as they do not add value to the textual analysis. Third, effective sentiment analyses also require considering negation. Since negation shifts the meaning of a word or even a whole sentence in the opposite direction, it leads to biased results. For example, adjectives with positive (e.g., *good, relevant, happy*) or negative (e.g., *bad, obsolete, frustrated*) connotations typically indicate the opposite sentiment. Words in the corpus that had been preceded by a negation word (e.g., *not, no, neither, never*) were identified and excluded from further analysis. Fourth, words that were not particularly relevant to the analysis because they were expletives or stop words were also filtered out. In addition to these stop words, a domain-specific corpus like the scientific KM corpus in this study might include specific words or word sequences that occur frequently. This affects the results of frequency counts and other analyses. For instance, many abstracts include the term sequence *research limitation*. Considering that the word *limitation* is also a negatively connoted sentiment word, this word and other similar specific words (sequences) were excluded from the corpus.

Before applying the dictionaries from step 1 to the corpus, some of the aforementioned preprocessing steps were also applied to the dictionaries to prevent the matching algorithm from leading to incorrect results. This concerned, in particular, spelling harmonization and the elimination of punctuation. Subsequently, the authors ran the sentiment analysis by applying the matching algorithm to examine and accumulate all occurrences of sentiment words in the corpus. Each dictionary entry was matched to the corpus, and the corresponding concept was stored once there was a match. Equal entries were automatically accumulated into a frequency count list. Finally, inflected word forms were harmonized by consolidating singular and plural word forms or merging degrees of comparison or derivatives into a single word form (e.g., *limitation* and *limitations* were consolidated to *limitation*; *good, better,* and *best* were consolidated to *good*; *enjoy, enjoyable,* and *enjoyment* were consolidated to *enjoy*).

CATEGORIZATION OF RESULTS INTO EMOTION SCALES

To identify the dominant emotions in KM research, the results of the preceding text-mining analysis were categorized in the final step according to the DES emotion scale (Izard, 1977). Based on the DES, sentiment words can be assigned to one of the following basic emotions: *interest, joy,* and *surprise* for the positively connoted emotions, and *anger, contempt, disgust, fear, guilt, sadness,* and *shame* for the negatively connoted emotions. All remaining emotions are assumed to be gradations of these 10 basic ones. As with the coding process undertaken in step 1 during the dictionary creation, two of the co-authors performed an independent categorization of the text-mining analysis results to assign each word to a basic sentiment category. To achieve a high degree of reliability, the individual main emotions' definitions and meanings were taken from The Oxford English Dictionary (2007) and used as coding guidelines. As the word lists also include synonyms, two thesauruses (http://www.thesaurus.com and https://www.dict.cc) were used to identify corresponding words, which helped avoid possible misinterpretation. After a first partial coding and subsequent discussion with both coders, the categorization continued for the remainder of the word list. All results were documented and compared, resulting in a significant intercoder-reliability value of 0.5 for the categorization of positive words and a weak value of 0.3 for the categorization of negative words. Where categorizations were ambiguous, a third person did additional coding, and the coders discussed these cases in more detail. Furthermore, the authors observed that some words, despite occurring in the corpus and the dictionaries, had no meaningful emotional connotation; thus, no categorization into an emotion scale could be made. Therefore, the category (N/A) was introduced. After several iterations, the results were consolidated and interpreted.

Sentiment analysis of knowledge management research

Applying the sentiment analysis to the corpus led to the identification of all occurring positive and negative sentiment words from the customized dictionaries, together with their corresponding frequencies. This revealed which emotions dominate KM research (RQ1). Next, these results were assigned to emotion scales (RQ2), thus moving the authors a step closer to a KM emotion taxonomy.

Most Dominant Positive and Negative Emotion Words In KM Research

Of the 1,911 positive terms listed in the developed KM dictionary, only 493 terms (26%) appear in the corpus after the merging of similar words. An even more drastic result can be seen concerning the negative words with 590 hits from the original 4,168 dictionary entries (14%). However, the frequency count analysis indicates that positively connoted words are used three times more frequently in scientific texts than those with negative connotations (78% vs. 22%). Table 2 provides a comparative list of the top 10 most frequent words from both the positive and the negative dictionary list, together with the corresponding frequency count. For each word, its original rank is shown according to its descending frequency count in the overall hit list (1,083 positive and negative words). For instance, the top 10 frequent words are all positively connoted words and followed by the first two negatively connoted words, *limit* and *critical.*

While the top 10 positively connoted words already account for 33% of the total frequency count, the 10 most frequently mentioned negatively connoted words account for only 9% of the total frequency count. It is also noteworthy that 39% of all positive and negative words are mentioned only once or twice in the whole corpus. Figure 3 depicts further statistical insights into the frequency count distributions of positively (left pie chart) and negatively (right pie chart) connoted sentiment words according to different frequency count categories.

For each category, the graph illustrates the absolute occurrence and, in brackets, relative frequency related to the total frequencies of all positive (or negative) words. For the positive words, the graph shows the most dominant category (36%) comprises words that were mentioned more than 100 but fewer than 1,000 times. The same applies to negative words, where this category accounts for a relative share of 13%.

Table 2. Comparative list of the top 10 most frequent positive and negative words in KM research

Rank	Positive Words	Frequency Count	Rank	Negative Words	Frequency Count
1	innovation	3,115	11	limit	879
2	originality	2,271	12	critical	824
3	support	1,848	14	problem	808
4	improve	1,543	24	risk	516
5	effective	1,521	28	complex	464
6	success	1,444	30	lack	385
7	good	1,209	35	regression	292
8	important	1,100	38	difficult	283
9	well	976	43	concern	238
10	competitive	945	44	exploitation	232

Figure 3. Frequency count share of positive words (left pie) and negative words (right pie)

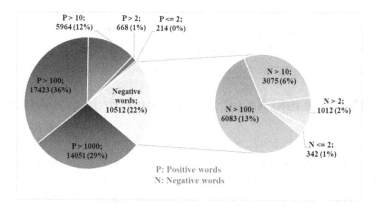

P: Positive words
N: Negative words

Emotion-Scale Categories of Positive and Negative Words

Based on the previous results, each of the 1,083 words was manually categorized according to one of the following 10 emotion categories: *interest, joy, surprise, anger, contempt, disgust, fear, guilt, sadness,* and *shame*. Additionally, the category *N/A* was introduced to account for ambiguous categorizations.

Figure 4 provides a meta-summary of the 11 emotion categories. For each category, the proportion of all its words out of the total number of all positive (or negative) words is specified as the word share.

The frequency count bars indicate the relative occurrence frequencies of all words in a particular category compared with the sum of all positive (or negative) occurrence frequencies.

After inspecting the results, the authors opted to merge the *contempt* and *disgust* (as well as *shame* and *guilt*) categories. This decision was taken as the categorization process had revealed that corresponding words could often not be assigned to a single category but are associated with both emotions. Additionally, the word share of the *disgust* and *guilt* categories is below 2%, which justifies this approach.

Figure 4. Meta-summary of emotion scales

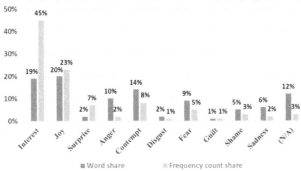

Positive Emotional Categories in KM Publications

Figure 5 shows a comparative word cloud for all three positive emotion categories (*interest, joy,* and *surprise*) and the words covered by these categories. The visualization also allows for a comparison concerning category size. For instance, the *surprise* category has the fewest words, while *interest* and *joy* are roughly equivalent. The illustration also makes it possible to show the relevance of a word in a particular category, based on its frequency count. For example, the word *originality* (2,271 counts) in the *surprise* category is mentioned less frequently over the whole corpus than the word *innovation* (3,115 counts) in the *interest* category. In relation to its own category, however, *originality* is more dominant, since the *surprise* category comprises a far smaller number of words than the *interest* category. Therefore, the weighting of the frequency count is considerably higher in the case of *originality* (69% vs. 14% for *innovation* in the *interest* category).

Regarding the individual categories, the results reveal that words in the *interest* category are mentioned twice as frequently as words in the *joy* category. *Interest* expresses an emotion associated with a helpful or important feeling and helps to draw particular attention: for instance, a *competitive* and business-aligned KM solution that provides *benefit* and enhances *trust, supports* organizations in achieving their business goals and, therefore, evokes the emotion of *interest*. Accordingly, words in the *joy* category are associated with an emotion of *happiness* and *satisfaction* that results from achieving particular *positive* effects. Words that express *joy* include *success, good, positive, advantage, intelligence, reputation, harmony,* and *motivate*. For example, *motivated* employees and a *harmonious* KM culture *positively* influence working outcomes and lead to more *success* with *happy* employees and a *satisfied* management.

Figure 5. Comparative word cloud of positive emotion categories

Figure 6. Comparative word cloud of negative emotion categories

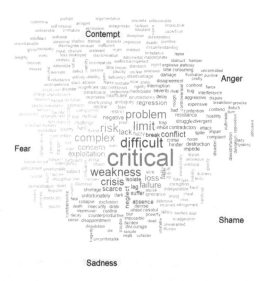

Negative Emotional Categories In KM Publications

Similar to the positive emotion categories, a comparative word cloud for the negative emotion categories was created from the *anger, contempt, fear, sadness*, and *shame* categories. Highly relevant negative words in their categories are *critical* (*shame* category), *difficult* (*anger* category), *problem* and *limit* (*contempt* category), *complex* and *risk* (*fear* category), and *weakness* and *crisis* (*shame* category). The category with the top word share is *contempt*, followed by *anger* and *fear*.

The most prominent negative emotion category is *contempt*, which the authors merged with *disgust*. With words from this category (e.g., *limit, problem, fuzzy, insufficient, poor, mistake, slow*), the emotion relates to something that is ignored or even despised and is, therefore, not worthwhile. Hence, *poorly* performing KM tools, *insufficient* KM activities, or frequently occurring *problems* in communication processes affect the quality of measures taken during KM implementation. Whereas *anger* is associated with annoyance and displeasure with a certain thing or situation, *fear* implies being scared or afraid because of an unwelcome event (*The Oxford English Dictionary*, 2007). Examples of words from the first category are *difficult, crime, hinder, bad, delay,* and *attack*, whereas fear is associated with words like *risk, error, radical, hard, chaos,* and *danger*. Applied to the KM context, *delays* in the delivery of project results or *attacks* on the KM system infrastructure can provoke *anger*, while *risks* or *dangers* arising from external environmental influences (e.g., job loss, knowledge gaps, introduction of new technologies) spread a feeling of *fear* unless suitable countermeasures are taken.

DISCUSSION

The authors find that emotions exist in KM research. While *joy* has the highest total word share of any emotion category, *interest* has the highest frequency count share, making the general emotional tone in KM a positive one. More specifically, particular terms (e.g., *success, innovation, trust* for the positive terms or *problem, risk, difficult* for the negative terms), which are highly associated with topics dealing with the successful or failed implementation of KM initiatives, processes, and systems, occur quite often in KM publications. Below is an example of a sentence from the corpus used in this study that contains three positive emotion categories, namely *joy* (represented by *genius, good/well, prosperity,* and *harmony*), *interest* (represented by *efficient, creative, value,* and *promote*), and *surprise* (represented by *spontaneous*):

*"**efficiency** on a par with nature's principle of least action; **spontaneous** and frictionless coordination; **creative** inspiration akin to artistic **genius**; doing **well** by doing good: **prosperity** and social **value**; **harmony** with the natural environment; **spontaneous** change in an evolutionary direction; and leadership which **promotes** full human development" (Heaton & Harung, 2011)*

To express negative emotions, the authors observed that KM researchers have primarily attempted to use words indicating an undesirable situation that, when related to KM, is associated with the deployment of technologies, the implementation of relating KM strategies, or the establishment of an organization-wide KM culture. Such feelings can occur when an unexpected outcome leads to disappointment, as shown in this sentence from the dataset used in the study, which displays *sadness* (represented by *traumatic*), *shame* (represented by *defenses*), *fear* (represented by *anxiety*), and a negative word assigned to no emotion category (*stress*):

*"The influence of unconscious factors was paramount, rooted in the re-stimulation of collective pre-**traumatic**-**stress** disorder, and mediated via a set of social **defenses** against **anxiety**" (Wasdell, 2011).*

Additionally, some positive (e.g., *beneficial, helpful, useful*) and many negative words (e.g., *problem, error, mistake*) are identified as synonyms, which makes it possible to draw conclusions on term diversity and the need for term consolidation in KM. This ambivalence is visible in the study's findings, which not only show that the top 10 most frequent emotion-related terms are all positive but also suggest a much higher frequency of positive emotion terms (78%) than negative emotion terms (22%) in

KM publications. Yet the negatively connoted sentiment dictionary (4,168 words) has more than twice as many expressions as its positively connoted counterpart. This imbalance also prevails in the chosen emotion scale, which offers more negative than positive basic emotions. Nonetheless, the DES (Izard, 1977) offers a good basis for emotion research in KM as many other emotion scales either provide an even stronger focus on negative sentiments (Kay & Loverock, 2008) or have many interpersonal emotions (Plutchik, 1980; Richins, 1997) unlikely to occur in scientific KM publications. However, positive basic emotions in the DES mostly occur in two categories, namely *interest* and *joy*, which suggests that KM ultimately needs its own taxonomy of emotions with more diverse and refined positive categories. Additionally, a KM-specific emotion taxonomy should encompass fewer negative categories than the DES suggests, as the authors merged *contempt* with *disgust* and *shame* with *guilt*. This may be the case because words describing *anger, fear*, and *sadness* are depicted less strongly in scientific texts, possibly because such emotions are more intense and expressive.

The findings reveal that some emotion categories, specifically those that are stronger and not typically researched but (as this study shows) are relevant to KM, are under-represented and provide examples for possible areas for future research. One example is the positive emotion category *surprise*, where few researchers have made attempts to research KM topics using surprise-connoted positive words such as *dynamic* leadership (Turner & Baker, 2017) or KM as an accelerator for *original* startup strategies (Bandera et al., 2018). To further investigate surprise in the context of KM, research regarding *dynamic*, *visionary*, or *original* KM initiatives and practices could be conducted. This could lead to important insights dealing with the emotion of surprise in a KM context since the negative counterpart emotion category *fear* has received such widespread attention through two of the top negative sentiment words, *complex* and *risk*. Such knowledge barriers, like the *risk* of losing power and appreciation, have been prominently researched by Khalil and Shea (2012), as well as Ardichvili et al. (2003). Furthermore, KM research on resistance to *radical* and *disruptive* change (Wasdell, 2011) has added the negative element of uncertainty to the framework of KM. Similarly, the relevance of holistic KM should be taken into account in future analyses by considering all the elements of KM systems and strategic initiatives, as well as a shared culture of knowledge exchange (Agrawal & Mukti, 2020) to build a bridge to an integrative relationship model for all the KM components involved. This aspect might, for instance, be covered by analyzing the context of the texts. In further studies, the authors of this paper intend to broaden their text-mining analysis to validate the manual results and develop a generalizable taxonomy of emotions in KM research. To this end, the authors will apply machine-learning techniques (e.g., classification algorithms) to their corpus and repeat the categorization for emotion scales. Aside from the comparison on a methodological level, machine learning can provide interesting insights and more reliable results than a manual classification technique in this context – for example, by building emotional topic categories that automatically group the related sentiment terms according to the documents' content.

CONCLUSION

As part of the overall research project to investigate the role of emotions in KM research and arrive at an overall taxonomy, this study aims to present the results of a KM-specific sentiment dictionary development process and its application to KM publications using text-mining methods. The first steps toward the intended emotions-in-KM taxonomy were taken by identifying positive and negative emotions in KM research and manually categorizing them according to the DES. In doing so, the study showed which emotions have dominated KM research and how they could be assigned to an emotion scale.

Lack of context during the text mining analysis is one of the limitations of this study. Some terms in the positive emotion categories can, depending on the context, also express a negative emotion or feeling (e.g., *enough, classic, simpler*), which can affect the interpretation and meaning of such terms. A statement like "*enough* liquid funds" may express *joy* but a feeling of *anger* or *contempt* in another context (e.g., "*enough* problems"). The same ambiguity applies to terms of the negative emotion categories, which, depending on the situation, may sometimes also be interpreted as a positive emotion ("*lower* costs" → *joy* vs. "*lower* motivation*" → *anger*). Furthermore, well-established sentiment dictionaries with a predefined categorization of positively and negatively connoted words were used for this study. For future research, a further refinement of these dictionaries can take place by omitting words expressing a cognitive cue rather than an emotion (e.g., *intelligence* or *unclean*). However, the existing sentiment dictionaries that were applied are widely used and proven across different application domains (Matthies, 2016), making the modification inherently biased through the manual approach – and, therefore, requiring careful and extensive validation. Another of this study's limitations is its manual aspect, especially the consolidation and coding of terms, which is time-consuming and relies solely on the judgment and efforts of all the coders involved.

With this attempt to highlight emotions in KM research, the authors have contributed to several research streams in IS. Despite the knowledge's strong ties to emotions and sentiments, this study fosters early research in the field and gains a better understanding of emotions research in KM. By adapting the sentiment dictionaries to a KM context and classifying them according to the DES, this study is also the first attempt to apply the DES to KM research. A comparison with the analyses' results of the machine-learning approach is currently underway. The authors have also contributed to emotion-related research in KM by providing a comprehensive overview of emotions in KM research. The authors reveal the need to consolidate emotions and emotion categories in KM, as well as the need for an emotions-in-KM-taxonomy to show relations and connections, especially in the KM context. A key implication for organizations is that, in addition to the traditional themes of KM, employees' feelings and emotions need to be considered to successfully implement KM initiatives. The presented text-mining approach constitutes a promising approach to analyze internal company text repositories such as discussion forums regarding employees' emotions.

As for the theoretical contribution in the general IS context, this study contributes to the analysis as described by Gregor's (2006) theory types in IS research. Developing a taxonomy and applying it to research objects generally serves the purpose of systematically describing how these research objects relate to specific common dimensions or attributes. In this context, the authors envision an emotions-in-KM taxonomy that is terminologically descriptive and allows for the classification of sentiment expressions. This study represents the first steps toward a comprehensive framework that will give causal explanations to make progress in said IS theory type taxonomy (Gregor, 2006).

ACKNOWLEDGMENT

The authors thank Nicolai Weiss for his valuable support during the preliminary data analysis phase.

REFERENCES

Aarrestad, M., Brøndbo, M. T., & Carlsen, A. (2015). When Stakes are High and Guards are Low: High-quality Connections in Knowledge Creation. *Knowledge and Process Management*, 22(2), 88–98. doi:10.1002/kpm.1469

Agrawal, A., & Mukti, S. K. (2020). Knowledge Management & It's Origin, Success Factors, Planning, Tools, Applications, Barriers and Enablers: A Review. *International Journal of Knowledge Management*, 16(1), 43–82. doi:10.4018/IJKM.2020010103

Alavi, M., & Leidner, D. E. (2001). Review: Knowledge Management and Knowledge Management Systems: Conceptual Foundations and Research Issues. *Management Information Systems Quarterly*, 25(1), 107. doi:10.2307/3250961

Ardichvili, A., Page, V., & Wentling, T. (2003). Motivation and barriers to participation in virtual knowledge-sharing communities of practice. *Journal of Knowledge Management*, 7(1), 64–77. doi:10.1108/13673270310463626

Aviezer, H., Trope, Y., & Todorov, A. (2012). Body cues, not facial expressions, discriminate between intense positive and negative emotions. *Science*, 338(6111), 1225–1229. https://www.ncbi.nlm.nih.gov/entrez/query.fcgi?cmd=Retrieve&db=PubMed&list_uids=23197536&dopt=Abstract doi:10.1126cience.1224313 PMID:23197536

Bandera, C., Keshtkar, F., & Passerini, K. (2018). Internalization among Technology Entrepreneurs: Looking to the Future While Grounded in the Past. *Hawaii International Conference on System Sciences 2018 (HICSS-51)*. https://aisel.aisnet.org/hicss-51/ks/entrepreneurship_and_knowledge_management/4

Beaudry, A., & Pinsonneault, A. (2010). The Other Side of Acceptance: Studying the Direct and Indirect Effects of Emotions on Information Technology Use. *Management Information Systems Quarterly*, 34(4), 689–710. doi:10.2307/25750701

Beedie, C., Terry, P., & Lane, A. (2005). Distinctions between emotion and mood. *Cognition and Emotion*, 19(6), 847–878. doi:10.1080/02699930541000057

Bojja, G. R., Ofori, M., Liu, J., & Ambati, L. S. (2020). Early Public Outlook on the Coronavirus Disease (COVID-19): A Social Media Study. *AMCIS 2020 Proceedings*.

Cao, X., Vogel, D. R., Guo, X., Liu, H., & Gu, J. (2012). Understanding the Influence of Social Media in the Workplace: An Integration of Media Synchronicity and Social Capital Theories. In R. H. Sprague (Ed.), *2012 45th Hawaii International Conference on System Science: (HICSS); USA, 4 - 7 Jan. 2012* (pp. 3938–3947). IEEE. 10.1109/HICSS.2012.618

Chaplin, J. S., & Krawiec, T. S. (1979). *Systems and Theories of Psychology*. University of Illinois Press.

Chau, M., Li, T. M., Wong, P. W., Xu, J. J., Yip, P. S., & Chen, H. (2020). Finding People with Emotional Distress in Online Social Media: A Design Combining Machine Learning and Rule-Based Classification. *Management Information Systems Quarterly*, 44(2), 933–955. doi:10.25300/MISQ/2020/14110

Clark, M. S., & Fiske, S. T. (1982). *Affect and cognition: The seventeenth annual Carnegie symposium on cognition* (Vol. 17). Psychology Press.

Davenport, T. H., & Prusak, L. (1998). *Working knowledge: How organizations manage what they know*. Harvard Business Press.

de Geofroy, Z., & Evans, M. M. (2017). Are Emotionally Intelligent Employees Less Likely to Hide Their Knowledge? *Knowledge and Process Management, 24*(2), 81–95. doi:10.1002/kpm.1532

Decker, B., Landaeta, R. E., & Kotnour, T. G. (2009). Exploring the relationships between emotional intelligence and the use of knowledge transfer methods in the project environment. *Knowledge Management Research and Practice, 7*(1), 15–36. doi:10.1057/kmrp.2008.29

Elder, J., Miner, G., & Nisbet, B. (2012). *Practical text mining and statistical analysis for non-structured text data applications* (1st ed.). Academic Press.

Elfenbein, H. A. (2007). Emotion in Organizations. *The Academy of Management Annals, 1*(1), 315–386. doi:10.5465/078559812

English, H. B., & English, A. C. (1958). *A comprehensive dictionary of psychological and psychoanalytical terms: A guide to usage*. Longmans, Green.

Fteimi, N., & Basten, D. (2015). Impact of Dictionaries on Automated Content Analysis - The Use of Compound Concepts in Analysing Knowledge Management Research. *European Conference on Information Systems (ECIS) 2015*. doi:10.18151/7217320

Fteimi, N., & Lehner, F. (2016). Main Research Topics in Knowledge Management: A Content Analysis of ECKM Publications. *Electronic Journal of Knowledge Management, 14*(1), 5–17.

Gregor, S. (2006). The Nature of Theory in Information Systems. *Management Information Systems Quarterly, 30*(3), 611. doi:10.2307/25148742

Gregor, S., Lin, A. C. H., Gedeon, T., Riaz, A., & Zhu, D. (2014). Neuroscience and a Nomological Network for the Understanding and Assessment of Emotions in Information Systems Research. *Journal of Management Information Systems, 30*(4), 13–48. doi:10.2753/MIS0742-1222300402

Guinea, A. O., Titah, R., & Léger, P.-M. (2014). Explicit and Implicit Antecedents of Users' Behavioral Beliefs in Information Systems: A Neuropsychological Investigation. *Journal of Management Information Systems, 30*(4), 179–210. doi:10.2753/MIS0742-1222300407

Holsapple, C. W., & Joshi, K. D. (2004). A formal knowledge management ontology: Conduct, activities, resources, and influences. *Journal of the American Society for Information Science and Technology, 55*(7), 593–612. doi:10.1002/asi.20007

Hornung, O., & Smolnik, S. (2018). It's Just Emotion Taking Me Over: Investigating the Role of Emotions in Knowledge Management Research. In T. Bui (Ed.), *Proceedings of the Annual Hawaii International Conference on System Sciences*. Hawaii International Conference on System Sciences. 10.24251/HICSS.2018.512

Hu, M., & Liu, B. (2004). Mining and summarizing customer reviews. In W. Kim (Ed.), *Proceedings of the tenth ACM SIGKDD international conference on Knowledge discovery and data mining* (p. 168). ACM. 10.1145/1014052.1014073

Ioannis, R., & Belias, D. (2020). Combining Strategic Management with Knowledge Management: Trends and International Perspectives. *International Review of Management and Marketing, 10*(3), 39–45. doi:10.32479/irmm.9621

Izard, C. E. (1977). Differential Emotions Theory. In *Human Emotions* (pp. 43–66). Springer US., doi:10.1007/978-1-4899-2209-0_3

Jennex, M. E., & Olfman, L. (2005). Assessing Knowledge Management Success. *International Journal of Knowledge Management, 1*(2), 33–49. doi:10.4018/jkm.2005040104

Jennex, M.E. and Olfman, L., (2006). A Model of Knowledge Management Success. International Journal of Knowledge Management, 2(3), pp. 51-68.

Kauffmann & Carmi. (2017). The Mediating Effect of Interpersonal Trust on Virtual Team's Collaboration. *International Journal of Knowledge Management, 13*(3), 20–37. doi:10.4018/IJKM.2017070102

Kay, R. H., & Loverock, S. (2008). Assessing emotions related to learning new software: The computer emotion scale. *Computers in Human Behavior, 24*(4), 1605–1623. doi:10.1016/j.chb.2007.06.002

Khalil, O. E. M., & Shea, T. (2012). Knowledge Sharing Barriers and Effectiveness at a Higher Education Institution. *International Journal of Knowledge Management, 8*(2), 43–64. doi:10.4018/jkm.2012040103

Krippendorff, K. (2013). *Content analysis: An introduction to its methodology* (3rd ed.). Sage.

Kuo, B., Young, M.-L., Hsu, M.-H., Lin, C., & Chiang, P.-C. (2003). A Study of the Cognition-Action Gap in Knowledge Management. *ICIS 2003 Proceedings*. https://aisel.aisnet.org/icis2003/36

Landis, J. R., & Koch, G. G. (1977). The Measurement of Observer Agreement for Categorical Data. *Biometrics, 33*(1), 159. doi:10.2307/2529310 PMID:843571

Leeper, R. W. (1948). A motivational theory of emotion to replace 'emotion as disorganized response.'. *Psychological Review, 55*(1), 5–21. doi:10.1037/h0061922 PMID:18910278

Li, F. (2010). The Information Content of Forward-Looking Statements in Corporate Filings-A Naïve Bayesian Machine Learning Approach. *Journal of Accounting Research, 48*(5), 1049–1102. doi:10.1111/j.1475-679X.2010.00382.x

Lin, J., Chan, H. C., & Wei, K. K. (2006). The effects of goal orientations on knowledge management system usage, knowledge sourcing and learning outcome. European Conference on Information Systems (ECIS) 2006.

Mandler, G. (1975). *Mind and emotion*. Krieger Publishing Company.

Marshall, J. (2000). Expanding the realm of organizational reasoning. *The Learning Organization, 7*(5), 244–251. doi:10.1108/09696470010353007

Martínez-Miranda, J., & Aldea, A. (2005). Emotions in human and artificial intelligence. *Computers in Human Behavior, 21*(2), 323–341. doi:10.1016/j.chb.2004.02.010

Matthies, B. (2016). Feature-based sentiment analysis of codified project knowledge: A dictionary approach. *PACIS 2016 Proceedings.* https://aisel.aisnet.org/pacis2016/144

Mowrer, O. H. (1960). *Learning theory and behavior.* John Wiley & Sons Inc. doi:10.1037/10802-000

Nonaka, I. (1994). A dynamic theory of organizational knowledge creation. *Organization Science, 5*(1), 14–37. doi:10.1287/orsc.5.1.14

Pemberton, J., Mavin, S., & Stalker, B. (2007). Scratching beneath the surface of communities of (mal) practice. *The Learning Organization, 14*(1), 62–73. doi:10.1108/09696470710718357

Peng, H. (2013). Why and when do people hide knowledge? *Journal of Knowledge Management, 17*(3), 398–415. doi:10.1108/JKM-12-2012-0380

Plutchik, R. (1980). *A general psychoevolutionary theory of emotion* (Vol. 1). Academic Press.

Plutchik, R. (1984). Emotions: A general psychoevolutionary theory. *Approaches to Emotion,* 197–219.

Qiu, J., & Lv, H. (2014). An overview of knowledge management research viewed through the web of science (1993-2012). *Aslib Journal of Information Management, 66*(4), 424–442. doi:10.1108/AJIM-12-2013-0133

Rice, R. E., & Love, G. (1987). Electronic Emotion: Socioemotional Content in a Computer-Mediated Communication Network. *Communication Research, 14*(1), 85–108. doi:10.1177/009365087014001005

Richins, M. L. (1997). Measuring Emotions in the Consumption Experience. *The Journal of Consumer Research, 24*(2), 127–146. doi:10.1086/209499

Rottenberg, J. (2005). Mood and Emotion in Major Depression. *Current Directions in Psychological Science, 14*(3), 167–170. doi:10.1111/j.0963-7214.2005.00354.x

Scherer, K. R., & Tran, V. (2003). Effects of Emotion on the Process of Organizational Learning. Handbook of Organizational Learning and Knowledge, Oxford Univ. Press.

Serenko, A., & Bontis, N. (2017). Global ranking of knowledge management and intellectual capital academic journals: 2017 update. *Journal of Knowledge Management, 21*(3), 675–692. doi:10.1108/JKM-11-2016-0490

Song, S., & Teng, J. T. C. (2008). An Exploratory Examination of Knowledge Sharing Behaviors: Voluntary vs. Solicited. In *Proceedings of the 41st Annual Hawaii International Conference on System Sciences (HICSS 2008)* (p. 342). IEEE. 10.1109/HICSS.2008.56

Swift, P. E., & Hwang, A. (2013). The impact of affective and cognitive trust on knowledge sharing and organizational learning. *The Learning Organization, 20*(1), 20–37. doi:10.1108/09696471311288500

Tenório, N., Ferrarezi Vidotti, A., Alaranta, M., & Fulk, H. K. (2017). The Influence of Positive Emotions on Knowledge Sharing. *AMCIS 2017 Proceedings,* 1–5.

The Oxford English Dictionary: On CD-ROM; including additions series volumes 1 - 3 (2. ed., Version 3.1, new user version). (2007). Oxford Univ. Press.

Trenck, A. d., Emamjome, F., Neben, T., & Heinzl, A. (2015). What's in it for Me? Conceptualizing the Perceived Value of Knowledge Sharing. In T. X. Bui & R. H. Sprague (Eds.), *48th Hawaii International Conference on System Sciences (HICSS), 2015: 5 - 8 Jan. 2015, Kauai, Hawaii* (pp. 3920–3928). IEEE. 10.1109/HICSS.2015.469

Trong Tuan, L. (2013). Leading to learning and competitive intelligence. *The Learning Organization*, *20*(3), 216–239. doi:10.1108/09696471311328460

Tuan, L. T. (2016). The chain effect from human resource-based clinical governance through emotional intelligence and CSR to knowledge sharing. *Knowledge Management Research and Practice*, *14*(1), 126–143. doi:10.1057/kmrp.2014.23

Turner, J. R., & Baker, R. (2017). Team Emergence Leadership Development and Evaluation: A Theoretical Model Using Complexity Theory. *Journal of Information & Knowledge Management*, *16*(02), 1750012. doi:10.1142/S0219649217500125

Ur-Rahman, N., & Harding, J. A. (2012). Textual data mining for industrial knowledge management and text classification: A business oriented approach. *Expert Systems with Applications*, *39*(5), 4729–4739. doi:10.1016/j.eswa.2011.09.124

Van den Hooff, B., Schouten, A. P., & Simonovski, S. (2012). What one feels and what one knows: The influence of emotions on attitudes and intentions towards knowledge sharing. *Journal of Knowledge Management*, *16*(1), 148–158. doi:10.1108/13673271211198990

Venables, W. N., Smith, D. M., & the R Core Team. (2014). *An introduction to R. Notes on R: A programming environment for data analysis and graphics version.* http://cran.r-project.org/doc/manuals/R-intro.pdf

Wasdell, D. (2011). The dynamics of climate change: A case study in organisational learning. *The Learning Organization*, *18*(1), 10–20. Advance online publication. doi:10.1108/09696471111095966

Yadollahi, A., Shahraki, A. G., & Zaiane, O. R. (2017). Current State of Text Sentiment Analysis from Opinion to Emotion Mining. *ACM Computing Surveys*, *50*(2), 1–33. doi:10.1145/3057270

Yassine, M., & Hajj, H. (2010). A Framework for Emotion Mining from Text in Online Social Networks. In W. Fan (Ed.), *IEEE International Conference on Data Mining workshops (ICDMW), 2010: Sydney, Australia, 13 [i.E. 14] Dec. 2010; proceedings* (pp. 1136–1142). IEEE. 10.1109/ICDMW.2010.75

This research was previously published in the International Journal of Knowledge Management (IJKM), 17(3); pages 1-16, copyright year 2021 by IGI Publishing (an imprint of IGI Global).

Chapter 91
Role of Educational Data Mining in Student Learning Processes With Sentiment Analysis:
A Survey

Amala Jayanthi M.

Kumaraguru College of Technology, India

Elizabeth Shanthi I.

Avinashilingam Institution for Home Science and Higher Education for Women, Avinashilingam University, India

ABSTRACT

Educational data mining is a research field that is used to enhance education system. Research studies using educational data mining are in increase because of the knowledge acquired for decision making to enhance the education process by the information retrieved by machine learning processes. Sentiment analysis is one of the most involved research fields of data mining in natural language processing, web mining, and text mining. It plays a vital role in many areas such as management sciences and social sciences, including education. In education, investigating students' opinions, emotions using techniques of sentiment analysis can understand the students' feelings that students experience in academic, personal, and societal environments. This investigation with sentiment analysis helps the academicians and other stakeholders to understand their motive on education is online. This article intends to explore different theories on education, students' learning process, and to study different approaches of sentiment analysis academics.

DOI: 10.4018/978-1-6684-6303-1.ch091

1. INTRODUCTION

Education is the continuous process of learning or ongoing development in abilities, values, attitudes, behaviours and intelligence. Types of Education include instruction, reading, narrative, debate, and guided study. Education is mostly provided under the inspection of teachers, and also but learners may undergo self-learning. The process of education can be done in a formal or informal environment. The definition of education differs between philosophers. Figure 1 shows some description of Education by various philosophers.

Figure 1. Definition of education

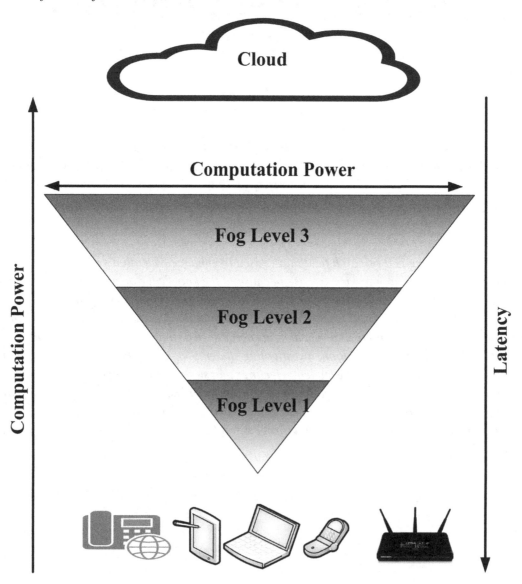

The essential motive of any academic program is to provide students with the required knowledge and skillsets to transform onto a productive professional within a given stipulated period. Using Data Mining (DM) strategies to evaluate knowledge about students may help establish potential explanations for learning. Educational Data Mining (EDM) is a data mining technology field developed to address educational problems (Altrabsheh et al., 2013). This contains a large volume of contextual information which offers a better understanding of learners based on their methods of learning. This utilizes DM methods to analyze data from the academic environment and to address academic problems that stop from achieving the motive of the educational programme. As with other extraction methods using DM techniques, EDM derives relevant, interpretable, valuable and novel information from educational data (Algarni 2016). Educational data mining researchers view the following as their work goals (T. E. D. Mining 2012):

- Predicting the potential learning behaviour of students by developing models of students that include such specific details as the experience, motivation, meta- cognition, and attitudes of students
- The discovery or development of domain structures characterizing the learning material and optimal instructional sequences.
- Investigating the influences of different kinds of pedagogical aid that learning applications can offer.
- Advancing empirical information about learning and learners by developing computational models that include student simulations, the environment and the pedagogy of the program

Sentiment analysis, also termed as opinion mining, is an application of natural language processing, computational linguistics, and content interpretation that, by analyzing the viewpoint, recognizes and retrieves emotion polarity from the content. The polarity of opinion is typically either positive (confident and enthusiastic) or negative (confused, boisterous, and furious), but often used as neutral (Altrabsheh et al., 2014). Mostly the sentiment analysis is applied in e-commerce, to analyze the customer reviews. Only a few articles (Altrabsheh et al., 2013; Altrabsheh et al., 2014) apply sentiment analysis in the education domain. This paper reviews sentiment analysis in the field of education.

The study is organized in this survey paper as the following. Section 2 gives the different definition of education Section 3 describes various theories on learning. It is based on emotion and academic performance of the student. Section 4 explains the research on Education, which mainly includes academic performance, student behaviour and emotions. The application of Education under computer science is described in Section 4. In section 5 the sentiment analysis and research in education using sentiment analysis is explored, and finally, section 5 concludes this paper.

2. WHAT IS EDUCATION?

Oxford definition of Education, Education is the process of acquiring or providing systematic instruction, especially at an academic environment like school, college or university. Education is the process of delivery of knowledge, skills and information to students by teachers.

According to Johann Heinrich Pestalozzi, a Swiss pedagogue and educational reformer, "Education is the natural, harmonious and progressive development of man's innate powers."

John Dewey, an American educational reformer who was also a philosopher and psychologist whose thoughts have been instrumental in Education and social reform. He stated, "Education is the development of all those capacities in the individual, which will enable him to control his environment and fulfil his possibilities".

Based on John Adams, was an American statesman, attorney, diplomat, writer, and the second president of the United States, "Education is a conscious and deliberate process in which one personality acts upon another to modify the development of that other by the communication and manipulation of knowledge."

3. THEORIES ON LEARNING

The philosophy of Education is the principle of intention, practice and perception of teaching and learning. Theory of learning explains the process of consuming, processing and maintaining information while learning. The factors of Cognitive, emotional and environmental and prior experience play a role in how opinion or a world view is gained or changed and information and skills conserved.

Theories of learning tend to fall under one of a variety of viewpoints or paradigms, including behaviourism, cognitivism, constructivism, humanism, connectivism, concise and others. This section discusses three fundamental theories shown in Figure 2 and also explains some taxonomy of learning theories.

Figure 2. Learning theories

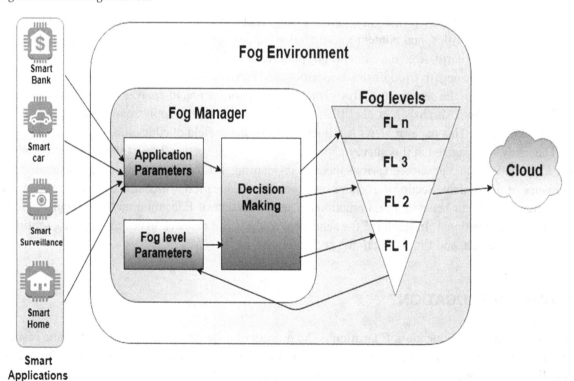

Behaviourism is a perspective of which contextual influences can describe behaviour, and behavioural conditioning should be seen as a primary learning mechanism. The principles of positive and negative feedback in behaviourism are essential methods for understanding and altering behaviour, as well as a method of discipline and reward. It involves repetitive actions, overt encouragement and participatory rewards. This is excellent for developing guidelines, especially for managing behaviour.

Cognitivism is a theory of learning by Jean Piaget. In this, he states that the child builds detailed neural processes and behavioural response to experiences. Students learn most efficiently in this theory by reading text and through teaching in lecture. In the opinion of cognitivism, learning comes about when the student reorganizes knowledge, either by seeking new approaches or by modifying old ones.

Constructivism believes that individuals are responsible for expanding their self-view on the environment by applying what they learned in the course of relating current knowledge to other experiences founded on previous experiences. People make use of those intercommunications and new knowledge to form their interpretation. Since students build their knowledge base, it is not always possible to predict outcomes, so the instructor will test and question the myths that may have arisen. A constructivistic approach may not be the best method to use where reliable outcomes are expected. Table 1 shows a short comparison of these three learning theories.

Table 1. Learning theories comparison

	Behaviourism	**Cognitivism**	**Constructivism**
Knowledge	Knowledge is a collection of behavioural responses to stimuli in the world	Learners are deliberately developing information systems with cognitive structures, built on pre-existing cognitive frameworks.	Knowledge is developed inside social contexts by experiences with a community of Knowledge
Learning	The Learner unconsciously consumes a predefined body of knowledge. Fostered by repetition and positive reinforcement	Effective assimilation of new knowledge and integration of existing cognitive systems. The learners stress discovery.	Integrating the students into a community of knowledge. Collaborative assimilation and absorption of new knowledge
Motivation	Extrinsic feedback, involving both positive and negative.	Intrinsic; the learners have their own goals and are motivated to understand.	Intrinsic and Extrinsic. Learning goals and motivations are decided by the intelligence group, both by learners and by extrinsic incentives.
Suggestion	The instructor conveys right interpersonal responses and is learned by the students.	The teacher makes learning possible by creating an atmosphere that facilitates experimentation and assimilation/ accommodation	The Instructor encourages and directs collective instruction. Encourage social practice.

3.1 Bloom's Taxonomy of Learning Domain

In 1956, Bloom's taxonomy was by developed by Dr Benjamin Bloom (Bloom n.d.) educational psychologist to promote higher modes concerning educational thought, such as evaluating and analysing, rather than merely memorising facts. The three types of knowledge, or domains, they describe are cognitive (knowledge), affective (attitudes), and psychomotor (physical abilities).

Cognitive Domain involves awareness, and analytical skills growth. This includes remembering or understanding basic facts, organizational habits and principles that help to improve analytical skills and competencies. The affective domain is concerned with emotions such as feelings, values, appreciation, enthusiasm, motivations and attitudes. The psychomotor environment applies to all aims related to the interpretive gestures and discrete physical processes of reflex actions (Figure 3).

Figure 3. Bloom's taxonomy

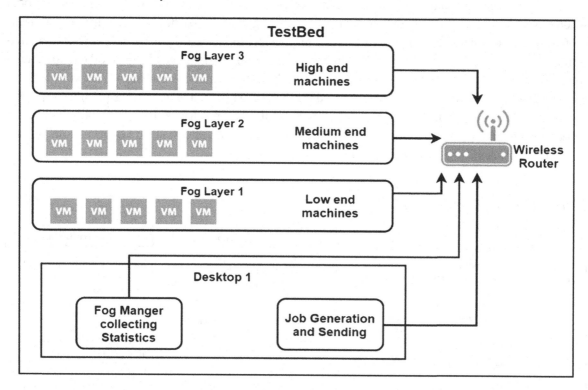

3.2 Gagné's Conditions of Learning

The book entitled "Robert Mills Gagné published the Conditions of Learning was an American educational psychologist in 1965. He has discussed the analysis of learning objectives and how the different classes of objective require specific teaching methods in his book.

He proposes five conditions of learning, which fall under the cognitive, affective and psycho-motor domains discussed by Bloom.

Gagné's Conditions of Learning are as follows:

- Verbal information (Cognitive domain)
- Intellectual skills (Cognitive domain)
- Cognitive strategies (Cognitive domain)
- Motor skills (Psycho-Motor domain)
- Attitudes (Affective domain)

3.2.1. Gagné's Levels of Learning

According to Gagne, to achieve the five conditions of learning, students progress through nine levels of learning, and any teaching session should make sure the class plan is planned according to nine levels. The idea was that the nine levels of learning activate the five conditions of learning and thus, learning will be achieved.

Gagne's nine levels of learning are listed below:

1. Gain attention.
2. Inform students of the objective.
3. Stimulate recall of prior learning.
4. Present the content.
5. Provide learning guidance.
6. Elicit performance (practice).
7. Provide feedback.
8. Assess performance.
9. Enhance retention and transfer to the job.

3.3 Maslow's Hierarchy of Needs

The basic idea for Maslow's hierarchy of needs is that students progress through a set of psychological needs to self-actualization (Figure 4).

Figure 4. Maslow's hierarchy of needs

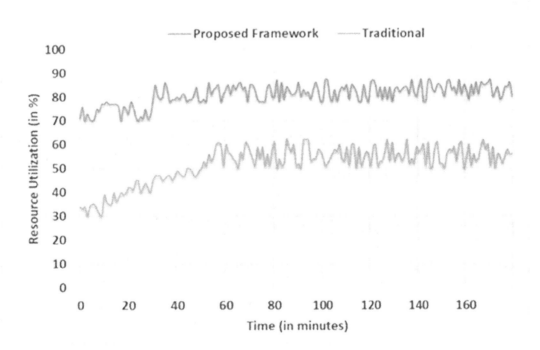

Maslow's theory is all about building student/teacher relationships rather than lesson or curriculum structure. He states that if the teacher does not show passion, enthusiasm and empathy, it is challenging for the students to meet their needs despite having the best resources and lesson plans."

3.4 Howard Gardner's Multiple Intelligences

Howard Gardner is an American psychologist who was working as a professor at Harvard University. In 1983 he published "Frames of Mind" where he laid out his theory of "multiple intelligences".

The Intelligences proposed by Gardner are as follows:

1. **Linguistic Intelligence:** The ability to understand and express one's thoughts by writing and speaking in a language
2. **Mathematical Intelligence:** The intelligence to solve scientific, mathematical problems logically and to perform experiments.
3. **Musical Intelligence:** Skill to appreciate, compose and perform musical notes and the ability to understand the sound of the tone, pitch and rhythm.
4. **Bodily-Kinesthetic Intelligence:** Ability to solve problems by coordinating mind and body movements.
5. **Spatial Intelligence:** Being able to understand and use patterns in a wide or restricted area.
6. **Interpersonal Intelligence:** The capacity to perceive others desires, motivations and intentions.
7. **Intrapersonal Intelligence:** The potential of understanding self fears, feelings and motivations.

Gardner suggested that the intelligence compliment each other when students learn new skills and solve problems and rarely occur independently.

3.5 Kolb's Experiential Theory

In 1984, four-stage experiential learning theory was proposed by an American education theorist named David Kolb (Figure 5). It is built based on:

"Learning is the process whereby knowledge is created through the transformation of experience."

Learning is fulfilled when all four stages have completed. Each step in the cycle both supported by and led into the next step. A learner may undergo the cycle any number of times so that he/she refine their understanding of the topic further.

4. RESEARCH PERSPECTIVES ON EDUCATION

Educational research refers to a concerted effort to achieve a deeper understanding of the method of schooling, usually to increase its performance. This is an extension of the scientific method to research the problems of Education. The educational analysis is the application of the scientific method to the study of issues in Education. Therefore the steps of educational research are more or less comparable with those in the scientific method. The measures commonly found in education research are as follows: Research problem, Formulation of hypothesis, methods to be used, data collection, analysis and interpretation of data, and reporting the results.

This section review some educational research based on student academic performance, behaviour and emotions.

Figure 5. Kolb's experiential theory

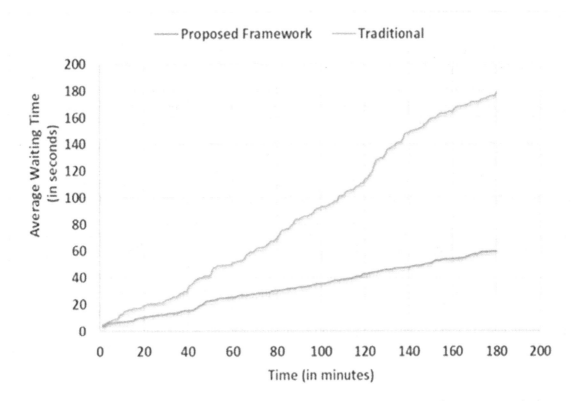

4.1 Students' Academic Performance

For an institution, academic success is critical for the positive results which will contribute to future job success. Arsenis and Flores (2019) study the relationship between the academic achievement of students and the possibility of gaining work experience as part of their undergraduate studies. Kostagiolas et al., (2019) provide evidence from the learning analytics to assess the effect of research satisfaction on academic self-efficacy and success of students. Academic achievement and student wellbeing are two ideal outcomes in phase-in learning and teaching. In a particular sense, the research in (Palos et al., 2019) measures the transient order of the link between educational success and two types of student progress. Path analysis models indicated that college grades could be considered a precedent of student participation and burnout, while wellbeing measures cannot be considered a precedent of academic success.

Budu et al., (2019) review the genesis of tension among midwife students in Ghana and its influence on their academic performance. The multivariate study showed that the responses of respondents when anxious had a significant effect on their academic success. However, having fewer holidays after accounting for the stressors had a substantial impact on the academic performance of the respondents. Meanwhile, the contact concept greatly enhances respondents who have had ample time to relax during their holidays. D'Alessio et al., (2019) examine the effect of critical thought on corporate Master of Business Administration (MBA) students ' academic achievement. Critical thinking has a positive impact on the average MBA student's academic success.

4.2 Students' Behavior

Student misbehaviour such as offensive speech, constant job evasion, clowning, dissatisfaction with instructional tasks, bullying peers, verbal abuse, instructor rudeness, defiance, and hatred, varying from rare to regular, moderate to severe, is a thorny problem in a daily classroom. Research has shown that school abuse has not only intensified over time but has also reduced academic performance and increased delinquency (Sun & Shek 2012).

Automatic review of the in-classroom behaviour of the students is useful for evaluating the teaching impact. Yang et al., (2020) aim to assess the degree of focus of the students concerning the instructor or quality of the instruction. Detect the faces of the students, map faces and evaluates the actions of the students, i.e. lift or bow faces and related instructor head orientations, teach material or not. In (Cantabella et al., 2019) case study undertaken at the Catholic University of Murcia, where student behaviour has been evaluated in the past four academic years based on learning modality, given the number of accesses to the Learning Management System, the resources used by students and their related behaviours.

The student behaviour analysis and prediction model focused on big data from the campus is developed in (Tu 2019), and the importance of big data produced by the behaviour of the campus students is analyzed. The behavioural data of the laws of consumption, living patterns and learning conditions of students are gathered, modelled, examined and excavated around the broad data sets, and the behaviour of the students is predicted and informed by the stratified model of behavioural characteristics of the students.

4.3 Students' Emotions

Through schooling and in all aspects of human life, feelings are of considerable value. It is understood that while people's backgrounds, the world in which they live, and the language they use vary, there are emotions that are regarded as universal. The students ' facial expressions were evaluated in (Tonguç & Ozkara 2020) and digitized in terms of feelings of dissatisfaction, disappointment, joy, anxiety, contempt, anger and surprise. The author also analyzed whether student emotions differed and how this difference was statistically meaningful based on their divisions, gender, lecture hours, machine position in the classroom, and style of lecture and session details.

Sahla and Kumar (2016) propose a deep learning method for emotion analysis. It focuses on students of a classroom and thus, understands their facial emotions. The neural networks of convolution estimate emotional groups with the highest likelihood as a consequence. An appraisal should include the user, for example, depending on the expected emotion; whether the students are satisfied and this class is interesting.

Concentration review of the students will help to strengthen the learning experience. Emotions are directly related and represent the attention of students closely. In (Sharma et al., 2019), a research program is introduced to assess the level of focus in real-time from the articulated facial emotions. The emotions conveyed was associated with the students ' concentration, and three distinct arousal levels (high, medium and low) were conceived. Bosch et al., (2016) using computer vision, learning analytics, and machine learning to predict the emotions of the students in a school computer lab's real-world environment. It succeeded in detecting fatigue, confusion, excitement, anger and focus in a way that was universal through pupils, time and demographics.

5. SENTIMENT ANALYSIS

It is recognized as a sentiment analysis (SA) to understand and categorize the emotions of users from a section of the text into specific emotions. For example, emotions such as joyful, depressed, angry or optimistic, negative or neutral to decide the mood of the users concerning a particular subject or event. This method of research is also called opinion mining (with an emphasis on extraction) or affective rating.

Sentiments refer to attitudes, opinions, and emotions. In other words, the interpretations are emotional as opposed to objective truth. Different forms of sentiment analysis use various methods and approaches to recognize the sentiments found in a given text.

5.1 Approaches of Sentiment Analysis

SA has three significant levels of classification (Medhat et al., 2014). In essence, document-level, sentence-level, and aspect-level SA. Document-level SA is aimed at classifying an opinion document as reflecting a positive or negative viewpoint or sentiment. This finds the whole text to be a simple unit of knowledge (talking of one subject). Sentence-level SA is aimed at classifying the emotions conveyed in each sentence. The first step is to see if the statement is subjective or objective. If the sentence is subjective, it will be determined by Sentence-level SA if the sentence expresses positive or negative opinions. Aspect-level SA is directed at classifying sentiment for the individual characteristics of individuals. The first step is to define the organizations and the facets thereof. The opinion holders will express different views on various aspects of the same organization.

Several algorithms, techniques are used to achieve sentiment analysis. Figure 6 shows the types of sentiment analysis approaches.

There are four necessary steps are used to analyze the sentiments D'Andrea et al., 2015). They are

1. **Data Collection:** The first phase of the sentiment analysis is to collect data from content created by users found in blogs, forums and social networks. These details are disorganized, articulated in multiple ways by the use of specific words, slangs, writing sense etc. Research by hand is almost impossible. Text mining and natural language modelling are also included in the retrieval and classification.

2. **Preprocessing:** Consists of cleaning before evaluating the extracted results. It detects and excludes non-textual contents and contents that are inappropriate for analysis.

Figure 6. Types of sentiment analysis approaches

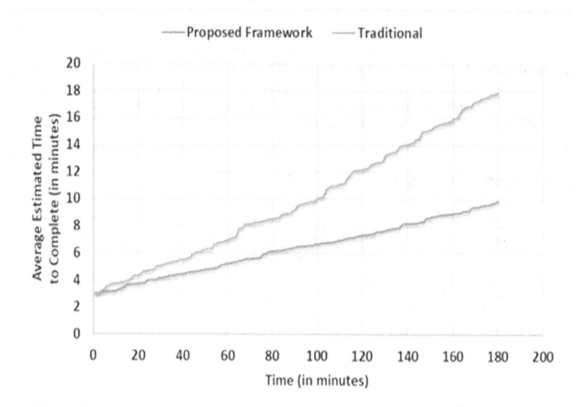

3. **Sentiment Detection:** Reviews and opinions extracted sentences are examined. Sentences with political statements (opinions, views, and beliefs) are preserved, and sentences of impartial communication (facts, truthful information) discarded.

4. **Sentiment Classification**: In this stage, subjective sentences are categorized as positive, negative, good, bad; like hate, but they can be categorized by several points.

5.2 Applications of Sentiment Analysis

Sentiment Analysis can be used in many applications. Some of the applications are listed below:

- **Market and FOREX Rate Prediction:** Foreign Currency Exchange plays an essential role in the financial market for currency trading. The market is predicted by analyzing the twitter sentiments on the commercial market.
- **Box Office Prediction:** Success of the upcoming movie is predicted using sentiment analysis on youtube comments, tweets, blogs etc.
- **Business:** Demand and Distribution choices should be taken depending on the user's perceptions of the product. Via these observations, the company can check the quality of the service it offers. Growing decisions in the market can be taken based on timely sentiments available.

- **Market Intelligence:** Designed to satisfy four needs of business managers likes (a) Possibilities and threat Determination, (b) Identifying opponents, (c) Help to acquire competitors' progress, and (d) aid great marketing decision making.
- **Politics:** Debated political issues on online forums. The public figure's positive and negative influence can be identified by examining people's thoughts on social media.
- **Recommenders System:** When customers use it enthusiastically, the good or service itself would have pleasant emotions. If the user considers the scores or emotions, these items may be highly recommended to a potential customer. Analysis of opinion also plays a critical role in supporting the system.
- **Summarization:** This is time-consuming for a reader to read all of the opinions about a particular institution and then judge. SA should give us every organization's general idea for a given period.
- **Government Intelligence:** The growth in violent behaviour can be monitored for tracking the sources. For making policies, the sentiments of people can be studied. This can be used for evaluating people's attitude about every SA conflict.
- **Education:** Analysis student behaviour, emotions based on the student feedback. In this educational framework, students provide feedback on Twitter at any time or at different time slots, as determined by the professor, to ensure that students observe the tempo of the lecture and provide assistance when faced with difficulties.

5.3 Research on Sentiment Analysis in Education

This section explains how sentiment analysis is used in Education. Rajput et al., (2016) suggested the sentiment analysis offered by students at the end of a course on faculty assessment. A Knime workflow was developed using its text processing feature for feel analysis of input from students. This method suggests a sentiment score measurement to identify the feedback as either positive, negative or neutral.

Nasim et al., (2017) propose a combination of machine learning and lexicon-based approaches to student input emotion analysis. The textual input, usually obtained at the end of a course, offers valuable insights into the general level of teaching and proposes useful ways to enhance teaching methods.

Aung and Myo (2017) plan to systematically evaluate the text feedback of the students using a lexicon-based approach to forecast the teaching performance levels. A dictionary of English sentiment terms is generated to get the polarity of terms as a lexical source.

Sujata Rani and Parteek Kumar (2017), proposed sentiment analysis system using performing temporal sentiment and emotion analysis of multilingual to enhance teaching and learning based on student feedback on teacher performance and course satisfaction.

Sultana et al., (2018) proposes a model based on Deep Learning approach to perform sentiment analysis on Educational data.

Featherstone and Botha (2015) reports on the teachers' experiences those who are participating in a professional development programme through sentiment analysis. It was inferred that those teachers were happy with the training, felt the course relevance strongly.

Sivakumar and Reddy (2017) using R tools, from Twitter API student feedbacks were collected for analysis. K-mean clustering and Naïve Bayes classification algorithm was used to perform sentiment analysis. The outcome of the proposed work will help the students to improve their learning skills and helps the academicians to enhance their teaching methodologies so that educational institutions can resolve the students' problems and attain their motto.

Nasim et al. (2017) proposes a combination of machine learning and lexicon-based methods to analyze the students feedback using sentiment analysis. With experimental results, it was inferred the performance of the proposed model is better than other methods.

Barron-Estrada et al. (2019) This paper presents a sentiment analyzer to detect student sentiment and/or emotions by recognizing the polarities and emotions on learning using textual phrases that are written in Spanish. The results obtained is 88.26% accuracy.

6. CONCLUSION

Education is concerned with methods of learning and teaching that facilitates the process of learning, or the acquisition of knowledge, skills, values, beliefs, and habits in the learning environments setup. The theories on education and learning process state that the motive of education is not that an individual grows successful as a professional but also as a complete person. That is, the student should grow himself in knowledge, behaviour, attitude, skills, emotions etc. through the learning process. The theories also state that education alone does not improve students skill, knowledge, behaviour, feelings, etc.,but also the environment and experiences he undergoes. This survey presents a brief background of Education with different learning theories. This paper describes various researches on Education using multiple methods of education data mining and sentiment analysis. It mainly focuses on student academic performance, behaviour and emotions in the academic environment and processes that assess these factors. It is inferred from the survey that education grooms a person in knowledge,skillset and emotions. The advances of computer technologies and research domains like educational data mining and sentiment analysis help out in identifying the issues in achieving the motive of education and satisfying the theories of learning by supporting in perfect decision making using machine learning algorithms.

REFERENCES

Algarni, A. (2016). Data Mining in Education. *International Journal of Advanced Computer Science and Applications*, 7(6).

Altrabsheh, N., Cocea, M., & Fallahkhair, S. (2014). Sentiment Analysis: Towards a Tool for Analysing Real-Time Students Feedback. *2014 IEEE 26th International Conference on Tools with Artificial Intelligence*, 419-423.

Altrabsheh, N., Gaber, M. M., & Cocea, M. (2013). SA-E; Sentiment analysis for education. *Frontiers in Artificial Intelligence and Applications*, *255*, 353–362.

Arsenis, P., & Flores, M. (2019). *Student academic performance and professional training year* (Vol. 30). International Review of Economics Education.

Aung, K. Z., & Myo, N. N. (2017). Sentiment analysis of students' comment using the lexicon-based approach. *2017 IEEE/ACIS 16th International Conference on Computer and Information Science (ICIS)*, 149-154. 10.1109/ICIS.2017.7959985

Barron-Estrada, M. L., Zatarain-Cabada, R., & Oramas-Bustillos, R. (2019). Emotion Recognition for Education using Sentiment Analysis. *Research in Computing Science, 148*(5), 71–80. doi:10.13053/rcs-148-5-8

Bloom. (n.d.). *Taxonomy of educational objectives*. New York, NY: David Mckay.

Bosch, N., D'Mello, S. K., Baker, R. S., Ocumpaugh, J., Shute, V., Ventura, M., Wang, L., & Zhao, W. (2016). Detecting StudentEmotions in Computer-Enabled Classrooms. *Proceedings of the Twenty-Fifth International Joint Conference on Artificial Intelligence*, 4125–4129.

Budu, H. I., Abalo, E. M., Bam, V., Budu, F. A., & Peprah, P. (2019). A survey of the genesis of stress and its effect on the academic performance of midwifery students in a college in Ghana. *Midwifery, 73*, 69–77. doi:10.1016/j.midw.2019.02.013 PMID:30903921

Cantabella, M., Martínez-España, R., Ayuso, B., Yáñez, J., & Muñoz, A. (2019). Analysis of student behavior in learning management systems through a Big Data framework. *Future Generation Computer Systems, 90*, 262–272. doi:10.1016/j.future.2018.08.003

D'Alessio, F. A., Avolio, B. E., & Charles, V. (2019). Studying the impact of critical thinking on the academic performance of executive MBA students. *Thinking Skills and Creativity, 31*, 275–283. doi:10.1016/j.tsc.2019.02.002

D'Andrea, A., Ferri, F., Grifoni, P., & Guzzo, T. (2015). Approaches Tools and Applications for Sentiment Analysis Implementation. *International Journal of Computers and Applications, 125*(3).

Featherstone, C., & Botha, A. (2015, May). Sentiment analysis of the ICT4Rural Education teacher professional development course. In *2015 IST-Africa Conference* (pp. 1-12). IEEE.

Kostagiolas, P., Lavranos, C., & Korfiatis, N. (2019). *Learning analytics: Survey data for measuring the impact of study satisfaction on students' academic self-efficacy and performance* (Vol. 25). Data in Brief.

Medhat, W., Hassan, A., & Korashy, H. (2014). Sentiment analysis algorithms and applications: A survey. *Ain Shams Engineering Journal, 5*(4), 1093–1113. doi:10.1016/j.asej.2014.04.011

Mining, T. E. D. (2012). Enhancing teaching and learning through educational data mining and learning analytics: An issue brief. *Proceedings of the conference on advanced technology for Education.*

Nasim, Z., Rajput, Q., & Haider, S. (2017, July). Sentiment analysis of student feedback using machine learning and lexicon-based approaches. In *2017 international conference on research and innovation in information systems (ICRIIS)* (pp. 1-6). IEEE.

Nasim, Z., Rajput, Q., & Haider, S. (2017). Sentiment analysis of student feedback using machine learning and lexicon-based approaches. *2017 International Conference on Research and Innovation in Information Systems (ICRIIS)*, 1-6. 10.1109/ICRIIS.2017.8002475

Paloş, R., Maricuţoiu, L. P., & Costea, I. (2019). engagement and student burnout: A cross-lagged analysis of a two-wave study. *Studies in Educational Evaluation, 60*, 199–204. doi:10.1016/j.stueduc.2019.01.005

Pekrun, R., Frenzel, A. C., Goetz, T., & Perry, R. P. (2007). *The Control-Value Theory of Achievement Emotions: An Integrative Approach to Emotions in Education*. Emotion in Education.

Pekrun, R., Goetz, T., Titz, W., & Perry, R. P. (2002). Academic Emotions in Students' Self-Regulated Learning and Achievement: A Program of Qualitative and Quantitative Research. *Educational Psychologist, 37*(2), 91–105.

Rajput, Q., Haider, S., & Ghani, S. (2016). Lexicon-based sentiment analysis of teachers evaluation. *Applied Computational Intelligence and Soft Computing, 2016*, 1–12. doi:10.1155/2016/2385429

Rani, S., & Kumar, P. (2017). A sentiment analysis system to improve teaching and learning. *Computer, 50*(5), 36–43. doi:10.1109/MC.2017.133

Sahla, K. S., & Kumar, T. S. (2016). Classroom Teaching Assessment Based on Student Emotions. *The International Symposium on Intelligent Systems Technologies and Applications*, 475-486. 10.1007/978-3-319-47952-1_37

Sharma, P., Esengönül, M., Khanal, S. R., Khanal, T. T., Filipe, V., & Reis, M. J. C. S. (2019). Student Concentration Evaluation Index in an E-learning Context Using Facial Emotion Analysis. *International Conference on Technology and Innovation in Learning, Teaching and Education*, 529-538. 10.1007/978-3-030-20954-4_40

Sivakumar, M., & Reddy, U. S. (2017, November). Aspect based sentiment analysis of students opinion using machine learning techniques. In *2017 International Conference on Inventive Computing and Informatics (ICICI)* (pp. 726-731). IEEE. 10.1109/ICICI.2017.8365231

Sultana, J., Sultana, N., Yadav, K., & AlFayez, F. (2018, April). Prediction of sentiment analysis on educational data based on deep learning approach. In *2018 21st Saudi Computer Society National Computer Conference (NCC)* (pp. 1-5). IEEE. 10.1109/NCG.2018.8593108

Sun, R. C. F., & Shek, D. T. L. (2012). *Student Classroom Misbehavior: An Exploratory Study Based on Teachers' Perceptions*. Developmental Issues in Chinese Adolescents.

Tonguç, G., & Ozkara, B. O. (2020). *Automatic recognition of student emotions from facial expressions during a lecture* (Vol. 148). Computers & Education.

Tu, L. (2019). Analysis and Prediction Method of Student Behavior Mining Based on Campus Big Data. *International Conference on Advanced Hybrid Information Processing*, 363-371. 10.1007/978-3-030-36405-2_36

Yang, B., Yao, Z., Lu, H., Zhou, Y., & Xu, J. (2020). In-classroom learning analytics based on student behavior, topic and teaching characteristic mining. *Pattern Recognition Letters, 129*, 224–231. doi:10.1016/j.patrec.2019.11.023

This research was previously published in the International Journal of Knowledge and Systems Science (IJKSS), 11(4); pages 31-44, copyright year 2020 by IGI Publishing (an imprint of IGI Global).

Chapter 92

Tracking How a Change in a Telecom Service Affects Its Customers Using Sentiment Analysis and Personality Insight

Ammar Adl

ⓘ https://orcid.org/0000-0001-5201-2116

Faculty of Computers and Information, Beni-Suef University, Egypt

Abdelsadeq Khamis Elfergany

Faculty of Computers and Information, Beni-Suef University, Egypt

ABSTRACT

Tracking the effect of change a telecom service on customer feeling is an important process for telecom companies. As a result of tangible growth and large competition among telecom companies, customer retention and satisfaction are the most important challenges faced by telecom companies nowadays. Customer retention can be achieved by identifying the feeling of the telecom customers after changing service and take care of the customers by modifying the services that aren't accepted by its customers. Hence, this article was done by using a combination of four stages of: text pre-processing, personality analysis, sentiment analysis, and a chatbot system. This article shows the effect of using the personality traits, agreeableness and emotional range, with sentiment analysis to help reaching a full description of customer feel. Combining the sentiment analysis Naïve Bayes technique in the natural language processing and personality insights pre-learning stage and adding feedback using the obtained results achieves higher accuracy than using the traditional sentiment analysis techniques.

DOI: 10.4018/978-1-6684-6303-1.ch092

1. INTRODUCTION

All companies depend on stakeholders, human resources, and customers as their backbone especially the telecom companies, that more interested to proactively interact with its customers on the significant increase in the number of telecom companies, that leads to customer migration from one company to another and create continuous warfare between companies. So, all these companies try not only to retain their current customers but also to increase them (Marchand et al., 2017). Prediction tasks have many useful applications ranging from tracking opinions about service to identifying the best and bad service and predicting of the telecom customer satisfaction, this prediction is based set of statistical studies.

Telecom companies may get a bad rap when it comes to customer experience. All too mostly customers feel that service inappropriate with their expectations, but those complaints useless as if it falls on deaf ears (Kasemsap, 2017; Aikhuele & Turan, 2018). Over the past years, there were trials for finding a solution to retain the telecom customer loyalty by found a positive correlation between service recovery and customer satisfaction (Ibrahim et al. 2018). A lot of companies are suffering from problems with integrating strategic planning into their daily works and promotional campaigns. There are many needs to suggest how strategic planning can solve these problems (Galli, 2018). But despite the poverty of the telecom companies in detecting customer sentiment, few companies have made the customer care as the first target and empirically test and evaluate the direct and indirect effects of service encounter constructs of service quality (Gera et al., 2017).

Hence, The proposed work tries to show how the use of customer textual data that come from an AI chatbot helps to determine if the telecom customers are willing or not with the new service, if not, how can we help them?, and helps to find a solution for a set of issues like what is the percent of success and acceptance of the new service? What are the services that a telecom customer does not need? And what the services that win the satisfaction of the customers? The proposed system can help the telecom companies to live day per day with its customers from the behavioral side; If it can predict and know the sentiment and behavioral meaning in each response. A question like what is the emotional affection that the change in a service lave? or do they really love the new feature added? Can be answered based on the proposed work in this paper.

The problem entities are how to understand and use the agreeableness and emotional range personality traits and its sub-traits with the sentiment analysis, emotional values of the telecom customer's conversations as shown in Figure 1, and how the use of this traits help for reaching to a detailed report about customer feel towards the telecom company.

1.1. Personality Traits

On the other hand, and based on (Sorić et al., 2017; Menidjel & Bilgihan, 2017), a common assumption is that personality traits act as a control system (Roberts & Woodman, 2017). People may stray briefly from their needs, but they will then tend to their needs by time or the change in the environment after defeating the outside pressure. Under this type of models, one could find a relationship between customer traits and customer behavior that helps in tracking the telecom customer feel. So, this work tries to use the customer personality insights and compute the agreeableness and emotional range traits that help in tracking customer feel (Abdulla & Suresh, 2017).

Figure 1. The cooperation between customer traits (agreeableness and Emotional range) and sentiment analysis in tracking telecom customer feel

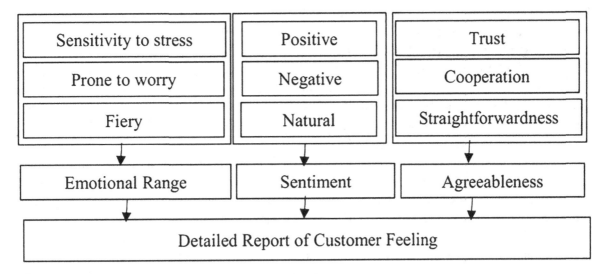

Figure 2. The four stages used in the proposed system

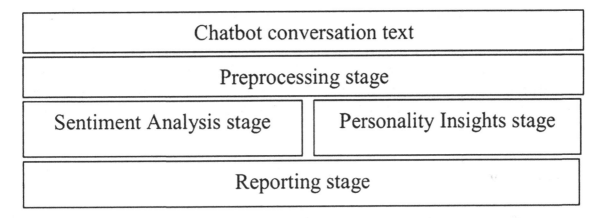

Personality means the characteristics and traits that make an individual unique. Despite there are many ways to determine personality traits (Rehman & Manjur, 2018), the proposed system deals with the popular five-factor model (or "Big 5"), which defines personality factors into five dimensions: extraversion (e.g. outgoing, talkative, active), agreeableness (e.g. trusting, kind, generous), conscientiousness (e.g. self-controlled, responsible, thorough), neuroticism (e.g. anxious, depressive, touchy), and openness (e.g. intellectual, artistic, insightful). the big five traits are a well-accepted definition of the human personality (Mäntylä et al., 2018). Referring to Figure 2; the proposed system is built over a state-of-the-art machine learning algorithm used for the learning process of sentiment analysis. It is developed by combining these four factors: (1) text preprocessing, (2) sentiment analysis, (3) personal analysis and (4) reporting stage and a chatbot system is created to achieve the needed task.

The proposed system uses the conversation data of telecom customers on the chatbot after changing a service to determine the success of the service and willing of the customers about it, how the success of change in a service can be seen in customer conversation text as we know that "The pen is mightier than the sword." So, what the proposed system trying to do is automatic recognition of the feeling of the telecom customer using a mix of personality analysis and some sort of ML sentiment analysis, NLP and textual AI algorithms; Figure 2 shows the relations between those processes.

Referring to Figure 2, after chatting with a customer, the textual data of telecom customer passing through a set of NLP algorithms to cover the needed data preprocessing, text vectorization, computing bag of words, TF-IDF, then entering it to the pre-trained naïve bays classifier that identifies the customer sentiment. On the other hand, using the IBM personality insights (PI) API for computing the customer big five traits, then feeding the result of the two stages to a pre-trained ML algorithm will increase the accuracy to reach to values higher than 92%.

This paper focuses exclusively on mean-level feeling and individual feeling of the telecom customers after any change, because these indices most directly reflect increases or decreases in telecom customer population, we show how to follow the customer feeling towards the new service, how to use the customer traits (agreeableness and emotional range) to track telecom customer's feeling from the textual data (Abdulla & Suresh, 2017; Cheng et al., 2017). Hence, the proposed system uses an AI chatbot (Weitzl et al., 2018) that uses a slang language in communication within the telecom customers to help all type of customers to communicate with the company. Using the chatbot as a data source of the telecom customers textual data that provides a deep view of the customer characteristics and behaviors. Humans may interact with chatbot but not a human partner (Andrei, 2018; Fryer et al., 2017). This paper shows how to improve correct measuring of telecom customer feeling by using the customer personality analysis with the sentiment analysis.

The proposed paper shows a set of related works, then provide a brief background about sentiment analysis, personality traits, and how to use customers personality traits for tracking their needs. The proposed paper shows the workflow and how we can use a hybrid of sentiment analysis and personality analysis to track the effect of change a service. Last, this article provides a conclusion, limitations, and a set of feature works to continue this research.

2. RELATED WORK

Sentiment analysis has gained much attention in investigating customer care in recent years (Agarwal et al. 2011). Really the proposed paper uses the Naïve Bayes (Song et al., 2017) in the sentiment analysis process of the customer conversation. There are many recent works prove that Naïve Bayes algorithm provides accurate result in the sentiment analysis (Srivastava et al. 2019). Kaur (2019) provide a full image of the MSA opportunities and difficulties and related field. Recent research worked by (Koutsothanassi et al., 2017) used the factor analysis; the results were enhanced a little but not enough to increase the performance. Using two established recurrent neural network algorithms, viz. Elman recurrent neural network (ERNN) and Jordan recurrent neural network (JRNN) by (Vijayaraman & Chellappa, 2016). Nowadays if you need to understand the customer personality you may target the personality insights that made a change from one person to another, the customer traits relate to the display of positive emotions by the service provider (Tan et al., 2017).

All the above along with (Sarker & Gonzalez, 2017; Onyibe & Habash, 2017) trial are the triggers for the methodology used in this paper. What has been done here is considered an innovative; a four-stages technique that made use of the above trials, by taking the accuracy of (Das & Kolya, 2017) and enhancing the algorithm to be faster and effective by adding the pre-learning step made by (Singh et al. 2017), stage is the post-identification process using nearest neighbor machine learning technique. Uniqueness comes from combining sentiment analysis, personality insights, and feedback processes together.

Until now all of the related research that studies the customer sentiment used the factor analysis or neural networks (Vijayaraman & Chellappa, 2016), but what have been done here is analyzing the telecom customer conversation using the IBM Watson personality insights service with sentiment analysis (Naïve Bayes) and learning process for identifying the telecom customer felling with changing a service. We used the Weka software tool for benchmark the used technique and reaching to the best algorithms.

The process of tracking the effect of change a service from telecom customer feeling implies finding a way by which we can communicate with the customers as we know that "The pen is mightier than the sword" so we have to create an AI chatbot and designing it to be near for all customer types by implementing it to use the slang language, by this way the proposed system can use it for offering the new service, then observe the customer conversation and analyze it from the Psychological, emotional side using the sentimental analysis and personality analysis then by this way we can correctly track the effect of change a service.

The proposed paper does not depend on sentiment analysis only but uses the personality traits as well. It was found that customer traits related to the display of positive emotions by the service provider (Tan et al., 2017). Personality traits can be used for tracking the user's behaviors and to discuss the emerging topic of information systems (Ong & Lin, 2018). By using the customer traits (Agreeableness, Emotional Range) and its sub-traits i.e.(Self-consciousness, Sensitivity to stress, Prone to worry ; Trust, Modesty, Sympathy) and mixing its result to the sentiment analysis process and feeding it to a pre-learned ML algorithm; It will help telecom companies to live day per day with its customer. The reporting stage based on the result of the first two processes result (sentiment analysis process and personality analysis). This processes with each other will give us a complete, accurate and detailed description of the telecom customer feeling about the new service or the telecom company generally.

The IBM Watson personality insights service (IBM PI API) has been used to compute the telecom customer personality traits. The sentiment analysis (Singh et al 2017; Onyibe & Habash, 2017) has been used to identify the telecom customer felling after changing a service.

With this in mind that the symptoms of this problem are very dangerous ones, telecom companies ignoring rate for the symptoms leads to the migration of its telecom customers. So, detecting the problem automatically from telecom customer conversation using sentiment analysis and personality behavior is a vital process to give early warnings before it gets dangerous. Helping telecom company to understand its weakness points for re-correcting it, help all kind of user to contact the telecom company by developing the slang language chatbot. Preventing telecom customers from leaving the telecom company to another one.

3. MATERIALS AND METHODS

These assumptions were set in order to start the experiment:

- Using the effective sub traits of the agreeableness (Agr_{sub}) and emotional range (ER_{sub}) will give a good description of customer feeling and needs;
- The mixing of sentiment analysis with personality analysis will give the best result;

- Using chatbot that used slang language will help all types of customers to easily communicate with telecoms and improving the efficiency by providing the textual data that needs about telecom customer.

The proposed paper used a combination of a set of stages as shown in Figure 3.

3.1. Preprocessing Stages

These stages prepare the text to feed to the classification algorithm in a set of sub-stages as shown in Figure 3 and Table 1, (1) tokenize the sentences within the text for splitting the text to a set of sentences, (2) tokenize and do minimal processing for words in each sentence, (3) elimination all of the stop words that do not affect the sentence meaning, (4) bag of words computation and text vectorization, where each unique word in a text will be represented by one number, (5) TF-IDF computation as shown in Equation 3. Based on TF-IDF documentation it stands for term frequency-inverse document frequency, and the TF-IDF weight is a weight that many times used in text mining and works with word generally. This weight is a statistical measure used to determine the importance of a selected word in a text document or corpus. The importance of the word increases by increasing its count in a document. For a term t in document d, the weight Wt,d of term t in document d is given by Equation 3, that represent multiplication of TF in Equation 1 by IDF in Equation 2. Then the data is ready to feed to Naïve Bayes classifier as shown in Table 1:

$$tf\left(t,d\right) = \frac{\left(\#\,of\,times\,term\,t\,appears\,in\,\,a\,document\,d\right)}{\left(total\,number\,of\,terms\,in\,the\,document\,d\right)} \tag{1}$$

$$idf\left(t,D\right) = \frac{\log\left(total\,number\,of\,documents\right)}{\left(\#\,of\,documents\,with\,term\,t\,in\,it\right)} \tag{2}$$

$$tfidf(t,\,d,\,D) = tf(t,\,d) \times idf(t,\,D) \tag{3}$$

Table 1. Model parameters

Model	Preprocessing	Sentiment Analysis	Personality Analysis	Reporting Stage
parameters	Slang Conversation text	TF-IDF, Bag of words, Tokenize text	Standard Conversation text	SA and PI result

Table 2. Shows the comparison among the results of using KNN, SVM, and NB classifiers

Classifier	KNN	SVM	Naïve Bays
Accuracy	85%	87%	91%

Figure 3. The general workflow

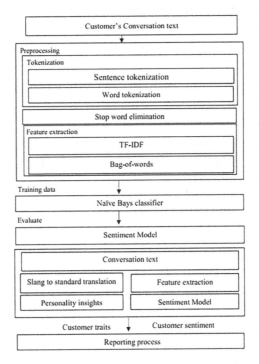

3.2. Sentiment Analysis

The sentiment analysis is also known as polarity classification. It is used to analyze in ample amount of text in which every sample is being determined as either positive, negative or neutral sample depending on the overall response received that is being expressed in that given textual data.

3.2.1. Sentence Level Sentiment Analysis

In this part of sentiment analysis (Singh et al. 2017), the sentiments are being analyzed in the level of text appearing at the sentence of the conversation. It is considered to fined grained classification as compared to the classification made at the document level in which the sentiment was expressed only in three forms either positive, negative or neutral format. This type of sentence classification can be done in the below mentioned 2 ways- grammatical syntactic approach or semantic approach. The former approach considers the grammatical hierarchy or structure of the various sentences occurring in the text by taking into consideration various parts of speech. And the latter one counts the occurrences of positive as well as negative words in order to propose the polarity of the analyzed sentence.

The assumption behind this methodology is that textual data, especially those expressing concerns, frustrations and acceptance from customers are rich in knowledge which needs to be mined for insights. Sentiment analysis is based on categorizations of particular words as 'positive' or negative. Algorithms based on presenting conversations in response to such emotional words have to be trained on this data. When working with sentiment analysis you may face many problems with training data because the procedure implies that the passing text has emotional meaning. Sentiment analysis algorithms cannot give good identifying when a word does not have emotional meaning. So, it is not like classical text mining which targets the topical text and picks only sentiment signals for real-time analysis (Hu & Kim, 2018).

By analyzing and tracking the customer sentiment more accurately and in particular finding the services that telecom customers are really unhappy about then telecoms can:

- Focus more on what differentiates it from the other telecom companies;
- Help users to find what they need; improve the increasing of the telecom customer's satisfaction;
- Produce the best service for its customers;
- Make the company work easier, help to retain its customers;
- Help telecom company to improve its customer care by keeping track of what the percent of acceptance that the new service generates;
- Know the aspects and themes in each response, that can also answer questions like: How long do people react negatively to a change in service, or do they really love the new feature added?

In the sentiment analysis stage, the proposed article uses the Naïve Bayes classifier for classification between the positive and negative (Hamoud et al., 2018) conversations that gives the best result with comparing with the supervised learning algorithms (SVM, KNN, and the neural network backpropagation). Referring to Table 2 that shows the comparison among the accuracy of the used algorithms in this process.

There is a tangible difference between these algorithms. Really the proposed system uses the Naïve Bayes (Song et al., 2017) to tack care of the sentiment of the last customer conversation not all of the text. This process passed through a set of subprocesses. First dataset collection. Second Preprocessing stage, Third and last train test split, this stage uses the K-fold algorithm for splitting the data into 10 folds, that goes in 10 iterations; in each iterate used 9 folds in training process and one fold for testing, this process increases the accuracy to be upper than 90%. All of this work was developed using python, and the processing is done on one machine.

3.3. Personality Analysis

The proposed system depends on the personality traits for tracking the customer sentiment after any change and in references (Mäntylä et al., 2018; Aarde et al., 2017). Hence, this paper uses the personality analysis process. But, which ones of the big five traits that will be useful? For answering this question depending on (Rehman & Manjur, 2018; McCarthy et al., 2017) that show that tracking the human satisfaction and willing need you to track her\his agreeableness and emotional range and referring to Table 4 there is a relation between the negative emotions and emotional range; on the other hand there is a relation between the positive emotions and the agreeableness. Agreeableness and Emotional range traits were helpful measures of the telecom customer's satisfaction towards a new service.

3.3.1. Effective Traits and Their Sub Traits

It was found that the agreeableness and emotional range will help in following customer feeling (Abdulla & Suresh, 2017; Cheng et al. 2017). The proposed system does not study the relation between the two traits only, but also it depends on the effective sub traits of each one as well (Straightforwardness, Cooperation, Trust) and (Fiery, Prone to Worry, Sensitivity to stress) respectively. For finding the effective sub-traits an experiment has been made; using a set of sentiment conversations and each time notes the result of each one. After hundreds of times it was found that (Straightforwardness, Cooperation, Trust, Fiery, Prone to Worry, Sensitivity to stress) are the most effective sub-traits that can be used for tracking the customer feeling as shown in Table 3 and shows the huge difference between the effective (Cooperation, trust, etc.) and not effective (Modesty, Altruism, etc.) sub-traits.

In the personality analysis process, the proposed system uses IBM Watson personality insights service for computing the big five traits of the telecom customers, referring to Table 1 the text comes from the telecom conversations on the AI chatbot. Because of the telecom customer used slang language in chatting in the chatbot, firstly the customer conversations pass through a set of processes convert it from slang to the standard language using slang to the standard dataset. Then sending the last 10 conversations to the IBM PI to compute the big five traits of the customer after that we extract the result of the effective traits (Agreeableness, Emotional range, and its sub-traits) from the returned JSON file. Figure 4 shows three cases of positive, negative and natural sentiment and customer effective sub-traits, improving the choice for the used sub-traits that give different and useful value with the difference of the customer sentiment. That was used with sentiment analysis in post-processing.

Table 3. The mean of the results of testing positive, negative and neutral conversation for finding the effective sub traits (the shaded ones)

Sub Traits		Conversation Type		
		Positive	Negative	Neutral
Agreeableness	Modesty	63%	55%	67%
	Straightforward	86%	35%	71%
	Altruism	20%	6%	45%
	Sympathy	44%	45%	40%
	Cooperation	94%	45%	85%
	Trust	86%	37%	80%
Emotional Range	Fiery	15%	55%	52%
	Prone to Worry	20%	51%	80%
	Sensitivity to stress	32%	63%	87%
	Impulsiveness	67%	69%	86%
	Self-consciousness	73%	94%	96%
	Melancholy	86%	93%	96%

Table 4. The mean of the agreeableness and emotional range effective sub-traits results of the customer conversation in case of positive, negative and natural conversations

		Negative	Positive	Neutral
Mean	Emotional Range (ER)	26%	74.7%	78.7%
	Agreeableness (Agr)	90%	13.7%	73%

3.4. Reporting the Result

In this last process, the result of sentiment analysis and personality analysis processes are fed to a pre-learned model that helps to find the meaning of these results. First, the negative sub treats need to be rearranged with the negative value and the positive sub traits with the positive value of the sentiment analysis then the mean for each set is calculated. It was found that in the positive cases the mean of agreeableness sub traits (Agr-sub) scores low value (Mean < 50) On the contrary the emotional range (ER-sub) scores high value in the same cases (Mean >= 50) as showing in Table 4 that calculated using Equations 4 and 5.

Figure 4. The result of the three cases of the customer feeling

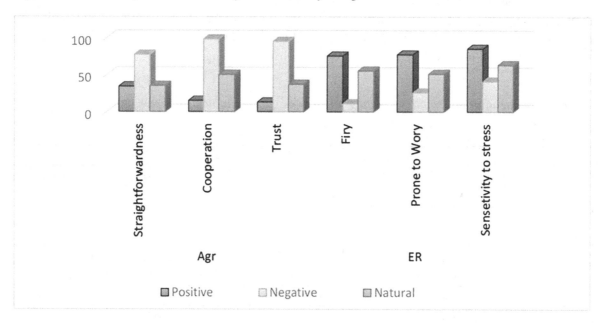

Then the mean of each trait is used with the result of the sentiment analysis to give the telecom company a detailed report about the customer feeling i.e. (this customer in first was happy and agree with the service features but after adding the last feature he/she was very angry and sad). Based on the result of the last stages we help the telecom companies to make a decision about the new service. Now the telecom company is able to understand its customer willing, sentiment, and emotions for predicting the fate of its customers in the coming days.

4. DATASET

Really in this article, using two dataset, because of the need to come closer to telecom customer, we have to use a chat system that understands the language and the accent that the most customer type so we used the slang language chatbot, on the other hand, we need to use the IBM personality insights service in telecom customer personal analysis process but this service need to take the string in a standard language, then we need to find a way to convert the string from slang to its standard, so we have created the slang dataset to help us in this process that works like a dictionary. The second dataset was the sentiment dataset that used for pre-learning the ML sentiment analysis algorithms. Coming, we will discuss the two in detail.

Table 5. Shows some samples of the slang to the standard dataset. Each word has its meaning in the standard.

Slang	Standard
R u here	Are you here
it's my cup of tea	describe something you like
Feeling blue	A feeling of depression or sadness.
For Real	A proclamation of honesty
Bob's your uncle	All is right

4.1. Slang to Standard Dataset

Referring to Table 5. The slang dataset used works as a dictionary that converts from slang to standard, such as "r u" to "are you" and so on. For collecting and building this dictionary, we target all of the common social media posts, plugs, tweets and comments related to telecom companies and customers. The data gathering process was not easy. This dictionary contains 3000 words in slang and its standard meaning.

4.2. Sentiment Analysis Dataset

In the sentiment analysis process, we have to collect as large as possible sentiment dataset that used for pre-learning the ML SA algorithms. The text come from three different fields/websites (imdb.com, amazon.com, and yelp.com). For each one, there are more than 600 positive and 600 negative sentences. Sentiment field is either 1 (for positive) or 0 (for negative). Those were selected randomly for larger datasets of reviews. We attempted to select sentences that have a clearly positive or negative meaning. It was a collection of more than 3600 labeled conversations, that have about 55% of the dataset have a positive meaning and 45% have a negative meaning. Table 6 shows some samples of the sentiment dataset. This dataset was taken from (Kotzias et al., 2015).

5. RESULTS AND DISCUSSION

Telecom companies use its web page to offer the new services, but it does not know what is the acceptance that is accurate. So we have proposed the chatbot system for communicating with customers and knowing their opinions towards these services. During the conversation between telecom customers and AI chatbot, the text of the conversation goes through a set of NLP (Ferrari, 2018) and machine learning algorithms. Then we can give the telecom company a full description of the effect of change a service on the telecom customer feeling, what the agreeableness and sadness that it create i.e. (this customer in first was happy and agree with the service features but after adding the last feature he/she was very angry and sad).

Table 6. Showing samples of sentiment analysis dataset

Id	Sentiment	Text
1	0	The only real effects work is the presence of all the animals, and the integration of those into the scenes is some of the worst and most obvious blue/green-screen work I've ever seen.
2	0	For a service that costs as much as this one does, I expect it to work far better and with greater ease than this thing does.
3	0	Not sure who was more lost - the flat characters or the audience, nearly half of whom walked out.
4	1	oh, thank you!
5	1	This review is long overdue since I consider A Tale of Two Sisters to be the single greatest film ever made.
6	1	Thanks, I need all the help I can get.

First, the use of the sentiment analysis process only was not helpful for a full description of the telecom customer besides, because of the difficulty of the working with text there are several problems when working with sentiment analysis. The first is an opinion sentence that is considered to be negative in one situation but may be classified as positive in another one. A second issue is that people do not always describe opinions in the same way. Most of the traditional text processing relies on the fact that small differences between the two parts of the text do not change the meaning very much. In SA, however, "the service was great" is very different from "the service was not great". People can be contradictory in their statements. Most conversations will have both positive and negative parts, which is somewhat manageable by analyzing conversation one at a time and analyzing the customer traits using all of the conversations. Firstly, and using the sentiment analysis only, accuracy was 89% that mean that there is 11% of the conversations that may not be classified if it is positive or negative but, after applying the personality analysis process to the conversation and computing the agreeableness and emotional range values the accuracy was improved to reach to more than 93%. So, the telecom company can depend on the proposed system to know the customer's impression. We use Weka tool for benchmarking all of these results.

5.1. Observations

- Naïve Bayes shows notable accuracy of 91% when the processing is done on a string less than 100 words;
- The use of personality analysis process helps in customer feeling report by using the agreeableness and emotional range traits;
- The learning curve is improved by time with the accuracy increase of 4% between the first and final run with the rate of .6% per trial;

- Using the IBM Watson PI in the personality analysis process is not optimum at a few words than 100 words, it is better to switch to the faster learning algorithm when the passing text has words less than 100 words;
- There are false positives reaching 6% occurring due to the text of telecom customer conversations, based on the interaction of the telecom customer with the new services.

The accuracy of the translation from slang to the standard in the chatbot improves with time, by increasing the slang to the standard dictionary, the accuracy of PI improves as well. While using the preprocessing learning was known to affect accuracy only with slowing down the performance, it was proved that using Naïve Bayes in this process does not affect performance much, on the other hand, it increases the total performance after successful learning process on the positive and negative emotions. By using the bag of words and text vectorization it is very simple to learn the Naïve Bayes classifier on the textual data.

Tracking the effect of change service on the telecom customer feeling using the sentiment analysis and personality analysis is a very effective process to help the telecom company to take care of its customers.

Now with new results, it is confirmed that the problem of tracking customer feeling was eliminated, and other researches can start from this point to focus on dynamic detection instead of using pattern matching techniques.

6. CONCLUSION AND FUTURE WORK

Using a machine learning algorithm in the preprocessing and post-processing stages with the personality insights service of the customer feeling analysis increases not only performance but also effectiveness. Emotional and sentimental conversations are vital for recognizing specific patterns e.g. loving, heating willing, felling, and acceptance towards the telecom service. Using the agreeableness and emotional range traits to track the telecom customer feeling helps to track the customer feeling and to understand the telecom customer needs. The accuracy level was increased to be 91% after using Naïve Bayes and SVM with the different stages of the identification process and increasing to reach to upper than 93% after using the personality analysis process. After hundreds of testing, was found that we can depend on (Straightforwardness, Cooperation, Trust, Fiery, Prone to Worry, Sensitivity to stress) sub-traits as the effective ones on the tracking of customer feel. But if we used the personality traits result, we will reach to accuracy increasing than 92%. But first, for moving the text through Naïve Bayes we must pass it through textual preprocessing such as using NLP for computing the bag of words. The communication between telecom companies and telecom customers has been improved by using the chatbot system that used slang and standard language.

All of the previous works were used English in chatbots, and they used standard English in the conversation with customers, but the proposed system used the English with standard and slang in the communication on the chatbot to be near as possible to all types of customers. What has been done here made it a sensitive and analytical chatbot that understand telecom customer emotions, characteristics and personality to give the telecom company a full description of its customers. The proposed study helps customers and preventing them from suffering from bad serving.

All companies depend on customers as its backbone especially the telecom companies on the significant increase in the number of telecom companies, that leads to the customer migration from one company to another and create continuous warfare between the companies. So, all these companies try not only to retain their current customers but also to attract them. When trying to find the solution for these problems we find that many of these companies do not know the feeling of the customers, so the proposed system provides an AI platform that analyzes the conversations of the customers from the sentimental and personal sides that successfully help on achieving the needed objectives by helping the telecom companies to easy track the effect of change an old service by adding new features or offering a new one. Telecom companies will not suffer from the customer migration and complain from bad of service by using the proposed system that helps to understand the personality characteristics and emotional values of its customers.

There are a set of suggested directions to continue this work in the future, first is to add the dynamic approach to the detection by testing either OneR or RNN to do this task. Second, is to test the effect of using a more accurate algorithm with a slower performance at low words count and switching it with a relative technique after passing a specific threshold. The third is to test the effect of adding the extra step as a deep learning step to run (LSTM) of RNN over Naïve Bayes results and see if this will enhance accuracy even if the passed text was small than 100 words. Developing a deep learning layer that would be able to compute the customer's personality traits without having to 100 words at least to define the customer's personality traits and using it instead of IBM Watson personality insights layer.

REFERENCES

Aarde, N. v., Meiring, D., & Wiernik, B. M. (2017). The validity of the Big Five personality traits for job performance: Meta-analyses of South African studies. *International journal of selection and assessment, 25*(3), 223-239.

Abdulla, A., & Suresh, K. (2017). Onward Ho! Studying Place Emotions, Language Style, and Social Tendencies in Travel Blogs. *Indian journal of management, 10*(6), 7-28.

Adamopoulos, P., Ghose, A., & Todri, V. (2018). The Impact of User Personality Traits on Word of Mouth: Text-Mining Social Media Platforms. *Information Systems Research, 29*(3), 3–6. doi:10.1287/isre.2017.0768

Agarwal, A., Xie, B., Vovsha, I., Rambow, O., & Passonneau, R. (2011). Entiment analysis of twitter data. In *Proceedings of the Workshop on Language in Social Media (LSM 2011)*. Academic Press.

Aikhuele, D., & Turan, F. (2018). A Conceptual Model for the Implementation of Lean Product Development. *International Journal of Service Science, Management, Engineering, and Technology, 9*(1), 1–9. doi:10.4018/IJSSMET.2018010101

Andrei, A. (2018). Chatbots for Education – Trends, Benefits and Challenges. In *Proceedings of the International scientific conference proceedings of eLearning and Software for Education (eLSE)* (Vol. 2, pp. 195-200). Academic Press.

Cheng, H., Green, A., Chapman, B. P., Treglown, L., & Furnham, A. (2017). Adrian Furnham Educational achievement and traits emotional stability and agreeableness as predictors of the occurrence of backache in adulthood. *Learning and Individual Differences, 117*(15), 205–209. doi:10.1016/j.paid.2017.06.008

Das, S., & Kolya, A. K. (2017). Sense GST: Text mining & sentiment analysis of GST tweets by Naive Bayes algorithm. In *Proceedings of the Third International Conference on Research in Computational Intelligence and Communication Networks (ICRCICN)*, (pp. 2996-3011). Academic Press. 10.1109/ICRCICN.2017.8234513

Ferrari, A. (2018). Natural language requirements processing: from research to practice. In *Proceedings of the 40th International Conference on Software Engineering: Companion Proceedings (ICSE '18)* (pp. 536-537). Academic Press. 10.1145/3183440.3183467

Fryer, L. K., Ainley, M., Thompson, A., Gibson, A., & Sherlock, Z. (2017). Stimulating and sustaining interest in a language course: An experimental comparison of Chatbot and Human task partners. *Journal of Computers in Human Behavior*, *75*(C), 461–468. doi:10.1016/j.chb.2017.05.045

Galli, B. J. (2018). Using Marketing to Implement a Strategic Plan: Reflection of Practiced Literature. *International Journal of Service Science, Management, Engineering, and Technology*, *9*(1), 41–54. doi:10.4018/IJSSMET.2018010104

Gera, R., Mittal, S., Batra, D. K., & Prasad, B. (2017). Evaluating the Effects of Service Quality, Customer Satisfaction, and Service Value on Behavioral Intentions with Life Insurance Customers in India. *International Journal of Service Science, Management, Engineering, and Technology*, *8*(3), 1–20. doi:10.4018/IJSSMET.2017070101

Hamoud, A. A., Alwehaibi, A., Roy, K., & Bikdash, M. (2018). Classifying Political Tweets Using Naïve Bayes and Support Vector Machines. *Recent Trends and Future Technology in Applied Intelligence*, *10868*, 736–744. doi:10.1007/978-3-319-92058-0_71

Hu, Y., & Kim, H. J. (2018). Positive and negative eWOM motivations and hotel customers' eWOM behavior: Does personality matter. *International Journal of Hospitality Management*, *75*, 27–37. doi:10.1016/j.ijhm.2018.03.004

Ibrahim, M., Abdallahamed, S., & Adam, D. R. (2018). Service Recovery, Perceived Fairness, and Customer Satisfaction in the Telecoms Sector in Ghana. *International Journal of Service Science, Management, Engineering, and Technology*, *9*(4), 73–89. doi:10.4018/IJSSMET.2018100105

Kasemsap, K. (2017). The Importance of Customer Satisfaction and Customer Loyalty in the Service Sector. In Handbook of Research on Strategic Alliances and Value Co-Creation in the Service Industry. Academic Press. doi:10.4018/978-1-5225-2084-9.ch004

Kaur, R., & Kautish, S. (2019). Multimodal Sentiment Analysis: A Survey and Comparison. *International Journal of Service Science, Management, Engineering, and Technology*, *10*(2), 38–58. doi:10.4018/IJSSMET.2019040103

Kotzias, D., Denil, M., Freitas, N. D., & Smyth, P. (2015). From Group to Individual Labels using Deep Features. In *Proceedings of the 21th ACM SIGKDD International Conference*. ACM. doi:10.1145/2783258.2783380

Koutsothanassi, E., Bouranta, N., & Psomas, E. (2017). Examining the relationships among service features, customer loyalty and switching barriers in the Greek banking sector. *International Journal of Quality and Service Sciences*, *9*(3), 425–440. doi:10.1108/IJQSS-02-2017-0013

Mäntylä, M. V., Graziotin, D., & Kuutila, M. (2018). he evolution of sentiment analysis—A review of research topics, venues, and top-cited papers. *Computer Science Review*, *27*, 16–32. doi:10.1016/j.cosrev.2017.10.002

Marchand, A., Thurau, T. H., & Wiertz, C. (2017). ot all digital word of mouth is created equal: Understanding the respective impact of consumer reviews and microblogs on new product success. *International Journal of Research in Marketing*, *34*(2), 336–354. doi:10.1016/j.ijresmar.2016.09.003

McCarthy, M. H., Wood, J. V., & Holmes, J. G. (2017). Dispositional pathways to trust: Self-esteem and agreeableness interact to predict trust and negative emotional disclosure. *Journal of Personality and Social Psychology*, *113*(1), 95–116. doi:10.1037/pspi0000093 PMID:28358543

Menidjel, C., & Bilgihan, A. (2017). Examining the moderating role of personality traits in the relationship between brand trust and brand loyalty. *Journal of Product and Brand Management*, *26*(6), 631–649. doi:10.1108/JPBM-05-2016-1163

Ong, C.-S., & Lin, M. Y.-C. (2018). Evaluating the Effects of Personality on Continuance Intention of Online User: An Empirical Study of Online Forum System in Taiwan. *International Journal of E-Adoption*, *10*(1), 19. doi:10.4018/IJEA.2018010103

Onyibe, C., & Habash, N. (2017). OMAM at SemEval-2017 Task 4: English sentiment analysis with conditional random fields. In *Proceedings of the 11th International Workshop on Semantic Evaluation* (pp. 670-674). Academic Press. 10.18653/v1/S17-2111

Rehman, H. U., & Manjur, K. I. (2018). Effects of Personality traits (Neuroticism, Agreeableness, Extraversion, Conscientiousness) on online impulse buying: Moderating role of hedonic motivation [Dissertation].

Roberts, R., & Woodman, T. (2017). Personality and performance: Moving beyond the Big 5. *Current Opinion in Psychology*, *16*, 104–108. doi:10.1016/j.copsyc.2017.03.033 PMID:28813330

Sarker, A., & Gonzalez, G. (2017). HLP@UPenn at SemEval-2017 Task 4A: A simple, self-optimizing text classification system combining dense and sparse vectors. In *Proceedings of the 11th International Workshop on Semantic Evaluation* (pp. 640-643). Academic Press. 10.18653/v1/S17-2105

Singh, J., Singh, G., & Singh, R. (2017). Optimization of sentiment analysis using machine learning classifiers. *Human-centric Computing and Information Sciences, 7*(1), 7-32.

Song, J., Kim, K. T., Lee, B., Kim, S., & Youn, H. Y. (2017). A novel classification approach based on Naïve Bayes for Twitter sentiment analysis. *Transactions on Internet and Information Systems (Seoul)*, *11*(6), 2996–3011.

Sorić, I., Penezić, Z., & Burić, I. (2017). The Big Five personality traits, goal orientations, and academic achievement. *Learning and Individual Differences*, *54*, 126–134. doi:10.1016/j.lindif.2017.01.024

Srivastava, A., Singh, V., & Drall, G. S. (2019). Sentiment Analysis of Twitter Data: A Hybrid Approach. *International Journal of Healthcare Information Systems and Informatics*, *14*(2), 16. doi:10.4018/IJHISI.2019040101

Tan, H. H., Foo, M.-D., & Kwek, M. H. (2017). The effects of customer personality traits on the display of positive emotions. *Academy of Management Journal, 47*(2), 287–296. doi:10.5465/20159579

Vijayaraman, B., & Chellappa, S. (2016). Analysing Customer Churn and Customer Attitude in Telecom Market. *Asian Journal of Research in Social Sciences and Humanities, 6*(6), 362–374. doi:10.5958/2249-7315.2016.00214.8

Weitzl, W., Hutzinger, C., & Einwiller, S. (2018). An empirical study on how webcare mitigates complainants' failure attributions and negative word-of-mouth. *Journal of Computers in Human Behavior, 89*, 316–327. doi:10.1016/j.chb.2018.07.012

This research was previously published in the International Journal of Service Science, Management, Engineering, and Technology (IJSSMET), 11(3); pages 33-46, copyright year 2020 by IGI Publishing (an imprint of IGI Global).

Chapter 93

Sentiment Analysis of Tweets on the COVID–19 Pandemic Using Machine Learning Techniques

Jothikumar R.
🔟 https://orcid.org/0000-0003-0806-7368
Shadan College of Engineering and Technology, India

Vijay Anand R.
Velloe Institute of Technology, India

Visu P.
Velammal Enginerring College, India

Kumar R.
National Institute of Technology, Nagaland, India

Susi S.
Shadan Women's College of Engineering and Technology, India

Kumar K. R.
Adhiyamaan College of Engineering, India

ABSTRACT

Sentiment evaluation alludes to separate the sentiments from the characteristic language and to perceive the mentality about the exact theme. Novel corona infection, a harmful malady ailment, is spreading out of the blue through the quarter, which thought processes respiratory tract diseases that can change from gentle to extraordinary levels. Because of its quick nature of spreading and no conceived cure, it ushered in a vibe of stress and pressure. In this chapter, a framework perusing principally based procedure is utilized to discover the musings of the tweets related to COVID and its effect lockdown. The chapter examines the tweets identified with the hash tags of crown infection and lockdown. The tweets were marked fabulous, negative, or fair, and a posting of classifiers has been utilized to investigate the precision and execution. The classifiers utilized have been under the four models which incorporate decision tree, regression, helpful asset vector framework, and naïve Bayes forms.

DOI: 10.4018/978-1-6684-6303-1.ch093

1. INTRODUCTION

Open thought, emotions and their readiness for the crisis conditions like pandemic is ordinarily fore-warned by method of aptitude of the print media, television, net posts, exchange sheets, interpersonal interaction destinations, thus forth Richardson, P et al (2020). Public wellness observing comprises of the wellness observation, following wellbeing dangers, occasional plague flare-ups and various crises consequently to restrict the risk of the famous open wellness. Generally wellbeing related overviews have been taken to secure sentiments of individuals on a wellness crisis. Celikyilmaz, A. (2010) The advancement of web and online life is an amazing flexibly for the wellbeing related information and cure data of the customary open which come to be named as 'Infodemiology'. Ji, X., Chun, S. A., et al (2016) Twitter, a smaller scale running a blog web page allows in customers to extent their considerations and feelings in a type of a message viewed as tweets, Liang, P. W., & Dai, B. R. (2013). The customers in this internet-based life webpage keeps up on developing and as of now the total vivacious clients are just about 330 million. Khatua, A., & Khatua, A. (2016) With this large assortment of clients, twitter has end up being a main gracefully for creating measurements which whenever examined, bears valuable bits of knowledge. Slant correlation and sentiment mining on twitter realities has risen path back in the beforehand years twitter. Piryani, R., et al (2017) A destructive malady is a sickness which spreads dur-ing the nations and affect a gigantic populace. Infirmity observation and early discovery may likewise be one of the significant bundles of e-wellbeing realities Li, L., Jin, X., et al (2012). Internet based life comprehensive of twitter can give crucial data comprising of open conversations on a topic alongside medical problems with longitudinal records which prompts expectation of flare-ups of scourges. Alessa, A., & Faezipour, M. (2018) Social media customers are sharing their wellness records and their assump-tions that may need to effectively go about as a machine for separating the general popular feeling on pandemic. Russell, C. D., et al (2020) the natural open gratefulness at the hour of pandemic flare-up is generally alluded to in the twitter and tweets goes about as an unmistakable flexibly of records in perusing the notion of the clients. Girotra, M., et al (2013) Twitter goes about as a viable device to get right of passage to open practices over pandemics, surveying the degrees of pandemic, content material exchange on infection episode issue reconnaissance and notion assessment/sentiment mining. Afrati, F. et al (2004) Corona Virus infirmity (COVID-19) is an irresistible medical issue realized by method of a recently discovered Corona infection. The flare-up spreads so quick from the tainted character to the diverse by method of bead sullying, surface contacts and has made a frenzy and crisis in numerous universal areas globally Blendon, R. J., et al (2003). Type procedures in data mining such Naïve Bayes, decision tree as are utilized to unharness the feelings of the clients as a segment of pandemic episode Taboada, M., et al (2011).

The Pediatric and geriatric immunity network mobile computational model for COVID-19 was pro-posed by the authors Mei, Q., et al (2007). The objective of the proposed methodology uses IoT devices for preventing the COVID-19. The IoT devices and sensors were used for data collection from the remote places Thelwall, M. (2010). The collected data was used by the machine learning algorithms to analyze and predict the chance of COVID-19 and prevention measures can be followed Priya, K. B., et al (2020).

The concept of Monitoring and sensing COVID-19 symptoms as a precaution using electronic wearable devices was proposed. The objective of this work is to observe and sense the different types of COVID-19 symptoms. This research has explained the different stages of COVID-19 along with the symptoms and the various mechanisms to observe the progress of this disease by many parameters. Risk aspects of the disease are sensibly analysed and equated with test results Josephine, M. S., (2020).

2. METHODOLGY USED

The dataset is taken and processed by using the above-mentioned algorithms. The overall process includes the data mining knowledge discovery steps. It needs preprocessing and cleansing of data before doing the process. These include lacking of attribute values having errors or outliers which do not belong to the given values. There are also possibilities of error in values or codes or names. The above said abnormalities are corrected before the record is taken for training the system. This process is referred to as data cleaning. The missing values in record can be either filled by studying the relevant records or can be removed if it's below 5%. The architecture of Tweets classification is shown in Fig 1.

Figure 1. Architecture of tweets classification

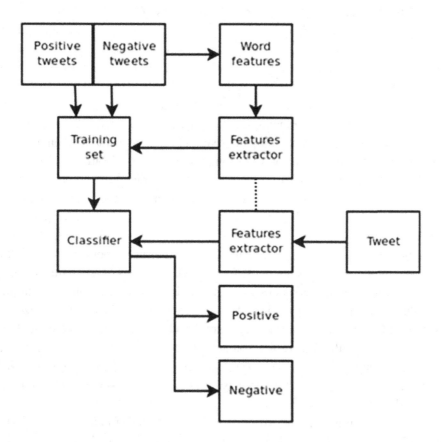

2.1 Collection of Tweets

We have aggregated our insights from Kaggle.com which contains nearly39455 tweets at the various hash labels identified with the sickness. Tweets extracted from the link given as follows:

https://www.kaggle.com/skylord/covid19-tweets.

Our work has been conceived in parts along with analyzing the notion of the COVID-19 related tweets and Public discernment at the lockdown or check in time executed for halting the unfurl of COVID-19. Our technique is to perform slant investigation on each tweet in the wake of cleaning and pre-preparing them.

2.2 Processing of Tweets

The section which contains the content of the tweet was taken for the examination. The superfluous segments were dropped and just the section containing the content of the tweets were put away in a csv document. The content of the tweet has numerous commotions, for example, username labels, hash labels, URLs and accentuations. The hash labels and other undesirable characters were expelled and supplanted with a clear space. Tokenization and stemming has been applied on the tweets and the English stop words have been expelled as a procedure on Natural Language Processing.

The cleaned tweet is utilized to examine and set the slant scores utilizing the bundle SentiWordNet in python which is solely utilized for supposition mining. The POS labeled words were utilized to set the positive and negative scores to the tweets. The NLTK toolbox in python is utilized for the procedure which is parting the tweets into important words and giving the objective scores for each word. The given document has been added with a section comprise of the notion scores of the tweet, for example, 0, 1 and - 1 under the arrangements negative, positive and impartial. Utilizing it, a well-known slant dictionary, the tweets were marked and the outcomes are appeared. The set of tweets used are listed as follows and shown in Fig 2.

Tweets Extracted : 43256
Tweets identified with sentiments : 42612
Classified Tweets
Positive Tweets : 10245
Negative Tweets : 13415
Neutral Tweets : 18952

Figure 2. Sentimental Classification of tweets

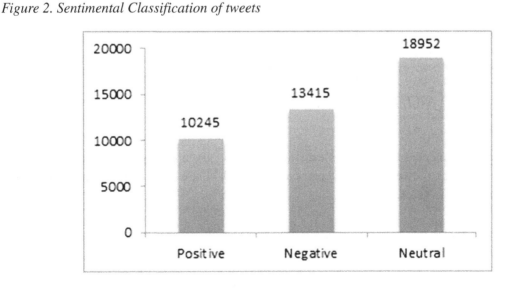

2.3 Analysis of Tweets

The total tweets are taken and splitted into various divisions. It includes train tweets and test tweets. Based on train tweets the model is designed and system is trained. The test data is validated based on trained model. Based on the analysis we come to an conclusion whether the model is fit or not. The validation results show the trained model efficiency. The percentage of tweets taken for validation differs from person to person. The ration of classification taken for our research is 80:20. Around 80% of data is taken as training data and remaining 20% of data is used for testing and validation purpose. The accuracy results based on the classification of tweets used for training and testing. The processing of data classification plays a major role in determining the performance of the algorithms used for prediction purposes

2.4 Performance Prediction by Classifiers

The unigram model is used to evaluate the performance of classifier after classification of the tweets. The tweets are processed by each of the classifier individually and listed out for validation purposes. Each of the validation is considered at various levels of classification. The final value detests the performance of different classifier. Four different algorithms are used for the tweets classification. The performance of the classifier is evaluated with time taken for classification and cross validation. The algorithm along with the type of classifier chosen for classification of tweets is listed as follows:

2.4.1 XG Boost

$$\hat{y}_i = \sum_{k=1}^{K} f_k(x_i), f_k \in F \tag{1}$$

This classification model is an ensemble approach that uses tree structure in which each step word is taken as attribute and resulting tweets are taken or considered as outcome. It is one of the models that is validated for weaker classification where data labels must be known to get a clear outcome.

The loss function retrieved at the end of the classifier can be further reduced by using the following equation.

$$L(\Phi) = \sum_i l\left(\hat{y}_i, y_i\right) + \sum \Omega(f_k) \text{ where } \Omega(f) = \gamma T + \frac{1}{2}\lambda \|w\|^2 \tag{2}$$

This classifier implemented from sklearn.ensemble which is given out by scikit-learn. The model supports the classification of tweets into different categories which are substantially classified to positive, negative and neutral.

2.4.2 Maximum Entropy

The primary thought here is, to pick the major uniform probabilistic model which amplifies the value of entropy, considering the imperatives. In contrast to other classifiers, it doesn't expect that highlights are restrictively free of one another. Along these lines, we can include highlights like bigrams without agonizing over component cover. In a twofold grouping issue as the one we are tending to, it is equivalent to utilizing Logistic Regression to discover dispersion over the classes.

$$P_{ME}(c \mid d, \lambda) = \frac{\exp\left[\sum_i \lambda_i f_i(c,d)\right]}{\sum_{c'} \exp\left[\sum_i \lambda_i f_i(c,d)\right]} \tag{3}$$

2.4.3 Support Vector Machine

It is a non-probabilistic binary linear classifier. It considers two coordinates x and y in which x is considered to be the vector denoting the features and y to be the class representation. After this identification of values, hyperplane is found out which divides with min and max value. Representation of hyperplane is stated as w.x-b=0. Classifier does this process is SVC classifier. The margin of hyperplane is maximized using the equation given below:

$$\max_{w,\gamma} \gamma, \text{ s.t. } \forall i, \gamma \le y_i(w \cdot x_i + b) \tag{4}$$

2.4.4 Naïve Bayes

$$\hat{c} = \arg\max_c P(c \mid t)$$

$$P(c \mid t) \propto P(c)\prod_{i=1}^{n} P(f_i \mid c) \tag{5}$$

The two different classifier supported through Naïve Bayes are Bernoulli Classifier and MultinomialNB Classifier. This can be used for text classification, in which c represents class that is assigned to tweet t.

The MultinomialNB Classifier is implemented using the package sklearn. naive Bayes from the scikitlearn. The Laplace method is used where α is represented as smoothing parameter that can set a default value to be 1. The sparse vector representation is used for classification and classified according to the features of frequency and presence. Adding to the results, bigram features make the accuracy to be improved.

3. EXPERIMENTAL RESULTS

Through different classifiers the experiments are performed. We take 10% of data for validation purpose from the dataset classified for training dataset that are used to check overfitting. Considering the above classifiers which are taken for experimenting, XGBoost, Maximum Entropy, SVM and Naïve Bayes sparse vector representation is used for tweets. The accuracy are checked out with various cross validation count. The same is implemented in python language by utilizing the packages available for each of the classification algorithm. The extractions of tweets are retrieved using the code:

Extracting tweets

```
ipfile = []
    with open(db,'rb') as csvfile:
        lineReader = csv.reader(csvfile,delimiter=',', quotechar="\"")
        for row in lineReader:
            ipfile.append({"tweet_id":row[2], "label":row[1], "topic":row[0]})
    rate_limit = 190
    sleep_time = 900/190
for tweet in infile:
        try:
            st = twitter_api.GetStatus(tweet["tweet_id"])
            print("fetched tweet" + st.text)
            tweet["text"] = status.text
            tds.append(tweet)
            time.sleep(sleep_time)
        except:
            continue
```

3.1 N-gram Model

The sparse vector representation is used here considering unigram, bigram and trigram along with vectorization. The frequency term is considered and referred as inverse document frequencies. It refereed as process of converting the text data into numerical form. These classifiers are estimated forming the three different frequencies as the base. The parameters are accuracy and time taken as parameters. It is shown in Table 1.

After attaining the classifier accuracy, n-gram analysis is carried out for unigram, bigram and trigram frequencies. Each of the accuracy values are validated before and after considering the stop words is shown in Table 2.

The MultinomialNB Classifier gives out accuracy of 69.12% which can be increased to 79.68% by adding bigram features. The SVC classifier is implemented using sklearn package. The term C is set to default value 0.1. The penalty parameter is represented as C, which is considered as error term. The objective function misclassification is considered. This SVC is executed using both unigram and bigram. Both the frequency and presence features are considered. The accuracy of 83.29% is achieved with both unigram and bigram features. The results are classified as train, test and validation data with the count of tweets is shown in Table 3.

Table 1. Classification Accuracy of Classifier

Classifier	Accuracy	Time Taken	Cross validation	Accuracy	Time Taken	Cross validation
	Cross fold - 15			Cross fold - 25		
XGBoost classifier	73.25%	4.0	3.5	74.75%	4.0	3.0
Maximum Entropy Classifier	84.3%	5.0	6.0	85.39%	6.0	5.0
SVC classifier	83.29%	2.0	8.0	85.67%	2.0	8.0
Multinomial NB classifier	67.24%	7.0	1.5	69.12%	8.0	1.5

Table 2. Validation of ngram Model

Model Used	Validation result – Count of features	Accuracy Score
Unigram – No Stop words	50000	81.92%
Unigram - Stop Words	20000	85.93%
Bigram - Stop Words	80000	83.91%
Trigram - Stop Words	90000	82.97%

Table 3. Classification of dataset

Dataset	Total tweets	Positive	Negative
Training set	39764	28.65%	49.32%
Validation set	2236	26.12%	43.09%
Test set	2236	27.32%	48.94%

The confusion Matrix is calculated through Naïve Bayes. The matrix is formed by calculating the total positive mapped with the predicted positive tweets. The variation in these values is termed to be misclassification rate. That is confusion matrix is shown in Table 4.

Table 4. Confusion Matrix

Confusion Matrix	Predicted Negative	Predicted Positive
Negative	845	42
Positive	102	337

3.2 Results, Discussion and Performance Analysis

Our model investigations on two classes, for example, "Positive" and "Negative". The exhibition measurements we have utilized is disarray lattice and order report. The disarray lattice speaks to Tp, Tn,

Fp and Fn which are True positive, True negative, False positive and False Negative. The Fn and Fp are considered as the mistakes. Accuracy uncovers the extent of right positive forecasts of the classifier and Recall uncovers the right positive expectations. The F1 measure is utilized to investigate how the accuracy and review performs with the order. The F1 score is 0.79 for 'negative' and 0.83 for 'positive' conclusion classifiers as shown in Table 5.

Precision = Tp/(Tp+Fp)

Recall = Tp/(Tp+Fn)

Table 5. Performance Analysis

	Precision	Recall	F1-score	Support
Negative	0.79	0.93	0.89	947
Positive	0.83	0.71	0.69	433
Average weighted mean	0.86	0.82	0.82	1432

4. CONCLUSION

For this research, tweet with the hash tags such as #lockdown, #covid, #corona, #lockdowncorona, #stay-home, #staysafe are considered. The total tweets are considered with these come around nearly 10245. These are considered as positive tweets and are further classified by using different classifiers. Hence by using machine learning algorithms the sentimental classification of tweets is carried out. As per the standard these tweets are extracted, preprocessed by considering retweets, irrelevant, emoticons etc., by using corpus-based standards. Further they are labeled as positive, negative and neutral tweets. The classifiers are used to analyze for different cross fold values. By using n-gram analysis model they are validated and measured by using precision and recall measures. The highest accuracy attained through this process seems to be 85.67%. The total consideration is said to be positive among the entire tweets. In Future, this research may be considered for analysis using deep learning algorithms for better accuracy.

REFERENCES

Afrati, F., Gionis, A., & Mannila, H. (2004, August). Approximating a collection of frequent sets. In *Proceedings of the tenth ACM SIGKDD international conference on Knowledge discovery and data mining* (pp. 12-19). ACM.

Alessa, A., & Faezipour, M. (2018, July). Tweet classification using sentiment analysis features and TF-IDF weighting for improved flu trend detection. In *International Conference on Machine Learning and Data Mining in Pattern Recognition* (pp. 174-186). Springer. 10.1007/978-3-319-96136-1_15

Blendon, R. J., Benson, J. M., Desroches, C. M., & Weldon, K. J. (2003). Using opinion surveys to track the public's response to a bioterrorist attack. *Journal of Health Communication*, *8*(sup1, S1), 83–92. doi:10.1080/713851964 PMID:14692573

Celikyilmaz, A., Hakkani-Tür, D., & Feng, J. (2010, December). *Probabilistic model-based sentiment analysis of twitter messages. In 2010 IEEE Spoken Language Technology Workshop*. IEEE.

Girotra, M., Nagpal, K., Minocha, S., & Sharma, N. (2013). Comparative survey on association rule mining algorithms. *International Journal of Computers and Applications*, *84*(10).

Ji, X., Chun, S. A., & Geller, J. (2016). Knowledge-based tweet classification for disease sentiment monitoring. In *Sentiment Analysis and Ontology Engineering* (pp. 425–454). Springer. doi:10.1007/978-3-319-30319-2_17

Josephine, M. S., Lakshmanan, L., Nair, R. R., Visu, P., Ganesan, R., & Jothikumar, R. (2020). Monitoring and sensing COVID-19 symptoms as a precaution using electronic wearable devices. *International Journal of Pervasive Computing and Communications*.

Khatua, A., & Khatua, A. (2016, September). Immediate and long-term effects of 2016 Zika Outbreak: A Twitter-based study. In *2016 IEEE 18th International Conference on e-Health Networking, Applications and Services (Healthcom)* (pp. 1-6). IEEE.

Li, L., Jin, X., Pan, S. J., & Sun, J. T. (2012, August). Multi-domain active learning for text classification. In *Proceedings of the 18th ACM SIGKDD international conference on Knowledge discovery and data mining* (pp. 1086-1094). 10.1145/2339530.2339701

Liang, P. W., & Dai, B. R. (2013, June). Opinion mining on social media data. In *2013 IEEE 14th international conference on mobile data management* (Vol. 2, pp. 91-96). IEEE. 10.1109/MDM.2013.73

Mei, Q., Ling, X., Wondra, M., Su, H., & Zhai, C. (2007, May). Topic sentiment mixture: modeling facets and opinions in weblogs. In *Proceedings of the 16th international conference on World Wide Web* (pp. 171-180). 10.1145/1242572.1242596

Piryani, R., Madhavi, D., & Singh, V. K. (2017). Analytical mapping of opinion mining and sentiment analysis research during 2000–2015. *Information Processing & Management*, *53*(1), 122–150. doi:10.1016/j.ipm.2016.07.001

. Priya, K. B., Rajendran, P., Kumar, S., Prabhu, J., Rajendran, S., Kumar, P. J., & Jothikumar, R. (2020). Pediatric and geriatric immunity network mobile computational model for COVID-19. *International Journal of Pervasive Computing and Communications*.

Richardson, P., Griffin, I., Tucker, C., Smith, D., Oechsle, O., Phelan, A., & Stebbing, J. (2020). Baricitinib as potential treatment for 2019-nCoV acute respiratory disease. *Lancet*, *395*(10223), e30–e31. doi:10.1016/S0140-6736(20)30304-4 PMID:32032529

Russell, C. D., Millar, J. E., & Baillie, J. K. (2020). Clinical evidence does not support corticosteroid treatment for 2019-nCoV lung injury. *Lancet*, *395*(10223), 473–475. doi:10.1016/S0140-6736(20)30317-2 PMID:32043983

Taboada, M., Brooke, J., Tofiloski, M., Voll, K., & Stede, M. (2011). Lexicon-based methods for sentiment analysis. *Computational Linguistics*, *37*(2), 267–307. doi:10.1162/COLI_a_00049

Thelwall, M. (2010). Emotion homophily in social network site messages. *First Monday*, *15*(4). Advance online publication. doi:10.5210/fm.v15i4.2897

This research was previously published in the Handbook of Research on Innovations and Applications of AI, IoT, and Cognitive Technologies; pages 310-320, copyright year 2021 by Engineering Science Reference (an imprint of IGI Global).

Chapter 94
Coronavirus Pandemic (COVID–19):
Emotional Toll Analysis on Twitter

Jalal S. Alowibdi
University of Jeddah, Saudi Arabia

Abdulrahman A. Alshdadi
University of Jeddah, Saudi Arabia

Ali Daud
University of Jeddah, Saudi Arabia

Mohamed M. Dessouky
University of Jeddah, Saudi Arabia

Essa Ali Alhazmi
Jazan University, Saudi Arabia

ABSTRACT

People are afraid about COVID-19 and are actively talking about it on social media platforms such as Twitter. People are showing their emotions openly in their tweets on Twitter. It's very important to perform sentiment analysis on these tweets for finding COVID-19's impact on people's lives. Natural language processing, textual processing, computational linguists, and biometrics are applied to perform sentiment analysis to identify and extract the emotions. In this work, sentiment analysis is carried out on a large Twitter dataset of English tweets. Ten emotional themes are investigated. Experimental results show that COVID-19 has spread fear/anxiety, gratitude, happiness and hope, and other mixed emotions among people for different reasons. Specifically, it is observed that positive news from top officials like Trump of chloroquine as cure to COVID-19 has suddenly lowered fear in sentiment, and happiness, gratitude, and hope started to rise. But, once FDA said, chloroquine is not effective cure, fear again started to rise.

DOI: 10.4018/978-1-6684-6303-1.ch094

1. INTRODUCTION

On Dec. 12th 2019, in Wuhan City, Hubei Province, China, the Wuhan Municipal Health Commission (WMHC) reported 27 individuals infected by a new coronavirus. The new coronavirus designated initially as 2019-novel coronavirus (2019-nCoV), and subsequently Coronavirus Disease 2019 (COVID-19) by the World Health Organization (WHO). The same symptoms had been suffered by the patients, such as hard breathing, dry cough, and high body temperature. These symptoms made the Centers for Disease Control and Prevention (CDC) to denominate this disease as "severe acute respiratory syndrome coronavirus 2" or SARS-CoV-2. Most cases from the primary group has epidemiological connections with a market of living animal in Wuhan. The virus that causes the pneumonia was concatenated and it was discovered that it is a one of beta-coronavirus family and extremely identical to SARS-like BAT coronaviruses bat-SL-CoVZC45 and bat-SL-CoVZXC21 with 88% similarity, 79.5% homology with SARS, and 50% with MERS (Lu et al., 2020; Wu et al., 2020). An early research has been proceeded in January 2020 stated that among 41 patients (with average age nearly 49 years), positive for COVID-19 infection, half of them have chronic diseases, including diabetes 20%, cardiovascular disease 15%, and hypertension 15%. The symptoms appear in them were at most high body temperature 98%, cough 76%, and tiredness 44%. The COVID-19 severe complications in such patients included respiratory distress syndrome 29%, RNAaemia 15%, acute cardiac injury 12%, and other secondary infections. Of the total infected patients, 32% were assumed to be accepted to Intensive Care Unit (ICU). The death rate was 15% by far (Bastola et al., 2020).

Social media provides very easy and useful means of communication between people, where they share information and exchange opinions and show their sentiments on social problems. Whole world in connected that's why people from different nations, cultures and beliefs can communicate. E.g. people may share their problems directly to the ministry of health or foreign affairs by using tweets as a medium. Social media platforms these days provide us with a great opportunity to perform analytics about any evert, such as, football world cup, launch of new technology product, opinion of people on educational policies, political events, tsunamis, earthquakes and spread of diseases, etc. Most of the information on social media platforms is unstructured and unmanageable. Information gathering on social media platforms is very fast that it results a trouble of "Social Media information overload" (Bright et al., 2015; Amjad et al., 2020) and difficulties and confront regarding information processing and analytics (Schuller et al., 2015; Amjad et al., 2020).

Social media platform information is processed and analyzed for the use by public sector organizations, news agencies, government officials, political leaders and parties due to presence of public emotions and opinion in that data. E.g. new agencies select topics of talk shows based on the hashtag trends on twitter and government revise their policies based on people opinion and sentiments. In this time of COVID-19, its really very important to process information available on the social platforms specifically twitter and convert it into knowledge to help government officials take timely decisions. Through effective use of social media analytics, government may make policies and take decisions for people in a more authoritative way (WeGov, 2016; Amjad et al., 2020).

Faces are the most applicable way to express different emotions. Words also is another way to represent the emotions. The emotions such as happiness indicates joyful and cheerful, sadness emotion represents dismal or scream and anger represents shout and ebullition, and so on (Saif et al., 2013; Amjad et al., 2020). Several tasks require automatic emotions' recognition such as (Saif et al., 2013): (a) Directing the relations to use the suitable behavior due to the emotion (such as displeasure, contentment, relief, sorrow, faith, expectancy, or indignation). (b) Monitoring emotions related to politicians, cinema, goods, cities, and other sides. (c) Improving developed search approaches that characterize among several emotions related to the output such as users perhaps look for hospitals, or doctors who has person confidence. (d) Establishing speech methods which reply correctly to various sentimental events of the people such as emotion-aware games. (e) Investigating smart tutoring systems which achieve the sentimental event of the user for better active learning. (f) Defining the hazard of iteration trials by analyzing the reasons of the suicide. (g) Realizing how genders connect in work-place and how they use the private emails. (h) Helping in writing several texts such as documents and e-mails to express the needed emotion. (i) Describing the sentiment in books or novels. (j) Specifying the emotions meant by the newspaper headline. (k) Re-arranging the answers and information of the questions or forums. (l) Revealing the usage of the emotion-bearing-words by persons and metaphors to encourage the others about one action. (m) Improving several text-to-speech algorithms. (n) Improving assistive robots that are sensitive to human sentiment.

Sentiments widespread among people, and several are natural. People debate in all field of life and could be with other cultures that they don't know how to contact. This is because all people have the same facial expressions, but there is a basic role played by language or culture in representing the emotions and how they express the facial expression.

This study proposes sentiment analysis method to analyze the emotions about COVID-19 on twitter social media. It's a challenging task to understand the dynamics of tweets as they are done by people from different demographic locations, races and religions. In start, the effective hashtags, such as corona, coronavirus, novel coronavirus, pandemic, etc. are specified to study the COVID-19 related sentiments. Then tweets related to these thirty hashtags are collected and stored in a large database of total 19,040,412 tweets, 4,635,074 users with total 355,555,573 engagements. Standard preprocessing is performed by lowercasing the tweet words, stemming and removing stops words. The tweets were in different languages, for ease of purpose we selected only English language tweets. Tweets emojis are also considered. All tweets are assigned to 10 emotions (fear/anxiety, gratitude, empathy, hope, happiness, depression/sadness, frustration/anger, shame/guilt/blame, loneliness, disgust) based on the highest percentage similarity with that emotion. Additionally, we have also calculated the overall sentiments for large set of collected tweets. Our salient contributions are as follows.

- Specification of 4 hashtags related to COVID-19 twitter which are: #COVID19, #COVID-19, #Covid_19 and #Corona
- Collection of large number of total 19,040,412 tweets, 4,635,074 users with total 355,555,573 engagements
- Classification of collected tweets in ten emotional themes
- Sentiment analysis of COVID-19 selected tweets to analyze ten emotions
- Consideration of emojis for all ten emotions analyzed
- Providing reasoning for high peaks through work cloud analysis

This paper is organized as following. Section 2, illustrates the related work of the sentiment analysis and emotions. Section 3, shows the proposed approach and all steps in details. Section 4, presents the results of analysis of emotions. Next, section 5, discusses the results. Last section 6, highlights this research work conclusions and future endeavors.

2. RELATED WORK

Social network platform Twitter has been increasingly used with more than 250 million users per month specially for the information related to public health (Scanfeld et al., 2010). Several published models had used and analyzed the Twitter data in projecting the propagation of influenza and other infectious news on time (Chorianopoulos et al., 2016). Several authors, in 2009, experimented the rapid concern with Influenza A news. They analyzed the activity of the disease and the efforts to stop the spread of it using several keywords (Signorini et al., 2011). Twitter had been utilized in 2014 during the spread of Ebola virus. The users had followed the outbreaks during 24 hours for any news of health information (Househ, 2016). The same thing had been done in 2015 with the spread of MERS. The Twitter at this time became as a monitoring method for the spread of the disease (Shin et al., 2016). Also, at the period of the spread of the epidemic Zika virus, different studies had been applied on Twitter on the behavior of the travel which was an important (Daughton et al., 2019).

Sentiment analysis is known as the procedure that automates mining of situations, thought, judgements and feelings from written words, spoken sentences, tweets and datasets origin from Natural Language Processing (NLP). Emotional analysis includes categorizing thoughts in text to classes such as "positive", "negative", and "neutral". It's may be known by personality analyzation, opinion mining, and evaluation extraction (Vishal et al., 2016).

Other research (Robert et al., 2019) made the sentiment analysis for inflammatory bowel disease. They depended on an unsupervised machine learning technique to recognize the content of 51,591 tweets from the Crohn's & Colitis Foundation Community Forum. They utilized the latent Dirichlet Allocation (LDA) algorithm to specify subjects in posts of different sentimental theme. They extracted 9 emotions (Gratitude, Scare, Sympathy, Outrage, Hope, Joy, Shame, Sorrow, and Loneliness).

This area is very important but there is a research gap with COVID-19. There are a few researches that depends on the emotional analysis of Indians after the full closure declaration had been done. They utilized twitter to gauge feelings of Indians towards the lockdown. They extract the tweets for only two hashtags (#IndiaLockdown and #IndiafightsCorona) for only three days (from Mar 25th to Mar 28th, 2020) with only 24,000 tweets (Gopalkrishna et al., 2020).

The authors in (Karishma et al., 2020) gather flowing data by the Twitter API from Mar 1st, 2020 to Mar 17th, 2020. They analyzed the social sentiment related to the policies such as "#socialdistancing" and "#workfromhome". They surveyed the obstacle of wrong information on social media and proposed an algorithm to specify wrong information from Twitter content. Their collected dataset contains 8.1M tweets but the English tweets was 4.7M. They only classify the tweets as positive or negative. They didn't make sentiment analysis on emotions.

In (Leonard et al., 2020), the authors survey the appearance of Sino-phobic attitude on the internet through the beginning of the new coronavirus pandemic. They collected two Twitter and /pol/ databases for nearly five months and proposed an algorithm to detect is there an increase about Sino-phobic or not. They found that the new coronavirus leads to the increase of the Sino-phobic on the internet and the spread of Sino-phobic posts is a cross-platform events. Also, they characterized the development of Sino-phobic defamation on both datasets. At last, they found variations in the posts in which posts attached to Chinese persons are used on the internet before and after the spread of the new coronavirus: on Twitter, there are upbraiding to China for this pandemic, but on /pol/ there are other Sino-phobic calumnies.

There are several other proposed algorithms that basically depends on emotions. In (Johnson-Laird et al., 1989), the authors proposed that there are only five basic emotions which are (joy, sorrow, terror, outrage, and disgust) and they analyzed the data around only these five emotions and corresponding verbs. In (Ekman, 1992), authors increased the analyzed emotions to six basic emotions: happiness, sorrow, outrage, terror, disgust, and surprise. In (Plutchik, 1994), authors expand the analyzed emotions to eight basic emotions which composed of the previous six and they added two emotions which are faith and anticipation.

There is also another research collected tweets keywords with respect to the new coronavirus and calculated number of hashtags due to contagion protection exercises, vaccination, and elemental fanaticism (Richard et al., 2020). They evaluated only 126,049 tweets from 53,196 users with engagements 114,635 replies, 1,248,118 retweets, and 1,680,253 likes. They extracted several keywords deo to the new coronavirus to find the related tweets during only two weeks from January 14th to 28th, 2020 by twitter API. They extracted only 6 emotions (outrage, disgust, sorrow, happiness, terror, or surprise). This proposed algorithm had different drawbacks. First, they didn't use a list of keywords. Second, they collected and analyzed very little number of all tweets. Finally, they collected the tweets at very little period only two weeks and before the high spread of the disease globally (Richard et al., 2020).

Existing work on COVID-19 lack in following things, which have motivated us to do this work.

- Limited number of tweets
- Limited number of hashtags
- Basic sentiment analysis in only positive, negative or neutral sentiments and ignored emotions detailed sentiment analysis
- Lower number of emotions sentiment analysis is performed up to 6 emotions
- Emojis are totally not considered

In this work, a large number of tweets are considered with thirty hashtags. And ten emotions sentiment analysis is performed with both textual content and emojis.

3. COVID-19 EMOTIONAL TOLL ANALYSIS APPROACH

The proposed approach for sentiment analysis of emotional themes in this research work is composed of following steps, which are presented in Figure 1. It starts by specifying Hashtags on Twitter to analyze the people's sentiments towards COVID-19. The hashtags selected are related to COVID-19, such as corona, coronavirus, stay home, lockdown, pandemic and other provided in Table 1 and Table 2. Subsequently, all tweets that are related to the hashtags were collected in and stored in database. All collected tweets have several languages, the proposed technique is focused on to collect only the tweets in English language. Later, preprocessing step is performed, which is aimed at to remove all unrelated contents from the tweets. After this step, each tweet was converted into some of keywords and some of emojis. The next step is assigning these keywords and emojis to one of basic 10 emotions. In next step, the percentage of each emotion in each tweet is calculated. Subsequently, each tweet was assigned to the related emotion with highest percentage. The final step was about getting the overall sentiment of all the collected tweets. The steps adopted in this research work are further elaborated in the following subsections.

Figure 1. COVID-19 Emotional Analysis approach

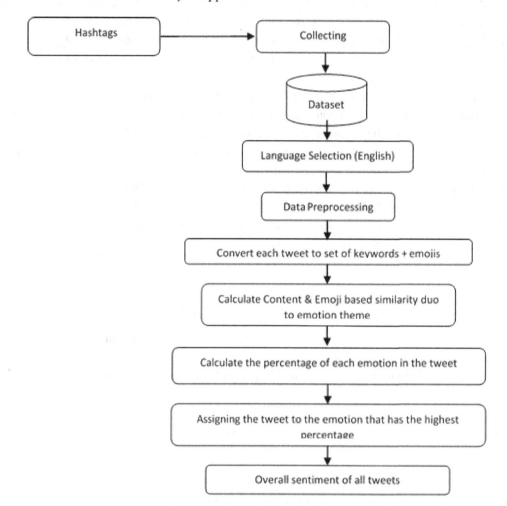

3.1 Hashtags

The first step in the proposed approach is specifying the hashtags related to COVID-19, for which the data is collected from twitter. There were several hashtags which are in several languages specially in English and other several languages, such as, Arabic, Spanish, French, German, Dutch, Italian, Hindi, Turkey which are #covid19, #covid_19, #covid-19, #corona, etc. The proposed approach concentrated on only English language and neglected all other languages. First, all hashtags that are related to the COVID-19 are collected using Twitter API. The sources of the collected tweets are derived from top thirty collected hashtags for all languages, which are presented in Table 1, with their number of repetitions. Also, top thirty English hashtags, with their number of repetitions, which are presented in Table 2.

Figure 2 illustrates the distribution of these languages, which clearly shows that English language is the dominating language in our collected tweets.

Table 1. Top 20 all languages hashtags and unique number of repetitions

Hashtag name	No. of repetition
'#covid19'	4099884
'#covid_19'	3547664
'#covid-19'	2541303
'#coronavirus'	2007005
'#corona'	1855508
'#covid2019'	270112
'#coronaviruspandemic'	247179
'#stayhome'	225122
'#covid'	212942
'#stayathome'	195039
'#coronavirusoutbreak'	177338
'#coronavirusupdate'	166235
'#quedateencasa'	150514
'#lockdown'	145431
'#socialdistancing'	113023
'#yomequedoencasa'	104607
'#staysafe'	87105
'#coronaoutbreak'	85668
'#quarantine'	84771
'#pandemic'	83926

Figure 2. Top languages distribution on the collected dataset

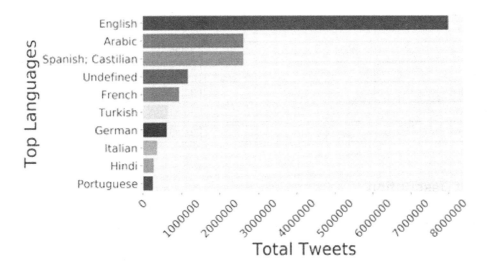

Table 2. Top 30 English hashtags and unique number of repetitions tweets

Hashtag name	No. of repetition
'#covid19'	2393798
'#covid_19'	1352520
'#covid-19'	1151756
'#coronavirus'	1000259
'#corona'	579726
'#coronaviruspandemic'	158713
'#stayhome'	136079
'#coronavirusoutbreak'	129121
'#covid'	112881
'#covid2019'	107165
'#stayathome'	101422
'#coronavirusupdate'	96297
'#lockdown'	92261
'#socialdistancing'	90937
'#pandemic'	71704
'#quarantine'	64405
'#staysafe'	63052
'#coronaoutbreak'	59175
'#coronavirusupdates'	51920
'#china'	47332
'#stayhomesavelives'	47081
'#trump'	42609
'#virus'	37408
'#covid19pandemic'	35652
'#coronavirususa'	32931
'#coronacrisis'	32337
'#quarantinelife'	31846
'#coronavirusindia'	30733
'#flattenthecurve'	30087
'#indiafightscorona'	28498

3.2 Dataset Description

All tweets that are related to the specified hashtags of COVID-19 were collected. Top 4 hashtags, such as, #COVID19, #COVID_19, #COVID-19 and #Corona are used in experiments to collect whole dataset. Twitter Application Program Interface (API) is used for collecting tweets. All collected tweets were stored in a database in order to perform the sentiment analysis on ten emotional themes. Number of collected tweets was more than 19 Million unique tweets and stored in nearly 500 Gigabytes. The data had been collected from Feb 29th, 2020 to May 1st, 2020. Table 3 shows the detailed description of the collected data.

Figure 3 shows the cumulative distribution function on the number of tweets per users. The vast majority of users (about 93%) posted less than 10 tweets including 56% of them tweeted once. In contrast, one user has tweeted 43,574 tweets during the observation period. Users less than 400 users of 4,635,074 users were highly active and published more than 1000 tweets. CDF distribution reflects the normal users' interactions in Twitter (Mendoza et al., 2010; Abel et al., 2011; Abel et al., 2011).

Table 3. Collected dataset specifications

Data description	Number of collected data
Total tweets	19,040,412
Total users	4,635,074
Total engagements • Total retweets • Total favorites • Total replies	355,555,573 • 91,973,323 • 223,418,558 • 21,123,280
Total hashtags	63,901,327
Total mentions	12,171,925
Total reply to	2403596
Total links	6228619
Total emojis	8922895
Total pictures	6504788
Total videos	1392449

Figure 3. The cumulative distribution function (CDF) of total tweets in English per users during the COVID-19

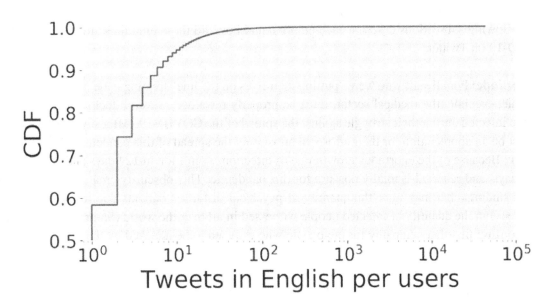

3.3 Data Preprocessing

Data Preprocessing is a technique used to clean text. Standard textual data preprocessing is applied, such as, all uppercase text is converted to lowercase for exact matchings, then stops words are removed (delete all words which has no effect on emotions' meanings) from dataset to get clear meaning from tweets, and stemming is performed to trim the words to their roots words for precise matching of words. Also, cleaning of text from nonemotionally contents, like usernames, photos, hashtags, URLs, and punctuation marks is carried out. This process is known as tagging which means signing nonemotionally content in a tweet which haven't any effect on the tweet emotion. This technique differs in kind and number. For example, a URL link could be exchanged with a URL tag, the username that shown after the character "@" in Twitter had been known as username and the word that shown next a hash "#" and not connected to the subject was labeled with hashtag. Also, Twitter users utilize characters like "1" and "12" to represent their feelings these sentimental express worthy information to the emotions. So, to observe the sentiment from the emotions they had been labeled as well. For instance, a feeling is labeled as joy if the person typed symbols: "12", ":')" and labeled as unhappy if the person typed symbols: "1", ":'(". Emotions tags were useful and affective in the classifying process since they hold a sentiment.

3.4 Defining Ten Emotions With Words and Emojis

In this research work, following ten basic emotions are considered which are: Gratitude, Anxiety/fear, Empathy, Frustration/anger, Hope, Happiness, Depression/sadness, Shame/guilt, Loneliness, and disgust. In the following, each emotion used to analyze sentiments is described.

A list of basic emotions had been manually discovered and collected which present the feelings of the patients, relatives and other surroundings. All of these collected emotions based on the estimation of the psychiatry literature. All keywords that best express these collected emotions had been also gathered by certified emotional libraries such as NRC Emotion Lexicon (Mohammad et al. 2013), WordNet (Lin, 1998) and an online thesaurus (Merriam-Webster et al., 2019). All these words had been selected to extract all words related to each emotion from all posts. Table 4 provides words and emojis defining ten emotional sentiments analyzed in this paper.

The following subsections describe each emotion and how did these emotions are basically related to COVID-19 on Twitter.

- **Gratitude:** For all staff who were "putting their lives on the line" treating patients during the pandemic, specially the medical sector, must be properly rewarded. Several doctors and nurses had been infected during their struggle against the spread of the COVID-19. After saying thanks, there must be an appreciation for their efforts in preventing the spread of this pandemic (Abi, 2020).
- **Fear:** Because of the enormous growth rate of infection, 1st million in 124 days and 2nd million in 12 days, and retrieval is totally obscure for this pandemic. This obscurity creates high exhausted surroundings that may raise the quantity of psychical disturbed patients due to the exponential increase in the quantity of infected people witnessed in all over the world (Samriti et al., 2020).
- **Empathy:** first that sympathy for the people who exposed to be attacked by the disease (e.g., the elderly, who are more likely to suffer from severe symptoms and have a higher mortality) is associated with increased physical distancing and, second, that experimentally induced (affective) empathy encourages the inducement to abide to physical distancing (Pfattheicher et al., 2020).

Table 4. Words and emojis defining ten emotion's symbols

Emotion	Keywords related to emotion	Emojis related to emotion
Gratitude	Thank, best, appreciate, enjoy, lucky, fortunate, gift, generous, delight, rejoice	
Anxiety/fear	Scare, worry, anxiety, afraid, fear, nervous, anxious, panic, doubt, nightmare, horror, fright, distress, uncertain, misery, restless, phobia, despair, suspicion, terror, shakes, dismay, distrust, cowardice, fainthearted, creeps, angst, mistrust	
Empathy	Understand, sorry, relate, definite, trust, sympathy, feel for, what you mean, how you feel	
Frustration/anger	Hate, frustrate, rage, hell, bother, anger, angry, spite, annoy, burden	
Hope	Hope, tough, encourage, bright, inspire, desire, conquer, empower	
Happiness	Love, happy, lol, glad, laugh, smile, excited, haha, cheer, optimistic, thrill, happiness, delighted, bliss, jolly	
Depression/ sadness	cry, sad, upset, miserable, feel bad, discourage, suicide, despair, unhappy, troubled, sorrow, low mood, glum, joyless	
Shame/guilt	Sin, guilt, embarrass, shame, blame, pity, stigma, disgrace, remorse	
Loneliness	Alone, empty, isolate, solo, lonely, withdraw, empty, neglect, forgot, desert, disconnect, seclusion, disjointed	
disgust	nausea, sickness, queasiness, disgust, qualm, squeamishness, revulsion, loathing	

- **Frustration / anger:** The great anger is against China. The most notorious example from a tweet of the WHO account on January 14: "Preliminary investigations by the Chinese haven't found any evidence of human-to-human transmission of the novel #coronavirus." The world know now that these statements were catastrophically untrue, the global pandemic killed more than 100,000 people. There is other anger against the WHO. Trump and his proponents thought that the WHO was tardy to alert about the danger of human-to-human movement. However, this is highly not proven by the proof because WHO technical orientation announced at the beginning of January the hazard of human-to-human transient (Gilsinan, 2020).

- **Hope:** The basic hope is that the numbers of recovered cases are very high and the number of death cases is very low. Other hope in the development of the diagnostics tests in little weeks and rolled out globally. Also, several studies provide hope that rapid control of COVID-19 spread might be possible, although with high economic and social costs (Giuseppe et al., 2020).

- **Happiness:** come from changing of people lifestyle such as washing hands with soup, wearing masks and keeping physical distance between others. Also, the reduction in emissions due to the lockdown all over the world. The dramatic drop in boat traffic in several lakes around the world caused clearing the water, fish are visibly swimming, and swans have taken to relaxing (Lauchli, 2020).

- **Depression/sadness:** Solitude, social distancing and highly alterations in everyday life are the primary reasons of the sadness and depression. The major pressure for all of people is monetary. Vac and economic damages will be serious. Surveys on previous stagnation offer that increasing vac and monetary instability result raised averages of gloominess and suicide. House isolation through the 2008 economic stagnation resulted a 62% raised gloominess (Kanter et al., 2020).
- **Shame/ guilt/ blame:** In the long term, individuals who recover from the novel coronavirus may be left with feelings of wrongdoing and trauma, a symptom called survivor's guilt. Survivor's guilt happened when someone thoughts like they have achieved wrong matter by remaining alive a traumatic condition while other people did not.
- **Loneliness:** Self-isolation is important to stop the propagation of COVID-19 but it may result severe psychological consequences. This self-preservation bias and implicit vigilance towards threats may in turn result in further disconnection from others and, in the longer term, may have a deleterious impact on mental and physical health. Lonely individuals may appraise the current outbreak situation more negatively and suffer from higher levels of distress (Okruszek et al., 2020).
- **Disgust:** COVID-19's misses of apparent or fluidic marks or signs which results that it is an easy to override, because it doesn't disgust us the same as other diseases do. It's also known that COVID-19 is minimal fatal than several of the actually "disgusting" diseases, like smallpox or Ebola (Neuroskeptic, 2020).

3.5 Assigning Words and Symbols to Emotion Themes

After data preprocessing and defining emotions each tweet is assigned to related emotion theme. The output from each tweet was composed of several words or symbols or both. In this step, each word and symbol are assigned to one of the basic 10 emotions that are described in Table 4 by calculating the percentage of each emotion in the tweet. It is done by calculating number of words and symbols for each emotion, divided by total number of words and symbols in that tweet. The tweet is classified to the emotion that has highest percentage as per following Equations 1 and 2.

Let i is an emotional theme that contains a list of terms w_i and emoji's e_i reflecting the emotion. For each tweet $t_j \in \{t_1, t_2, t_3, ..., t_n\}$, where n is the total number of tweets, it contains a list of terms w_j and emoji's e_j. We define two metrics that calculate content-based emotional similarity score and emoji-based similarity score across all emotions i and tweets j as follows:

$$ContentScore(i,j) = \frac{w_i \cap w_j}{w_i} \tag{1}$$

$$EmohiScore(i,j) = \frac{e_i \cap e_j}{e_i} \tag{2}$$

The resulting similarity ranges from 0 (meaning not similar) to (1 meaning perfectly similar), while in-between values indicate intermediate similarity or dissimilarity. In order to label each tweet by a specific theme, we omit all tweets that have zero score. Then, we label the tweet based on the maximum score among themes. In case multiple themes have same scores, we omit them as well due to the ambiguity of theme.

4. RESULTS AND DISCUSSION

This section presents the results and discussion of the proposed research methodology to perform sentiment analysis for different emotions. Here, detailed analysis of large number of tweets 19,040,412 with 4,635,074 users and 355,555,573 engagements (retweets, favorites and replies) is provided. Tweets data from Feb 29th, 2020 to May 1st, 2020 and engagements for all languages (nine languages here) and separately for English language are provided. Date-wise frequency analyses of tweets is also provided. General word cloud analysis, specifically reasoning for higher peaks is provided. Percentage analysis of content-based and Emoji-based tweets and engagements emotional themes is provided, show which emotions have been dominating. Finally, date-wise analysis of content-based and emoji-based tweets is shown to understand how social media platforms can influence human emotions.

4.1 Date-Wise Analysis of Total Tweets and Total Engagements for English Language Only

Figure 4 presents date-wise distribution of total tweets collected about COVID-19 over the period from Feb 29th, 2020 to Apr 27th, 2020 in all languages. One can see, from the figure that tweets suddenly increased from about Mar 11th, 2020, when deaths in different countries specially in Italy were on the raise. Later on, one can see social media has got attention of people from all over the world. There are sudden spikes Mar 11th, 2020 to Mar 24th, 2020 because of many different reasons, such as, too many numbers of people dying, diagnosed positive, lock downs started in different parts of the world and press conferences and news about cure and vaccine trials related announcements for COVID-19. From Mar 25th, 2020 there is a leisureliness in number of tweets and then again, few spikes and again reduction in tweets and engagements trends observed due to people starting to accept the reality of COVID-19 not going anywhere soon. E.g. one can see spikes on Mar 18th, 2020, which is due the press conference held by Trump (Factbase, 2020) about chloroquine cure found for coronavirus and FDA was asked to perform trials, which was proved wrong later in the medical trials by FDA. Mar 19th, 2020 (Reuters, 2020) Italy government has ordered the army to move bodies to northern town, which is at the heart of the coronavirus outbreak. As, regular funerals were not possible and more due to prolonged emergency lockdown measures across the county, which left people with sad, angry and mixed emotions on twitter. Figure 4 presents date-wise distribution of total tweets engagements collected of English language about COVID-19 over the period from Feb 29th, 2020 until Apr 15th, 2020. One can see, that the overall trend is like all language's tweets, but the retweets seems much less as compared to all languages. As in English language major focus was USA president Trump and people are trolling about his press conference about chloroquine hype (Robertson, 2020) and stating in tweets it as bigger misinformation problem than social media platforms. The (Intercept, 2020) also reported Trumps ridiculous behavior at COVID-19 White House briefings by talking about himself mostly and distracting people from vital real updates from WHO or medical scientists, unlike in other democracies. E.g., in Greece, Dr. Sotirios Tsiodras, who is leading Greek government COVID-19 task force and is graduate of Harvard in infectious diseases briefs the nation at 6 Pm. He helped the nation to calm down and stay home during lock down and show love to their elders which are more prone to infection and death. While, on the other hand Trumps briefings are attention divertors from real issues which can be seen in the word cloud sections below.

Figure 4. Date-wise distribution of total tweets for English language only about COVID-19

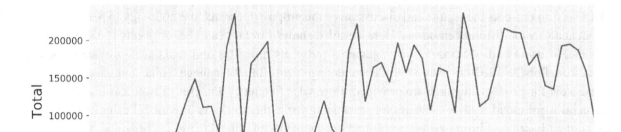

Figure 5 presents date-wise distribution of total tweets engagements collected about COVID-19 over the period from Feb 29th, 2020 until May 1th, 2020 in all languages. One can see that the favorites, and re-tweets have similar frequency to tweets, but people were not much interested in replying tweets with similar spikes of tweets.

Figure 5. Date-wise distribution of total engagements for English language only about COVID-19

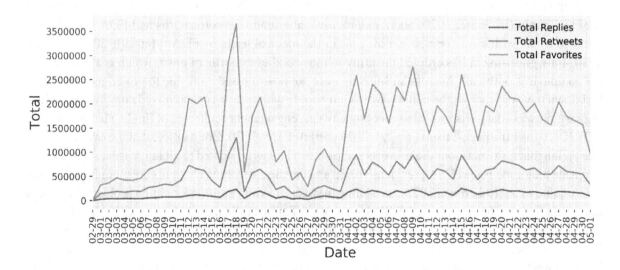

4.2 Word Clouds Analysis Expressing All Emotional Themes

Word cloud analysis provides us with the topic discussed during the time span under discussion. One can see from Figure 6, that stay home, self-isolate, COVID, Trump, work, shame, quarantine, love, social distancing, sad, pandemic, stay safe, wash hands, hospital. Lock down, crises, fear, government, corona virus, panic buying, crises, china, corona virus, trust are the prominent words in the general word cloud. It is telling us that people are talking about saying home and stay safe to save yourself and especially isolate yourself or quarantine yourself in case you have infection. A very clear keyword is wash hand which is suggested while you go out and come back home. There are mixed emotions as well of fear, sad, love, hope shame, etc., which shows that people are stressed but also are happy and hoping for life and asking their loved ones to stay safe.

Figure 6. General words cloud for tweets expressing all of the emotional themes

Figure 4 shows first peak, for which the word cloud is given in Figure 7. On analysis it is found that at night of Mar 17th, 2020 American president Trump (Factbase, 2020) did a press conference from white house about a drug usefulness for coronavirus, which is later found in-effective by FDA during the trials. Once Trump has announced press conference all the world was on their feet. They were expecting something really hopeful, but all resulted in nothing. People also stated to call this diseases Chinese virus although it has become a pandemic very soon after its occurrence.

Figure 8 shows the unigrams words been popular during the time period under consideration. It is seen that, thank word (which belongs to gratitude emotional theme) is even more used on the twitter as compared to coronavirus, with people, corona, hope, time and love afterwards. It is clear that as coronavirus and corona are treated as two words, that's why thanks are most frequent word. Figure 8 also shows that people have been thanking and were hopeful with different news like the news of chloroquine as a cure for COVID-19.

Figure 7. Word Cloud Mar 18th, 2020 about COVID-19 of English Language

Figure 8. Unigram word histogram

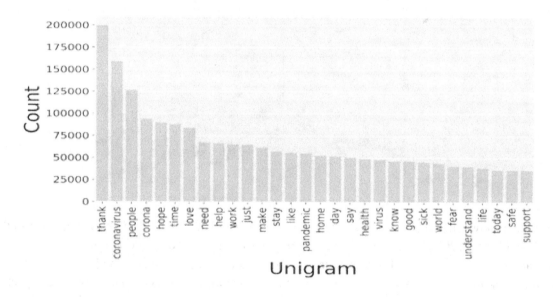

Figure 9 shows the bi-grams words been popular during the time period under consideration. It is seen that, stay home is most popular bigram as all people are requested to stay at home, followed by stay safe. People are also advised a lot in tweets by government officials to have social distancing, wash hands, save life's and be helpful to health workers. Also, from coronavirus disease to coronavirus pandemic new naming of COVID-19, panic buying of people from superstores and shortage of supplies, toilet paper shortage in western countries, testing positive of famous people and thanking God in tough time are among most popular keywords due to getting some hopeful news. Bigrams are mostly reflecting that governments and people are advising each other to protect themselves and unify the whole society to fight with this pandemic.

Figure 9. Bi-gram word histogram

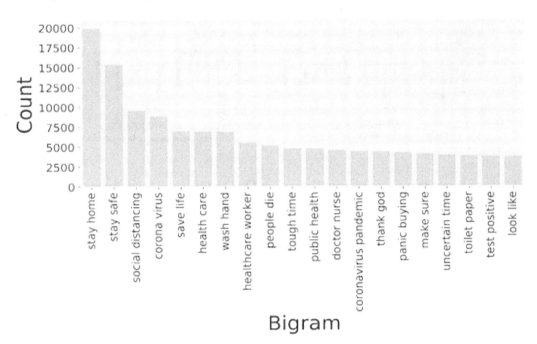

4.3 Percentage Analysis of Content-Based and Emoji-Based Total Tweets and Engagements of Emotional Themes

Percentage for all ten emotions is calculated for each tweet, by calculating number of words and symbols for each emotion divided by the number of words and symbols in that tweet. The tweet was assigned to the emotion with highest percentage. Figure 10 and 11 shows the percentage of tweet and engagement distribution for English language for ten emotions. One can see, most percentage of tweets is assigned to gratitude as people are being nice, humble and helping in this time of disaster and are trying to fight with it with positive attitude. Secondly, both happiness and anxiety/fear have almost similar percentages of tweets. It shows people get happy with announcement of cure or vaccines as well are they are in fear due to lock down and people dying in each part of the world, especially in English speaking countries. But it is good symbol that people are showing empathy and are more hopeful as compared to shame, anger, guilt, frustration, loneliness, etc.

One can see from the Figure 10 (b) that when people are happy, they use emojis more. They do not use emojis much in case of gratitude and fear as compared to content-based emotions analysis of tweets. Similar type of trend is followed for tweets engagement percentages given in Figure 11.

Figure 10. The percentage of tweet distribution on English language for the content-based emotions (left) and emoji-based emotions (right)

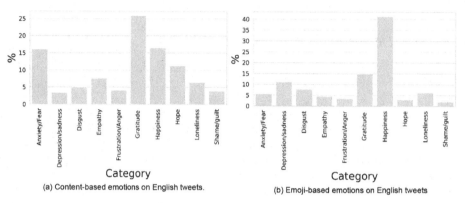

(a) Content-based emotions on English tweets.

(b) Emoji-based emotions on English tweets

Figure 11. The percentage of engagements' tweets on English language for the content-based emotions (a) and emoji-based emotions (b)

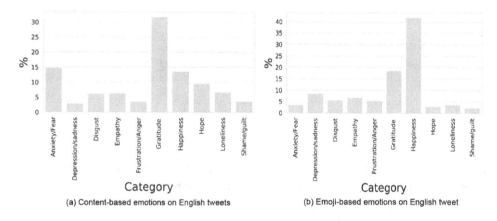

(a) Content-based emotions on English tweets

(b) Emoji-based emotions on English tweet

4.4 Date-Wise Analysis of Content-Based and Emoji-Based Total Tweets and Engagements of Emotional Themes

Figure 12 shows date-wise content-based emotions in all English tweets for the selected time period. One can see that in start fear was dominating all over the English tweets, but on around 14th or 15th, March when there was news in the media that chloroquine is useful in curing the COVID-19. Suddenly, the fear pattern lowered as compared to gratitude, also happiness among people started to raise on social media platforms. That just happened due to reacting to positive news more and reacting to negative news less. Like fear, disgust was higher but with the time people started to feel more hopeful and disgust has lowered.

Emoji-based emotions always is dominated by happiness as most people use emojis for happiness, and very les people use these emojis for gratitude or anxiety / fear. One can see, even emojis are more used to express depression/sadness as its pattern is above fear pattern in Figure 13. While, disgust emotions show higher pattern in emojis and shame guilt is the lowest pattern represented by emojis.

Figure 12. Content-based emotions in all English tweets

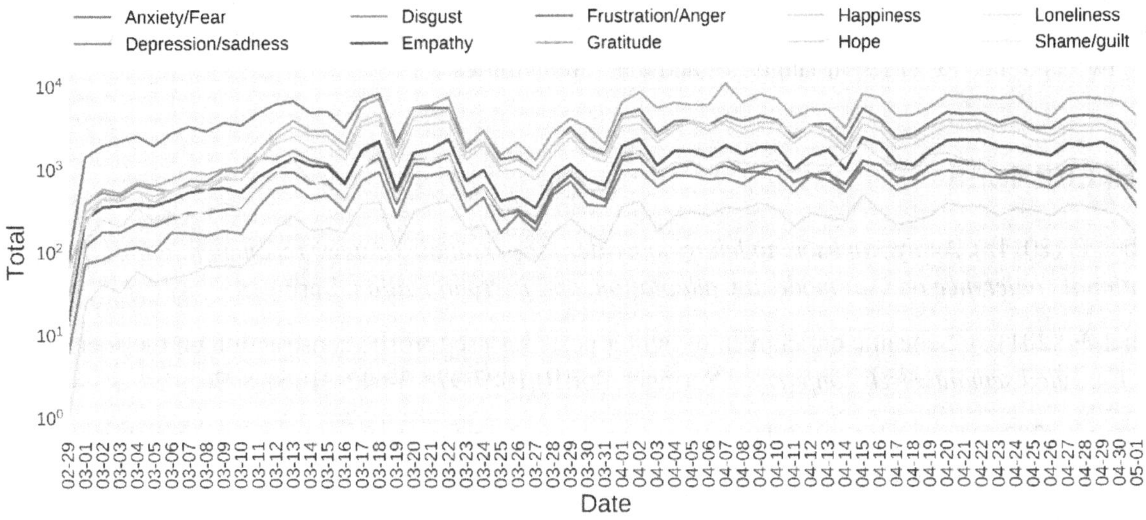

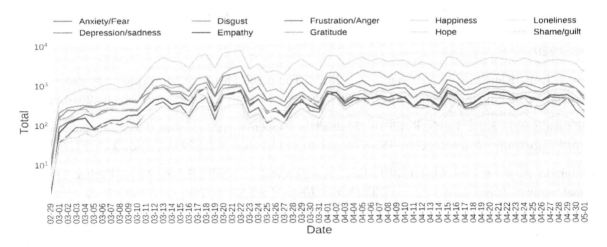

Figure 13. Emoji-based emotions in all English tweets

5. CONCLUSION

In this study, ten emotional themes are explored. On can conclude that social media platform is playing very active role in human lives during COVID-19. People are suddenly engaged in more tweets and engagements with the occurrence of event such as, when chloroquine medicine was announced as a cure and Italian government announced quick burials through army. It is also observed that people have shown much more fear than that of current situation, as gratitude and happiness is increasing, and anxiety/fear is decreasing. One can also conclude that emojis are more used for happiness and less used for anxiety/ fear and hope, as for hope the emojis list is also small. Finally, it is concluded that analysis social media provided us with insightful thoughts about sentiment analysis and emotional themes for COVID-19.

The analysis can be used to take timely decisions and amend government health policies. Specially, by providing people with correct good news the fear, stress, depression, anxiety can be removed from people and happiness, hope, gratitude can be introduced. As a future work, it could be nice to compare the tweets trends for different languages and their anonymities.

REFERENCES

Abel, F. (2011a). *Analyzing user modeling on twitter for personalized news recommendations. In International conference on user modeling, adaptation, and personalization.* Springer.

Abel, F. (2011b). Semantic enrichment of twitter posts for user profile construction on the social web. In *Extended semantic web conference.* Springer. doi:10.1007/978-3-642-21064-8_26

Rimmer. (2020). Covid-19: give NHS staff rest spaces and free parking not thank you, says doctor. *BMJ.* doi:10.1136/bmj.m1171

Amjad, T., Daud, A., Hayat, M. K., Afzal, M. T., & Dawood, H. (2020). *Coronavirus Pandemic (COVID-19): A Survey of Analysis.* Modeling and Recommendations.

Bastola, A., Sah, R., Rodriguez-Morales, A. J., Lal, B. K., Jha, R., Ojha, H. C., Shrestha, B., Chu, D. K. W., Poon, L. L. M., Costello, A., Morita, K., & Pandey, B. D. (2020). The first 2019 novel coronavirus case in Nepal. *The Lancet. Infectious Diseases*, *20*(3), 279–280. doi:10.1016/S1473-3099(20)30067-0 PMID:32057299

Bright, L. F., Kleiser, S. B., & Grau, S. L. (2015). Too much Facebook? an exploratory examination of social media fatigue. *Computers in Human Behavior*, *44*, 148–155. doi:10.1016/j.chb.2014.11.048

Chorianopoulos, K., & Talvis, K. (2016). Flutrack.org: Open-source and linked data for epidemiology. *Health Informatics Journal*, *22*(4), 962–974. doi:10.1177/1460458215599822 PMID:26351261

Daughton, A. R., & Paul, M. J. (2019). Identifying Protective Health Behaviors on Twitter: Observational Study of Travel Advisories and Zika Virus. *Journal of Medical Internet Research*, *21*(5), e13090. doi:10.2196/13090 PMID:31094347

Ekman, P. (1992). An argument for basic emotions. *Cognition and Emotion*, *6*(3), 169–200. doi:10.1080/02699939208411068

Factbase. (2020). *Press Conference: Donald Trump Joins the Daily Coronavirus Pandemic Briefing - March 17, 2020.* https://factba.se/transcript/donald-trump-press-conference-coronavirus-briefing-march-17-2020

Gilsinan, K. (n.d.). *How China Deceived the WHO?* https://www.theatlantic.com/politics/archive/2020/04/world-health-organization-blame-pandemic-coronavirus/609820/

Gopalkrishna Barkur, V., & Kamath, G. B. (2020). Sentiment analysis of nationwide lockdown due to COVID 19 outbreak: Evidence from India. *Asian Journal of Psychiatry*, *51*, 102089. doi:10.1016/j.ajp.2020.102089 PMID:32305035

Ippolito, Hui, Ntoumi, Maeurer, & Zumla. (2020). Toning down the 2019-nCoV media hype—and restoring hope. *The Lancet Respiratory Medicine, 8*(3), 230-231.

Househ, M. (2016). Communicating Ebola through social media and electronic news media outlets: A cross-sectional study. *Health Informatics Journal*, 22(3), 470–478. doi:10.1177/1460458214568037 PMID:25656678

Intercept. (2020). *Trump's Ridiculous Behavior at Pandemic Briefings Baffles a Watching World.* https://theintercept.com/2020/04/10/trumps-ridiculously-political-briefings-pandemic-unique-democratic-world/?comments=1

Johnson-laird, P. N., & Oatley, K. (1989). The Language of Emotions: An Analysis of a Semantic Field. *Cognition and Emotion*, 3(2), 81–123. doi:10.1080/02699938908408075

Kanter, J., & Manbeck, K. (n.d.). *COVID-19 could lead to an epidemic of clinical depression, and the health care system isn't ready for that, either.* https://theconversation.com/covid-19-could-lead-to-an-epidemic-of-clinical-depression-and-the-health-care-system-isnt-ready-for-that-either-134528

Sharma, K., Seo, S., Meng, C., Rambhatla, S., Dua, A., & Liu, Y. (2020). *Coronavirus on social media: Analyzing misinformation in twitter conversations.* arXiv:2003.12309v1.

Lauchli Di villa. (n.d.). *A Positive Side Effect of COVID-19.* https://www.wantedinrome.com/news/a-positive-side-effect-of-covid-19.html

Schild, L., & Blackburn, S. Zhang, & Zannettou. (2020). *"Go eat a bat, Chang!": An Early Look on the Emergence of Sinophobic Behavior on Web Communities in the Face of COVID-19.* arXiv:2004.04046v1.

Lin, D. (1998). WordNet: an electronic lexical database. In Language, Speech, and Communication. Cambridge, MA: MIT Press.

Lu, R., Zhao, X., Li, J., Niu, P., Yang, B., Wu, H., Wang, W., Song, H., Huang, B., Zhu, N., Bi, Y., Ma, X., Zhan, F., Wang, L., Hu, T., Zhou, H., Hu, Z., Zhou, W., Zhao, L., ... Tan, W. (2020). Genomic characterisation and epidemiology of 2019 novel coronavirus: Implications for virus origins and receptor binding. *Lancet*, 395(10224), 565–574. doi:10.1016/S0140-6736(20)30251-8 PMID:32007145

Mendoza, M., Poblete, B., & Castillo, C. (2010). Twitter under crisis: Can we trust what we RT? *Proceedings of the first workshop on social media analytics.* 10.1145/1964858.1964869

Merriam-Webster Thesaurus. (2019). https://www.merriam-webster.com/thesaurus

Mohammad, S. M., & Turney, P. D. (2013). Crowdsourcing a word-emotion association lexicon. *Computational Intelligence*, 29(3), 436–465. doi:10.1111/j.1467-8640.2012.00460.x

Neuroskeptic. (n.d.). *Is COVID-19 Not Disgusting Enough?* https://www.discovermagazine.com/mind/is-covid-19-not-disgusting-enough

Okruszek, Ł., Aniszewska-Stańczuk, A., Piejka, A., Wiśniewska, M., & Żurek, K. (2020). *Safe but lonely? Loneliness, mental health symptoms and COVID-19.* 10.31234/ doi:osf.io/9njps

Pfattheicher, S., Nockur, L., Böhm, R., Sassenrath, C., & Petersen, M. (2020). *The emotional path to action: Empathy promotes physical distancing during the COVID-19 pandemic.* 10.31234/, doi:osf.io/y2cg5

Plutchik, R. (1994). *The psychology and biology of emotion.* Harper Collins.

Reuters. (n.d.). *COVID-19 Italy videos show military fleet transporting coffins of coronavirus victims out of overwhelmed town.* https://nationalpost.com/news/world/covid-19-italy-videos-show-military-fleet-transporting-coffins-of-coronavirus-victims-out-of-overwhelmed-town

Medford, Saleh, Sumarsono, Perl, & Lehmann. (n.d.). *An "Infodemic": Leveraging High-Volume Twitter Data to Understand Public Sentiment for the COVID-19 Outbreak.* doi:10.1101/2020.04.03.20052936

Lerrigo, R., Coffey, J. T. R., Kravitz, J. L., Jadhav, P., Nikfarjam, A., Shah, N. H., Jurafsky, D., & Sinha, S. R. (2019). The Emotional Toll of Inflammatory Bowel Disease: Using Machine Learning to Analyze Online Community Forum Discourse. *Crohn's & Colitis, 360*(2), otz011. Advance online publication. doi:10.1093/crocol/otz011

Robertson, A. (n.d.). *Trump's chloroquine hype is a misinformation problem bigger than social media.* https://www.theverge.com/2020/4/9/21209797/trump-chloroquine-hydroxychloroquine-medication-social-media-misinformation

Mohammad & Turney. (2013). Crowdsourcing a Word-Emotion Association Lexicon. [cs.CL]. *Computational Intelligence, 29*(3), 436–465. arXiv1308.6297v1

Sharma, S., Sharma, M., & Singh, G. (2020). A chaotic and stressed environment for 2019-nCoV suspected, infected and other people in India: Fear of mass destruction and causality. *Asian Journal of Psychiatry, 51*(June), 102049. doi:10.1016/j.ajp.2020.102049 PMID:32278890

Scanfeld, D., Scanfeld, V., & Larson, E. L. (2010). Dissemination of health information through social networks: Twitter and antibiotics. *American Journal of Infection Control, 38*(3), 182–188. doi:10.1016/j.ajic.2009.11.004 PMID:20347636

Schuller, B., Mousa, A., & Vryniotis, V. (2015). Sentiment analysis and opinion mining: On optimal parameters and performances. *Data Mining and Knowledge Discovery, 5*(5), 255–263. doi:10.1002/widm.1159

Shin, S.-Y., Seo, D.-W., An, J., Kwak, H., Kim, S.-H., Gwack, J., & Jo, M.-W. (2016). High correlation of Middle East respiratory syndrome spread with Google search and Twitter trends in Korea. *Scientific Reports, 6*(1), 32920. doi:10.1038rep32920 PMID:27595921

Signorini, A., Segre, A. M., & Polgreen, P. M. (2011). The Use of Twitter to Track Levels of Disease Activity and Public Concern in the U.S. during the Influenza a H1N1 Pandemic. *PLoS One, 6*(5), e19467. doi:10.1371/journal.pone.0019467 PMID:21573238

Kharde & Sonawane. (2016). Sentiment Analysis of Twitter Data: A Survey of Techniques. *International Journal of Computer Applications, 139*(11), 5-15.

WeGov. (2016). *Where eGovernment meets the eSociety.* Retrieved from http://www.wegovproject.eu

Wu F. Zhao S. Yu B. Chen Y.-M. Wang W. Hu Y. (2020). *Complete genome characterisation of a novel coronavirus associated with severe human respiratory disease in Wuhan, China.* doi:10.1101/2020.01.24.919183

This research was previously published in the International Journal on Semantic Web and Information Systems (IJSWIS), 17(2); pages 1-21, copyright year 2021 by IGI Publishing (an imprint of IGI Global).

Chapter 95
General Awareness and Responses to COVID-19 Crisis:
A Sentiment Analysis of Twitter Updates

Dipima Buragohain
Jilin University, China

ABSTRACT

The ongoing pandemic situation of COVID-19 has impacted people across nations while taking social media by storm with its massive pool of information. As social media platforms are full of horserace reporting and uncritical or even fake updates most of the time, users should respond carefully during a crisis like COVID-19 pandemic while consuming and sharing updates. The current study presents an exploratory analysis of and highlights language use in terms of users' general awareness of the crisis and their responses on social media platforms through a sentiment analysis of 805 Twitter messages related to the COVID-19 pandemic in India. The findings reported users' varied sentiments while expressing their general awareness about the crisis and its widespread outbreak. It also reported their use of cognizant verbal expressions and abusive words as an expression for dealing with panic of the crisis.

INTRODUCTION

The ongoing pandemic situation of COVID-19 has impacted people across nations at so many levels of everyday life. World Health Organization (WHO) has defined COVID-19 or the coronavirus disease as an infectious disease of respiratory illness caused by the most recently discovered corona virus. The common symptoms of COVID-19 include fever, fatigue, dry cough, nasal congestion, runny nose, sore throat, body pain, headache, and diarrhea. It can cause a range of symptoms from mild illness to even pneumonia or in extreme cases, difficulty in breathing and death. While constant medical attempts of controlling the situation are on the go, the global outbreak of COVID-19 is taking social media by storm with its massive pool of information. There are numerous COVID-19 information updates on various social media platforms such as Facebook, Instagram, and Twitter. There are information, misinformation,

DOI: 10.4018/978-1-6684-6303-1.ch095

rumors, and hoaxes being written, updated, and circulated on these platforms regarding the outbreak, outcomes, prevention, and cure of this disease. This further raises pertinent questions on the nature and authenticity of the information that has been circulated across these platforms. It is undeniably true that these social media platforms are full of horse-race reporting and uncritical or even fake updates at times, or most of the times. What is even worse is the fact that such fake news spread faster on social media than the updates from reliable sources, which can adversely impact the authenticity of reliable sources. That is why it is important for the users of social media platforms to respond carefully and responsibly during a crisis like COVID-19 pandemic when it comes to consuming and sharing updates related to the pandemic situation. Apart from the concern of the accuracy of disseminated information on various social media platforms regarding the ongoing situation, another issue to take into serious account is the need for constant monitoring of the expressions and stylistics of the content used, posted, and shared on these platforms. It is important to identify whether and how language is utilized or misused in the communication process on such social media platforms.

One of the primary challenges of receiving and sharing information on various social media platforms during a pandemic outbreak is to react and respond to the panic associated with the adverse health outcomes. Panic among public during a pandemic outbreak is common, but it may further influence the dissemination of information on social media platforms in both positive and negative sentiments. To be specific, such news gets more media attention and coverage due to which these updates become most or frequently searched trending topics on the internet along with more shares and tweets on social media. This further can help health authorities as well as public to identify real-time prediction of the outbreak. However, the viral updates can adversely impact health systems by spreading fake news, misinformation, and hoaxes on the pandemic, thus instigating more panic. In other words, such posts or tweets on social media can identify multiple issues that the outbreak may prompt. Such concerns are of grave nature during the time of any epidemic or pandemic outbreak. Fu et al. (2016) reported several issues which were identified from the tweets during the outbreak of the Zika virus in early 2016 when it first spread outside of Africa and Asia regions where the virus had formerly been restricted. This has led to a variety of information and misinformation disseminated across social media platforms. However, it also spreads information through tweets raising various concerns, including social impact of the outbreak, issues of pregnancy and unborn child, actions of government and health authorities, and geographical expansion of the virus across regions.

In the light of this introduction, the current study explores and highlights several concerns of Twitter users related to the virus outbreak and other health information caused or impacted by it. While Twitter users across India demanded the practices of social distancing and lockdown extension, they were found to be misinformed about the causes and cures of the pandemic outbreak as well. While lockdown hampered the economy of the country, people were heard advocating as well as discouraging an extension. Twitter updates showed that Assam and most of the northeastern states demanded an extended lockdown since they believed it would curb the pandemic from outbreaking in that region which still showed low intensity and across the country as it will be addressed and discussed later in the study.

Social media platforms play a significant source for disseminating, collecting, and updating information when it comes to updating public knowledge on a pandemic or any infectious disease outbreak. While public health authorities can utilize these platforms for notifying people on health hazard prevention notices and recommendations to avoid travelling to the virus-affected sensitive areas, dissemination of misinformation on the same can result in adverse consequences. The content posted and shared on Twitter is viewed widely across the Internet by a sizeable global human population on a daily basis.

Therefore, it is important to study the types of content updated on other social media platforms during an infectious disease and pandemic outbreak.

Previous studies on crises have reported Twitter users updating and sharing information along with their opinions related to such outbreaks while voicing their concerns. In the light of this, a study by Chew and Eysenbach (2010) analyzed the tweets related to H1N1 or swine flu outbreak in 2009. It conducted a content analysis of tweets containing keywords such as 'swine flu', 'swineflu', and 'H1N1' and found that the increased use of 'H1N1' indicated a gradual adoption of WHO-recommended terminology by public. The study also reported the use of Twitter by credible and popular sources to share outbreak updates and to raise their concerns. It found Twitter as one of the reliable social media platforms for spreading knowledge on outbreak situations. Based on their findings, the study further suggested that governments and health authorities should use Twitter for sharing updates and raising concerns for such situations. This suggestion is pertinent to the current study in which the government health authorities of the concerned region use Twitter to inform and update information on COVID-19 outbreak, thus making Twitter a conscious choice for information dissemination during a crisis-like situation. This platform was used as the authentic and confidential source of information related to the COVID-19 updates by the government as well as the people of Assam during the initial phase of the pandemic outbreak.

Another issue of concern is the negativity about infectious disease outbreaks spread on various social media platforms. Most of the previous studies discussed above highlighted that negative emotions are evident in the Twitter updates whenever there is a situation of infectious disease or pandemic outbreak. Researchers have addressed and discussed such instances. Users tweeted and shared misinformation during the Zika virus outbreak which had negative outcomes. This explains why there were inaccurate updates on advice around the prevention and transmission of the virus (Fu et al., 2016). Moreover, such updates can evoke negative emotions indicating varied sentiments such as anxiety, anger, abuse, and even death. Therefore, exploring sentiments, emotions, reactions, and responses of Twitter users is a subject of immense significance in terms of scientific inquiry. In the light of this, the current study focuses on exploring the sentiments of Twitter users regarding the dissemination of information related to COVID-19 which will be discussed in detail later in the study.

Based on the previous introduction, this study, therefore, is structured as follows:

- The background of the study including existing literature is discussed in the following section,
- The primary concern along with the research method,
- Methodology, participants, and research questions and objectives,
- Detailed discussion of the findings,
- Results and recommendations section,
- Scope for future research and research directions,
- Summarized discussion of the study in the conclusion section.

Background

The ongoing COVID-19 pandemic outbreak has not only brought havoc and public health challenge to the health systems across nations but also created panic among people over the world which is evident in the massive pool of information being floated on different social media platforms. This further signals the alarming concern of misinformation on COVID-19 being spread across these platforms in an enormous amount. Dissemination of misinformation and wrong updates during a pandemic situation is not a new phenomenon as observed by previous studies (Liu, 2011; Collinson et al., 2015; Kaila & Prasad, 2020; Raman, 2020). Liang et al. (2019) reported about the broadcasting or viral spreading of misinformation as a common phenomenon on Twitter during the time of Ebola outbreak in 2014-15. The study also highlighted that Twitter updates of influential users can be considered as a source of reliability and authenticity of the outbreak-related information. The study categorized users with fewer followers but more retweets as "hidden influential users". It further found that, "Although the media and health organization accounts were influential users, they accounted for only a small proportion of the cascade dynamics directly. Many other Twitter users, who served as influential users, triggered most information cascades" (Liang et al., 2019, p.7). However, updates of misinformation and fake news are relatively more frequent which can impact in adverse manner as supported by Shu et al. (2017).

Similarly, Fung et al. (2014) reported high levels of anxiety related to Ebola outbreak which was evident in tweets. The study found that misinformation related to health. During public health events or emergencies include false remedies for illness, incorrect information on disease transmission, or allegations that the disease is associated with a government conspiracy (Fung et al., 2014). This further fueled high levels of anxiety on tweets with a lot of negative emotions including anger, anxiety, abuse, and death. During the COVID-19 pandemic outbreak, people living in quarantine, isolation, or at risk of the outbreak are more likely to experience stress, anxiety, and panic which may evoke interests in looking for more updates on the disease (Ahmed et al., 2020). It is important to highlight panic and the related concerns to identify the authenticity of information during a pandemic outbreak as "Infectious disease outbreaks may cause fear and panic among the public making it important to study these phenomena" (Ahmed et al., 2020, p 449).

Fake news and misinformation can misguide them in this concern while aggravating the health hazards. Therefore, not only common public should be careful while receiving and sharing information and post responsibly on social media platforms, but governments and health authorities should also take responsible initiatives by implementing policies and guidelines to handle the spread of misinformation during such situations. According to Oyeyemi et al. (2014), there was widespread broadcasting of misinformation on social media platforms during the Ebola outbreak compared to the accurate and correct updates. This is also relevant to the outbreak of COVID-19 which requires similar guidelines from reliable authorities. World Health Organization (WHO) has already implemented strict and clear instructions for organizations, social media platforms, authorities, nations, and people to deal with the ongoing pandemic situation. Updates from reliable sources are important for dealing with stress and panic. This is supported by Fung et al. (2014) who found that accurate update of information by concerned authorities and health practitioners can help reduce the panic and anxiety especially in places where the intensity of the outbreak is low or zero. Further, this finding is also relevant for the current study which focuses on the COVID-19 Twitter updates, mainly on Assam, India where the intensity of the outbreak was comparatively very low at the time of research than the rest of the country. It is important to note that the present study focuses on the data collected during the initial period of the pandemic outbreak of COVID-19 in Assam, India, as will be discussed later in the study.

BACKGROUND INFORMATION

The current study provides a sentiment analysis of 805 randomly selected Twitter messages related to COVID-19 pandemic in Assam, India during the initial period of its outbreak. Sentiment analysis is a significant technique used for analyzing and determining a text in terms of positive, negative, or neutral sentiments it carries. It is further used for assessing public opinion based on the analysis. Public opinions as well as human sentiments expressed and shared on a social media platform like Twitter are mostly unstructured in nature as individual opinions are unique to each social media user (Rout et al., 2017). This is why computational strategies, such as sentiment analysis, are required for identifying opinions and sentiments of Twitter users. Detailed discussion on sentiment analysis is included in this section.

Methodology of the Study

The current study uses sentiment analysis to find out the general awareness of Twitter users about the ongoing COVID-19 pandemic outbreak along with their reactions and responses to the situation in Assam, India during the initial phase of the pandemic outbreak. Sentiment analysis is an approach for analyzing people's sentiments, opinions, attitudes, viewpoints, and emotions towards something which further can be effective in the decision-making process of people. Sentiment analysis helps collect and evaluate precise and timely information on a certain topic.

It is relevant to mention that previous studies have recognized Twitter as a crucial social media platform for political information seeking and dissemination (Ahmed et al., 2018) which further validates the information source as authentic and reliable since the concerned government authority in the current study used this platform for updating COVID-19 outbreak information. Choosing Twitter and sentiment analysis to explore, understand, and evaluate emotions, opinions, and sentiments of the people for the current study has its reasonable ground. People of the researched region along with the rest of India were mostly confined to their homes due to the enforced lockdown. It further made them rely more on social media platforms for expressing and perceiving various feelings and attitudes concerning the pandemic.

The current study chose Twitter as it was used by the government authorities and officials to disseminate information and updates on the pandemic outbreak and related aspects. The COVID-19 pandemic has caused unprecedented losses to the lives and economy of India as well as to the world. While it has turned India to be the second worst-hit nation after the US, it caused widespread anxiety and fear among the people of India which was apparent in their expressions, opinions, and attitudes on various social media platforms including Twitter. Therefore, conducting a sentiment analysis is of utmost significance to understand their concerns of mental well-being as well as how they react to any potential threat or respond to precautionary measures.

The current study thus used two applications to collect data from Twitter and explore and analyze it. These are:

- Sentiment Analysis Tool on danielsoper.com.
- Text Analysis Tool of IntenCheck software.

The analysis includes six main categories of sentiment parameters for data interpretation containing positive, negative, strong, weak, active, and passive sentiments. The scale of grades for these parameters vary between High, Normal, and Low. The value for the parameters is calculated between 0 and 100.

Participants of the Study

The data for the study were collected through random selection from Twitter users particularly responding to COVID-19 updates of the concerned government. With a population over 36 million, Assam is one of the frontier states of India's northeastern region and considered as the gateway to northeast India. The northeast India comprises of eight states and the region shares international border with China, Tibet Autonomous Region, Myanmar, Bangladesh, Nepal, and Bhutan, thus making it a sensitive region. The region features a pool of diverse languages, cultures, and social systems totally different from the rest of India, or rather the 'mainland' India. This is also evident from the fact that the region is geographically located away from the mainland India.

During the initial phase of the pandemic outbreak, India witnessed gradual increase in the confirmed cases from January 2020 onwards whereas its northeastern region had zero cases till Assam witnessed the first confirmed case on 31st March 2020. It is important to understand the peoples (netizens), the sensitivity, and their reactions in particular. While the country was going through bouts of information, misinformation, and disinformation on the pandemic outbreak on different social media platforms, Twitter users expressed their reactions and responses. Leading news channels constantly telecasted infringement of social distancing in several Indian cities where people were seen observing rituals, performing *puja*, and hosting marches to 'ward off' Coronavirus. Leading newspaper Deccan Chronicle reported performing of *puja* in a Hyderabad temple by reciting shlokas to ward off Coronavirus which was attended by 2000-odd devotees with no norms of social distancing in February 2020 (Deccan Chronicle, 2020). Reuters reported hosting of *gaumutra* (cow urine) party by some 200 members of All India Hindu Mahasabha to ward off Coronavirus in New Delhi in March 2020 (Reuters, 2020). Such instances were not witnessed as such in the northeastern region of India and particularly in Assam. Twitter updates showed awareness of Assamese people about the rising concerns of the pandemic including the need of social distancing, lockdown extension, and other precautionary measures to be taken to prevent any potential threat.

A total of 805 tweets were collected for this study that were responded to the COVID-19 updates on the Twitter account of the Health Minister of Assam, Mr Himanta Biswa Sharma who regularly tweeted with the pandemic updates in the state since the beginning of its outbreak. Regarding the current study, the tweets of the State Health Minister included regular and specific details on the total number of infected cases in COVID-19, their names, and locations. The tweets collected for the study were posted in between the timeframe of three months, from March 2020 to May 2020, which was the initial period of the pandemic outbreak in the region. It is important to note that there was not a single confirmed case of COVID-19 in Assam during the initial stage of its outbreak in the country. The first confirmed case in India was reported on 30 January 2020 whereas the first positive case of COVID-19 pandemic in Assam was reported on 31 March 2020. A nationwide rigid lockdown was first implemented on 24 March 2020 as a preventive measure against the COVID-19 pandemic in India. Even though there were no COVID-19 positive cases in Assam in March and a few in the following month, netizens were vocal about the outbreak in the region on Twitter since the Health Minister tweeted daily updating the situation. The current study involves research of this timespan of the initial phase of COVID-19 pandemic outbreak in the concerned region.

Purpose of the Study

The current study aims at providing an exploratory study analyzing how language is used on social media platforms at the times of crisis like this and how the users react to pandemic updates in their posts and updates. The study particularly focuses on the use of language on social media platforms especially on Twitter in order to investigate users' general awareness of the ongoing health crisis and their responses. It has chosen Twitter which is one of the most popular social media platforms in which people share and post news, information, opinions, and updates through text regarding various global issues. Having a wide user base, Twitter, along with Facebook, has become an important political information source (Ahmed et al., 2018). Therefore, choosing Twitter as the database source for the current research is relevant since the study aims at focusing on Twitter messages addressing information and updates on the ongoing pandemic outbreak of COVID-19. Based on the discussion above, the current study attempts to find answers to the following research questions:

- How do the Twitter users react and respond to the ongoing situation of the COVID-19 pandemic outbreak and its related concerns?
- How well are the Twitter users aware of the authenticity and accuracy of information they update and share on the outbreak?
- How do the Twitter users react to the negativity and panic related to the pandemic outbreak?

In order to find answers to the research questions above along with the objectives to fulfil, the current study attempts at exploring the general awareness of Twitter users and their reactions to COVID-19 crisis through their tweet responses. It provides a sentiment analysis of Twitter messages related to COVID-19 pandemic in India.

ANALYSIS AND DISCUSSION

The study investigated COVID-19 tweet responses to the regular tweets of the State Health Minister of Assam, India posted during the initial phase of its outbreak in the region. The findings reported varied sentiments and attitudes expressed by the Twitter users while voicing out their concerns about the crisis and its widespread outbreak. These findings are aligned with the research objectives and questions which will be discussed in detail in the following sections.

General Concern Over the Pandemic Situation

The study reported public concerns over the pandemic situation raising various issues related to the outbreak which was evident in the tweets and the keywords used. This finding, which aligns with the first research question and objective, explains the concerned issues. The researched region witnessed a relatively low intensity of strong emotions regarding the COVID-19 outbreak during its initial stage. It is important to note that India reported more than 100,000 active cases and over 6,000 deaths due to COVID-19 on the 11th of March 2020, the day it was declared a pandemic by WHO. But Assam did not have a single case till the last week of March. Its first confirmed case was reported after the enforcement of the first phase of countrywide lockdown in the same week, thus indicating the intensity of the situation across India. While the Twitter users responded to the daily updates of the State Health Minister's tweets on the pandemic situation, the most frequent keywords used in the response tweets included 'action', 'administration', 'assistance', and 'community'. The tweets showed users' knowledge and understanding of the pandemic situation in the researched region while they demanded swift action from the administration to handle the initial situation which further resulted in the announcement of state-level lockdown. Some of the tweets are mentioned below.

We need more strict action against those people who went out during LOCK DOWN unnecessary otherwise the situation goes out of control... (Thakuria, 2020)

Sir please look into the matter that some people are breaking the LOCKDOWN at evry steps and roaming freely where and there in our karimganj Honourable sir please talk to our karimganj administration. (Biddu, 2020)

The earliest confirmed case in Assam was notified on the last week of March 2020. However, this made the public stay alert and careful regarding the possible outbreak of COVID-19 which made them aware of notions like community spread much ahead of the full-grown outbreak and demand more action from the government and concerned health authorities. *Figure 1* below describes the Twitter users' sentiments on their general concerns over the pandemic situation in the highlighted region. Users were aware of the severity of the outbreak in the rest of the country since January while it affected Assam only in March with a single infected case.

Use of keywords like 'careful', 'functional', and 'essential' represents the cautious attitude of people during the tense situation of the pandemic across the country. While demanding more watchfulness of the authorities in the state situation which was relatively safer and a green zone at that time, keywords like 'blunder', 'dangerous', 'disastrous', and 'accountable' represent the somewhat negative aspects of Twitter users indicating the element of panic to some extent. Through the response tweets, users seemed to highlight public as the primary reason for not following the new normal practices like social distancing and wearing masks, which could be dangerous to expose them to COVID-19.

User Awareness of the Widespread Outbreak of the Pandemic

This finding also explains the concerned issues. It is important to note that people in Assam were well aware of the widespread outbreak of COVID-19 across the country as well as in other nations such as China, Italy, and Spain while the state was going through its initial outbreak. This was evident in the following tweets,

Hope now people realise that religious practice won't just help in fighting covid-19. Let the senses prevail and those coming from Nizamuddin and other parts of India voluntarily submits themselves for examination. Let's help @himantabiswa to end this crisis in Assam. (Chachan, 2020)

Sir please stop mentioning "Patient is related to Nizamuddin event" in every tweet. This will create more hatred among the different communities. I don't think that is helping us anyway. We should try to face the situation with peace and love. Jai Hind @himantabiswa (Deep, 2020)

Figure 1. User sentiment on general concern over the pandemic situation
Source: IntenCheck software report

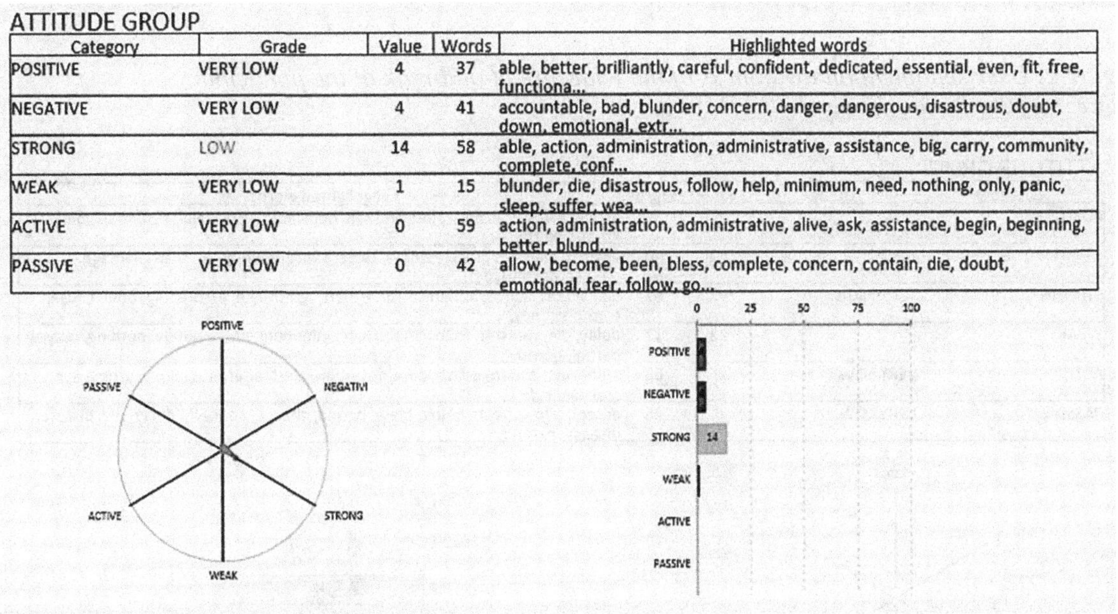

ATTITUDE GROUP

Category	Grade	Value	Words	Highlighted words
POSITIVE	VERY LOW	4	37	able, better, brilliantly, careful, confident, dedicated, essential, even, fit, free, functiona...
NEGATIVE	VERY LOW	4	41	accountable, bad, blunder, concern, danger, dangerous, disastrous, doubt, down, emotional, extr...
STRONG	LOW	14	58	able, action, administration, administrative, assistance, big, carry, community, complete, conf...
WEAK	VERY LOW	1	15	blunder, die, disastrous, follow, help, minimum, need, nothing, only, panic, sleep, suffer, wea...
ACTIVE	VERY LOW	0	59	action, administration, administrative, alive, ask, assistance, begin, beginning, better, blund...
PASSIVE	VERY LOW	0	42	allow, become, been, bless, complete, concern, contain, die, doubt, emotional, fear, follow, go...

While reading about the graveness of the situation in the mentioned countries, Twitter users (Ali, 2020; Rajbongshi, 2020) expressed strong sentiments demanding stringent guidelines and instructions on social interaction of people and even stricter guidelines and COVID-19 protocols from the government authorities. This was manifested in the frequently used keywords like 'action', 'alert', 'assistance', and 'administration' as shown in *Figure 2* below. There was also a negative flow of emotions with frequently used keywords such as 'carelessness', 'alarming', 'criminal', 'crisis', and 'danger' which were primarily used for criticizing public who disregarded the basic protocols of social distancing and wearing masks in public places. For example,

It's a very sad news and danger situation for assam.. People assam please lockdown is not a joke.. It's a a very critical situation for us.. Please take it seriously.. And support our #Assamgovt #assampolice .. #assam_fight_against_covid19. (Rajbongshi, 2020)

It is important to note that the Prime Minister of India announced the first nationwide lockdown on March 24 for 21 days sensing the impending outbreak of COVID-19 in the country. It limited the movement of the entire 1.3 billion population of the country violating which was subject to severe penalties. The alarming situation was perceived by the users on Twitter as well who expressed their concerns by using those negative emotions. There was also the looming element of panic among Twitter users visible in a sizeable amount keyword frequency of 'delay', 'die', 'disaster', 'help', and 'lose'. This aligns with the findings of Fung et al. (2014) which supported that the regular update on the outbreak from the concerned authorities can reduce panic and anxiety among people in places where the intensity of the pandemic is very low. The awareness of COVID-19 outbreak across the world and the nationwide lockdown by the government as a precautionary measure helped the Twitter users to feel less panic and anxiety particularly in Assam where the infected cases were very few in the initial phase of its outbreak.

Figure 2. User sentiment on awareness of the widespread outbreak of the pandemic
Source: IntenCheck software report

ATTITUDE GROUP

Category	Grade	Value	Words	Highlighted words
POSITIVE	LOW	6	36	active, awesome, basic, better, bold, dedicated, especially, essential, good, great, healthy, h...
NEGATIVE	NORM	62	40	against, alarming, carelessness, close, concern, criminal, crisis, damage, danger, despite, det...
STRONG	VERY HIGH	97	67	act, action, active, administration, alert, assistance, assure, big, bold, cause, commissioner,...
WEAK	NORM	32	17	delay, die, disaster, follow, help, lose, minimum, need, needy, nothing, only, partial, pause, ...
ACTIVE	VERY LOW	0	63	abide, act, action, active, administration, alert, alternate, apply, arrive, ask, assistance, b...
PASSIVE	VERY LOW	0	36	accept, allow, been, being, bless, bound, chance, concern, delay, die, disaster, disease, exten...

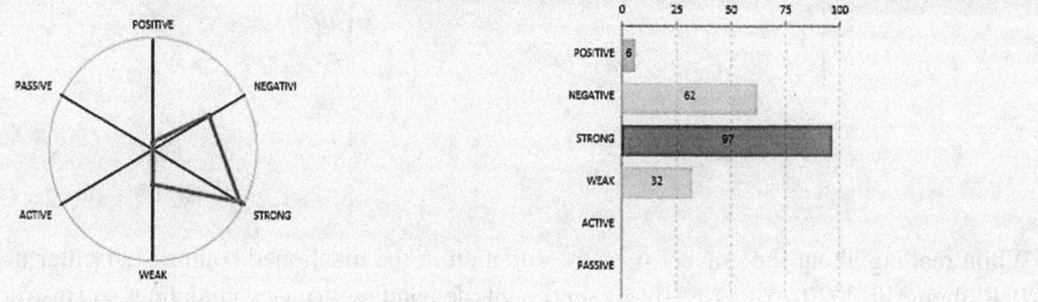

Suggestions for Social Distancing

With the pandemic outbreak of COVID-19 slowly spreading across various parts of India by April, the government authorities implemented stricter guidelines to follow social distancing, wearing masks and using hand sanitizers across the country. Assam was not an exception as well which was informed and updated by the State Health Minister's Twitter account. In response to those and other COVID-19 related tweets, users expressed strong opinions with frequent use of keywords like 'community', 'decision', 'active', 'action', and 'central' as shown in *Figure 3* below. Users requested the Health Minister to implement stricter actions against defaulters of the new normal practices and protocols implemented by the government. The efforts of the State Government of Assam for taking appropriate measures to contain the outbreak in its initial phase were also appreciated widely by the Twitter users who responded with 'Thank you' tweets to the Health Minister's updates. Those response tweets included the presence of positive sentiment with keywords like 'accurate', 'extraordinary', 'active', and 'calm'. For example,

Sir respect to your hard work n dedication. It's your hard work n forsightedness that is making everyone calm n stay at peace indoors. Sir there should be a big applause for the committment you have shown for the people of assam. We know Assam is in safe hands.... (Anks, 2020)

Figure 3. User sentiment on social distancing practices
Source: IntenCheck software report

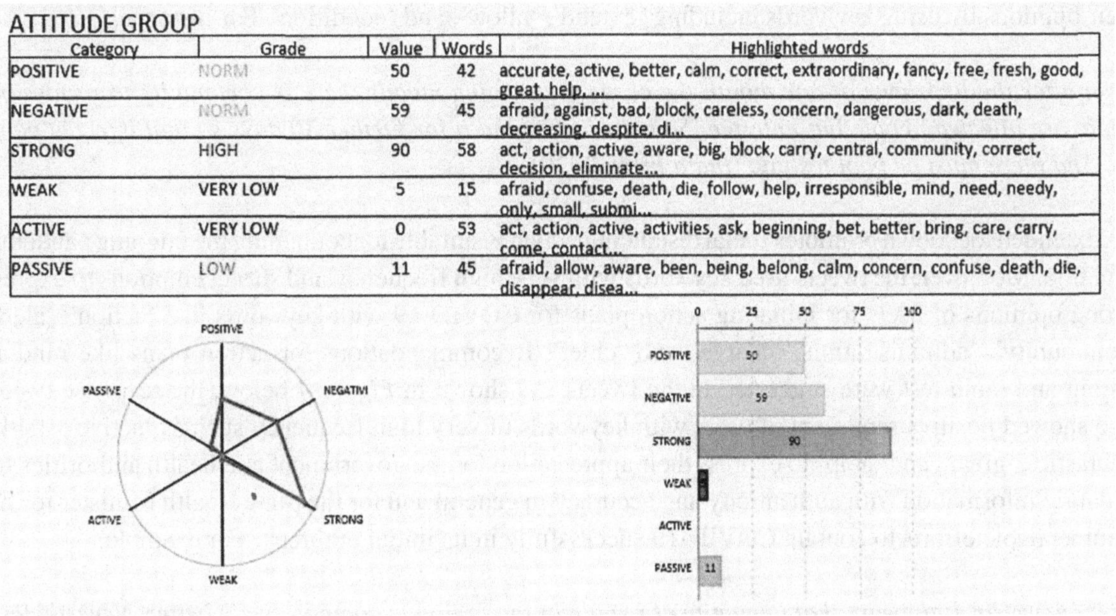

ATTITUDE GROUP

Category	Grade	Value	Words	Highlighted words
POSITIVE	NORM	50	42	accurate, active, better, calm, correct, extraordinary, fancy, free, fresh, good, great, help, ...
NEGATIVE	NORM	59	45	afraid, against, bad, block, careless, concern, dangerous, dark, death, decreasing, despite, di...
STRONG	HIGH	90	58	act, action, active, aware, big, block, carry, central, community, correct, decision, eliminate...
WEAK	VERY LOW	5	15	afraid, confuse, death, die, follow, help, irresponsible, mind, need, needy, only, small, submi...
ACTIVE	VERY LOW	0	53	act, action, active, activities, ask, beginning, bet, better, bring, care, carry, come, contact...
PASSIVE	LOW	11	45	afraid, allow, aware, been, being, belong, calm, concern, confuse, death, die, disappear, disea...

The health authorities of the state were successful in containing the outbreak of COVID-19 in its initial phase which was much appreciated on Twitter and other social media platforms. However, negative sentiment was evident with high frequency of keywords like 'careless', 'dangerous', 'death', 'dark', and 'afraid' which showed not only the panic and anxiety of people but also user concern for public to stay safe and follow the guidelines mandated by the government. Moreover, suggestions of Twitter users for social distancing indicated their knowledge on the seriousness of the pandemic situation across the country and worldwide which could be considered as one of the deciding factors of the virus containment and prevention in the researched region during its initial phase.

Public Demand for Lockdown Extension

The study reported public awareness on the causes and effects of the COVID-19 pandemic. Even though Assam witnessed a relatively low flow of the outbreak than the rest of India at the time of research, people were watchful enough to comprehend the gravity of the situation and reacted accordingly. This was evident in their Twitter updates as well. While the users highly appreciated the regular updates and remarkable steps taken by the State Health Minister, they demanded extension of lockdown which was for 21 days at the initial phase for the entire country. It is important to note that while the rigid lockdown across the country was successful and widely appreciated, it did not go well with countries outside India. As researchers studied and found, an adverse scenario was observed in the United States where rumors about a national lockdown fueled panic buying of groceries and stationaries (Spencer, 2020). This further led to disruption in supply chain resulting in widening demand-supply gaps and increasing food insecurities among the people with low socioeconomic status and other vulnerable population. People in the researched region were fully aware of the intensity of this and similar situations across the world.

Hence, the demand for extension was made by the Twitter users for the researched region where they felt extended lockdown would be crucial in containing the region as a green zone. The users expressed their opinions by using keywords including 'extend', 'allow', and 'condition'. For instance,

Even after the lockdown of one month the cases are coming means there is community transmission. There are infected people but untested. So better to extend it for further 30 days so that infected come up. And there must be pool testing. (India First, 2020)

Extended lockdown promotes social distancing which is suitable for containing the ongoing pandemic situation. Moreover, the tweets used keywords with very high frequency and strong emotions to express strong opinions of users for initiating action plans for COVID-19 with keywords like 'action', 'alert', 'community', 'administration', 'charge', and 'chief'. Recommendations for action plans like random testing and rapid test were suggested in the tweets. As shown in *Figure 4* below, the response tweets also showed positive sentiment of users with keywords of very high frequency such as 'active', 'faith', 'fantastic', 'great', and 'help' to express their appreciation for the government and health authorities for updating information with authenticity and accuracy in general and for the State Health Minister for his commendable efforts to contain COVID-19 successfully in its initial outbreak. For example,

Great news sir. It appears that immunity of people in the region is comparatively better. Nevertheless, the effort put in by you and the entire Health Department is commendable. Jai Hind. (Arup, 2020)

However, the demand for lockdown extension was also evident as a crucial one with the negative opinions being expressed by keywords like 'blame', 'condolences', 'deadly', and 'destruction' indicating the anguish and panic of users about the ongoing situation. This was mainly caused by the widespread outbreak of COVID-19 and its extremely adverse outcomes in the intensively affected regions across the world. Looking at the global situation of the pandemic, the suggestion for extended lockdown was a valid one in the researched region for its continuous successful containment.

Regular Updates on Localities and Problems Caused by the Pandemic Situation

The results reported the use of cognizant verbal expressions by the Twitter users while preferring and engaging in direct interaction with and regular updates to the concerned authority. This finding aligns with the second research question and objective and explains the concerned issues. This finding is in contrast with the study of Fu et al. (2016) which reported the Twitter users' reliance on user-generated content rather than the content updated by the government or concerned authorities. It is important to note that the State Health Minister took to his Twitter account for updating the COVID-19 situations of Assam regularly which gave Twitter users a perfect platform for directly interacting with him. This is in line with the suggestions recommended by Chew and Eysenbach (2010) and Fung et al. (2014) who found Twitter as a reliable social media platform for knowledge dissemination on pandemic outbreak and suggested its use by governments and health authorities sharing updates and raising concerns in such situations. Ahmed et al. (2018) also found it to be a reliable source for political information seeking and dissemination, thus facilitating connections with political leaders. This directly aligns with the current study which connected general public with the State Health Minister for directly communicating their information and concerns through their retweets and responses to the former's tweet updates on the pandemic outbreak.

Figure 4. User sentiment on demand for lockdown extension
Source: IntenCheck software report

ATTITUDE GROUP				
Category	Grade	Value	Words	Highlighted words
POSITIVE	VERY HIGH	98	39	active, basic, especially, even, faith, fantastic, free, gain, good, great, help, honorable, ho...
NEGATIVE	NORM	64	37	against, black, blame, condolences, deadly, deep, defeat, destruction, disease, down, failure, ...
STRONG	VERY HIGH	98	53	action, active, administration, aggressive, alert, army, charge, chief, community, deadly, deep...
WEAK	NORM	36	15	admit, common, failure, follow, help, hide, loss, minimum, need, needy, nothing, only, private,...
ACTIVE	LOW	8	59	action, active, administration, aggressive, alert, care, charge, come, contact, control, credit...
PASSIVE	NORM	21	43	admit, agree, allow, been, being, believe, common, condition, disease, emotion, extend, failure...

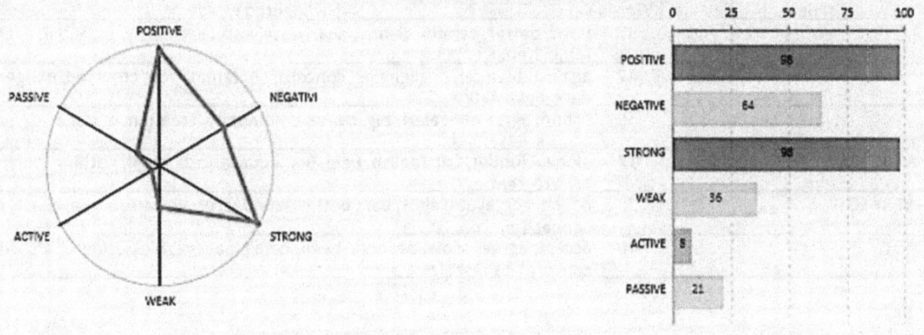

In light of this discussion, the current study found that users acknowledged the Twitter updates of the State health authorities credible to receive latest updates on the outbreak of COVID-19. Therefore, they used the Twitter account of the State Health Minister for raising their varied concerns and issues caused by the pandemic situation while responding directly to his regular tweets. Apart from their problems, the Twitter users also provided latest updates on their respective localities due to COVID-19. As shown in *Figure 5* below, users demonstrated strong expressions on the awareness of the situation with keywords like 'action', 'alert', 'community', 'decision', and 'demand' while updating the Health Minister on the conditions of their respective localities. For example,

Sir,as still lockdown seems as the best way to fight against Corona than is it necessary to open wine shops risking spread of the same. If not when agricultural goods start decomposing in fields it is better to rethink the decision please.All hv faith in u. (Sarma, 2020)

There were positive reactions from some users with the use of keywords like 'essential', 'ease', 'careful', 'basic', and 'better' to appreciate the effort of the government. However, negative sentiments were equally voiced out by using keywords like 'blunder', 'challenging', 'contamination', 'crowded', and 'dangerous' mainly to raise alarming concerns about defaulters who did not follow the COVID-19 health and hygiene instructions properly or not at all. Twitter users were aware that those defaulters are an obvious threat to the ongoing pandemic situation possibly causing to its outbreak. For example,

Sir who all hiding their identity please don't give them treatment also let them go for die. They will become dangerous for entire humanity. (Alam, 2020)

The tweet above indicates a grave concern that reported there were people who were exposed to the pandemic-hit areas, the red zones, or infected individuals but chose to refrain from checking and updating their health status mainly due to the fear of getting infected with the virus. But most importantly, they were scared of being socially isolated from their respective societies or communities. This has made the Twitter users of the researched region demand more health checkups by the health authorities and identify the 'defaulters' who did not follow health measures.

Figure 5. User sentiment on regular pandemic updates from authorities
Source: IntenCheck software report

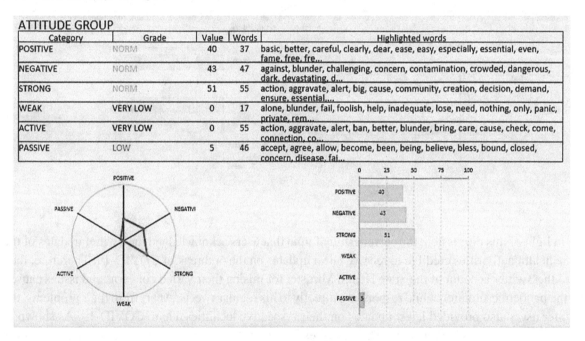

Use of Abusive Words Expressing Panic among the Public

The results found the use of abusive words by Twitter users as an expression for dealing with panic regarding the COVID-19 crisis. This finding aligns with the third research question and objective. At the same time, the use of abusive language also hinted tinge of communal nationalism at play. This aligns with previous studies (Oyeyemi et al., 2014) that reported the likely impacts of panic during a pandemic outbreak. It further reported two outcomes that panic can evoke. It can instigate the flow of misinformation on social media while giving way to frequent use of abusive language in the user content.

In the context of the current study, the twitter users were angry and disappointed due to the panic created on social media about the gradual pandemic outbreak across India and almost a hysterical situation across the world which was strongly evident in the tweets. Studies reported that misinformation related to the diagnosis and treatment of COVID-19 disseminated on social media and other online media confused people and healthcare providers across the world who are dealing with relatively less researched diseases (Spencer, 2020). Thus, creating rumors and hoaxes on social media may not only evoke panic among general population but also create social stigma around the disease resulting in discreet home quarantine and social isolation practices. This was evident in many countries including India that reported hundreds of confirmed cases infected by a single individual who visited their mosque or church despite their doctor's advice to remain on home isolation or without notifying their respective health authorities about their visit (Kasulis, 2020). While such rumors and misinformation created panic and hysteria among general population making it difficult for health authorities to contain the infection or control the pandemic across populations, it gave way to the spreading of fraud and negativity across social media platforms. As shown in *Figure 6* below, there was a very high frequency of negative sentiments among Twitter users evident through their use of keywords like 'alarming', 'anarchy', 'adversity', 'catastrophe', 'challenging', and 'block'. Such various abuses were hurled mainly at the government and concerned health authorities to criticize their lenient approach towards defaulters as well as the precautionary measures to be taken for the outbreak containment. Moreover, the panic evident from their response tweets entailed their watchfulness of the situation and their readiness to face it with any consequence. This was further evident from their strong opinions and sentiments with their highly frequent use of keywords like 'action', 'administration', 'alert', 'army', 'appropriate', and 'authority'. For example,

Figure 6. User sentiment on expressions for panic
Source: IntenCheck software report

ATTITUDE GROUP

Category	Grade	Value	Words	Highlighted words
POSITIVE	NORM	30	68	above, adequate, appropriate, beautiful, better, calm, cooperation, courage, dear, easy, econom...
NEGATIVE	VERY HIGH	97	89	abuses, adversity, against, alarming, anarchy, bad, blind, block, catastrophe, challenging, con...
STRONG	HIGH	95	104	action, administration, afford, alert, appropriate, army, authority, battle, bear, big, block, ...
WEAK	VERY LOW	0	33	apart, breakdown, decrease, desperate, diminish, disastrous, fall, follow, foolish, handful, he...
ACTIVE	VERY LOW	0	74	action, administration, alert, arrangement, ask, battle, better, bomb, bring, build, care, catc...
PASSIVE	VERY LOW	0	76	attention, become, been, being, believe, bless, bound, calm, coincidence, complete, decrease, d...

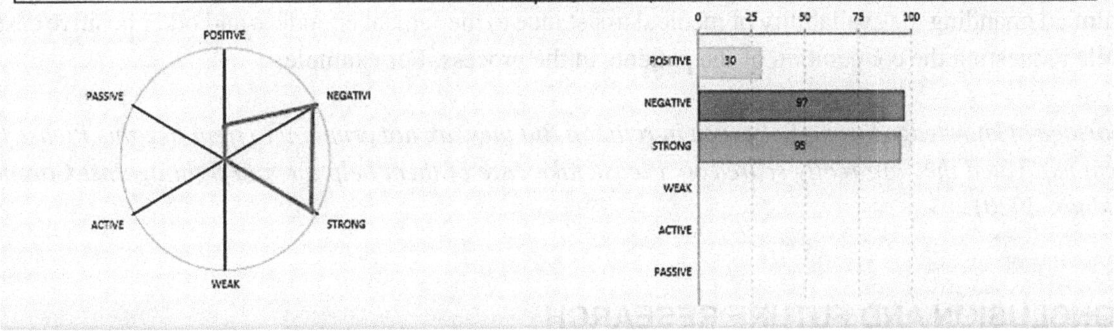

Sad news. This should alert us .Let good civic sense prevails .Let us help the administration by abiding the directions and stay home. Hon'ble Himantada is toiling hard and doing the best he can do. We should not undo his efforts. (Duronto, 2020)

Further, their response tweets continuously demanded stricter action from the authorities in order to contain the gradual outbreak of the pandemic. It is important to note that during the months of the initial outbreak of COVID-19 in Assam (March-May, 2020), most of the positive cases found in the region were attendees of the Tablighi Jamaat; a religious gathering practiced by the Muslim community in the nation as well as abroad, organized in Nizamuddin Markaz, New Delhi as updated in the newspapers, media reports, and social media. The Health Minister of Assam updated the details daily on his Twitter account.

This further led to a public outrage on social media due to which the pandemic outbreak in the researched region received a religious and/or communal outcry among public in Assam. It was evident in the use of abusive and hate words on Twitter as well as on other social media platforms. It is important to note that incitement of hate words and speech on various social media platforms are caused by massive online offensives as reported by previous studies (Vigna et al., 2017) which is evident in the current study as well. The study also reported that the hate can be directed towards individuals or wide groups, usually discriminated for some features such as race or gender. The current study reported a similar finding when the Twitter updates were flooded with selective attacks at the Jamaat attendees mainly for religious and communal reasons. Some of the response tweets in the study used keywords like 'breakdown', 'diminish', 'disastrous', and 'foolish' to express their opinion towards this religious and communal uproar. For example,

Sir please declare all those people who r hiding irrespective of religion as criminal and strict action like shoot and sight should be implemented. They are now become virus for us. extremely sorry sir if I. Wrong. (Deka, 2020)

The courage we get few days back to fight against covid19 will diminish becoz of these kind of blind religious freaks..destroying d society, destroing d nation..its time to stand 2gethr, fight 2gethr.. (Rupjit, 2020)

However, it did not outgrow as the Jamaat participants from the researched region returning home were attended with proper medical care, and they eventually came negative. While the religious and communal outcry was beginning to make noise, Twitter users were prompt enough to stifle it by using keywords with positive sentiment, including 'adequate', 'appropriate', 'cooperation', 'courage', and 'calm', demanding the availability of medical assistance to the Jamaat attendees and other positive cases while requesting the cooperation of the patients in the process. For example,

Shortage of knowledge Strong Believe in in religion But they are not criminal to treat like this Please let them motivated they are really scared sir Please take care of them help them to fight against Corona. (Akhtar, 2020)

CONCLUSION AND FUTURE RESEARCH

The current study provided an exploratory research of the Twitter messages on COVID-19 in its initial outbreak in Assam, India by employing sentiment analysis. The results reported three main findings:

- General awareness of Twitter users on the pandemic outbreak in the researched region.
- Their reactions and responses to the outbreak of Covid-19 as well as panic and negativity.

- Their knowledge and responses to the authenticity and reliability of information sources about COVID-19 pandemic outbreak.

However, this study focused on the time of the initial phase of the pandemic outbreak which limited the scope of research for the current study. The ongoing pandemic situation is witnessing a sea of information floating on various social media platforms which requires further investigation for observing and analyzing different perspectives and possibilities on the use of content and language to disseminate information and knowledge on the pandemic.

The current study also provided a sentiment analysis of tweets responded to the COVID-19 updates by the Health Minister of Assam, India during the initial period of the pandemic outbreak in the region. The study particularly explored the reactions and responses of the Twitter users in relation to their knowledge dissemination on the pandemic outbreak. It also explored their reactions to panic and negativity through use of language and content, and their responses to the authenticity and reliability of information on Twitter regarding the pandemic. The findings reported the response tweets to the COVID-19 updates showing users' varied attitudes and sentiments while expressing their general awareness about the crisis and its widespread outbreak.

In the context of expressing their concerns about the ongoing pandemic situation, the study found the Twitter users to be well-aware of the seriousness of the infectious disease and its gradual outbreak. Their awareness was evident in the response tweets to the health authority's regular updates. Previous studies discussed earlier have informed how a pandemic outbreak can evoke panic and create hysteria among people in places where the outbreak flow is high as well as in those areas where its occurrence is relatively low or zero. The aspect of panic can further be fueled by the nonstop flow of information, misinformation, and disinformation on various social media platforms. Twitter, being one of the most widely used social media platforms, is no exception to it. Since users are exposed to a wide range of information, being updated by reliable sources or sources from government or concerned authorities is highly recommended.

The current study concludes that there has been relatively less panic and hysteria among the Twitter users responding to the Health Minister's tweets in Assam compared to the rest of India during the initial phase of the pandemic outbreak. While more of performing *puja* and observing rituals were reported from various parts of India by news channels, the people of Assam seem to have relatively more patience and practical attitudes towards the various aspects of the ongoing pandemic. Their tweets indicated less panic and more awareness about the situation with frequently used keywords like 'action', 'alert', 'assistance', and 'administration' demanding cooperation from people as well as from government authorities. Moreover, regular and at times daily updates by the Health Minister or health authorities made the pandemic-related information and updates more reliable and authentic for users to believe and follow due to which it was relevant and easier for people to stay aware of the ongoing crisis-like situation. The ongoing pandemic situation has already created havoc across the world by infecting millions and killing thousands, and the numbers are still growing. In the light of this grave situation, it is important to exchange correct information and regular updates, implement and follow precautionary health measures, and react and respond to the situation with less panic and negativity for both government authorities and public. Therefore, using the appropriate choice of words is crucial for both general users and government authorities in disseminating information related to COVID-19 particularly on social media platforms.

Since Twitter is one of the most popular and widely used social media platforms and previous studies advocated for its reliability as the dependable source of information for knowledge dissemination during such pandemic situations (Chew & Eysenbach, 2010; Fung et al., 2014; Ahmed et al., 2018), there is considerable room for rational inquiries into the use of language, types and style of content, and the analysis of expressions and opinions posted and updated on Twitter. Regarding the broadcasting of misinformation and disinformation, further research is required to address and analyze the measures adopted by the government and health authorities as well as online platforms to identify and eliminate potentially harmful misinformation, hoaxes, and rumors. Further research on these aspects will be effective in finding and understanding Twitter users' sentiments and attitudes towards the ongoing pandemic outbreak and the situations caused by it. Moreover, there is adequate scope for further research on how frontline healthcare providers find and receive accurate and reliable information online regarding the outbreak, its containment, and possibility of vaccine availability and how they respond. The use of language can further be explored and evaluated to check if the updates and other authentic information are circulated proficiently and accurately among population in places where the outbreak intensity is relatively less, whether online or offline, so that the validated information is communicated across platforms efficiently. Moreover, there can be a comparative study on these aspects between the initial and later phases of the outbreak.

REFERENCES

Agarwal, A., Xie, B., Vovsha, I., Rambow, O., & Passonneau, R. J. (2011). Sentiment analysis of Twitter data. In *Proceedings of the Workshop on Language in Social Media (LSM 2011)* (pp. 30-38). Academic Press.

Ahmed, S., Jaidka, K., & Cho, J. (2018). Do birds of different feather flock together? Analyzing the political use of social media through a language-based approach in a multilingual context. *Computers in Human Behavior, 86*, 299–310. doi:10.1016/j.chb.2018.04.051

Ahmed, W., Bath, P. A., Sbaffi, L., & Demartini, G. (2020). Zika outbreak of 2016: Insights from Twitter. In Social Computing and Social Media. Participation, User Experience, Consumer Experience, and Applications of Social Computing (pp. 447-458). Springer. doi:10.1007/978-3-030-49576-3_32

Akhtar, J. [@JavedAk32243808]. (2020, April 2). *Shortage of knowledge Strong Believe in in religion But they are not criminal to treat like this Please let them motivated they are really scared sir Please take care of them help them to fight against Corona* [Tweet]. Twitter. https://twitter.com/JavedAk32243808/status/1245524943606972417

Alam, A. [@AzarAlam0]. (2020, April 2). *SIR WHO ALL HIDING THEIR IDENTITY PLEASE DON'T GIVE THEM TREATMENT ALSO LET THEM GO FOR DIE. THEY WILL BECOME DANGEROUS FOR ENTIRE HUMANITY* [Tweet]. Twitter. https://twitter.com/AzarAlam0/status/1245596317444747264

Anks. [@Anks60869416]. (2020, April 2). *Sir respect to your hard work n dedication. Its your hard work n forsightedness that is making everyone calm n stay at peace indoors. Sir there should be a big applause for the committment you have shown for the people of assam. We know Assam is in safe hands....* [Tweet]. Twitter. https://twitter.com/Anks60869416/status/1245545457184641024

Arup. [@Arup64094929]. (2020, April 26). *Great news sir. It appears that immunity of people in the region is comparatively better. Nevertheless, the effort put in by you and the entire Health Department is commendable. Jai Hind* [Tweet]. Twitter. https://twitter.com/Arup64094929/status/1254364488381464576

Biddu, S. N. [@BidduSaugat]. (2020, March 31). *Sir please look into the matter that some people are breaking the LOCKDOWN at evry steps and roaming freely where and there in our karimganj Honourable sir please talk to our karimganj administration* [Tweet]. Twitter. https://twitter.com/BidduSaugat/status/1244992392425439232

Chachan, M. [@chachan_mukesh]. (2020, April 4). *Hope now people realise that religious practice won't just help in fighting covid-19. Let the senses prevail and those coming from Nizamuddin and other parts of India voluntarily submits themselves for examination. Let's help @himantabiswa to end this crisis in Assam* [Tweet]. Twitter. https://twitter.com/chachan_mukesh/status/1246317359956017152

Chew, C., & Eysenbach, G. (2010). Pandemics in the age of Twitter: Content analysis of tweets during the 2009 H1N1 outbreak. *PLoS One, 5*(11), e14118. doi:10.1371/journal.pone.0014118 PMID:21124761

Collinson, S., Khan, K., & Heffernan, J. M. (2015). The effects of media reports on disease spread and important public health measurements. *PLoS One, 10*(11), e0141423. Advance online publication. doi:10.1371/journal.pone.0141423 PMID:26528909

Deccan Chronicle. (2020, February 8). *Pooja to ward off Corona virus.* http://www.deccanchronicle.com/amp/lifestyle/viral-and-trending/080220/pooja-to-ward-off-corona-virus.html

Deep. [@Deep57358864]. (2020, April 4). *Sir please stop mentioning "Patient is related to Nizamuddin event" in every tweet. This will create more hatred among the different communities. I don't think that is helping us anyway. We should try to face the situation with peace and love. Jai Hind @himantabiswa* [Tweet]. Twitter. https://twitter.com/Deep57358864/status/1246325314663284736

Deka, B. [@BIPULDEKA1]. (2020, April 2). *Sir please declare all those people who r hiding irrespective of religion as criminal and strict action like shoot and sight should be implemented.they are now become virus for us.extreamly sorry sir if I. Wrong* [Tweet]. Twitter. https://twitter.com/BIPULDEKA1/status/1245584368241766400

Duronto. [@Duronto31440015]. (2020, April 10). *Sad news.This should alert us. Let good civic sense prevails. Let us help the administration by abiding the directions and stay home.Hon'ble Himantada is toiling hard and doing the best he can do.We should not undo his efforts* [Tweet]. Twitter. https://twitter.com/Duronto31440015/status/1248469859265961985

Fu, K. W., Liang, H., Saroha, N., Tse, Z. T. H., Ip, P., & Fung, I. C. H. (2016). How people react to Zika virus outbreaks on Twitter? A computational content analysis. *American Journal of Infection Control, 44*(12), 1700–1702. doi:10.1016/j.ajic.2016.04.253 PMID:27566874

Fung, I. C. H., Tse, Z. T. H., Cheung, C. N., Miu, A. S., & Fu, K. W. (2014). Ebola and the social media. *Lancet, 384*(9961), 2207. Advance online publication. doi:10.1016/S0140-6736(14)62418-1 PMID:25625391

India First. [@VoiceOfIndia007]. (2020, April 28). *Even after the lockdown of one month the cases are coming means there is community transmission. There are infected people but untested. So better to extend it for further 30 days so that infected come up. And there must be pool testing* [Tweet]. Twitter. https://twitter.com/VoiceOfIndia007/status/1255128482243198976

Kaila, R. P., & Prasad, A. V. K. (2020). Informational flow on Twitter – Coronavirus outbreak topic modelling approach. *International Journal of Advanced Research in Engineering and Technology, 11*(3), 128–134.

Kasulis, K. (2020). "Patient 31" and South Korea's sudden spike in coronavirus cases. *Aljazeera*. https://www.aljazeera.com/news/2020/03/31-south-korea-sudden-spike-coronavirus-cases-200303065953841.html

Liang, H., Fung, I. C. H., Tse, Z. T. H., Yin, J., Chan, C.-H., Pechta, L. E., Smith, B. J., Marquez-Lameda, R. D., Meltzer, M. I., Lubell, K. M., & Fu, K.-W. (2019). How did Ebola information spread on Twitter: Broadcasting or viral spreading? *BMC Public Health, 19*(438), 438. Advance online publication. doi:10.118612889-019-6747-8 PMID:31023299

Liu, B. (2011). Opinion mining and sentiment analysis. Web data mining: Exploring hyperlinks, contents, and usage data, 459-526. doi:10.1007/978-3-642-19460-3_11

Oyeyemi, S. O., Gabarron, E., & Wynn, R. (2014). Ebola, Twitter, and misinformation: A dangerous combination? *BMJ (Clinical Research Ed.), 349*(oct145), g6178. doi:10.1136/bmj.g6178 PMID:25315514

Raman, S. (2020). *Public health experts worry about spread of COVID-19 misinformation*. https://www.rollcall.com/2020/03/18/public-health-experts-worry-abuout-spread-of-covid-19-misinformation/

Rajbongshi, M. P. [@ManashPratimRa3]. (2020, March 31). *It's a very sad news and danger situation for assam. People assam please lockdown is not a joke. It's a a very critical situation for us. Please take it seriously. And support our #Assamgovt #assampolice. #assam_fight_against_covid19* [Tweet]. Twitter. https://twitter.com/ManashPratimRa3/status/1244994393255235585

Reuters. (2020, March 14). *Hindu group offers cow urine in a bid to ward off coronavirus*. https://www.reuters.com/article/amp/idINKBN2110CF

Rout, J. K., Choo, K. R., Dash, A. K., Bakshi, S., Jena, S. K., & Williams, K. L. (2017). A model for sentiment and emotion analysis of unstructured social media text. *Electronic Commerce Research, 2018*(18), 181–199.

Rupjit. [@Rupbarsha1]. (2020, April 3). *The courage we get few days back to fight against covid19 will diminish becoz of these kind of blind religious freaks.destroing d society, destroing d nation.its time to stand 2gethr, fight 2gethr* [Tweet]. Twitter. https://twitter.com/Rupbarsha1/status/1246088359274930176

Sarma, M. [@MANABENDRASAR19]. (2020, April 14). *Sir,as still lockdown seems as the best way to fight against Corona than is it necessary to open wine shops risking spread of the same. If not when agricultural goods start decomposing in fields it is better to rethink the decision please.All hv faith in u* [Tweet]. Twitter. https://twitter.com/MANABENDRASAR19/status/1250126223218315264

Shu, K., Sliva, A., Wang, S., Tang, J., & Liu, H. (2017). *Fake News Detection on Social Media.* ACM SIGKDD Explore News., doi:10.1145/3137597.3137600

Spencer, S. H. (2020, March 16). *False claims of nationwide lockdown for COVID-19.* https://factcheck.org/2020/03/false-claims-of-nationwide-lockdown-for-covid-19/

Thakuria, M. [@MrinalThakuri12]. (2020, March 31). *We need more strict action against those people who went out during LOCK DOWN unnecessary otherwise the situation goes out of control...* [Tweet]. Twitter. https://twitter.com/MrinalThakuri12/status/1244981120543764480

Vigna, F. D., Cimino, A., Dell'Orletta, F., Petrocchi, M., & Tesconi, M. (2017). Hate me, hate me not: Hate speech detection on Facebook. *Proceedings of the First Italian Conference on Cybersecurity (ITA-SEC17),* 86-95. http://ceur-ws.org/Vol-1816/paper-09.pdf

ADDITIONAL READING

Abd-Alrazaq, A., Alhuwail, D., Househ, M., Hamdi, M., & Shah, Z. (2020). Top concerns of tweeters during the COVID-19 pandemic: Infoveillance study. *Journal of Medical Internet Research, 22*(4), e19016. doi:10.2196/19016 PMID:32287039

Alhajji, M., Al Khalifah, A., Aljubran, M., & Alkhalifah, M. (2020). Sentiment Analysis of Tweets in Saudi Arabia Regarding Governmental Preventive Measures to Contain COVID-19. Preprints 2020, 2020040031. http://doi:doi:10.20944/preprints202004.0031.v1

Belli, B. (2020, March 24). Yale webinars: Using emotional intelligence to combat COVID-19 anxiety. https://news.yale.edu/2020/03/24/yale-webinars-using-emotional-intelligence-combat-covid-19-anxiety

Kumar, A., Khan, S. U., & Kalra, A. (2020). COVID-19 pandemic: a sentiment analysis: A short review of the emotional effects produced by social media posts during this global crisis. *European Heart Journal, 41*(39), 3782–3783. doi:10.1093/eurheartj/ehaa597 PMID:32678890

Kruspe, A., Häberle, M., Kuhn, I., & Zhu, X. X. (2020). Cross-language sentiment analysis of European Twitter messages during the COVID-19 pandemic. *arXiv preprint arXiv:2008.12172.*

Lwin, M. O., Lu, J., Sheldenkar, A., Schulz, P. J., Shin, W., Gupta, R., & Yang, Y. (2020). Global sentiments surrounding the COVID-19 pandemic on Twitter: Analysis of Twitter trends. *JMIR Public Health and Surveillance, 6*(2), e19447. doi:10.2196/19447 PMID:32412418

Signorini, A., Segre, A. M., & Polgreen, P. M. (2011). The use of Twitter to track levels of disease activity and public concern in the US during the influenza A H1N1 pandemic. *PLoS One, 6*(5), e19467. doi:10.1371/journal.pone.0019467 PMID:21573238

Sooknanan, J., & Comissiong, D. M. G. (2020). Trending on social media: Integrating social media into infectious disease dynamics. *Bulletin of Mathematical Biology, 82*(7), 86. doi:10.100711538-020-00757-4 PMID:32617673

KEY TERMS AND DEFINITIONS

COVID-19: A disease caused by a new strain of coronavirus.

Crisis: A time of intense difficulty or danger, particularly addressing the ongoing pandemic outbreak of COVID-19.

Pandemic: An epidemic or disease occurring worldwide or over a very wide area while crossing international boundaries and affecting a large number of people.

Sentiment Analysis: An application for systematically identifying, extracting, quantifying, and studying affective states and subjective information.

Text Analysis: The process of automatically extracting high-quality information from text or different written sources.

This research was previously published in Rhetoric and Sociolinguistics in Times of Global Crisis; pages 320-341, copyright year 2021 by Information Science Reference (an imprint of IGI Global).

Chapter 96
Analyzing the Impact of e–WOM Text on Overall Hotel Performances:
A Text Analytics Approach

Aakash Aakash
https://orcid.org/0000-0002-3900-4215
University of Delhi, India

Anu G. Aggarwal
https://orcid.org/0000-0001-5448-9540
University of Delhi, India

Sanchita Aggarwal
University of Delhi, India

ABSTRACT

A flourishing of the importance of customer reviews has been observed in this digital era. This is especially true in hotel sector, which allows guests to express their satisfaction towards the service in the form of open-structured online reviews and overall ratings over travel agency websites. Using reviews data of 2001 hotels from Tripadvisor.com, the chapter analyzes the overall hotel performances through linguistic features of e-WOM such as its length, readability, sentiment, and volume. The chapter develops a regression model for evaluating guest satisfaction by using overall ratings as its measure, validated through hotel review data. Data analysis result shows that review volume, sentiment index, and readability have significant positive affect over guest satisfaction whereas length shows the negative influence. This chapter discusses beneficial implications for researchers and practitioners working in this field.

DOI: 10.4018/978-1-6684-6303-1.ch096

INTRODUCTION

In the times of emerging technologies, digitalization has perforated every field. To survive in present marketing environment, practitioners need to have an edge over their competitors at all times. Businesses have the tendency to easily adapt to the environment like a malleable alloy, which is also a need of the hour. Majority of the customer base is turning tech-savvy, which in turn creates a necessity for the companies to keep up with their dynamic customer landscape. Market practitioners are now realigning their businesses to online domain in order to streamline their everyday operations. Automation of operations comes with its own set of benefits. Besides indulging digital customer at all touch points during customer experience lifecycle, it effectively leads to increased efficiency, reduced related cost, enables better analysis and downsizes humanly error.

Recreation and tourism is a major sector of consideration for a majority of economies around the world. It contributes in innumerable ways to social, economic and other intangible benefits to them (Wood, Guerry, Silver, & Lacayo, 2013). Information on tourist trends and behavior in this realm is collected using user generated content on social platforms. With the emergence of cybernated environment, service industry has ventured into online marketing in full bloom. In the Online Travel Agencies, provision of hotel booking and other services through online mode has given rise to an ever-increasing amount of online textual data in the form of feedbacks and reviews (Tandon, Sharma, & Aggarwal, 2019). With the technological advancements, Word of Mouth (WOM) has taken the electronic form (EWOM) with an additional benefit on businesses in the form of wide reach among audience beyond the geographical and time constraints (Yen & Tang, 2019). EWOM can be described as a form of casual information exchange with other consumers through online technological platforms talking about usage and characteristics of a product or service or their seller (De Pelsmacker, van Tilburg, & Holthof, 2018).

User Generated Content (UGC) on the websites provides travelers with non- commercial information and travel experiences shared by fellow travelers. These uncensored, straight from the reviewers, expressions of experience are considered to be more reliable and current (Gretzel & Yoo, 2008). Customers perceive the information provided by the members of travel fraternity to be more trustworthy and influential as compared to that provided by the service providers (Fotis, Buhalis, & Rossides, 2012). A recent survey report by Nielsen states that 63% of the travel services and product customers, did a prior online investigation before the purchase of product or service (McKenzie & Adams, 2018).These results bespeak of the emerging trend of traveler's reliance on content available online as a part of decision making process. Today, these websites have become an important source of information for the travel destinations as well as the choice of activities to be conducted there (Xiang & Gretzel, 2010). A number of researchers have shown that EWOM axiomatically affect the product sales like books (Hong, Xu, Xu, Wang, & Fan, 2017), cars (Fan, Che, & Chen, 2017), movies (Duan, Gu, & Whinston, 2008), and cameras (Gu, Park, & Konana, 2012).

Since the nature of hospitality industry matches that of experiential goods, these studies strongly suggest that EWOM holds particular importance for experiential products as their quality level is obscured before consumption (Klein, 1998). Online reviews have notable effect in hotel sector when compared to other tourism segments as these are overwhelmingly referred by majority of users for "where to stay" decisions (Gretzel & Yoo, 2008). This customer-generated data is a rich source of information for the marketers as these reviews can be analyzed in depth to understand the customer psychology and their satisfaction level. To evaluate the role of travel reviews in decision making procedure, we need to find out the interpretation derived by users from the available EWOM. Existing research has shown that it's a human tendency to solicit viewpoint of peers in order to reduce the probability of making a bad decision (Goldsmith & Horowitz, 2006). Considering the abundant increase in the volume of EWOM available, conducting a deep analysis of text has become a pivotal task of data mining.

A recent report revealed that guest review websites are another most commonly used information source (first being the online search engines) for the travelers planning a trip. Service providers have therefore started utilizing EWOM as a advertising tool by encouraging consumers to share their feedback online (Yang, Park, & Hu, 2018). In this chapter, we are utilizing EWOM in the form of reviews. Few studies in the past have applied different methods to understand the factors affecting hotel ratings and in turn affecting the guest satisfaction level. Study of guests' opinions, rationales, details, and feelings, personalization or projection were taken up using Stance-shift analysis (Crotts, Mason, & Davis, 2009). Another study took into account average EWOM ratings, variation of ratings among EWOMs, price, city rank, official star rating category of the hotel as the factors affecting hotel sales (Ye, Law, & Gu, 2009). They considered review volume as a proxy of online bookings. Another approach in understanding these trivial issues was adopted which assessed the effect of deals, amenities, family friendliness, core product, staff and a hybrid of other factors on guest experience and satisfaction (Stringam & Gerdes Jr, 2010). Number of expert reviews and reviewing expertise level were studied to find out their effect on traveler's rating (Zhang, Zhang, & Yang, 2016). In this chapter, we propose to understand the impact of review volume, length, sentiment index and readability on hotel ratings, which is basically an indicator of guest experience.

Guest satisfaction is the main aim of the hotel industry. It is the evaluation of how many of the customers' expectation parameters are fulfilled by the service provider. Satisfaction is a feeling which is hard to express. OTA websites provide its users with the facility to rate the hotel and share their experience in the form of reviews. These overall ratings and textual reviews are the empirical representation of guest experience which are referred by people from travel community as well as the hotel industry to make informed decisions. Guest experience hold the ability to affect broadly all the factors of hotel business. Reviews in themselves influence the purchase decisions of other customers (Guo, Barnes, & Jia, 2017). Satisfaction of the guest affects the sales, revisit intension, positive EWOM probability and market reputation to name a few.

Consumer textual review analysis draws its strength from its ability to exhibit guest consumption experience, highlight key features of product and services people are talking about, and providing customers' mindset, notion, demand and inclination (Chau & Xu, 2012). Personnel from research community as well as the hotel industry want to know about (a) minutiae of guest experience in order to enhance product as well as service quality and (b) assessment of guest experience to get the idea of overall performance of the hotels. This can be utilized to make improved promotion strategies (Cantallops & Salvi, 2014). Review volume talks about the number of reviews posted on the OTA websites by the guests. Volume of EWOM have been found to have a direct relationship with awareness, hotel performance and hotel popularity (Viglia, Minazzi, & Buhalis, 2016; Zhao, Wang, Guo, & Law, 2015). The review volume of a product/service is considered to be one of the most crucial review facets. Reviews posted online, whether positive or negative are the indicator of hotel popularity and thus attract curious travelers, and serves to keep the product longer in limelight. It depicts the market reach of the product, reduces the uncertainty associated with it and motivates peer behavior ("Go with the flow") (De Pelsmacker et al., 2018).

One of the key features allied with EWOM is the review length. It is typically the measurement of number of characters contained in a EWOM posted about a specific product or service. Since EWOM is an unfiltered expression by the experience holder himself, it tends to be the most raw form of guests' feelings about the service or product availed by him. Thus, these reviews are often found to be a concoction of neutral, positive and negative words resulting in a lengthy review (Bradley, Sparks, & Weber, 2015). Moreover, a meticulous review containing considerable number of arguments is expected to provide a better picture of the product reviewed. Also, the length of review is an indicator of reviewers' involvement in writing it, and thus depicts his dedication to the travel community.

A focal objective of Lodging sector being experience based strives hard to capture customer experiences. Hotels have always employed the concept of customer feedbacks (earlier in the form of comment cards, feedback forms or market survey) and utilized it as a basis for amendments in hotels' operational framework. Guest experience is an intangible characteristic which is a challenge in itself to capture. To understand the mindset of the customer and get an insight into their sentiments associated with the hotel experience is the current field of interest. A sentiment is a thought, view, attitude or opinions which are rooted in feelings. Unlike physical goods, which comprise of characteristics that can be objectified, hotel experience is an experience good that contains the dimensions "good" or "bad". These are often difficult to quantify and extract empirical values from. Therefore, the subjective opinions of uses that are embedded in their review is a critical source of information. These can be mined extensively for sentiment analysis and draw implementable insights (Mankad, Han, Goh, & Gavirneni, 2016).

The effectiveness of a review is highly affected by its ability to be meaningful to the reader. This in literature is termed as review readability which refers to the ease of understanding and ability to fathom the judgment related to a review posted online (M. Smith & Taffler, 1992). Readability of a review is viably defined as 'how easy is to read and comprehend a textual content that carry the judgements related to the product/service being analyzed' (Calderón, Morales, Liu, & Hays, 2006). The linguistic style of a review clearly portrays the education level of the reviewer (Geetha, Singha, & Sinha, 2017). The highly educated peoples are more accurate in their expression of opinions. A well-written review can be considered more reliable and influential.

The chapter attempts to study a conceptual relationship between the overall hotel ratings and EWOM measures namely number of reviews, review length, sentiment index and readability through econometric modelling. This modelling enables the marketer to understand the impact of each independent variable onto the dependent variable. These models are applied on secondary data collected from an online travel agency (OTA). We have developed a python program to process the data for the hypotheses testing.

The remaining chapter is organized as follows: next section provides a comprehensive literature review related to EWOM in e-services and hotel guest satisfaction. Then development of the hypotheses are provided, next we present the methodology of the study. The data analysis results are provided in subsequent section. Then discussion related to the results and their managerial implication is provided. Final section comprises of the limitations and the future scope of the study.

LITERATURE REVIEW

EWOM in E-Service

Due to the innate uncertainty associated with an untried product or service, consumer often bank upon WOM for making related decisions (Laroche, McDougall, Bergeron, & Yang, 2004). Before the advancement of technology and emergence of Web 2.0, there was a notion of traditional marketing, but with the spread of internet communication, EWOM has gained significant importance. EWOM is defined "any positive/negative sentiments expressed by potential/actual/former customers related to the product or overall firm, which is online available for multitude of peoples and institutions" (Vermeulen & Seegers, 2009). The anomalousness of EWOM lies in its reach of the reviewers' impact i.e. number of people that can be influenced and the speed of interaction (Cantallops & Salvi, 2014). This evolution of customers' decision-making cycle (information sharing, acquiring of knowledge, decision making) has presented the market professionals with an opportunity to augment their communication effectiveness and thus target a broader market than ever before. However, in this new age electronically interactive world, where communication of individuals' opinions knows no bounds, the 'customer turned reviewers' have dethroned the hoteliers from the role of travel opinion leaders (Litvin, Goldsmith, & Pan, 2008).

From marketers' viewpoint, utilization of customer reviews to make buying decisions is a two way opportunity. Firstly, a positive review highlights their good services. Secondly, though a negative review may stake the hotels' reputation but it provides them with the problem areas which can be worked upon to improve the satisfaction level. Prior studies have focused on this problem along with additional variables like ego, vengeance and help to decipher the customers' intention to write a review (Dixit, Badgaiyan, & Khare, 2019). Purchase involvement and service experience have also been identified as momentous antecedents of review providing motivation (E. E. K. Kim, 2017).Further,studies have been able to identify information and e- service quality to be the driving measures of guest satisfaction. A satisfied customer is more inclined towards providing EWOM to the hotel (Rizal, Yussof, Amin, & Chen-Jung, 2018). The language in which a review is written has also been established as an influential factor on service rating provided by the guest These studies clearly depict the importance of customer feedback in the hotel sector. Also, impact of EWOM in e-services can be clearly identified from the previous literature.

Hotel Guest Experience and Satisfaction

A travel trip whether for the recreational purpose or for the work purpose is always followed by an experience which the traveler felt or encountered. These guest experiences are the major source of information for the service provider. It can provide a snapshot of hotel performance, which can be evaluated and analyzed for various managerial purposes. Understanding of customer experience involves various intricate factors majorly because of its personal nature. Due to the competitive nature of hospitality industry, it is vital for the hoteliers to understand guest experience and improve their satisfaction level. High guest satisfaction level has been associated with positive hotel image, willingness to make recommendation and revisit intention (Hu, Kandampully, & Juwaheer, 2009; Velázquez, Blasco, & Gil Saura, 2015). The amount of distance travelled by a tourist to reach the hotel has been studied to understand how it shapes their experience and thus their satisfaction at a destination (Park, Yang, & Wang, 2019). Hotel property's accessibility to various attraction points, airports, public transportation and local businesses was found to be a significant determinant of guest satisfaction (Yang, Mao, & Tang, 2018). Tourist satisfaction has also been studied in combination with hotels' event experience. This delivered a clear understanding about guest experience in a gust driven environment (Boo & Busser, 2018). Linguistic knowledge of the traveler has been found to influence their key satisfaction factor. It was found that customers who spoke diverse languages, emphasized on different hotel attributes in forming their overall satisfaction rating (Y. Liu, Teichert, Rossi, Li, & Hu, 2017). Prior studies have also proved guest satisfaction to be an antecedent of guest return intention (Susskind, Kacmar, & Borchgrevink, 2018). Further, guests' demographic profile and hotel class has been found to affect the satisfaction level (Fernandes & Fernandes, 2018). Also, in another study, he determinants of customer satisfaction or dissatisfaction were found to be unique and for different variety of hotels, namely full-service hotels, limited service hotels, suite hotels with and without food and beverages (Xu & Li, 2016). So it won't be incorrect to say that guest satisfaction is the key element of study for the all the aspects of hotel industry. As the customer satisfaction directly controls a hotels' market position.

EWOM, Text and Statistical Analysis for Guest Satisfaction

Table 1. Shows the relevant literature comprising the techniques used for review text analysis.

S. No.	Author	Antecedent	Technique Used	Endogenous Variable
1	(Anu G. Aggarwal & Aakash, 2018)	Sentiment index, product rating, review volume, length and price	Econometric modelling and text analytics	Sales rank
2.	(Rizal et al., 2018)	Information, e-service, system quality	Partial least squares – structural equation modeling	EWOM intention
3	(Y. Liu et al., 2017)	User language and hotel attributes	Regression Analysis	Hotel star rating
4	(Xu & Li, 2016)	Hotel attributes	LSA	Guest satisfaction and dissatisfaction
5	(Z. Liu & Park, 2015)	Messenger and message factors	TOBIT regression model	Review helpfulness
6	(Marinkovic, Senic, Ivkov, Dimitrovski, & Bjelic, 2014)	Hotel atmosphere, quality, price	Structural Equation Modeling (SEM)	Customer satisfaction and revisit intention
7	(Qi & Qiang, 2013)	Review volume and overall hotel ratings	Econometric modelling	Hotel sales
8	(Öğüt & Onur Taş, 2012)	Customer rating and star rating	Linear regression	Hotel sales and Price
9	(Nam, Ekinci, & Whyatt, 2011)	Hotel brand equity	SEM	Hotel brand loyalty
10	(Chand, 2010)	Human resource management (HRM) practices	SEM	Customer satisfaction and Hotel Performance
11	(Wu & Liang, 2009)	Environment, interaction with employees and fellow customers	Regression analysis	Customer satisfaction with luxury hotels.
12	(Jeong & Mindy Jeon, 2008)	Hotel characteristics	Descriptive analysis and ANOVA	Return intention

Guest satisfaction is the key factor in hospitality industry. The sole purpose of marketers and practitioners in lodging sector is related to the psychological, emotional and physical satisfaction of their guests. Customers' intention to post EWOMs has been worked upon in the past and it was observed that quality of the information provided, e-service and system quality have significant impact on intention to provide EWOM (Rizal et al., 2018). Impact of EWOM on the sale of product is a hot topic in this industry (Anu G. Aggarwal & Aakash, 2018). Sales rank along with the price factor has also been studied. Higher customer rating was observed to result in higher sales and high pricing of hotels result (Öğüt & Onur Taş, 2012). People in research community have studied the effect of difference in spoken language of the customers on the hotel rating provided by them using regression analysis(Y. Liu et al., 2017). Study of the determinants of guest satisfaction has received considerable limelight. A study of luxury hotels was done and its results indicated that restaurant environment directly and positively affects the customer satisfaction where as interaction with staff and other customers had an indirect and positive impact on satisfaction level (Wu & Liang, 2009) Satisfaction and dissatisfaction determinants have been found to be different for different types of hotels by employing LSA text mining technique (Xu & Li, 2016). Another area which has been worked on is the customer satisfaction and the subsequent revisit intention associated with it. They took into account various factors namely atmosphere, quality of interaction and pricing to understand satisfaction(Marinkovic et al., 2014).

The effect of various reviewer characteristics (messenger factors) and both qualitative and quantitative review attributes (message factors) on the helpfulness of a review has also been studied(Z. Liu & Park, 2015) . They used TOBIT regression model to find that a combination of reviewer and review content factors positively influence the said reviews' helpfulness(Z. Liu & Park, 2015). Another study found that overall hotel ratings positively influence the hotel sales (Qi & Qiang, 2013). Further, a path model was proposed to study the effect of brand equity on brand loyalty in hospitality industry. Customer satisfaction was taken as mediating factor between hotel brand equity and hotel brand loyalty for the study conducted(Nam et al., 2011). Human resource management practices have been concluded to improve service quality, thus in turn enhancing hotel customer satisfaction and organizational performance (Chand, 2010). Another study engaged descriptive analysis and ANOVA technique to study the effect of hotel characteristics on guest satisfaction which in turn had an impact on return intention of the customer(Jeong & Mindy Jeon, 2008). Hence, it could be significant to analyze the impact of review (EWOM) characteristics on hotel guest satisfaction.

HYPOTHESES DEVELOPMENT

One significant feature of electronic-word-of-mouth (EWOM) is the way in which it has shown to the users. Electronic service marketplace such as TripAdvisor had more than 460 million reviews (EWOM) of activities, hotels, and restaurants which help them to see progress in enhancing unique visitors as well as reviews each quarter (ComScore, 2017). The EWOM interface contains four significant information: (1) The hotel's meta characteristics such as: address, hotel-ID, hotel-URL, imgURL, name, price. (2) The overall ratings to the hotel on a 1-5 Likert scale given by the reviewer. (3) The EWOM characteristics such as EWOM text, reviewer, reviewer's location, date, star-ratings (value, location, service, rooms, cleanliness, sleep quality), EWOM-ID, EWOM-title. Figure 1, shows an example of EWOM at TripAdvisor.in.

The guest satisfaction is a tedious task within the hotel industry. The concept of guest satisfaction was introduced in the late 1970s. The guest satisfaction is the evaluation on which customers feel that service is as excellent as supposed to be (Hunt, 1975). The emotional response after using a service is known as guest satisfaction (Oliver, 1981). According to Yoon and Uysal (2005), the tourist satisfaction involves the views (i.e. equity and norms), expectation towards service, and also the perceived overall performance. Hence, there is a growing need to understand the antecedents of hotel guest satisfaction. Many services provided by hotels are intangible this indicates an information disparity amog customers and hotels related to the hotels' service quality. Customers give their feedback in terms of electronic word of mouth (EWOM) after staying in the hotel. The linguistic characteristics of EWOM text help future customers as well as hotel managers to analyze the perception of guests towards that hotel (Geetha et al., 2017). Therefore, not only customers' writing style, but also the linguistic features of EWOM signals the perception of customers towards that hotel services. The sentiment and emotional expression of EWOM help to evaluate the customer satisfaction (Mady, 2011). In this chapter, we considered readability and EWOM length as key attributes of linguistic features of EWOMs. We use Naïve Bayes (NB) sentiment analysis technique to calculate the sentiment index of each EWOM text. Additionally, Ye et al. (2009) examined that the number of online reviews influence the hotel room sales. Thus, number of EWOMs is also a significant measure for analyzing the customers' perception towards the hotel services. As an indirect interaction with previous and prospect customers, EWOM powerfully improve the impact of information asymmetry and intensely stimulus hotel sales.

Figure 1. Example of EWOM at TripAdvisor

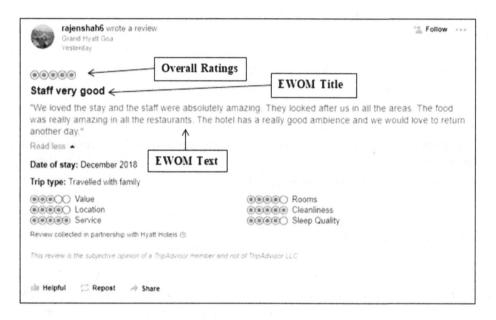

According to W. G. Kim, Lim, and Brymer (2015), overall ratings is associated with hotel performance. Therefore, overall ratings represent the customers' past experience or satisfaction with that hotel. If perceived performance is higher than their evaluation, then the customer will satisfied otherwise dissatisfied (Berezina, Bilgihan, Cobanoglu, & Okumus, 2016). In EWOMs, customer disscuss the perceived hotel performance, their pre-assessment, or both to highlight why they are pleased or frustrated.

Volume of Electronic-Word-Of-Mouth (EWOM Volume) and Overall Hotel Ratings

The EWOM Volume refers to the number of reviews posted online by different users over time. With the enhancement of social media, EWOMs act as an important source to gain knowledge about any product/service for customers. Hyan Yoo and Gretzel (2008) highlighted that 75% customers read user generated content (EWOM) for collecting the information before they travel. As EWOMs increase, customers get more and more knowledge about the product/service quality as well as its actual performance. Although customers can get product/service related specification from other variety of sources but the information generated by EWOMs is considered to be more reliable as compared to the information given by seller (Anu G Aggarwal & Aakash, 2018; Cantallops & Salvi, 2014).

According to Ye, Law, Gu, and Chen (2011), as the volume of EWOMs increases they become trustworthy indicator of hotel performance and reduce the uncertainty related to hotel services which in turn positively affects the hotel online bookings . Mauri and Minazzi (2013) proposed that the volume of EWOMs is significantly correlated with the buying intention of potential hotel customers. Brandes and Nolte (2011) examined that EWOM volume positively influence the hotel demand. The volume of EWOMs is shown to enhance customer awareness about service/product and produce higher sales (Öğüt & Onur Taş, 2012; Qi & Qiang, 2013). Therefore, the higher number of EWOMs towards any hotel impact customer buying decisions by affecting both their awareness of the hotel and the perception of its services. Hence, we posit the following hypothesis.

H₁: WOM volume has a significant impact on overall hotel ratings.

EWOM Length and Overall Hotel Ratings

The EWOM length refers to the number of characters included in the review text. Customers write more elaborated EWOMs with extensive information about hotels by comparing their positive aspects with negative aspects of hotels' product and services (Ngo-Ye & Sinha, 2014). Shelat and Egger (2002) examined that EWOM length positively influence the buying intention. Mudambi and Schuff (2010) highlighted that lengthy EWOMs provide detailed information about product/service, but usually happens when a customer feel negative about product/service is offered to him (Verhagen, Nauta, & Feldberg, 2013). Customers put extra efforts to explain their disappointment, temper, and dissatisfaction when they highlight the negative aspects of products/services (Cantallops & Salvi, 2014). Customer with nasty feelings tend to post lengthy EWOMs to endeavor recognition and help from the tourism society and label their EWOM more helpful (Hong, Xu, Wang, & Fan, 2017). Thus:

H₂: WOM length has a significant impact on overall hotel ratings.

EWOM Sentiment and Overall Hotel Ratings

EWOM sentiment basically refers to the reviewer's emotions expressed through words and other verbal cues. EWOM contains substantial amount of information which influence the customer in his 'to buy' or 'not to buy' decisions (Geetha et al., 2017). In e-service sector, it is important to understand the sentiment of the EWOMs using mining of EWOM text and NPL (natural language processing) techniques, not only from marketing point of view but also to take strategies decisions.

The EWOM sentiment is the level of satisfaction in terms of positive, negative or neutral sentiments that customers showed at the time of posting EWOMs. Good experience about product/service can increase the perception towards product/service quality, which is the antecedents for guest satisfaction, while bad experience is an antecedent of guest dissatisfaction (Dai, Luo, Liao, & Cao, 2015). Customers can judge their experience towards product/service clearly when they are in satisfied sentimental phase as compared to the dissatisfied emotional state (Isen, 1987).

Using NPL techniques, the EWOM text may be classified as positive, negative or on n-point scale as very good, good, average, bad, very bad. Higher percentage of sentiment shows more positive EWOMs. Through sentiment analysis, e-service industry may frame their key marketing decisions with respect to the hoteliers, delivery/payment mechanism, hotel's service quality, future hotel bookings, hotel recommendation etc. Therefore, we set:

H₃: WOM sentiment has a significant impact on overall hotel ratings.

Extraction of EWOM Sentiment

Sentiment analysis is the process of recognizing and classifying emotions expressed through a piece of text or *emoji*. It is a method for understanding the reviewers' attitude towards a product/service and classifying it as positive, negative, or neutral.

Numeric values which we get after performing sentiment analysis are known as "Sentiment Index". Sentiment Index represents how pessimist or optimist a reviewer is with respect to the quality of a hotel. The sentiment of a review goes a long way in forming the customer perception towards a hotel as customer tend to trust the information provided by the fellow users more as compared to the information provided by the seller.

In this chapter, we use the Naïve Bayes (NB) classifier through Natural Language Toolkit (NLTK) for calculating the sentiment index of each hotel review (EWOM) because NLTK is an efficient way to understand the human language such as hotel EWOMs. This method is based upon Bayes theorem which states that

$$P\left(E_2|E_1\right) = \frac{P\left(E_1|E_2\right) * P\left(E_2\right)}{P\left(E_1\right)}.$$

The Naïve Bayes (NB) algorithm is applied for polarity classification and calculating the sentiment index for each electronic-word-of-mouth (EWOM). Here, the EWOMs have been classified as positive (S_+) and negative (S_-) and belongs either to the set of two classes as S_j where $j \in \{-,+\}$.

Let E represent set of emotive words; $E \in R^\eta$ where η represents number of emotive words. Let $nk._b$e the number of emotive words in the k*th* EWOM of each hotel. Let $N_k \in R^{\eta_k}\left(k = 1,2,....,n\right)$.be the set of emotive word for k*t*ʰ EWOM, where n is total number of EWOMs. Let wi_k represent i*t*ʰ emotive word in N*k*

The likelihood of N_k.is in the class S_j. where $j \in \{-,+\}$ is calculated using NB method as follows:

$$argmax_{s_j}\left(P\left(S_j|N_k\right)\right) = argmax_{s_j}\left(\frac{P(N_k \mid S_j) \times P\left(S_j\right)}{P\left(N_k\right)}\right), \tag{1}$$

Here $P(S_+)$ and $P(S_-)$ represents the chances of positive & negative class. These probabilities may be obtained from the number of words belonging to positive & negative class in the training set. $P(N_k)$

represents the likelihood of a particular set of emotive words in a class, $P(N_k|S_j)$ represents the likelihood that N_k comes under the class S_j. Here, $P(N_k|S_j)$ is calculated as follows:

$$P\left(N_k|S_j\right) = P\left(w_{1k}, w_{2k}, \ldots, w_{nk}|S_j\right), \tag{2}$$

can be written as

$$P\left(N_k|S_j\right) = P\left(w_{1k}|S_j\right) \times P\left(w_{2k}|S_j\right) \ldots\ldots\ldots \times P\left(w_{ik}|S_j\right), \tag{3}$$

(It has been assumed that emotive words are independent of each other)

Here $P(w_{i,k}|S_j)$ is the likelihood that the word w_{ik} appears in the class S_j. It is calculated by dividing the number of times word w_{ik} occurs in class S_j by the total number of words in that class. Hence, $P(w_{ik}|S_j)$ is calculated as:

$$P\left(w_{ik}|S_j\right) = \frac{t_{ij} + 1}{\sum_{w'_j \in V} t_{i'j} + K}, \tag{4}$$

where t_{ij} be the number of times w_{jk} occurs in training set belonging to class S_j. $t_{i'j}$ is the number of times $w_{i'k}$ occurs in the training set related to class S_j and K is the number of words in the sentiment wordlist.

After obtaining $P(S_j|N_k)$ using Naïve Bayes technique, the sentiment index for time t, SI_t, calculated as follows:

$$SI_t = \sum_{Rev}\left(P\left(S_j|N_k\right) \times s\right) = \sum_{Rev}\left(SI_{tk} \times s\right) \tag{5}$$

where *Rev* represents the volume of EWOMs within time t and the constant (s) is either -1 or 1 its value based on the class of SI_{tk}. If it lies in positive category then $s=1$ otherwise s will be -1 for negative category. Hence, the sentiment index for each hotel can be calculated with the help of Eq. (1) to (5).

Readability and Overall Hotel Ratings

The level of education and effort needed to understand a piece of text defines the concept of readability (Zakaluk & Samuels, 1988). The objective of readability measures is to provide a scale-based signal of how hard a piece of textual content is for readers to interpret on the basis of linguistic features of that content. Therefore, a readability score can only give a signal of how much easy or difficult a piece of text is for readers on the basis of its style and syntactical elements. In addition, the readability measures have also been used in that case when a reader wants to read a particular text for making decisions or to comprehend the reason behind that text. For example, financial statements (M. Smith & Taffler, 1992).

Readability measures have been used to analyze the qualitative features of different types of text and there are many readability formulas have been proposed in the past studies (Paasche-Orlow, Taylor,

& Brancati, 2003). In this chapter, we choose four key readability measures which have been applied widely to estimate the text readability by individuals with different educational standards. One specific reason for choosing readability measures an ideal tool for analyzing the customers' performance towards the hotels on the basis of overall ratings stems from theoretical basis provide in the previous sections. According to the Calderón et al. (2006), an easily readable text gives better comprehensible to readers, thus those who understand a textual content better will create a better justified attitude towards it.

Table 2 gives the readability measures used in this chapter, these include the Dale Chall Readability Score (DCRS), the Flesch Kincaid Grade Level (FKGL), the Smog Index (SMOG) and the Gunning Fog index (GFI). All four measures calculate the readability of a review text by dividing the review text into basic structural features, which are then integrated through an empirical regression technique. However, it is significant to understand that all the indexes calculate the same characteristics.

Table 2. Readability measures

Readability Index	Description
Gunning Fog Index	The gunning fog index is indirectly proportional to the readability level. The lower the value of gunning fog index, the more readable the text.
Smog Index	The SMOG index is based on polysyllable word in the text. Therefore, the total polysyllable word count directly related to the educational grade level.
Flesch Kincaid Grade Level	The Flesch Kincaid Grade level is directly correlated with the educational grade level required to read the given textual content.
Dale Chall Readability Score	The Dale Chall Readability score directly proportional to the educational grade level.

Gunning Fog Index (Gfi)

GFI represents a level of the extent to which a reader with a mean educational grade level (i.e. 10th standard) would be able to understand a textual content (Gunning, 1969). The formula for calculating the GFI score is as follows:

$$\text{GFI} = 0.4 \left(\frac{words}{sentences} + 100 * \left(\frac{difficult\,words}{words} \right) \right).$$

The tedious task in calculating the GFI score is to find difficult words in a given piece of text. In this study, we form a word as difficult whenever it has greater than three syllables.

Smog Index (Smog)

The Smog Index (Mc Laughlin, 1969) combines various mainly two aspects of text such as number of pollysyllables and sentences to estimate the comprehensibility with respect to each EWOM text. In precise, the SMOG index of EWOM text is estimated through the formula given by Contreras, Garcia-Alonso, Echenique, and Daye-Contreras (1999):

$$\text{SMOG} = 1.0430\sqrt{\frac{30 * \left(pollysyllables\right)}{sentence}} + 3.1291 \, .$$

Furthermore, the calculation of SMOG index with less than thirty sentences for a piece of text are statistically insignificant because SMOG measure was normed on thirty-sentence samples (Contreras et al., 1999).

Flesch-Kincaid Grade Level (Fkgl)

The Flesch-Kincaid Grade Level (Kincaid, Fishburne Jr, Rogers, & Chissom, 1975) combines various aspects of text such as number of words, sentences, and syllables to estimate the comprehensibility with respect to each EWOM text. In precise, the grade level of EWOM text is estimated through the formula given by Kincaid et al. (1975).

$$\text{FKGL} = 0.39\left(\frac{words}{sentences}\right) + 11.8\left(\frac{syllables}{words}\right) - 15.59 \, .$$

FKGL is frequently used readability measure due to their calculation speed and past support for their reliable results (Kincaid et al., 1975). We also used this readability measure because FKGL weights are calibrated with the U.S. grade levels.

Dale Chall Readability Score (Dcrs)

The Dale Chall Readability Score (Dale & Chall, 1948) combines various aspects of text such as number of difficult words, words, and sentences to calculate the comprehensibility with respect to each EWOM text. The formula for measuring the DCRS score is given by Dale and Chall (1948):

$$\text{DCRS} = 0.1579\left(\frac{difficult\,words}{words} * 100\right) + 0.0496\left(\frac{words}{sentences}\right).$$

According to Korfiatis el al. (2012), the level of readability of text affects the level of understanding of the reader (Korfiatis, GarcíA-Bariocanal, & SáNchez-Alonso, 2012). Ghose and Ipeirotis (2011) proposed that readability score affect the product sales (Ghose & Ipeirotis, 2011). Additionally, Chua and Banerjee (2016), readability score is a measure of review helpfulness (Chua & Banerjee, 2016). Therefore, we hypothesize:

H_4: Readability of the review has a significant impact on overall hotel ratings.

DATA ANALYSIS

Data Description

We used the data of Tripadvisor.com because it is world biggest social media platform specific to e-services and also it has more than 460 millions EWOM related to hotels, restaurants, and other e-services. We used set of EWOMs extracted from Tripadviosr webiste and originally crawled by Wang, Lu, and Zhai (2011). The dataset contains 12,782 json files in which each file holds the information with respect to different hotel. We accessed 2001 hotels out of 12,782 for our analysis. We extracted 27,3599 number of EWOMs with respect to 2001 hotels. Each EWOM contains the name of associated hotels, EWOM Title, and overall hotel ratings. The flow diagram of our analysis is give in Figure 2.

Figure 2. Flow diagram of research

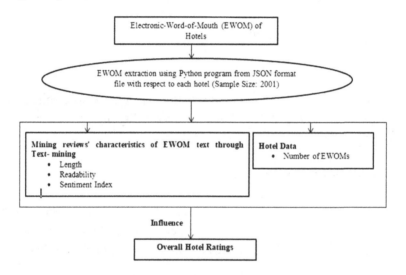

Figure 3. Number of e-WOM per unit of the guest ratings

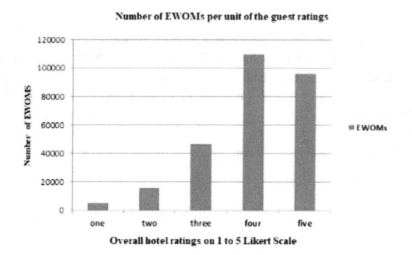

For statistical analysis, we have extracted the linguistic features of EWOM text such as readability and EWOM length. We have also extracted the EWOM sentiment through Naïve Bayes (NB) sentiment analysis approach. The overall ratings for each hotel is based on one to five Likert scale where one-star represents minimum and five-star for maximum satisfied experience with the hotel. Some summary statistics for the data included in our analysis is given in Table 3. Figure 3 represents the frequency distribution for the overall hotel ratings or guest ratings. Figure 4 represents the frequency distribution EWOMs volume.

Table 3. Summary Statistics of Hotel review data included in the study

Independent Variable	Mean	Median	Std. Dev.	Min.	Max.
EWOM_Volume	136.73	131	25.982	100	190
EWOM_length	396.29	278.82	370.59	22.59	2991.65
Sentiment_index	20.72	19.34	12.37	3.27	95.24
Flesch_Kincaid_Grade	8.87	8.1	4.24	-0.4	58.7
Dale_Chall_Readability_Score	6.96	6.87	1.08	0.74	13.82
Smog_Index	9.95	10.1	2.71	0	19.6
Gunning_Fog	14.3	13.54	4.69	3.51	64.62
			2001		
Total Number of EWOMs			273599		
Dep. Variable			Overall hotel ratings		

Significance: ***$p<0.001$; **$p<0.01$; *$p<0.05$

Figure 4. e-WOM volume

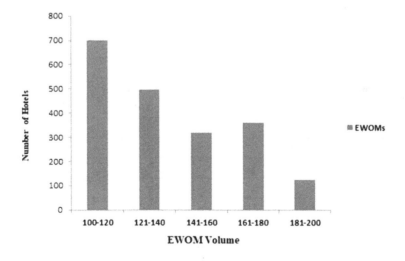

EMPIRICAL MODEL AND RESULTS

We applied a multivariate linear regression technique for analyzing the impact of EWOM text on overall hotel performances through two models as provided by Eq. (6) and (7). In first model, we analyze the impact of EWOM_Volume(EV_i) EWOM_Length(EL_i) and EWOM_Sentiment(ES_i) on overall_ratings (*overall_ratings_i*) of hotel (*i*) by estimating model of the form:

$$overall\_ratings_i = \alpha_0 + \alpha_1 EV_i + \alpha_2 EL_i + \alpha_3 ES_i + \varepsilon_i \qquad (6)$$

In the second model, we include additional variables related to the review readability name as the Flesch Kincaid Grade Level ($FKGL_i$). Dale Chall Readability Score ($DCRS_i$) the Smog Index ($SMOG_i$) and the Gunning Fog index (GFI_i).

$$overall\_ratings_i =$$
$$\beta_0 + \beta_1 EV_i + \beta_2 EL_i + \beta_3 ES_i + \beta_4 FKGL_i + \beta_5 DCRS_i + \beta_6 SMOG_i + \beta_7 GFI_i + \varepsilon_i \qquad (7)$$

In addition, we used an endogenous variable (εi_i or incorporating all other environmental factors which may influence the performance of the hotel (i) (Ye et al., 2009). First, to analyze the impact of EWOM sentiment on hotels performances, we have estimated the basic model in which the information related to the EWOM sentiment is included (Eq. (6)). Later on to study the impact of EWOM readability on the overall hotel satisfaction, we estimate the multivariate linear regression model with four readability indexes (Eq. (7)). The empirical results for both models are represented in Table 4, including the number of hotels (N) adjusted R2 values, standardized coefficient of the key variables, standard errors of estimation.

Table 4. Empirical results for both models

Independent variables	Model-I		Model-II	
	coef.	std. err.	coef.	std. err.
EWOM_Volume		0.000		0.001
EWOM_Length		0.001		0.000
EWOM_Sentiment		0.002		0.002
Flesch_Kincaid_Grade				0.026
Dale_Chall_Readability_Score				0.045
Smog_Index				0.009
Gunning_Fog			-0.1119***	0.029
Adj. R-squared	0.951		0.954	
Df	3		4	
Number of Hotels (*N*)	2001		2001	
Dep. Variable	Overall hotel ratings			

Significance: ***p<0.001; **p<0.01; *p<0.05

The overall ratings of the hotel is directly related to the overall hotel performances such that one-star rating represents least and five-star for most satisfied experience of the guest with the hotel. Therefore, positive correlation between any independent variable and overall hotel ratings represents positive impact on hotel performances. In other words, higher value of that variable corresponds to higher level of guest satisfaction towards that hotel.

This model gives a flexibility to analyse percentage change in overall hotel ratings with respect to given level of change in EWOMs variables. From the regression results it may be observed that *EWOM_Volume* influence overall_ratings significantly ($p<0.001$) across both models. This outcome is in agreement with many other past studies (Brandes & Nolte, 2011; Zhu & Lai, 2009). In both models, *EWOM_Length*, has a negative impact on overall hotel performances, which means higher are the EWOM_Length, the lower are the satisfaction level towards that hotel. These results were also reported in previous studies (Bradley et al., 2015; Sparks & Browning, 2010). It shows that review length is not positively related to the hotel performance, on the contrary the hotels having relatively more lengthy reviews have poor guest experience (Berezina et al., 2016). The coefficient of, *EWOM_Sentiment*, is positive in model-I as well as II, This implies that the higher EWOM_Sentiment percentage leads to greater overall hotel ratings. EWOM_Sentiment reflects guests' emotions when they share their experiences towards that hotel. Higher positive sentiment shows that guest used more positive words as compare to negative in their feedback through EWOM (Geetha et al., 2017).

The proposed relationship between *EWOM_Volume* and overall_ratings is significant in both of the models ($\alpha1\_0.0275$, $\beta1=_0.0152$, $p<0.001$), which supports H1 $_H2$ investigates the relationship between the overall_ratings and EW*OM_Length*. Our findings show that the coefficient of EW*OM_Length* is significant with a negative sign for both models ($\alpha2=-_0.0015$, $\beta2=-0.0007$, $p<0.001$). Thus, lengthy EWOMs will negatively affect the guest satisfaction. The relationship between the EWOM_*sentiment and* overall_*ratings was* significant for both models ($\alpha3=0.0_385$, $\beta3=0.03_56$, $p<0.001$). Hence, our results support H3.

The model-II contained the readability metrices which measure the difficulty level of the EWOM text. By comparing the results obtained from model-I and II, we observe that model-II (Adjus*tedR2=0.9*54) is better than model-I (Adjus*tedR2=0.9*51). It reinforces that the readability of the EWOM text significantly influences the mood of customers and gives better results for analyzing the overall hotel performances. These findings, together with the value of coefficients ($\beta4$, $\beta5$, $\beta6$, and β_7) supports H4. Hence, the qualitative characteristics of EWOMs will impact on overall hotel ratings. One of the crucial points we noted that the coefficient of all four readability measures showed a higher value as compared to EWOM_Length. This implies that the readability of the EWOM text had a higher impact than EWOM_Length on overall guest satisfaction.

CONCLUSION AND MANAGERIAL IMPLICATION

Online user generated content (EWOM) act as an excellent source of information for both customer as well as the marketer in hospitality industry. The marketer analyzes EWOMs to extract useful information regarding customer preferences, feedback and satisfaction analysis it also helps the marketer to connect with its customer base in cost and time effective manner. The prospective customers' access and read online customer content to judge the service quality and performance on the basis of overall ratings and the verbal cues posted online by previous customers. EWOMs act as word of mouth available electronically and influence the purchasing intention of imitator class of adopters. E-services giants like Tripadvisor, and Yelp etc. maintain online review system to monitor the market pulse so as to design key marketing strategies with respect to promotion, advertising, vendor monitoring, service quality etc. In spite of this, it is an interesting area of research to examine the extent of relation that EWOMs has on the usage experiences of the customers. In this chapter, we identify the key variables related with EWOM text which affects the performances of the hotel opportunity conversion for the marketer.

Major Findings

This study provides insight about the effects of EWOMs, and its measures on the buying intention of customers through multivariate linear regression modeling. We have constructed two multivariate regression models- one which includes the effect of EWOM_Volume, EWOM_Length, and EWOM_Sentiment on the hotel performances (measured through overall hotel ratings); the second which includes readability measures in addition to the above mention variables. The models were validated on review data of 2001 hotels available on Tripadvisor.com. From the regression results, the key findings are as follows:

First, EWOM_Volume and EWOM_Sentiment have positive relation with overall hotel ratings. This indicates that a hotel whose EWOM text holds positive emotions, opinions and behavior, impact performance positively and large number of EWOMs has higher guest satisfaction. In contrast, EWOM_Length have negative regression coefficient with overall hotel ratings. It means that lengthy reviews indicate low hotel performance or customer overall ratings.

Third, readability matrices enhance the accuracy of the model as represented by higher value of adjusted R2($A^djustedR2=0.954$) as compared to model without readability metrices (Adj$ustedR2=0.951$). The incorporation of readability measures in the model building not only helps in analyzing the actual hotel performance but it also provides a medium to measure the satisfaction level of the customer with respect to e-service platform, its vendors, payment mechanism, complaint handling, and market positioning.

Theoretical Contribution

This study adds a value to the literature of marketing as well as social science in many ways. First, from social aspect, the method gives a technique to relate hotel performance with a customer feedback given in terms of verbal text/emoji/pictures. It helps us to understand how the people are influenced by the opinion, judgments of others.

Second, from marketing aspect, in this chapter, we have used an integrated approach for investigating the influence of different EWOMs measures on overall hotel ratings, which incorporate statistics, text mining, and sentiment analysis simultaneously. The previous studies reported in the literature focused only on one technique at a time (Berezina et al., 2016; Bradley et al., 2015; Sparks & Browning, 2010).

Third, Naive Bayes (NB) sentiment analysis has been used to capture positive, negative and neutral polarity as a combined opinion. Although, sentiment analysis has been used to examine EWOMs by many previous researchers also but NB methods give better results for the same (Fan et al., 2017).

Fourth, this chapter represents the connection between linguistic features of electronic-word-of-mouth (EWOM) and overall ratings. As compared with overall hotel ratings, linguistic features can highly reflect the guest's feelings and opinion in detail due to their profoundness. This chapter concentrates on the linguistic features such as readability and review length servers as a pointer to analyze the overall guest perceptions towards that hotel.

Finally, by incorporating readability measures in our analysis, we were able to study the impact of review language on the overall hotel ratings.

Managerial Implication

Overall hotel ratings are directly related with the guest experience. EWOM text measures the customers experience with verbal protocols, which are indirectly related to customer perception and satisfaction (A. K. Smith & Bolton, 2002). In this way, guests' feedback in terms of EWOMs affects the perception and satisfaction towards that hotel.

The results of this chapter can encourage hoteliers to extract other features from the textual content of EWOMs and to analyse the impact of these features on overall hotel ratings. These EWOMs generate a greater impact that influences future hotel bookings. However, electronic-word-of-mouth analysis remains challenging.

This chapter used a text analytics approach that provides a real-world technique for hoteliers to analyse that how linguistic features of EWOM text as well as EWOM sentiment related to the overall hotel ratings. Giving quick and effective reply to reviewers' negative comments is an efficient technique to apply service recovery activities and maintaining customers (Chevalier, Dover, & Mayzlin, 2018). Hotels may attempt to study the poor experiences of customers through EWOM text for future enhancements.

This chapter gives new direction in terms of detecting the EWOM sentiment as well as linguistic features of EWOM. This work uses a Naïve Bayes (NB) algorithm for analyzing sentiment polarity not only for each review but also in respect of each hotel. Lastly, our study confirms previous studies that lengthy reviews affects guest satisfaction negatively and also the readability of EWOM text significantly influences the overall hotel performances. We also noted that the review readability had a greater impact than review length on overall hotel ratings.

LIMITATIONS AND FUTURE SCOPE

Even though the chapter represents a comprehensive and well explained study, there are some limitations of the research. Firstly, the non-English words were counted as wrong words in the study, however, the non-English words may have a say in the sentiment analysis. These non-English words may be considered for analysis in future work. Secondly, the analysis is based on the review text obtained from only one OTA website i.e. Tripadvisor.com. Therefore, research findings should be generalized to other domains also. Thirdly, this study considers reviews data of only 2001 hotels to evaluate their overall performance based on only four technical characteristics of reviews. Future research can consider more volume of reviews and additional technical characteristics to converge towards high level big data analysis. Also, machine learning techniques can be used to judge hotel guest satisfaction. Moreover, future work can also examine the helpfulness of the reviews with the available ratings.

REFERENCES

Aggarwal, A. G., & Aakash. (2018). Analyzing the Interrelationship between Online Reviews and Sales: The Role of Review Length and Sentiment Index in Electronic Markets. *International Journal of Internet Marketing and Advertising*.

Aggarwal, A. G., & Aakash, N. A. (2018). Multi-criteria-based prioritisation of B2C e-commerce website. *International Journal of Society Systems Science*, *10*(3), 201–222. doi:10.1504/IJSSS.2018.093940

Berezina, K., Bilgihan, A., Cobanoglu, C., & Okumus, F. (2016). Understanding satisfied and dissatisfied hotel customers: Text mining of online hotel reviews. *Journal of Hospitality Marketing & Management*, *25*(1), 1–24. doi:10.1080/19368623.2015.983631

Boo, S., & Busser, J. A. (2018). Tourists' hotel event experience and satisfaction: An integrative approach. *Journal of Travel & Tourism Marketing*, 1–14.

Bradley, G. L., Sparks, B. A., & Weber, K. (2015). The stress of anonymous online reviews: A conceptual model and research agenda. *International Journal of Contemporary Hospitality Management*, *27*(5), 739–755. doi:10.1108/IJCHM-01-2014-0005

Brandes, L., & Nolte, I. (2011). *Where Do the Joneses Go on Vacation?* Social Distance and the Influence of Online Reviews on Product Sales.

Calderón, J. L., Morales, L. S., Liu, H., & Hays, R. D. (2006). Variation in the readability of items within surveys. *American Journal of Medical Quality*, *21*(1), 49–56. doi:10.1177/1062860605283572 PMID:16401705

Cantallops, A. S., & Salvi, F. (2014). New consumer behavior: A review of research on eWOM and hotels. *International Journal of Hospitality Management*, *36*, 41–51. doi:10.1016/j.ijhm.2013.08.007

Chand, M. (2010). The impact of HRM practices on service quality, customer satisfaction and performance in the Indian hotel industry. *International Journal of Human Resource Management*, *21*(4), 551–566. doi:10.1080/09585191003612059

Chau, M., & Xu, J. (2012). Business intelligence in blogs: Understanding consumer interactions and communities. *Management Information Systems Quarterly*, *36*(4), 1189–1216. doi:10.2307/41703504

Chevalier, J. A., Dover, Y., & Mayzlin, D. (2018). Channels of Impact: User reviews when quality is dynamic and managers respond. *Marketing Science*, *37*(5), 688–709. doi:10.1287/mksc.2018.1090

Chua, A. Y., & Banerjee, S. (2016). Helpfulness of user-generated reviews as a function of review sentiment, product type and information quality. *Computers in Human Behavior*, *54*, 547–554. doi:10.1016/j.chb.2015.08.057

ComScore. (2017). *Is TripAdvisor's Business Model Broken?* Author.

Contreras, A., Garcia-Alonso, R., Echenique, M., & Daye-Contreras, F. (1999). The SOL formulas for converting SMOG readability scores between health education materials written in Spanish, English, and French. *Journal of Health Communication*, *4*(1), 21–29.

Crotts, J. C., Mason, P. R., & Davis, B. (2009). Measuring guest satisfaction and competitive position in the hospitality and tourism industry: An application of stance-shift analysis to travel blog narratives. *Journal of Travel Research, 48*(2), 139–151. doi:10.1177/0047287508328795

Dai, H., Luo, X. R., Liao, Q., & Cao, M. (2015). Explaining consumer satisfaction of services: The role of innovativeness and emotion in an electronic mediated environment. *Decision Support Systems, 70*, 97–106. doi:10.1016/j.dss.2014.12.003

Dale, E., & Chall, J. S. (1948). A formula for predicting readability: Instructions. *Educational Research Bulletin*, 37-54.

De Pelsmacker, P., van Tilburg, S., & Holthof, C. (2018). Digital marketing strategies, online reviews and hotel performance. *International Journal of Hospitality Management, 72*, 47–55. doi:10.1016/j.ijhm.2018.01.003

Dixit, S., Badgaiyan, A. J., & Khare, A. (2019). An integrated model for predicting consumer's intention to write online reviews. *Journal of Retailing and Consumer Services, 46*, 112–120. doi:10.1016/j.jretconser.2017.10.001

Duan, W., Gu, B., & Whinston, A. B. (2008). Do online reviews matter?—An empirical investigation of panel data. *Decision Support Systems, 45*(4), 1007–1016. doi:10.1016/j.dss.2008.04.001

Fan, Z.-P., Che, Y.-J., & Chen, Z.-Y. (2017). Product sales forecasting using online reviews and historical sales data: A method combining the Bass model and sentiment analysis. *Journal of Business Research, 74*, 90–100. doi:10.1016/j.jbusres.2017.01.010

Fernandes, T., & Fernandes, F. (2018). Sharing Dissatisfaction Online: Analyzing the Nature and Predictors of Hotel Guests Negative Reviews. *Journal of Hospitality Marketing & Management, 27*(2), 127–150. doi:10.1080/19368623.2017.1337540

Fotis, J., Buhalis, D., & Rossides, N. (2012). *Social media use and impact during the holiday travel planning process.* Springer-Verlag. doi:10.1007/978-3-7091-1142-0_2

Geetha, M., Singha, P., & Sinha, S. (2017). Relationship between customer sentiment and online customer ratings for hotels-An empirical analysis. *Tourism Management, 61*, 43–54. doi:10.1016/j.tourman.2016.12.022

Ghose, A., & Ipeirotis, P. G. (2011). Estimating the helpfulness and economic impact of product reviews: Mining text and reviewer characteristics. *IEEE Transactions on Knowledge and Data Engineering, 23*(10), 1498–1512. doi:10.1109/TKDE.2010.188

Goldsmith, R. E., & Horowitz, D. (2006). Measuring motivations for online opinion seeking. *Journal of Interactive Advertising, 6*(2), 2–14. doi:10.1080/15252019.2006.10722114

Gretzel, U., & Yoo, K. H. (2008). Use and impact of online travel reviews. *Information and communication technologies in tourism 2008*, 35-46.

Gu, B., Park, J., & Konana, P. (2012). Research note—The impact of external word-of-mouth sources on retailer sales of high-involvement products. *Information Systems Research, 23*(1), 182–196. doi:10.1287/isre.1100.0343

Gunning, R. (1969). The fog index after twenty years. *Journal of Business Communication*, 6(2), 3–13. doi:10.1177/002194366900600202

Guo, Y., Barnes, S. J., & Jia, Q. (2017). Mining meaning from online ratings and reviews: Tourist satisfaction analysis using latent dirichlet allocation. *Tourism Management*, 59, 467–483. doi:10.1016/j.tourman.2016.09.009

Hong, H., Xu, D., Wang, G. A., & Fan, W. (2017). Understanding the determinants of online review helpfulness: A meta-analytic investigation. *Decision Support Systems*, 102, 1–11. doi:10.1016/j.dss.2017.06.007

Hong, H., Xu, D., Xu, D., Wang, G. A., & Fan, W. (2017). An empirical study on the impact of online word-of-mouth sources on retail sales. *Information Discovery and Delivery*, 45(1), 30–35. doi:10.1108/IDD-11-2016-0039

Hu, H.-H., Kandampully, J., & Juwaheer, T. D. (2009). Relationships and impacts of service quality, perceived value, customer satisfaction, and image: An empirical study. *Service Industries Journal*, 29(2), 111–125. doi:10.1080/02642060802292932

Hunt, J. D. (1975). Image as a factor in tourism development. *Journal of Travel Research*, 13(3), 1–7. doi:10.1177/004728757501300301

Hyan Yoo, K., & Gretzel, U. (2008). The influence of perceived credibility on preferences for recommender systems as sources of advice. *Information Technology & Tourism*, 10(2), 133–146. doi:10.3727/109830508784913059

Isen, A. M. (1987). Advances in experimental social psychology: Vol. 20. *Positive affect, cognitive processes, and social behavior*. Elsevier. doi:10.1016/S0065-2601(08)60415-3

Jeong, M., & Mindy Jeon, M. (2008). Customer reviews of hotel experiences through consumer generated media (CGM). *Journal of Hospitality & Leisure Marketing*, 17(1-2), 121–138. doi:10.1080/10507050801978265

Kim, E. E. K. (2017). The Impact of Restaurant Service Experience Valence and Purchase Involvement on Consumer Motivation and Intention to Engage in eWOM. *Journal of Quality Assurance in Hospitality & Tourism*, 18(3), 259–281. doi:10.1080/1528008X.2016.1213687

Kim, W. G., Lim, H., & Brymer, R. A. (2015). The effectiveness of managing social media on hotel performance. *International Journal of Hospitality Management*, 44, 165–171. doi:10.1016/j.ijhm.2014.10.014

Kincaid, J. P., Fishburne, R. P., Jr., Rogers, R. L., & Chissom, B. S. (1975). *Derivation of new readability formulas (automated readability index, fog count and flesch reading ease formula) for navy enlisted personnel*. Academic Press.

Klein, L. R. (1998). Evaluating the potential of interactive media through a new lens: Search versus experience goods. *Journal of Business Research*, 41(3), 195–203. doi:10.1016/S0148-2963(97)00062-3

Korfiatis, N., García-Bariocanal, E., & Sánchez-Alonso, S. (2012). Evaluating content quality and helpfulness of online product reviews: The interplay of review helpfulness vs. review content. *Electronic Commerce Research and Applications*, 11(3), 205–217. doi:10.1016/j.elerap.2011.10.003

Laroche, M., McDougall, G. H., Bergeron, J., & Yang, Z. (2004). Exploring how intangibility affects perceived risk. *Journal of Service Research, 6*(4), 373–389. doi:10.1177/1094670503262955

Litvin, S. W., Goldsmith, R. E., & Pan, B. (2008). Electronic word-of-mouth in hospitality and tourism management. *Tourism Management, 29*(3), 458–468. doi:10.1016/j.tourman.2007.05.011

Liu, Y., Teichert, T., Rossi, M., Li, H., & Hu, F. (2017). Big data for big insights: Investigating language-specific drivers of hotel satisfaction with 412,784 user-generated reviews. *Tourism Management, 59*, 554–563. doi:10.1016/j.tourman.2016.08.012

Liu, Z., & Park, S. (2015). What makes a useful online review? Implication for travel product websites. *Tourism Management, 47*, 140–151. doi:10.1016/j.tourman.2014.09.020

Mady, T. T. (2011). Sentiment toward marketing: Should we care about consumer alienation and readiness to use technology? *Journal of Consumer Behaviour, 10*(4), 192–204. doi:10.1002/cb.329

Mankad, S., Han, H. S., Goh, J., & Gavirneni, S. (2016). Understanding online hotel reviews through automated text analysis. *Service Science, 8*(2), 124–138. doi:10.1287erv.2016.0126

Marinkovic, V., Senic, V., Ivkov, D., Dimitrovski, D., & Bjelic, M. (2014). The antecedents of satisfaction and revisit intentions for full-service restaurants. *Marketing Intelligence & Planning, 32*(3), 311–327. doi:10.1108/MIP-01-2013-0017

Mauri, A. G., & Minazzi, R. (2013). Web reviews influence on expectations and purchasing intentions of hotel potential customers. *International Journal of Hospitality Management, 34*, 99–107. doi:10.1016/j.ijhm.2013.02.012

McLaughlin, G. H. (1969). SMOG grading-a new readability formula. *Journal of Reading, 12*(8), 639–646.

McKenzie, G., & Adams, B. (2018). A data-driven approach to exploring similarities of tourist attractions through online reviews. *Journal of Location Based Services, 12*(2), 94–118. doi:10.1080/17489725.2018.1493548

Mudambi, S. M., & Schuff, D. (2010). Research note: What makes a helpful online review? A study of customer reviews on Amazon. com. *MIS Quarterly*, 185-200.

Nam, J., Ekinci, Y., & Whyatt, G. (2011). Brand equity, brand loyalty and consumer satisfaction. *Annals of Tourism Research, 38*(3), 1009–1030. doi:10.1016/j.annals.2011.01.015

Ngo-Ye, T. L., & Sinha, A. P. (2014). The influence of reviewer engagement characteristics on online review helpfulness: A text regression model. *Decision Support Systems, 61*, 47–58. doi:10.1016/j.dss.2014.01.011

Öğüt, H., & Onur Taş, B. K. (2012). The influence of internet customer reviews on the online sales and prices in hotel industry. *Service Industries Journal, 32*(2), 197–214. doi:10.1080/02642069.2010.529436

Oliver, R. L. (1981). Measurement and evaluation of satisfaction processes in retail settings. *Journal of Retailing*.

Paasche-Orlow, M. K., Taylor, H. A., & Brancati, F. L. (2003). Readability standards for informed-consent forms as compared with actual readability. *The New England Journal of Medicine, 348*(8), 721–726. doi:10.1056/NEJMsa021212 PMID:12594317

Park, S., Yang, Y., & Wang, M. (2019). Travel distance and hotel service satisfaction: An inverted U-shaped relationship. *International Journal of Hospitality Management, 76*, 261–270. doi:10.1016/j.ijhm.2018.05.015

Qi, L., & Qiang, Y. (2013). *How hotel star rating moderates online word-of-mouth effect: A difference-in-difference approach.* Paper presented at the Management Science and Engineering (ICMSE), 2013 International Conference on. 10.1109/ICMSE.2013.6586254

Rizal, H., Yussof, S., Amin, H., & Chen-Jung, K. (2018). EWOM towards homestays lodging: Extending the information system success model. *Journal of Hospitality and Tourism Technology, 9*(1), 94–108. doi:10.1108/JHTT-12-2016-0084

Shelat, B., & Egger, F. N. (2002). *What makes people trust online gambling sites?* Paper presented at the CHI'02 Extended Abstracts on Human Factors in Computing Systems. 10.1145/506443.506631

Smith, A. K., & Bolton, R. N. (2002). The effect of customers' emotional responses to service failures on their recovery effort evaluations and satisfaction judgments. *Journal of the Academy of Marketing Science, 30*(1), 5–23. doi:10.1177/03079450094298

Smith, M., & Taffler, R. (1992). Readability and understandability: Different measures of the textual complexity of accounting narrative. *Accounting, Auditing & Accountability Journal, 5*(4). doi:10.1108/09513579210019549

Sparks, B. A., & Browning, V. (2010). Complaining in cyberspace: The motives and forms of hotel guests' complaints online. *Journal of Hospitality Marketing & Management, 19*(7), 797–818. doi:10.1080/19368623.2010.508010

Stringam, B. B., & Gerdes, J. Jr. (2010). An analysis of word-of-mouse ratings and guest comments of online hotel distribution sites. *Journal of Hospitality Marketing & Management, 19*(7), 773–796. doi:10.1080/19368623.2010.508009

Susskind, A. M., Kacmar, K. M., & Borchgrevink, C. P. (2018). The Relationship of Service Providers' Perceptions of Service Climate to Guest Satisfaction, Return Intentions, and Firm Performance. *Cornell Hospitality Quarterly.*

Tandon, A., Sharma, H., & Aggarwal, A. G. (2019). Assessing Travel Websites Based on Service Quality Attributes Under Intuitionistic Environment. *International Journal of Knowledge-Based Organizations, 9*(1), 66–75. doi:10.4018/IJKBO.2019010106

Velázquez, B. M., Blasco, M. F., & Gil Saura, I. (2015). ICT adoption in hotels and electronic word-of-mouth. *Academia (Caracas), 28*(2), 227–250. doi:10.1108/ARLA-10-2013-0164

Verhagen, T., Nauta, A., & Feldberg, F. (2013). Negative online word-of-mouth: Behavioral indicator or emotional release? *Computers in Human Behavior, 29*(4), 1430–1440. doi:10.1016/j.chb.2013.01.043

Vermeulen, I. E., & Seegers, D. (2009). Tried and tested: The impact of online hotel reviews on consumer consideration. *Tourism Management, 30*(1), 123–127. doi:10.1016/j.tourman.2008.04.008

Viglia, G., Minazzi, R., & Buhalis, D. (2016). The influence of e-word-of-mouth on hotel occupancy rate. *International Journal of Contemporary Hospitality Management, 28*(9), 2035–2051. doi:10.1108/IJCHM-05-2015-0238

Wang, H., Lu, Y., & Zhai, C. (2011). Latent aspect rating analysis without aspect keyword supervision. *Proceedings of the 17th ACM SIGKDD international conference on Knowledge discovery and data mining.* 10.1145/2020408.2020505

Wood, S. A., Guerry, A. D., Silver, J. M., & Lacayo, M. (2013). Using social media to quantify nature-based tourism and recreation. *Scientific Reports, 3*(1), 2976. doi:10.1038rep02976 PMID:24131963

Wu, C. H.-J., & Liang, R.-D. (2009). Effect of experiential value on customer satisfaction with service encounters in luxury-hotel restaurants. *International Journal of Hospitality Management, 28*(4), 586–593. doi:10.1016/j.ijhm.2009.03.008

Xiang, Z., & Gretzel, U. (2010). Role of social media in online travel information search. *Tourism Management, 31*(2), 179–188. doi:10.1016/j.tourman.2009.02.016

Xu, X., & Li, Y. (2016). The antecedents of customer satisfaction and dissatisfaction toward various types of hotels: A text mining approach. *International Journal of Hospitality Management, 55*, 57–69. doi:10.1016/j.ijhm.2016.03.003

Yang, Y., Mao, Z., & Tang, J. (2018). Understanding guest satisfaction with urban hotel location. *Journal of Travel Research, 57*(2), 243–259. doi:10.1177/0047287517691153

Yang, Y., Park, S., & Hu, X. (2018). Electronic word of mouth and hotel performance: A meta-analysis. *Tourism Management, 67*, 248–260. doi:10.1016/j.tourman.2018.01.015

Ye, Q., Law, R., & Gu, B. (2009). The impact of online user reviews on hotel room sales. *International Journal of Hospitality Management, 28*(1), 180–182. doi:10.1016/j.ijhm.2008.06.011

Ye, Q., Law, R., Gu, B., & Chen, W. (2011). The influence of user-generated content on traveler behavior: An empirical investigation on the effects of e-word-of-mouth to hotel online bookings. *Computers in Human Behavior, 27*(2), 634–639. doi:10.1016/j.chb.2010.04.014

Yen, C.-L. A., & Tang, C.-H. H. (2019). The effects of hotel attribute performance on electronic word-of-mouth (eWOM) behaviors. *International Journal of Hospitality Management, 76*, 9–18. doi:10.1016/j.ijhm.2018.03.006

Yoon, Y., & Uysal, M. (2005). An examination of the effects of motivation and satisfaction on destination loyalty: A structural model. *Tourism Management, 26*(1), 45–56. doi:10.1016/j.tourman.2003.08.016

Zakaluk, B. L., & Samuels, S. J. (1988). *Readability: Its Past, Present, and Future.* ERIC.

Zhang, Z., Zhang, Z., & Yang, Y. (2016). The power of expert identity: How website-recognized expert reviews influence travelers' online rating behavior. *Tourism Management, 55*, 15–24. doi:10.1016/j.tourman.2016.01.004

Zhao, X., Wang, L., Guo, X., & Law, R. (2015). The influence of online reviews to online hotel booking intentions. *International Journal of Contemporary Hospitality Management*, 27(6), 1343–1364. doi:10.1108/IJCHM-12-2013-0542

Zhu, M., & Lai, S.-q. (2009). *A study about the WOM influence on tourism destination choice*. Paper presented at the Electronic Commerce and Business Intelligence, 2009. ECBI 2009. International Conference on. 10.1109/ECBI.2009.104

Chapter 97

eWOW of Guests Regarding Their Hotel Experience:
Sentiment Analysis of TripAdvisor Reviews

Zelia Breda
https://orcid.org/0000-0002-5882-063X
GOVCOPP, University of Aveiro, Portugal

Rui Costa
https://orcid.org/0000-0002-4044-0030
GOVCOPP, University of Aveiro, Portugal

Gorete Dinis
GOVCOPP, Polytechnic Institute of Portalegre, Portugal

Amandine Angie Martins
University of Aveiro, Portugal

ABSTRACT

Online comments are increasingly mentioned as an important source of information, simplifying consumers' buying decisions. Online user-generated content has become one of the main sources of information for tourists, who themselves become creators of their own online content. This chapter focuses on sentiment analysis of comments made on TripAdvisor regarding one resort located in the Algarve region, in Portugal. The resort has good reviews, which means that the eWOM is positive. The highest scores relate to the resort's cleanliness, location and quality of sleep, and those that were less relevant were the value for money, the rooms and the service. The most dominant emotion is joy, followed by an analytical response. Negative emotions, such as sadness and anger, were not found very often in the online reviews. These results could be explained by the quality of the service, the kindness of the staff, the facilities for children, the entertainment, and the location, attributes that were often highlighted in the comments.

DOI: 10.4018/978-1-6684-6303-1.ch097

INTRODUCTION

The Internet has become an essential tool for any user, either on a personal or on a professional level. The rapid evolution of information and communication technologies (ICT) has given rise to Web 2.0, mainly characterized by user-generated content (UGC), or electronic word of mouth (eWOM). Companies used to control the information they wanted to share, now users determine the information they want to see and to consume (Limberger, Anjos, Meira, & Anjos, 2014).

In tourism, social media predominates in terms of knowledge and information sharing, being recognized as an innovative knowledge sharing tool (e.g. product reviews, market trends, restaurant and hotel reviews, and travel blogs), allowing users to interconnect, share the desired information and interact with other users (Gaál, Szabó, Obermayer-Kovács, & Csepregi, 2015). This type of user-generated content allows to reach a greater number of users in a shorter time, eliminating restrictions of time, location and speed during the exchange of information. On the other hand, it can affect purchasing decisions, as well as consumer perceptions of product quality, since most of the comments on online platforms serve to recommend or discourage a product (Limberger et al., 2014).

Sentiment analysis can be applied to user-generated content, such as online reviews, survey responses and social media, aiming to identify ideas and opinions about a particular subject or event, classifying and quantifying them as positive, negative or neutral (Liu, 2015). Pang and Lee (2008) state that there are numerous companies in the world, especially in the United States, that provide sentiment analysis services on the Internet. It is considered that through sentimental analysis, e-commerce benefits can be realized, and companies tend to promote their products more on a website, blog or social networks. Organizations will have other benefits such as ease of designing marketing strategies, improved security policies, accurate perception of a product / service by a customer, among others.

Studies on sentiment analysis are still relatively scarce (e.g. Freitas & Vieira, 2015; Neethu & Rajasree, 2013; Pak & Paroubek, 2010; Serrano-Guerrero, Olivas, Romero, & Herrera-Viedma, 2015; Valdivia, Luzón, & Herrera, 2017), thus, this study aims to provide a contribution in the tourism sector. This chapter focuses on sentiment analysis of comments made on TripAdvisor regarding one resort located in the Algarve region, in Portugal. In general, this study aims to identify: (i) the profile of the visitor; (ii) the general and specific evaluation for each category of the resort; and (iii) the emotional intonations of the visitors' comments. The methodology of the study is based on qualitative and quantitative analysis of secondary sources, i.e. comments posted by customers on TripAdvisor. A sample of 294 comments was used to perform the sentiment analysis, using IBM Watson Tone Analyzer. After this analysis, results were imported on IBM SPSS v. 25, where univariate and bivariate analyses were performed.

The chapter is organized as follows: first, the literature on social media and tourism is reviewed, following which user-generated content and eWOM are addressed. Subsequently, the methodology used for the empirical study is described in more detail. Finally, research findings are reported and discussed, and their implications for further research and applications are highlighted.

LITERATURE REVIEW

Social Media and Tourism

The availability of the Internet through various platforms allows users to access, in real time, a large amount of information, such as maps, information about a particular destination, attraction or service, among others. It is inevitable that people's behaviour has influenced the form of communication (Afonso & Borges, 2013).

In Portugal, the number of residents aged 15 and above accessing social networks increased significantly from 1,417 thousand (17.1%) in 2008 to 5,064 thousand (59.1%) in 2017 (Marktest, 2017). According to the same study, the proportion of users in the 15-24 age group is not much higher than that of users between 45 and 64 years old. However, the reason why young people are connected is mainly because entertainment and leisure, while adults, in addition to this, use more social networks to search for health information, opinions on articles, among others. Facebook (95.3%), WhatsApp (74.2%) and Instagram (67.9%) are the most used social networks in Portugal (Marktest, 2019).

Technological advances influence the way companies and consumers relate to each other, undermining traditional communication management models of transactional marketing processes. Interest in social networking systems is growing as industries have to consider new forms of planning, marketing of tourism products and services (Di Pietro, Di Virgilio, & Pantano, 2012).

Social networks have become increasingly relevant and are generally used to: (i) improve product / service and brand awareness, thereby managing reputation; (ii) increase customer loyalty, that is, the customer is more exposed to publications and these may affect the feeling of loyalty to the product or service; (iii) simplify market research through the creation of new ideas, also helping in the projection of new products or services; and (iv) emphasize eWOM, stimulating users' trust among themselves (Berthon, Pitt, Plangger, & Shapiro, 2012; Vermeulen & Seegers, 2009; Vlachvei & Notta, 2014).

For marketers, social networks have advantages such as: (i) simple and instant information update; (ii) greater freedom and efficacy in measuring the results of a marketing campaign; (iii) marketing strategies aimed at triggering a viral result; (iv) plurilateral and participatory communication in order to create greater contact with the public; (v) user interaction and learning about the particularities of products, services, news; (vi) reduced marketing costs; (vii) insight into customer needs to take into account in future strategies; (viii) direct traffic to the company's website, blog, articles, among others; (ix) campaigns aimed at a certain audience; (x) real time market perception; (xi) input of ideas by users; and (xii) improved customer service through closer relationships (Afonso & Borges, 2013; Hays, Page, & Buhalis, 2013; Leung, Law, Van Hoof, & Buhalis, 2013; Sigala, Christou, & Gretzel, 2012). However, social networks have also some disadvantages that should be taken into account when the manager or marketer decides whether or not to be present on social networks. These usually refer to the visibility and reach of the social network, which, in case of negative comments generated by users, it will contribute to a pejorative image of the company; and the need to have employees with availability and with specific knowledge for effective social network management (Afonso & Borges, 2013; Hays, Page, & Buhalis, 2013; Leung, Law, Van Hoof, & Buhalis, 2013; Sigala, Christou, & Gretzel, 2012).

Regarding the organization and fruition of travel, the desire to use social networks is directly related to the user's perception of their benefits (Wang, Yu, & Fesenmaier, 2002). However, the process of identifying the benefits of using social networks is complex, since there are so many travellers and not everyone is looking for the same information, which also depends on their ability to use it. According to Munar and Jacobsen (2014), altruistic and community-related motivations are most relevant for information sharing, differing depending on the type of content and type of social media. Other authors (Hsu & Lin, 2008; Wang & Fesenmaier, 2004; Wang, Yu, & Fesenmaier, 2002) also report that tourists can enjoy positive dynamics in using social networks depending on the functional, social, psychological and hedonic benefits of their use.

In the case of tourism, in terms of functional benefits, the use of social networks is effective because it allows travellers to keep up to date on tourist sites they want to visit and the activities of interest (Yoo & Gretzel, 2008). Since the price of travel arrangements is one of the motivations for seeking online reviews (Goldsmith & Horowitz, 2006), active Internet collaboration certainly helps tourists save money; and the exchange of information between social network users provides mutual benefits (Wang & Fesenmaier, 2004).

With regard to social benefits, social networks allow: (i) visitors to always share and maintain contact with others who share the same interests in travel; (ii) increase interpersonal relationships between people who have the same motivations for travel, further emphasizing interest; (iii) develop a strong feeling in the users that they belong to a group with the same interest (Leung et al., 2013; Wang & Fesenmaier, 2004).

Regarding psychological and hedonic benefits, online travel communities, in addition to meeting functional requirements and social needs, also meet basic psychological needs (Wang & Fesenmaier, 2004). The psychological benefits are related to users' trust in social networks and belonging to a particular group. These benefits can be achieved through persistent communication and participatory activity in a fully collaborative environment, meeting social benefits (Bressler & Grantham, 2000, cited by Chung & Buhalis, 2008). On the other hand, community members want not only functional, social and psychological benefits, but also fun and enjoyment, which fit the hedonic benefits. Using social media is fun and enjoyable, and travellers who participate in online communities to voice their opinions and share their tourist experiences are proud to do so (Wang & Fesenmaier, 2004).

TripAdvisor does not offer any kind of reward but a recognition for its loyal users. This form of gamification of the interaction with the platform becomes, in a way, a motivation for its use, since, when giving their opinion, users accumulate more points and "climb up the hierarchy", thus achieving the desired merit and notoriety among other members (Mkono, 2012; Yoo & Gretzel, 2010). Similar to the motivations for using social networks, the drive comes from the need for social recognition and is also a psychological incentive (Chen, Fay, & Wang 2011; Lecture, Fehr & Falk, 2002). Thus, the motivation results in the search for this social status that has as its principle to achieve more economic and social power (externally) and is also stimulated by psychological and emotional reasons (internally) (Perretti & Negro, 2006). However, the essence and main objective of this platform is to spread the experience of each user as their social status increases, which is important for virtual communities (Chen et al., 2011). The form of expressing feelings or something that may be happening through the publication of comments posted on other users' pages or on their own profile is also pointed out by Brandtzaeg and Heim (2009) as a reason for using social networks.

User-generated Content and eWOM

Today, WOM has moved from an informal conversation between people who get the word out about a product or service to sharing opinions / information on online platforms, such as social networks, blogs, review websites, discussion boards, among others (Cheung, Chiu, & Lee, 2012; Litvin, Goldsmith, & Pan, 2018). A retrospective view of electronic word-of-mouth in hospitality and tourism management.

International Journal of Contemporary Hospitality Management, 30(1), 313-325.). Online comments are increasingly mentioned as an important source of information, simplifying consumers' buying decisions (Zhang et al., 2014). Online user-generated content becomes one of the main sources of information for tourists, who themselves become creators and users of their own online content (Marchiori & Cantoni, 2015). In addition, this type of communication allows to reach a larger number of users in a shorter time, eliminating time, location and speed constraints during information exchange (Chaves, Gomes, & Pedron, n.d.).

According to a Skift.com report, overall, 89% of travellers and 64% of the hotel industry believe online reviews have an influence on reservations (Skift, 2014). In addition, 95% of travellers report they would rather read online reviews before making a reservation as they became a deciding factor in hotel selection (Ady & Quadri-Felitti, 2015). Thus, online content not only highlights opinions, but encompasses legitimacy and power of influence for other consumers, whether positively or negatively (Sales, Carvalho, Arruda, & Albuquerque, 2015). The online opinions of experienced and trusted users have a significant influence on the purchasing decisions of other travel consumers (Litvin, Goldsmith, & Pan, 2008, 2018). Today, online content influences other consumers' opinions, and numerical ratings are an important tool that can measure the value of comments themselves without having to read them in full (Godes & Mayzlin, 2004).

Thus, eWOM may, according to Stringam and Gerdes (2010), affect consumers' purchasing decisions and product quality perceptions, as most comments on online platforms provide information about the recommendation or discouragement of a product to other consumers. Cantallops and Salvi (2013) argue that eWOM includes various forms of online communication, such as opinions, recommendations and comments. This means that the type of information is both informative, providing additional information as a way to complement and guide the consumer's decision, as well as advisory, where the popularity of the product is indicated by a positive or negative score (Jalilvand, Esfahani, & Samiei, 2011).

There are many online platforms that allow users to interact and provide reviews on tourism services, namely TravBuddy, Travellerspoint, WAYN, Woophy, Wheretostay, Zoomandgo, Passportstamp, and TripAdvisor (Jeong & Jeong, 2008; Miguéns, Baggio, & Costa, 2008). The latter is probably the most recognized online review platform in the tourism and hospitality industry. It provides reviews (both quantitative and qualitative) from millions of users and a wide range of destination choices and planning features with built-in links to booking tools that check hundreds of websites to find the best prices. Studies addressing user-generated content and eWOM have already focused on TripAdvisor as a social media platform in travel content (e.g. Barcala, Díaz, & Rodriguez, 2009; Huang, Basu, & Hsu, 2010; Jeong & Jeon, 2008; Lei, & Law, 2015; Limberger et al., 2014; O'Connor, 2010; Sparks & Browning, 2010; Weilin & Svetlana, 2012).

METHODOLOGY

The main purpose of this study is to analyse the opinions shared by guests of a resort on the TripAdvisor online platform, in order to identify the emotion associated with these comments and therefore the experience gained during their stay. The specific objectives are to identify: (i) the profile of the visitor; (ii) the general and specific evaluation made for each category; and (iii) the emotional intonations of the visitors' comments. Thus, it is intended to qualify the comments separately by categories and to identify the type of traveller, and to quantify and analyse the emotion present in each one.

The study was applied to a resort located in the Algarve region, which is the only development of a renowned French hotel group existing in Portugal. This hotel is made up of 389 rooms, divided into 3 buildings, and has various activities available for its guests (tennis, trapeze, archery, fitness, golf, ping pong and mini golf). Being a family-oriented resort, it is suitable for children from 4 months to 17 years old, with special food services for babies and various activities for all children. In this resort there are two restaurants and three bars, as well as a spa service with different packages for its guests. It should also be noted that the resort is not open all year round, it closes from November to mid-February.

The data used in this study was collected on TripAdvisor. TripAdvisor is, in part, similar to a social network, a virtual community, and a blog, being hard to categorize its type (O'Connor, 2010). It is, therefore, considered a multifaceted platform, recognized for providing information and user feedback, where it is possible to respond to each user comment (not being able to remove or edit comments). This platform was chosen for this study because it is the world's largest travel website that allows easy interaction with travellers, and with more user-generated content, including comments, ratings, photos and videos (TripAdvisor, 2017).

The study collected a sample of 294 comments from September 1, 2017 to April 15, 2018, to provide a sample of comments from visitors who had stayed until Easter. Data extraction from guest posts on TripAdvisor was possible using filters, namely the language filter. Since most reviews for resort are available in French (2,719 reviews), which may be due to the nationality of the hotel chain, and since 75% of French people use TripAdvisor reviews for the choice of destination (Wesgro, 2017), it was decided to choose to analyse only the comments of the francophone public.

The comments were collected individually through manual extraction into an Excel file. Along with the comment, elements that allow a characterization of the visitor (gender, city and country of residence) and the trip (month and year, and type of trip) were also collected. In addition, the overall rating and rating by category (value for money, location, sleep quality, rooms, cleanliness and service) were collected, being the TripAdvisor rating on a scale of 1 to 5.

After data collection, the comments were manually entered individually into an artificial intelligence software, the IBM Watson Tone Analyzer. This tool analyses feelings automatically, based on algorithms designed to extract feelings in a similar way to humans. That is, the software "questions / identifies" the feeling(s) present in each comment, regarding terms and topics, making a classification taking into account its polarity (positive, neutral and negative). This software, in its context, identifies emotional intonations (anger, fear, joy, sadness, analytical, confident and tentative), which are classified by a score. The score may be less than 0.5 (none or weak intonation), between 0.5 and 0.75 (median intonation) and greater than 0.75 (strong intonation). The program assigns a colour to sentences according to the punctuation. Usually if there is more than one emotion extracted, the score shown will be the strongest. Emotion results were also integrated into the Excel database, which later were imported and analysed on the IBM SPSS Statistics v.25 statistical program. In this study, univariate and bivariate analysis were performed.

RESULTS

Profile of the Guests

From the analysis of the reviews, it was found that the profile of guests was mostly female (46%), 35% were male and 19% did not specify their gender. Guests live predominantly in France (44.9%), Belgium

(10.9%) and Switzerland (3.1%). Other countries represent only 2.7% of the comments (Luxembourg, Portugal, Canada and Russia). From 38.4% of the comments it was not possible to identify the users' country of origin. Regarding the cities of origin, there is a large dispersion. It is found that, generally, guests come from the main cities of each country, however, users did not insert their city of residence in 39.1% of the comments. It was also found that, from the French guests, 44.7% are residents of the Île-de-France, 13.6% of the Provence-Alpes-Côte d'Azur region, 10.6% of the Hautes de France, and 7.6% from Auvergne-Rhône-Alpes, with the other regions having a reduced expression.

Regarding the characteristics of the trip, it was found that 69.7% of the guests travelled in 2017, having commented mostly on September (30.6%), October (20.7%) and August 2017 (13.6%), and 30.3% in 2018, mainly in March (14.3%). Most guests (55.7%) travel with their families, 26.2% travel as a couple or with friends (11.8%), 5.9% travel alone and only 0.5% travelled for business reasons. People from the Île-de-France and Hautes-de-France regions travelled mostly with their families (57.9% and 64.3%, respectively), while people from Provence-Alpes-Côte d'Azur travelled mostly as a couple (50%) and in family (38.9%).

Review of the Guests' Ratings

The resort scored an average rating of 4.3 out of 5, with a standard deviation of 0.896 (Table 1); 53.7% of the guests rate it as excellent, 32.7% give it a very good rating and 1.7% give it a terrible rating.

Table 1. Descriptive frequency of the 'general classification'

Classification	Frequency	%	Average	Standard Deviation
Terrible	5	1,7		
Weak	10	3,4		
Average	25	8,5	4,3	0,896
Good	96	32,7		
Excellent	158	53,7		
Total	294	100		

Source: Own construction

In this context, Cantallops and Salvi (2013) argue that the type of information is both informative, helping to complement and guide the consumer's decision, as well as advisory, where the popularity of the product is indicated by a positive or negative score (Jalilvand et al., 2011). The comments in which tourists rated the resort are mostly positive (86.4%), showing their relevance.

Regarding the classification by parameter, measured on a 5-point scale, it was found that the highest emphasis goes to the cleanliness and location with an average of 4.30, while the least rated attribute was the value for money, with an average of 4.0, which, although with a lower rating, is a good reference for the quality / price ratio (Figure 1).

Figure 1. Ratings by category
Source: Own construction

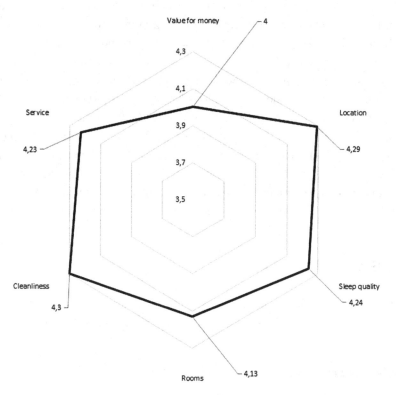

There was a high frequency of comments regarding the service (mentioned 159 times), with a strong correlation coefficient regarding the total rating (> 0.8). Other frequently mentioned categories are rooms (109 times) and location (106 times), which show a moderate (> 0.6) and strong (> 0.7) correlation, respectively (Table 2).

Table 2. Pearson correlation

Specific Classifications	Coefficients	Number of Comments	p-Value
Value for money	0.701	95	
Location	0.722	106	
Sleep quality	0.564	106	
Bedrooms	0.656	109	0.000
Cleanliness	0.635	102	
Service	0.828	159	

Source: Own construction

Overall, the guests greatly appreciate the strategic positioning of the resort and rate the location as one of the service's key points. They also refer to the kindness of staff, both in the bar and restaurant, as well as in the personalized attention and care of children. The results obtained are in line with other studies, namely Ong (2012), who argue that the location and distance from the hotel to the most well-known attractions, the cleanliness of the room and the value for money are important attributes as well. According to Öğüt and Taş (2012), the most mentioned attributes were the location, service, price, room and features of the hotel, safety, reputation and category. In the case of the resort under study, the most relevant attributes were the service, the cleanliness, the location and the sleep quality.

Sentiment Analysis of the Comments

Regarding the sentiment analysis of the comments, it was found that "joy" is the most relevant emotion, with a strong intonation of 73.8% (Table 3). Joy can be explained by the many services and features that the resort offers, such as: (i) the all-inclusive regime; the kindness of the staff, since they have the duty to interact with customers and always be available; (ii) the childcare setting where parents can rest while enjoying the pool or spa because their children are busy with activities with a team of certified educators; (iii) the entertainment in which thematic shows are presented every night; and (iv) prime location.

Table 3. Descriptive frequency of the emotions

	Analytical	**Confident**	**Joy**	**Sadness**	**Tentative**	**Anger**
No emotions	184 62.6%	256 87.1%	18 6.1%	242 82.3%	268 91.2%	253 86.1%
Weak	-	-	1 0.3%	-	-	
Medium	68 23.1%	17 5.8%	58 19.7%	42 14.3%	9 3.1%	35 11.9%
Strong	42 14.3%	21 7.1%	217 73.8%	10 3.4%	17 5.8%	6 2%
Mean	0.263	0.096	0.743	0.114	0.067	0.085
Median	0.00	0.00	0.80	0.00	0.00	0.00
Standard deviation	0.349	0.255	0.211	0.251	0.219	0.216

Source: Own construction

Following is "analytical", with 23.1% of medium intonation and 14.3% with strong intonation. However, "confident" and "tentative" also stood out with 7.1% and 5.8% of strong intonation, and 5.8% and 3.1% with medium intonation. Finally, the emotions "sadness" and "anger" had 14.3% and 11.9% medium intonation, and 3.4% and 2.0% referred to strong intonation.

This resort is characterized as being enjoyable for holidays, the emotions that stand out mainly are those related to joy and analytical, as it may mean that people feel happiness when staying at the resort.

CONCLUSION

Technological advances in recent years have had a significant impact on the tourism sector. Social media has become a powerful tool to leverage services for the tourism industry and, therefore, caused a change in the role of traditional intermediaries (Buhalis & Law, 2008). The online environment enables the effective exchange of information between users, allowing them to access information faster, easier and more conveniently (Wang & Fesenmaier, 2004). Today, Internet users contribute significantly to the generation of online content and information. They share their experiences, describing their levels of satisfaction with various services in order to inform and help other visitors. It is the consumer who manages the information, sharing it easily in an informal way and influencing the choice of other consumers. Therefore, user-generated content has been identified as an important source of information, influencing consumer choice and decision.

Overall, this study allowed to identify a resort's rating assigned by tourists on TripAdvisor and the emotions associated with the comments. Regarding the profile of visitors to the resort under analysis, they are mostly women, French, and from the Île-de-France region. The date of the trip and the comments on TripAdvisor were mainly September and October 2017. Concerning the travel typology, most visitors are accompanied by their family or travel as a couple. In addition, the results show that the resort has a strongly positive rating from guests who visited it, meaning that eWOW and influence on other potential consumers is positive. The most relevant criteria for guests were the cleanliness, location and sleep quality, and the ones that obtained lower ratings, although they may be considered good, were the value for money, the rooms and the service. As far as emotions were concerned, the ones that were most evident were joy and the analytical, and the less strong were sadness and anger.

This study, while focusing on a case study in the hospitality industry, allowed to reflect on how user-generated content on online platforms, such as TripAdvisor, can provide relevant data and information for tourism companies, which should be seen as a competitive advantage and incorporated into their online marketing strategies. It showed that it is possible to group different opinions and understand the consumers' needs through the emotional intonations of each comment and, therefore, be able to improve the service quality. For companies starting their business or those looking to embrace digital technologies, given that many of the tourists' experiences are shared on online social networks and online booking platforms, this kind of information becomes increasingly important. It is, therefore, relevant to realize the potential of this data, which may impact on several areas, such as customer loyalty, making predictions in order to study the popularity or introduction of a new product or service, and understanding the profile of customers who express opinions about the company. Thus, eWOM must be seen as an opportunity rather than a threat. As a result, tourism companies increasingly have to adapt, create and / or streamline user-generated content-based strategies.

The study presents some limitations, namely the limited time period for data collection, as well as the fact that certain comments did not have complete information about the guests' profile, and the lack of classifications in the different categories. In future research, it is suggested that the study integrates comments published at other times of the year, in order to assess the impact of seasonality, as well as comments from guests from other countries, on the other hand, it would be interesting to make a comparative study with other similar hotels of the same group.

REFERENCES

Ady, M., & Quadri-Felitti, D. (2015). Consumer research identifies how to present travel review content for more bookings. Retrieved from https://static1.squarespace.com/static/56dd934137013bc69c80ae95/t/56e6c50462cd94987f7ad826/1457964296558/Consumer+Research+Identifies+How+To+Present+Travel+Review+Content+for+More+Bookings.pdf

Afonso, C., & Borges, L. (2013). *Social target: Da estratégia à implementação – Como tirar partido das redes sociais e potenciar o negócio.* Top Books.

Barcala, M. F., Díaz, M. G., & Rodriguez, J. P. (2009). Factors influencing guests' hotel quality appraisals. *European Journal of Tourism Research, 2*(1), 25–40.

Berthon, P. R., Pitt, L. F., Plangger, K., & Shapiro, D. (2012). Marketing meets Web 2.0, social media, and creative consumers: Implications for international marketing strategy. *Business Horizons, 55*(3), 261–271. doi:10.1016/j.bushor.2012.01.007

Brandtzaeg, P., & Heim, J. (2009). Why people use social networking sites. In A. A. Ozok & P. Zaphiris (Eds.), *Online Communities and Social Computing (OCSC 2009).* Berlin: Springer. doi:10.1007/978-3-642-02774-1_16

Buhalis, D., & Law, R. (2008). Progress in tourism management progress in information technology and tourism management: 20 years on and 10 years after the Internet – The state of eTourism research. *Tourism Management, 29*(4), 609–623. doi:10.1016/j.tourman.2008.01.005

Cantallops, A. S., & Salvi, F. (2014). New consumer behavior: A review of research on eWOM and hotels. *International Journal of Hospitality Management, 36*, 41–51. doi:10.1016/j.ijhm.2013.08.007

Chaves, M. S., Gomes, R., & Pedron, C. (n.d.). Decision-making based on online reviews: The small and medium hotels management. Retrieved from https://repositorio-cientifico.essatla.pt/bitstream/20.500.12253/639/1/ecis-2012-mchaves-etal-cr.pdf

Chen, Y., Fay, S., & Wang, Q. (2011). The role of marketing in social media: How online consumer reviews evolve. *Journal of Interactive Marketing, 25*(2), 85–94. doi:10.1016/j.intmar.2011.01.003

Cheung, C. M. K., Chiu, P.-Y., & Lee, M. K. O. (2011). Online social networks: Why do students use Facebook? *Computers in Human Behavior, 27*(4), 1337–1343. doi:10.1016/j.chb.2010.07.028

Chung, J. Y., & Buhalis, D. (2008). Information needs in online social networks. *Information Technology & Tourism, 10*(4), 267–281. doi:10.3727/109830508788403123

Di Pietro, L., Di Virgilio, F., & Pantano, E. (2012). Social network for the choice of tourist destination: Attitude and behavioural intention. *Journal of Hospitality and Tourism Technology, 3*(1), 60–76. doi:10.1108/17579881211206543

Freitas, L., & Vieira, R. (2015). Exploring resources for sentiment analysis in Portuguese Language. *Brazilian Conference on Intelligent Systems.* Retrieved from https://www.researchgate.net/publication/300409116_Exploring_Resources_for_Sentiment_Analysis_in_Portuguese_Language

Gaál, Z., Szabó, L., Obermayer-Kovács, N., & Csepregi, A. (2015). Exploring the role of social media in knowledge sharing. *Electronic Journal of Knowledge Management, 13*(3), 185–197.

Gallegos, J. A. (August 23, 2016). What is user generated content (and why you should be using it). Tintup. Retrieved from https://www.tintup.com/blog/user-generated-content-definition/

Godes, D., & Mayzlin, D. (2004). Using online conversations to study word-of-mouth communication. *Marketing Science, 23*(4), 545–560. doi:10.1287/mksc.1040.0071

Goldsmith, R. E., & Horowitz, D. (2006). Measuring motivations for online opinion seeking. *Journal of Interactive Advertising, 6*(2), 2–14. doi:10.1080/15252019.2006.10722114

Hays, S., Page, S. J., & Buhalis, D. (2013). Social media as a destination marketing tool: Its use by national tourism organisations. *Current Issues in Tourism, 16*(3), 211–239. doi:10.1080/13683500.2012.662215

Hsu, C.-L., & Lin, J. C.-C. (2008). Acceptance of blog usage: The roles of technology acceptance, social influence and knowledge sharing motivation. *Information & Management, 45*(1), 65–74. doi:10.1016/j.im.2007.11.001

Huang, Y., Basu, C., & Hsu, M. K. (2010). Exploring motivations of travel knowledge sharing on social network sites: An empirical investigation of U.S. college students. *Journal of Hospitality Marketing & Management, 19*(7), 717–734. doi:10.1080/19368623.2010.508002

Jalilvand, M. R., Esfahani, S. S., & Samiei, N. (2011). Electronic word-of-mouth: Challenges and opportunities. *Procedia Computer Science, 3*, 42–46. doi:10.1016/j.procs.2010.12.008

Lecture, J. S., Fehr, E., & Falk, A. (2002). Psychological foundations of incentives. *European Economic Review, 46*(4-5), 687–724. doi:10.1016/S0014-2921(01)00208-2

Lei, S., & Law, R. (2015). Content Analysis of Tripadvisor Reviews on Restaurants: A Case Study of Macau. *Journal of tourism, 16*(1), 17–28.

Leung, D., Law, R., Van Hoof, H., & Buhalis, D. (2013). Social media in tourism and hospitality: A literature review. *Journal of Travel & Tourism Marketing, 30*(1-2), 3–22. doi:10.1080/10548408.2013.750919

Limberger, P. F., Anjos, F. A., Meira, J. V., & Anjos, S. J. (2014). Satisfaction in hospitality on TripAdvisor.com: An analysis of the correlation between evaluation criteria and overall satisfaction. *Tourism & Management Studies, 10*(1), 59–65.

Litvin, S. W., Goldsmith, R. E., & Pan, B. (2008). Electronic word-of-mouth in hospitality and tourism management. *Tourism Management, 29*(3), 458–468. doi:10.1016/j.tourman.2007.05.011

Litvin, S. W., Goldsmith, R. E., & Pan, B. (2018). A retrospective view of electronic word-of-mouth in hospitality and tourism management. *International Journal of Contemporary Hospitality Management, 30*(1), 313–325. doi:10.1108/IJCHM-08-2016-0461

Liu, B. (2015). *Sentiment analysis: Mining opinions, sentiments, and emotions.* New York: Cambridge University Press. doi:10.1017/CBO9781139084789

Marchiori, E., & Cantoni, L. (2015). The role of prior experience in the perception of a tourism destination in user-generated content. *Journal of Destination Marketing & Management, 4*(3), 194–201. doi:10.1016/j.jdmm.2015.06.001

Marktest. (2017). Os portugueses e as redes sociais 2017. Retrieved from http://www.marktest.com/wap/a/grp/p~96.aspx

Marktest. (2019). Os portugueses e as redes sociais 2019. Retrieved from http://www.marktest.com/wap/a/grp/p~96.aspx

Miguéns, J., Baggio, R., & Costa, C. (2008). Social media and tourism destinations: TripAdvisor case study. *Advances in tourism research, 26*(28), 1–6.

Mkono, M. (2012). Netnographic tourist research: The Internet as a virtual fieldwork site. *Tourism Analysis, 17*(4), 553–555. doi:10.3727/108354212X13473157390966

Munar, A. M., & Jacobsen, J. K. S. (2014). Motivations for sharing tourism experiences through social media. *Tourism Management, 43*, 46–54. doi:10.1016/j.tourman.2014.01.012

Neethu, M. S., & Rajasree, R. (2013). Sentiment analysis in Twitter using machine learning techniques. *Proceedings of the 2013 Fourth International Conference on Computing, Communications and Networking Technologies (ICCCNT)* (pp. 1–5). IEEE. 10.1109/ICCCNT.2013.6726818

O'Connor, P. (2010). Managing a hotel's image on TripAdvisor. *Journal of Hospitality Marketing & Management, 19*(7), 754–772. doi:10.1080/19368623.2010.508007

Öğüt, H., & Onur Taş, B. K. (2012). The influence of Internet customer reviews on the online sales and prices in hotel industry. *Service Industries Journal, 32*(2), 197–214. doi:10.1080/02642069.2010.529436

Pak, A., & Paroubek, P. (n.d.). Twitter as a corpus for sentiment analysis and opinion mining. *LREC*, 1320–1326. Retrieved from https://pdfs.semanticscholar.org/ad8a/7f620a57478ff70045f97abc7aec9687ccbd.pdf

Pang, B., & Lee, L. (2008). Opinion mining and sentiment analysis. *Foundations and Trends in Information Retrieval, 2*(12), 1–135. doi:10.1561/1500000011

Perretti, F., & Negro, G. (2006). Filling empty seats: How status and organizational hierarchies affect exploration versus exploitation in team design. *Academy of Management Journal, 49*(4), 759–777. doi:10.5465/amj.2006.22083032

Sales, R., Carvalho, C., Arruda, D., & Albuquerque, J. (2015). Clique aqui para decidir: As recomendações online na decisão de compra dos serviços hoteleiros. *Revista de Turismo y Patrimónío Cultural, 13*(3), 541–550. doi:10.25145/j.pasos.2015.13.038

Serrano-Guerrero, J., Olivas, J. A., Romero, F. P., & Herrera-Viedma, E. (2015). Sentiment analysis: A review and comparative analysis of web services. *Information Sciences, 311*, 18–38. doi:10.1016/j.ins.2015.03.040

Sigala, M., Christou, E., & Gretzel, U. (Eds.). (2012). *Social media in travel, tourism and hospitality: Theory, practice and cases.* Ashgate Publishing, Ltd.

Skift.com. (2014). State of travel: 2014. Retrieved from http://skift.com/wp-content/uploads/2014/08/Skift-2014-State-of-Travel-Report-Full.pdf

Sparks, B. A., & Browning, V. (2010). Complaining in cyberspace: The motive and forms of hotel guests' complaints online. *Journal of Hospitality Marketing & Management*, *19*(7), 797–818. doi:10.1 080/19368623.2010.508010

Stringam, B. B., & Gerdes, J. Jr. (2010). An analysis of word-of-mouse ratings and guest comments of online hotel distribution sites. *Journal of Hospitality Marketing & Management*, *19*(7), 773–796. doi :10.1080/19368623.2010.508009

TripAdvisor. (2017). PT Media Center | About TripAdvisor. Retrieved from https://tripadvisor.media-room.com/pt-about-us

Valdivia, A., Luzón, M. V., & Herrera, F. (2017). Sentiment analysis on TripAdvisor: Are there inconsistencies in user reviews? In F. Martínez de Pisón, R. Urraca, H. Quintián, & E. Corchado (Eds.), *Hybrid artificial intelligent systems*. Cham: Springer. doi:10.1007/978-3-319-59650-1_2

Vermeulen, I. E., & Seegers, D. (2009). Tried and tested: The impact of online hotel reviews on consumer consideration. *Tourism Management*, *30*(1), 123–127. doi:10.1016/j.tourman.2008.04.008

Vlachvei, A., & Notta, O. (2014). Social Media adoption and managers' perceptions. *International Journal of Strategic Innovative Marketing*, *1*(2), 61–73. doi:10.15556/IJSIM.01.02.001

Wang, Y., & Fesenmaier, D. R. (2004). Modeling participation in an online travel community. *Journal of Travel Research*, *42*(3), 261–270. doi:10.1177/0047287503258824

Wang, Y., Yu, Q., & Fesenmaier, D. R. (2002). Defining the virtual tourist community: Implications for tourism marketing. *Tourism Management*, *23*(4), 407–417. doi:10.1016/S0261-5177(01)00093-0

Wang, Y., Yu, Q., & Fesenmaier, D. R. (2002). Defining the virtual tourist community: Implications for tourism marketing. *Tourism Management*, *23*(4), 407–417. doi:10.1016/S0261-5177(01)00093-0

Weilin, L., & Svetlana, S. (2012). Ecoturism experiences reported online: Classification of satisfaction attributes. *Tourism Management*, *33*(3), 702–712. doi:10.1016/j.tourman.2011.08.003

Wesgro. (2017). France: Tourism Market Insights 2017. Retrieved from http://www.wesgro.co.za/ pdf_repository/Tourism Market Insights_France.pdf

Yoo, K. H., & Gretzel, U. (2008). The influence of perceived credibility on preferences for recommender systems as sources of advice. *Information Technology & Tourism*, *10*(2), 133–146. doi:10.3727/109830508784913059

Yoo, K. H., Gretzel, U., Yoo, K.-H., Lee, Y., & Fesenmaier, D. R. (2010). Antecedents and impacts of trust in travel-related consumer-generated media. *Journal of Information Technology and Tourism*, *12*(2), 139–152. doi:10.3727/109830510X12887971002701

Zhang, K. Z. K., Zhao, S. J., Cheung, C. M. K., & Lee, M. K. O. (2014). Examining the influence of online reviews on consumers' decision-making: A heuristic–systematic model. *Decision Support Systems*, *67*, 78–89. doi:10.1016/j.dss.2014.08.005

This research was previously published in the Handbook of Research on Social Media Applications for the Tourism and Hospitality Sector; pages 295-308, copyright year 2020 by Business Science Reference (an imprint of IGI Global).

Section 6
Critical Issues and Challenges

Chapter 98

Multimodal Sentiment Analysis:
A Survey and Comparison

Ramandeep Kaur

https://orcid.org/0000-0003-4732-5710

Guru Kashi University, Talwandi Sabo, India

Sandeep Kautish

Guru Kashi University, Talwandi Sabo, India

ABSTRACT

Multimodal sentiments have become the challenge for the researchers and are equally sophisticated for an appliance to understand. One of the studies that support MS problems is a MSA, which is the training of emotions, attitude, and opinion from the audiovisual format. This survey article covers the comprehensive overview of the last update in this field. Many recently proposed algorithms and various MSA applications are presented briefly in this survey. The article is categorized according to their contributions in the various MSA techniques. The main purpose of this survey is to provide a full image of the MSA opportunities and difficulties and related field with brief details. The main contribution of this article includes the sophisticated categorizations of a large number of recent articles and the illustration of the recent trend of research in the MSA and its related areas.

INTRODUCTION

"Sentiment analysis," productions a substantial protagonist in fields in "affective computing," refers to all the parts of detecting, analyzing and evaluating humans' frame of cognizance towards different events, issues, services, or any other interest. More precisely, this field aims to mine sentiments, interpretations, and sensations based on observations of people's actions can be captured using their writings, facial expressions, speech, music, movements etc. Below is the Exploration of sentiments from each one of these media is a specific field (Yang & Chen, 2012; Ayadi, Kamel & Karray, 2011).

DOI: 10.4018/978-1-6684-6303-1.ch098

Manuscript sentiment exploration has been an attractive topic of study since the mid-1990s; however, there barely exists a systematic organization of tasks under this area and people use different terms to mention to different tasks. For example, sentiment analysis, opinion mining, and polarity classification, which are define below, are rummage-sale to discourse the same concept. Sentiment is a thought, attitude or judgment provoked by a feeling. However, sentiment is a view colored by an emotion. It is not grim to confuse opinion and emotion; subsequently they have a well-built correlation. For instance, in many situations emotion stimulates a person to judge an entity and build opinions about it. Additionally, opinion of a soul can cause emotions in others. Based on the aforementioned reasons, the categorization of sentiment exploration is done into two chunks: Opinion mining, distributed with the manifestation of opinions, and Emotion mining, distributed with the articulation of emotions. Figure 1 that shows the categorization of sentiment exploration to these 2 tasks and the subtasks of each.

Figure 1. Taxonomy of sentiment exploration tasks (Source: Yadollahi, Shahraki & Zaiane, 2017)

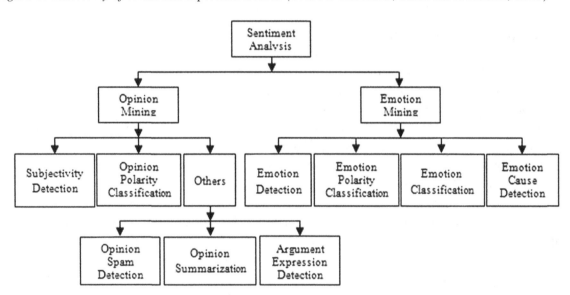

Opinion Mining

Estimation excavating is more anxious with the clue of opinions uttered in texts which can be positive, negative, or neutral and various Opinion-mining tasks are:

- **Subjectivity Detection:** The mission of detecting if a text is unprejudiced or idiosyncratic. Objective texts carry some factual information, while subjective texts express somebody's personal views or opinions, for example, (Liu, 2011);
- **Opinion Polarity Classification:** The chore of determining whether the typescript expresses either affirmative or deleterious (or sometimes neutral) opinion;

- **Estimation Unsolicited Mail Concealment:** The chore of detecting fake opinions in favor of or against a merchandise or amenity that malicious users intentionally write to variety their target popular or unpopular. (Jindal & Liu, 2008);
- **Opinion Summarization:** The chore of summarizing a large bunch of opinions toward a topic, encompassing different perspectives, aspects, and polarities. The drudgery of (Hu & Liu, 2004), is an example of opinion summarization on product reviews;
- **Argument Expression Detection:** The chore of identifying argumentative structures and the inextricable between different arguments within a manuscript, the drudgery of (Lin et al., 2006), is solitary of the interesting previous works for one to read.

Emotion Mining

Emotion mining is the learning of emotions (e.g., joy, sadness) reflected in a portion of text and various emotion-mining tasks are:

- **Emotion Detection:** The chore of detecting if a text conveys any type of sensation or not. This is analogous to subjectivity detection for opinions and is lectured in (Gupta et al., 2013);
- **Emotion Polarity Classification:** The chore of influential the schism of the prevailing emotion in a text, assuming that it has some. This is comparable to guesstimates chemotaxonomy. Examples of this study can be predictable in (Hancock et al., 2007);
- **Emotion Classification:** The chore of fine-grained classification of existing emotion in a manuscript into one (or more) of a customary of defined emotions;
- **Emotion Cause Detection:** The chore of mining factors for eliciting some kinds of emotions is pronounced in the work (Gao et al., 2015).

Figure 2 shows some illustrations of multimodal tweets. Both image and text present positive sentiment in (a); while in (b), image and text bear an obvious negative sentiment. The text in (c) is neutral, but we can distinguish the negative emotion from the image (c) built on the scene of the poor child lying on the beach together with "REFUSE" in the image.

Besides the outmoded contrivance learning-based methods, subterranean neural grid has extended raising attention in extracting textual representation (Zhang & Wallace, 2015), Meanwhile, motivated by their bigger enactment in image classification, CNNs (You, 2015), have also been jumble-sale in image sentiment analysis. For multimodal sentiment exploration chore, one key problem is the merging of all modalities of samples, including text, image, video or speech. Although related deep neural network-based methods have achieved fairly good performance, their fusion model underlying CNNs as thriving as their single image processing model are still relatively simple and essential to be further refined. Sentiment analysis is divided into two main processes: the collection of data sets (corpus) and the categorization of the data depending on their sentiments.

LITERATURE SURVEY

Table 1 Shows various existing techniques used. Most existing methods fluctuate in rapports of topographies and accentuate on dissimilar traits of the problem.

Figure 2. Examples of multimodal tweets from Twitter (Source: Xu & Mao, 2017)

I ruminate it's anodyne to say I've under no circumstances been so infatuated and in adoration with someone. Never want another Valentine.

UPDATED: Police: 2 dead, 3 gammy in police-involved bombardment in River Forest.

Harper Government Refugee

Era: 2003-2008

In the paper, (Pantic & Rothkrantz, 2003), developed multimodal distress penetrating HCI riggings which will be capable to check human non-verbal performance and to get used to the present user, to his context, and to the predominant scenario. Make those adaptive tools commercially accessible to the users who will profile them in the situation in the tools are to be used. Withdraw the systems of trained later than some time and inextricable the stored information such that derive generic statistical rules/models for interpretation of human nonverbal performance in the given context/environment. As, (Lisetti et al., 2003), main penalty area is at constructing a tool that can gather patterns, forecast, and some suggestions are thru for the patients such that capable to progress from one emotional position to another. Integrating MOUE with skilled systems that could cooperatively evaluate patterns and health indicators for analytical, predictive and dictatorial purposes is also on their research plan. Looking forward, (Ishizuka & Prendinger, 2006), described an outline of their drudgery of exploration and developments on the multimodal means and contents with embodied lifelike agents, particularly the research focused on their MPML. While the efficiency of lifelike agents has been perceptible in their explore and developments of the preceding decade, and they sometimes see multimodal contents utilizing character agents on the Network and elsewhere nowadays, their popularity still remains low. Moving further, (Raaijmakers et al., 2008), described the exploitation of prosodic types, phoneme n-grams, character n-grams, and word n-grams for subjectivity recognition and categorize of polarization of dialog performances in dual discussion. It shows that character n-grams outperform prosodic topographies, phoneme n-grams and word n-grams in subjectivity recognition and divergence classification. Combining these features significantly improves performance. Equate the additive value of four information sources available, prosodic information seem to be least informative while character-level information indeed proves to a very valuable source.

Era: 2009-2012

However, (Jansen et al., 2009), examined the utilization of microblogging for eWOM imprinting. Examining several datasets from a amalgamation of angles, their research has shed bright on critical features of their phenomenon. Their work includes micro blogging, which is a potentially affluent way for organizations to. Consumer product observations and buying choices seem increasingly swayed by Web interactions and community network services, as users steadily more use these communication technologies for feasible sources of opinions, information and insights. Their trend offers new prospects to physique marquee associations with probable customers and eWOM communication platforms. Given the comfort of monitoring any brand's sentiment, one can view microblogging as a competitive intelligence source. Whereas, (Bower & Hedberg, 2010), presented the multimodal discourse analysis (MDA) approach that delivered a calculating of the superfluous involvement gave by adopting student-centered learning voguish in the conference of web situation, with a greater than 6 fold enhance in involvement as associated to teacher-centered methods. The MDA enabled motifs in the environment of discourse to be detected, with more student-centered strategies that outcome in more student argument particularly linked to the content and less student ripostes to teacher questions. As, (Soleymani et al., 2012) recorded and made vacant a multimodal affective database to the sentimental computing community. The huge group of modalities logged (multi-camera video of face, head, speech, eye gaze, pupil size, ECG, GSR, respiration amplitude, and skin temperature) and the extraordinary synchronization accuracy between them makes their database a valuable involvement to the enduring development and benchmarking of emotion-related algorithms that exploit data fusion, as thriving as to studies on human emotion and emotional expression. Whereas, (Stieglitz & Dang-Xuan, 2012), proposed an agenda for social media logical in dogmatic situation. More particularly, they summarize different kind of strategies of data tracking and data analysis as thriving as consequent analysis techniques that might help gains a deeper approaching into political negotiations in societal means. The structure should provide a principle for the growth of toolsets goal at gathering, holding, examining, evaluating, and summarizing politically appropriate user-generated content from societal means for dogmatic administrations. Their drudgery is fixated on considering public data exclusively; they recommend that political actors should also replicate on ethical concerns which might become applicable when considering conversation in societal means. Moving further, Mohammad (Soleymani et al., 2012) determine the deed of an inter-participant emotion recognition tagging strategy using participants' EEG signals, gaze distance and papillary reaction as sentimental responses. The sustainability of a technique to classify emotion in imperative to respond to videos is shown. Though the outcomes were constructed on a justly minor video data set due to experimental drawbacks, the promising exactitude can be scalable to more models from a larger population. The improved enactment using multimodal fusion procedures information to the decision that by add other expressions, such as facial expressions, accuracy as thriving as robustness should further improve.

Era: 2013-2015

In spite of, (Suthers & Verbert, 2013), presented an order of proof-of- concept studies for what I termed "multimodal learning analytics:" a conventional of procedures can be usage to gather numerous sources of data in high rate (video, logs, audio, gestures, biosensors), coordinate and cipher the data, and observe learning in accurate, economically effective, community, mixed-media learning atmospheres. Whereas, (Perez-Rosas et al., 2013), explained a multimodal method for level of utterance in classification of sentiment. They presented a new multimodal dataset comprehending of sensation annotated expressions mined from video appraisals, where each expression is concomitant with a video, audio, and linguistic DataStream However, (Alonso-Martin et al., 2013), a multimodal and spontaneous sentiment recognition system realistic to the HRI has been designated. Their grind has been realistic in a general interface (or dialog) system, called RDS. Using the sentiment recognition system, the customer sentiment can be encompassed in the information swapped flanked by the manipulator and the robot during a dialog turn, called a communicative act (CA). The manifestation of their emotive information will benefit to grow the version and naturalness of the dialog. The detected sentiments are: pleasure, grief, impartial and amazement. The sentiment recognition method has been combined as a chunk in the RDS, and it has been tremendously defined. In mandate to designate the user emotion, two information channels have been used: the audio and the visual ones. The system, GEVA, is the chief aim of their exertion. Their method examines the user speech to quotation its features using the Debauched Fourier Transmute and the Wavelet Transform. Once these topographies have been attained, 2 classifiers are used (J48 and JRIP) to define which sentiment links to these topographies. Furthermore, GEVA has a refined appliance to explain the starting and the finishing point of the speech sign, being capable to distinguish it from noise. On the jesting side, alternative part has been thru to classify the sentiments through the face expression analysis: the system, GEFA. Their method is made by 2 third-party software packages that are capable to define the user sentiment using simulated idea: SHORE and CERT. In the paper, (Jindal & Singh, 2015), propose to attention on the scrutiny of images, solitary of the dominant media types of online micro blogging services. They have used convolutional neural grids to solve their problem. They have premeditated a new training strategy to overcome small scale training samples. To appraisal the presented method on real-world data, they constructed a sentiment benchmark from the photo posts on Flickr, which has a rich repository of images and associated tags reflecting user's emotions. They have also presented a 7-scale granularity of sentiment rating, which is more inclusive allied with the bi-polar category system in the current datasets. Both transfer learning and progressive training invested by a lesser number of confidently considered images have produced notable improvements. As, (Poria et al., 2015), propose a novel technique for determining sentiment polarity in video clips of people speaking. They combine evidence from the confrontations they utter, the facial expression, and the speech sound. The chief invention of their paper consists in using profound CNN to citation topographies from type-script and in using MKL to identify the multimodal heterogeneous fused feature vectors. And, (Fang et al., 2015), proposed a multimodal possibility graphical model to report the delinquent of multimodal aspect-opinion excavating for stuffs in societal means. The proposed mmAOM captures the connections between verbatim and graphic modalities as thriving as the correlations between features and sentiments in a principled way, which is informative and functional. The derived multimodal aspects and corresponding opinions have demonstrated its effectiveness in applications of entity connotation imagining and multimodal aspect-opinion salvage tasks.

Era: 2016-2017

Scientometric as well as meticulous brochure exploration of study out- put in OMSA published in SCIE journals. The research publication dataset has been computationally and manually analyzed to map the OMSA research landscape during last 16 years. The scientometric analysis helped in classify year-wise numeral and amount of evolution of publications, categories of invention of papers on OMSA, association forms in publications on OMSA, most productive nations, organizations, papers and writers, quotation forms and a year-wise allusion system, and refrain mass subversions and keyword eruptions in OMSA publications during the era. The manual analysis helped in identifying popular methods (lexicon-based and lexicon-based machine) used in these periodicals, stages (text, aspect-level or sentence) of sentiment exploration drudgery completed and chief application parts of OMSA. Whereas, (Singh, Khushwaha & Vyas, 2016), studied two categories of methods that have been exploited for sentiment types: semantic analysis and contraption erudition. In the contraption learning approaches, evaluations are gathering from altered web sites and train the dataset according to a particular classifier. They implemented sentiment analysis through proposed technique, which offers a realistic explanation to contribution the perception of business analysis, and thus consequences in product improvement. However, (Islam & Zhang, 2016), introduced an innovative pictorial sentiment analysis structure using a very unfathomable convolutional neural web that beats preceding state-of- the-art in the normal dataset. Their archetypal can be cast-off to examine large-scale big data multimedia gratified for understanding user feedback, advertising, and predictive modeling. It can be useful for monitoring emotional states of individuals anguish from cere-bral disorder. They have established how CNN can perform well with a smaller dataset with the help of transfer learning. Moving further, (Ji et al., 2016), introduce the up-to-the-minute enquiry works in their related stream and detail some state-of- the-art approaches. To push forward their field, there are 2 chief directions: 1) visual ontology construction. Although VSO and GSO have been studied, there are still certain interesting problems. 2) Deep-level learning and understanding. To recognize the emotion of an image, both the deep visual structure and the deep visual semantic are needed. Besides this, (Caschera et al., 2016) provided an excursus in the main techniques used for identifying sentiments from data mined from text, videos and audio. The discussion on these techniques has underlined the imperative role of contrivance erudition approaches for the emotion identification, and the chief contests addressed by these techniques. In addition, the analysis has steered to underline the foremost disputes connected to statistics mined from multiple media sources, and, therefore, the limitation to overcome in edict to mend the right considerate of the sentimental ceremonial of the users form videos and/or audios and/or texts. Starting from these findings, they have anticipated a technique for extracting emotion from multimodal statistics formal concluded a multimodal linguistic. The proposed method associates a machine wisdom method with a language-based formalization. The anticipated method structures data mined from video, audio and text by a language-based approach including information about language semantics and syntax, but also including the chronological kindred between the modalities and their cooperation. In the grind of (Niu et al., 2016), presented a new dataset called MVSA containing of multi-view tweets for sentiment exploration. To the preeminent of their knowledge, it is now the chief dataset devotedly built for multi-view sentiment analysis. Whereas present dataset only contains numerous thousands of observations, they will continuously amend the data and frequently relief the explanations on the utmost up-to- date tweets in the forthcoming. With their dataset, they have presented a pipeline for sentiment exploration on multi-view and single-view data. In addition to all, (Katsurai & Satoh, 2016), describe a new dop-pelganger sentiment exploration method that usages the latent associations amongst many views of training images. In the proposed technique, they 1st extract features from graphic, textual, and sentiment views. Then, to scheme the topographies from these views, they follow the outline of multi-view CCA using obvious feature mappings. Finally, in the embedding space, a sentiment polarization classifier is qualified established on the probable features. To ratify the effectiveness of the proposed technique, they constructed image datasets via crowd sourcing. Moreover, (Ullah et al., 2017), summarizes some of those opportunities such as exploring the current datasets with different approaches, amendment the method of preprocessing combinations, etc. and difficulties such as co-reference resolution, video summarization, and exploration of more feature points etc. from the most recent articles and provide necessary guidelines to the future researchers. Their research also offers a single vivid exemplification of MSA tasks and approaches. As, (Poria et al., 2017), concluded a generous periodical of the fundamental stages of a multimodal affect recognition framework. They started by discussing available benchmark datasets, followed by an outline of the ceremonial of the art in audio-, visual- and textual- based affect recognition. In particular, they highlighted prominent studies in unimodal affect recognition, which they consider crucial components of a multimodal have emotional impact gauge framework. For example, without efficient unimodal affect classifiers or feature extractors, it is not possible to make a well-performing multimodal have emotional impact gauge. Looking forward, (Yadav & Pandya, 2017), summarizes existing approaches for sentiment scrutiny. Text pre-processing, feature mining and chin miscellany plays a substantial role for analyzing sentiments efficiently. Various issues such as sarcasm, dynamic dictionary handling, acronyms and language slangs, lexical variations have been discussed in brief. Furthermore, (Yadollahi et al., 2017) introduced state-of- the-art methods and improvements on text sentiment analysis. Sentiment scrutiny refers to all the zones of detecting, analyzing, and evaluating humans' state of mind towards different topics of interest. In particular, text sentiment scrutiny goals to mine people's opinions, emotions, and sentiments based on their writings. Personal notes, emails, news headlines, blogs, tales, novels, chat messages, and social schmoozing websites like Twitter, Facebook, and MySpace are some types of text that can convey emotions. On the flip side, (Xu & Mao, 2017), propose an end-to- end deep neural network framework MNN for multimodal sentiment scrutiny. Their presented technique relies on convolutional architectures to extract and learn the demonstrations of text and image. They further introduce the new residua model to merge multimodal features and propose two combined merged strategies for a deeper and more differentiate feature depiction. At last, (Xu et al., 2017), proposed a hierarchical semantic attention network grounded on image caption for multimodal sentiment exploration. To best of their knowledge, is the first time that using image slogan extracts visual semantic feature as the additional information for text in multimodal sentiment exploration task.

COMPUTATIONAL APPROACHES OF SENTIMENT ANALYSIS

Sentiment in Text

Sentiment scrutiny has been extensively studied as computational handling of feelings, sentiment and bias in typescript (Pang & Lee, 2008). It is done on basis of schism and concentration of lexicon, and it makes use of techniques for Data Mining and Natural Languages Processing (NLP) devoted to tracking the mood and opinion of people about a merchandise or a topic in blog stakes, tweets, reviews and annotations in a text. Text-oriented Sentiment scrutiny is mainly addressed by two main approaches:

- **Lexicon-Based:** Both sentiment dictionary and opinion words are used by Lexicon-based, after that, it matches them with data to pronounce the polarity. There is no necessity of prior training in Lexicon-based techniques such that to categorize data and the classification process is obtained by matching the topographies of a given text with sentiment bilingual dictionary whose emotion standards are concluded proceeding to their custom;

Table 1. Survey for the popular methods studied out from literature is as follows

Ref. No	Year	Algorithm Used	Advantages	Limitations	Applications	Domain Oriented	DataSet
(Lisetti et al., 2003)	2002	MOUE (a Model Of User's Emotions)		MOUE could not collectively assess health indicators and patterns for diagnostic.	Observing the user (e.g. patient) via multi-sensory devices	No	Collect their own dataset.
(Bower & Hedberg, 2010)	2010		Embrace student-centered learning strategies		Allows the nature of philosophy and erudition skills	NA	NA
(Soleymani et al., 2012)	2012	Recorded modalities and excitement elicitation etiquette.	Data fusion.	Limited to the static images only.		No	MAHNOB-HCI
(Stieglitz & Dang-Xuan, 2013)	2012	Analysis methods (Content analysis/text mining, trend analysis, opinion mining/ sentiment analysis, social network analysis)	The structure is of high relevance for the academic discussion.	Restricted. Interval of 140 charms in tweets	Business and marketing.	No	Twitter, Facebook, and weblogs
(Soleymani et al., 2012)	2012	Multimodal fusion techniques	Emotion recognition enactment and no necessity of direct user inputs.	It is applicable to fairly small video data set		Yes	youtube.com
(Perez Rosas et al., 2013)	2013		A layered approach works better in three-way classification.			Yes	YouTube
(Alonso-Martun et al., 2013)	2013	SHORE and CERT	In the occasion of adding new material frequencies with new classifiers, it does not need to be rewritten.	Dialog context are not used.	Computer game, software/ hardware and cataloguing babies 'emotions	No	(EmoDB), (LDC), (HUMANAINE), FAU Aibo Emotion Corpus.
(Jindal & Singh, 2015)	2015	Convolutional neural grids	Exploit the supremacy of the pre-trained Convolutional Neural Complex	Stand with small scale dataset	Sentiment exploration with user-tagged data on societal means locates.	Yes	Flickr image
(Poria et al., 2015)	2015	Used to TGV a classifier with a MKL algorithm		Lack of parameter miscellany for verdict level fusion to give optimal result		Yes	YouTube
(Fang et al., 2015)	2015	Kinship proliferation algorithm	Multimodal probabilistic graphical exemplary is used	Not used to advance the exertion of multimodal at ease modeling and sentiment scrutiny	Enable two approaches: entity connotation conception, and multimodal aspect-opinion reclamation	No	Flickr photos, Trip advisor reviews, and news articles.

continues on following page

Table 1. Continued

Ref. No	Year	Algorithm Used	Advantages	Limitations	Applications	Domain Oriented	DataSet
(Yuan et al., 2015)	2015	Image sentiment exploration algorithm based on mid-level attributes, Asymmetric bagging approach, eigenface-based sentiment recognition algorithm	Discover the connotation flanked by the sentiment uttered by text tweets and image tweets.	The sentiment analyses of images are still not mature.		Yes	Twitter
(Singh et al., 2016)	2016	LESK algorithm	Provides a graphical interpretation.	it needs more period to process and to transfer queries to a web search engine	Business intelligence	No	Blogs, Review sites
(Islam & Zhang, 2016)	2016	Deep convolutional neural grid	It leaves behind previous state-of-the- art in the stock dataset.	Work with integrated textual tags related with images only.	Understanding user feedback, advertising, and predictive modeling	Yes	Twitter image
(Caschera et al., 2016)	2016	A machine erudition methodology with a language-based formalization	Extract sentiment from multimodal data pompous through a multimodal linguistic	It needs to be trained	Analyze sentiment and emotion from text, video and audio on social media sites.	No	Social networks
(Niu et al. 2016)	2016	Fusion strategies and an advanced multi-view feature extraction method	The enactment can be improved by mutually examine the textual and visual views	No differentiation incompatible labels between the text view and image view		No	HCR, STS, SemEval, STS-Gold, Sanders, ImgTweet, Sentibank, MVSA
(Katsurai & Satoh, 2016)	2016	Multi-view embedding-based approach	Multi-view embedding space is more operative for classifying image sentiment polarity	Do not characterize facial expression, letters and drawings in the images.	Flicker dataset	No	Flickr and Instagram
(Xu & Mao, 2017)	2017	Merged Neural Network (MNN) model, and Early-RMNN (i.e. Early Residual MNN) and Late-RMNN (i.e. Late Residual MNN)	Get a better fusion feature.	Used for low datasets only.		Yes	Twitter
(Xu et al. 2017)	2017	Hierarchical Semantic Attention Network HSAN	Image caption extracts visual semantic feature	Only public available datasets be used.		Yes	Twitter
(Amencheria & Varshney, 2017)	2017	Cumulative distribution functions (cdfs) and Kolmogorov-Smirnov (K-S) test	Refine opposing hedonic psycho visual principles	Generalization error of 14%	Color-based hedonometer, color-based transportation paths.	No	Instagram API, capturing 2580, 1470, and 1744 images for the hashtags happy, awesome, and sad, respectively.
(Huang et al., 2017)	2017	PKInitializer, MJST_Gibbs and MJST_Analyzer	MJST can discriminate sentiment polarity with higher accuracy.	It can work on small dataset only.	Identify more explainable topics in messages.	Yes	weibo.com

- **Machine Learning-Based:** This technique uses classification methods to categorize text (Medhat et al., 2014) Many instances include in this brand of method include decision tree classifier, linear classifier, rule-based classifier and probabilistic classifier are supervised learning approaches.

Sentiment in Visual

This brand of data includes more signals to classify sentiments and opinions since they include information about eminence of the narrator contained in the audio data and movement of face, i.e. expressions sent by visual data. Detection named as human face recognition plays a vivacious protagonist in which it includes huge variety of application such as video conferencing, HCI, human face recognition surveillance, and many more. The continued improvement in the quantity of multimedia data, especially images, led to a large mass of image databases which results two major challenge: image processing (Zekri et al., 2017). Facial expressions allow understanding the present emotion of human. The human's emotions are mainly divided in 6 simple sentiments (i.e. anger, sadness, surprise, fear, disgust, and joy), and non-basic emotions (e.g. fatigue, pain, agreeing, engaged, curiosity, irritation and thinking) (Sikandar, 2014). For recognizing emotions, the typically used features are grounded on indigenous special position, movement of both regions and points of the face like include and eyebrows, edge of the mouth, lip, nasolabial furrow and wrinkles (Pantic & Rothkrantz, 2003). Several methods address the association of typical part of face and movement of specific point with different emotional states. The most conjoint method to divide physical expression of emotions in a definite manner is FACS (Facial Action Coding System) (Ekman & Oster, 1979) that has the capability to produce temporary outlines of each facial movement from video by coding facial expressions into a conventional of facial action units (AUs). During pattern discovery phase various statistical and data mining techniques are applied on collected and available data to mine useful and novel patterns with the help of visual sentiment study (Singh et al., 2015).

Sentiment in Speech

Audio data are important for achieving the aim of emotion recognition, even if the emotion recognition from the communication is an intricate process due to different voice features that are influenced by speaking styles, speakers, sentences and languages. These variances in voice features lead to complications in peculiar amid various emotions. Moreover, the same utterance may mention to dissimilar sentiments and it may be associated to emotional states which are not correct. Several challenges have been thru to extract emotions by examining explicit messages (linguistic) and implicit messages (paralinguistic). The discourse sentiment appreciation process consists of extracting the suitable feature from the available speech data and deciding the underlining emotions of the speech expression.

Multimodal Sentiment Analysis Research

MSA is an important area of research. (Truta et al., 2018) Facebook, LinkedIn, Twitter and many others, social networks have grown tremendously in size and a new path of research that focus on developing fast and accurate solutions for very large social networks has increased in importance. Sentiment scrutiny (Pak & Paroubek, 2010), is the method which rises to the application of (NLP), computational theory. Basically, Estimation excavating is categorize into three foremost type along with linguistic i.e. resources which refers the appraisal theory of any document, second is the sentiment taxonomy which refers how can a review take place for any kind of review analysis, and last one is opinion summarization. Task of opinion summarization has been reputable as a category of procedures which are used to eliminate duplicate data and contribute appropriate and best outcome for review mining. Linguistic resource theory (Pang & Lee, 2008), is grounded on the defined well set of data and appraisal theory previously (Martin, 1992) is grounded on how a comment or review strongly done with the subjectivity analysis. Main persistence of this way is to novelty a proper and suitable approach to determined reviews which might be a part of any sentiment classification. In this, the foremost goal mouth is to find how a user or developer put their thinking in the procedure of a review or comment (J. Martin, 1992). J.R. Martin (computer linguistic researcher) proposed a theory which is known as appraisal theory, an alternate name of this theory. Figure 3 shows the idea unconscious analyzer of human sentimental.

Subjectivity analysis (Fujii & Ishikawa, 2006), of any review refers to check statistics whether inapposite for consideration. In this, data is commonly depicted in the technique of comment. Its main aim is to bargain out data and check whether is intensely commented for appraisal theory, for example: "fine", "good" and "best" is the example of positive comment or review and "bad", "worst" are strongly shows negative words. In referred work (Cambria & White, 2014), authors used classifier named as ingenuous bayes exhausting incremental learning technique to perform analysis in hourly, weekly and monthly pattern. Table 2 Shows the Summary of existing methods in sentiment scrutiny.

Figure 3. Architecture of an "ideal" unconscious analyzer of human sentimental criticism. Source: (Pantic & Rothkrantz, 2003).

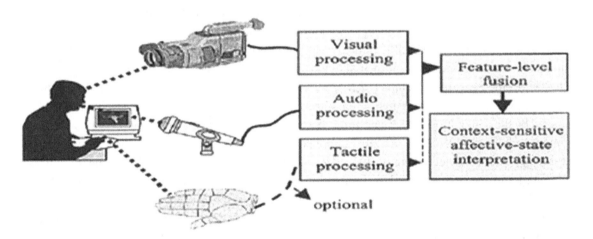

MSA RESEARCH OPPORTUNITIES

Facial commotion centered methodology on videos and image were smeared by (Joho et al., 2011), for tracing motion vectors on a human face. This exploration constructs a new prospect to the academics to explore more key arguments from the aspect as it only traces twelve key points consuming more techniques. For classification of sentiments using rectilinear and Facial Part Actions model from facial exterior was applied by (Ahn et al., 2012). The prospect creates by their research are- use of nonlinear exemplary in the analogous domain, and identifying incessant changing sentiments such as iris movement etc. more accurately. (Dumoulin et al., 2015), used categorized methodology for distress appreciation from the hominoid face, where, they habitually detect sensations from the hominoid face in the flicks. But, the main use of chronological smoothing for the enlargement of sensation revealing from pictures will be the future research prospect. (Dupplaw et al., 2012), used Tested Podium agenda for extracting sentimentalities of image data and text. But, both the upshot of image and text sentiment exploration could be deepened using Future Conjecturer Applications (FPA) and Media at ease Exploration (MCA), which would be the imminent prospect. (Chen et al., 2014), used Slanted SVM and Proportion-SVM for sentiment concept cataloguing from image and text data and achieved performance enhancement from state-of-art exploration by 50%. They craft the unpremeditated to smear the similar approach to voluminous domains as they only smeared to the dogmatic domain. Akin modality data were reconnoitered by (Baecchi et al., 2016), for aspect extraction using some models of neural network, for example: Frisk gram and De-noising Auto-encoders. As these mockups were applied to twitter data, it could also be smeared to other social media data. S. (Leeman-Munk et al., 2015), used yawning learning based and topology-based models on same modality data to bargain the consequence of multimode over single mode data in student debt and got better enactment. As per them, the future prospect is to reconnoiter more modality for creating bespoke scaffolding. Kernel-based evidence fusion method (KCFA) and Thrilling Wisdom Machine (ELM) were used by (Poria et al., 2016), to pigeon-hole sentiments from a video, audio and text. Their research outpaced the state-of-art method by 22.90%. On other arrow, forthcoming forecasts pretended by them are the enlargement of sentiment taxonomy using more perceptive amended fusion engine, and some unsubstantiated, and semi-supervised wisdom algorithms. (Siddiquie et al., 2015), also reconnoitered the same modality to quota "Review" expediency by the routine of SLIC Algorithm, SVM, and Convolution Neural Networks (CNNs) and found, diplomatically attached videos benevolences violently negative viewer annotations than non-persuasive videos. Investigation of intents and aesthetics would be the possible future prospects. (Poria et al, 2013) used decision and feature-level fusion slants to conglomerate sentimental evidence from video, audio and text by applying classifiers such as Extreme Learning Machine (ELM), SVM, Naïve Bayes, and Neural Networks algorithms and amended performance of ceremonial of the knack investigation by 20%. The enactment could be more amended by the exploration of gaze and smile-based facial appearance, 3D face appreciation, also applying more techniques. (Pereira et al., 2015), applied content-based multimodal sentiment exploration on text, image, video, and audio data on TV videos and got reasonable result and poses the possibilities of applying the similar technique in the investigation of general videos. (Liu et al., 2015), used Multimodal Deep Belief Networks (MDBN) model for unraveling link prognostication with the auspicious result, which can be then extended by applying the similar exemplary to other domains. For subjectivity classification from the text, image, and video, (Maynard et al., 2013), applied Active Shape Models, Active Appearance Models, Constrained Local Model, and Semantic and Rule-based approaches. Prospects happen in their work are-an in-depth use of dissertation exploration and scorn revealing. (Rho & Yeo, 2013), used Thayer's model and TWC model to identify emotions from images, videos and audios. But using GMM and SVM may attain more correct outcomes.

Table 2. Summary of existing techniques

Referred Work	Data Sources	Pre-Processing	Technique Used
Datar & Kosamkar (2016)	Online Survey on application reviewing	Blank space and punctuation removal	Dictionary based Lexicon Approach
Anwar Hridoy et al. (2015)	Twitter Oauth	POS Tagging	Corpus based Lexicon Approach
Hogenboom, et al. (2013)	Dutch Tweets	Segmentation	Dictionary based Lexicon Approach
Zhao et al. (2012)	Weibo Tweets	Bag of Word	Incremental Naïve Bayes Classifier
Rosa et al. (2016)	Social Network Posts	Filtering using Machine Erudition (SVM)	Corpus based Lexicon Approach
Boia et al. (2013)	Twitter API	Case Conversion, Remove Non-alphabetic characters, Stemming	Pointwise Reciprocated Gen
Wang et al. (2014)	Tweets related to public transportation	Segmentation	Adaptive Fuzzy Inference method with linguistics processors
Solakidis et al. (2014)	Geek forums	Stemming, Stop word Removal	K-Nearest Neighbor, SVM, Logistic Regression, Multinomial naïve bayes classifier
Wang & Castanon, (2015)	Twitter Decahose API	Filtering based on frequency	Word2Vec (Deep Learning) and KMeans clustering

MSA RESEARCH LIMITATIONS

Acc. to (Lisetti et al., 2003), while developing system below are the characteristic problems in identifying human emotions from physiological signals, which address in future research:

- Project studies that produce modest degrees of emotional intensity in single elicitations for minimum duration such that further confidently characteristic rises in arousal to the emotion except specious artifacts (e.g. fatigue, irrelevant emotional states, movement, compensation mechanisms, habituation) (Levenson, 1988);
- Collect baseline data that includes an evenhanded notch of physical production such that (a) capture emotional-physiological events in a more realistic way and (b) examine declines in stimulation without a floor limit;
- Baseline information and/or No emotion variance is subtracted by emotion statistics in mandate to clean up the problems related with differences in mood and physiology, particularly when gathering statistics from the identical subjects over numerous days (Picard et al., 2001);
- Because the steadiness of ANS activity may fluctuate for each physiological response, collect multiple baseline data and provide adequate stint for subjects to regulate to the tentative eminence quo and after finishing each exercise (Levenson, 1988);
- Confirm that subjects experience the intended emotion(s) via self-report and/or CDs of facial jargons (Levenson, 1988). The multimedia nature of our system provides the perfect tool for such estimation and verification;

- Because the field is in its beginning, being able to bear studies and/or also, keep up to date on new findings about the start and period of each emotion such that to ensure about (a) physiological data is gathered at the right time and (b) combined data does not embrace unrelated time durations (Levenson, 1988);
- In edict to additional the arena and measure appropriate elements of physiological events, conduct studies and/or keep up to date on (a) the relationship(s) between bodily and emotional events and (b) whether these relations are limited (e.g. context bound) can be generalized (Cacioppo & Tassinary, 1990);
- For the tenacity to manage for regulate the approaches used for hand washing, measurement artifacts, and gel application, placement of electrodes, movement and gel application (Picard et al., 2001).

As per (Bhat et al., 2014), complications in MSA exploration are crafting multimodal data set, recognizing undetected emotions from multimodal data, and fusing multimode sentiments results. Microblog text, images, and painterly satisfied cataloguing were being done by (Zhao et al, 2014), using SVM. Their Topographies removed are high-level semantic image and low-level painterly topographies and TF-IDF text features. The difficulties still need to co-relate with are shortness between visual content and text, incompatibility and diversity of data in a microblog. (Wang et al., 2015), deals with the hitches of the semantic gap between low-level visual sentiments and high-level image topographies in the social images with the expenditure of unendorsed SA model. But, SA for geo-location, link evidence, and user history are several of the complications that still vital to be addressed. (Maynard & Hare, 2015), handled the SA difficulties for example: use of execrate words, loud inaccurate text, sarcasm, face model arrangement inaccuracies from image and text with the consumption of rule-based approach and LSH respectively. More difficulties need to discourse are Co-reference doggedness, short exclamations, and brochures with inherent acquaintance, pinpointing couched and multi-dimensional tokens in images. As per (Ji et al., 2016), the imminent teething troubles in Visual Sentiment expectation are fabrication and deep indulgent of visual and GIF ontology. (Sikandar, 2014), piloted a appraisal and initiate the succeeding imminent hitches that prerequisite to be addressed sensibly for MSA, such as Recognizing images with Hand obstruction, noise, low tenacities and crusade of objects, enlargement of affect recognizer for recognition of multimodal human sentimental deeds, Fusing dissimilar modality topographies with esteem to fluctuating dynamic structure, time scale and metric levels, Mining philological and paralinguistic topographies steadfastly from audio channel, building context model with dissimilar fields such as one's ID, speech etc. As per (Saif et al., 2016), hitches in MSA exploration are Colloquial language, Short texts, Platform-specific rudiments, and Real-time Big Data. (Panda et al., 2013), anticipated a model to co-relate with the hitches related with multimodal music sentiment recognition. Some other difficulties need to address in their work are- growing size of the dataset uniting customary, using semantic topographies in the tougher emotive state of song lyrics, melodic, MIDI and demonstrative features of audio. (Cambria et al., 2013), anticipated a method to work with the incessant elucidation of multimodal hypothetical and sentimental evidence in some domains. But, this work poses some other difficulties such as discrete elucidation of multimodal conjectural and sentimental evidence and including the different domain of multi-modality in the revision of advantageous evidence. The teething troubles as per (Langlet & Clavel, 2015), in commerce with human-agent collaboration sentiments are- supervision speech disfluencies and peculiar amongst embedded and unambiguous sentiments of likes and dislikes. According to (A. Zadeh et al., 2016), existing and the forthcoming hitches in MSA exploration are the foundation of the dataset. They have bent aspect level dataset correlating sentiment concentration and prejudice interpretations. On the other hand, still there happen complications in crafting the dataset of multimodality in the script and ruling level. In a study (B. Schuller et al., 2016) originate that, the key complications related to MSA exploration is to virtuously collect, interpreted and exploit the sentimental and negotiating corpus. From an exploration by (Fulse et al, 2014), on dissimilar input modes, their conclusion on each other, and fusion techniques and got multiple modalities as a whole benevolences the better results than single mode. As per them, MSA exploration difficulties include- dealing with Cultural effects, philological variation, diverse contexts, and moving from single modal to multimodal itself. A study was done by (Yadav et al., 2015), in the cinematic format to explore sentiments and got highly incredible improvement in routine than in text. Some other hitches in a kin exploration are uniting more feature points in scrutinizing sentiments from the face, survey of larger videos, the merging of communication topographies with facial sentiments, and summarization of videos.

APPLICATIONS OF SENTIMENT ANALYSIS

In footings of both products sale and review analysis, (Liu et al. 2007), presented a sentiment model to forecast trades enactment; (McGlohon et al., 2010), used analyses by different authors in order to study about ranking system of products and merchants; (Joshi et al., 2010), discussed the sentiment of flick reviews in edict to prediction about box-office proceeds of movies; (Feldman et al., 2011), considered the sentiment of store; (Zhang & Skiena, 2010), used sentiment outcomes to identify about exchange approaches. In public sentiment poll, (Tumasjan et al., 2010) proposed a model named as learning model; in which it learned how to use emotion outcomes to forecast election consequences; (Chen et al., 2010) used sentimentality to forecast administrative positions; (Yano & Smith, 2010), proposed a novel method to forecast comment volumes of political blogs. In academic (Baporikar, 2016) help students know what to expect, make understanding more efficient. In social relation scrutiny (Hauffa et al., 2012), deliberates the social next of kin from a sentiment analysis opinion. There are many application areas, where MSA could be smeared such as Student feedback analysis, market prediction, etc. With the growth of internet technologies, e-commerce activities are growing exponentially. It is being used in different IT applications (Tripathy & Mishra, 2017) Figure 4 shows various other applications of MSA.

CONCLUSION

With the passageway of interval, Sentiment exploration research has gone as far away in the improvement of required tools, algorithms, and techniques, but is still a lengthy way in an event of such development for multimodal sentiment scrutiny. For multimodal sentiment scrutiny task, one key problem is the fusion of all modalities of samples, including text, image, video or speech. The study has providing a deep description on the main techniques used for detecting feelings from data mined from text, video and audio. The discussion on these techniques has underlined the vital role of machine wisdom methods for the emotion identification, and the key defies addressed by these techniques. In addition, the analysis has steered to underline the main disputes connected to statistics mined from multiple media sources, and, therefore, the limitation to overcome in edict to progress the right indulgent of the sentimental ceremonial of the users form videos and/or audios and/or texts. From the above study, it has been concluded that

Among existing methods in sentiment scrutiny, Machine erudition ways and means are domain specific and work well for a explicit domain (Movie or product reviews) but not in general approaches such as sentiment scrutiny on social schmoosing data or twitter dataset. Lexicon based approach are convenient for all domains as it emphasis on part of text present in the bilingual dictionary. Innumerable machine erudition modus operandi and lexicon based techniques can be collected to form an amalgam methodology which may result into more accurate sentiment analysis.

Figure 4. Multimodal sentiment analysis applications (Source: Ullah, Islam, Azman & Zaki, 2017)

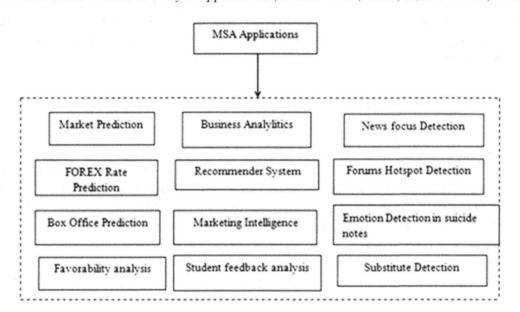

REFERENCES

Ahn, J., Gobron, S., Thalmann, D., & Boulic, R. (2012, November). Conveying real-time ambivalent feelings through asymmetric facial expressions. In International Conference on Motion in Games (pp. 122-133). Springer. doi:10.1007/978-3-642-34710-8_12

Alonso-Martín, F., Malfaz, M., Sequeira, J., Gorostiza, J., & Salichs, M. (2013). A Multimodal Emotion Detection System during Human–Robot Interaction. *Sensors (Basel)*, *13*(11), 15549–15581. doi:10.3390131115549 PMID:24240598

Amencherla, M., & Varshney, L. R. (2017). Color-based visual sentiment for social communication. In *15th Canadian Workshop on Information Theory (CWIT)*. Quebec City, Canada. doi:10.1109/cwit.2017.7994829

Anwar Hridoy, S. A., Ekram, M. T., Islam, M. S., Ahmed, F., & Rahman, R. M. (2015). Localized twitter opinion mining using sentiment analysis. *Decision Analysis*, *2*(1). doi:10.118640165-015-0016-4

ElAyadi, M., Kamel, M. S., & Karray, F. (2011). Survey on speech emotion recognition: Features, classification schemes, and databases. *Pattern Recognition*, *44*(3), 572–587. doi:10.1016/j.patcog.2010.09.020

Baecchi, C., Uricchio, T., Bertini, M., & Del Bimbo, A. (2015). A multimodal feature learning approach for sentiment analysis of social network multimedia. *Multimedia Tools and Applications*, 75(5), 2507–2525. doi:10.100711042-015-2646-x

Baporikar, N. (2016). Student Learning and Information Technology Nexus. *International Journal of Service Science, Management, Engineering, and Technology*, 7(2), 35–47. doi:10.4018/IJSSMET.2016040103

Bhat, V. D., Deshpande, V. S., & Sugandhi, R. (2015). A Multimodal Sentiment Analysis Scheme to Detect Hidden Sentiments. In *Fourth Post Graduate Conference iPGCON*.

Boia, M., Faltings, B., Musat, C., & Pu, P. (2013a). A:) Is Worth a Thousand Words: How People Attach Sentiment to Emoticons and Words in Tweets. In *2013 International Conference on Social Computing* (pp. 345-350). 10.1109/SocialCom.2013.54

Bower, M., & Hedberg, J. G. (2010). A quantitative multimodal discourse analysis of teaching and learning in a web-conferencing environment – The efficacy of student-centred learning designs. *Computers & Education*, 54(2), 462–478. doi:10.1016/j.compedu.2009.08.030

Cacioppo, J. T., & Tassinary, L. G. (1990). Inferring psychological significance from physiological signals. *The American Psychologist*, 45(1), 16–28. doi:10.1037/0003-066X.45.1.16 PMID:2297166

Cambria, E., Howard, N., Hsu, J., & Hussain, A. (2013). Sentic blending: Scalable multimodal fusion for the continuous interpretation of semantics and sentics. In *2013 IEEE Symposium on Computational Intelligence for Human-like Intelligence (CIHLI)*, Singapore (pp. 108-117). 10.1109/CIHLI.2013.6613272

Cambria, E., & White, B. (2014). Jumping NLP Curves: A review of natural language processing research [Review Article]. *IEEE Computational Intelligence Magazine*, 9(2), 48–57. doi:10.1109/MCI.2014.2307227

Caschera, M. C., Ferri, F., & Grifoni, P. (2016). Sentiment analysis from textual to multimodal features in digital environments. In *Proceedings of the 8th International Conference on Management of Digital EcoSystems - MEDES* (pp. 137-144). 10.1145/3012071.3012089

Chen, B., Zhu, L., Kifer, D., & Lee, D. (2010). What is an opinion about? exploring political standpoints using opinion scoring model. In *AAAI'10 Proceedings of the Twenty-Fourth AAAI Conference on Artificial Intelligence*, Atlanta, GA (pp. 1007-1012).

Chen, T., Yu, F. X., Chen, J., Cui, Y., Chen, Y., & Chang, S. (2014). Object-Based Visual Sentiment Concept Analysis and Application. In *Proceedings of the ACM International Conference on Multimedia - MM '14* (pp. 367-376). 10.1145/2647868.2654935

Datar, M., & Kosamkar, P. (2016). A novel approach for polarity determination using emoticons: emoticon-graph. In Advances in Intelligent Systems and Computing (pp. 481-489). doi:10.1007/978-981-10-0135-2_47

Deshmukh, P. G., & Ublae, V. (2017). HSI Classification [Review]. *International Journal of Advanced Research in Computer Science and Software Engineering*, 7(5), 951–954. doi:10.23956/ijarcsse/V7I4/0185

Dumoulin, J., Affi, D., Mugellini, E., Abou Khaled, O., Bertini, M., & Del Bimbo, A. (2015). Movie's Affect Communication Using Multisensory Modalities. In *Proceedings of the 23rd ACM international conference on Multimedia - MM '15* (pp. 739-740). 10.1145/2733373.2807965

Dupplaw, D., Matthews, M., Johansson, R., & Lewis, P. (2012). LivingKnowledge: A Platform and Testbed for Fact and Opinion Extraction from Multimodal Data. *Communications in Computer and Information Science, 255*, 100–115. doi:10.1007/978-3-642-28033-7_9

Ekman, P., & Oster, H. (1979). Facial expressions of emotion. *Annual Review of Psychology, 30*(1), 527–554. doi:10.1146/annurev.ps.30.020179.002523

Fang, Q., Xu, C., Sang, J., Hossain, M. S., & Muhammad, G. (2015). Word-of-mouth understanding: entity-centric multimodal aspect-opinion mining in social media. *IEEE Transactions on Multimedia, 17*(12), 2281–2296. doi:10.1109/TMM.2015.2491019

Feldman, R., Rosenfeld, B., Bar-Haim, R., & Fresko, M. (2011). The Stock Sonar - Sentiment Analysis of Stocks Based on a Hybrid Approach. In *Proceedings of the Twenty-Third Conference on Innovative Applications of Artificial Intelligence* (Vol. 2, pp. 642-1647).

Fujii, A., & Ishikawa, T. (2006). A system for summarizing and visualizing arguments in subjective documents. In *Proceedings of the Workshop on Sentiment and Subjectivity in Text - SST '06* (pp. 15-22). 10.3115/1654641.1654644

Fulse, S. J., Sugandhi, R., & Mahajan, A. (2014). A Survey on Multimodal Sentiment Analysis. *International Journal of Engineering Research and Technology, 3*(11), 3–14.

Gao, K., Xu, H., & Wang, J. (2015). Emotion Cause Detection for Chinese Micro-Blogs Based on ECOCC Model. In *Pacific-Asia Conference on Knowledge Discovery and Data Mining* (pp. 3-14). Springer. doi:10.1007/978-3-319-18032-8_1

Gupta, N., Gilbert, M., & Fabbrizio, G. D. (2013). Emotion detection in email customer care. *Computational Intelligence, 29*(3), 489–505. doi:10.1111/j.1467-8640.2012.00454.x

Hancock, J. T., Landrigan, C., & Silver, C. (2007). Expressing emotion in text-based communication. In *Proceedings of the SIGCHI conference on Human factors in computing systems - CHI '07* (pp. 929-932). 10.1145/1240624.1240764

Hathlian, N.F., B., & Hafez, A. M. (2017). Subjective Text Mining for Arabic Social Media. *International Journal on Semantic Web and Information Systems, 13*(2), 1–13. doi:10.4018/IJSWIS.2017040101

Hauffa, J., Lichtenberg, T., & Groh, G. (2012). Towards an NLP-Based Topic Characterization of Social Relations. In *2012 International Conference on Social Informatics* (pp. 289-294). 10.1109/SocialInformatics.2012.80

Hogenboom, A., Bal, D., Frasincar, F., Bal, M., de Jong, F., & Kaymak, U. (2013). Exploiting emoticons in sentiment analysis. In *Proceedings of the 28th Annual ACM Symposium on Applied Computing - SAC 13* (pp. 703-771). 10.1145/2480362.2480498

Hu, M., & Liu, B. (2004). Mining and summarizing customer reviews. In *Proceedings of the 2004 ACM SIGKDD International Conference on Knowledge Discovery and Data Mining - KDD 04* (pp. 168-177). 10.1145/1014052.1014073

Huang, F., Zhang, S., Zhang, J., & Yu, G. (2017). Multimodal learning for topic sentiment analysis in microblogging. *Neurocomputing, 253*, 144–153. doi:10.1016/j.neucom.2016.10.086

Ishizuka, M., & Prendinger, H. (2006). Describing and generating multimodal contents featuring affective lifelike agents with MPML. *New Generation Computing, 24*(2), 97–128. doi:10.1007/BF03037295

Islam, J., & Zhang, Y. (2016). Visual Sentiment Analysis for Social Images Using Transfer Learning Approach. In *2016 IEEE International Conferences on Big Data and Cloud Computing (BDCloud), Social Computing and Networking (SocialCom), Sustainable Computing and Communications (SustainCom) (BDCloud-SocialCom-SustainCom)* (pp. 124-130). doi:10.1109/bdcloud-socialcom-sustaincom.2016.29

Jansen, B. J., Zhang, M., Sobel, K., & Chowdury, A. (2009). Twitter power: Tweets as electronic word of mouth. *Journal of the American Society for Information Science and Technology, 60*(11), 2169–2188. doi:10.1002/asi.21149

Ji, R., Cao, D., Zhou, Y., & Chen, F. (2016). Survey of visual sentiment prediction for social media analysis. *Frontiers of Computer Science, 10*(4), 602–611. doi:10.100711704-016-5453-2

Jindal, N., & Liu, B. (2008). Opinion spam and analysis. In *Proceedings of the International Conference on Web Search and Web Data Mining - WSDM 08* (pp. 219-230). 10.1145/1341531.1341560

Jindal, S., & Singh, S. (2015). Image sentiment analysis using deep convolutional neural networks with domain specific fine tuning. In *2015 International Conference on Information Processing (ICIP)*. 10.1109/INFOP.2015.7489424

Joho, H., Staiano, J., Sebe, N., & Jose, J. M. (2010). Looking at the viewer: Analysing facial activity to detect personal highlights of multimedia contents. *Multimedia Tools and Applications, 51*(2), 505–523. doi:10.100711042-010-0632-x

Joshi, M., Das, D., Gimpel, K., & Smith, N. (2010). Movie reviews and revenues: An experiment intext regression. In *Proceedings of the 2010 Annual Conference of the North American Chapter of the Association of Computational Linguistics* (pp. 293-296). Los Angeles, California: Association for Computational Linguistics.

Katsurai, M., & Satoh, S. (2016). Image sentiment analysis using latent correlations among visual, textual, and sentiment views. In *2016 IEEE International Conference on Acoustics, Speech and Signal Processing (ICASSP)*. 10.1109/ICASSP.2016.7472195

Langlet, C., & Clavel, C. (2015). Adapting sentiment analysis to face-to-face human-agent interactions: From the detection to the evaluation issues. In *2015 International Conference on Affective Computing and Intelligent Interaction (ACII)* (pp. 14-20). 10.1109/ACII.2015.7344545

Leeman-Munk, S., Smith, A., Mott, B., Wiebe, E., & Lester, J. (2015). Two Modes are Better Than One: A Multimodal Assessment Framework Integrating Student Writing and Drawing. *Lecture Notes in Computer Science, 9112*, 205–215. doi:10.1007/978-3-319-19773-9_21

Levenson, R. W. (2014). The Autonomic Nervous System and Emotion. *Emotion Review*, *6*(2), 100–112. doi:10.1177/1754073913512003

Lin, W., Wilson, T., Wiebe, J., & Hauptmann, A. (2006). Which side are you on?: identifying perspectives at the document and sentence levels. In *Proceedings of the Tenth Conference on Computational Natural Language Learning - CoNLL-X '06* (pp. 109-116). 10.3115/1596276.1596297

Lisetti, C., Nasoz, F., Lerouge, C., Ozyer, O., & Alvarez, K. (2003). Developing multimodal intelligent affective interfaces for tele-home health care. *International Journal of Human-Computer Studies*, *59*(1-2), 245–255. doi:10.1016/S1071-5819(03)00051-X

Liu, B. (2011). Opinion Mining and Sentiment Analysis. In Web Data Mining (pp. 459-526). doi:10.1007/978-3-642-19460-3_11

Liu, F., Liu, B., Sun, C., Liu, M., & Wang, X. (2015). Multimodal Learning Based Approaches for Link Prediction in Social Networks. In Natural Language Processing and Chinese Computing (pp. 123-133). Springer. doi:10.1007/978-3-319-25207-0_11

Liu, J. J., Cao, Y. B., Lin, C. Y., Huang, Y. L., & Zhou, M. (2007). Low-quality product review detection in sentiment summarization. In *Proceedings of the 2007 Joint Conference on Empirical Methods in Natural Language Processing and Computational Natural Language Learning* (pp. 334-342). Prague, Czech.

Lokhande, B., & Dhavale, S. (2014). Overview of information flow tracking techniques based on taint analysis for Android. In *2014 International Conference on Computing for Sustainable Global Development (INDIACom)* (pp. 749-753). 10.1109/IndiaCom.2014.6828062

Martin, J. (1992). *System and structure*. John Benjamins. doi:10.1075/z.59

Maynard, D., Dupplaw, D., & Hare, J. (2013, December 10). *Multimodal Sentiment Analysis of Social Media*. ePrints Soton. Retrieved from https://eprints.soton.ac.uk/360546/

Maynard, D., & Hare, J. (2015). Entity-Based Opinion Mining from Text and Multimedia. In Advances in Social Media Analysis (pp. 65-86). doi:10.1007/978-3-319-18458-6_4

McGlohon, M., Glance, N., & Reiter, Z. (2010). Star quality: Aggregating reviews to rank products and merchants. In *Proceedings of the Fourth International AAAI Conference on Weblogs and Social Media* (pp. 114-121).

Medhat, W., Hassan, A., & Korashy, H. (2014). Sentiment analysis algorithms and applications: A survey. *Ain Shams Engineering Journal*, *5*(4), 1093–1113. doi:10.1016/j.asej.2014.04.011

Niu, T., Zhu, S., Pang, L., & El Saddik, A. (2016, January). Sentiment analysis on multi-view social data. In *International Conference on Multimedia Modeling* (pp. 15-27). Cham: Springer. doi:10.1007/978-3-319-27674-8_2

Pak, A., & Paroubek, P. (2011). Twitter for Sentiment Analysis: When Language Resources are Not Available. In *2011 22nd International Workshop on Database and Expert Systems Applications* (pp. 111-115). doi:10.1109/dexa.2011.86

Panda, R., Malherio, R., Bruno, R., & Pavia, R. P. (2013). Multi-Modal Music Emotion Recognition: A New Dataset, Methodology and Comparative Analysis. In *10th International Symposium on Computer Music Multidisciplinary Research – CMMR'*. Marseille, France.

Pang, B., & Lee, L. (2008). Opinion Mining and Sentiment Analysis. *Foundations and Trends® in Information Retrieval, 2*(1–2), 1-135. doi:10.1561/1500000011

Pantic, M., & Rothkrantz, L. (2003). Toward an affect-sensitive multimodal human-computer interaction. *Proceedings of the IEEE, 91*(9), 1370–1390. doi:10.1109/JPROC.2003.817122

Pereira, M., Pádua, F. L., Pereira, A. C., Silva, G. D., & Souza, F. B. (2015). Multimodal Sentiment Analysis for Automatic Estimation of Polarity Tension of TV News in TV Newscasts Videos. In *Proceedings of the 21st Brazilian Symposium on Multimedia and the Web - WebMedia '15* (pp. 157-160). 10.1145/2820426.2820461

Perez Rosas, V., Mihalcea, R., & Morency, L. (2013). Multimodal Sentiment Analysis of Spanish Online Videos. *IEEE Intelligent Systems, 28*(3), 38–45. doi:10.1109/MIS.2013.9

Picard, R., Vyzas, E., & Healey, J. (2001). Toward machine emotional intelligence: Analysis of affective physiological state. *IEEE Transactions on Pattern Analysis and Machine Intelligence, 23*(10), 1175–1191. doi:10.1109/34.954607

Piryani, R., Madhavi, D., & Singh, V. (2017). Analytical mapping of opinion mining and sentiment analysis research during 2000–2015. *Information Processing & Management, 53*(1), 122–150. doi:10.1016/j.ipm.2016.07.001

Poria, S., Cambria, E., Bajpai, R., & Hussain, A. (2017). A review of affective computing: From unimodal analysis to multimodal fusion. *Information Fusion, 37*, 98–125. doi:10.1016/j.inffus.2017.02.003

Poria, S., Cambria, E., & Gelbukh, A. (2015). Deep convolutional neural network textual features and multiple kernel learning for utterance-level multimodal sentiment analysis. In *Proceedings of the 2015 Conference on Empirical Methods in Natural Language Processing* (pp. 2539–2544). 10.18653/v1/D15-1303

Poria, S., Cambria, E., Howard, N., Huang, G., & Hussain, A. (2016). Fusing audio, visual and textual clues for sentiment analysis from multimodal content. *Neurocomputing, 174*, 50–59. doi:10.1016/j.neucom.2015.01.095

Poria, S., Chaturvedi, I., Cambria, E., & Hussain, A. (2016). Convolutional MKL Based Multimodal Emotion Recognition and Sentiment Analysis. In *2016 IEEE 16th International Conference on Data Mining (ICDM)* (pp. 439-448). doi:10.1109/icdm.2016.0055

Raaijmakers, S., Truong, K., & Wilson, T. (2008). Multimodal subjectivity analysis of multiparty conversation. In *Proceedings of the Conference on Empirical Methods in Natural Language Processing - EMNLP '08* (pp. 466–474). 10.3115/1613715.1613774

Rho, S., & Yeo, S. (2010). Bridging the semantic gap in multimedia emotion/mood recognition for ubiquitous computing environment. *The Journal of Supercomputing, 65*(1), 274–286. doi:10.100711227-010-0447-6

Rosa, R. L., Rodriguez, D. Z., Schwartz, G. M., De Campos Ribeiro, I., & Bressan, G. (2016). Monitoring system for potential users with depression using sentiment analysis. In *2016 IEEE International Conference on Consumer Electronics (ICCE)*. 10.1109/ICCE.2016.7430656

Saif, H., Ortega, F. J., Fernández, M., & Cantador, I. (2016). Sentiment Analysis in Social Streams. In *International Conference on Multimedia Modeling* (pp. 15-27). Cham; Springer. doi:10.1007/978-3-319-31413-6_7

Siddiquie, B., Chisholm, D., & Divakaran, A. (2015). Exploiting multimodal affect and semantics to identify politically persuasive web videos. In *Proceedings of the 2015 ACM on International Conference on Multimodal Interaction - ICMI '15* (pp. 203-210). 10.1145/2818346.2820732

Sikander, M. (2014). A Survey for Multimodal Sentiment Analysis Methods. *Int. J. of Computer Technology and Application*, *5*(4), 1470–1476.

Singh, A., Sharma, A., & Dey, N. (2015). Semantics and agents oriented web personalization: state of the art. *International Journal of Service Science, Management, Engineering, and Technology*, *6*(2), 35–49. doi:10.4018/ijssmet.2015040103

Singh, B., Kushwaha, N., & Vyas, O. P. (2016, November). An interpretation of sentiment analysis for enrichment of Business Intelligence. In 2016 IEEE Region 10 Conference (TENCON) (pp. 18-23). IEEE. doi:10.1109/tencon.2016.7847950

Solakidis, G. S., Vavliakis, K. N., & Mitkas, P. A. (2014). Multilingual Sentiment Analysis Using Emoticons and Keywords. *2014 IEEE/WIC/ACM International Joint Conferences on Web Intelligence (WI) and Intelligent Agent Technologies (IAT)* (Vol. 2, pp. 102-109). doi:10.1109/wi-iat.2014.86

Soleymani, M., Garcia, D., Jou, B., Schuller, B., Chang, S., & Pantic, M. (2017). A survey of multimodal sentiment analysis. *Image and Vision Computing*, *65*, 3–14. doi:10.1016/j.imavis.2017.08.003

Soleymani, M., Lichtenauer, J., Pun, T., & Pantic, M. (2012). A Multimodal Database for Affect Recognition and Implicit Tagging. *IEEE Transactions on Affective Computing*, *3*(1), 42–55. doi:10.1109/T-AFFC.2011.25

Soleymani, M., Pantic, M., & Pun, T. (2012). Multimodal Emotion Recognition in Response to Videos. *IEEE Transactions on Affective Computing*, *3*(2), 211–223. doi:10.1109/T-AFFC.2011.37

Soleymani, M., Schuller, B., & Chang, S. (2017). Guest editorial: Multimodal sentiment analysis and mining in the wild. *Image and Vision Computing*, *65*, 1–2. doi:10.1016/j.imavis.2017.09.001

Stieglitz, S., & Dang-Xuan, L. (2012). Social media and political communication: A social media analytics framework. *Social Network Analysis and Mining*, *3*(4), 1277–1291. doi:10.100713278-012-0079-3

Suthers, D., & Verbert, K. (2013). Learning analytics as a "middle space." In *Proceedings of the Third International Conference on Learning Analytics and Knowledge - LAK '13*. doi:10.1145/2460296.2460298

Tripathy, B., & Mishra, J. (2017). A generalized framework for e-contract. *International Journal of Service Science, Management, Engineering, and Technology*, *8*(4), 1–18. doi:10.4018/IJSSMET.2017100101

Truta, T. M., Campan, A., & Beckerich, M. (2018). Efficient approximation algorithms for minimum dominating sets in social networks. *International Journal of Service Science, Management, Engineering, and Technology, 9*(2), 1–32. doi:10.4018/IJSSMET.2018040101

Tumasjan, A., Sprenger, T. O., Sandner, P. G., & Welpe, I. M. (2010). Predicting elections with twitter: what 140 characters reveal about political sentiment. In *Proceedings of the International Conference on Weblogs and Social Media* (pp. 178-185).

Ullah, M. A., Islam, M. M., Azman, N. B., & Zaki, Z. M. (2017). An overview of Multimodal Sentiment Analysis research: Opportunities and Difficulties. In *2017 IEEE International Conference on Imaging, Vision & Pattern Recognition (icIVPR)*. 10.1109/ICIVPR.2017.7890858

Wang, H., & Castanon, J. A. (2015). Sentiment expression via emoticons on social media. In *2015 IEEE International Conference on Big Data (Big Data)*. 10.1109/BigData.2015.7364034

Wang, Y., & Li, B. (2015). Sentiment Analysis for Social Media Images. In *2015 IEEE International Conference on Data Mining Workshop (ICDMW)* (pp. 1584-1591). 10.1109/ICDMW.2015.142

Wang, Y., Wang, S., Tang, J., Liu, H., & Li, B. (2015). Unsupervised sentiment analysis for social media images. In *Proceedings of the Twenty-Fourth International Joint Conference on Artificial Intelligence*, Buenos Aires, Argentina.

Wang, Z., Joo, V., Tong, C., & Chan, D. (2014). Issues of Social Data Analytics with a New Method for Sentiment Analysis of Social Media Data. *2014 IEEE 6th International Conference on Cloud Computing Technology and Science*. doi:10.1109/cloudcom.2014.40

Xu, N. (2017). Analyzing multimodal public sentiment based on hierarchical semantic attentional network. In *2017 IEEE International Conference on Intelligence and Security Informatics (ISI)* (pp. 152-154). 10.1109/ISI.2017.8004895

Xu, N., & Mao, W. (2017). A residual merged neutral network for multimodal sentiment analysis. In *2017 IEEE 2nd International Conference on Big Data Analysis (ICBDA)*. doi:10.1109/icbda.2017.8078794

Yadav, P., & Pandya, D. (2017). SentiReview: Sentiment analysis based on text and emoticons. In *2017 International Conference on Innovative Mechanisms for Industry Applications (ICIMIA)*. 10.1109/ICIMIA.2017.7975659

Yadav, S. K., Bhusan, M., & Gupta, S. (2015). Multimodal sentiment analysis: Sentiment analysis using audiovisual format. Computing for Sustainable Global Development. In *Proceedings of the second International Conference on Innovative Mechanisms for Industry Applications (ICIMIA)* (pp. 1415-1419). New Delhi, India: IEEE.

Yadollahi, A., Shahraki, A. G., & Zaiane, O. R. (2017). Current State of Text Sentiment Analysis from Opinion to Emotion Mining. *ACM Computing Surveys, 50*(2), 1–33. doi:10.1145/3057270

Yang, Y., & Chen, H. H. (2012). Machine Recognition of Music Emotion. *ACM Transactions on Intelligent Systems and Technology, 3*(3), 1–30. doi:10.1145/2168752.2168754

Yano, T., & Smith, N. A. (2010). What's worthy of comment? content and comment volume in political blogs. In *Proceedings of the International AAAI Conference on Weblogs and Social Media*, 359-362.

You, Q., Luo, J., Jin, H., & Yang, J. (2015). Robust image sentiment analysis using progressively trained and domain transferred deep networks. In *Proceedings of the Twenty-Ninth AAAI Conference on Artificial Intelligence* (pp. 381-388).

Yuan, J., You, Q., & Luo, J. (2015). Sentiment Analysis Using Social Multimedia. In Multimedia Data Mining and Analytics (pp. 31-59). doi:10.1007/978-3-319-14998-1_2

Zadeh, A., Zellers, R., Pincus, E., & Morency, L. (2016). Multimodal sentiment intensity analysis in videos: facial gestures and verbal messages. *IEEE Intelligent Systems*, *31*(6), 82–88. doi:10.1109/MIS.2016.94

Zekri, K., Touzi, A. G., & Ellouze, N. (2017). Optimized image retrieval system in Oracle DBMS. *International Journal of Service Science, Management, Engineering, and Technology*, *8*(1), 1–17. doi:10.4018/IJSSMET.2017010101

Zhang, W., & Skiena, S. (2010). Trading Strategies to Exploit Blog and News Sentiment. In *Proceedings of the Fourth International AAAI Conference on Weblogs and Social Media ICWSM '10* (pp. 375-378).

Zhang, Y., & Wallace, B. (2015). A Sensitivity Analysis of (and Practitioners' Guide to) Convolutional Neural Networks for Sentence Classification. arXiv:1510.03820

Zhao, J., Dong, L., Wu, J., & Xu, K. (2012). MoodLens: An Emoticon-Based Sentiment Analysis System for Chinese Tweets. In *Proceedings of the 18th ACM SIGKDD international conference on Knowledge discovery and data mining - KDD '12* (pp. 1528-1531). 10.1145/2339530.2339772

Zhao, S., Yao, H., Zhao, S., Jiang, X., & Jiang, X. (2016). Multi-modal microblog classification via multi-task learning. *Multimedia Tools and Applications*, *75*(15), 8921–8938. doi:10.100711042-014-2342-2

Zhou, L. (2009). Survey on research of sentiment analysis. *Jisuanji Yingyong*, *28*(11), 2725–2728. doi:10.3724/SP.J.1087.2008.02725

This research was previously published in the International Journal of Service Science, Management, Engineering, and Technology (IJSSMET), 10(2); pages 38-58, copyright year 2019 by IGI Publishing (an imprint of IGI Global).

Chapter 99

A Literature Review on Cross Domain Sentiment Analysis Using Machine learning

Nancy Kansal

Ajay Kumar Garg Engineering College Ghaziabad, India

Lipika Goel

Ajay Kumar Garg Engineering College Ghaziabad, India

Sonam Gupta

Ajay Kumar Garg Engineering College Ghaziabad, India

ABSTRACT

Sentiment analysis is the field of NLP which analyzes the sentiments of text written by users on online sites in the form of reviews. These reviews may be either in the form of a word, sentence, document, or ratings. These reviews are used as datasets when applied to train a classifier. These datasets are applied in the annotated form with the positive, negative or neutral labels as an input to train the classifier. This trained classifier is used to test other reviews, either in the same or different domains to know like or dislike of the user for the related field. Various researches have been done in single and cross domain sentiment analysis. The new methods proposed are overcoming the previous ones but according to this survey, no methods best suit the proposed work. In this article, the authors review the methods and techniques that are given by various researchers in cross domain sentiment analysis and how those are compared with the pre-existing methods for the related work.

1. INTRODUCTION

Sentiment analysis is also called opinion mining or emotion AI. Sentiment Analysis is used to know about what people think about things they are consuming from watching a movie to purchasing an AC. On the basis of their thinking either positive or negative, producer or holders of service or product get to know whether the given service/product has the future scope or not. For example, there is a new movie released; various social networking sites are the source of thoughts of people who have seen the movie. On the basis of those reviews, publicity of the movie reaches to the makers of the movie and related

DOI: 10.4018/978-1-6684-6303-1.ch099

trend goes on. Whenever there are elections to be held, election outcomes are predicted on the basis of the analysis of sentiments, opinion, and thoughts those are shared by public on various online portals or social networking sites or news. Sentiment Analysis is the study of attitudes of the holder of service towards the consumed service either in the form of love or hate; like or dislike; positive or negative (polarity). This attitude is analyzed from the text that is presented in the form of reviews in word form, sentence form or document form or in the form of ratings given by holder.

Sentiment Analysis can be done using various machine learning algorithms in which a model/classifier is trained using reviews that are annotated with the polarity positive or negative. These annotated reviews can be taken from any domain to train the classifier and the trained classifier is tested for the orientation of text or reviews in same or different domain.

While doing sentiment analysis in single domain, classifier is trained in single domain and is tested for the same domain thus only problem is to annotate the dataset but in cross domain sentiment analysis problem arises that any word/feature having positive meaning in one domain may have negative meaning in other domain; or in one domain, positive sentiments are expressed by some words and in other domain those positive sentiments are expressed using different words(domain specific words in different domains). In the cross domain, the problem of dataset labeling may be a time-consuming and costly process as it is done manually. SentiWordNet can also be a solution as it is an opinion Lexicon derived from WordNet database which is having scores of positive and negative for attributes and hence can tell polarity of the document on the basis of overall polarity of words written in the document, but it is also having a limitation of words. Various methods and techniques have been proposed recently to overcome this problem of labeling of dataset. The aim of the study is to put some relevant studies together in this paper to help the researchers, by comparing the methods proposed in various studies and by also giving a performance comparison of techniques used in studies. This study aims to focus only on the most recent works published during the period 2010 to 2019.

The remainder of this paper is as follows: Section 2 defines some key Terminologies used to understand the study on cross domain sentiment analysis. Section 3 describes some challenges and issues related to sentiment analysis in the cross domain. Section 4 demonstrates the methodology for this study purpose followed by a brief discussion of methods used in researches those the authors have used in this study. Section 5 demonstrates various datasets used by different researches on cross domain sentiment analysis. Section 6 defines some of the baseline methods used to compare performances of their proposed methods by various scholars. Section 7 gives answers to the questions that are aimed at this survey study. It compares the performance of all the baselines proposed by various researches. Section 8 is about some discussion on methods given to the problem of sentiment analysis in the cross domain and the Section 9 concludes the paper.

2. KEY TERMINOLOGY

Here, the authors define some basic terminologies that are used for this review purpose.

2.1 Domain

With respect to this research, the domain is such collection where all the entities have similar characteristics like in electronics products, DVD is one domain and AC is a different domain. In social networking sites, Twitter is one domain and Facebook is a different domain.

2.2 Sentiment Analysis

Sentiment analysis is the field of natural language processing in which unstructured online public opinions about any product, social media, brand, news, or research and so on presented in the form of reviews, are transformed in structural information that is annotated dataset having the positive, negative, neutral or mixed polarity of sentiments.

Sentiments can be represented in word, sentence or document form and accordingly, analysis is applied on the stated.

2.2.1 Aspect Based Sentiment Analysis

When a researcher is interested in the particular feature/aspect along with positive, negative and neutral sentiments of product, to which users are interested in; it is called Aspect Based Sentiment Analysis. For Ex- if someone says "battery of the new phone is short term" then the negative sentiment is shown for the battery of the phone, not for the phone, hence here battery is one aspect of sentence-level sentiment.

2.3 Sentiment Analysis Methods

2.3.1 *Rule/Lexicon-Based Approach*

A lexicon is a collection of words associated with their individual polarity. In this approach, a lexicon is used to detect the polarity of sentiment documents. Like someof the popular lexicons are: AFINN-11, SentiWordNet, and SenticNet. The words of AFINN-11 are manually labeled by Finn Arup Neilsen in 2009-2010, SentiWordNet is augmented form of WordNet having sentiment information of each word, SenticNet provides orientataion associated with nearly 50,000 natural languages concepts.

2.3.2 Machine Learning-Based Approach

It has a machine learning classifier that is trained by first input the labeled features then polarity/label of unlabeled features are predicted, either in the same domain or in different domains. The output of this classifier is the polarity of sentiment features of the output domain.

2.3.3 Cross Domain Sentiment Analysis

While applying machine learning algorithms for sentiment analysis if model/classifier is trained using the dataset of one domain (called input domain) but is tested with the dataset for a different domain (called output domain), whether that dataset is labeled or unlabeled, then such analysis is called cross domain sentiment analysis. If the dataset is labeled overall sentiment polarity can be found easily but if the dataset is unlabeled, it is tough to predict the overall sentiment of a document. Sentiment analysis is a predominant task in every field that too when it is a smart era of the internet. But it is economically unreliable to do sentiment analysis in every domain, so cross domain sentiment analysis is performed in which classifier is trained in input domain using annotated dataset of that domain and is tested on output domain to annotate the sentiment polarity expressed by the sentiments presented in form of reviews (words, sentences or documents) or ratings as well.

3. CHALLENGES AND ISSUES IN CROSS DOMAIN SENTIMENT ANALYSIS

3.1 Feature Meagerness

It is the problem when feature those are expressed in the output domain is not found in the input domain. Due to which classifier trained in the input domain is not sufficiently trained for sentiment analysis in the output domain.

3.2 Polarity Deviation

When any word in one domain has either positive or negative polarity but in other domains, the same word has opposite polarity then it may cause bad results of the trained classifier as actual sentiments are opposed by the classifier.

3.3 Lexical Ambiguity

When a word/feature has different meanings due to different contexts of different domains (as a word has many different meanings based on the context they are being used to) hence classifier trained for input domain may not be accurate for testing in the output domain.

4. SYSTEMATIC LITERATURE REVIEW

The authors have performed a systematic literature review to survey current state-of-the-art around cross domain sentiment analysis and based on that work the authors tried to seek the answer to the following two questions.

Question 1: which method is widely used as a baseline to compare the performance of proposed methods by different authors?
Question 2: which baseline method gives the best comparison results among all the baselines on the basis of their compared performance analysis?

The authors performed this survey on cross domain sentiment analysis, for which the authors followed the following steps:

4.1 Searching Process

The authors started this survey by searching for relevant topics for cross domain sentiment analysis. The authors used the Google search engine for this searching process.

4.2 Sources

The authors search for digital libraries like IEEE. Google Scholar and ScienceDirect using keywords sentiment analysis cross domain sentiment analysis and cross domain sentiment analysis techniques, as these are keywords to this related review.

4.3 Study Inclusion Criteria

The authors have taken research papers mainly during the period 2010 to 2019, related to cross domain sentiment analysis. Table 1 shows a brief discussion of all the studies that the authors have taken for this review.

4.4 Research Focus

The authors have performed this research in order to give the answer to two above mentioned questions so that it might aid to researchers to enhance their research in respected field of cross domain sentiment analysis.

The authors have considered all the mentioned papers to give answers to the above questions.

5. DATASETS TAKEN BY STUDIES

Datasets collected for most studies (P1, P2, P3, P4, P5, P6, P7, P8, and P9) are in the English language. This one selected study has a Chinese dataset of reviews of restaurants and cameras from the Dianping website. Reviews from the camera are labeled by three experienced persons. The authors have not considered the part of the study related to that dataset for this review process.

Amazon product dataset is mostly used in research studies as this dataset is widely used to perform cross domain sentiment analysis. Table 2 shows a hetero domain dataset of Amazon product reviews.

Other studies are done on different datasets taken from various domains; those are presented in Table 3.

6. BASELINE METHODS TAKEN BY STUDIES FOR COMPARISON WITH THE PROPOSED

Various baseline methods are chosen by various research scholars for their studies which the authors have taken for this review process. Those baseline methods are discussed in Table 4. And some of the baseline methods are discussed below.

Table 1. *Summary of selected studies related to Cross Domain Sentiment Analysis*

Publication (Year)	Methodology/Finding	Proposed Classifiers	Performance/ Result	Natural Language Processing	Key
Cross domain sentiment classification via spectral feature alignment (2010)	SFA algorithm is proposed to reduce the gap between cross domain sentiment data. The co-occurrence matrix is used to gap between domain-specific words to domain-independent words. Features are represented in the form of a collection of words (Ngrams) that are labeled with +1(positive) and -1(negative) polarity based on all words in Ngrams. A bipartite graph is constructed to co-align domain-independent features to domain-specific features to find a new feature space. The spectral clustering algorithm is applied on feature bipartite graph to align domain-specific words if they have more common domain independent words and vice-versa. These clusters then represent a new dataset which is used to train sentiment classifier.	SFA, LSA, NoTransf, LSA,FALSA	Accuracy of SFA is compared with NoTransf, LSA, FALSA, SCL by 24 tasks on 2 datasets. the t-test is done on the comparison results of two datasets and SFA out-performs other methods with 0.95 confidence interval.	n-gram	P1
Cross domain sentiment classification using sentiment sensitive thesaurus (2013)	Sentiment sensitive thesaurus (SST) is created to align words having the same sentiments from different domains. SST is used to expand feature vector (training set) and using this L1 Logistic regression based binary classifier is trained which is used to predict the sentiment of the target domain.	L1 Regularized logistic Regression.	Performance varies with varying thesaurus size. Accuracy increases with an increase in thesaurus size. After saturation, it decreases with an increase in size. Trained Classifier is compared with SentiWordNet, and it performs better grouping of words that expresses similar sentiments.	Unigrams and bigrams (called lexicon elements), ratings (called sentiment elements).	P2
Cross domain sentiment classification using sensitive sentiment embeddings (2016)	The unsupervised classification method is used using spectral embeddings. Domain dependent features (pivots) are selected to map in embedded space as close as possible. Documents having the same polarity should be embedded close to each other than a document with different polarities.	Composite optimization model using OO matrices.	Performance is comparable to SCL and SFA.	pointwise mutual information (PMI) method is used for selecting pivots from the document.	P3
Cross-domain sentiment classification: An empirical investigation (2016)	Three datasets are used to compare performance using three different classifiers. Datasets are taken as the first dataset is created using sentiment 140 corpus, second is SemVal dataset and the third is dataset as three review domains. The performance of cross domain classification is determined by using these datasets by training the models. Supervised learning was applied as classifiers were tested on manually labeled tweets. 8 types of Emoticons were used to label tweets	SVM, NB, MNB	Best performance is gained using MNB trained by tweets dataset to determine sentiment in reviews. The best performance was gained using SVM with unigrams and ME with unigrams and bigrams.	Unigram, bigram, unigram and bigrams, unigrams with parts-of-speech (POS) bags.	P4
Cross-domain sentiment classification based on transfer learning and adversarial network (2018)	The shared knowledge Learning and transfer (SKLT) model is introduced based on Transfer Learning and adversarial Networks. Shared and Private models (bi-GRU) are used to learn shared sentiment knowledge and domain-specific knowledge.	SKLT, bi-GRU	Single bi-GRU, SKLT- frozen, SKLT-adaptation are the contrast models to compare with. And SKLT domain adaptation outperforms.	n-grams	P5
Hierarchical attention transfer network (HATN) for cross product sentiment classification (2018)	HATN automatically captures pivot and non-pivots elements. P-nets and NP-nets conduct Attention learning to find pivots and non-pivots elements. It provides a hierarchical attention transfer mechanism that automatically transfers the attention of emotions in both word and sentence levels across domains. HATNh is a proposed model that has hierarchical positional encoding.	NLTK used for tokenization, HATN, HATNh	Comparison is done with the baseline models like SFA, DANN, DAmSDA, CNN-aux, AMN, P-net, NP-net. And it is found that representation of P-net and NP-net are complementary. HATNh improves the performance of HATN by 0.41% on average.	Document-based features.	P6

continues on following page

Table 1. Continued

Publication (Year)	Methodology/Finding	Proposed Classifiers	Performance/ Result	Natural Language Processing	Key
Cross Domain sentiment classification by Capsule network with semantic rules (2018)	CapsuleDAR Model consist of two capsules is used. (Called Base Network and Rule Network). Rule Network to integrate semantic rule to capsule network to capture common knowledge of different domains. Base Network is having an embedding layer to convert word into a low dimensional vector representation, convolutional layer to extract n-gram features. Pivot Based Filter Initialization method is introduced. SCL is used to select pivot features. The K-means method is used to cluster the features. Incaps, Outcaps, and classcaps layers are used in Base Network. Rulecaps layer is used in Rule network. CORAL LOSS is used to minimize the feature difference between the source and target domain.	CapsuleDAR (capsule network in Domain Adaptation with semantic Rule)	The model outperforms various methods like SCL-MI,SS-FE,DANN, SVM, DACNN, DAmSDA, AE-SCL-SR, PBLM, and CapsuleNoDA. It gives a 7.9% improvement over its best competitor (AMN).	n-grams	P7
Adding prior knowledge In hierarchical attention neural network (HANP) for cross domain sentiment classification (2019)	Sentiment Dictionary Layer is used to identify all sentiment words in the context of pivots, non-pivots, and dis-pivots. 3-Layer CNN is used for contextual preservation from source Domain to target Domain. HANP is tested on various datasets for classification.	HANP	It is compared to HAN, CNN-aux, AMN, HATNh, HAN+CNN, HAN+CNN+pivots, HAN+CNN+pivots+non-pivots and gives a state-of-the-art performance with the max. average accuracy of 5.78% when compared with the CNN-aux.	n-grams	P8
CCHAN: An end-to-end model for cross domain sentiment classification (2019)	CTN + CTAN = CCHAN. Cloze Task Network (CTN) is used to obtain word embeddings and also matching is done between document and candidate answer.(to update word embeddings in the source as well as target domains). CTAN is used for sentiment classification.	CCHAN	Model is compared with HAN, CNN-aux, AMN, HATNh, CHAN, CCHAN-pivots, and it outperforms all the models.	n-gram	P9
Neural attentive network for cross-domain aspect level sentiment classification (2019)	It uses a weekly supervised Latent Dirichlet Allocation Model (Wilda) to learn Domain-specific Aspect and sentiment Lexicon representations. Aspect level sentiment classifier uses domain classification results and aspect document representation to classify aspect level sentiments in the target domain. LSTM is used to encode the input document. NAACL transforms document embeddings to domain-specific document embeddings.	Bi-directional LSTM	NAACL is superior to compared baseline methods in terms of classification accuracy and F1 score. And also it is shown that it can also find the words that are important to judge the polarity of the source text. Baseline methods are SVM. SVM feature, LSTM, TD-LSTM, JST, SFA, SDA-LSS, ATAE-LSTM, MemNET, RAM, IAM.	wsLDA (weakly supervised latent Drichilit Allocation) is used to finddomain-specific aspects from documents.	P10
Cross-domain co-extraction of sentiment and topic lexicons (2012)	A new bootstrapping-based method, Realtional Adaptive Bootstrapping (RAP) is proposed for expanding lexicon to retrain the classifier. Transfer Adaboost learning (TrAdaBoost) algorithm (Dai et al., 2007) is used for learning in RAP. They have used SVM as a base classifier in Tr-AdaBoost.	Relational Adaptive Bootstrapping(RAP), Tr-AdaBoost, SVM	The relational bootstrapping method(RAP) performs better than the TrAdaBoost and the cross-domain CRF algorithm, and achieves comparable results with the semi-supervised method.	POS tagging is used to represent previous, current and next words.	P11

Table 2. Research studies based on Amazon Product dataset

Dataset	Domain	Key: Year	Author
Amazon product reviews	DVD, Kitchen, Books, Electronics	P1: 2010	Pan et al.
		P2: 2013	Bollegala et al.
		P3: 2016	Bollegala et al.
		P5: 2018	Xiaoyu Duan et al.
		P6: 2018	Li et al.
		P7:2018	Zhang et al.
		P8:2019	Tu Manshu and Wang Bing
		P9:2019	Tu Manshu and Zhao Xuemin

Table 3. Dataset taken by selected research studies

Key	Author(year)	Dataset	Domain	Description
P1	Pan et al.(2010)	Yelp and Citysearch reviews dataset Amazon product reviews dataset	Hotel Videogames Software Electronics	12000 reviews from www.yelp.com and www.citysearch.com 8000 review from each domain are taken from www.amazon.com
P4	Brian et al.(2016)	Sentiment140 corpus dataset SemEval dataset Reviews and rating dataset	Twitter tweets (emotions) Tweets (emotions) Hotels Doctors Restaurant	From 1.6 million tweets from www.twitter.com labeled with emoticons, 10000 were used for the study. Manually annotated tweets Were taken. 2836 annotated reviews were taken from.
P5	Xiaoyu Duan et al.(2018)	IMDB reviews dataset	Movies	Labeled English sentences are taken.
P10	Tang et al.(2019)	Semeval14, SemEval15 SemEval16 datasets	Restaurant Laptop	Five aspect based categories are used, those are price, food, service, ambiance and miscellaneous. Categorized on the basis of performance, price, quality, and appearance.

6.1 NoTransf

Transfer learning is the process where a model is trained using a large amount of annotated dataset and this model is used as a baseline to train other data. In (Pan et al., 2010) pan et al. has used the NoTransf classifier that is trained only by training data of the source domain. And is used to test the target domain.

6.2 LSA

LSA is used to find the features having the same meaning in a review text document. Pan et al. (Pan et al., 2010) used LSA as a baseline method to train the classifier by applying LSA in domain-specific features.

Table 4. Baseline methods used in studies

Baseline comparison methods	Elision	Key	Author (year)
No transfer	No-Transf	P1	Pan et al. (2010)
Latent semantic Analysis	LSA	P1	Thomas Hofmann (2001)
Featured latent semantic Analysis	FALSA	P1	Serafin and Di Eugenio (2004)
Negative adaptation	No adapt	P2,P3	
Spectral Feature Alignment	SFA	P3, P6, P10	Pen et al. (2010)
Structured Correspondence Learning	SCL	P1, P3	Blitzar et al. (2016)
Support Vector Machine	SVM	P4, P7, P10	Vladimir Vapnik and Hava Siegelmann (2001)
Naïve Bayes	NB	P4	(1960)
Discriminant Adaptive Nearest Neighbor	DANN	P6, P7	Ganin et al. (2016)
DANN+mSDA	DAmSD	P6,P7	Ganin et al. (2016)
Convolutional Neural Network auxiliary	CNN-aux	P6, P8, P9	Yu and Jiang (2016)
Adversarial Memory Network	AMN	P6, P8, P9	Li et al. (2017)
SCL Mutual Information	SCL-MI	P7	Blitzar et al. (2007)
Hierarchical attention Network	HAN	P8, P9	Yang et al. (2016)
Joint Sentiment Topic/Model	JST	P10	Lin et al. (2012)
Long Short Term Memory	LSTM	P10	S. Hochreiter and J. Schmidhuber (1997)
Stacked Denoising Autoencoder with Domain and Sentiment Supervision	SDA-DSS	P10	Liu and Huang (2015)
Transfer Ada-Boost	Tr-AdaBoost	P11	Dai et al. (2007)

6.3 FALSA

Pan et al. (Pan et al., 2010) used FALSA as the base method that works in the same way as LSA except that it applies LSA on the co-occurrence matrix of domain-specific and domain-independent features.

6.4 No Adapt

When a classifier is trained, feature expansion is done as preprocessing step to train the classifier but in No adapt baseline method feature extraction is not performed but binary classifier is trained only by using unigram and bigram features from annotated source domain and classifier is tested for the dataset of the target domain.

Table 5. Performance comparisons of baselines proposed in different researches taken for this study

Baselines	Key	Accuracy (%)	F-Score	AUC-Score	Description	Average Accuracies
SFA(Spectral Feature Alignment)	P1 P2 P3 P6 P10	86.75 77.73 65.47 78.69 78.6	78.4		The highest accuracy achieved when comparing SFA with different datasets in the cross domain aspect. SFA when compared to the baseline in SST (Bollegala et al.2013). With the dimensionality set to 30, experimented on the Amazon dataset. Average acc. On Amazon reviews dataset.	77.44%
SCL(Structural Correspondence Learning)	P3	66.04			Average accuracy on target domain when different source domains are used.	66.04%
NoAdapt (Negative Adaptation)	P3	62.91			The average accuracy of the baseline when different source domains are used to compare the performance of the proposed methods.	62.91%
NB(Naïve Bayes)	P4	-		0.764	When using the sentiment140 Amazon reviews dataset.	
SVM(Support Vector Machine)	P4 P7 P10	- 80.2 72.7	70.9	0.780	Using sentiment140 corpus Amazon reviews dataset. Zhang et al. selected hyperparameter c between 10^-5 to 1.	76.45%
SKLT	P5	87.98			Average accuracy to compare performance in adversarial networks.(Duan et al.2019)	87.98%
DANN(Discriminant Adaptive Nearest Neighbor)	P6 P7	79.00 74.8			Average classification accuracy on Amazon review datasets. Encoded in 5000 dimension feature vector. Average accuracy When tested on 12 different sets of domains using the adaptation parameter between 0.001 and 1 with learning rate 0.001.	76.9%
DANN+mSDA	P6 P7	82.36 76.2			Average acc. Using Amazon review dataset with 5 output layers and a vector of 30000 dimensions. Average accuracy on 12 different domain sets with every instance encoded in a vector of 3000 dimensions.	79.28%
CNN-aux	P6 P8 P9	81.98 81.98 81.98			Average accuracy for Amazon reviews dataset to induce sentiment embeddings using two auxiliary tasks. Average accuracy when using 20 sets of different source and target domains. Average accuracy for 20 transfer pairs of Amazon review dataset.	81.98%

continues on following page

Table 5. Continued

Baselines	Key	Accuracy (%)	F-Score	AUC-Score	Description	Average Accuracies
AMN(Adversarial Neural Network)	P6 P8 P9	82.79 82.79 82.79			Average classification accuracy for Amazon review dataset by learning domain shared representations. Average acc. When taken 20 different domain pairs for study. Average acc. For 20 transfer pairs on Amazon review dataset.	82.79%
HAN(Hierarchical Attention Network)	P8 P9	81.07 81.07			Average acc. When taken 20 different domain pairs for study. Average acc. For 20 transfer pairs on Amazon review dataset.	81.07%
JST	P10	79.3			The performance of this baseline is used for comparing performance of NAACL. Performance(given average accuracy) is measured by varying percentage of labeled data in target domain. Labeled data from source domain and labeled/ unlabeled data from target domain are used as training set.	79.3%
LSTM	P10	78.6			Average accuracy while taking the SemEval-14 S-res./Dianping D-res. as the source domains and use SemEval-14 S-laptop/ Dianping D-camera as the target domains,by varying percentage of labeled data in target domain.	78.6%
SDA-DSS	P10	81.5			Average accuracy while taking the SemEval-14 S-res./Dianping D-res. as the source domains and use SemEval-14 S-laptop/ Dianping D-camera as the target domains,by varying percentage of labeled data in target domain.	81.5%
Tr-AdaBoost	P11		0.51		Average F-Score while taking two tasks: Sentiment Lexicon extraction and Topic Lexicon extraction, on product and movie review datasets.	

6.5 SFA

SFA aligns domain-specific features/words from different domains and forms a cluster of those aligned features. In (Bollegala et al., 2016; Li et al., 2018) authors have used SFA as a baseline method on their dataset to compare their proposed method's performances.

6.6 SVM

SVM is a discriminant also called hyperplane that separates the annotated features in two different classes in a multidimensional space. A-line/ discriminator is drawn between the two classes. Regularization parameter (c) is used to set the margin of the discriminator such that smaller c value, higher the margin and vice-versa. In (Heredia et al., 2016), Brian et al. have set c to 5.0 for their study and in (Zhang et al., 2018), Zhang et al. has used SVM with RBM kernel.

6.7 NAÏVE BAYES

In general, naïve Bayes classifier works on Bayes theorem which works on the relative probability of an outcome (p (x/E) means the probability of x while event E occurs). In sentiment analysis, it calculates the probability for features to belong in a particular class/polarity (positive and negative). It is called naïve as it assumes features/input words to be independent of each other. In (Heredia et al., 2016) Brian et al. used NB as a baseline as it can give good performance and shows dependencies of features on local as well as global level.

6.8 CNN-aux

It is CNN with two auxiliary tasks to aid sentence embedding. It is used by (Li et al., 2018; Manshu et al., 2019) as their baseline method for the same purpose. (Tu Manshu and Wang Bing, 2019) have also used it for sentiment classifiers.

6.9 AMN

(Li et al. 2017) proposed AMN that automatically captures pivots using an attention mechanism. It does not need a manual selection of pivots. It consists of two memory networks that were sharing parameter, one for sentiment classification and other for domain Classification. And both networks were jointly trained. Thus AMN was focused to learn pivots only (Li et al. 2017). AMN is used by (Tu and Wang, 2019) as the baseline for their study.

6.10 JST

JST is the extension of latent dirichlet allocation (LDA) that is used for document-level classification as it constructs an additional sentiment layer (Lin et al., 2012). JST is used by (Yang et al., 2019) with the same parameter as taken in its original paper.

6.11 HAN

It is used for document classification as it constructs a document vector. For this it first selects important words to form a sentence vector, the sentence vectors are aggregated to form the document vector. (Tu and Wang, 2019) have used HAN in their studies to compare the performance of their proposed models.

6.12 DANN

DANN can be applied to almost any feed-forward model by increasing a few standard layers and a gradient reversal layer and the resulting layer is trained (Ganin et al., 2016).

7. PERFORMANCE COMPARISON OF BASELINES PROPOSED IN STUDIES

Based on this comparison study of performance measures of various baselines it is found that all methods taken as baselines give accuracy according to the different parameters and datasets on which those are applied. The performance of methods varies with variation in parameter values and selection of source and target domain combinations. They also depend upon the different feature selection methods applied by different researches. Table 5. shows the values of performance matrices of different baseline methods that are calculated by researchers in their proposed papers. Performance comparison results pictured in Figure 1 show that although SFA is a widely used method in various studies SKLT gives the best accuracy in all the methods that the authors have studied for sentiment analysis in cross-domain.

Figure 1. Performance comparison of baselines using the line graph

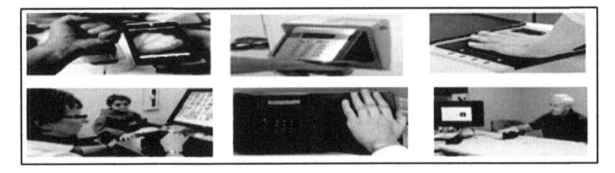

8. DISCUSSION

Most of the techniques of cross domain sentiment analysis depend upon the similarity of source and target domains. During study an over belief is made upon the similarity of features of source and target domains however as there is meagerness between the features of source and target domains, the techniques give poor results with less accuracy. Furthermore, more accurate results can be found while using labeled datasets to train different models for classification. Labeling dataset manually is costly as well as time-consuming, hence various techniques are being applied by different researches in the last few years. The attention mechanism is introduced that automatically captures pivot features without human intervention. Based on that attentive network is proposed that selects important sentiment from the whole document dynamically and give higher word attention to only domain-specific and domain-independent or pivot whole-part relationships. Based on this review research the authors can classify cross domain sentiment analysis methods or techniques into two classes. The first method is based on the transfer of training data features to testing data features. Example studies of this class are feature-based and thesaurus based researches. The second class is the transfer of the complete document from the target domain to the source domain to work as a training dataset to train the model. An example under this class is active learning-based techniques.

There are different challenges that still need to overcome like polarity deviation and lexical ambiguity. Sentiments in different languages, mixed polarity sentiments, differences in contexts, etc are yet to be faced by the techniques introduced by different researches.

9. CONCLUSION

Sentiment analysis has gained a lot of attention from researchers as it is in demand with the increasing online sentiments of users on different topics as it gives the ability to extract insights from the opinions, sentiments, thoughts reviews and online response that is being given by users. **Cross domain sentiment analysis** is a relevant topic about the same application in which one topic can be used to predict certain decisions about other topics as it provides the facility to train and test sentiments behind heterogeneous topics that can be used to make decisions. Hence, sentiment analysis in the cross domain is widely used as their research topic by many researchers those all to give the solution to this problem by giving models for testing and training based on different methods and techniques to improve the accuracy of results.

The authors have performed this study on a systematic literature review on previous researches related to the same to help the researchers in their respective fields to build a model that gives better performance by knowing the pros and cons of previous related methods proposed. As per this study no technique or method yet proposed gives the perfect solution but later methods proposed are always better than former methods proposed in terms of accuracy. Performance of cross domain sentiment analysis depends on the proper selection of source domain to train the classifier to test the target domain hence proper identification of source domain for a particular domain is most important for feature similarity of domains. The study should be done to select the proper source domain for the adaptation of the target domain.

Techniques should be chosen such as to face all the challenges for sentiment analysis in the cross domain. The most important in which is lexical ambiguity in which word/sentiment's meaning changes with context, hence proper domain selection is required to minimize this ambiguity.

REFERENCES

Ben-Hur, A., Horn, D., Siegelmann, H. T., & Vapnik, V. (2001). Support vector clustering. *Journal of Machine Learning Research*, 2(December), 125–137.

Bollegala, D., Mu, T., & Goulermas, J. Y. (2016). Cross-Domain Sentiment Classification Using Sentiment Sensitive Embeddings. *IEEE Transactions on Knowledge and Data Engineering*, 28(2), 398–410. doi:10.1109/TKDE.2015.2475761

Bollegala, D., Weir, D., & Carroll, J. (2013). Cross-Domain Sentiment Classification Using a Sentiment Sensitive Thesaurus. *IEEE Transactions on Knowledge and Data Engineering*, 25(8), 1719–1731. doi:10.1109/TKDE.2012.103

Dai, W., Yang, Q., Xue, G., & Yu, Y. (2007). Boosting for transfer learning. In *Proceedings of the 24th International Conference on Machine Learning* (pp. 193–200). ACM.

Duan, X., Zhou, Y., Jing, C., Zhang, L., & Chen, R. (2018). Cross-domain Sentiment Classification Based on Transfer Learning and Adversarial Network. In *Proceedings of the 2018 IEEE 4th International Conference on Computer and Communications (ICCC)* (pp. 2302-2306). IEEE Press. doi:10.1109/CompComm.2018.8780771

Ganin, Y., Hana, A. H. L., Laviolette, F., & Lempitsky, V. (2016). Domain-Adversarial Training of Neural Networks. *Journal of Machine Learning Research*, 17, 1–35.

Heredia, B., Khoshgoftaar, T. M., Prusa, J., & Crawford, M. (2016). Cross-Domain Sentiment Analysis: An Empirical Investigation. In *Proceedings of the 2016 IEEE 17th International Conference on Information Reuse and Integration (IRI)* (pp. 160-165). IEEE Press. doi:10.1109/IRI.2016.28

Hochreiter, S., & Schmidhuber, J. (1997). Long Short Term Memory. *Journal Neural Computation*, 9(8), 1735–1780. doi:10.1162/neco.1997.9.8.1735

Hofmann, T. (2001). Unsupervised Learning by Probabilistic Latent Semantic Analysis. *Machine Learning*, 42(1-2), 177.

Li, F., Pan, S. J., Jin, O., Yang, Q., & Zhu, X. (2012, July). Cross-domain co-extraction of sentiment and topic lexicons. In *Proceedings of the 50th Annual Meeting of the Association for Computational Linguistics* (Vol. 1, pp. 410-419). Association for Computational Linguistics.

Li, Z., Wei, Y., Zhang, Y., & Yang, Q. (2018, April). Hierarchical attention transfer network for cross-domain sentiment classification. In *Proceedings of the Thirty-Second AAAI Conference on Artificial Intelligence*. AAAI Press.

Li, Z., Zhang, Y., Wei, Y., Wu, Y., & Yang, Q. (2017, August). End-to-End Adversarial Memory Network for Cross-domain Sentiment Classification. In IJCAI (pp. 2237-2243). Academic Press.

Lin, C., He, Y., Everson, R., & Ruger, S. (2012, June). Weakly Supervised Joint Sentiment-Topic Detection from Text. *IEEE Transactions on Knowledge and Data Engineering*, 24(6), 1134–1145. doi:10.1109/TKDE.2011.48

Manshu, T., & Bing, W. (2019). Adding Prior Knowledge in Hierarchical Attention Neural Network for Cross Domain Sentiment Classification. *IEEE Access : Practical Innovations, Open Solutions*, 7, 32578–32588. doi:10.1109/ACCESS.2019.2901929

Manshu, T., & Xuemin, Z. (2019). CCHAN: An End to End Model for Cross Domain Sentiment Classification. *IEEE Access : Practical Innovations, Open Solutions*, 7, 50232–50239. doi:10.1109/ACCESS.2019.2910300

Pan, S. J., Ni, X., Sun, J. T., Yang, Q., & Chen, Z. (2010, April). Cross-domain sentiment classification via spectral feature alignment. In *Proceedings of the 19th international conference on World wide web* (pp. 751-760). Academic Press.

Serafin, R., & Eugenio, B. D. (2004). FLSA: Extending Latent Semantic Analysis with Features for Dialogue Act Classification. ACL. doi:10.3115/1218955.1219043

Yang, M., Yin, W., Qu, Q., Tu, W., Shen, Y., & Chen, X. (2019). *Neural attentive network for cross-domain aspect-level sentiment classification*. IEEE Transactions on Affective Computing.

Zhang, B., Xu, X., Yang, M., Chen, X., & Ye, Y. (2018). Cross-Domain Sentiment Classification by Capsule Network with Semantic Rules. *IEEE Access : Practical Innovations, Open Solutions*, 6, 58284–58294. doi:10.1109/ACCESS.2018.2874623

This research was previously published in the International Journal of Artificial Intelligence and Machine Learning (IJAIML), 10(2); pages 43-56, copyright year 2020 by IGI Publishing (an imprint of IGI Global).

Chapter 100
Microblog Sentiment Analysis Using User Similarity and Interaction–Based Social Relations

Chuanmin Mi

iD https://orcid.org/0000-0002-9211-0332

College of Economics and Management, Nanjing University of Aeronautics and Astronautics, China

Xiaoyan Ruan

College of Economics and Management, Nanjing University of Aeronautics and Astronautics, Nanjing, China

Lin Xiao

College of Economics and Management, Nanjing University of Aeronautics and Astronautics, Nanjing, China

ABSTRACT

With the rapid development of information technology, microblog sentiment analysis (MSA) has become a popular research topic extensively examined in the literature. Microblogging messages are usually short, unstructured, contain less information, creating a significant challenge for the application of traditional content-based methods. In this study, the authors propose a novel method, MSA-USSR, in which user similarity information and interaction-based social relations information are combined to build sentiment relationships between microblogging data. They make use of these microblog–microblog sentiment relations to train the sentiment polarity classification classifier. Two Sina-Weibo datasets were utilized to verify the proposed model. The experimental results show that the proposed method has a better sentiment classification accuracy and F1-score than the content-based support vector machine (SVM) method and the state-of-the-art supervised model known as SANT.

DOI: 10.4018/978-1-6684-6303-1.ch100

1. INTRODUCTION

Sentiment Analysis (SA), also known as opinion mining or opinion analysis, is a process of detecting, extracting, analyzing, and classifying subjective and objective texts by using text mining and natural language processing techniques (Ravi and Ravi 2015). Along with the development of online social networks, especially the emergence of microblogging platforms such as Twitter and Sina-Weibo, users can easily produce blogs and distribute their feelings, emotions, and attitudes on breaking news, public events, or products. The massive amount of microblogging data is a useful and timely source that carries mass sentiments and opinions on various topics related to political, economic, and social life, among other topics. Effectively mining the information within this text data, which is full of opinions and senti-ments, is of great practical value for market intelligence (Li and Li 2013), recommendations (Ren and Wu 2013), information prediction (Rui et al. 2012), and public opinion monitoring (Shi et al. 2013). Therefore, in recent years, Microblog Sentiment Analysis (MSA) has attracted an increasing number of researchers' attention and become a hot research area.

Two main SA techniques have been intensively applied: lexicon-based approaches and machine learning. Studies tend to apply these two techniques directly to the content of microblogging text (Go et al. 2009; Bermingham and Smeaton 2010; Kiritchenko et al. 2014). However, the microblogging texts are characterized by their short length, low information content, unstructured nature, and high data noise, resulting in poor accuracy for MSA using content-based machine learning methods. Moreover, the complexity and diversity of microblogging data, as well as the characteristics of certain informal words, such as acronyms or new abbreviations, also requires the construction of a wide range of domain dictionaries for lexicon-based approaches. Thus, it is a challenge to apply traditional pure content-based methods to MSA.

In fact, microblogs are networks, with users being nodes in social network, and based on the "mu-tual follow" link structure in the social network, users' sentiments are easily unconsciously influenced by other nodes in the social network. Research carried out on SA for a friendship relations network on Myspace indicated that linked users usually tend to have the same emotional tendencies (Thelwall 2010). Meanwhile, some recent studies have pointed out that certain sociological theories, such as sentiment consistency (Abelson 1983) and emotional contagion (Hatfreld et al. 1993), can be usefully applied to social networks. Moreover, based on emotional contagion between friends, researchers have reported the phenomenon of sentiment diffusion (Miller et al. 2011) in the "follower/followee" relations (also called friend relations) in social networks. Therefore, researchers have increasingly realized that MSA is no longer confined to traditional content-based analysis, and that incorporating the users' friend re-lationship information into the analysis process may be useful to improve the accuracy of MSA (Tan et al. 2011; Hu et al. 2013).

With the arrival of Web 2.0, interactive behavior has become a basic characteristic of users. In ad-dition to the user relationship of "follower/followee", users' interactive behaviors, such as retweeting, pressing a "like" button, or commenting on other people's posts, may also reflect emotional contagion (Hatfreld et al. 1993) to a certain extent. Based on the enormous volume of data on Twitter, a study of the homogeneity of happiness in social networks indicates that users are more likely to choose people with the same index of happiness to interact with (Bollen et al. 2011). Although some researchers have been aware of the importance of user interaction information, only a small number of researchers in-corporate this information into MSA (Deng et al. 2014; So and Were 2016). Moreover, when mining social network data, research usually considers the similarity of the nodes. According to the sociological theory that "birds of a feather flock together" (Mcpherson et al. 2003), users who are similar to others in some way, such as by education or location, tend to hold similar attitudes or express the same sentiment on a particular topic. However, research incorporating user similarity information in MSA is lacking.

To fill these aforementioned gaps, we propose a method for MSA that incorporates user similarity information and interaction-based social relation information (MSA-USSR). In particular, we first introduce the concepts of the new model that we build in this paper. Secondly, we describe the methods used to measure user similarities and discuss how they are employed for MSA. After modeling social relations based on considering user interactions, we put forward our new model that integrates user similarity and interaction-based user social relations to enhance the original model. Finally, we use real-world datasets to verify the proposed model.

2. LITERATURE REVIEW

SA has been extensively studied over the past decade because of its potential challenges and wide range of applications (Yu et al. 2012; Li et al. 2014; Nassirtoussi et al. 2015). Two main SA techniques have been widely used in the literature. The first is the lexicon-based approaches, which use a constructed sentiment lexicon to determine overall sentiment polarity of a document (Wilson et al. 2005; O'Connor et al. 2010). The other is machine learning, in which the classifiers are trained on a particular data set by using valuable features such as unigrams or bigrams (Go et al. 2009). While lexicon-based approaches and machine learning methods have been shown to be effective for many types of textual documents, microblog posts are very short and informal, reducing the effectiveness of these traditional purely content-based methods. To overcome this drawback, non-textual or other useful features such as emoticons, pictures, and social network information have been incorporated in the SA process. For example, Read (2005) and Go et al. (2009) collected Twitter messages with emoticons like "☺" and "☹" as training data sets for MSA, in which the emoticons are regarded as noisy labels. Since the emoticons are widely available, this data collection method not only effectively enlarges the scale of training set, but also reduces the cost of manual labeling. Consequently, the experimental results of SA show high classification accuracy (Read 2005; Go et al. 2009). Subsequently, the Emoticon Space Model (ESM), which exploits a large number of emoticons with and without clear emotional meanings in microblogging data, has been proven to help achieve the tasks for subjectivity, polarity, and emotion (Jiang et al. 2014).

Some recent studies have pointed out that utilizing social relations such as "follower/followee" relations could be helpful in MSA (Tan et al. 2011; Hu et al. 2013). For example, it has been demonstrated that two connected users are more likely to hold the same sentiment on a particular topic than two users selected by chance (Tan et al. 2011). Furthermore, experimental results show that integrating this "follower/followee" or "mention" relationship information into sentiment classification increases the accuracy of MSA by approximately 5–10% (Tan et al. 2011). Moreover, based on the sociological theories of sentiment consistency (Abelson 1983) and emotional contagion (Hatfreld et al. 1993), the role of social relations has been explored in MSA. In Hu et al.'s (2013) study, T hypothesis tests were used on two publicly available Twitter datasets to verify that these two social theories hold true for microblogging data, and a novel supervised graph-regularization model was proposed to deal with noisy and short texts for sentiment polarity classification. This model, known as SANT, integrates user social relations into the process of sentiment classification model learning. The results of comparative experiments showed that the SANT model significantly outperforms several representative sentiment classification methods, such as MinCuts and LexRatio.

Although the above-mentioned work of Tan et al. (2011) and Hu et al. (2013) suggests that user-centric social relations are helpful for sentiment classification of microblogging messages, they only use the form of "follower/followee" to measure users' social relations, ignoring other useful information. Specifically, there are still some limitations to the SANT model. For instance, Hu et al. (2013) only captures the point that the sentiments of two messages posted by users with a "follower/followee" relationship (also called a friend relationship in microblogs) are more likely to be similar than those of two randomly selected messages on a given topic, while ignoring the influence of the interactions between these friends.

Social network platforms, like Facebook, Twitter, and Sina-Weibo, allow users to set up personal profiles that include basic information such as their name, birth date, gender, location, home town, and interests, among others (Bhattacharyya et al. 2011; Tang et al. 2015). Exploiting user similarity helps to achieving goals such as community recommendations (Han et al. 2016) and predicting individual retweeting behavior (Ren and Wu 2013) in online social networks. According to the "birds of a feather flock together" theory (Mcpherson et al. 2003), users who are similar to others in certain ways may have similar attitudes or express the same sentiments on a particular topic. Thus, user similarity information may also be a useful non-textual feature and may play an important role in SA tasks. However, little research has incorporated user similarity information into MSA.

3. NOTATION AND PRELIMINARIES

In order to construct a state-of-the-art model, apart from considering and modeling the "mutual follow" relations between users, we further propose a new model for the polarity classification of microblog text by incorporating user similarity information and interaction-based social relation information (MSA-USSR). Hence, we first provide some notation and preliminaries about the MSA-USSR model in this section.

Boldface uppercase letters (e.g., P) are used to denote matrices; boldface lowercase letters (e.g., p) are used to denote vectors; and lowercase letters (p) to denote scalars. Letters such as P_{i*} are used to denote the ***ith*** row of P and P_{*j} are used to denote the ***jth*** column of P so the element at the ***ith*** row and ***jth*** column is denoted as P_{ij}. The formula $P_1 = \sum_{i=1}^{m} \sum_{j=1}^{n} |P_{ij}|$ represents the l_1 norm and $P_F = \sqrt{\sum_{i=1}^{m} \sum_{j=1}^{n} |P_{ij}|^2}$ represents the Frobenius norm of P. The transposition of matrix P is denoted as P^T.

Given a corpus of microblogging messages $\mathbf{T} = [X,Y]$ in which $\mathbf{X} \in R^{k \times n}$ represents the content matrix, $\mathbf{Y} \in R^{n \times c}$ represents the sentiment label matrix, k is the number of features, n is the total number of microblogging messages and c is the number of sentiments. For each message in the corpus $\mathbf{T} = \{t_1, t_2, \ldots, t_n\}$ $t_i = \left(x_i^{(k)}, y_i^{(c)} \right)$ consists of microblogging message content and sentiment labels, in which the former $x_i^{(k)}$ is the message feature vector and the latter $y_i^{(c)}$ is the sentiment label vector. In this paper, we study the polarity classification, so c = 2. It is practical to extend this setting to a multi-dimension sentiment classification task. As the user set is denoted by $\mathbf{u} = \{u_1, u_2, \ldots, u_d\}$ where d is the number of distinct users in the corpus, $\mathbf{U} \in R^{d \times n}$ represents the user–message matrix, the element $U_{ij} = 1$ in the matrix suggests that message t_j is posted by user u_i. $\mathbf{F} \in R^{d \times d}$ represents the user–user matrix, and the element $F_{ij} = 1$ in the matrix indicates that user u_i is connected by user u_j. $\mathbf{S} \in R^{d \times d}$ represents the user–user similarity matrix, the value of element $S_{ij} \in [0,1]$. The higher this value, the greater the similarities are between user u_i and user u_j.

4. PROPOSED MODEL

In this section, we introduce the methods employed to measure user similarities and discuss how we use them to model relations between messages based on user similarities. Then we employ a user interaction factor to enable the calculation of social relations in this state-of-the-art model. Finally, we incorporate user similarities and interaction-based social relations into the content-based model and adopt sparse learning to deal with the sparse and high-dimensional data so as to obtain better performance.

4.1. Modeling User Similarity

Users who are connected in some way are likely to have similar attitudes or express similar sentiments on a particular topic. Thus, before conducting MSA, we first determine the similarity between users, and then define the sentiment relations among the microblogging messages they post according to their degree of user similarity.

The main user similarity Ziegler et al. (2011) employed to predict individual retweet behavior in social network was the users' own profile similarities, especially the profiles of interest. When measuring the similarity between two users, Tang et al. (2015) divided user similarity into three parts: basic information similarity, mutual following similarity (network similarity), and tweets' topic similarity. In addition, Akcora et al. (2011) combined user similarity with trust, and approached user similarity measures from two angles: network similarity and semantic similarity. Network similarity measures both the direct and indirect connections between two users, while sematic similarity is mainly based on user profile information. Thus, in this paper we calculate user similarity from two aspects: user network structure similarity and user semantic similarity, with the former indicating user mutual following similarity, while the latter indicates user basic information similarity and user interest similarity. The specific procedures employed to calculate these two similarities are summarized in the following sections.

4.2. User Network Structure Similarity

In social networks, the "mutual follow" relationship between users is representative of the users' friendship. The so-called "birds of a feather flock together" theory posits that the more mutual friends are shared between two users, the more consistent their emotions are likely to be. Hence, we use the ratio of mutual friends to all friends between users as a measure of network structure similarity. As a microblog social network is built by characterizing the behaviors of following and being followed as out-degree and in-degree respectively (Yan et al. 2013), we also use out-degree **out** (u_i to denote the number of friends user u_i follows, and **out** (u_j to denote the number of friends user u_j follows. Thus, the formula to denote the user network structure similarity is as follows:

$$\text{Sim}_{\text{net}}\left(u_i, u_j\right) = \frac{\left|\text{out}(u_i) \cap \text{out}(u_j)\right|}{\sqrt{\left|\text{out}(u_i)\right| \times \left|\text{out}(u_j)\right|}} \tag{1}$$

4.3. User Semantic Similarity

As social network platforms allow users to set up personal profiles that include basic user information, when measuring user similarity, gender and location were used (Tang et al. 2015). Since the values of users' birth dates may lead to complicated calculations, we constructed the age attribute based on discretizing the attribute of users' birth dates by using Formula (2):

$$F\left(\text{age}\right) = \begin{cases} \text{Child} & 0 < \text{age} \leq 6 \\ \text{Teenage} & 7 \leq \text{age} \leq 17 \\ \text{Youth} & 18 \leq \text{age} \leq 40 \\ \text{Middle-aged} & 41 \leq \text{age} \leq 65 \\ \text{Old} & \text{age} \geq 66 \end{cases} \tag{2}$$

In order to obtain a more accurate value of user similarity, we chose gender, age, education, and location to measure user basic information similarity. The value space of gender is U_gender={F,M] the value space of age is U_age= {Child, Teenage, Youth, Middle-aged, Old} and the value space of education is U_education= {Primary, Junior_high, Secondary_technical, Senior_high, College}. However, since the value of location has the characteristic of a multi-level hierarchy, to reduce the complexity of the calculation, we only select the value form of a two-level hierarchy; that is, the provincial–municipal level (for example: Jiangsu Nanjing).

To consider the existence of missing features, we filled the missing value with a null value. Thus, the gender similarity, age similarity, and education similarity between user u_i and user u_j can be defined as follows, while the location similarity between user u_i and user u_j is defined in a slightly different way:

$$\text{Sim}_g\left(u_i, u_j\right) = \begin{cases} 1 & \text{if } u_{i\text{gender}} = u_{j\text{gender}} \text{ and } u_{i\text{gender}} = u_{j\text{gender}} \neq \text{null}, \\ 0 & \text{if } u_{i\text{gender}} \neq u_{j\text{gender}} \text{ or } u_{i\text{gender}} = u_{j\text{gender}} = \text{null}. \end{cases}$$

$$\text{Sim}_a\left(u_i, u_j\right) = \begin{cases} 1 & \text{if } u_{i\text{age}} = u_{j\text{age}} \text{ and } u_{i\text{age}} = u_{j\text{age}} \neq \text{null}, \\ 0 & \text{if } u_{i\text{age}} \neq u_{j\text{age}} \text{ or } u_{i\text{age}} = u_{j\text{age}} = \text{null}. \end{cases}$$

$$\text{Sim}_e\left(u_i, u_j\right) = \begin{cases} 1 & \text{if } u_{i\text{education}} = u_{j\text{education}} \text{ and } u_{i\text{education}} = u_{j\text{education}} \neq \text{null}, \\ 0 & \text{if } u_{i\text{education}} \neq u_{j\text{education}} \text{ or } u_{i\text{education}} = u_{j\text{education}} = \text{null}. \end{cases}$$

$$\text{Sim}_l\left(u_i, u_j\right) = \begin{cases} 1 & \text{if } u_{i\text{loc}\_p} = u_{j\text{loc}\_p} \neq \text{null and } u_{i\text{loc}\_m} = u_{j\text{loc}\_m} \neq \text{null}, \\ 0.5 & \text{if } u_{i\text{loc}\_p} = u_{j\text{loc}\_p} \neq \text{null but } u_{i\text{loc}\_m} \neq u_{j\text{loc}\_m}, \\ 0 & \text{if } u_{i\text{loc}\_p} \neq u_{j\text{loc}\_p} \text{ or } u_{i\text{loc}} = u_{j\text{loc}} = \text{null}. \end{cases}$$

Therefore, the formula to denote basic information similarity between user u_i and user u_j is as follows:

$$\text{Sim}_{\text{basic}}\left(u_i, u_j\right) = \frac{\left(\text{Sim}_g\left(u_i, u_j\right) + \text{Sim}_a\left(u_i, u_j\right) + \text{Sim}_e\left(u_i, u_j\right) + \text{Sim}_l\left(u_i, u_j\right)\right)}{\text{The total number of features}} \tag{3}$$

Each user has his/her own interests in a social network, which can be collected from the user's tag information. We use vector $T_{u_j} = \left(t_{u_j}\left(\omega_1\right), t_{u_j}\left(\omega_2\right), \cdots, t_{u_j}\left(\omega_n\right)\right)$ to denote the tag data of user u_j, where n represents the total dimension of the user's tags, $t_{u_j}\left(\omega_i\right)$ represents the preference support strength of user u_j to tag i, which is calculated by **TF-IDF** method as follows:

$$TF_{u_j}\left(\omega_i\right) = \frac{The\,number\,of\,tag\,i\,used\,by\,u_j}{The\,number\,of\,all\,tags\,used\,by\,u_j} \tag{4}$$

$$IDF_{u_j}\left(\omega_i\right) = \log\left(\frac{The\,number\,of\,all\,users}{The\,total\,number\,of\,the\,users\,who\,used\,tag\,i + 1}\right) \tag{5}$$

$$t_{u_j}\left(\omega_i\right) = TF_{u_j}\left(\omega_i\right) \times IDF_{u_j}\left(\omega_i\right) \tag{6}$$

The tag information vectors of user u_i and u_j, T_{u_i} and T_{u_j} can be constructed by the above formulas. The similarity of interest between user u_i and u_j can be measured by cosine similarity as follows:

$$\text{Sim}_{\text{interest}}\left(u_i, u_j\right) = \cos\left(\overrightarrow{T_{u_i}}, \overrightarrow{T_{u_j}}\right) = \frac{\overrightarrow{T_{u_i}} \cdot \overrightarrow{T_{u_j}}}{\overrightarrow{T_{u_i}}_2 \times \overrightarrow{T_{u_j}}_2} \tag{7}$$

After calculating each user's similarity with all other users with Formulas (1), (3), and (7), we can obtain the user network structure similarity matrix S_{net}, user basic information similarity matrix S_{basic}, and user interest similarity matrix S_{interest}, and then the total user similarity matrix $S = \alpha_1 S_{\text{net}} + \alpha_2 S_{\text{basic}} + \alpha_3 S_{\text{interest}}$, where $\alpha_1 + \alpha_2 + \alpha_3 = 1$ and $\alpha_1, \alpha_2, \alpha_3 \in R^+$. The selection of these three weights is based on the data analysis and ensures the user similarity value is in the range [0, 1]. The higher the value is, the greater the user similarities are. The microblogs' sentiment relations of user similarity can be built based on the user–microblog matrix **U** and the user similarity matrix **S** as follows, where $R_{\text{simij}} \in [0,1]$, and reflect the degree of sentiment similarity between message t_i and message t_j:

$$R_{\text{sim}} = U^T \times S \times U \tag{8}$$

4.4. Modeling Social Relations by Considering User Interactions

Recently, researchers have proposed two important social theories: sentiment consistency and emotional contagion, which can be usefully applied in MSA (Hu et al. 2013; Lu 2015; Wu et al. 2016). Specifically, in the SANT model, Hu et al. (2013) adopted $Asc=U^{T}\times U$ and $Aec=U^{T}\times F\times U$ to define the message–message sentiment relation matrix for sentiment consistency and emotional contagion, respectively. In this paper, for sentiment consistency, we retain the argument that microblogs posted by the same author are more likely to maintain consistency in sentiment polarity than two randomly selected microblogs. However, for emotional contagion, in addition to friend relations, users' interactive behaviors, such as retweeting, "liking" other people's tweets, also reflect emotional contagion. We presume that the sentiments of microblogs posted by friends with more interactive behaviors are more likely to be similar than those of two microblogs selected from friends who have no interaction. Hence, we append the information of users' interactive behaviors to measure social relations. In this section, we construct a new user–user influence matrix, NF, which represents the degree of emotional influence between users to replace the original user–user matrix F.

The general interactive behaviors in social media that we employ as measures are "retweet" and "like". From the perspective of retweet and like, we use matrix $\mathbf{R}\in R^{d\times d}$ to represent the retweet relationship between users, where R_{ij} indicates the frequency that user u_i retweets the posts of user u_j; and matrix $\mathbf{L}\in R^{d\times d}$ to represent the like relationship between users, where L_{ij} indicates the frequency that user u_i likes the posts of user u_j. We then construct the matrix $\mathbf{H}\in R^{d\times d}$ to represent the interactions between users comprehensively, in which:

$$H_{ij}=\frac{R_{ij}+L_{ij}}{\sum\left(R_{i*}+L_{i*}\right)} \tag{9}$$

Based on the user–user interactive relation matrix $\mathbf{H}$ and the user–user friend relation matrix F, while also considering the possibility of, and existence of, interactions between non-friends, the new user–user influence matrix NF we construct is as follows, where the operation symbol (*) represents the element-by-element multiplication of the two matrices, and θ is the parameter to control the weight of the interaction between non-friends:

$$F*H=\begin{bmatrix} F_{11}*H_{11} & F_{12}*H_{12} & \cdots & F_{1d}*H_{1d} \\ F_{21}*H_{21} & F_{22}*H_{22} & \cdots & F_{2d}*H_{2d} \\ \vdots & \vdots & \ddots & \vdots \\ F_{d1}*H_{d1} & F_{d2}*H_{d2} & \cdots & F_{dd}*H_{dd} \end{bmatrix} \tag{10}$$

$$NF = F * H + \theta \times H \tag{11}$$

The microblogs' sentiment relations of interaction-based social relation and user's own consistency can be built based on the user–microblog matrix $\mathbf{U}$ and the user–user influence matrix NF as follows:

$$R_{sr} = U^{T} \times NF \times U + U^{T} \times U \tag{12}$$

4.5. Merging User Similarity and Interaction-Based Social Relations

We employ the unigram model to construct the term–feature space X, and use term presence as the feature weight. Following previous studies (Lawson and Hanson 1974; Hu et al. 2013), we also adopt the least squares method to achieve sentiment classification based on the textual information, which can be formulated as the following optimization problem, where W represents the learned classifiers:

$$\min_{W} \frac{1}{2} X^T W - Y_F^2 \tag{13}$$

Next, based on Formula (13), to incorporate the microblogs' sentiment relations factors based on user similarity and user interaction-based social relations into the classification task, we established a connection to represent the sentiment difference between two messages. Specifically, this is to ensure the sentiment of two messages is as similar as possible if their holders have high similarity, as well as to make the sentiment of two messages as similar as possible if their holders have a strong social relationship. Due to the characteristics of microblog messages, this classification model will be characterized by high dimensionality and sparseness. To solve this problem, based on the Lasso theory (Bühlmann and Geer 2011), we add the l_1- norm regularization of the model parameters into the objective function, which will constrain certain of the insignificant parameters to be exactly zero, an accordingly, will effectively reduce the dimension of the model and improve its robustness. Ultimately, the sentiment classification of microblogging data can be formulated as the following optimization problem:

$$\min_{W} \frac{1}{2} X^T W - Y_F^2 + \frac{\lambda_1}{2} \sum_{i=1}^{n} \sum_{j=1}^{n} R_{ij} x_i^T W - x_j^T W^2 + \lambda_2 W_1 \tag{14}$$

in which $R = \sigma_1 R_{sim} + \sigma_2 R_{sr}$, $\sigma_1 + \sigma_2 = 1$ control the weight of two different types of microblogs' sentiment relations in the model, and λ_1 and λ_2 are positive regularization parameters.

5. EXPERIMENTS

In this section, we conduct experiments on two real-world Sina-Weibo datasets to assess our proposed MSA-USSR model. We briefly introduce the datasets and some preprocessing steps first. Then we evaluate the performance of our proposed model by comparing the experiment results with extant SA approaches, including the SVM method and the supervised SANT model.

5.1. Datasets and Preprocessing

The datasets used in our experiments were collected from Sina-Weibo, the largest microblogging platform in China. We developed a web crawler program to fetch the required data by visiting the Sina Open API. Among the hot topics in 2016, we select **#IPhone7#** and **#RIO2016#** as the keywords for the search API. We obtained one dataset for each topic. The first dataset consists of users and their tweets, which indicate their attitudes and sentiments toward a new product, the IPhone7. The second dataset is based on the 31st Summer Olympic Games that was organized in Rio, a major international event in 2016. The data set contains the tweets related to the word "RIO2016", as well as the messages' posters. We also obtained other relevant data that the experimental models require, including basic personal information, followee and follower status, as well as users' interests and the interactive behaviors between users.

To facilitate the subsequent experiments, preprocessing of the microblog data was conducted. Specifically, we removed certain useless information, including URL links, special characters, and emoticons to improve the classification quality. Meanwhile, we filtered repeated tweets to prevent duplicated data from lending extra weight to particular features. We then manually labeled each tweet with a polarity sentiment label, since supervised methods use labeled data to train models. After filtering and labeling the data, we segmented the microblog data from sentences to words so as to construct the term–feature space. We choose the JieBa word segmentation software to preprocess the textual data after comparing several word segmentation systems. The descriptive statistics of the datasets are summarized in Table 1.

Table 1. Statistics of the two datasets

	IPhone7	RIO2016
Number of Tweets	13,026	7,971
Number of Users	7,685	5,124
Number of Words	6,789	5,734
Number of Positives	7,208	4,782
Number of Negatives	5,818	3,189
Number of Retweets	4,385	3,247
Number of Likes	3,942	2,856
Number of Friend Relations	1,092	623

5.2. Comparison With Other Supervised Methods

We compared the proposed MSA-USSR framework with the following state-of-the-art supervised methods:

- **SVM:** Support vector machines are supervised learning models with associated learning algorithms that analyze data used for classification and regression analysis (Wang et al. 2009);
- **SANT:** A sociological supervised model proposed by Hu and Tang (2013), which employs social relations to handle networked texts in microblogging.

To compare the performance of the models, we adopted four metrics: accuracy, precision, recall, and F1-score, which are standard metrics for classification performance (Han and Kamber 2006). These metrics, defined for polarity sentiment classification, are as follows:

$$\text{Accuracy} = \frac{\#\text{correctly classified as positive} + \#\text{correctly classified as negative}}{\#\text{true positive} + \#\text{true negative}} \quad (15)$$

$$\text{Precision} = \frac{\#\text{correctly classified as positive}}{\#\text{ classified as positive}} \qquad (16)$$

$$\text{Recall} = \frac{\#\text{ correctly classified as positive}}{\#\text{ true positive}} \qquad (17)$$

$$\text{F1-score} = \frac{2 \times \text{precision} \times \text{recall}}{\text{precision} + \text{recall}} \qquad (18)$$

Several parameters are critical in our experiments, including α_1, α_2, and α_3 which control the weight of three different types of user similarity; σ_1, σ_2, which control the weight of user similarities and interaction-based social relations in the model; and λ_1 and λ_2 in Equation (14). λ_1 is the parameter to control the contribution of the sentiment relation information, while λ_2 is the sparse regularization parameter. All of these parameters are positive. Commonly, λ_1 and λ_2 are adjusted via cross validation. In the experiments, we set $\lambda_1 = 0.05$ and $\lambda_2 = 0.1$ for general experimental purposes. We set $\alpha_1 = \alpha_2 = \alpha_3 = 1/3$, which means that the three types of user similarity matrices are simply combined with equal weight. Setting $\sigma_1 = \sigma_2 = 0.5$ means that the two matrices of user similarities and interaction-based social relations are simply combined with equal weights.

The experimental results of the three methods on the two datasets are reported in Figures 1 and 2. In the experiments, we used five-fold cross validation. In each round of the experiment, 80% of the whole dataset was used for training and the rest was used for testing. We used F1-score, precision, accuracy, and recall to measure the performance of the three methods. In each round of the experiment, the result denotes the average score of ten test runs. By comparing the results of the different methods, we found that compared to the SANT and SVM methods, the MAS-USSR model consistently achieved better performance for four metrics with both datasets.

Through the above experiments, we verified that our proposed model MSA-USSR is able to improve the classification accuracy of both datasets. As we merged the user similarity information and users' interaction-based social relations in the proposed model, in order to elaborate the effects of these two factors in improving the sentiment classification accuracy respectively, we conducted more experiments to compare them. Specifically, we construct two new models based on MSA-USSR, named MSA-US and MSA-SR, by setting the values of σ_1 and σ_2; that is:

- **MSA-US:** The model is built only on user similarity, with the parameter settings of $\sigma_1 = 1$ and $\sigma_2 = 0$;
- **MSA-SR:** In turns, the model is built only on users' interaction-based social relations, with the parameter settings of $\sigma_1 = 0$ and $\sigma_2 = 1$.

We used five-fold cross validation on both datasets and chose the SANT model as the baseline for these experiments. Since the F1-score considers both the precision P and the recall R, it can be interpreted as a weighted average of precision and recall (Crestani and Rijsbergen 1998; Powers 2011). In order to investigate the intuitive results, we calculated the actual value of the accuracy and F1-score, as well as the gain value of these two indicators on the three new models. The specific experimental results are summarized in Table 2:

Figure 1. Experimental results for the IPhone7 dataset

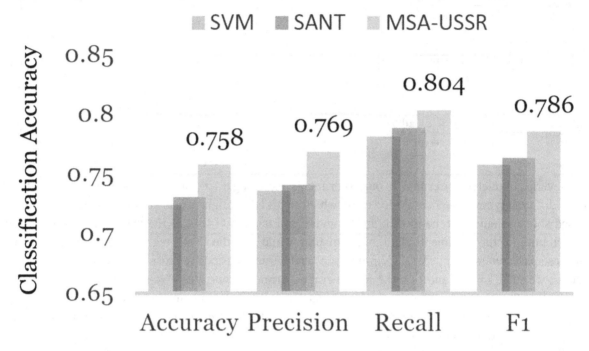

Figure 2. Experimental results for the RIO2016 dataset

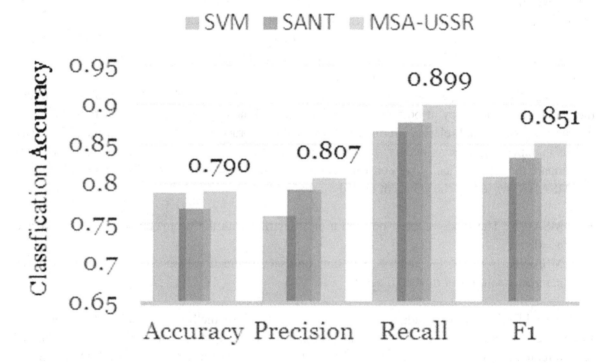

- Compared to the SANT model, the performance of the MSA-US was less accurate and gave a lower F1-score. By only considering user similarity, it leads to excessive noise in the training process, which reduces the accuracy and F1-score of the sentiment classification;
- In contrast to MSA-US, the performance of MSA-SR on both datasets showed an obvious increased in accuracy and F1-score compared to the SANT model;
- When considering both user similarity information and users' interaction-based social relations, the performance of the MSA-USSR model is better than the SANT model in terms of accuracy and F1-score. However, the performance of the MSA-USSR model is poorer than that of the MSA-SR model, which considers users' interaction-based social relations alone.

Table 2. Experimental results for both datasets

Methods	IPhone7		RIO2016	
	Accuracy (Gain)	F1-Score (Gain)	Accuracy (Gain)	F1-Score (Gain)
SANT	0.731 (N.A.)	0.764 (N.A.)	0.769 (N.A.)	0.817 (N.A.)
MSA-US	0.671 (-8.21%)	0.705 (-7.72%)	0.724 (-5.85%)	0.780 (-4.53%)
MSA-SR	0.774 (+5.88%)	0.798 (+4.45%)	0.800 (+4.03%)	0.843 (+3.18%)
MSA-USSR ($\sigma_1 = \sigma_2 = 0.5$)	0.758 (+3.69%)	0.786 (+2.88%)	0.790 (+2.73%)	0.835 (+2.20%)

In order to explore the best performance of MSA-USSR model, we conducted more experiments to determine the optimized combination of σ_1 and σ_2. The results are shown in Figures 3 and 4.

Figure 3. Experimental results for the accuracy on both datasets under different sets of values for σ_1 and σ_2

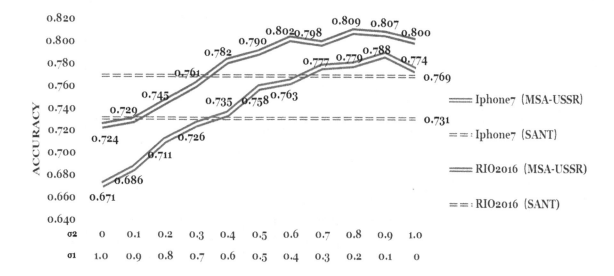

Figure 4. Experimental results of the f1-score on both datasets under different sets of values for σ_1 and σ_2

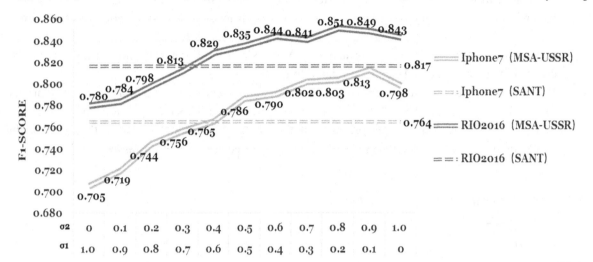

We can draw the following observations based on the experiment results:

- Generally, it is noted that the sentiment classification accuracy and the F1-score of our proposed model increases with increasing of weights of σ_2; that is, the weight of users' interaction-based social relations;
- On the IPhone7 dataset, the best performance of MSA-USSR showed an accuracy of 78.8% and a F1-score of 81.3%, when $\sigma_1=0.1$ and $\sigma_2=0.9$, while on the RIO2016 dataset, the best performance was seen when $\sigma_1=0.2$ and $\sigma_2=0.8$, giving an accuracy of 80.9% and a F1-score of 85.1%.

In summary, the MSA-USSR model performed differently under the different sets of weights on user similarity information and users' interaction-based social relations, and achieved the best performance when both user similarity information and users' interaction-based social relations are incorporated.

Table 3. Summary of experimental results for both datasets

Methods	IPhone7		RIO2016	
	Accuracy (Gain)	F1-Score (Gain)	Accuracy (Gain)	F1-Score (Gain)
SANT	0.731 (N.A.)	0.764 (N.A.)	0.769 (N.A.)	0.817 (N.A.)
MSA-US	0.671 (-8.21%)	0.705 (-7.72%)	0.724 (-5.85%)	0.780 (-4.53%)
MSA-SR	0.774 (+5.88%)	0.798 (+4.45%)	0.800 (+4.03%)	0.843 (+3.18%)
MSA-USSR	0.788 (+7.80%)	0.813 (+6.41%)	0.809 (+5.20%)	0.851 (+4.16%)

6. CONCLUSION AND FUTURE WORK

In this paper, we have proposed a novel supervised method, MSA-USSR. Our method can effectively analyze topic-dependent labeled data for MSA. By employing two real-world datasets to verify the proposed model, we have demonstrated that incorporating user similarity information and interaction-based social relation information enables a significant improvement in supervised MSA. Although the results of the experiment show that the improvement in the accuracy and F1-scores of microblog sentiment classification brought by interaction-based social relation information is greater than that when considering the information on user similarity, we still cannot ignore the subtle improvements brought by the latter, especially in the current "big data" environment. The MSA-USSR model achieved the best performance when incorporating both user similarity information and users' interaction-based social relations.

For future work, our model can be tested on a large-scale dataset in different domains and extended to multiple emotion classifications. Moreover, according to the sociological theory of sentiment consistency, future studies can further explore the impact and significance of individual historical behavior and historical sentiments on determining the microblog sentiments of individuals in the future. It is possible that the individual's history can also be used as a good indicator in the measurement of user similarity.

ACKNOWLEDGMENT

This work was financially supported by the Project of National Social Science Foundation of China (17BGL055), Young Scientists Fund from Ministry of Education in China Project of Humanities and Social Sciences (20YJC630163), China Postdoctoral Science Foundation [grant number 2019M650078], Fundamental Research Funds for the Central Universities [grant number NJ2019021, NJ2020044], Jangsu Province Graduate Education Teaching Reform Project [grant number JGLX19_014], Nanjing University of Aeronautics and Astronautics Graduate Education Teaching Reform Research Project [grant number 2018YJXGG17].

REFERENCES

Abelson, R. P. (1983). Whatever Became of Consistency Theory? *Personality & Social Psychology Bulletin*, *9*(1), 37-64.

Akcora, C. G., Carminati, B., & Ferrari, E. (2011). Network and profile based measures for user similarities on social networks. *IEEE International Conference on Information Reuse and Integration*, 292-298. 10.1109/IRI.2011.6009562

Bermingham, A., & Smeaton, A. F. (2010). Classifying sentiment in microblogs: is brevity an advantage? *ACM International Conference on Information and Knowledge Management*, 1833-1836. 10.1145/1871437.1871741

Bhattacharyya, Garg, & Wu. (2011). Analysis of user keyword similarity in online social networks. *Social Network Analysis and Mining*, *1*(3), 143-158.

Bollen, Gonçalves, Ruan, & Mao. (2011). Happiness Is Assortative in Online Social Networks. *Artificial Life*, *17*(3), 237-251.

Bühlmann, P., & Geer, S. V. D. (2011). *Theory for the Lasso*. Springer Berlin Heidelberg.

Crestani & Rijsbergen. (1998). A Study of Probability Kinematics in Information Retrieval. *ACM Transactions on Information Systems*, *16*(3), 225-255.

Deng, Han, Li, Ji, Wang, & Lu. (2014). Exploring and inferring user-user pseudo-friendship for sentiment analysis with heterogeneous networks. *Statistical Analysis & Data Mining: The ASA Data Science Journal*, *7*(4), 308-321.

Go, A., Bhayani, R., & Huang, L. (2009). Twitter sentiment classification using distant supervision. Cs224n Project Report.

Han, J., & Kamber, M. (2006). *Data Mining Concepts and Techniques* (2nd ed.). San Francisco: Morgan Kaufmann.

Han, X., Wang, L., Farahbakhsh, R., Cuevas, Á., Cuevas, R., Crespi, N., & He, L. (2016). CSD: A multiuser similarity metric for community recommendation in online social networks. *Expert Systems with Applications*, *53*, 14–26. doi:10.1016/j.eswa.2016.01.003

Hatfreld, Cacioppo, & Rapson. (1993). Emotional Contagion. *Current Directions in Psychological Science*, *2*(3), 96-99.

Hu, X., Tang, L., Tang, J., & Liu, H. (2013). Exploiting social relations for sentiment analysis in microblogging. *ACM International Conference on Web Search and Data Mining*, 537-546. 10.1145/2433396.2433465

Jiang, F., Liu, Y., Luan, H., Zhang, M., & Ma, S. (2014). *Microblog Sentiment Analysis with Emoticon Space Model*. Springer Berlin Heidelberg. doi:10.1007/978-3-662-45558-6_7

Kiritchenko, S., Zhu, X., & Mohammad, S. M. (2014). Sentiment Analysis of Short Informal Text. *Journal of Artificial Intelligence Research*, *50*, 723–762. doi:10.1613/jair.4272

Lawson, C. L., & Hanson, R. J. (1974). *Solving least squares problems*. SIAM.

Li & Li. (2013). Deriving market intelligence from microblogs. *Decision Support Systems*, *55*, 206-217.

Li, Xie, Chen, Wang, & Deng. (2014). News impact on stock price return via sentiment analysis. *Knowledge-Based Systems*, *69*(1), 14-23.

Lu, T. J. (2015). Semi-supervised microblog sentiment analysis using social relation and text similarity. *International Conference on Big Data and Smart Computing*, 194-201. 10.1109/35021BIGCOMP.2015.7072831

Mcpherson, Smithlovin, & Cook. (2003). Birds of a feather: Homophily in social networks. *Annual Review of Sociology*, *27*(1), 415-444.

Miller, M., Sathi, C., Wiesenthal, D., Leskovec, J., & Potts, C. (2011). Sentiment Flow through Hyperlink Networks. *International Conference on Weblogs and Social Media*.

Nassirtoussi, Aghabozorgi, Wah, & Ngo. (2015). Text mining of news-headlines for FOREX market prediction: A Multi-layer Dimension Reduction Algorithm with semantics and sentiment. *Expert Systems with Applications*, *42*(1), 306-324.

O'Connor, B., Balasubramanyan, R., Routledge, B. R., & Smith, N. A. (2010). From Tweets to Polls: Linking Text Sentiment to Public Opinion Time Series. *International Conference on Weblogs and Social Media*.

Powers, D. M. W. (2011). Evaluation: From Precision, Recall and F-Factor to ROC, Informedness, Markedness & Correlation. *Journal of Machine Learning Technologies*, *2*(1), 37-63.

Ravi, K., & Ravi, V. (2015). A survey on opinion mining and sentiment analysis. Knowledge-Based Systems, 89(C), 14-46.

Read, J. (2005). Using Emoticons to reduce Dependency in Machine Learning Techniques for Sentiment Classification. The Student Research Workshop at the 2005 Meeting of the Association for Computational Linguistics. doi:10.3115/1628960.1628969

Ren & Wu. (2013). Predicting User-Topic Opinions in Twitter with Social and Topical Context. *IEEE Transactions on Affective Computing*, *4*(4), 412-424.

Rui, Liu, & Whinston. (2012). *Whose and what chatter matters? The effect of tweets on movie sales.* Social Science Electronic Publishing.

Shi, Wang, & He. (2013). Sentiment analysis of Chinese microblogging based on sentiment ontology: a case study of '7.23 Wenzhou Train Collision'. *Connection Science*, *25*(4), 161-178.

So & Were. (2016). Microblog Sentiment Orientation Detection Using User Interactive Relationship. *Journal of Electrical & Computer Engineering* (3), 1-6.

Tan, C., Lee, L., Tang, J., Jiang, L., Zhou, M., & Li, P. (2011). User-level sentiment analysis incorporating social networks. *International Conference on Knowledge Discovery & Data Mining*, 1397–1405.

Tang, X., Miao, Q., Quan, Y., Tang, J., & Deng, K. (2015). Predicting individual retweet behavior by user similarity. Knowledge-Based Systems, 89(C), 681-688.

Thelwall, M. (2010). Emotion Homophily in Social Network Site Messages. *First Monday*, *15*(4), 4. doi:10.5210/fm.v15i4.2897

Wang, Li, Song, Wei, & Li. (2009). A feature selection method based on improved fisher's discriminant ratio for text sentiment classification. *Expert Systems with Applications*, *5854*(7), 8696-8702.

Wilson, Wiebe, & Hoffmann. (2005). Recognizing contextual polarity in phrase-level sentiment analysis. *International Journal of Computer Applications*, *7*(5), 347-354.

Wu, F., Huang, Y., & Song, Y. (2016). Structured microblog sentiment classification via social context regularization. Neurocomputing, 175, 599-609. doi:10.1016/j.neucom.2015.10.101

Yan, Wu, & Zheng. (2013). Social network based microblog user behavior analysis. *Physica A Statistical Mechanics & Its Applications*, *392*(7), 1712-1723.

Yu, Liu, Huang, & An. (2012). Mining Online Reviews for Predicting Sales Performance: A Case Study in the Movie Domain. *Knowledge & Data Engineering IEEE Transactions*, 24(4), 720-734.

Ziegler, C. N., & Lausen, G. (2004). *Analyzing Correlation between Trust and User Similarity in Online Communities*. Springer Berlin Heidelberg. doi:10.1007/978-3-540-24747-0_19

This research was previously published in the International Journal of Web Services Research (IJWSR), 17(3); pages 39-55, copyright year 2020 by IGI Publishing (an imprint of IGI Global).

Chapter 101
Sentiment Analysis of Twitter Data:
A Hybrid Approach

Ankit Srivastava
The NorthCap University, Gurgaon, India

Vijendra Singh
The NorthCap University, Gurgaon, India

Gurdeep Singh Drall
The NorthCap University, Gurgaon, India

ABSTRACT

Over the past few years, the novel appeal and increasing popularity of social networks as a medium for users to express their opinions and views have created an accumulation of a massive amount of data. This evolving mountain of data is commonly termed Big Data. Accordingly, one area in which the application of new techniques in data mining research has significant potential to achieve more precise classification of hidden knowledge in Big Data is sentiment analysis (aka optimal mining). A hybrid approach using Naïve Bayes and Random Forest on mining Twitter datasets is presented here as an extension of previous work. Briefly, relevant data sets are collected from Twitter using Twitter API; then, use of the hybrid methodology is illustrated and evaluated against one with only Naïve Bayes classifier. Results show better accuracy and efficiency in the sentiment classification for the hybrid approach.

1. INTRODUCTION

Nowadays, one way to aid individuals and/or organizations in making intelligent decisions such as choosing among available options wisely is to draw upon the opinion of the crowd. Traditionally, many of us have depended on other people's opinions, particularly those of family members, friends and relatives, when making decisions on critical issues (Pang & Lee, 2008; Saif, He, & Alani, 2012; Kharde &

DOI: 10.4018/978-1-6684-6303-1.ch101

Sonawane, 2016; Xia, Zong, & Li, 2011; Cambria, Schuller, Xia, & Havasi, 2013). However, with rapid technological advances and the increasing ubiquity of the Internet in all corners of the world, many of us are now showing interests in social platforms, as these have made it relatively easy for us to know the thinking of not only family members and friends, but also of strangers around us (including willing experts who do not mind providing their educated advice) (Godbole, Srinivasaiah, & Skiena, 2007; Tan, Lee, Tang, Jiang, Zhou, & Li, 2011).

Accordingly, around 6,000 tweets are generally disseminated on Twitter every second; on average, this amounts to 500 million tweets daily or, 200 billion tweets annually. Platforms such as Facebook, Yelp and Amazon have accumulated a huge traffic of texts and opinions being generated daily. Such huge numbers means a lot of texts and data from all around the globe. Consequently, it has become crucial for individuals and/or organizations to be able to analyze these data meaningfully so as to be able to profit from, and/or capitalize on, these opinions to enhance one's reputation (Balahur & Jacquet, 2015; Kumar, Morstatter, & Liu, 2014; Isah, Trundle, & Neagu, 2014; Jiang & Kotzias, 2016).

Sentiment analysis (SA), a process by which sentiment over the accumulated tweets can be automatically detected, is an increasingly popular means of analyzing "big data" such as "tweets" arising from the use of Twitter. Furthermore, such analysis allows the text polarity (whether it is neutral, positive or good, negative or bad), to be aggregated. Briefly, in order to classify the polarity of the accumulated text via sentiment classification (West, Paskov, Leskovec, & Potts, 2014; Cogburn & Espinoza-Vasquez, 2011; Gamallo & Garcia, n.d.), SA entails five fundamental steps: (1) collecting the data to be analyzed; (2) preprocessing the data; (3) extracting feature(s) linked to the data; (4) performing sentiment classification on the data; and (5) presenting result(s).

In essence, SA can be conducted at four different levels: Word, Sentence, Document and/or the Feature/Aspect level (Karlgren & Ericsson, 2013; Recupero & Cambria, 2014; Irsov & Cardie, 2014). At the Document level, the aim will be to aggregate the single sentiment polarity of the entire document by seeking out the sentiment polarities of all sentences combined in the document and then summarizing them. At the Sentence level, sentiment polarity of a sentence is first computed by identifying the sentiment polarity of each and every word in the sentence. These are then aggregated (Tan et al., 2011; Vijendra & Laxman, 2013; Vijendra, Sahoo, & Ashwini, 2010). At the Word level, sentiment polarity of each and every word is determined. At the Aspect/Feature level, the main concern will be to identify and extract product features from the source data. In this approach, the entities for which the sentiment may be directed will have to be identified, for example, if the sentiment analysis encompasses that of phone reviews, the differing aspects/features may include the camera, the screen, and the phone speaker.

In Twitter data, tweets often contain noises, incomplete data, slangs, unstructured sentences and many irregular expressions. Before preforming classification analysis, a preprocessing of the text is needed such as the removal of URLs (Uniform Resource Locators), numbers, stop words and the like (Feldman, 2013; Vinodhini & Chandrasekaran, 2012; Vijendra & Laxman, 2015; Quadri, Prashanth, Pongpaichet, Esmin, & Jain, 2017). In an earlier work, six different pre-processing methods were used to filter out the necessary and useful data from the complete dataset with a series of experiments using four classifiers conducted to verify the effectiveness of several pre-processing methods on Twitter datasets. Results indicate that in N-grams model, removing URLs and stop words reduce the vocabulary size while no change in the performance of all of the classifier approaches was observed. In this follow up work, we aim to improve the performance by incorporating a hybrid model.

The rest of this paper is organized as follows. Section 2 describes the background or related work. Section 3 presents the hybrid methodology for the suggested evaluation approach. Section 4 details the experimental procedures and results while concluding remarks and future work will be highlighted in section 5.

2. RELATED WORK

In an earlier work, Wilson et al. (2011) investigate the utility of linguistic features for capturing the sentiment of twitter messages. Part of Speech (POS) features, they conclude, are not much helpful when used in the area of microblogging for sentiment analysis (SA); instead, they observe that using hashtags for collecting training dataset would be quite useful given that the data are collected based on positive vs. negative emotions. In the end, it is concluded that the efficiency of the best approach for classifying sentiment may well depend on the type and/or mix of feature(s) chosen for the analysis.

Following the Wilson et al. (2011) publication, Bollegala et al. (2013) propose a method to address the complication of cross-domain sentiment classification. Cross-domain sentiment classification entails resolving the wrongful assumption of simply applying supervised learning via labeled data from the source domain to the target domain, especially when human factor is also neglected. Briefly, when the training dataset is aligned for a specific input dataset domain in supervised machine learning for classification purpose, using this same training dataset for other input dataset domain may in fact reduce the efficiency and accuracy of the system. Hence, Bollegala et al. suggest first developing a distributional thesaurus, which is sentiment sensitive by using labeled data from the source domain and then using the unlabeled data from both the target and source domains to resolve the cross-domain sentiment classification problem. They advocate recording the sensitivity of the sentiment in the thesaurus by using sentiment labels at the Document level in the context vectors used so as to measure the distributional similarity among the words. After this, they advise using the constructed thesaurus to expand feature vectors in the process of testing-training times in a binary classifier. The proposed system is argued to perform better then the baseline models. The dataset here entails user reviews on different type of products (on Amazon). The proposed system has been tested on various adaptations such as single vs. multi-source domain adaptation and on supervised v. unsupervised domain adaptations.

More recently, new works in the field of SA and hybrid algorithmic approaches have appeared in the consumer review literature. Zha et al. (2014), present a product aspect-ranking framework, which automatically identify the important aspect of a product, which is also the key component of a product. For example, the various aspects of a phone are camera, screen, design, apps and the like. Two observational criteria to aid in identifying the important aspects of a product are noted by Zha et al. (2014): (1) It is typical for a large number of consumers to comment on the important aspect of a product vis-à-vis other non-important aspects; and (2) A customer review on an important aspect of a product is expected to greatly influence the overall opinion of the product. In this work, a shallow dependency parser is first used to identify all aspects of a product; then, a probabilistic aspect-ranking algorithm is used to identify the aspects of the products that are important. All in all, the Zha et al. algorithm examines the aspects frequency together with a consumer review influence about each aspect, which makes up the overall opinion of the product. Dengel et al. (2013) evaluate the dataset of 940 tweets to compare some PD (pattern decomposition) algorithms and an automatic aspect detection algorithm. They collected the dataset using the word "iPhone" and apply a hybrid approach of different algorithms and methods with a built-in sentiment summarization system. Their result indicates that the hybrid method performed better than their unigram baseline method; moreover, the authors observe that adding sarcasm detection and using more features can also increase the performance of the system. Saif et al. (2012) examine six different stopwords removal method and evaluate their effect on sentiment classification. Performing analysis on twitter data, the authors observe that most, if not all, the stopwords removal methods have somewhat similar affects but a better performance can generally be expected for Naïve Bayes (NB) than for Maximum Entropy. Dhande et al. (2014) took the dataset of movie review and trained the dataset using the NB Classifier v. Neural Network (NN) classifier. After training the data, the authors classify the data using NB, NN classifier, and Naïve Bayes Neural (NBN) hybrid classifier. The accuracy of the NBN approach outperforms the other two methods with an accuracy of 80.65% as compared to 62.35% for NB and 49.95% for NN respectively.

Incorporating a similar line of thinking, Dahiya et al. (2015) look at mobile reviews via a hybrid method using NB with modified k-means (MKM) clustering. Accordingly, the authors observe that the proposed system is more accurate than Support Vector Machine (SVM) and NB taken individually. On 1000 mobile reviews, for example, the authors get an overall accuracy of around 90%. In addition, they observe that NB with MKM is more suited for text-based classification whereas SVM is more suited for interpreting social media data. Dey et al. (2016) compare two supervised machine-learning algorithms NB v. K-NN (k-nearest neighbor) and evaluated the sentiment classification accuracy, recall and precision. These authors focus on hotel and movie reviews. When they consider movie reviews, NB outperformed K-NN and showed accuracy of around 80% whereas when hotel reviews are compared, the accuracy declined and NB v. K-NN both showed almost similar results. In the end, they conclude that for movie reviews, the NB classifier can be used successfully. Mishra et al. (2016) propose a novel system to work on movie reviews for feature level SA. These authors focus on various problems such as negation, synonyms, intensifier, and more. Their study applies four methodologies after the collected data are cleaned for analysis to yield an 81% accuracy at the most; afterwards, the accuracy decreases as their system could not handle the True Negative (TN) reviews correctly.

In one of the more interesting SA works, Mirani et al. (2016) analyze the sentiments of the tweets related to ISIS (the Islamic State in Iraq and Syria). The authors jointly recognize the need to use hashtags, which are related to ISIS tags. Following data collection, data are cleaned via two processes: (1) Regular expressions, tokenization and commonly shared wordings are identified to create the dictionary; and (2) Frequently occurring words associated with ISIS are noted with the most frequent words computed to be Isil, Younus AlGohar, isi, Libya, Daesh and Iraqi. At the classification level, linear SVM, Maximum Entropy (ME), Bagging, Decision Tress (DT) and Random Forest (RF) are applied. It is concluded that all of the deployed classification algorithms averages an accuracy of 90% after 10-fold cross-validation. After validating using #isil, ME yields the best result at 99% accuracy. It is further noted that collecting data in different languages with more dictionaries might yield better results. Hiai et al. (2016) analyze 10,000 reviews of a Japanese product with data comprising 70 sarcastic sentences after manually going through each sentence. These authors use three types of rules (Rejection rules, Boosting rules and Rules for eight classes) to evaluate expressions for the classification of sentences into eight groups. First, they apply the rules to each sentence in the input data, emphasizing rejection rules; later on, if the sentences are still having the expressions for the rejection, then that particular sentence is removed from the final list. It is found that the proposed method improved only with increasing number of sarcastic tweets. In fact, sarcasm in tweets is found to be of significance even if the dataset or sentences are small in numbers. Zhao et al. (2017) study six different preprocessing techniques on 5 different Twitter datasets. These authors employ two feature models (N-gram and prior polarity model) to check the effectiveness of these models on four different classifiers (SVM, NB, Logistic Regression (LR), and RF). They conclude that removing stop words, URLs and numbers is useful to reduce noise in the dataset while these steps do not fundamentally affect the performance of the sentiment classification system.

Most recently, Kharde et al. (2016) provide a detailed review and comparative analysis of various existing opinion-mining techniques such as lexicon-based approaches v. machine learning approaches. They highlight the challenges and applications of sentiment analysis on Twitter with brief explanations of various words/terms such as opinion, view, belief, sentiment, object, feature, opinion orientation or polarity and opinion holder. Essentially, these authors provide a general SA architecture as follows: (a) In the data pre-processing step, datasets are cleaned include spelling correction, the removal of URLs, stopwords, punctuation marks, and more; (b) In the feature extraction step, the features related to the documents are extracted by using techniques such as words and their frequencies, tagging, negation, position of terms, etc; (c) In the training step, a technique for training the dataset for classification purpose is performed - such techniques include supervised machine learning classifier algorithms; the lexicon-based approach, which is performed by using the dictionary-based approach; and the corpus-based approach. These authors note that SA can be performed at different level(s) and that various sentiment classification algorithms may yield different percentages of accuracy as computed by taking into consideration different pre-processing steps each time. As well, Bharti et al. [34] compare Hadoop v. non-Hadoop frameworks to implement sarcasm detection. These authors use the twitter streaming API to retrieve tweets while deploying the Hadoop Distributed File System (HDFS) to store the data using Apache Flume; they use POS tagger as well as the Map Reduce functions to detect Sarcasm in tweets. The study results lead them to conclude that the Hadoop framework, as compared to non-Hadoop Framework, can reduce processing time up to 66%. These authors also employ 2 algorithms to identify sarcasm for two different types of tweet structures: (1) A parse-based lexical generation algorithm (PBLGA), whose input is a Tweet Corpus; and (2) The Interjection Word Start (IWS), which takes input tweets that begins with interjection words. The authors conclude that IWS algorithm proves that if the text uses interjecting words, then it is more likely that the text in the tweet is sarcastic.

Finally, a 2017 study by Chen et al. (2017) working on Chinese social media data reveals that the effectiveness of the feature extraction method chosen depends largely upon POS tagging. It is found that NB generally performs better than ME methods. Additionally, NB feature extraction method is superior to classic N-grams feature extraction methods and when compared to a bigrams having a lower complexity.

3. METHODOLOGY

SA is a process by which one can get useful insights from large amount of data. As aforementioned, the key SA tasks include data collection (dataset); data preprocessing; feature selection/extraction; sentiment classification algorithmic processing; and result presentation.

3.1. Data Collection

Data collection in SA is the first step; specifically, the amount of data required for the analysis is collected. Three (3) datasets are collected from Twitter by using Twitter API, which helps to fetch tweets from the twitter. In this work, as Twitter is largely used by the public to share different opinions, we focus on the keywords "Amazon" v. "Hachette" to build up the twitter datasets for the intended SA. Our system uses the "twitty" object, which stores tweets in structure array created from the API response in JSON format.

3.2. Data Pre-Processing

For extracting useful sentiments from the raw dataset, our proposed system has to first filter out the raw data set in order to remove the useless information. This step may be noted as the most crucial stage of the complete SA process (Kouloumpis, Wilson, & Moore, 2011; Nozza, Maccagonla, Guigue, Messina, & Gallinari, 2014; Liu, 2012). In the proposed system, we performed the following 4 pre-processing techniques on the three datasets: (1) Tokenization; (2) Removal of Numbers, Special Characters and URLs; (3) Removal of Stopwords; and (4) Stemming. Figure 1 illustrates the "pseudocode" for preprocessing.

Figure 1. Pseudocode for preprocessing

```
Procedure for data preprocessing:
{
    Input = dataset
    tokens = words_tokenize(Input)
    tokens = regexprep(tokens)
    tokens = tokens(~cellfun('isempty',tokens));
    tokens = tokens(~is member(tokens, stopWords))
    tokens = tokens(cellfun('length',tokens)>1)
    word_list = [word_list; tokens]
    function s = porterstemmer();


}
```

3.2.1. Tokenization

In the proposed work, word tokenization performed on the proposed system means we have to tokenize particular words for the tweets. As the proposed system cut off the sentences in smaller pieces, the collection of tokens can then be identified for further processing. In word tokenization, each word is independent of the other word and thus a word polarity will not affect the polarity of other word (not considering the case of negation and n-gram approach).

The process of tokenization mainly works on the principle of division of a big problem into subproblems.

3.2.2. Removal of Numbers, Special Characters and URLs

From the datasets, the next step is the removal of the unnecessary data, which we considered irrelevant to the analysis in the proposed system. Numbers, URLs and Special Characters mainly do not have any subjectivity that is useful for SA; therefore, these elements are removed.

3.2.3. Removal of Stopwords

In this stopword removal process, the proposed system removes all the unwanted and useless words from the collection of words which we have identified in the first step (Zha et al., 2014; Pak & Paroubek, 2010; Balahur, 2013). These stopwords are mainly words which do not add meaning to a sentence or documents and are considered useless for SA purpose, for example, "both", "same", "will", "such", "up", "can", "does", "a", your etc.]. To remove stop words the proposed system has used AFINN and online English stopwords list in order to remove the stopwords.

3.2.4. Stemming

Stemming is a process to reduce the word to its stem, for example, words like play, plays and playing have the play as the stem word so the system will remove "ing", "s" to get the stem which will further simplify the data for analysis. The proposed system has stemming performed on words.

3.3. Feature Extraction

From the pre-processed data, the proposed system identifies and extracts the features sets. The feature is described as a part or attribute of an object for which the intended evaluation is to be performed. It is these feature sets that are being used to classify the data; therefore, to perform feature extraction, the proposed system makes use of the N- Gram technique. Figure 2 illustrates the "pseudocode" for feature extraction.

In this work, the proposed system has used N-gram approach for performing unigram and bigram on the pre-processed data. In the bigram approach, the proposed system divide the complete sentence in grouping of 2 words to check if there may be any change in the meaning of any of the grouped word whereas, in the unigram approach, each individual word is only taken into consideration. A tri-gram approach can also be used, but using tri-gram reduces the efficiency of the system.

3.4. Classification

The proposed system uses Term Frequency – Inverse term frequency, to make a word count matrix. In this Tf measures the frequency of the term occurrence in a document. Its formula is:

$$Tf(t) = \frac{\text{No. of times term t occurs in a document}}{\text{Total no. of terms in the document}} \tag{1}$$

Figure 2. Pseudocode for feature extraction

Procedure for feature extraction:

```
{

        // Applying N-gram Approach
        NGRAM_set = dataset('fileA', 'fileB');
        X = double (NGRAM_set(:,1:11));
        Y = double (NGRAM_set(:,12));
        Gamma = 2;


}
```

Even so, inverse document frequency (IDF) tells us about the importance of the terms as in term frequency all terms are considered equally important. Therefore, IDF scales up the rare terms and weigh down the frequent terms and it is calculated as:

$$\text{IDF}\left(t\right) = \log_e\left(\frac{\text{Total no. of documents}}{\text{No. of document with term t in it}}\right) \tag{2}$$

Now, Tf-Idf of the term is the product of its Tf and Idf weights i.e.:

$$W_{t,d} = (1 + \log tf_{t,d}) * \log_{10}(N / df_t) \tag{3}$$

Using Singular value decomposition (SVD), the proposed system decomposes the general matrix, which can be used on any m x n Matrix, and then we performed the Principal Component analysis.

The equation for singular value decomposition of X is as followed:

$$X = USV^T \tag{4}$$

Using principal component analysis (PCA), our proposed system will identify directions in which the data has the most variation; that is, the eigenvectors corresponding to the largest eigenvalues of the covariance matrix, and project the data onto these directions. The proposed system uses SVD to perform PCA. The proposed system decomposes X using SVD, i.e. $X = X = USV^T$, and finds that the covariance matrix can be written as $C = 1/n\ XX^T = 1/n\ U\ S^2\ U^T$ and then the transformed data can be presented as:

$$Y = \tilde{U}^T X = \tilde{U}^T USV^T \tag{5}$$

Equation (1) and (2) is used to calculate Tf and Idf respectively whereas Equation (3) is used to calculate Tf-Idf. Equation (4) and (5) is used to calculate SVD and PCA. The architecture of our proposed system is shown in Figure 3 while pseudocode for sentiment classification is illustrated in Figure 4.

Figure 3. Architecture of the proposed system

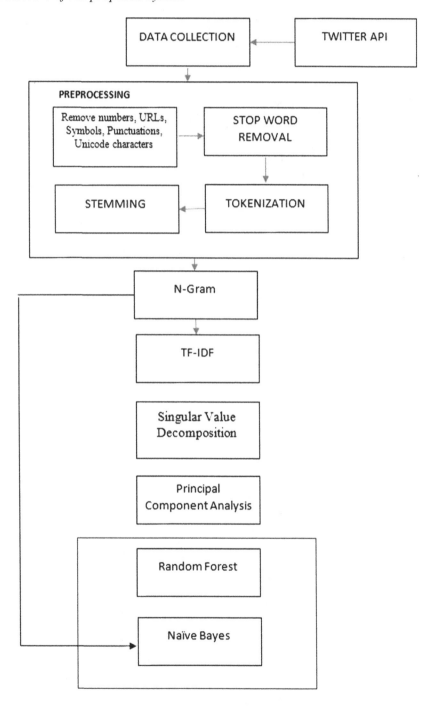

Figure 4. Pseudocode for sentiment classification

```
Procedure for Sentiment Classification (Tf-idf, svd, pca, nbrf)
{
        //create a word count matrix for document freq
                getIDF = log10( size(dict,2) ./ (bothNSR(:) + 1) );
        //Apply SVD
                [U S V] = svd(getIDF)
                U=diag(U);
        //Get the maximum eigenvalue for PCA
                maxEigval=V(:,find(U==max(U)));
        // train treebagger data
                TreeBagger_userTwt=data(nTree,dataColumn);
                TreeBagger_userTwt=diff(TreeBagger_userTwt);
        //use trained decision forest id for refined users
                id = iddata(TreeBagger_userTwt,[],1);
        //covariance matrix
                rhod=xcov(ddata,'coeff');
                rhod=rhod(nd:nd+floor(nd/2));
                nrho=length(maxEigval+rhod);
        //Create a training set
        // compute class probability
            fy(i)=sum(double(y==yu(i)))/length(y);
                switch distr
                case 'normal'
        // probability for test set
        fu=normcdf(ones(nc,1)*u(j,:),mu,sigma);
        P(j,:)=fy.*prod(fu,2)';
                case 'kernel'
        //probability of test set estimated from training set
        for i=1:nc
                for k=1:ni
                        xi=x(y==yu(i),k);
                        ui=u(:,k);
                        fuStruct(i,k).f=ksdensity(xi,ui);
        // get predicted output for test set
                [pv0,id]=max(P,[],2);
                for i=1:length(id)
                pv(i,1) = yu(id(i));
        //Use confusion matrix for accuracy
                confMat=sentimentcf(v,pv);
                conf=sum(pv==v)/length(pv);
                base=conf*gamma;
}
```

Subsequently, the proposed system has applied the Naïve Bayes (NB) and Random Forest (RF) to classify the data. NB is one of the simplest classification models, which works well for the categorization of text. NB classifier takes into assumption that the effect of a variable value on a given class is not dependent on the values of other variable in the given class - an assumption known as *class conditional independence.*

RF is one of the best in classification algorithms and can classify accurately large amount of data. It is an ensemble-learning method; specifically, a combination of tree predictors where every tree relies on the values of a random vector, which is independently sampled with the same distribution for all trees in the forest. The accuracy is calculated using the confusion matrix.

4. EXPERIMENTAL RESULTS

In this work, our proposed system has used three (3) datasets. All of these datasets are applied on the existing and the proposed work. The datasets details are as followed:

Dataset 1: A file of tweets related to the keyword 'Amazon'.
Dataset 2: A file of tweets related to the keyword 'Hachette'.
Dataset 3: A file of tweets, which is the combination of both.

In dataset one, we have collected the tweets using the keyword 'Amazon' whereas in second dataset we collected the datasets using the keyword 'Hachette'. In the third dataset, we have combined both. We have also computed the accuracy using the datasets with 100 tweets, 250 tweets and 500 tweets. We have pre-processed the data by performing tokenization, removing numbers, symbols, and URLs as well as stopwords via stopwords list. Following the successful application of both the proposed system and the existing system on the three data set, we get the following results as provided in Table 1:

Table 1. Comparing accuracy of the existing and proposed system on different datasets

Data Set Number	Data Set Size (words)	Existing System	Proposed System
		Accuracy (%)	Accuracy (%)
1	100	48.3164%	95.6292
2	250	46.1696%	92.3991
3	500	47.5996%	94.1992

Table 1 unveils that the accuracy of the proposed system is high as compared to that of the existing system. The accuracy table represents the accuracy obtained by both the proposed and the existing system on the given three datasets. The accuracy of the proposed system for the datasets with 100 tweets is 95.62% whereas the existing system only has the accuracy of 48.31%. The accuracy of the proposed system for datasets with 250 and 500 tweets each is 92.39% and 94.19% respectively whereas the accuracy of the existing system is 46.16% and 47.59% respectively.

Figures 5 and 6 represent the positive and negative sentiment scores of the datasets. In other words, however many positive and negative tweets there are in each dataset associated with different score.

Figure 5. Negative sentiment score for datasets

Figure 6. Positive sentiment score for datasets

Figure 7 represents the accuracy of the proposed system for the datasets with 100 tweets each to be 95.62% whereas in the existing system (Jianqiang et al., 2017), the accuracy is only that of 48.31%. The accuracy of the proposed system for datasets with 250 v. 500 tweets each is 92.39% and 94.19% respectively whereas the accuracy of the existing system is 46.16% and 47.59% respectively.

Figure 7. Accuracy of varying datasets of existing and proposed system

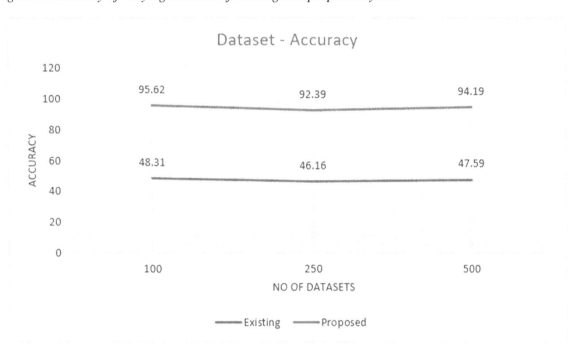

Figure 8 depicts the redundancy comparison of the base v. proposed system. In Figure 8, each dot represents the number of tweets, and the larger distance between them shows that the data is less redundant whereas the smaller distance represents data is somewhat more redundant. The output is presented in four iterations by taking 250 tweets at a time. The figure represents that in the proposed system, the redundancy of the data is very low when compared to the redundancy of the data in the existing system (Jianqiang et al., 2017).

5. CONCLUSION AND FUTURE WORK

In the existing work, applying stopwords removal on NB classifier while taking N-gram as a feature model does not affect much of the performance of the classification system. This paper has evaluated three datasets along a five-step SA process: Data Collection (Dataset), Pre-Processing of Data, Feature Selection and Extraction, Sentiment Classification, Sentiment Score Calculation and output representation.

Figure 8. Redundancy comparison of base and proposed system

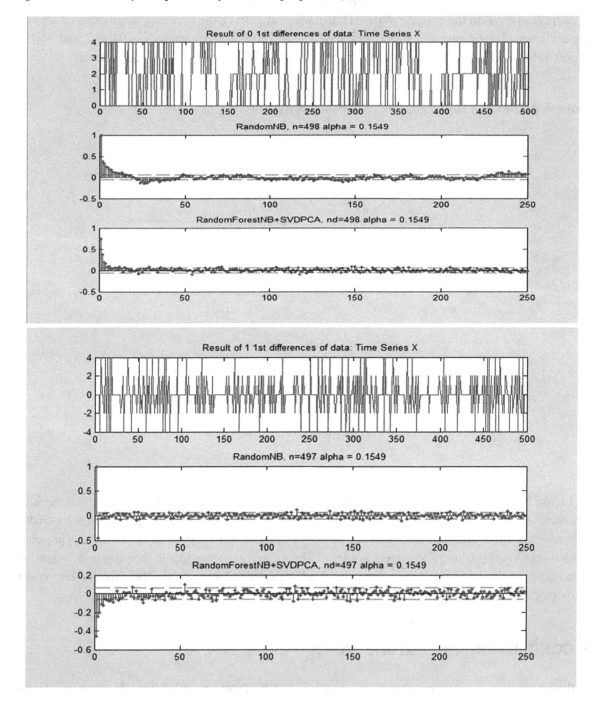

Using N-gram model as the feature model with the classification performed using PCA via SVD and using NB-RF hybrids, it is observed that accuracy is improved when compared with using NB alone on the same dataset and an N-Gram model although time efficiency may have decreased. It is argued that future work of this SA process can be effectively applied to many health informatics and information systems research domains other than publishing as illustrated by the focus on the keywords of "Amazon" v. "Hachette." For example, several recent papers have appeared in the evaluation of tweets on Zika virus and other diseases (Quadri et al., 2017; Muppalla et al., 2017). Tweets are also used for real-time analysis of health care sector to understand the various developments in health care sector (Ta, Liu, & Nkabinde, 2016). Research work is also focused on to understand the impact of social media networks on healthcare process knowledge management and Enhancing Twitter data analysis with simple semantic filtering (Fareedi & Hassan, 2014; Beykikhoshk, Arandjelovic, Phung, & Venkatesh, 2015; Nair & Ganesh, 2016). Finally, this paper can also be improved by taking larger dataset and by applying more pre-processing techniques.

REFERENCES

Pang, B., & Lee, L. (2008). Opinion mining and sentiment analysis. *Foundations and Trends in Information Retrieval*, 2(1–2), 1–135.

Saif, H., He, Y., & Alani, H. (2012, November). Semantic sentiment analysis of twitter. In *International semantic web conference* (pp. 508-524). Springer. 10.1007/978-3-642-35176-1_32

Kharde, V., & Sonawane, P. (2016). Sentiment analysis of twitter data: A survey of techniques. arXiv:1601.06971

Xia, R., Zong, C., & Li, S. (2011). Ensemble of feature sets and classification algorithms for sentiment classification. *Information Sciences*, 181(6), 1138–1152. doi:10.1016/j.ins.2010.11.023

Cambria, E., Schuller, B., Xia, Y., & Havasi, C. (2013). New avenues in opinion mining and sentiment analysis. *IEEE Intelligent Systems*, 28(2), 15–21. doi:10.1109/MIS.2013.30

Godbole, N., Srinivasaiah, M., & Skiena, S. (2007). Large-Scale Sentiment Analysis for News and Blogs. *Icwsm*, 7(21), 219–222.

Tan, C., Lee, L., Tang, J., Jiang, L., Zhou, M., & Li, P. (2011, August). User-level sentiment analysis incorporating social networks. In *Proceedings of the 17th ACM SIGKDD international conference on Knowledge discovery and data mining* (pp. 1397-1405). ACM.

Balahur, A., & Jacquet, G. (2015). Sentiment analysis meets social media–Challenges and solutions of the field in view of the current information sharing context.

Kumar, S., Morstatter, F., & Liu, H. (2014). *Twitter data analytics* (pp. 1041–4347). New York: Springer. doi:10.1007/978-1-4614-9372-3

Isah, H., Trundle, P., & Neagu, D. (2014, September). Social media analysis for product safety using text mining and sentiment analysis. In *2014 14th UK Workshop on Computational Intelligence (UKCI)* (pp. 1-7). IEEE. 10.1109/UKCI.2014.6930158

Jiang, S., & Kotzias, D. (2016). Assessing the Use of Social Media in Massive Open Online Courses. arXiv:1608.05668

West, R., Paskov, H. S., Leskovec, J., & Potts, C. (2014). Exploiting social network structure for person-to-person sentiment analysis. arXiv:1409.2450

Cogburn, D. L., & Espinoza-Vasquez, F. K. (2011). From networked nominee to networked nation: Examining the impact of Web 2.0 and social media on political participation and civic engagement in the 2008 Obama campaign. *Journal of Political Marketing, 10*(1-2), 189–213. doi:10.1080/15377857 .2011.540224

Gamallo, P., & Garcia, M. A Naive-Bayes Strategy for Sentiment Analysis on English Tweets. In *Proceedings of the 8th International Workshop on Semantic Evaluation, SemEval.* 10.3115/v1/S14-2026

Karlgren, J., & Ericsson, L. (2013). Semantic Space Models for Profiling Reputation of Corporate Entities. In CLEF 2013 Conference and Labs of the Evaluation Forum Information Access Evaluation meets Multilinguality, Multimodality, and Visualization, Valencia, Spain, September 23-26. CLEF.

Recupero, D. R., & Cambria, E. (2014, May). Eswc'14 challenge on concept-level sentiment analysis. In *Semantic Web Evaluation Challenge* (pp. 3–20). Cham: Springer.

Irsoy, O., & Cardie, C. (2014). Opinion mining with deep recurrent neural networks. In *Proceedings of the 2014 conference on empirical methods in natural language processing (EMNLP)* (pp. 720-728). 10.3115/v1/D14-1080

Vijendra, S., & Laxman, S. (2013). Subspace clustering of high-dimensional data: An evolutionary approach. *Applied Computational Intelligence and Soft Computing, 2013*, 16. doi:10.1155/2013/863146

Vijendra, S., Sahoo, L., & Ashwini, K. (2010, February). An effective clustering algorithm for data mining. In *2010 International Conference on Data Storage and Data Engineering (DSDE)* (pp. 250-253). IEEE. 10.1109/DSDE.2010.34

Feldman, R. (2013). Techniques and applications for sentiment analysis. *Communications of the ACM, 56*(4), 82–89. doi:10.1145/2436256.2436274

Vinodhini, G., & Chandrasekaran, R. M. (2012). Sentiment analysis and opinion mining: A survey. *International Journal (Toronto, Ont.), 2*(6), 282–292.

Vijendra, S., & Laxman, S. (2015). Symmetry based automatic evolution of clusters: A new approach to data clustering. *Computational Intelligence and Neuroscience, 2015*, 13. doi:10.1155/2015/796276 PMID:26339233

Kouloumpis, E., Wilson, T., & Moore, J. D. (2011). Twitter sentiment analysis: The good the bad and the omg! *ICWSM, 11*(538-541), 164.

Bollegala, D., Weir, D., & Carroll, J. (2013). Cross-domain sentiment classification using a sentiment sensitive thesaurus. *IEEE Transactions on Knowledge and Data Engineering, 25*(8), 1719–1731. doi:10.1109/TKDE.2012.103

Zha, Z. J., Yu, J., Tang, J., Wang, M., & Chua, T. S. (2014). Product aspect ranking and its applications. *IEEE Transactions on Knowledge and Data Engineering, 26*(5), 1211–1224. doi:10.1109/TKDE.2013.136

Bahrainian, S. A., & Dengel, A. (2013, December). Sentiment analysis and summarization of twitter data. In *2013 IEEE 16th International Conference on Computational Science and Engineering (CSE)* (pp. 227-234). IEEE. 10.1109/CSE.2013.44

Dhande, L. L., & Patnaik, G. K. (2014). Analyzing sentiment of movie review data using Naive Bayes neural classifier. *International Journal of Emerging Trends & Technology in Computer Science*, *3*(4), 313–320.

Preety, S. D., & Dahiya, S. (2015). Sentiment Analysis using svm and naive bayes algorithm. *International Journal of Computer Science and Mobile Computing*, *4*(9), 212–219.

Dey, L., Chakraborty, S., Biswas, A., Bose, B., & Tiwari, S. (2016). Sentiment Analysis of Review Datasets Using Naive Bayes and K-NN Classifier. arXiv:1610.09982

Sharma, P., & Mishra, N. (2016, October). Feature level sentiment analysis on movie reviews. In *2016 2nd International Conference on Next Generation Computing Technologies (NGCT)* (pp. 306-311). IEEE. 10.1109/NGCT.2016.7877432

Mirani, T. B., & Sasi, S. (2016, December). Sentiment Analysis of ISIS Related Tweets Using Absolute Location. In *2016 International Conference on Computational Science and Computational Intelligence (CSCI)* (pp. 1140-1145). IEEE. 10.1109/CSCI.2016.0216

Hiai, S., & Shimada, K. (2016, July). A Sarcasm Extraction Method Based on Patterns of Evaluation Expressions. In *2016 5th IIAI International Congress on Advanced Applied Informatics (IIAI-AAI)* (pp. 31-36). IEEE. 10.1109/IIAI-AAI.2016.198

Jianqiang, Z., & Xiaolin, G. (2017). Comparison Research on Text Pre-processing Methods on Twitter Sentiment Analysis. *IEEE Access: Practical Innovations, Open Solutions*, *5*, 2870–2879. doi:10.1109/ACCESS.2017.2672677

Bharti, S. K., Vachha, B., Pradhan, R. K., Babu, K. S., & Jena, S. K. (2016). Sarcastic sentiment detection in tweets streamed in real time: A big data approach. *Digital Communications and Networks*, *2*(3), 108–121. doi:10.1016/j.dcan.2016.06.002

Ficamos, P., Liu, Y., & Chen, W. (2017, February). A Naive Bayes and Maximum Entropy approach to sentiment analysis: Capturing domain-specific data in Weibo. In *2017 IEEE International Conference on Big Data and Smart Computing (BigComp)* (pp. 336-339). IEEE.

Nozza, D., Maccagnola, D., Guigue, V., Messina, E., & Gallinari, P. (2014, September). A latent representation model for sentiment analysis in heterogeneous social networks. In *International Conference on Software Engineering and Formal Methods* (pp. 201-213). Springer, Cham.

Liu, B. (2012). *Sentiment analysis and opinion mining, synthesis lectures on human language technologies Morgan & Claypool published*. Google Scholar.

Pak, A., & Paroubek, P. (2010, July). Twitter based system: Using Twitter for disambiguating sentiment ambiguous adjectives. In *Proceedings of the 5th International Workshop on Semantic Evaluation* (pp. 436-439). Association for Computational Linguistics.

Balahur, A. (2013, June). Sentiment analysis in social media texts. In *4th workshop on Computational Approaches to Subjectivity, Sentiment and Social Media Analysis* (pp. 120-128).

Quadri, S. M., Prashanth, T. K., Pongpaichet, S., Esmin, A. A., & Jain, R. (2017, August). TargetZIKA: Epidemic situation detection and risk preparedness for ZIKA virus. In *2017 10th International Conference on Ubi-media Computing and Workshops (Ubi-Media)* (pp. 1-6). IEEE.

Muppalla, R., Miller, M., Banerjee, T., & Romine, W. (2017, July). Discovering explanatory models to identify relevant tweets on Zika. In *2017 39th Annual International Conference of the Engineering in Medicine and Biology Society (EMBC)* (pp. 1194-1197). IEEE. 10.1109/EMBC.2017.8037044

Ta, V. D., Liu, C. M., & Nkabinde, G. W. (2016, July). Big data stream computing in healthcare real-time analytics. In *2016 IEEE International Conference on Cloud Computing and Big Data Analysis (ICCCBDA)* (pp. 37-42). IEEE.

Fareedi, A. A., & Hassan, S. (2014, October). The impact of social media networks on healthcare process knowledge management (using of semantic web platforms). In *2014 14th International Conference on Control, Automation and Systems (ICCAS)* (pp. 1514-1519). IEEE.

Beykikhoshk, A., Arandjelović, O., Phung, D., & Venkatesh, S. (2015, August). Overcoming data scarcity of Twitter: using tweets as bootstrap with application to autism-related topic content analysis. In *2015 IEEE/ACM International Conference on Advances in Social Networks Analysis and Mining (ASONAM)* (pp. 1354-1361). IEEE. 10.1145/2808797.2808908

Nair, S. S. K., & Ganesh, N. (2016, March). An exploratory study on big data processing: A case study from a biomedical informatics. In *2016 3rd MEC International Conference on Big Data and Smart City (ICBDSC)* (pp. 1-4). IEEE. 10.1109/ICBDSC.2016.7460338

Doan, S., Ohno-Machado, L., & Collier, N. (2012, September). Enhancing Twitter data analysis with simple semantic filtering: Example in tracking influenza-like illnesses. In *2012 IEEE Second International Conference on Healthcare Informatics, Imaging and Systems Biology (HISB)* (pp. 62-71). IEEE.

This research was previously published in the International Journal of Healthcare Information Systems and Informatics (IJHISI), 14(2); pages 1-16, copyright year 2019 by IGI Publishing (an imprint of IGI Global).

Chapter 102
A Sentiment Analysis of the 2014–15 Ebola Outbreak in the Media and Social Media

Blooma John
https://orcid.org/0000-0001-6725-6025
University of Canberra, Australia

Bob Baulch
International Food Policy Research Institute, Malawi

Nilmini Wickramasinghe
https://orcid.org/0000-0002-1314-8843
Swinburne University of Technology, Australia & Epworth HealthCare, Australia

ABSTRACT

The negative and unbalanced nature of media and social media coverage has amplified anxieties and fears about the Ebola outbreak. The authors analyse news articles on the Ebola outbreak from two leading news outlets, together with comments on the articles from a well-known social media platform, from March 2014 to July 2015. The volume of news articles was greatest between August 2014 and January 2015, with a spike in October 2014, and was driven by the few cases of transmission in Europe and the USA. Sentiment analysis reveals coverage and commentary on the small number of Ebola cases in Europe and the USA were much more extensive than coverage and commentary on the outbreak in West Africa. Articles expressing negative sentiments were more common in the USA and also received more comments than those expressing positive sentiments. The negative sentiments expressed in the media and social media amplified fears about an Ebola outbreak outside West Africa, which increased pressure for unwarranted and wasteful precautionary measures.

DOI: 10.4018/978-1-6684-6303-1.ch102

INTRODUCTION

The Ebola outbreak in West Africa began in late 2013, and was declared as an international public health emergency by the World Health Organization (WHO) on 8th August 2014 (WHO 2014). A total of 28,616 cases of Ebola virus disease (EVD) and 11,310 deaths were reported in Guinea, Liberia, and Sierra Leone (WHO, 2016). There were an additional 36 cases and 15 deaths that occurred when the outbreak spread outside of these three countries that include Italy, Mali, Nigeria, Senegal, Spain, United Kingdom and United States. By 7th October 2015, the WHO reported its first week with any new Ebola cases, and on 26 March 2016, it lifted the Public Health Emergencies of International Concern (PHEIC) status of West Africa.

In the 2014 – 2015 outbreak, coverage of Ebola was extensive in the media and social media but was also narrow, negative, and unbalanced (Funge et al., 2014). As mentioned in a Lancet editorial of November 2014, a "disproportionate airtime has been given to the nine confirmed American cases of Ebola compared with the massive human crisis unfolding in Liberia, Guinea, and Sierra Leone" (Lancet, 2014, pg 1). While Europe and the USA demonstrated preparedness by identifying cases, isolating them, treating and quarantining contacts, media coverage of the outbreak created a parallel epidemic of fear and fueled demand for additional, ineffective and unnecessary precautionary measures (Mira et al., 2015). These measures included temperature screening at airports, the cancellation of flights to West Africa, and the isolation and quarantining of asymptomatic health workers and other returning from the region (Mello et al., 2005).

However, evidence is missing on the role played by the social media in molding public perceptions about the risks of Ebola. The research problem addressed in this study is to determine how the attitudes of writers of news articles and comments on the Ebola outbreak influenced public perceptions towards it in Europe and America, thereby amplifying fears about an Ebola outbreak in the West. This paper employs sentiment analysis (Deng et al., 2018; Lak et al., 2017), a textual analysis method originating in the computational linguistics and natural language processing literature, to determine the attitudes of writers of news articles and comments toward the Ebola outbreak. We applied design science steps to plot and present the findings from the sentiment analysis based on the six activities of design science research (Baskerville et al., 2018). Thus, to analyse the research question, we collected coverage on the Ebola outbreak from two leading news services on either side of the Atlantic (the British Broadcasting Corporation (BBC) and the US-based Cable Network News (CNN), together with follow-up comments from a well-known social media platform (Reddit), and conducted an in-depth sentiment analysis. Our findings suggest that the negative and unbalanced nature of news coverage in Europe and the USA amplified public anxieties and fears about the Ebola outbreak outside West Africa.

Literature Review

From the start of Ebola in August 2014 till to its official end in March 2016, most studies focused on how to handle Ebola (Kruk, 2015; Gostin, 2015). The loss of life, social disruption, and failure of health-care systems demonstrate what happens when a crisis like Ebola hits the world (Peterson, 2015; Asamoah at al., 2015). Ebola is covered as an emerging social issue often led to rumors breeding and propagation in social media in various parts of the world (Ye et al., 2018). Guah (2017) presents the resilience during Liberia's Ebola epidemic while, Ding et al., (2016) investigates people's online prosocial microlending decision making after a natural disaster like Ebola in Africa. Chung et al., (2015) visualized Ebola outbreak discussions on Twitter by presenting an approach to social-media-based public health informatics by using 255,118 tweets posted by 210,900 users in January 2015. The Western media's coverage of the Ebola outbreak in West Africa in mid-2014 has been compared to their response to avian influenza, H1N1, SARS, and even the early years of the HIV-AIDS pandemic (Honigsbaum, 2017). Another study analyzed 2,276 unique tweets about Ebola in twitter and showed the use design science methodology that provides direct guidelines for better understanding the problem (Chatterjee et al., 2017).

Sentiment analysis is an area that is active in the field of information systems, computer science and media studies (Deng et al., 2018; Lak et al., 2017). Media and social media plays an important role in sentiment analysis of the content shared specially, due to the recent growth of social media platforms through numerous blogs, microblogs, forums, and social networks (Riloff et al., 2003; Yu & Hatzivassiloglou 2003). Sentiment analysis are important tools used today for understanding large amounts of social media data (Abbasi et al. 2008; Mohammad et al. 2013). Social media are increasingly important information sources for understanding public sentiments by identifying opinion leaders in discussion forums (Song et al. 2007) and visualizing networked relationships of infectious disease transmission. However, very little work is found in analyzing emotion to support public health policy decision making in situation like Ebola in Africa.

Design science is a new research paradigm in information systems (Gregor & Hevner, 2013). Design science is used to solve an identified problem by building socio-technical artefacts (Myers & Venable, 2014). Seven guidelines presented by Hevner et al. (2004) originated from information-systems design theory originally proposed by Walls et al. (1992). The six steps proposed by Peffers et al. (2007) are problem identification and motivation, definition of the objectives for a solution, design and development, demonstration, evaluation, and communication. The design science theory as a methodology needs to be incorporating these steps. There is also a need to give a minimal procedure and a mental model for offering and assessing the design science research (Peffers et al., 2007). As we propose sentiment analysis, the design science theory provides a groundwork for thoroughly specifying its design. Thus, this paper presents an instantiation of solving the problem of sentiment analysis of media and social media by developing a computational model for sentimental analysis. This is a classic example of computational genre of design science research (Rai, 2017).

Data and Methodology

To identify news coverage on Ebola outbreak, we used two leading news services, the BCC and CNN. This selection was based on Alexa's rankings of the top 15 news sites, in which BBC and CNN scored the top global ranks among reputable news outlets. We then downloaded all news headlines in 2014 and the first half of 2015 from these news services with the search term 'Ebola'. For BBC, we filtered to 'News' and for CNN, we filtered to 'Story and article' in English. This resulted in 889 unique news headlines from BBC and 486 unique news headlines from CNN.

To capture the perceptions and the sentiments generated in the social media by the news articles, we collected comments from Reddit.com. Reddit is the top news social media ranked by Alexa where registered members can submit content such as text posts or direct links. Reddit comments are the follow up discussions to news articles posted by users. We located 502 articles with the word 'Ebola' in the title that has been shared and discussed in Reddit, of which 276 were BBC articles and 226 from CNN. A total of 26,948 comments were made on these 502 articles.

Sentiment analysis involves calculating polarity scores—which show whether the opinions expressed in the text are positive, negative or neutral—for pieces of text (such as sentences or paragraphs) using an algorithm and sentiment dictionary (Pang & Lilian, 2005; Liu, 2015) This article employs the widely used R package qdap to code the algorithm for analyzing the sentiments of the articles together with the sentiment dictionary developed by Hu and Liu, 2004. Polarizing words, such as 'contagious' or 'epidemic' (negative) or 'recovery' and 'treatment' (positive), are identified in each sentence.

The cluster of neighboring words is then examined to see how valence shifters (such as 'highly',' partially', or 'never') act as amplifiers, deamplifier or negators of the polarized words. By identifying positive or negative words and weighting using the neighboring valence shifters, a polarity score between minus one and plus one is assigned to each sentence. For example, the sentence, 'If I contracted Ebola, I'd definitely kill myself.' has two negative words ('contracted' and 'kill'), one valence shifter ('definitely') and results in a polarity score of -0·458. In contrast the sentence, "This is good news for getting an effective vaccine for Ebola." has three positive words ('good', effective' and 'vaccine') and a polarity score of +0·424. The polarity scores assigned to each sentence are then summed and averaged over the number of sentences to give a total polarity score for the article or comment. Table 1 gives a list of the top twenty articles about Ebola based on the number of social media comments.

To identify news coverage on Ebola outbreak, we used two leading news services, the BCC and CNN. This selection was based on Alexa's rankings of the top 15 news sites, in which BBC and CNN scored the top global ranks among reputable news outlets. We then downloaded all news headlines in 2014 and the first half of 2015 from these news services with the search term 'Ebola'. For BBC, we filtered to 'News' and for CNN, we filtered to 'Story and article' in English. This resulted in 889 unique news headlines from BBC and 486 unique news headlines from CNN.

To capture the social media's perceptions and the sentiments generated by the news articles, we collected comments from Reddit.com. Reddit is the top news social media ranked by Alexa where registered members can submit content such as text posts or direct links. Reddit comments are the follow up discussions to news articles posted by users. We located 502 articles with the word 'Ebola' in the title that has been shared and discussed in Reddit, of which 276 were BBC articles and 226 from CNN. A total of 26,948 comments were made on these 502 articles.

We applied design science to plot and present the findings from the sentiment analysis based on the six activities of design science research as detailed by Peffers et al. (2007). These are:

- Problem identification and motivation: The problem identified in this paper is to determine how the attitudes of writers of news articles and comments on the Ebola outbreak influenced public perceptions towards it in Europe and America, thereby amplifying fears about an Ebola outbreak in the West. The problem identified will help in understanding the linkage between the digital artefact designed for conducting sentiment analysis by embracing design thinking practices.
- Define the objective of a solution: Developing sentiment analysis and applying to the data collected from various news and social media defines the objective of the solution that result in a viable artefact.
- Design and Development: The designed artefact in this paper is an instantiation of sentiment analysis as evidenced in the figure 2 and 3.
- Evaluation: We evaluated the artefact based on data collected from BBC, CNN and Reddit.com. The evaluation demonstrated clear evidence of improved precision of sentiment analysis.

- Communication: We published the findings and its applicability on media and social media. This study can be extended to apply and evaluate the sentiments of other types of content in social media, like tweets and comments in social media.

Table 1: List of top twenty articles (2014 – 2015) about Ebola based on number of social media comments

Headline	Source	Date	Total Article Polarity Score	Number of Comments
A 2nd American has now tested positive for Ebola	CNN	27/07/2014	-0·17893	2356
People actively resisting Ebola Treatment	BBC	28/07/2014	-0·74212	213
Liberia closes borders. Trying to stop spread of the Ebola Virus	BBC	28/07/2014	-0·89686	425
Ebola 'spreading too fast' – WHO	BBC	1/08/2014	-0·75898	1426
Ebola is declared an international health emergency	BBC	8/08/2014	-1·22527	1249
A Spanish missionary who contracted the Ebola virus while working in West Africa has died in hospital in Madrid	BBC	12/08/2014	-1·45326	561
Blood-stained bedding looted from Ebola quarantine centre	BBC	17/08/2014	-3·05078	929
Ebola Doctor to be released from Atlanta hospital after tests show he has recovered	CNN	21/08/2014	1·756349	192
Ebola outbreak "threatens Liberia's national existence"	BBC	10/09/2014	-4·02918	171
Ebola Patients Buying Survivors' Blood from Black Market, WHO Warns	CNN	20/09/2014	-2·16222	377
Woman saves three relatives from Ebola. Her protection method is being taught to others in West Africa	CNN	29/09/2014	-0·27185	471
Ebola outbreak: '80 monitored' in Dallas, Texas	BBC	2/10/2014	-1·12334	341
Four People Still Living Inside Apartment of U.S. Ebola Patient	CNN	3/10/2014	0·960795	222
Nurse 'infected with Ebola' in Spain	BBC	6/10/2014	-2·46897	2548
Texas healthcare worker tests positive for Ebola	CNN	12/10/2014	-4·37207	4323
The Ebola epidemic threatens the "very survival" of societies and could lead to failed states	BBC	13/10/2014	-1·69021	165
Ebola cases now over 8900, death toll rises to 4,447, says WHO	BBC	14/10/2014	-1·25622	326
Spanish nurse who became first person to contract Ebola outside Africa tests negative for the virus	BBC	19/10/2014	-1·13586	164
Patient in NYC Tests Positive for Ebola	CNN	24/10/2014	-2·40009	5830
Quarantined nurse who tested negative twice for Ebola said that her human rights were violated	CNN	26/10/2014	0·30013	456

RESULTS

Figure 1 plots the number of news articles on Ebola on a fortnightly basis between January 2014 and July 2015. In the four months following the WHO's declaration of the Ebola outbreak in Guinea (23rd March 2014), there were just 47 articles published by the BBC and 32 articles published by the CNN. However, once an American doctor with Ebola virus diseases arrived in the USA and was confined in isolation at

Atlanta (2nd August 2014), news coverage of Ebola increased more than tenfold. News coverage then spiked in October, when healthcare workers in Madrid and Dallas tested positive for Ebola, and a doctor was diagnosed with Ebola in New York. With no further cases recorded in Europe and the US, and declining rates of infection and improved survivals rates in West Africa, subsequent news coverage of Ebola was less extensive. However, a confirmed Ebola case in Glasgow led to a sudden increase in the number of BBC, though not CNN, articles in late December and mid-January. The declaration of end of the Ebola outbreak in April 2015 and a few new Ebola cases in Liberia in June/July 2015 generated very little news coverage.

Thus, Figure 1 provides strong evidence of a news 'bubble' generated by the four confirmed American and two confirmed European cases of Ebola in third and fourth quarters of 2014. This is the same period during which an 'epidemic of fear' concerning Ebola occurred in the USA, which led to the quarantining of asymptomatic health workers and travelers in at least eight US states plus the District of Colombia (Gonsalves et al., 2014). At this time, several European countries (including Belgium, France and the United Kingdom), introduced airport screening of travelers arriving from West Africa, despite disagreements among European Union health ministers about the need for such measures. An opinion poll in November 2014 revealed that the American public ranked Ebola as the third most urgent health problem in the country, after cost and access and above cancer and heart-diseases.

The sentiment analysis was performed on a total of 14,327 comments for 502 articles during the period of intense media interest concerning Ebola that occurred between July and November 2014. The sentiment analysis illustrates the flow of sentiments demonstrated by users in Reddit, with the average total polarity of the comments posted, reported on a daily basis. The average polarity score (-0·118) of the 6,403 comments on CNN articles were more negative than the average polarity score (-0·088) of the 7,924 comments on BBC articles. Social media sentiment started out as highly negative and remained negative, with an average score of -0·1 until October but started to neutralize during November based on the recovery of healthcare workers in the US and Europe and the news of declining rates of infection in Guinea and Liberia. However, as can be seen from the analysis that, there was a wide variation in the average polarity scores on the daily comments, with 83% of days attracting negative comments on average.

Figure 1. Number of BBC and CNN news articles concerning Ebola, 2014-15

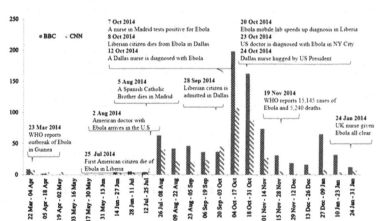

To understand the relationship between the sentiments of the articles in the media and related discussion by the community in the social media, we selected the 20 articles with the highest number of social media comments. Table 1 gives the list of twenty articles sorted according to the chronological order. Among the twenty articles, twelve articles are from BBC and eight articles are from CNN. It is interesting to note that the article on "Patient in NYC tests positive for Ebola" (24th October 2014) received the highest number of comments (5830 comments), followed by "Texas healthcare worker tests positive for Ebola" (12th October 2014) with 4323 comments, and "Nurse infected with Ebola in Spain" (6th October 2014) with 2548 comments. It should be noted that articles with positive polarity are both rarer (3 articles among the top 20 articles) and attracted fewer comments (an average of 290 comments for positive articles compared to 1215 comments for negative articles).

Articles with the most negative or positive polarity scores did not receive the most comments. The article with the lowest negative polarity score is "Texas healthcare worker tests positive for Ebola" (CNN, 12th October 2014) which is the second most commented article with 4,323 comments. However, the article with the second most negative polarity score is "Ebola outbreak threatens Liberia's national existence" (BBC, 10th September 2014), and received just 171 comments and is one of the least commented articles among the top 20 articles. The two articles with the highest positive polarity scores are "Ebola Doctor to be released from Atlanta hospital (CNN, 21st August 2014) and "Four people still living inside apartment of U.S. Ebola patient" (CNN, 3rd October 2014). Both these articles received less than 225 comments.

Articles on the small number of Ebola cases in Europe and the USA received far more comments, and comments of a more negative nature, than those on the Ebola outbreak in West Africa. The ten top articles on Ebola in Europe and the USA received a total of 16,993 comments while the ten articles on the Ebola in West Africa received a total of 5,753 comments. Furthermore, the total polarity of all comments on the European and US articles was - 785·1 compared to -383·8 for comments on the outbreak in West Africa. This suggests it was fears of an Ebola outbreak outside Africa, in particular news that healthcare workers in Europe and the USA had contracted the disease, which drove the wave of negative sentiments in the Western social media.

Figure 2: Polarity scores of articles and their comments

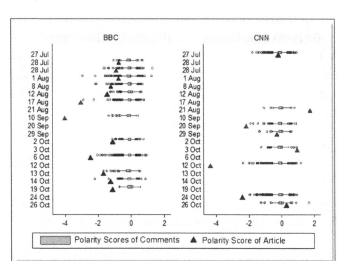

Figure 2 compares the polarity scores of the original news articles and the social media comments they generated. The triangles show the polarity scores of the original articles. The box plots show the interquartile range, outer quartiles and outliers for the polarity scores of the comments on each news article. There is very low correlation between the polarity scores of the article and comments ($\rho < 0.06$) with a slightly higher correlation found for the comments on CNN articles. It is interesting to note that the polarity of the comments on BBC articles were generally more positive than those for the original articles, while those for CNN articles were more one-sided. This may indicate a more optimistic and independent stance among commentators of the BBC articles. The BBC articles were also generally reporting on different events than the CNN's and contained more detailed coverage of the situation in West Africa. Figure 3 gives the sentiments of the comments for the top 20 most commented articles. It is evident that the comments were negative.

CONCLUSION

In this paper, we have conducted a sentiment analysis of BBC and CNN news articles and social media comments during the Ebola outbreak in West Africa from 2014-15. By using a sentiment analysis combined with a design science approach, we show that the volume of news articles and comments peaked between August 2014 and January 2015, with a marked spike in October 2014. Both news articles and comments were heavily biased towards the few cases of Ebola transmission in Europe and the USA (Peterson, 2015). While there was a wide variation of polarity scores of comments on these articles, more than four-fifths were dominated by negative comments. This is similar to the Western Media's response to avian influenza, H1N1, SARS, and even the early years of the HIV-AIDS pandemic (Honigsbaum, 2017). Articles expressing positive sentiments about Ebola received substantially fewer comments than articles expressing negative sentiments, with the commentary on BBC news articles being generally more positive than those on CNN articles.

Thus, largely unwarranted public fears about an Ebola outbreak outside West Africa appear to have been amplified by negative sentiments in the media and social media, especially in the United States. In the absence of prompt and effective communication by public health agencies, this led to a series of unwarranted and wasteful preventative measures being implemented at the state and national levels. To add on, as reported on 7th April 2019, in the recent outbreak, the number of Ebola virus disease (EVD) cases in the North Kivu provinces of the Democratic Republic of the Congo is 1156 cases and 731 deaths (WHO, 2019). However, the recent outbreak is well handled when compared to the earlier outbreak. As part of future work, there is a need to examine the second Ebola outbreak in the Democratic Republic of the Congo, in media and in social media and how the lessons learnt from 2014-2015 Ebola outbreak improved the situation.

REFERENCES

Abbasi, A., Chen, H., Thoms, S., & Fu, T. (2008). Affect analysis of web forums and blogs using correlation ensembles. *IEEE Transactions on Knowledge and Data Engineering, 20*(9), 1168-1180.

Asamoah, D., Sharda, R., & Thandapani Kumarasamy, A. (2015). Can Social Media Support Public Health? Demonstrating Disease Surveillance using Big Data Analytics. *Proceedings of the Twenty-first Americas Conference on Information Systems.*

Baskerville, R., Baiyere, A., Gregor, S., Hevner, A., & Rossi, M. (2018). Design science research contributions: finding a balance between artifact and theory. *Journal of the Association for Information Systems, 19*(5), 358-376.

Chatterjee, S., Deng, S., & Liu, J. (2017). Improving Opinion Mining by Classifying Facts and Opinions in Twitter. *Proceedings of the American Conference on Information Systems,* 2017

Chung, W., He, S., & Zeng, D. (2015). emood: Modeling emotion for social media analytics on Ebola disease outbreak. *Proceedings of the International Conference on Information Systems.*

Dempsey, L. A. (2018). *Targeting Ebola.* Nature Microbiology.

Deng, S., Huang, Z., Sinha, AP, & Zhao, H. (2018). The Interaction Between Microblog Sentiment and Stock Returns: An Empirical Examination. *MIS Quarterly, 42*(3), 895-918.

Ding, Y., Xu, H., Yang, L., & Tan, B. C. (2016). Online Prosocial Microlending Decision Making: A Natural Experiment of Ebola Outbreak. *Proceedings of the International Conference on Information Systems.*

Funge, I., Zion, T., Chi-Ngai, C., Adriana, S., & King-Wa, F. (2014). Ebola and the social media. *Lancet, 384,* 207.

Gonsalves, G., & Staley, P. (2014, December). Panic, Paranoia, and Public Health— The AIDS Epidemic's Lessons for Ebola. *The New England Journal of Medicine, 371*(25), 2348–2349. doi:10.1056/NEJMp1413425 PMID:25372947

Gostin, L.O., & Friedman, E.A. (2015). A retrospective and prospective analysis of the west African Ebola virus disease epidemic: robust national health systems at the foundation and an empowered WHO at the apex. *Lancet, 385*(9980), 1902-1909.

Gregor, S., & Hevner, A. R. (2013). Positioning and presenting design science research for maximum impact. *Management Information Systems Quarterly, 37*(2), 337–355. doi:10.25300/MISQ/2013/37.2.01

Guah, M. W. (2017). Resilience in the Gaze of Ebola: Analysis from a Developing Country. *Proceedings of the 50th Hawaii International Conference on System Sciences.* 10.24251/HICSS.2017.304

Hevner, A., March, S.T., Park, J., & Ram, S. (2004). Design science research in information systems. *MIS Quarterly, 28*(1), 75-105.

Honigsbaum, M. (2017). Between securitisation and neglect: managing Ebola at the borders of global health. *Medical History, 61*(2), 270-294.

Hu, M., & Liu. (2004). *Mining and summarizing customer reviews.* Paper presented at the ACM SIGKDD International Conference on Knowledge Discovery and Data Mining, Seattle, WA.

Kruk, M.E., Myers, M., Varpilah, S.T., & Dahn, B.T. (2015). What is a resilient health system? Lessons from Ebola. *Lancet, 385*(9980), 1910-1912.

Lak, P., & Turetken, O. (2017). The Impact of Sentiment Analysis Output on Decision Outcomes: An Empirical Evaluation. *AIS Transactions on Human-Computer Interaction, 1*(9), 1–22. doi:10.17705/1thci.00086

Liu, B. (2015). Sentiment analysis and subjectivity. In N. Indurkhya & F. Dameraua (Eds.), *Handbook of Natural Language Processing* (2nd ed.; pp. 627–666). Boca Raton, FL: CRC.

Mello, M., Merritt, M., & Halpern, S. (2015). Supporting those who go to fight Ebola. *PLOS Medicine, 12*(1).

Mira, J.J., Susana, L., María, T.G., Jesús, A., & Carlos, A. (2015). Ebola's media outbreak: lessons for the future. *European Journal of Public Health, 25*(2), 188-189.

Mohammad, S. M., Kiritchenko, S., & Zhu, X. (2013). NRC-Canada: Building the state-of-the-art in sentiment analysis of tweets. *Proceedings of the seventh international workshop on Semantic Evaluation Exercises.*

Myers, M.D., & Venable, J.R. (2014). A set of ethical principles for design science research in information systems. *Information & Management, 51*(6), 801-809.

Pang, B., & Lilian, L. (2005). Seeing stars: Exploring class relationships for sentiment categorization with respect to rating scales. *Proceedings of the Association for Computational Lingustics, 2005*, 417–424.

Peffers, K., Tuunanen, T., Rothenberger, M.A., & Chatterjee, S. (2007). A design science research methodology for information systems research. *Journal of Management Information Systems, 24*(3), 45-77.

Peterson, A. T. (2015). Good and bad news about Ebola. *PLoS Neglected Tropical Diseases, 9*(3), e0003509. doi:10.1371/journal.pntd.0003509 PMID:25764305

Rai, A. (2017). Editor's comments: Diversity of Design Science Research. *Management Information Systems Quarterly, 41*, 1.

Riloff, E., Wiebe, J., & Wilson, T. (2003). Learning Subjective Nouns Using Extraction Pattern Bootstrapping. in *Proceedings of the seventh conference on Natural language learning at HLTNAACL 2003*. Association for Computational Linguistics. 10.3115/1119176.1119180

Song, X., Chi, Y., Hino, K., & Tseng, B. (2007, November). Identifying opinion leaders in the blogosphere. In *Proceedings of the sixteenth ACM conference on Conference on information and knowledge management* (pp. 971-974). ACM.

The medium and the message of Ebola. (2014). *Lancet, 2014*, 384–9955.

Timen, A., Sprenger, M., Edelstein, M., Martin-Moreno, J., & McKee, M. (2015). The Ebola crisis: Perspectives from European Public Health. *European Journal of Public Health, 25*(2), 187–188. doi:10.1093/eurpub/cku236 PMID:25583039

Walls, J.G., Widmeyer, G.R., & El Sawy, O.A. (1992). Building an information system design theory for vigilant EIS. *Information Systems Research, 3*(1), 36-59.

WHO. (2014). *Statement on the meeting of the international health regulations emergency committee regarding the 2014 Ebola outbreak in West Africa*. Geneva: World Health Organization. Retrieved from http://www.who.int/mediacentre/news/statements/2014/ebola-20140808/en/

WHO. (2016b). *Ebola data and statistics – 11 May 2016.* Retrieved from http://apps.who.int/gho/data/node.ebola-sitrep.quick-downloads?lang=en

WHO. (2019). *Ebola situation report - 24 April 2019.* Retrieved from https://www.who.int/ebola/situation-reports/drc-2018/en/

Ye, X., Li, S., Yang, X., Lee, J., & Wu, L. (2018). The fear of Ebola: A tale of two cities in China. In *Big data support of urban planning and management* (pp. 113–132). Cham: Springer. doi:10.1007/978-3-319-51929-6_7

Yu, H., & Hatzivassiloglou, V. (2003). Towards answering opinion questions: Separating facts from opinions and identifying the polarity of opinion sentences. In *Proceedings of the 2003 conference on Empirical methods in natural language processing.* Association for Computational Linguistics. 10.3115/1119355.1119372

Index

A

Acronyms 18, 20-21, 24-25, 187, 791, 836, 840, 842, 848-849, 1457, 1474, 1618, 1853, 1888

Activation Function 165, 369, 375, 423, 626, 631, 877, 881-882, 891, 1347, 1638

Active citizenship 1530, 1536-1537

AdaBoost 503-504, 508-509, 514-515, 867

Adversarial Learning 27, 47, 49, 61

Agglutination 1247, 1258, 1265

Airbnb 996, 1380, 1494-1499, 1502-1505

Algerian dialect 1248, 1256, 1262, 1264-1267, 1269-1270, 1272, 1276

analytical process 268-271, 281-283

Apple 112, 201, 208, 485, 487, 494, 1123, 1229, 1602, 1659-1660, 1667

Applications Of Opinion Mining 1, 1240, 1563, 1565

Arabic Language 643, 666, 1034-1035, 1056, 1237-1239, 1243-1248, 1250, 1252-1254, 1258, 1264-1268, 1364, 1480-1481, 1483-1484, 1486, 1490, 1493, 1550

Arabic Sentiment Analysis 195, 998, 1035, 1056, 1147, 1237, 1239, 1242-1243, 1247, 1249, 1251-1252, 1254, 1483, 1486

Artificial Neural Network (ANN) 176, 864, 877, 1192

Aspect Based 55, 266, 311, 314-318, 321, 325, 327, 446, 448, 461, 577, 824, 1029, 1218, 1234, 1332-1333, 1481, 1483, 1485, 1490, 1492-1493, 1508, 1514, 1525, 1732, 1873

Aspect Extraction 81-82, 318, 500, 520, 537, 824, 828, 833, 902, 1314-1320, 1322-1332, 1335-1336, 1484, 1510, 1636, 1858

Aspect Level 29-30, 58, 186, 316, 465, 837, 969, 1037, 1123, 1241, 1298-1299, 1315-1316, 1318, 1322, 1326-1328, 1330-1332, 1336, 1340-1342, 1350, 1442, 1480-1481, 1861, 1906

Aspect Oriented Sentiment Analysis 562, 1492

Aspect-Based Sentiment Analysis 26, 102, 200, 290-293, 311, 328, 453, 456, 459-460, 519-521, 537, 902, 1221, 1253, 1331, 1335-1336, 1398, 1435, 1480-1481, 1483-1485, 1491, 1506-1508, 1511, 1513-1515, 1522, 1526-1527, 1543, 1636, 1648-1649

author detection 690, 703

Autoencoder 27, 33-34, 51, 55, 60-61, 819, 835, 883

Automated System 198-199, 384, 395, 1006, 1050

automatic clustering 446, 448, 455, 459-461

Aylien 1196-1199, 1506, 1513-1514

B

Bag Of Words Model 263, 634, 1170

Big Data 25, 50, 53, 58-59, 106, 171, 196, 199, 230, 234, 247, 249, 255, 262, 266, 268-269, 277, 281, 286-289, 326, 410, 428, 432, 434-435, 463, 475, 495, 615, 634, 642, 677-678, 687, 689, 719, 721, 759, 762, 777-778, 795, 819, 821, 834-835, 891, 901, 917, 947, 950-951, 963, 971, 996, 1001, 1010, 1028, 1056, 1060, 1099, 1107, 1116, 1118, 1156, 1169, 1171, 1189-1191, 1193-1197, 1199, 1201-1202, 1216, 1233, 1236, 1294, 1308, 1311, 1338-1339, 1355, 1358, 1377, 1380-1381, 1391, 1399-1400, 1494-1497, 1502-1505, 1524, 1526, 1550, 1570, 1599, 1635, 1647, 1649, 1651-1652, 1659, 1673, 1675-1678, 1680, 1690, 1698, 1726, 1731-1732, 1823, 1827, 1852, 1860, 1865, 1869, 1901-1902, 1905-1906, 1921-1922, 1931, 1933

Bigram 176, 191, 205, 365, 559, 619, 625, 629-634, 636, 724, 787, 924-925, 1299, 1346, 1350, 1684, 1755-1756, 1776, 1879, 1911

Bilstm 416, 419-420, 423, 427, 814

Binary Cuckoo Search 1203-1206, 1208, 1210, 1214, 1216-1217

biogeography based optimizer 1219, 1221

bi-partite graph 1174, 1176-1178

brand marketing 199, 211

brand personality positioning 852-854

bureaucratic reform 1189-1190, 1198

bureaucrats 1189-1190, 1193-1194, 1196, 1198-1199

business modeling 1101-1102, 1112

C

Chatbots 141, 692, 933-940, 944-947, 1574, 1652, 1745-1746

chronic-degenerative diseases 637, 639, 647-648, 650, 658, 665

citizen centricity 116-117, 134

close-ended questions 342, 345-346, 350, 354, 360, 365

cloud service 1000-1001, 1008, 1027, 1201

Cluster Analysis 277, 342-343, 358, 365, 1101, 1333, 1435-1436, 1654, 1676, 1686, 1695

Clustering 33, 69, 102, 110, 176, 189-190, 196, 208, 222, 225, 233, 237-238, 241, 244-246, 249-250, 254-255, 276, 288, 342, 358, 436, 440, 442, 446, 448, 452, 455, 459-461, 475, 503, 561, 622-623, 691, 694, 718, 722-723, 728, 738-739, 747-749, 758, 789, 791, 799, 816, 894, 900, 1003, 1043, 1059, 1066, 1080-1081, 1084, 1094-1095, 1098, 1117, 1124, 1219, 1221-1222, 1225-1227, 1230, 1233-1236, 1282, 1319, 1324, 1326, 1332-1333, 1384, 1423, 1429, 1434, 1439, 1507, 1544, 1549, 1551, 1555, 1564, 1599, 1609, 1647, 1654, 1675, 1684, 1686, 1698, 1729, 1884, 1908, 1920

Codebook (Codeframe) 365

code-mixed phonetic text 598, 600-601, 613

colloquial words 1032-1033, 1050, 1053, 1055

community graph 1172, 1174-1175, 1178, 1186-1187

Community Members-Opinion Matrix 1172

Comparative Approach 761

computational text analysis 342-343, 350, 356-357, 359, 361, 365

Concept Map 357, 365

Concept Models 342

Conceptnet 160, 1220, 1401-1402, 1404, 1407, 1409, 1412, 1414-1415, 1417, 1419-1420

connected government 116-118, 122, 132, 134-135

Consumer Reviews 15, 133, 482, 813, 971, 997, 1001, 1105, 1112, 1114, 1337, 1363, 1382, 1424, 1556, 1633, 1635, 1648-1649, 1748, 1841

Convolution Neural Network 159, 165, 190, 256, 263, 1217, 1316, 1570

Convolutional Neural Network (CNN) 38, 96, 159-161, 165-166, 171-172, 256, 261-262, 267, 367-371, 376, 379, 441, 624, 639, 696, 817, 820, 833, 864, 880, 890, 1054, 1057-1058, 1060, 1348, 1588, 1637-1638, 1681, 1867

Coronavirus Pandemic (COVID-19) 1761, 1780

Corpus 17, 22, 24-25, 31-32, 35, 42, 45, 69, 74, 80, 86-87, 89-90, 95-98, 102-105, 110, 126, 138, 145-150, 153, 155, 160, 162, 164, 182, 199-200, 208, 216, 221, 239, 241, 248, 250, 289, 305, 308, 324-325, 343, 366, 370-374, 382-386, 389-391, 394, 396-397, 402, 404, 411, 435, 437-439, 498-500, 502-504, 506, 508-509, 514, 516, 540, 553, 561-562, 579, 582-583, 594-595, 621, 623, 625-626, 634, 645, 647, 649, 656-657, 662, 665, 667-668, 671, 673, 676, 678-680, 682-687, 702, 721, 723, 732, 749, 763-765, 770-771, 773-774, 784, 789-790, 806, 837, 850, 872, 875, 887, 904, 916, 920-922, 924, 926, 930-931, 1001, 1003, 1044, 1051, 1065, 1078, 1081, 1087, 1094, 1124, 1133, 1195, 1205, 1208-1209, 1212, 1229, 1241-1243, 1248-1249, 1252-1255, 1257, 1264-1266, 1269-1272, 1274, 1277, 1286-1287, 1303-1304, 1319-1320, 1342, 1350, 1352-1353, 1358, 1380, 1382, 1400, 1408, 1413, 1424, 1427, 1449, 1452, 1468, 1473, 1481, 1485-1486, 1509, 1541-1542, 1548, 1550, 1571, 1578-1582, 1586-1587, 1601, 1610, 1613, 1617, 1619, 1656, 1658, 1684, 1687, 1691, 1694, 1696, 1704-1705, 1707, 1709-1710, 1738, 1843, 1848, 1861, 1890, 1909

Corpus-Based 19, 25, 31, 93, 146, 199, 208, 216, 250, 582, 597, 686, 702, 721, 765, 838, 920-922, 924, 930, 1001-1003, 1034, 1044, 1237, 1241, 1265, 1424, 1449, 1509, 1578, 1601, 1684, 1758, 1909

Coverage Error 347, 365

Crisis Communication 1529, 1531, 1538-1539

Crisis Management 116, 215, 1528, 1536, 1538

Cross-Domain 43-44, 47, 49, 51-52, 54-57, 60, 75, 157-159, 170-173, 221, 616-617, 813, 833, 835, 1081, 1352, 1356, 1358, 1452, 1454, 1550-1551, 1883, 1885-1886, 1907, 1920

CTM 433, 437-438, 560

Customer Satisfaction 6, 109, 144, 439, 801, 967, 1027, 1103-1106, 1113, 1115, 1117, 1308, 1338, 1365, 1379, 1444, 1471, 1497, 1554, 1577, 1652, 1654-1655, 1658-1659, 1674-1675, 1733-1734, 1747, 1810-1812, 1824, 1826, 1829

D

Dale Chall Readability Score 1816-1817, 1820

data augmentation 27, 29, 46-47, 49, 57, 61, 412, 415, 418-419, 425-427, 429-432

Data compression 949, 954-955, 958

Data Goodness 761-762

Data Mining 14, 53, 57-58, 75, 78, 93, 110, 140, 183, 195-196, 220, 224, 230, 244, 247, 250, 252-253, 276, 285, 315-316, 326-328, 340, 379, 381,

383-384, 395-396, 430, 435, 442-444, 464-465, 473-474, 481-483, 497, 514, 516-517, 536-537, 553, 580, 594, 615, 666-668, 677, 691-692, 718-720, 737-738, 762, 797-798, 803, 821, 833, 849, 855-856, 860, 902, 916, 948, 1029-1030, 1033, 1046, 1058-1059, 1061-1062, 1065, 1097, 1124, 1148-1150, 1156, 1168, 1175, 1187, 1196, 1202, 1217-1220, 1233-1234, 1238, 1255, 1271-1272, 1289, 1310, 1313, 1333-1334, 1338-1339, 1355, 1357, 1360, 1376, 1379-1381, 1385, 1387, 1400, 1413-1414, 1426, 1435-1436, 1453-1454, 1456-1457, 1468, 1497, 1506-1507, 1513, 1524, 1526, 1542, 1551, 1553, 1563-1565, 1567, 1572, 1630, 1636, 1659, 1675-1677, 1681-1683, 1714, 1716-1717, 1719, 1730-1731, 1751-1752, 1758-1759, 1782, 1802, 1807, 1829, 1853, 1856, 1864-1867, 1869-1870, 1902-1903, 1905, 1919-1920, 1931

Datasets 1, 18, 24, 34, 37, 44, 46-48, 62, 95-101, 103, 105, 107, 110, 127, 140, 163, 165-169, 192, 195, 262-263, 265, 335, 365, 367-368, 370-371, 373-376, 378, 380, 406, 416, 418, 420, 425, 427, 429-430, 455, 475, 485, 500, 502-504, 508-510, 513, 515, 525, 527-529, 535, 558, 560, 563, 596-601, 609-611, 613, 625, 629-630, 633, 643, 697, 726, 731, 738, 740, 747, 755, 776, 778, 792, 800, 807, 812, 838, 843-845, 848, 927, 930, 936, 945, 966-967, 971-973, 975-976, 981-985, 988-989, 991-992, 994, 1035, 1040, 1071, 1178, 1184, 1186, 1205-1206, 1219, 1221-1222, 1229-1230, 1242-1243, 1250, 1264, 1266, 1345, 1347-1348, 1350, 1355, 1364, 1388, 1391, 1405, 1414, 1417, 1419, 1461-1462, 1471-1472, 1484, 1513, 1572, 1595, 1597, 1617, 1636, 1659, 1684, 1703, 1743, 1764, 1850-1853, 1871-1872, 1875, 1883, 1887, 1889, 1895-1897, 1899-1901, 1905-1906, 1908-1911, 1915-1917, 1921

Decision Making 5, 28, 49-50, 63, 117, 131, 140, 259, 367, 413, 433, 471, 496-497, 514, 641, 645, 663, 665, 678, 747, 757-758, 777, 900, 1001-1002, 1046, 1107, 1119-1120, 1146, 1219, 1237, 1336, 1360-1362, 1364, 1366-1369, 1371-1372, 1374-1377, 1402-1403, 1423, 1461, 1543, 1553-1554, 1558-1560, 1563, 1566, 1572, 1629, 1651, 1660, 1717, 1729-1730, 1806, 1809, 1924-1925, 1931

Decision Support System 286-287, 289, 443, 918-921, 1262, 1267

Decision Tree (DT) 66, 68, 93, 97, 110, 174-176, 178-179, 188-190, 196, 223, 263, 330, 410, 526, 538, 540-541, 543-553, 559, 586, 589, 591-593, 704, 739, 763, 767, 771-772, 776, 807, 812, 877-880, 887, 891, 902-903, 906, 908-916, 971, 1003-1004,

1125, 1195, 1205, 1214-1216, 1218, 1265, 1290, 1349, 1405, 1414, 1470, 1475, 1477, 1484, 1498, 1640, 1642, 1750-1751, 1856

Deep Learning (DL) 27-29, 34-36, 42, 46, 48-50, 52-55, 57, 62, 95-97, 100, 102, 105-108, 114-115, 141, 157, 159-160, 166, 171, 186, 190, 196, 221, 223, 256-257, 259, 261-267, 279-280, 288, 292, 363, 367-371, 375-376, 378-379, 381, 384, 396, 400-401, 414-416, 418-419, 423, 426, 428-430, 440, 464, 474, 497, 517-518, 598, 619-620, 623, 627, 633-634, 694-697, 716, 718-720, 723, 738, 816-821, 823-826, 828, 831-835, 865-866, 880, 883, 888-891, 917, 951, 963, 1004, 1033-1035, 1054-1056, 1059-1060, 1062, 1097, 1153, 1159, 1192, 1199, 1202, 1237, 1250, 1252, 1277, 1298, 1306-1307, 1310, 1316, 1322, 1324-1325, 1329, 1336, 1348, 1381, 1387, 1471, 1569-1571, 1573, 1587, 1589, 1633-1634, 1637-1638, 1641, 1643, 1697, 1726, 1729, 1732, 1746, 1758

Dendrogram 357, 365

Dependency Rules 290-292, 305, 311, 1316, 1320-1322, 1329

Depressive 581, 584, 588-589, 591-592, 1735

Description Logic 1480-1483, 1485

diacritic 1243-1244, 1247, 1258

Differential Evolution 446, 448-450, 452-453, 455-456, 459-462, 502, 504, 514, 516-518

Diglossia 1244-1245, 1254, 1258

Dimensionality 33, 66, 95, 191, 201-202, 224, 245, 365, 421, 500, 502, 749, 802-804, 811, 814, 823, 832, 894, 898, 1087, 1287, 1289-1290, 1292, 1327, 1642, 1698, 1895

Disaster Management 133, 793, 1539

Discourse Relation 519

Document-Term Matrix (DTM) 127, 134

Domain Adaptation 43, 50, 52, 55, 60, 171, 182, 615, 721, 1153, 1356, 1548, 1676, 1871, 1907

Drugs Opinion 637

Duolingo 933, 935, 938-939, 944, 946, 948

E

Earthquake 100-101, 116-124, 128-133, 279, 1529

Ebola 1764, 1772, 1781, 1786, 1801-1802, 1923-1933

E-Commerce Websites 199-200, 970, 1029, 1119, 1146, 1338

Eggbun 933, 935-936, 941-942, 945-947

Electronic Word-Of-Mouth 76, 433-434, 443, 445, 798, 1117, 1376, 1378-1381, 1383, 1495, 1504, 1506, 1539, 1827-1830, 1834, 1842

Electronic Word-Of-Mouth (Ewom) 76, 433-434, 443,

445, 798, 1117, 1376, 1378-1381, 1383, 1495, 1504, 1506, 1539, 1827-1830, 1834, 1842

Elicitation 365-366, 1191, 1193, 1195, 1201

emoji classification 398, 410

Emojis 17-18, 20-22, 24, 98, 398, 402-403, 405-410, 416, 419, 421-422, 1034, 1286, 1369, 1602-1603, 1763, 1765, 1770-1771, 1777-1779

Emoticons 24, 26, 68, 87, 98, 119, 127, 142, 185, 191, 222, 335, 384, 398-402, 410, 416, 419, 421-422, 467, 500, 540, 553, 558, 577, 661, 669, 683, 781, 785, 861, 904, 920, 922-924, 951, 953-954, 1009-1011, 1018, 1027, 1037, 1054, 1075, 1122, 1158, 1220, 1226, 1354, 1423, 1498-1499, 1574, 1592, 1600-1606, 1609-1610, 1618-1619, 1758, 1863-1864, 1868-1869, 1889, 1896, 1903

Emotion Analysis 77-81, 83-84, 108, 110-111, 114, 119, 133, 402, 412-416, 418, 423, 431, 476, 653, 693, 695, 716-717, 856, 858-859, 1065, 1067, 1172, 1217, 1307-1308, 1313, 1636, 1726, 1729, 1732, 1802

Emotion Detection 58, 79, 89, 105-108, 110-111, 330, 385, 400, 410, 415-417, 419, 426-428, 430, 432, 789, 793, 903, 1050, 1074, 1205, 1442, 1451-1452, 1596, 1848, 1862, 1864

emotion scales 1699-1700, 1705, 1707, 1710

emotion taxonomy 1699, 1705, 1710

Emotional Factors 291, 1696

Emotional Fingerprints 1076, 1094

emotional range 1733-1737, 1740-1742, 1744-1745

E-reputation 1384-1387, 1396, 1398-1400

Euclidean Distance 417, 458, 561, 1043, 1138, 1150, 1222, 1227, 1234, 1290, 1429, 1439

Evaluation Metrics 181, 263, 406, 408, 425, 1290, 1611, 1621

explainable AI 27, 29, 48-49, 62

Explicit Aspect 315, 1314, 1480, 1483

Explicit Opinions 1462, 1480

F

feasibility analyzer 1553

Feature Based Opinion Mining 315, 1404, 1553-1559, 1562, 1566

Feature Engineering,Bag-of.word model 619

Feature Extraction 17-18, 20, 22, 38-39, 46, 185, 190, 195, 201-202, 211, 214-215, 218-220, 227, 230, 257, 265, 288, 318, 388, 428, 502, 559, 577, 622, 643, 666, 693, 698, 713, 716, 721, 724, 740, 770, 779, 801-802, 818-820, 831, 838-839, 880, 951, 995, 1007-1008, 1010, 1033, 1045, 1050, 1125, 1128, 1133, 1195, 1204-1205, 1225, 1307, 1312,

1334-1335, 1337, 1391, 1402, 1408, 1442, 1445, 1523, 1526, 1545, 1555-1557, 1563, 1566, 1649, 1661, 1879, 1909, 1911-1912

Feature Selection 19, 106, 113, 190-192, 199, 202-203, 211, 245, 261, 327, 385, 389, 496-497, 499-502, 506, 509, 514-518, 541, 544, 553, 559, 690-691, 693-696, 699, 701-702, 706, 709-717, 719-724, 738, 800-805, 811-815, 905, 908, 916, 972, 975-977, 992, 994, 996-997, 1056, 1060, 1066, 1075, 1149, 1195, 1203-1206, 1208-1209, 1212, 1214-1218, 1234, 1277, 1299, 1302, 1324, 1331, 1333, 1335, 1347, 1355, 1404, 1415, 1445, 1460, 1524, 1542, 1598-1599, 1883, 1903, 1909, 1917

Feature set summary 1553

Feature Space 31, 42-43, 99, 190-191, 224, 417-418, 424, 499, 788, 802-803, 894, 1041-1042, 1133, 1151, 1619, 1895-1896

Features Selection 382, 987-989, 993, 1214

Figurative Language 634, 1611, 1630

File-Upload Questions 365

Flesch Kincaid Grade Level 1816, 1820

Fuzzy Inference System (FIS) 1064-1065, 1067, 1074

fuzzy logical relationships 446, 448, 452, 455, 460

Fuzzy-Logic 1000

G

game review 463-464, 476

Gated Recurrent Unit 59, 891

Generalization 423, 498, 635, 781-782, 790, 803, 893, 1522, 1545, 1640, 1657

Genetic Algorithm 222, 231, 461, 499, 1099, 1146, 1216, 1221, 1236, 1298, 1306-1307, 1311, 1328

genetic rank aggregation 496-497, 500, 509, 513-515, 517

Graph Based Co-Ranking 329, 332-333, 336-337

Graph Mining 440, 444, 1172, 1174-1175, 1186-1187

Gunning Fog index 1805, 1816, 1820

H

Hadoop 190, 463, 475-476, 901, 949-950, 952-956, 958-959, 962-963, 1201-1202, 1219, 1221-1222, 1228-1230, 1234, 1307-1308, 1310-1311, 1387, 1680, 1689-1690, 1909

Hadoop Distributed File System 190, 949-950, 1221-1222, 1690, 1909

Harmonic Mean 248, 392, 425, 685, 1142, 1151, 1351, 1619, 1622

Hashtag 23, 128-129, 134, 153, 488, 1000, 1008-1009, 1011, 1019, 1027, 1367, 1369, 1533, 1535, 1586,

1604-1605, 1616, 1618, 1621, 1762, 1770

Health Care 7, 375, 638, 640, 665, 753, 807, 1307, 1423, 1781, 1866, 1919

High-Burden 345, 365

Holon 1536, 1539

hotel rating 1805, 1810

Human Behavior Analysis 1846

Hybrid Approach 19, 222, 265, 311, 313, 379, 540, 614, 637, 639, 645, 647, 665, 904, 918, 922, 926, 930, 1000-1003, 1007, 1028, 1039, 1055, 1074, 1221, 1233, 1241-1242, 1257-1258, 1265, 1267, 1270, 1278, 1354, 1364, 1368, 1748, 1864, 1905, 1907

Hybrid recommender systems 1076

I

Imbalance classes 412

Implicit Aspect 318, 921, 1314, 1330-1331, 1480, 1483, 1493

Implicit Opinions 645, 1330

Informal Language Learning 933-934, 944-947

Informal Text 798, 900, 930, 1050, 1065-1066, 1354, 1902

Information Extraction 15, 78, 155, 619, 650, 667, 722, 750, 755, 782, 795, 797-798, 849, 931, 1064-1065, 1401, 1407, 1418, 1526, 1588, 1614, 1761

instance selection 800-809, 811-812, 815

K

K Nearest Neighbor 224, 544, 585, 907, 1130, 1137-1138

Kaggle 142, 406, 417, 420, 427, 429-431, 864, 872, 1128, 1131, 1150, 1203, 1205-1208, 1215-1216, 1218, 1372, 1378, 1575, 1639, 1649, 1658, 1679, 1752

Kappa 90, 104, 107, 121, 125, 134, 178-182, 356, 587

keyword selection 694, 721

K-Nearest Neighbor (KNN) 214, 220, 223, 225, 227, 230, 538, 540-541, 543-544, 694-695, 758, 895, 902-903, 906-907, 1119, 1121, 1138, 1265, 1317, 1326, 1406, 1414, 1484, 1908

Knowledge Base 143, 233, 285, 308, 378, 765, 1133-1136, 1332, 1452, 1576, 1721

Knowledge Discovery 14, 53, 57-58, 109-110, 172, 213, 247, 249, 251-252, 255, 269, 288, 327-328, 381, 430, 435, 465, 481-482, 516-517, 536, 578, 718, 849, 1029, 1058, 1061-1062, 1065, 1097, 1148-1150, 1153, 1155, 1187, 1313, 1333, 1356-1357, 1380, 1435-1436, 1453-1454, 1467-1469, 1524, 1526-1527, 1567, 1648, 1659, 1677, 1703, 1714,

1752, 1758-1759, 1782, 1829, 1864-1865, 1870, 1903, 1919, 1931

Knowledge Management Research 1699, 1705, 1713, 1715-1716

L

Language Identification 620, 622, 644, 691, 717, 1282, 1470-1476, 1478-1479

Language Models 51, 56, 171, 416, 431, 619-620, 623, 625, 696, 793, 1472

Language Use 1690, 1783

LDA 99-100, 292, 330-332, 334, 336, 339, 433, 437-438, 520, 537, 562, 697, 765, 1155, 1334, 1510, 1546, 1764, 1882

Learning System 159, 239, 518, 790, 1069, 1266, 1680-1683, 1687

learning theories 1717, 1720-1721, 1730

Lemmatization 91, 98, 421, 436, 474, 556, 563, 577, 621, 771, 785, 875, 892-894, 896, 899, 901, 975, 1037, 1317, 1321, 1390, 1606, 1654

Lexical Analysis 219, 643, 751-753, 1595

Lexicon 2, 12, 19, 25, 31, 40, 51, 69, 74, 83, 86-90, 98, 103-105, 108, 111, 137, 141, 145, 147-148, 185-186, 190-191, 199, 207-209, 211-212, 216, 222, 230-231, 261-263, 266, 279, 286, 312, 315-317, 332, 340, 375-376, 379-380, 382, 385, 388-389, 391, 394, 415, 428, 439, 441, 443, 498, 504-507, 556, 560, 562, 595, 644, 686, 762, 764, 776, 783, 789, 836, 838-840, 842, 844-845, 848, 857, 859, 921-922, 951-952, 1002-1003, 1027, 1030, 1034, 1044, 1057, 1062, 1125, 1149, 1158, 1205, 1220, 1235, 1239, 1241-1243, 1249, 1252-1255, 1264-1266, 1287, 1299, 1303, 1307, 1312, 1316-1318, 1320-1322, 1326, 1331, 1334-1335, 1338, 1342-1343, 1351-1353, 1355, 1357, 1364, 1368, 1376, 1379, 1402, 1405-1407, 1409, 1414, 1425, 1434, 1436, 1445-1446, 1448-1449, 1452-1454, 1467, 1481, 1483-1486, 1489, 1492-1493, 1499, 1501, 1503, 1505, 1508, 1526, 1546, 1550, 1561, 1569, 1573-1574, 1578, 1580, 1610, 1617-1619, 1621, 1627, 1631, 1658, 1679, 1684, 1697, 1770, 1781-1782, 1853, 1862, 1872-1873, 1889

Lexicon Adaptation 137, 147, 1569, 1580

Lexicon generation 382, 385, 388, 428

lexicon resource 840, 842, 845

Lexicon-Based 14, 18-19, 22, 24, 31, 44, 58, 65, 69, 93, 98, 104, 141, 198-199, 207, 220, 222, 231, 313, 326, 368, 379, 415, 498, 516, 518, 520, 536, 554, 560, 597-598, 615-617, 666, 679, 764, 779, 784-785, 789, 838, 857, 917, 1001-1003, 1030, 1034,

1044, 1054, 1122, 1205, 1220, 1235, 1237, 1241,
1250, 1252, 1256, 1265-1266, 1278-1279, 1358,
1364, 1381, 1405, 1424-1425, 1481, 1484, 1492,
1509, 1567, 1573, 1632, 1658, 1682, 1685, 1729-
1732, 1760, 1852-1853, 1873, 1888-1889, 1909

Linear Classifier 31, 66-67, 788, 817, 883, 1041, 1346,
1447, 1755, 1856

Linguistic Analysis 89, 250, 342-343, 359, 365, 383-
384, 848, 922, 1029, 1158, 1525, 1567, 1614

Literature Review 8, 18, 50, 56, 106, 110, 118, 175,
220-221, 268-272, 274, 276-277, 281, 283-285,
361, 400, 414-415, 449-450, 461, 558, 582, 615,
802, 853, 1002-1004, 1028, 1103, 1112, 1155-
1156, 1171, 1173, 1216, 1239, 1264, 1266, 1362,
1472, 1492, 1524, 1531, 1537-1538, 1634, 1808,
1833, 1842, 1871, 1874, 1884, 1889, 1924

Logistic Regression (LR) 126-127, 174-176, 178-182,
184, 194, 262, 369, 375, 401, 455, 598, 643, 676,
684, 690, 704-705, 763, 766, 768, 771, 776, 807,
812, 964, 966-967, 971-972, 976-977, 980-981,
985, 987, 989, 992, 994, 1125, 1137-1138, 1337,
1384, 1391, 1395-1396, 1470, 1472, 1475-1476,
1527, 1640-1642, 1755, 1908

Long Short-Term Memory 37, 53, 95-96, 105, 173,
370, 420, 429, 486, 696, 830-832, 834, 891,
1054, 1333, 1639

M

Machine Learning 1-2, 18-19, 25, 28, 31, 35, 42-43,
52, 56-57, 59, 62-63, 65-66, 68-69, 75, 78, 80,
93-94, 97, 99, 101-102, 107-108, 111-113, 126,
131-133, 137, 141-142, 146, 155-156, 171, 174-
175, 182-184, 186-187, 189-190, 192, 194-199,
202-204, 211-212, 214, 216-218, 220, 222-224,
227, 230-231, 233-234, 244, 246-250, 256-267,
276, 279-280, 286, 288, 291, 312, 315-316, 327,
330-331, 339-340, 355-356, 369, 373, 375-376,
378-380, 383-384, 395-397, 399-400, 412-413,
415, 426, 428, 430-431, 435, 439-442, 448,
463-464, 473-474, 485-486, 494, 497, 503, 514,
516-517, 536-538, 540-541, 553, 555, 558-561,
579-581, 595, 597-598, 619, 623-624, 627,
630, 633-634, 637, 639, 641, 643-644, 647,
649, 673-674, 676-677, 679-680, 684, 689-690,
692, 694-701, 704-705, 716, 718-720, 722-724,
729, 737-738, 750, 757, 761-766, 768-770, 776,
778-780, 786, 794-795, 797-799, 812-817, 831-
833, 836-837, 843, 848-850, 857, 864-866, 877,
889-890, 902-904, 916, 945, 951, 963-964, 966,
969, 971-972, 975, 981, 996, 1001-1004, 1029-

1030, 1032, 1034-1035, 1039, 1041-1042, 1044,
1056, 1058, 1060, 1065, 1067, 1069, 1102-1103,
1108, 1115, 1119, 1122-1125, 1137, 1147, 1149-
1151, 1165-1166, 1205, 1207, 1216-1217, 1220,
1241-1243, 1250, 1252, 1258, 1262, 1264-1265,
1272, 1278, 1298-1299, 1302, 1308-1309, 1312,
1316, 1322-1323, 1331, 1333-1336, 1342-1343,
1350-1351, 1353, 1355-1357, 1359, 1364, 1376-
1379, 1381, 1384, 1387-1388, 1390-1392, 1395,
1397-1398, 1400, 1405-1406, 1413, 1419-1420,
1424-1425, 1446, 1452, 1458, 1461-1462, 1467-
1468, 1470, 1472-1473, 1479, 1481, 1484, 1496-
1497, 1508-1511, 1513, 1523-1524, 1527, 1532,
1544-1545, 1549, 1569-1570, 1573-1574, 1578,
1587-1589, 1595-1596, 1599, 1601, 1609-1610,
1617, 1619, 1631, 1633-1637, 1640-1643, 1647-
1648, 1655-1658, 1661, 1675, 1677-1678, 1681,
1698, 1710, 1712, 1714, 1717, 1727, 1729-1732,
1735, 1737, 1743, 1745, 1748, 1750-1751, 1758,
1764, 1782, 1823, 1843, 1871-1873, 1884-1886,
1888-1889, 1903, 1905, 1907, 1909

Majority Rule 184, 194

Mapreduce 100, 182, 949-952, 955, 962-963, 1202,
1219, 1221-1223, 1227, 1229-1230, 1234-1236

Marketing Decision Making 1360, 1362, 1364, 1366-
1369, 1371-1372, 1374-1377, 1729

Marketing Team 199, 211, 1375

markov assumption 625, 631, 635

matrix query 342, 357

Media 1, 3, 5-7, 9, 16-18, 24, 26-28, 34, 49, 53, 55-56,
63, 74, 77-79, 97, 101-103, 105-110, 112-117,
129-134, 137, 144, 172, 174-175, 184-185, 195,
197, 199, 215, 218, 220-222, 230, 233, 247,
256-257, 262, 277, 279-281, 286-290, 311, 314,
331-332, 339-340, 342, 358, 368, 380, 382, 384,
395, 398-399, 409-411, 416, 430, 434-435, 443,
447, 461, 463-465, 467-476, 480-486, 491, 495,
497, 527, 538, 555-556, 580-582, 595-596, 610,
615, 617, 637, 640-641, 651, 673-675, 683,
687-689, 695, 697, 721, 723, 749, 758-760,
762, 776-780, 782-784, 787, 789-799, 801, 812,
815-818, 833, 852-853, 855, 859, 862, 889, 893,
896, 902, 918, 921, 931, 936, 947, 952, 995-997,
1000-1003, 1006, 1032-1033, 1037, 1046-1047,
1049-1050, 1056-1058, 1060-1062, 1080, 1098,
1102-1103, 1106, 1112-1113, 1115, 1117, 1119,
1121, 1128, 1146, 1148, 1150, 1153-1158, 1160,
1166-1171, 1190-1191, 1193, 1195, 1199-1200,
1204, 1220, 1233, 1235, 1238-1239, 1243-1246,
1248, 1252, 1254, 1256, 1259, 1262-1263,
1270, 1276-1278, 1298-1299, 1308-1309, 1313,

1334-1335, 1338-1339, 1353, 1356, 1360-1361,
1363-1369, 1376-1377, 1379-1383, 1385-1387,
1399, 1402-1403, 1418-1420, 1432, 1434-1435,
1437, 1443, 1449, 1452, 1454-1457, 1459, 1461,
1468-1469, 1470-1471, 1476, 1478-1479, 1481,
1483, 1494-1497, 1503-1505, 1513, 1524, 1526,
1528-1529, 1531-1532, 1536-1539, 1541-1544,
1547-1552, 1566, 1569, 1576, 1590, 1596-1597,
1600, 1611-1614, 1618, 1629-1631, 1651-1653,
1655, 1674-1675, 1677, 1697, 1700, 1702, 1712,
1729, 1743, 1746, 1751, 1759, 1761-1764, 1773,
1778-1789, 1793-1794, 1796-1803, 1812, 1818,
1825-1826, 1829, 1831-1835, 1840-1844, 1846,
1850-1852, 1858, 1861, 1864-1866, 1868-1870,
1873, 1894, 1902-1903, 1908-1909, 1919-1920,
1922-1932

Memrise 933, 935-936, 939-940, 944, 947

Message Length 215, 884, 886, 891

Microblog Sentiment Analysis 399, 815, 1887-1888,
1902

Micro-Blogging 65, 117, 135, 186, 464, 551, 558, 784,
793-794, 915, 1037, 1461, 1549

Mining 1-3, 5-9, 11-12, 14-16, 18, 24-25, 28, 30, 53,
57-58, 61, 64-66, 70-71, 73-81, 83-84, 86, 93,
97, 102-111, 114, 132-133, 137, 140-141, 155-
156, 174-175, 182-183, 185, 195-196, 199, 201,
211-212, 214, 218, 220-224, 230-233, 241-242,
244-245, 247, 249-250, 252-257, 261, 265-266,
268-272, 276-277, 279-281, 283-292, 311-318,
324-330, 336, 340, 367, 378-379, 381-385, 389,
391, 394-399, 401-402, 410-411, 430-431, 433,
435, 437, 439-445, 461, 464-465, 467, 473-476,
480-483, 496-497, 499-500, 514, 516-517, 520,
536-539, 552-553, 555-556, 560-561, 578-582,
594, 597-598, 614-616, 637-645, 647, 649, 653,
665-668, 677, 687-697, 699-700, 716-720, 722-
724, 726-728, 737-739, 747-750, 753, 757-760,
762, 778-780, 782-783, 789, 794-798, 800-803,
807, 811-816, 821, 827-828, 833, 838, 840, 848-
850, 852-853, 855-857, 860, 862, 867, 872, 890,
892-896, 900-903, 916, 918, 921, 931-932, 945,
948, 951, 962-964, 968, 971, 973, 995-999, 1001-
1003, 1006, 1027, 1029-1030, 1032-1033, 1036,
1046-1047, 1050, 1056, 1058-1062, 1064-1068,
1074-1075, 1080, 1087, 1096-1098, 1101-1102,
1106-1108, 1112, 1116-1119, 1121, 1124-1126,
1146, 1148-1151, 1153, 1155-1156, 1168-1169,
1171-1175, 1186-1189, 1191, 1195-1196, 1200-
1202, 1204-1205, 1216-1221, 1233-1234, 1237-
1238, 1240-1241, 1245, 1247, 1252-1255, 1258,
1262-1263, 1271-1272, 1278-1283, 1289, 1294-

1296, 1298, 1303, 1306, 1310-1315, 1317-1318,
1331, 1333-1335, 1337-1340, 1350, 1355-1358,
1360, 1362-1366, 1369, 1374-1376, 1378-1382,
1385-1387, 1400-1409, 1412-1414, 1417-1422,
1424-1428, 1434-1437, 1441-1442, 1452-1457,
1459-1462, 1467-1468, 1480-1481, 1484, 1492-
1494, 1497-1498, 1502, 1504, 1506-1511, 1513,
1521-1528, 1532, 1537, 1541-1569, 1572-1573,
1587-1588, 1596, 1598, 1600-1601, 1603, 1609,
1612, 1614, 1629-1630, 1634-1636, 1646-1651,
1653-1654, 1656, 1658-1659, 1673-1679, 1681-
1683, 1700, 1703, 1711, 1713-1714, 1716-1717,
1719, 1727, 1730-1732, 1738, 1740, 1747, 1751-
1753, 1758-1759, 1764, 1782, 1802, 1807, 1811,
1813, 1822, 1824-1826, 1829, 1842-1843, 1847-
1848, 1853, 1856-1857, 1860, 1862, 1864-1871,
1888, 1901-1905, 1919-1922, 1931

Mondly 933, 935, 942-945, 947

MongoDB 892-893, 895-896, 900-901

Movie Reviews 18, 44-45, 65, 87, 97, 196, 203, 207,
231, 257-258, 312, 316, 327-328, 383-384, 482,
508-509, 553, 556, 559-560, 580, 596, 598, 600-
601, 610, 613, 619-620, 629-630, 633, 739-740,
749, 836, 849, 857, 916, 1065, 1088, 1096, 1119,
1121-1122, 1124, 1128, 1131, 1137, 1146, 1149-
1150, 1206, 1263, 1299, 1302, 1307, 1313, 1324,
1335, 1345, 1347, 1355, 1358, 1403, 1419, 1436,
1454-1456, 1460-1461, 1467, 1526, 1681, 1698,
1865, 1908, 1921

Movies Recommender Systems 1076

Multimodal Sentiment Analysis 49, 1747, 1846, 1856,
1862-1864, 1866-1869

Multivariate Analysis of Variance (MANOVA) 1117

Multivariate Sentiment Analysis 1101

N

Natural Language 9, 12-13, 15, 18, 25-28, 42, 49-51, 53-
55, 57-63, 66-67, 75-79, 89, 95, 98, 104, 109-110,
112-113, 131, 139-140, 158, 172-173, 176, 182,
199, 205, 211-212, 214, 216-217, 221, 245, 250,
254, 256-257, 259, 261, 264-265, 269, 279, 290,
293, 312-313, 326-328, 330, 339, 341, 356, 358,
361, 365, 367-369, 378, 381, 383, 396, 400-402,
410-412, 415, 419, 428, 430-433, 435, 439, 441-
442, 444, 464, 474, 481-484, 489, 497, 516, 518,
536-538, 554-556, 560, 563-564, 579, 595, 597,
602, 619-621, 623-624, 627, 634-639, 666, 668,
678-680, 684, 687, 690-694, 696-697, 699-700,
703-704, 707-715, 717-724, 728-729, 748-750,
759, 762-764, 776, 778, 780, 783, 795, 797-798,

801, 814, 816-817, 821, 832-835, 848-850, 893, 901, 903, 917-920, 922, 927, 930, 933-934, 936, 946, 948, 950, 968, 975, 994, 1032-1033, 1045-1046, 1053-1061, 1063, 1065-1066, 1120, 1124, 1146, 1148-1151, 1153-1154, 1169-1171, 1218, 1220, 1234, 1238, 1240, 1243-1245, 1252-1259, 1263, 1278-1282, 1294-1296, 1300, 1307, 1310, 1312, 1332-1338, 1354, 1358-1359, 1364, 1377, 1380-1381, 1386, 1403, 1419-1421, 1424, 1451, 1454, 1457, 1460, 1462, 1464, 1468, 1478, 1492-1493, 1498, 1507-1508, 1526-1527, 1541-1542, 1551, 1563, 1565, 1567, 1570-1572, 1589, 1592, 1610, 1612, 1614, 1617, 1619, 1630, 1637-1638, 1675-1676, 1678, 1717, 1719, 1727, 1733, 1747, 1753, 1761, 1764, 1813-1814, 1863, 1866-1867, 1873, 1888, 1920, 1924, 1932-1933

Natural Language Processing (NLP) 12, 15, 18, 25-28, 49-51, 53-55, 57-63, 66-67, 75-78, 89, 104, 109, 112-113, 131, 140, 158, 172-173, 176, 182, 199, 211-212, 214, 216-217, 221, 250, 254, 256-257, 261, 265, 269, 279, 290, 312-313, 326-328, 330, 341, 361, 367-369, 378, 381, 383, 396, 400-401, 410-412, 415, 419, 428, 431-433, 435, 439, 441-442, 444, 464, 474, 481-484, 489, 497, 516, 518, 536-538, 555-556, 560, 595, 597, 602, 619-621, 623-624, 627, 634-639, 668, 678-680, 687, 690-693, 696-697, 699-700, 703-704, 707-715, 717-724, 729, 748-750, 759, 762-764, 776, 778, 780, 795, 797-798, 801, 814, 816-817, 821, 832-835, 848-850, 893, 903, 918-920, 922, 927, 934, 936, 950, 968, 975, 994, 1032, 1046, 1053-1061, 1063, 1065-1066, 1120, 1124, 1146, 1148-1151, 1153-1154, 1169-1171, 1220, 1234, 1238, 1240, 1243-1245, 1252-1259, 1263, 1278-1282, 1294-1296, 1300, 1307, 1312, 1332, 1334-1338, 1354, 1358-1359, 1364, 1377, 1380-1381, 1386, 1403, 1419-1421, 1424, 1451, 1454, 1457, 1460, 1462, 1468, 1478, 1493, 1498, 1507-1508, 1526-1527, 1541-1542, 1551, 1563, 1567, 1570, 1572, 1592, 1610, 1614, 1617, 1619, 1630, 1638, 1675-1676, 1678, 1717, 1719, 1733, 1753, 1761, 1764, 1813, 1863, 1866-1867, 1873, 1888, 1920, 1924, 1932-1933

NBC 66, 766, 787, 1338, 1344-1345, 1347, 1350-1351, 1353

Network Analysis 132, 276, 342-343, 360, 365, 395, 441, 794, 796, 971, 996, 1062, 1173, 1187, 1253-1254, 1492, 1630, 1682, 1868, 1901

Networks Analysis 265, 285, 395, 667, 945, 1233, 1310, 1312-1313, 1922

Neural Network 19, 27-28, 36, 38-39, 44, 56-59, 68, 95-96, 105-106, 157, 159-161, 165-167, 171-172, 176, 190, 196, 247, 256, 261-263, 265-267, 289, 311, 313, 316, 326, 367-371, 376, 378-380, 395, 398, 405, 411, 419, 423, 441, 460-461, 486, 493, 500, 619, 622-624, 627-630, 633-634, 639, 695-696, 720, 778, 796, 816-822, 832-835, 864, 876-877, 880, 882-883, 889-891, 997, 1004, 1041-1042, 1054, 1057-1058, 1060, 1192, 1195, 1205, 1217, 1220, 1236, 1253, 1279, 1306, 1312, 1316, 1324, 1328, 1338, 1347-1348, 1379, 1391, 1398, 1551, 1569-1570, 1588, 1617, 1637-1638, 1648, 1676, 1681, 1736, 1740, 1853, 1858, 1867, 1885, 1908

New Public Service 1189-1190

news classification 690-691, 693, 716

NGO 135, 1903

N-Gram 66, 99, 111, 160, 195, 214, 220, 223, 227, 230, 263, 266, 291, 326, 365, 401, 485, 496-497, 500-507, 514, 540, 558, 560, 584, 589, 593-594, 620, 622-626, 629, 631, 634, 636, 644-645, 695, 716, 724, 781, 796, 814, 904, 975, 1066, 1125, 1195, 1243, 1264, 1319, 1345, 1348, 1350, 1356, 1369, 1379, 1470, 1472-1473, 1475-1476, 1479, 1510, 1656-1657, 1676-1677, 1756, 1758, 1908, 1910-1911, 1917-1918

NIRF rankings 555-556, 562, 575, 577

NLTK 17-18, 22, 24, 142, 373, 425, 488, 494, 562-564, 577, 601, 676, 679-680, 684, 726, 728-733, 737, 747, 895, 898, 1218, 1269, 1286-1287, 1317, 1335, 1462, 1464, 1574, 1604-1606, 1641, 1677-1678, 1753, 1814

NLTK Corpus 17, 22, 24, 1286

Non-Substantive Option 366

Normalization 98, 205, 259, 373, 441, 472-473, 556, 615, 621, 642, 648, 720, 750, 876, 879, 893, 918-924, 926-927, 930-931, 975, 1017, 1153, 1155, 1158, 1243, 1247, 1270, 1285, 1288, 1322, 1473, 1545, 1661

O

Online Reviews 6, 15, 76, 107, 112, 156, 201, 212, 232, 293, 313, 444, 452, 462, 555-556, 562, 565, 577-578, 597, 620, 629, 634, 728, 782, 784, 790, 836, 855, 862, 1033, 1046, 1055, 1057, 1096, 1099, 1101-1106, 1108-1115, 1117, 1120, 1334, 1359, 1378, 1380, 1424, 1426, 1435, 1471, 1494-1496, 1498-1502, 1505, 1509-1510, 1523, 1525, 1542, 1549, 1551, 1589, 1599, 1633-1635, 1647-1648, 1805-1806, 1812, 1824-1825, 1827, 1830-1832, 1834-1835, 1841, 1844, 1904 online tourist reviews 1494, 1506, 1521-1523

Ontology Learning 210, 233, 237-241, 244, 249-251, 253-255, 1630

open-ended questions 342, 344-350, 353-354, 360-366

Opinion Extraction 311, 391, 395, 476, 643, 645, 653, 824, 828, 848, 1148-1149, 1172, 1262, 1356, 1401, 1413, 1416-1418, 1522, 1557, 1614, 1864

Opinion Holder 4, 30, 81-82, 654, 828, 1009, 1259, 1340, 1480, 1554, 1560, 1909

Opinion Mining 1-3, 5-9, 11-12, 14-16, 18, 25, 28, 30, 57, 61, 64-65, 70-71, 73-81, 84, 105-106, 108, 111, 132, 137, 140-141, 155-156, 174-175, 182, 185, 195, 199, 211-212, 214, 220-222, 230-233, 249, 255-257, 261, 266, 272, 280-281, 287-291, 311-312, 314-318, 325-327, 330, 336, 340, 367, 378, 382-385, 391, 394, 396-397, 401-402, 410-411, 430, 441, 443, 461, 465, 467, 476, 480, 496-497, 499, 514, 516-517, 520, 536-537, 539, 553, 555-556, 560-561, 578-582, 597-598, 614-616, 637-645, 647, 649, 653, 665-668, 687-689, 726-728, 739, 747-748, 750, 757-760, 778, 795, 800-803, 807, 811-814, 821, 827-828, 833, 840, 848, 855, 862, 892, 916, 918, 921, 931-932, 951, 962-964, 968, 971, 995-998, 1001-1003, 1006, 1027, 1047, 1056, 1060-1061, 1065-1066, 1075, 1080, 1121, 1126, 1146, 1148-1151, 1153, 1168, 1172-1174, 1186-1189, 1191, 1200, 1204-1205, 1216-1218, 1220, 1233, 1237-1238, 1240-1241, 1245, 1247, 1252-1253, 1255, 1258, 1263, 1278, 1280-1283, 1294-1296, 1298, 1303, 1306, 1310, 1312, 1314, 1331, 1333-1334, 1337, 1340, 1357-1358, 1364, 1378, 1380-1382, 1386, 1401-1409, 1412, 1417-1421, 1425-1428, 1434-1436, 1441-1442, 1453-1456, 1459-1461, 1468, 1481, 1484, 1492-1493, 1504, 1506-1511, 1522-1523, 1525, 1527-1528, 1532, 1537, 1541-1563, 1565-1569, 1573, 1587-1588, 1598, 1601, 1609, 1612, 1630, 1675, 1678, 1681, 1719, 1727, 1759, 1764, 1782, 1802, 1843, 1847, 1862, 1866-1867, 1871, 1888, 1903, 1919-1921, 1931

Opinion Spam 441, 1243, 1246, 1250, 1255, 1259, 1295, 1331, 1546, 1551-1552, 1566, 1608, 1865

Opinion Summarization 313, 482, 1315, 1341, 1848, 1857

opinion verb 596-597, 599, 607, 609

Opinionated Text 15, 1037, 1049, 1063, 1340-1341

Opinionated Words 1119

Optimal Feature Selection 496, 501, 506, 509, 812, 994, 1203

P

PANAS 119, 132, 135, 1632

Pandemic 770, 1102, 1105, 1750-1751, 1761, 1763-1765, 1770-1771, 1775-1777, 1780-1800, 1803-1804, 1925, 1930

Part-Of-Speech Tagging 18, 112, 135, 293, 435, 540, 620, 733, 892-894, 896, 899, 904, 938, 1255

Performance Measures 179, 199, 209, 237, 248-249, 423, 645, 703, 836, 844, 1631, 1883

performance metrics of classification 1130, 1151

Personality Insight 1733

Personality Traits 854, 1733-1737, 1740, 1745-1746, 1748-1749

pharmacovigilance 637-638, 640, 665, 668

Polarity 17, 20-22, 26, 30-31, 42, 45, 62-63, 69-70, 78, 81, 101, 117, 120, 129, 135, 137, 140-141, 145-147, 157, 186, 199-200, 207-209, 215-218, 221-222, 227, 256-257, 259, 261, 263, 269, 282, 290-292, 302, 311, 313, 316, 319, 325, 327, 331-333, 341, 368, 384, 399, 401-402, 439, 444, 446, 448, 450, 452-453, 455-456, 459, 498, 501, 504, 507-508, 514-515, 519-530, 533, 535-536, 538-541, 554, 556, 562, 582, 595, 597-598, 606-607, 616, 618, 630-631, 637, 642-644, 649-650, 656-659, 662-663, 665, 667, 671, 674, 678-679, 684, 686, 697, 721, 735, 757, 762-765, 781, 789, 798, 800, 802, 813, 815, 836-842, 848-850, 855, 857, 859, 894, 903-905, 917-918, 931, 951-952, 964, 982, 1000, 1002-1004, 1006, 1010-1011, 1016-1020, 1032-1037, 1044, 1048, 1050-1054, 1063, 1066, 1088, 1108-1109, 1121-1126, 1128, 1131, 1133-1137, 1146, 1150-1151, 1153, 1155-1159, 1163, 1167, 1171, 1220, 1226, 1229, 1238, 1240, 1243, 1256, 1262, 1264-1266, 1268-1269, 1271-1272, 1274, 1276-1277, 1299, 1303-1304, 1306-1308, 1314-1316, 1318, 1322, 1328, 1341-1342, 1354-1355, 1366, 1369, 1372-1373, 1375, 1377, 1381, 1401, 1404-1405, 1407-1408, 1411-1413, 1416-1417, 1421-1423, 1425, 1433-1434, 1442-1443, 1448-1450, 1454, 1456, 1458, 1460, 1468, 1480-1486, 1489-1490, 1493, 1498, 1508-1509, 1511, 1514-1515, 1517, 1523, 1526-1527, 1531-1533, 1543, 1548-1549, 1552, 1554-1555, 1557-1558, 1566, 1569, 1573-1574, 1577-1580, 1590, 1592-1595, 1604-1605, 1608, 1611, 1613-1614, 1616-1617, 1619-1624, 1627, 1629, 1635-1637, 1648, 1658, 1661, 1663, 1667, 1669, 1671-1673, 1682, 1684, 1719, 1729, 1739, 1814, 1822-1823, 1836, 1847-1848, 1851, 1853, 1863, 1867, 1872-1874, 1882, 1884, 1887, 1889-1890, 1894, 1896,

1903, 1906, 1908-1910, 1926, 1928-1930, 1933

Polarity Classification 45, 70, 399, 536, 644, 697, 721, 798, 815, 1034, 1125, 1220, 1240, 1269, 1272, 1277, 1355, 1372, 1523, 1611, 1617, 1621, 1623, 1637, 1739, 1814, 1847-1848, 1887, 1889-1890

Policy-Opinion Matrix 1172

Polysemous 354, 366

Pooling 38-39, 165, 262, 369-371, 376, 817-818, 820, 881, 887, 891, 1324, 1570, 1638

Population Segmentation 346, 366

Positive Predictive Value 209, 1151

Pos-Tagging (Part-Of-Speech Tagging) 18, 112, 127, 135, 293, 435, 540, 559, 620, 733, 892-894, 896, 899, 904, 938, 1255

Pre-Processing 18, 21, 23, 86, 114, 126, 140, 161-162, 177, 181, 185, 194, 218, 227, 264, 372, 382, 385, 413, 416, 419, 421-422, 453, 455, 473, 485-486, 488, 501-502, 508-509, 540, 556, 563, 577, 620-621, 629, 647-648, 691, 693, 695, 697-699, 701, 727, 737, 743, 750, 771, 777, 780-782, 784-786, 789, 791, 794, 796, 816, 838-839, 848, 855, 875, 892-895, 898, 900-901, 904, 918, 920-922, 952-953, 973, 975, 1007-1010, 1027, 1127-1128, 1131, 1195, 1200-1201, 1205-1206, 1209, 1211, 1225, 1242-1243, 1248, 1265-1266, 1350-1351, 1369, 1384, 1388, 1394, 1460, 1463, 1467, 1542, 1573, 1605, 1609, 1614, 1620, 1637, 1641, 1684, 1689, 1691, 1695, 1733, 1853, 1906, 1909-1910, 1917, 1919, 1921

Probabilistic Classifier 32, 63, 66, 100, 543, 787, 807, 906, 1042, 1344, 1856

Product Development 1305, 1422-1424, 1433-1434, 1436, 1746

Psychology 132-133, 279, 357, 363, 413, 581, 833, 863, 932, 945, 1503, 1505, 1618, 1632, 1701, 1712-1713, 1748, 1781, 1806, 1826, 1864, 1901

psychometrics 342-343, 356, 359

Public Administration 134, 222, 276, 1200, 1528-1529, 1531-1532, 1536-1538

public perception 484, 555, 557, 571, 575-577

public security 268-272, 275-279, 281-286

Public Sentiment 3, 40, 49, 60, 272, 329, 331, 339-340, 484-485, 779, 1306, 1312, 1460-1461, 1782, 1861, 1869

Punctuation Count 884, 886, 891

Python 18, 109, 141-142, 179, 197, 214, 220, 223, 227, 273, 280, 373, 419, 421-422, 425, 455, 487-488, 494, 562-564, 578, 601, 629, 643, 668, 676, 681, 684, 687, 726, 728, 730-732, 895, 966, 972, 975, 981, 1206, 1209, 1211, 1269, 1286, 1317, 1389, 1392-1393, 1395, 1462-1464, 1498, 1513, 1574,

1603, 1619, 1648, 1653-1654, 1659, 1675-1676, 1678, 1740, 1753, 1756, 1808

Q

qualitative cross-tabulation analysis 342-343, 355, 358-359, 366

R

Random Forest 97, 101, 119, 126-127, 184, 188, 190, 194, 197, 484, 486, 490-491, 559, 690, 696, 704, 788, 877, 879, 1004, 1029, 1125, 1137-1138, 1221, 1527, 1640, 1642-1643, 1648, 1656, 1905, 1908, 1914

Rapidminer 155, 759, 1189, 1196-1197, 1202, 1414, 1506, 1513-1514, 1521, 1524, 1588, 1678

Recommendation Algorithm 1083, 1098-1099, 1633, 1635-1636, 1640-1642, 1645, 1647

Recurrent Neural Network 36, 58-59, 105, 160, 190, 256, 262-263, 265, 267, 369, 380, 398, 405, 419, 623, 627, 629-630, 634, 818, 821-822, 833-834, 880, 882, 1253, 1348, 1398, 1638, 1648, 1736

reputation systems 964-969, 971, 992, 995-998

resampling 364, 412, 414-415, 417-419, 426-427

Research Agenda 268, 270-271, 283-284, 287, 1824

Review Analysis 176, 379, 536, 619, 995, 1148, 1307, 1313, 1350, 1461, 1510, 1524, 1550, 1634, 1807, 1857, 1861

review length 1660, 1663-1665, 1805, 1807-1808, 1821-1824

Review Volume 1367, 1805, 1807

rhetorical structure theory 519-521, 536-537

R-Language 1680, 1689, 1696

RNN 36-37, 39, 96, 190, 262-263, 369, 371, 400-403, 405-406, 418-420, 486, 495, 623, 629-630, 818, 828-830, 880, 882, 891, 1054, 1250, 1332, 1348, 1570, 1633, 1638-1639, 1641, 1643, 1645, 1746

Romanized text 1470, 1472, 1474, 1479

Rule Mining 233, 241-242, 254, 1315, 1317-1318, 1453, 1462, 1759

Rule-Based Classification 98, 519, 527, 529-530, 1446, 1712

S

Sarcasm Detection 110, 263, 443, 500, 793, 795, 848, 1032, 1035, 1049-1050, 1053-1055, 1234, 1305-1306, 1310, 1543, 1598, 1600, 1609, 1630-1631, 1907, 1909

Scarce Resource language 1051, 1063

Science Communication 673-674, 688

scoring method 631, 633

Semantic Analysis 19, 52, 87, 114, 143-144, 208, 265, 331-332, 340, 384, 429, 432, 442, 556, 694, 719, 726, 749, 751-753, 862, 891, 1103, 1108, 1169, 1332, 1357, 1388, 1453, 1467, 1513, 1576-1577, 1697, 1852, 1885-1886

Semantic Orientation 14-15, 18, 26, 31, 52, 58-59, 69, 114, 145-146, 211, 213, 328, 340, 381, 384, 397, 481, 498, 518, 595, 597, 617, 645, 721, 727, 850, 921, 925, 1002, 1061, 1102, 1122, 1150-1151, 1241, 1299, 1311, 1313, 1324, 1342, 1357, 1359, 1406, 1419-1420, 1448, 1453-1454, 1469, 1578, 1618

Semantic Relations 104, 277, 290, 292-293, 303, 306, 310, 441, 1316

Semantic Web 137-140, 233-235, 237, 239, 243, 249-255, 396, 614, 618, 641-642, 647, 1031, 1045, 1105, 1257, 1492, 1569, 1571-1572, 1648, 1780, 1782, 1864, 1919-1920, 1922

Sensitivity 209-210, 263, 509, 685, 768, 887, 1021, 1045, 1142, 1151, 1380, 1413, 1432, 1440, 1615, 1737, 1740-1741, 1745, 1788, 1870, 1907

sentence modeling 1347

sentence modelling 27-29, 32, 37, 62

Sentiment Analysis (SA) 1-3, 6, 11-12, 14-19, 21, 24-29, 31, 33, 36-37, 39-40, 42-43, 46-59, 61-67, 69-71, 73-78, 80, 90-91, 93, 97-98, 101-103, 105-121, 124, 126, 129-130, 132-133, 135, 137-138, 140-143, 145-146, 148, 151-160, 162, 171-172, 174-176, 181-182, 184-186, 189-190, 192-203, 205, 207-224, 227, 230-234, 247, 252, 256-272, 276-277, 279-293, 307, 309, 311-313, 316, 326-332, 334, 339-343, 355-358, 366-371, 374, 376, 378-382, 384-385, 395-397, 399, 401-402, 410-413, 415, 422, 428, 430, 433, 435, 439, 441-444, 446-448, 450, 453, 456, 459-462, 463-465, 467, 475-476, 480-481, 484-486, 489, 494-500, 508, 514, 516-522, 535-541, 550-562, 564, 567, 570-571, 573, 575-581, 595-597, 599, 613-617, 619-620, 628-630, 632-634, 636, 638, 640-644, 649, 653, 666-668, 673, 678-679, 682, 686-691, 693-694, 696-697, 703, 716-720, 722, 726, 728, 735, 747-748, 750, 755-759, 761-768, 776-780, 792, 794-797, 799, 801-802, 811-815, 817, 821, 823-824, 831-838, 841-842, 848-850, 852, 855, 857, 862, 864-865, 872, 889, 891, 893, 895-896, 900, 902-905, 915-922, 926, 930-933, 935-939, 945-948, 949-956, 959-964, 968, 971-972, 975, 984, 994-1007, 1011, 1014, 1020, 1026-1063, 1065-1066, 1075-1076, 1078, 1081, 1087, 1097, 1101, 1108-1109, 1112, 1115, 1117, 1119-1126, 1128, 1130, 1133-1134, 1137, 1140, 1146-1150, 1153-1155, 1157-1159, 1166-1168, 1170-1173, 1187, 1189, 1192-1193, 1195-1199, 1203-1205, 1216-1221, 1227, 1230, 1233-1243, 1247, 1249-1258, 1262-1270, 1276-1284, 1295, 1298-1301, 1303, 1306-1316, 1328, 1330, 1333-1336, 1338-1345, 1347-1350, 1352-1355, 1357-1360, 1362-1366, 1368-1370, 1372-1388, 1390-1391, 1398-1403, 1418-1420, 1422-1427, 1430-1437, 1439, 1441-1446, 1449-1463, 1466-1469, 1470-1471, 1476, 1480-1486, 1490-1499, 1502, 1504-1511, 1513-1515, 1522-1523, 1525-1529, 1532, 1536-1537, 1541, 1543, 1547-1552, 1554, 1564-1567, 1569-1574, 1576-1578, 1581, 1583, 1585-1590, 1592-1598, 1600, 1608-1615, 1618, 1621, 1630-1637, 1639-1640, 1642, 1645-1651, 1654, 1656, 1658-1659, 1661, 1666, 1672, 1674-1684, 1686-1687, 1690, 1696-1702, 1704-1705, 1715-1717, 1719, 1727-1737, 1739-1745, 1747-1748, 1750, 1758-1761, 1763-1765, 1768, 1773, 1779-1780, 1782-1783, 1786-1787, 1789, 1798-1800, 1802-1805, 1808, 1812, 1814, 1819, 1822-1823, 1825, 1831-1832, 1839, 1841-1844, 1846-1848, 1852-1853, 1856, 1861-1876, 1882-1885, 1887-1888, 1902-1903, 1905-1907, 1909, 1919-1926, 1928, 1930, 1932

Sentiment Analysis Model (SAM) 98, 157, 159, 213, 290-293, 494, 964, 971, 1087, 1355, 1381, 1492-1493, 1508, 1636, 1647, 1681

Sentiment Analysis of the Text 1117

Sentiment Benefits 214

Sentiment Classification 11, 17, 25-26, 30-31, 40, 42-44, 47, 51-52, 54-58, 60-61, 68-70, 75, 81-82, 98-99, 102-103, 105, 112-114, 145, 156, 158-160, 171-173, 182, 189-190, 195-196, 202, 212, 216, 218, 220-221, 223, 227, 230-231, 265-266, 286-287, 289, 312, 315-316, 327, 380-381, 395-396, 411, 461, 496, 514, 517-518, 520, 522, 535, 553-554, 560-561, 577-580, 595, 597-598, 615-617, 638, 647, 654, 723, 739, 762, 764-765, 778-779, 781-782, 787-790, 796-798, 813, 823-827, 832-835, 837, 840, 843, 848-851, 857, 916-917, 966-968, 971-972, 975-976, 994-995, 997, 1016, 1029-1031, 1034-1037, 1039, 1041, 1056-1057, 1059, 1062, 1075, 1101, 1121, 1123-1126, 1147, 1149-1150, 1171, 1205-1208, 1216-1218, 1236, 1253, 1256-1257, 1266, 1278, 1295, 1299, 1306-1308, 1310, 1312, 1316-1318, 1322, 1324-1328, 1330-1331, 1336, 1340, 1342-1344, 1349-1352, 1355-1359, 1408, 1420, 1424, 1436, 1441-1442,

1445-1448, 1450, 1452, 1454-1455, 1461-1462, 1467-1468, 1481, 1508, 1511, 1523, 1526, 1551, 1570, 1578, 1589, 1594, 1598, 1631, 1633, 1657, 1678-1679, 1728, 1857, 1882, 1885-1887, 1889-1890, 1895-1897, 1899-1903, 1905-1909, 1913-1914, 1917, 1919-1920

Sentiment Dictionaries 290, 292, 1006, 1044, 1702-1703, 1711

Sentiment Inference 1314-1315, 1330

Sentiment Labelled Data Set 1153, 1159, 1162, 1166, 1171

Sentiment Lexicons 2, 102, 147, 291, 399, 442, 497-498, 500-502, 504, 506-507, 509, 514, 641, 789, 1044, 1109-1110, 1148, 1241, 1253, 1256, 1298-1299, 1303, 1309-1310, 1342, 1400, 1483, 1497, 1580

Sentiment Polarity 69, 137, 200, 207-208, 216, 261, 263, 290-292, 333, 384, 498, 507, 514-515, 667, 813, 931, 951, 1032-1033, 1036, 1044, 1052, 1063, 1066, 1088, 1125, 1220, 1256, 1262, 1314, 1316, 1322, 1354, 1422, 1425, 1468, 1485, 1511, 1514, 1527, 1543, 1552, 1569, 1635-1637, 1661, 1823, 1851, 1873-1874, 1887, 1889, 1894, 1906

Sentiment Score 98, 153, 199, 222, 261, 318-319, 322, 334, 450, 452-453, 520, 524, 555, 562-564, 571-575, 577, 596-597, 606-609, 613, 737, 765, 789, 840, 938-940, 942, 944, 1043, 1125, 1425, 1433, 1451, 1458, 1460, 1462, 1583, 1585, 1603, 1605, 1650-1651, 1656, 1658, 1661, 1665-1666, 1671, 1729, 1916-1917

Sentimental Analysis 78, 80, 96, 100, 105-106, 112, 143, 215-216, 430, 620, 1004-1006, 1028, 1045, 1125, 1166, 1314, 1338, 1365, 1442, 1444, 1451, 1463, 1467, 1554, 1576, 1593-1595, 1603, 1681-1682, 1684-1685, 1687, 1689, 1691, 1696-1698, 1737, 1831-1832, 1925

Sentimental analyzer 1553

Sentistrength 332, 335, 597, 687, 789, 925, 1001-1003, 1017-1018, 1027, 1493, 1619, 1621, 1624-1627, 1629, 1632

Sentiwordnet 146, 160, 190, 314-317, 319, 322, 325-326, 333, 378, 418, 453, 521, 524, 536, 560, 564, 577-579, 597-598, 607, 614, 638, 641-642, 644, 666, 686, 765, 785, 789-790, 795-796, 801-802, 804, 815, 837-840, 844-845, 848, 857, 925-926, 931-932, 955, 1001-1004, 1017-1018, 1153, 1158, 1168, 1303, 1306, 1310, 1329, 1342, 1353, 1382, 1423, 1425, 1430, 1434-1436, 1439, 1483, 1492, 1579, 1609, 1617-1619, 1621, 1753, 1872-1873

service format 1101, 1104, 1106, 1108, 1112, 1117

Service Industry 1360, 1362, 1364, 1368, 1375, 1377, 1747, 1806

Smog Index 1816-1817, 1820

Social Media 1, 3, 5-7, 9, 16-18, 24, 26-28, 34, 49, 53, 55-56, 63, 74, 77-79, 97, 101-103, 105-110, 112-117, 131-134, 137, 144, 172, 174-175, 184-185, 195, 197, 199, 215, 218, 220-222, 230, 233, 247, 256-257, 262, 280-281, 286-289, 331, 339-340, 342, 358, 368, 380, 384, 395, 398-399, 409-411, 416, 430, 434, 443, 447, 463-465, 467-476, 480-486, 491, 495, 497, 538, 555-556, 580-582, 596, 610, 615, 617, 637, 640-641, 673-674, 687-689, 695, 697, 721, 749, 758-760, 762, 776-778, 780, 782-784, 787, 789-799, 801, 812, 815-818, 833, 852-853, 855, 859, 862, 889, 893, 896, 902, 918, 921, 931, 936, 952, 995-997, 1000-1003, 1032-1033, 1037, 1046-1047, 1050, 1056-1058, 1060-1062, 1080, 1098, 1102-1103, 1112-1113, 1115, 1117, 1119, 1121, 1128, 1146, 1148, 1150, 1153-1158, 1160, 1166-1171, 1190-1191, 1193, 1195, 1199-1200, 1204, 1220, 1233, 1235, 1238, 1243-1246, 1248, 1252, 1254, 1256, 1262-1263, 1270, 1276-1278, 1298-1299, 1308-1309, 1313, 1335, 1338-1339, 1353, 1356, 1360-1361, 1363-1369, 1376-1377, 1379-1383, 1385-1386, 1399, 1402-1403, 1418-1420, 1432, 1434-1435, 1437, 1443, 1449, 1452, 1455-1457, 1459, 1461, 1468-1469, 1470-1471, 1476, 1478-1479, 1481, 1483, 1494-1497, 1503-1505, 1513, 1524, 1526, 1528-1529, 1531-1532, 1536-1539, 1541-1544, 1547-1552, 1566, 1569, 1576, 1590, 1596-1597, 1600, 1611-1614, 1618, 1629-1631, 1651-1653, 1655, 1674, 1677, 1697, 1700, 1702, 1712, 1729, 1743, 1746, 1751, 1759, 1761-1764, 1773, 1778-1789, 1793-1794, 1796-1803, 1812, 1818, 1825-1826, 1829, 1831-1835, 1840-1844, 1850, 1858, 1864-1866, 1868-1870, 1873, 1894, 1902-1903, 1908-1909, 1919-1920, 1922-1931

Social Media Analysis 380, 430, 495, 777, 780, 817, 833, 1058, 1153, 1155-1156, 1254, 1456, 1496, 1550, 1629, 1865-1866, 1919, 1922

Social Media Analytics 113, 185, 288, 463-464, 471-472, 474-476, 480, 1434, 1503, 1526, 1761-1762, 1781, 1868, 1931

Social Media Marketing 852, 1113, 1356

Social Media Platforms 17-18, 24, 368, 464, 467, 471, 474-475, 480, 555, 790, 1037, 1113, 1653, 1746, 1761-1762, 1773, 1778, 1783-1789, 1793, 1797-1799, 1925

Social Network 1, 24, 100, 119, 132, 135, 276, 279, 285, 329, 383, 395, 398-400, 441-442, 465, 470, 582, 640-641, 643, 645-646, 674-676, 678, 680, 685, 688, 794, 796, 801, 813, 853, 862, 951,

971, 996, 1062, 1097, 1151, 1156, 1166, 1173, 1187-1188, 1205, 1254, 1264, 1269, 1312, 1377, 1385, 1396, 1435, 1492, 1529, 1536, 1620, 1630, 1632, 1681-1682, 1698, 1760, 1764, 1833-1834, 1836, 1841-1842, 1863, 1868, 1887-1893, 1901, 1903, 1920

Social Networking Sites 185, 231, 259, 596, 837, 853, 950, 1047, 1063, 1120, 1314, 1363, 1388, 1422-1428, 1433, 1452, 1612, 1683, 1688, 1841, 1871-1873

Social Relations 481, 1095, 1234, 1403, 1418, 1864, 1887, 1889-1891, 1894-1897, 1899-1902

Social Web 268-272, 276-277, 279-283, 285-286, 334, 336-337, 383, 518, 1027, 1045, 1048, 1057-1058, 1217, 1632, 1780

Spanish Language Analysis 637

Spark-ALS 1633-1634, 1636

Stemmer 388, 502, 542, 561, 596, 600, 602, 611, 699, 721, 741-742, 785, 906, 1211, 1604

Stock Market 13, 18, 58, 70, 110, 257, 339, 368, 399, 409, 461, 464, 481, 484-487, 494-495, 692-693, 717, 720, 793, 1028, 1033, 1043, 1047, 1125, 1148-1149, 1298, 1353, 1367, 1378, 1403, 1418, 1459

Stop Words 18-20, 22, 24, 91, 96, 142, 149, 201, 245, 388, 422, 453, 485, 488, 502, 542, 600, 602, 609, 613, 616, 621, 630, 636, 699, 701, 710, 724, 741, 750, 771, 838, 841-842, 893, 898, 906, 1009, 1225, 1242-1243, 1269, 1282, 1286, 1317, 1326, 1351, 1372, 1427, 1445, 1463, 1517, 1575, 1582, 1606, 1637, 1641, 1657-1658, 1678, 1704, 1738, 1753, 1756, 1906, 1909, 1911

student behaviour 1680-1681, 1683, 1685, 1719, 1726, 1729

student emotions 1717, 1726, 1732

stylometry 342-343, 356-357, 359, 366

subjective reviews 1553, 1566

Subjectivity Detection 113, 718, 1037, 1039, 1052, 1063, 1119, 1122, 1127-1128, 1130, 1135-1136, 1140, 1147, 1614, 1847-1848

Supervised Machine Learning 63, 66, 141, 156, 214, 216, 220, 246, 316, 399, 538, 540-541, 553, 639, 647, 649, 674, 676, 679, 689, 694, 705, 720, 768-769, 817, 857, 902-903, 916, 1029, 1041-1042, 1044, 1058, 1060, 1119, 1137, 1149, 1166, 1205, 1316, 1343, 1359, 1405, 1472-1473, 1510, 1573, 1589, 1656, 1907, 1909

Support Vector Machine (SVM) 18-19, 31, 67-69, 93, 95-96, 98, 101-102, 115, 174-175, 178-179, 188, 190, 196, 199, 203, 205, 214, 223, 249, 255, 315, 330-331, 375, 385, 391, 462, 536, 541, 558-560,

641, 694, 705, 722, 749, 807, 843, 864, 877, 879, 895, 904, 971, 1001, 1003-1004, 1041, 1064-1067, 1069, 1074, 1124, 1148, 1200, 1205, 1216, 1218, 1221, 1233, 1253, 1262, 1265, 1301, 1308, 1346, 1395, 1398, 1497, 1510, 1527, 1594, 1619-1620, 1626, 1678, 1755, 1887, 1908

sustainable transport 1153-1155, 1160-1161, 1166, 1171

Swarm Intelligence 450, 462, 1203-1204, 1206, 1217-1218, 1311, 1333

Synonyms 12, 19, 31, 46, 69, 121-122, 143, 146, 157-158, 160-161, 163-165, 169-171, 207, 216, 238, 316, 418, 425-426, 439, 583, 700, 749, 765, 776, 802, 838, 856, 1001-1002, 1158, 1265, 1299, 1304, 1321, 1328, 1409-1411, 1424, 1487, 1507-1509, 1546, 1561, 1575, 1579, 1617-1618, 1705, 1709, 1908

syntactic analysis 699, 751-753

T

Tagger 78, 95, 125-126, 135, 202, 211, 312, 317, 605, 733, 751, 1287, 1303, 1328, 1332, 1409, 1489, 1605, 1909

Task Of Opinion Mining 1, 3, 11, 1252, 1561, 1567

telecom customers 1733-1737, 1740-1741, 1743, 1745

Text Analysis 3, 28, 63, 65, 149, 216, 218, 330, 342-343, 348-350, 355-357, 359-363, 365, 626, 748, 753, 756, 758-759, 762-763, 776, 778-779, 801-802, 856, 858, 865, 890, 936, 1033, 1101, 1107-1108, 1117, 1122, 1124, 1312, 1441, 1458, 1494-1495, 1510, 1513-1514, 1522, 1582, 1635, 1646, 1650, 1689, 1691, 1698, 1702, 1787, 1804, 1810, 1827

Text Classification 35, 51, 53, 55-58, 60-61, 67-68, 78, 81, 97, 113, 115, 141, 171, 246, 250, 254-255, 259, 369, 401, 419, 428, 432, 460, 542, 586, 597, 620-621, 625, 629, 690-691, 693-701, 703, 716-723, 757, 762-763, 788-789, 800-801, 803, 811, 813-816, 820, 832, 835-836, 864-865, 894, 906, 971-972, 1042, 1067, 1072, 1075, 1121, 1124, 1150, 1169-1170, 1233, 1282, 1299, 1302, 1333, 1335, 1341-1342, 1347, 1349, 1358, 1380, 1420, 1424-1425, 1446, 1448, 1507-1509, 1524, 1564, 1572, 1574, 1613, 1637, 1669, 1677, 1716, 1748, 1755, 1759

Text Corpus 343, 366, 680, 1087, 1094, 1541-1542

Text Mining 66, 77, 97, 107, 109, 133, 201, 221, 223, 245, 256, 269, 276-277, 285, 288, 367, 396, 398, 431, 433, 435, 437, 439, 442, 444-445, 465, 500, 516, 539, 552, 556, 581, 597, 690-697, 699-700, 716-718, 722, 724, 748-749, 753, 758-759, 762,

779, 783, 801, 814, 816, 821, 838, 850, 852-853,
855-857, 860, 872, 893-894, 900-901, 903, 916,
968, 973, 997, 1033, 1066, 1075, 1096, 1101-
1102, 1106-1108, 1112, 1116-1119, 1124-1126,
1148, 1156, 1169, 1171, 1196, 1201, 1238, 1240,
1262, 1280, 1362-1366, 1369, 1374-1375, 1378-
1379, 1400, 1424, 1426, 1434, 1437, 1442, 1461,
1480, 1494, 1497, 1502, 1504, 1506-1507, 1509,
1513, 1521-1525, 1527, 1541-1542, 1547, 1563-
1565, 1567, 1614, 1629, 1646-1647, 1650-1651,
1653-1654, 1656, 1658-1659, 1673-1675, 1677,
1682, 1700, 1703, 1711, 1713, 1717, 1727, 1738,
1740, 1747, 1811, 1822, 1824, 1829, 1864, 1888,
1903, 1919

Text mining systems 1108, 1280

Text Mining Technologies 1118

Textblob 18, 22, 24, 141, 1382, 1430, 1498, 1504, 1574,
1600, 1606-1609, 1661, 1665, 1677

Textual information mining 1064

Theme Extraction 342-343, 356-357, 366

thwarted words 1119, 1122, 1128-1129, 1133, 1140,
1147

time series analysis 485-486, 494

Tokenization 18, 78, 88, 91, 95, 98, 162, 201, 211, 281,
372, 435-436, 442, 474, 501, 504, 540, 563, 577,
600-601, 620-621, 643, 669, 683, 696, 698, 724,
728-729, 750, 781, 831, 838, 875, 892, 894, 896,
898, 901, 904, 922, 925, 975, 1054, 1242-1244,
1247, 1253, 1265, 1269, 1286, 1351, 1384, 1388,
1390, 1394, 1402, 1404, 1472, 1485, 1498, 1515,
1653-1654, 1661, 1753, 1908, 1910, 1915

Tokens 17, 19-22, 42, 46, 84, 87, 91, 104, 142, 162,
176, 201, 373, 423, 426, 436, 473, 501, 556,
620-621, 630, 635, 669, 681, 683, 724, 729, 733,
751-752, 876, 898, 922-925, 1009, 1244, 1247,
1269-1270, 1286, 1288, 1404, 1409, 1474-1475,
1517, 1557, 1575, 1620, 1658, 1685, 1860, 1910

Tools Of Opinion Mining 155, 726, 728, 1587

Topic Modeling 283, 335, 342-343, 356-357, 366, 498,
1002, 1167, 1454, 1526

Topic Models 436-438, 441-442, 445, 475, 778, 1435

Tourism Domain 314-317, 324-327, 1080

Transcription 1259

Transfer Learning 27-28, 42-43, 47, 49, 51, 55, 57,
59, 62, 113, 159, 172, 423, 790, 796, 1061, 1205,
1242, 1252, 1442, 1452, 1681, 1851-1852, 1865,
1871, 1878, 1885

Transliteration 577, 601, 617, 1242-1243, 1245-1246,
1248, 1252-1260, 1262, 1264, 1267-1272, 1274,
1276-1279, 1478-1479

Transportation 7, 111, 277, 287, 798, 862, 1153-1154,

1156, 1158, 1160, 1167-1171, 1308, 1310, 1366,
1434, 1809

Treemap Diagram 366

trending topic 121, 123, 128-129, 135

Tripadvisor 315, 317, 322, 434, 792, 966, 998, 1047,
1101-1102, 1106, 1108-1114, 1153-1155, 1157-
1158, 1160, 1166-1168, 1250, 1336, 1420, 1497,
1510, 1513, 1521, 1523-1526, 1805, 1811-1812,
1818, 1822-1824, 1831-1832, 1834-1836, 1840,
1842-1844

Tweets 17-18, 20-24, 27-28, 32, 45, 54, 68, 78, 95-98,
107, 111, 118-131, 153, 159, 174, 176, 184-186,
190-191, 194-196, 199, 210, 215, 217-218, 221,
223, 227, 230-231, 256, 263, 265-266, 315-316,
328-335, 340, 368, 370, 375, 382-383, 385-388,
390-391, 396-403, 405-406, 408-410, 412-414,
416-427, 432, 435, 443, 469, 472, 485-487, 489-
490, 494-495, 498, 500, 509, 517, 538-543, 546-
547, 549-552, 556, 558-562, 581-586, 588-594,
598, 616, 639-644, 646, 667-668, 673, 675-676,
680-682, 686-689, 704, 708-709, 713-714, 721-
722, 753, 757-758, 761-763, 769-774, 776-777,
779-780, 783-784, 789, 793, 797, 807, 823, 834,
836, 843, 850, 872, 889, 892-893, 895-896, 902-
904, 906, 909-910, 912-915, 930, 949-957, 963,
1000-1002, 1004, 1006, 1008-1010, 1018-1020,
1022, 1027-1028, 1034, 1046, 1057, 1060, 1125,
1149, 1155-1156, 1197, 1203, 1205-1209, 1212,
1216, 1219-1221, 1225-1227, 1229, 1233, 1235,
1242, 1252, 1254, 1257, 1264, 1266-1267, 1278-
1279, 1283, 1295, 1307-1308, 1317, 1346, 1350,
1353, 1355, 1358, 1367, 1377, 1386-1387, 1389,
1393-1397, 1419, 1425, 1444, 1449-1450, 1459-
1461, 1463, 1466-1467, 1472-1473, 1479, 1484,
1492, 1533-1534, 1539, 1548, 1550, 1566, 1586,
1590, 1596, 1601, 1603-1606, 1609, 1613, 1616,
1618-1621, 1623-1631, 1657, 1697, 1728, 1743,
1747, 1750-1754, 1756-1758, 1761-1766, 1768-
1770, 1772-1780, 1783-1786, 1788-1790, 1792,
1794-1799, 1801, 1803, 1848-1849, 1852-1853,
1863, 1865, 1870, 1891, 1894-1896, 1903, 1906-
1910, 1915, 1917, 1919-1922, 1925, 1927, 1932

Twitter 2, 5, 7, 9, 13, 15-21, 23-28, 45, 50, 52-53,
55-56, 58, 61, 65, 96-98, 106-108, 110, 112-114,
116-117, 120-122, 127-133, 135, 137-138, 148-
150, 153-155, 176, 181-186, 189-190, 192-194,
196, 198-199, 210-214, 218, 220-221, 223, 227,
230-232, 256-257, 261-263, 265-267, 276, 281,
285, 288, 314-316, 326, 329-332, 334-335, 339-
340, 367-368, 375, 378-385, 387-388, 395-399,
401-403, 406, 409-413, 415, 417, 419, 421, 423,

426-433, 441, 464, 473, 475, 481, 484-489, 494-495, 498, 500, 508-509, 518, 537-540, 542, 551, 553-554, 556, 558, 560-562, 578-583, 593, 595-596, 614, 617, 639-647, 667, 673-681, 683-689, 697, 703, 710, 726, 728, 749, 757, 761, 778-780, 782-784, 789, 793, 795-801, 807-808, 812-817, 823, 832, 834, 836-837, 843-844, 847, 850, 853, 865-867, 892-893, 895-896, 899-900, 902, 915-917, 937, 949-953, 955, 958, 962-963, 995, 1000-1001, 1006, 1009, 1027, 1029-1030, 1034, 1047, 1057-1058, 1062, 1066, 1074-1075, 1120, 1125-1126, 1148-1149, 1156, 1165, 1168, 1173, 1187, 1191, 1195-1197, 1200-1201, 1205-1206, 1211, 1217-1221, 1225, 1227, 1229-1230, 1232-1233, 1235-1236, 1242, 1252, 1266, 1298, 1306-1308, 1310-1312, 1338, 1345, 1347, 1350, 1353, 1355, 1357-1358, 1364, 1367, 1369, 1371, 1378-1380, 1382, 1384-1389, 1393, 1396, 1400, 1403, 1418, 1420, 1426, 1436, 1444, 1449, 1452, 1455-1457, 1460-1464, 1467-1469, 1470, 1472, 1474, 1478, 1492, 1505, 1529, 1532-1534, 1536, 1539, 1542, 1544, 1548, 1550, 1552, 1569, 1571, 1581, 1583, 1586-1587, 1589, 1596-1600, 1603, 1606, 1608, 1610, 1613-1614, 1618, 1620, 1628-1631, 1648, 1676, 1681-1682, 1684, 1697, 1728-1729, 1746, 1748, 1751, 1756, 1759, 1761-1766, 1768-1770, 1773, 1775, 1780-1803, 1843, 1849, 1853, 1856, 1858, 1862, 1865-1866, 1869, 1873, 1888-1890, 1902-1903, 1905-1909, 1919-1922, 1925, 1931

Twitter Analysis 184, 189, 1350

Twitter API 17-18, 20-21, 23-24, 96, 153, 210, 473, 542, 562, 892-893, 895-896, 899-900, 953, 1350, 1389, 1462-1463, 1470, 1474, 1586, 1729, 1764-1766, 1905, 1909

Twitter Clustering 1384

Twitter Corpus 383, 595, 1229, 1400

Twitter Events 382, 815

Twitter Sentiment 25, 61, 97-98, 110, 113, 184-186, 189-190, 192-193, 196, 211, 218, 230, 266-267, 288, 335, 339, 367, 375, 378-381, 395-396, 411, 441, 518, 537, 553-554, 578-579, 667, 678, 687, 796-797, 807, 813, 832, 834, 900, 902, 916-917, 963, 1029-1030, 1062, 1075, 1218-1220, 1227, 1230, 1233, 1235, 1307-1308, 1310-1312, 1379, 1382, 1400, 1436, 1463, 1467-1468, 1598, 1610, 1748, 1902, 1920-1921

U

Unsupervised Learning 2, 18, 35, 42, 69, 93, 102, 131, 187, 189, 198-200, 203, 206-207, 211, 216, 221, 225, 263, 411, 677, 691, 724, 765, 778, 786, 789, 815, 818, 832, 883, 1003, 1039, 1043, 1069, 1124, 1171, 1342, 1422, 1425-1426, 1446, 1448, 1453, 1509, 1513, 1527, 1543, 1617, 1637, 1885

Unsupervised Machine Learning 63, 68, 102, 107, 203, 233, 677, 694, 797, 1497, 1513, 1764

user similarity 1887, 1889-1893, 1895, 1897, 1899-1901, 1903-1904

User-Generated Content 18, 105, 137, 497, 653, 759, 788, 797, 1032, 1035, 1037, 1045-1046, 1116, 1149, 1246, 1422-1424, 1428, 1433-1434, 1495, 1541, 1557, 1570, 1794, 1829, 1831-1832, 1834-1836, 1840, 1842, 1850

V

value co-production 1528, 1530-1531, 1537

value proposition 1101-1106, 1108, 1110, 1112-1115, 1118

visual question answering 361-362, 365-366, 430

W

Web 2.0 17-18, 25-26, 133, 135, 137, 198, 211, 234, 276, 434, 467, 643, 673-674, 726, 780, 1064, 1066, 1361, 1363, 1385, 1541, 1549, 1570, 1590, 1597, 1808, 1832, 1841, 1888, 1920

Web Content Mining 780, 794, 1564-1565

Web Mining 268-272, 276-277, 279-280, 283-284, 286, 395, 442, 465, 497, 782, 821, 867, 890, 1065, 1187, 1253, 1564-1566, 1717

Web Scraping 637, 639, 647, 650-651, 947, 1389, 1513

WEKA 395, 526, 536, 726, 728, 737-741, 743-744, 747, 807, 1264, 1288-1290, 1296, 1513, 1737, 1744

Word Embedding 28, 43-44, 52, 95, 113, 157-158, 160, 162-163, 165, 170, 257, 261-264, 398, 400, 402-403, 405-406, 409-410, 418, 423, 518, 621, 627-628, 642, 814, 938, 997, 1167, 1257, 1637

Word Frequency Count 366

Word Polarity 439, 644, 1000, 1493, 1555, 1910

Word Sense Disambiguation 144, 380, 440, 620, 718, 747, 749, 751, 785, 798, 952, 963, 1003, 1006, 1033, 1063, 1158, 1167, 1493, 1545, 1577

Word Tree 356, 366

Word2vec 28, 34, 39, 45, 62, 90, 102, 162-163, 168, 170, 262, 279, 384, 388, 391, 394, 417, 485-486, 489, 494, 718, 1125, 1391, 1637, 1641, 1648

Wordclouds 433, 436

Wordnet 12, 15, 19, 86, 89, 104-105, 111, 143, 146, 160, 163-165, 172, 207-209, 212, 236, 251, 316, 340, 380, 388, 396, 418, 439, 442, 541, 560, 564, 579,

583, 621, 638, 645, 686, 728, 753, 765, 794, 838, 840, 848, 904, 923-924, 1002, 1034, 1066, 1125, 1158, 1168-1169, 1241, 1252, 1304, 1316-1317, 1321, 1331, 1333, 1387, 1401, 1404-1405, 1407, 1409, 1417, 1420, 1453, 1575, 1579, 1618-1619, 1631, 1770, 1781, 1872-1873

Word-Of-Mouth 2, 14-15, 76, 133, 433-434, 443, 445, 481-482, 798, 1117, 1376, 1378-1383, 1495, 1504, 1506-1507, 1525, 1531, 1539, 1749, 1825-1830, 1834, 1842, 1864

working professionals 1680, 1683, 1688, 1696

World Knowledge 1033, 1052, 1119, 1122, 1127-1129, 1134-1135, 1140, 1147, 1546, 1549

Y

YARN 950

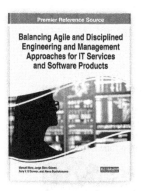

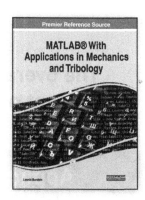

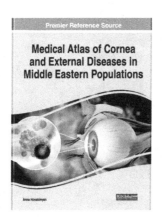
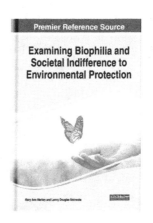
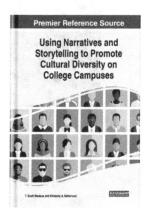

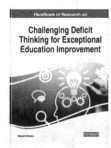

Printed in the United States
by Baker & Taylor Publisher Services